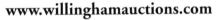

MILLER'S

collectibles

collectibles

MADELEINE MARSH *GENERAL EDITOR*

2006
VOLUME XVIII

MILLER'S COLLECTIBLES PRICE GUIDE 2006

Created and designed by
Miller's
The Cellars, High Street
Tenterden, Kent, TN30 6BN
Tel: +44 (0)1580 766411
Fax: +44 (0)1580 766100

First published in Great Britain in 2005
by Miller's, a division of Mitchell Beazley,
imprints of Octopus Publishing Group Ltd,
2–4 Heron Quays, London E14 4JP
Miller's is a registered trademark of
Octopus Publishing Group Ltd

ISBN 1845331869

A CIP record for this book is
available from the British Library

Set in Frutiger

Colour origination by One Thirteen Ltd, Whitstable, Kent, England
Advert reproduction: Ian Williamson, Pevensey Scanning
Printed and bound by Rotolito Lombarda, Italy

General Editor: Madeleine Marsh
Managing Editor: Valerie Lewis
Production Co-ordinator: Philip Hannath
Editorial Co-ordinator: Deborah Wanstall
Editorial Assistants: Melissa Hall, Joanna Hill
Production Assistants: Natasha Hamblin, Charlotte Smith,
Mel Smith, Ethne Tragett
Advertising Co-ordinator & Administrator: Melinda Williams
Advertising Executives: Emma Gillingham, Michael Webb
Designer: Nick Harris
Advertisement Designer: Kari Moody
Indexer: Hilary Bird
Jacket Design: Rhonda Summerbell
Production Controller: Jane Rogers
Additional Photography: Emma Gillingham, Paul Harding, Dennis O'Reilly,
Robin Saker, Neville Woodcock
North American Consultants: Marilynn and Sheila Brass

Front Cover Illustrations:
Chuck Berry, 'Rhythm and Blues with Chuck Berry', 1956. **£150–170 / €220–250 / $290–330** ⊞ BNO
A Goebel figure, early 1930s, 10½in (26.5cm) high. **£490–550 / €710–800 / $940–1,050** ⊞ BEV
A pair of sunglasses, by Jean Patou, 1960s. **£35–40 / €50–60 / $65–75** ⊞ DRE

Title page Illustrations:
A bronze table lighter, 1940s, 6in (15cm) high. **£50–60 / €75–85 / $100–115** ⊞ COB
A wooden model of a soldier, 1960s, 20in (51cm) high. **£55–65 / €80–95 / $105–125** ⊞ LAS
A T. G. Green Blue Domino teapot, early 1950s, 7in (18cm) high. **£70–80 / €100–115 / $135–155** ⊞ JWK

Contents

Acknowledgments

We would like to acknowledge the great assistance given by our consultants who are listed below. We would also like to extend our thanks to all the auction houses, their press offices, dealers and collectors who have assisted us in the production of this book.

DANIEL AGNEW
Christie's
85 Old Brompton Road
London SW7 3LD
020 7752 3335
(Teddy Bears)

GRAHAM BUDD
Budd Auctions Ltd
London
gb@grahmbuddauctions.co
(Football)

GRAHAM COOLEY
07968 722269
(Glass)

JOHN CORNISH
Denim Junkies
www.denimjunkies.com
(Costume)

MARTYN MOORE
Classic Cars Magazine
Media House
Lynchwood
Peterborough Business Park
Peterborough
Cambridgeshire PE2 6EA
01733 468219
(Automobilia)

MALCOM PHILLIPS
Comic Book Postal Auctions
40–42 Osnaburgh Street
London NW1 3ND
(Comics)

STEPHEN PHILLIPS
Rellik Antiques
248 Camden High Street
London NW1 8QS
(Costume)

GEOFF PRINGLE
Old Nautibits
P O Box 67
Langport
Somerset TA10 9WJ
(Aeronautica)

SKIP SMITHSON
Skip and Janie Smithson Antiques
Lincolnshire
01754 810265
(Kitchenware)

DAVID STANLEY
David Stanley Auctions
Stordon Grange
Osgathorpe
Leicestershire LE12 9SR
(Tools)

How To Use This Book

It is our aim to make this guide easy to use. In order to find a particular item, turn to the contents list on page 7 to find the main heading, for example, Jewellery. Having located your area of interest, you will see that larger sections may be sub-divided by subject or maker. If you are looking for a particular factory, maker or object, consult the index which starts on page 453.

Caption
provides a brief description of the item including the maker's name, medium, date, measurements and in some instances condition.

Information Box
covers relevant collecting information on factories, makers, care, restoration, fakes and alterations.

Cross Reference
directs the reader to where other related items may be found.

Price Guide
these are based on actual prices realized at auction or offered for sale by a dealer, shown in £sterling, Euros and $US. Remember that Miller's is a PRICE GUIDE not a PRICE LIST and prices are affected by many variables such as location, condition, desirability and so on. Don't forget that if you are selling, it is quite likely you will be offered less than the price range. Price ranges for items sold at auction tend to include the buyer's premium and VAT if applicable. The exchange rate used in this edition is 1.92 for $ and 1.45 for €.

Further Reading
directs the reader towards additional sources of information.

Source Code
refers to the 'Key to Illustrations' on page 443 that lists the details of where the item was sourced. The ✗ icon indicates the item was sold at auction. The ⊞ icon indicates the item originated from a dealer.

Introduction

Collecting appears to be a universal passion and at some stage in their lives most people have collected something. For many of us, the habit begins in childhood and often our adult collecting is shaped by these juvenile experiences. Over the decades, the objects that delight each generation will change: cigarette cards, lead soldiers and tinplate toys have been superseded by trading cards, computer games and teenage fashion dolls with supermodel wardrobes. However, the basic urge to acquire, swap and build up sets remains the same. As shown in our sections devoted to comics, dolls, toys, games and children's books, many of these playthings can command high prices (see Record Breakers page 428) and over the past year toys have been one of the strongest performing areas in the adult collectors' market.

Nostalgia is not the only factor that makes objects collectable. This year we include an expanded section devoted to vintage tools. On the one hand, these are collected as reminders of a long-vanished world where every village had its cooper, blacksmith and wheelwright and where everything was made by hand. Equally, however, vintage tools are purchased by modern-day craftsmen to use, because they claim these antique implements are often better made and easier to work with than their 21st-century equivalents.

Many of the objects illustrated in this book still fulfil their original function. Collectors of classic and vintage cars will look for period motor accessories and perhaps a matching suitcase or picnic set to put in the boot (see Automobilia and Luggage pages 47 & 272). In this year's Aeronautica section we devote a special section to air force uniforms, which are collected not just as display items but also by people involved in World War re-enactment groups and those who fly vintage planes.

Vintage costume in general is another area that has expanded rapidly in recent times, largely because people enjoy wearing the clothes. Some will collect because of interest in a particular period, others might become involved through music and dance (for example Lindy Hop or Mod enthusiasts), but many will buy a vintage item simply as an addition to their contemporary wardrobe. It's become fashionable, and not just with women.

Alongside the 1920s' beaded flapper dresses and vintage high-heeled shoes we also devote a section to men's fashion. This includes collectable denim jeans, US flying jackets, and even a vintage hoodie, today famously associated with 'chav' style and juvenile delinquency, but which started out as a piece of sensible sports wear, designed for clean-cut American youth.

One of the attractions of collectables is that these everyday items provide us with a little piece of 3-D history that we can hold in our hands and which can be far more immediate and evocative than simply reading facts or dates in a book. This year we include a large section devoted to antique kitchenware. The objects not only show us the elaboration of Victorian eating habits when the emerging middle classes demonstrated their new-found status with countless dishes on the table, but also the huge amount of labour that was required to produce food and drink.

As well as reminding us of the attractions of the past, the collectables shown in this book can also reveal a world that we probably wouldn't care to return to. Many of the objects in our scientific instruments section are undoubtedly fascinating and beautifully crafted, but very few people would want their internal organs removed and ailments doctored with the implements in our medical section pages 333–335.

As we at Miller's know, there is a collector for everything. *Miller's Collectables Price Guide* covers a huge variety of objects from pocket money collectables to rare pieces worth thousands. Now in its 18th edition, this is the most established guide in its field. Each entry is given a price range that reflects the current state of the market and sections are supplemented with introductions and fact boxes that provide useful historical and market information. Subjects covered in this year's book range from desirable dogs to collectable quilts, from 20th-century glass to vintage Christmas decorations, sporting memorabilia and prehistoric fossils. If you have any further subjects you would like to see included please contact us. Our aim is to reflect your passions and to celebrate collectables in their infinite and endlessly fascinating variety. **Madeleine Marsh**

Advertising & Packaging

A Bailey & Thomas Hatchett's Hotel meat plate, by Spode, ceramic, 19thC, 14¾in (37.5cm) wide.
£300–360 / €440–520
$580–690 ✦ G(L)

An H. Adams Ship Tavern plate, ceramic, transfer-printed with a ship, c1835, 10in (25.5cm) diam.
£360–400 / €520–580
$690–770 ⊞ COB

A set of Joseph & Jesse Siddons butter scales, cast-iron, with a porcelain plate, c1850, 14in (35.5cm) wide.
£130–150 / €190–220
$250–290 ⊞ SMI

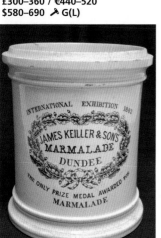

A James Keiller & Sons shop display marmalade jar, ceramic, Scottish, 1860s, 10in (25.5cm) high.
£270–300 / €390–440
$520–580 ⊞ SMI

A Thomas Glover Gas Meter Manufacturer paperweight, ceramic, c1890, 4in (10cm) diam.
£85–95 / €125–140
$165–185 ⊞ BS

A Jonas Wood Family Grocer calendar, depicting two girls and a dog in the countryside, 1892, 23 x 27in (58.5 x 68.5cm).
£45–50 / €65–75
$85–95 ✦ BBR

A Blue Ridge Household Chemicals advertising poster, depicting the Libbey Glass Co factory, slight damage, late 19thC, 21 x 29in (53.5 x 73.5cm).
£370–440 / €540–640
$710–840 ✦ JDJ

A Horniman's Pure Tea ashtray, tin, depicting an Edwardian lady, c1900, 4¾in (12cm) diam.
£65–75 / €95–105
$125–145 ⊞ HUX

A William Millar's Stores 6lb butter crock, ceramic, Scottish, c1900, 8in (20.5cm) diam.
£110–125 / €160–180
$210–240 ⊞ Cot

A Cleverley's Hatters hat brush, wood, c1900, 10in (25.5cm) long.
£10–15 / €15–22
$19–28 ⊞ Cot

A Coon & Co Brand Collars & Cuffs dressing mirror, on a bronzed-metal frame, c1900, 16in (40.5cm) high.
£250–300 / €370–440
$480–580 ➶ JAA

A J. & R. Coats Sewing Cotton display cabinet, wood, knobs replaced, 1900, 19in (48.5cm) wide.
£140–155 / €200–220
$270–300 ⊞ Cot

A Cincinnati Ice-Coal Company sign, paper, American, early 1900s, framed, 18¼ x 24¼in (46.5 x 61.5cm).
£115–130 / €165–190
$220–250 ⊞ MSB

A Joseph Thorley measuring cup, ceramic, c1900, 2½in (6.5cm) high.
£135–150 / €195–220
$260–290 ⊞ SMI

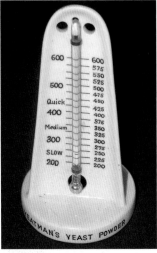

A Yeatman's Yeast Powder kitchen thermometer, ceramic, early 20thC, 6½in (16.5cm) high.
£105–120 / €150–170
$200–230 ⊞ WeA

A Kiwi Polish stand, metal, early 20thC, 15in (38cm) wide.
£145–165 / €210–240
$280–310 ⊞ SMI

A Fry's Cocoa Caracas Chocolate promotional folding ruler, tin, 1905, 12in (30.5cm) long.
£80–90 / €115–130
$155–175 ⊞ HUX

A Keen's Mustard glove button hook, 1905, 2½in (6.5cm) long.
£20–25 / €30–35
$40–45 ⊞ HUX

A C. A. Wedderburn & Co margarine slab, ceramic, c1910, 13in (33cm) diam.
£450–500 / €650–730
$860–960 ⊞ B&R

A Domex Housemaids cleaning box, pine, metal handle, c1910, 16in (40.5cm) wide.
£115–130 / €165–190
$220–250 ⊞ Cot

A Coca-Cola tip tray, tin, slight damage, 1910, 4¼in (11cm) wide.
£420–470 / €610–680
$810–900 ➴ JDJ

A Coca-Cola tip tray, tin, slight damage, 1913, 4¼in (11cm) wide.
£400–480 / €580–700
$770–920 ➴ JDJ

A Harris's Sausages plate, ceramic, transfer-printed with a man riding a pig, inscribed 'Winner of the Pork Sausage Derby', c1920, 9in (23cm) diam.
£135–150 / €195–220
$260–290 ⊞ B&R

Coca-Cola

Coca-Cola syrup was developed in America in 1886 by Atlanta pharmacist John S. Pemberton and was initially intended as an over-the-counter medicine to be taken mixed with water. The following year, carbonated water was added to the mixture. Pemberton sold his interests in the company and in 1891 fellow druggist Asa G. Candler became sole proprietor of Coca-Cola for an investment of just over £1,200 / €1,750 / $2,300. The drink was marketed for pleasure as well as for health and sales boomed, rising from 1,300 gallons (5,900 litres) per day in 1901 to 11,500 gallons (52,279 litres) in 1910. As well as supplying the beverage to soda fountains, Coca-Cola began producing bottled Coke from the 1890s so that customers could take the drink home. In the early years a range of different bottles were used, but in 1915 the Root Glass Company came up with the famous 'contour' or 'hobble skirt' bottle, allegedly inspired by the line-drawing of a cocoa pod, which went on to become one of the most recognized bottle designs in the world.

From the earliest years, heavy advertising contributed to the success of the brand. Tin trays were supplied to soda fountains and drug stores and the earliest recorded example dates from 1897. As these models decorated with beauties show, trays from the first part of the 20th century can command high prices. However, condition is crucial to value and buyers should also take care as many reproductions have been manufactured since the 1970s.

A Quaker Oats bowl, ceramic, c1920, 7¾in (19.5cm) diam.
£25–30 / €40–45
$50–55 ⊞ AL

A millinery head, papier-mâché, c1920, 14in (35.5cm) high.
£230–270 / €330–390
$440–520 ➴ DuM

A J. & B. Cordials & Fruit Squashes jug, ceramic, c1920, 11in (28cm) high.
£180–200 / €260–290
$340–380 ⊞ SMI

A Mitchell's Tobacco display cabinet, wooden, c1920, 23in (58.5cm) wide.
£360–400 / €520–580
$690–770 ⊞ JUN

A Calders Yeast plate, ceramic, c1920, 12in (30.5cm) wide.
£180–200 / €260–290
$340–380 ⊞ SMI

A Shelley Girl advertising figure, porcelain, modelled as a lady with a cup of tea, marked, c1926, 12in (30.5cm) high.
£1,750–2,100
€2,550–3,050
$3,350–4,000 ♣ AH
The Shelley Girl figure – used to advertise Shelley china, is much sought after by Shelley enthusiasts.

A Mazda Man display dummy, gesso and wood, the articulated arms and legs with slots to display cards, his head in the form of a valve, c1929, 14in (35.5cm) high.
£155–175 / €220–250
$300–340 ⊞ LFi

◄ **A Battersby hat box,** cardboard, 1920s, 13in (33cm) high.
£15–20
€22–29
$29–38 ⊞ OH

A Bovril spoon, marked 'Pelican Silver JGNS' 1920s, 5¾in (14.5cm) long.
£6–10 / €9–15
$12–19 ⊞ WeA
Pelican silver was a trade name for nickel silver, a nickel alloy containing copper, nickel and zinc.

A Crone & Taylor's Fertilisers ashtray, steel, 1920s, 4½in (11.5cm) diam.
£35–40 / €50–60
$65–75 ⊞ BS

A Cow & Gate Milk Food figure, plaster, in the form of a mother holding a baby, 1920–30, 10in (25.5cm) high.
£80–90 / €115–130
$155–175 ♣ BBR

An F. S. Plumpton Bread and Cake delivery basket, by Vanesta Fitted Cases, wood with wicker base, with drawer for fancy cakes, c1930, 14in (35.5cm) wide.
£270–300 / €390–440
$520–580 ⊞ B&R

A Bisto postcard, by J. Clutterbuck, original artwork, signed and dated 7 December 1933, 6½ x 4½in (16.5 x 11.5cm).
£310–370 / €450–540
$600–710 ♣ VS

Bisto

From the words Browns, Seasons and Thickens all In One came the acronym Bisto, the name given to the gravy powder invented in 1908 by Messrs Roberts & Patterson in response to their wives' pleas to find an easier way to make gravy. Both Mr Roberts and Mr Patterson worked at the Cerebos Company which produced salt and other food products, and soon they persuaded their employer to start making Bisto commercially. The Bisto Kids were originally created by the famous cartoonist Will Owen in 1919 and were subsequently depicted by various commercial artists; they remained on the packs until the early 1990s. The ragamuffin children, with their famous slogan 'Ah! Bisto' were hugely popular in the interwar years and over the decades have inspired a wealth of advertisements and collectables. In 1979, Bisto updated their famous product and launched gravy granules. Today, Bisto gravy is served over 3.4 billion times a year in the UK.

◀ **A Vim kaleidoscope,** cardboard and tin, 1930s, 2¼in (5.5cm) high.
£35–40 / €50–60
$65–75 ⊞ HUX

▶ **A Chiver's Olde English Marmalade calendar advert,** card, 1945, framed, 22 x 17in (56 x 43cm).
£60–70 / €85–100
$115–135 ✕ BBR

A Coca-Cola ice chest, 1940s, 36in (91.5cm) high.
£390–460 / €570–670
$750–880 ✕ JAA

◀ **A box of three Fairy Household Soaps,** 1940s, 7in (18cm) wide.
£6–10 / €9–15
$12–19 ⊞ NFR

A Peter's Ideal Milk Chocolate dummy chocolate bar, c1955, 4½in (11.5cm) wide.
£8–12 / €12–18
$16–23 ⊞ HUX

A packet of Sprinko tile and paint cleaner, cardboard and tin, 1950s, 9in (23cm) high.
£10–15 / €15–22
$19–28 ⊞ RTT

A packet of Co-Op 99 Tea, 1940s, 5in (12.5cm) high.
£8–12 / €12–18
$16–23 ⊞ NFR

A Wall's Snocreme Lolly advertisement, 1957, 5 x 10in (12.5 x 25.5cm).
£15–20 / €22–29
$29–38 ⊞ RUSS

◀ **A Christian Dior advertising model of a female head supported by two hands,** pottery, 1950s, 22in (56cm) high.
£240–280 / €350–410
$460–540 ✕ DD

◀ **A Blue Bird Toffees box,** cardboard, 1950s, 9in (23cm) wide.
£8–12 / €12–18
$16–23 ⊞ DaM

A set of eight Robertson's Golly musicians, hand-painted pottery, 1950s, 3in (7.5cm) high.
£75–85 / €110–125
$145–165 ⊞ TASV

A Suchard de Luxe display chocolate bar, tin, late 1950s, 6½in (16.5cm) wide.
£10–15 / €15–22
$19–28 ⊞ HUX

◀ **A Lever's Feed ashtray,** ceramic, c1960, 4in (10cm) diam.
£3–7 / €4–10
$6–13 ⊞ JUN

A Tough Guy Grub advertising pamphlet, printed by A. Smith & Son, 1960s, 7¼ x 5in (18.5 x 12.5cm).
£1–5 / €2–7
$3–9 ⊞ TWI

A Robertson's Golly book marker, plastic, 1960s, 4in (10cm) long.
£30–35
€45–50
$55–65 ⊞ UD

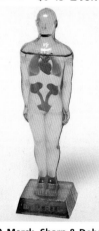

A Merck, Sharp & Dohme Diuril drug advertising figure, plastic, 1960s, 7in (18cm) high.
£25–30 / €40–45
$50–55 ⊞ HUX

A child shop mannequin, fibreglass, 1960s, 33in (84cm) high.
£70–80 / €100–115
$135–155 ⊞ JUN

A set of four Express Dairy Milk drinking glasses, 1970s, 4½in (11.5cm) high.
£15–20 / €22–29
$29–38 ⊞ TWI

▶ **A Robertson's Golly toast rack,** ceramic, 1980s–90s, 5in (12.5cm) wide.
£45–50 / €65–75
$85–95 ⊞ HYP

▶ **A Dulux Paints advertising figure,** by Beswick, ceramic, in the form of an Old English Sheepdog, 1990, 12½in (32cm) high.
£400–480 / €580–690
$770–920 ⋗ Ben

Enamel & Tin Signs

Also known as street jewellery, enamel signs date from the 19th century. Their boom in popularity coincided with the expansion of the railways, thus providing means to transport the heavy signs around the country, and a perfect location for advertising to a wide number of people. In addition to stations and alongside railway tracks, shop fronts, garages and public houses were favourite sites, while omnibuses, trams and commercial vehicles provided the opportunity for mobile advertising.

Vitreous enamel signs were extremely durable. They could be produced in different sizes and shapes, depending on location, and took bright, strong colours. Enamel signs were commonplace until WWII when steel was rationed. After the war, tin, paper and cardboard signs provided a cheaper alternative to expensive enamel, and large hoardings, which sprung up to conceal bombsites, were covered with posters. Small shops were being replaced by supermarkets; new planning regulations made it difficult to affix signs to buildings and, in the age of television, advertising itself had changed, focusing on quick-fire campaigns with changing imagery. The golden age of street jewellery was over; many signs were removed and scrapped or simply left to rust.

Vintage signs can command high prices today, and an attractive image is all-important; however, as an advertising image may have been used over a considerable period of time, signs can be difficult to date. The fixing holes and edges of signs are particularly susceptible to damage, and condition can affect the value.

A Kingov Flour double-sided sign, enamel, c1900, 8½ x 12in (21.5 x 30.5cm).
£360–400 / €520–580
$690–770 ⊞ AAA

A Jones' Sewing Machines sign, enamel, c1900, 34in (86.5cm) wide.
£450–500 / €650–730
$860–960 ⊞ JUN

▶ A Ripe Bananas price sign, tin, c1910, 7in (18cm) wide.
£45–50 / €65–75
$85–95 ⊞ SMI

A Van Houten's Cocoa sign, enamel, c1900, 59in (150cm) wide.
£135–150 / €195–220
$260–290 ⊞ JUN

A De Laval Cream Separator sign, tin, early 1900s, 12 x 15¾in (30.5 x 40cm).
£75–85 / €110–125
$150–165 ⊞ MSB

A Swan Collars sign, enamel, c1905, 30in (76cm) wide.
£450–500 / €650–730
$860–960 ⊞ JUN

A Dairy Fed and Farm Fed display sign, tin, c1910, 6in (15cm) wide.
£45–50 / €65–75
$85–95 ⊞ SMI

A Rowntree's Chocolates and Pastilles sign, enamel, c1910, 69in (175.5cm) wide.
£155–175 / €220–250
$300–340 ⊞ JUN

A Wills's Gold Flake Cigarettes sign, enamel, c1910, 48in (122cm) wide.
£85–95 / €125–140
$165–185 ⊞ JUN

◄ **A Brooke Bond Tea sign,** enamel, c1920, 30in (76cm) high.
£70–80 / €100–115
$135–155 ⊞ JUN

A Sun Insurance Office sign, enamel, slight damage, 1910–20, 18 x 24in (45.5 x 61cm), framed.
£100–120 / €145–175
$195–230 ✂ BBR

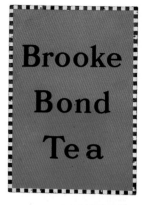

► **A Dennis's Pig Powders sign,** tin, 1920s–30s, 18in (45.5cm) wide.
£270–300 / €390–440
$520–580 ⊞ BS

An Imperial Roll Films double-sided hanging sign, enamel, 1920s, 10 x 14in (25.5 x 35.5cm).
£310–350 / €450–510
$600–670 ⊞ AAA

► **A Selo Film sign,** enamel, 1920s, 18in (45.5cm) high.
£220–250
€320–360
$430–480
⊞ JUN

◄ **A Fry's Chocolate sign,** enamel,1920s–30s, 22 x 30in (56 x 76cm).
£720–800
€1,000–1,150
$1,400–1,550
⊞ AAA

► **A Portsmouth & Gosport Gas Company sign,** enamel, 1930s, 6in (15cm) square.
£20–25 / €30–35
$40–50 ⊞ COB

Showcards

A Corbo Nero Velveteen showcard, late 19thC, 23 x 17in (58.5 x 43cm).
£65–75 / €95–105
$125–145 ⊞ RTT

▶ **Mrs S. A. Allen's World's Hair Restorer showcard,** 1890–1910, 20 x 14¾in (51 x 37.5cm).
£70–80 / €100–115
$135–155 ⋏ BBR

An Andersons' Waterproofs showcard, depicting Lord and Lady Randolph Churchill, 1885–90, 12 x 18in (30.5 x 45.5cm).
£270–300 / €390–440
$520–580 ⊞ MURR

▶ **A Carr's Biscuits showcard,** depicting Piccadilly Circus, 1925, 21in (53.5cm) high.
£340–380 / €490–550
$650–730 ⊞ HUX

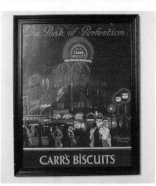

◀ **A Borax Starch Glaze showcard,** c1910, 23in (58.5cm) high.
£220–250
€320–360
$420–480
⊞ JUN

A Bird's Custard showcard, stonelitho, framed and glazed, 1920s, 19 x 11in (48.5 x 28cm).
£180–200 / €260–290
$340–380 ⊞ AAA

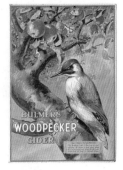

A Bulmer's Woodpecker Cider showcard, 1920–30, 19in (48.5cm) high.
£180–200 / €260–290
$340–380 ⊞ MRW

A Wills's Star Cigarettes showcard, framed and glazed, 1920–30, 21 x 15in (53.5 x 38cm).
£670–750 / €970–1,100
$1,300–1,450 ⊞ AAA

A Coca-Cola soda fountain window display, cardboard with satin ribbon garlands, 1932, largest image 33in (84cm) wide.
£850–1,000 / €1,250–1,450
$1,600–1,900 ✗ JDJ

A Daws Lemon Squash and Orange Squash showcard, 1930s, 12½ x 9in (32 x 23cm).
£20–25 / €30–35
$40–50 ⊞ RTT

A Nugget Boot Polish showcard, framed and glazed, 1930s, 9 x 6in (23 x 15cm).
£155–175 / €220–250
$300–340 ⊞ AAA

A Be-Ro Self-Raising Flour showcard, decorated with a Mabel Lucie Attwell figure, 1930s, 12 x 8in (30.5 x 20.5cm).
£35–40 / €50–60
$65–75 ⊞ MURR

A Singer Sewing Machines Re-Dress your Rooms showcard, late 1930s, 9 x 6in (23 x 15cm).
£2–6 / €3–9
$4–11 ⊞ RTT

◀ **A Hires Root Beer showcard,** 1940s–50s, 15 x 24in (38 x 61cm).
£45–50 / €65–75
$90–100 ⊞ MSB

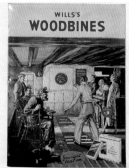

A Wills's Woodbines showcard, plastic on metal, 1950s, 20in (51cm) high.
£100–120 / €145–175
$190–230 ⊞ HUX

Three Good Year Stick-on-Soles hanging showcards, 1950s, 15 x 19in (38 x 48.5cm).
£65–75 / €95–105
$125–145 each ⊞ Do

◀ **A Bulmer's Cider 3-D showcard,** cardboard, 1950s, 12in (30.5cm) wide.
£40–45 / €60–70
$75–85 ⊞ LAS

Tins

A **Victorian Murray & Co Japanese Cocoanut tin,** 9in (23cm) wide.
£35–40 / €50–60
$65–75 ⊞ AL

A **Huntley & Palmer's biscuit tin,** decorated with a mosaic pattern, 1899–1901, 8¼in (21cm) wide.
£80–90 / €115–130
$155–175 ⊞ HUX

A **Huntley & Palmer's biscuit tin,** in the form of eight books held together with a strap, c1900, 6¼in (16cm) wide.
£140–165 / €200–240
$270–320 ⚒ L

◀ A **Chocolat Ibled tin,** French, c1905, 8in (20.5cm) wide.
£65–75 / €95–105
$125–140 ⊞ HUX

A **Mazawattee Tea tin,** decorated with scenes from *Alice in Wonderland*, 1895, 8½in (21.5cm) high.
£220–250 / €330–370
$430–480 ⊞ HUX

A **Mackenzie & Mackenzie biscuit tin,** c1900, 10in (25.5cm) wide.
£300–350 / €440–500
$590–670 ⊞ HUX

A **Dalu-Kula Tea tin,** 1895, 7in (18cm) wide.
£500–550 / €730–810
$950–1,050 ⊞ HUX

A **Golden Syrup dispenser,** tin, c1900, 20in (51cm) high.
£270–300 / €390–440
$520–580 ⊞ JUN

◀ A **D. Leonardt & Co, Birmingham nibs and matchstriker tin,** 1900, 2½in (6.5cm) wide.
£55–65 / €80–95
$105–125 ⊞ HUX

A **Boyle's Jap Nuggets tin,** 1905, 2½in (6.5cm) wide.
£100–120 / €145–175
$190–220 ⊞ HUX

A Huntley & Palmer's biscuit tin, in the form of a bookcase, 1905, 6in (15cm) high.
£135–150 / €195–220
$260–290 ⊞ JUN
Approximately 140,000 examples of this tin were produced.

A Dr Bengué sample matches tin and striker, French, 1910, 2in (5cm) wide.
£65–75 / €95–105
$125–140 ⊞ HUX

A biscuit tin, German, 1910–20, 4¾in (12cm) high.
£12–15 / €15–22
$19–28 ⊞ RTT

A Köhler sewing machine accessories tin, German, c1910, 6¾in (17cm) wide.
£40–45 / €60–70
$75–85 ⊞ HUX

A Nicholls & Coombs Clarnico toffee tin, 1910, 9in (23cm) wide.
£50–60 / €75–85
$100–110 ⊞ HUX

Five hook and eye tins, decorated with sporting women, French, 1915, 2in (5cm) wide.
£20–25 / €30–35
$40–45 each ⊞ HUX

◀ A Charlot Shoe Polish tin, depicting Charlie Chaplin, c1920, 1¾in (4.5cm) diam.
£20–25 / €30–35
$40–50 ⊞ HUX

A Noah's Ark tin, 1910, 5in (12.5cm) high.
£30–35 / €45–50
$60–70 ⊞ HUX

A Rowntree's tin, depicting the State Entry into London by Queen Elizabeth I, together with a letter of introduction, 1915, 7in (18cm) wide.
£30–35 / €45–50
$60–70 ⊞ HUX

A Rowntree's chocolate tin, in the form of a lantern, 1910–18, 3in (7.5cm) high.
£115–130 / €170–190
$220–250 ⊞ MURR

A Confiture au Sirop de Fruits Confits tin, in the form of a child's bucket and lid, French, c1925, 4½in (11.5cm) high.
£45–50 / €65–75
$85–95 ⊞ HUX

A Mackintosh's Toffee de Luxe tin, 1925, 6in (15cm) wide.
£100–120 / €145–175
$190–220 ⊞ HUX

A Mohar Selected Turkish Tobacco tin, 1920s, 3½in (9cm) wide.
£65–75 / €95–105
$125–140 ⊞ HUX

◄ **A Cocoa Bendsor tin,** made in Holland for the French market, 1920s, 6in (15cm) high.
£30–35 / €45–50
$55–65 ⊞ HUX

► **A Lambert & Butler Log Cabin tobacco tin,** 1920–30, 4¾in (12cm) wide.
£15–20 / €22–29
$29–38 ⊞ RTT

A Callard & Bowser's Peter Pandies tin, with a paper label, 1920s, 5½in (14cm) wide.
£25–30 / €40–45
$50–55 ⊞ c20th

A Brompton Hospital Lozenges tin, 1920s, 3¾in (9.5cm) wide.
£15–20 / €22–29
$29–38 ⊞ HUX

A Sto-Mike Coffee tin, c1930, 5in (12.5cm) high.
£25–30 / €40–45
$50–55 ⊞ HUX

African American collectables

A number of tins in this section fall into the category of African American collectables. In the first half of the 20th century, African American imagery was used by what were predominantly white manufacturers in the USA and Europe to advertise their products. Typically, African Americans are shown in stereotypical roles and occupations: servants, musicians, nursemaids or plantation workers. Particularly in the USA, African American collectables can fetch high prices. Many collectors are African American; celebrity enthusiasts include Oprah Winfrey and Spike Lee, both of whom have formed collections of material documenting America's racist past. The objects illustrated pre-date WWII; after the war, the Civil Rights Movement and growing political awareness made such imagery unacceptable. People were embarrassed to own items which caricatured the African American race and there was little demand for vintage material, much of which was simply discarded. By the late 1970s, however, attitudes had shifted and memorabilia was becoming sought after. The 1980s saw the publication of several price guides on the subject, and today it is an established area of the collectors' market.

A Lyle's Golden Syrup free sample tin, 1930, 2in (5cm) high.
£35–40 / €50–60
$65–75 ⊞ HUX

A Huntley & Palmer's biscuit tin, in the form of a farmhouse and farmyard, c1931, 12in (30.5cm) wide.
£270–300 / €390–440
$520–580 ⊞ MURR

A William Crawford & Sons Fairy House Biscuit and Money Box, by Mabel Lucie Attwell, produced for Christmas 1934, 8in (20.5cm) high.
£75–85 / €110–125
$145–165 ✗ SWO

A Dresdner cigarette paper tin, German, 1935, 3in (7.5cm) wide.
£30–35 / €45–50
$55–65 ⊞ HUX

A McVitie & Price Sing-a-Song-of-Sixpence tin, possibly by Randolph Caldecote, c1937, 6in (15cm) high.
£60–70 / €85–100
$115–135 ⊞ HUX

A Zut sweet tin, decorated with tennis players, French, 1930s, 3in (7.5cm) diam.
£25–30 / €40–45
$50–55 ⊞ HUX

Four Huntley & Palmer's miniature biscuit tins, 1930s, 2¼in (5.5cm) high.
£40–45 / €60–70
$75–85 each ⊞ HUX
Huntley & Palmer's produced a variety of small tins. Sample tins, containing three or four biscuits, were given away free to boost sales at the launch of a new product. From 1922, the company also retailed miniature tins filled with miniature biscuits – tiny replicas of the large shop display tins, complete with the company's garter and buckle motif – which were marketed as gifts and stocking fillers.

A Genatosan Sanatogen tin, c1940, 5½in (14cm) high.
£15–20 / €22–29
$29–38 ⊞ HUX

A Thorne's Assorted Toffee tin, 1930s, 6½in (16.5cm) wide.
£20–25 / €30–35
$40–50 ⊞ RTT

Two Blitz Nadeln gramophone needle tins, German, 1930s, 2in (5cm) wide.
£50–60 / €75–85
$100–115 each ⊞ HUX

▶ A Lébène polish tin, French, 1930s, 1½in (4cm) diam.
£20–25 / €30–35
$40–50 ⊞ HUX

◄ A Cadette Baby Talc tin, in the form of a soldier, American, 1940s, 7½in (19cm) high.
£115–130 / €170–190
$220–250 ⊞ HUX

A set of three biscuit tins, in the form of a fairground steamroller with a menagerie, a trailer and a caravan, 1950, 24in (61cm) long.
£850–950 / €1,250–1,400
$1,650–1,800 ⊞ HUX
Tins in the form of toys tend to command the highest prices. Impressive results achieved at auction in Philadelphia, USA include £10,900 / €15,800 / $20,900 for a Gray Dunn's racing car biscuit tin and £5,400 / €7,800 / $10,400 for a Crawford's Sedan biscuit tin.

A Brasso sample tin, 1950, 2in (5cm) high.
£15–20 / €22–29
$29–38 ⊞ HUX

A Welfare Foods Service National Dried Milk tin, 1950s, 7in (18cm) high.
£5–10 / €9–15
$12–19 ⊞ DaM

A Bird's Custard sample tin, 1950s, 2in (5cm) high.
£15–20 / €22–29
$29–38 ⊞ HUX

A Cote d'Or Chocolat tin, in the form of a bucket, 1950s, 5½in (14cm) high.
£25–30 / €40–45
$50–55 ⊞ HUX

A Bahlsen Express Biscuits sample tin, German, 1950s, 1½in (4cm) high.
£15–20 / €22–29
$29–38 ⊞ HUX

A Huntley & Palmer's Big-Ears picnic biscuit tin, 1965, 5in (12.5cm) diam.
£20–25 / €30–35
$40–50 ⊞ HUX

A Negro Spiritual Cachou tin, French, 1960s, 1¾in (4.5cm) diam.
£15–20 / €22–29
$29–38 ⊞ HUX

A Mackintosh's Quality Street 50th Anniversary tin, c1986, 5in (12.5cm) diam.
£1–5 / €2–7
$3–9 ⊞ DaM

Aeronautica

In this year's Aeronautica section, we feature flying clothing, particularly focusing on WWII. 'Aviation collectables and uniforms are attracting increasing interest around the world,' says dealer Geoff Pringle, from Oldnautibits. According to Geoff, some buyers are dedicated collectors, purchasing uniforms to decorate a dummy; others buy to wear themselves either because they are part of re-enactment groups or because they have a vintage plane or related vehicle, and want the matching kit. 'This makes condition and quality very important,' notes Geoff. 'A WWII re-enactment enthusiast would rather pay more for period goggles in good, useable condition than less for a pair in which the face padding has fallen apart.'

Practicality was crucial when it came to designing flying clothing. Air crews faced two major hazards: cold and lack of oxygen. 'RAF oxygen masks came complete with a microphone but the Germans and Americans had separate throat-sensor microphones that were far easier to use,' says Geoff. Bomber crews wore fleece-lined leather jackets and trousers over their uniforms and flying jackets are very sought after by collectors today. 'In the USA, after the war, decommissioned uniforms were degraded by the armed forces. A flight jacket might have its zip cut out so that in theory it couldn't be used again, but people simply put in another one. 'British uniforms were the property of the state and were exchanged at the end of service for a demob suit. In practice however,

many people hung on to their uniforms and material still turns up. 'I went to a house the other day where the owners had found a Battle of Britain flying suit being used as loft insulation!' says Geoff. Some garments are rarer than others. 'RAF trousers were made from thick serge, they were warm and practical and a lot of people bought them from army surplus stores after the war. They wore them out then threw them out, so trousers can be harder to find and more valuable than a battledress top. In order to help identify clothing, look for a mark or label,' advises Geoff. 'RAF clothing was marked with the store's reference code 22C followed by a serial number. There are good reference books that can help you to date objects such as goggles and relevant museums can also be very helpful.'

Certain areas are particularly sought after in the current market such as pilot log books, Battle of Britain material and items related to escape, including silk maps that could be worn as scarves and compasses concealed inside buttons. Shown on page 29 is a pair of WWII RAF escape boots. 'They came with a small knife concealed in the back and the idea was that if you landed in enemy territory you cut off the soft upper part of the boot so that it would look like you were wearing ordinary, civilian shoes.' Historical interest is all-important to collectors – the better the provenance and the fact that an object is linked with a particular raid or major event, the more desirable it will be.

A **Coupe de Berlin poster,** by Gamy, a colour lithograph, French, 1909, 13½ x 29in (34.5 x 73.5cm).
£420–500 / €610–730
$810–960 ✈ DW

▶ **Four sweet tins,** each decorated with aircraft, c1910, 2½in (6.5cm) wide.
£65–75 / €95–105
$125–145 each ⊞ HUX

◀ **A Eugen Riemer tin,** decorated with an airship, c1910, 3in (7.5cm) wide.
£180–200
€260–290
$340–380
⊞ HUX

A silver cigarette box, in the form of an aeroplane, with embossed decoration, the wings with compartments for cigarettes, the tailplane with a matchstriker and compartment for matches, German, c1912, 8½in (21.5cm) wide.
£2,000–2,250 / €2,900–3,250 $3,850–4,300 ⊞ AU
Pre-war silver aviation items are rare.

A London Aerodrome First Annual Dinner menu and souvenir, the cover with a mounted colour illustration, ink inscription to autograph sheet, 26 pages, dated 1914, 4°.
£200–240 / €290–350 $380–450 ➤ DW

A Brighton-Shoreham Aerodrome Second Summer Meeting programme, 16 pages, slight damage, 1914, 8°.
£210–250 / €300–360 $400–480 ➤ DW

A Vickers Oleo aluminium and wood hand pump, 1916, 26in (66cm) long.
£130–145 €190–210 $250–280 ⊞ OLD

◄ **A leather civilian pattern flying helmet,** with Gosport tubes, c1930.
£110–125 €160–180 $210–240 ⊞ OLD

◄ **A pair of RAF Mark II glass and leather flying goggles,** c1930, 6in (15cm) wide.
£200–230 €290–330 $380–430 ⊞ OLD

► **An RAF B-type leather flying helmet,** c1930.
£290–330 €420–480 $560–630 ⊞ OLD

◄ **A pair of RAF leather flying gauntlets,** c1933, 14in (35.5cm) long.
£130–145 €190–210 $250–280 ⊞ OLD

An RAF D-Type cloth oxygen mask, with a Type E carbon microphone, wiring loom and receivers, c1935.
**£900–1,000 / €1,300–1,450
$1,700–1,900 ⊞ OLD**

A pair of RAF Mark III Perspex and leather goggles, c1935, 8in (20.5cm) wide.
**£200–230 / €290–330
$380–430 ⊞ OLD**

A pair of RAF Mark VIII leather flying goggles, with spare lenses, c1933, 7in (18cm) wide, with original box.
**£130–145 / €190–210
$250–280 ⊞ OLD**

A laminated mahogany and brass Gypsy Minor propellor, 1939, 71in (180.5cm) long.
**£500–550 / €720–800
$950–1,050 ⊞ OLD**

An Air Ministry navigator's stopwatch, named to Sergeant Lupton, 1938, 2in (5cm) diam, together with a photograph and Notification of Death.
**£220–250 / €320–360
$420–480 ⊞ OLD**

A wood and metal model of a de Haviland Gipsy Moth, G-ABJT, 1/48th scale, with a rotating propeller, in an inscribed and glazed display case.
**£160–190 / €230–270
$300–360 ⋌ DW**

A pair of RAF 1939 pattern canvas and leather flying boots, lined with fleece, c1939.
**£310–350 / €450–510
$600–670 ⊞ OLD**

A Poole Pottery Port of Poole Empire Airways charger, designed by Arthur Bradbury and painted by Margaret Holder, impressed mark, painted inscription, 1940, 14½in (37cm) diam.
**£2,500–3,000 / €3,650–4,350
$4,800–5,800 ⋌ WW**
This is a very rare charger and one of only about six examples. It depicts the Empire flying boat that provided a scheduled service from Poole harbour between 1939 and 1948.

A brass and Perspex model of a Hawker Typhoon aeroplane, modelled from aircraft materials, c1940, 7in (18cm) wide.
**£75–85 / €110–125
$145–165 ⊞ GBM**

An RAF leather Irvin flying jacket, lined with sheepskin, c1940.
**£450–500 / €650–730
$860–960 ⊞ OLD**

The Aeroplane magazine, September 1941, 11 x 8in (28 x 20.5cm).
£1–5 / €2–7
$3–9 ⊞ HOM

An RAF cloth Pathfinders Service dress tunic, named to Sergeant Williams, c1942.
£130–145 / €190–210
$250–280 ⊞ OLD

A Luftwaffe plastic AK39 wrist compass, with a leather strap, c1942, 2in (5cm) diam.
£110–125 / €160–180
$210–240 ⊞ OLD

 ◀ An RAF brass 06A hand bearing compass, c1942.
£65–75
€95–105
$125–145
⊞ OLD

A pair of RAF leather and suede escape boots, with fleece lining, concealed knife missing, c1942.
£200–220 / €290–320
$380–420 ⊞ OLD

A pair of US AAF gunners goggles, with Polaroid lenses and tracer shield, c1942, 6in (15cm) wide, c1942.
£85–95 / €125–140
$165–185 ⊞ OLD

An RAAF cotton summer flying suit, c1942.
£130–145 / €190–210
$250–280 ⊞ OLD

◀ A pair of US AAF A-9 leather and sheepskin flying gauntlets, 1942.
£130–145 / €190–210
$250–280 ⊞ OLD

A pair of RAF Mark VII glass and metal flying goggles, with a fabric strap, c1942, 7in (18cm) wide.
£110–125 / €160–180
$210–240 ⊞ OLD

An RAF G-Type oxygen mask and tube, with a Type 48 microphone, c1943, 5in (12.5cm) diam.
£200–220 / €290–320
$380–420 ⊞ OLD

A US AAF officer's tunic and 'pinks', with original badges, c1943.
£200–220 / €290–320
$380–420 ⊞ OLD

A pair of Luftwaffe flying goggles, with spare lenses and original tin, c1943, 8in (20.5cm) wide.
£175–195 / €250–280
$340–380 ⊞ OLD

An aircraft clock, 1943, 3in (7.5cm) wide.
£100–120 / €145–175
$190–220 ⊞ COB

A model of a P51 fighter aeroplane, modelled from aircraft material, mounted on a propeller base, 1943.
£65–75 / €95–105
$125–145 ⊞ OLD

◄ **An anti-aircraft scramble bell,** by Gillett & Johnson, London, with a later clapper, stamped 'AATW', Air Ministry stamp dated 1943, 10½in (26.5cm) high.
£50–60 / €75–85
$100–115 ⚒ DW

A Super Marine Spitfire propeller blade, c1944, 60in (152.5cm) long.
£310–350 / €450–510
$600–670 ⊞ OLD

▶ **A Fleet Air Arm C-type leather flying helmet,** with wiring and loom, 1944.
£200–220 / €290–320
$380–420 ⊞ OLD

A pair of RAF D-type leather flying gauntlets, 1944, 14in (35.5cm) long.
£85–95 / €125–140
$165–185 ⊞ OLD
In order to avoid pilfering in WWII, separate factories were given the commission to produce either right-hand or left-hand gloves, which would only be brought together as a pair when the uniform was ready to be distributed.

A chromed-brass model of a P-38 Lightning aeroplane, the base formed as a map of Australia, 1947, 6in (15cm) wide.
£80–90 / €115–130
$155–175 ⊞ OLD

A US AAF cloth air crew cap, c1948.
£45–50 / €65–75
$85–95 ⊞ OLD

◄ **An Air Ministry metal oxygen regulator,** c1949, 9in (23cm) wide.
£25–30 / €40–45
$50–55 ⊞ OLD

A **BOAC biscuit tin,** 1950s, 7in (18cm) wide.
£10–15 / €15–22
$19–28 ⊞ HeA

A **BOAC magazine advertisement,** 1953, 10 x 8in (25.5 x 20.5cm).
£6–10 / €9–15
$12–19 ⊞ RTT

Four books of BOAC matches, unused, c1958, 1½in (4cm) wide.
£6–10 / €9–15
$12–19 ⊞ RTT

An **aluminium Sea Princess propeller blade,** c1960, 52in (132cm) long.
£85–95 / €125–140
$165–185 ⊞ OLD

◄ **A chrome table lighter,** in the form of an aeroplane, c1960, 5in (12.5cm) wide.
£75–85 / €110–125
$145–165 ⊞ TOP

► **A chrome ashtray,** surmounted by a model of an aeroplane, 1960s, 8in (20.5cm) high.
£50–60 / €75–85
$100–115 ⊞ COB

► **A Concorde nylon bag strap,** 1990s, 12in (30.5cm), boxed.
£10–15 / €15–22
$19–28 ⊞ COB

A **plastic model of a Lufthansa DC10 aircraft,** 1980, 29in (73.5cm) long.
£65–75 / €95–105
$125–145 ⊞ GTM

► **A Sokol KV2 leather and nylon cosmonaut's space suit glove,** 1980s.
£270–300 / €390–440
$520–580 ⊞ IQ

Amusement & Slot Machines

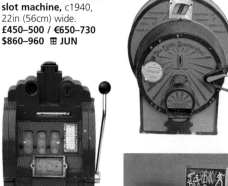

▶ **A Little Stockbroker slot machine,** c1940, 22in (56cm) wide.
£450–500 / €650–730
$860–960 ⊞ JUN

A New Polyphon Supply Co penny slot machine, 'Winter's Sport, The Running Hare', in an oak case, c1910, 21in (53.5cm) high.
£360–430 / €520–620
$690–830 ↗ GH

▶ **A penny-play one-armed bandit,** c1930, 28in (71cm) high.
£400–450 / €580–650
$770–860 ⊞ JUN

▶ **A Williams Perky pinball machine,** with painted glass scoreboard, 1950s, 52in (132cm) long.
£115–135 / €165–195
$220–260 ↗ JAA

A Whales Redcar Have A Go Allwin machine, c1950, 32in (81.5cm) high.
£400–450 / €580–650
$770–860 ⊞ JUN

A Parkers Carousel All Winners machine, c1960, 33in (84cm) high.
£450–500 / €650–730
$860–960 ⊞ JUN

A Dean Brothers metal and chrome cigarette dispenser, 1950s, 13½in (34.5cm) wide.
£70–80 / €100–115
$135–155 ↗ BBR

▶ **A Williams Smarty pinball machine,** American, 1962, 53in (134.5cm) long.
£450–500 / €650–730
$860–960 ⊞ Pin

◄ A Sega Lucky Devil one-armed bandit, 1960s, 32in (81.5cm) high.
£720–800 / €1,000–1,150 $1,300–1,450 ⊞ Pin

◄ A Golden Star slot machine, 1960s, 28in (71cm) high.
£860–880 / €900–1,000 $1,200–1,350 ⊞ AME

A Jubilee Riviera one-armed bandit, 1970, 30in (76cm) wide.
£720–800 / €1,000–1,150 $1,300–1,450 ⊞ Pin

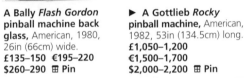

A Bally Flash Gordon pinball machine back glass, American, 1980, 26in (66cm) wide.
£135–150 €195–220 $260–290 ⊞ Pin

► A Gottlieb Rocky pinball machine, American, 1982, 53in (134.5cm) long.
£1,050–1,200 €1,500–1,700 $2,000–2,200 ⊞ Pin

A Data East Playboy 35th Anniversary pinball machine, 1989, 53in (134.5cm) long.
£1,150–1,300 €1,650–1,900 $2,200–2,500 ⊞ Pin

◄ A Data East
*Teenage Mutant
Ninja Turtles*
pinball machine
back glass,
American, 1991,
26in (66cm) wide.
£135–150
€195–220
$260–290 ⊞ Pin

A Bally *Dr Who* pinball
machine, American,
1992, 53in (135cm) long.
£900–1,000
€1,300–1,450
$1,600–1,800 ⊞ Pin

A Data East *Star Wars*
pinball machine, American,
1992, 53in (134.5cm) long.
£1,000–1,200
€1,450–1,700
$1,950–2,300 ⊞ Pin

► A Data East *Star Trek*
25th Anniversary
pinball machine,
American, 1990s,
53in (135cm) long.
£1,200–1,400
€1,750–2,050
$2,300–2,700 ⊞ Pin

A Williams F-14 Tomcat
pinball machine, 1990s,
52in (132cm) long.
£1,000–1,200
€1,450–1,700
$1,950–2,300 ⊞ AME

An Electrocoin
Automatics Century 21
slot machine, 1990s,
32in (81.5cm) high.
£350–400 / €500–580
$670–770 ⊞ Pin

A Bally Creature from the Black
Lagoon pinball machine, American,
1992, 53in (134.5cm) long.
£900–1,000 / €1,300–1,450
$1,600–1,800 ⊞ Pin

A Sega Mary Shelley's
Frankenstein pinball machine,
1994, 53in (134.5cm) long.
£810–900 / €1,150–1,300
$1,550–1,750 ⊞ Pin

A Gottlieb *Waterworld* pinball
machine, American, 1995,
53in (134.5cm) long.
£900–1,000 / €1,300–1,450
$1,600–1,800 ⊞ Pin

Architectural Antiques

A cast-iron ring handle, 18thC, 7in (18cm) diam.
£490–550 / €710–800
$940–1,050 ⊞ DRU

A Victorian terracotta ridge tile, decorated with a gargoyle, 16in (40.5cm) high.
£60–70 / €85–100
$115–135 ⊞ DEB

◄ A metal servant's bell, 19thC, 9in (23cm) high.
£250–280 / €360–410
$480–540 ⊞ DRU

◄ A pair of polished steel hinges, 19thC, 5in (12.5cm) long.
£80–90 / €115–130
$150–175 each ⊞ DRU

A pair of Victorian terracotta chimney pots, 14in (35.5cm) high.
£110–125 / €160–180
$210–240 ⊞ DEB

◄ A cast-iron grille, cast with a portrait silhouette of Queen Victoria, c1880, 25in (63.5cm) high.
£20–25 / €30–35
$40–50 ⊞ DEB

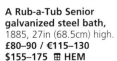

A Rub-a-Tub Senior galvanized steel bath, 1885, 27in (68.5cm) high.
£80–90 / €115–130
$155–175 ⊞ HEM

A pair of Art Nouveau brass door handles, 15in (38cm) long.
£360–400 / €520–580
$690–770 ⊞ SAT

A pair of terracotta corbels, late 19thC, 11in (28cm) high.
£85–95 / €125–140
$165–185 ⊞ DEB

A brass drop handle, c1900, 3½in (9cm) high.
£20–25 / €30–35
$40–50 ⊞ Penn

▶ **A copper exterior electric bell push,** 1904, 4in (10cm) square.
£110–125 / €160–180
$210–240 ⊞ BS

A carved stone corbel, late 19thC, 11in (28cm) high.
£110–125 / €160–180
$210–240 ⊞ DEB

A pair of cast-iron window grilles, French, c1920, 36in (91.5cm) high.
£175–195 / €250–280
$330–370 ⊞ DEB

An Ashwell's System brass vacant/ engaged lavatory door bolt, 1920s, 4in (10cm) long.
£135–155 / €195–220
$260–300 ⊞ BS

▶ **A George VI cast-iron post box,** 24in (61cm) high.
£250–280
€360–410
$480–540 ⊞ JUN

A brass door knob, c1900, 3½in (9cm) high.
£20–25 / €30–35
$40–50 ⊞ Penn
Single door knobs are less valuable than pairs as it is unlikely that a matching knob for the other side of the door will be found.

A pair of brass hinges, c1910, 8in (20.5cm) long.
£45–50 / €65–75
$85–95 ⊞ HO

A George VI cast-iron letter box, 22in (56cm) high.
£400–450 / €580–650
$770–860 ⊞ JUN
The first British post box was installed on Guernsey in 1852 by post office official and subsequent novelist Anthony Trollope. Since that time, 365 variations have been produced. Traditionally made from cast iron, boxes bear the insignia of the reigning monarch at the time of their manufacture, although those installed during the brief reign of King Edward VIII had doors bearing his insignia replaced with that of King George VI.

Art Deco

A silver-plated figure of an archer, by Pierre le Faguays, c1930, 17in (43cm) high.
£400–480 / €580–700 $770–920 ✗ AH

A glass vase, with enamel floral decoration, signed, Continental, c1930, 8in (20.5cm) high.
£150–170 / €220–250 $290–330 ⊞ HEW

► **A metal figure of a dancer,** on a marble stand, signed 'Deremme', c1930, 8in (20.5cm) high.
£350–410 / €510–600 $670–790 ✗ BERN

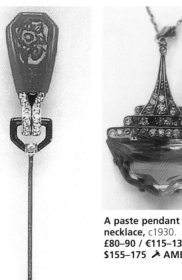

A paste pendant necklace, c1930.
£80–90 / €115–130 $155–175 ✗ AMB

◄ **An agate and enamel pin,** set with diamonds, c1930, 2¾in (7cm) long.
£480–570 / €700–830 $920–1,100 ✗ LAY

A fish service, with bone handles, in original case, 1930, 8in (20.5cm) wide.
£50–60 / €76–85 $100–115 ⊞ SAT

◄ **A silver toast rack,** by Deakin & Francis, Birmingham 1932, 5in (12.5cm) long.
£70–80 €100–115 $135–155 ⊞ WAC

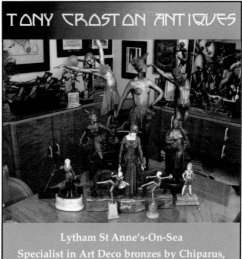

A Shelley Queen Anne tea service, comprising 25 pieces, c1935.
£130–155 / €190–220
$250–300 ⚹ GAK

A chrome timepiece, in the form of a tennis racket, 1930s, 8¾in (22cm) long.
£500–600 / €730–870
$960–1,150 ⚹ SWO

A set of four liqueur glasses, 1930s, 2½in (6.5cm) high.
£240–270 / €350–390
$460–520 ⊞ JAS

▶ **A metal and Bakelite desk lamp,** by Christian Dell for Kaiser & Co, German, 1930s, 17¾in (45cm) high.
£240–290
€350–420
$470–560 ⚹ SK

◀ **A chrome tea service,** comprising teapot and six cups and saucers, 1940s, teapot 7in (18cm) high.
£85–95 / €125–140
$165–185 ⊞ SAT

Ceramics

◀ **A Royal Dux wall mask,** c1930, 9in (23cm) high.
£400–450 / €580–650
$770–860 ⊞ HEW

▶ **A Myott jug,** with hand-painted decoration, c1930, 9in (23cm) high.
£55–65 / €80–95
$105–125 ⊞ BET

◀ **A Gustavsberg Argenta ware vase,** by Wilhelm Kage, with silver-leaf decoration, marked, 1920s, 10¾in (27.5cm) high.
£250–300 / €370–440
$480–580 ⚹ G(L)

◀ **A Myott vase,** with hand-painted decoration, c1930, 7in (18cm) high.
£360–400 / €520–580
$690–770 ⊞ BEV

A Keramis vase, marked, Belgian, c1930, 8in (20.5cm) high.
£400–450 / €580–650
$770–860 ⊞ HEW

A Clews Chameleon ware vase, c1930, 10in (25.5cm) high.
£270–300 / €390–440
$520–580 ⊞ HEW

A Thomas Forester jug, with hand-painted and incised decoration, c1930, 8in (20.5cm) high.
£220–250 / €320–360
$420–480 ⊞ HEW

A Gray's Pottery cream jug, with hand-painted decoration, c1930, 5in (12.5cm) high.
£100–115 / €145–165
$190–220 ⊞ BEV

A tea service, by Margarete Heymann, comprising 16 pieces, slight damage, marked, German, c1930, teapot 5¼in (13.5cm) high.
£460–550 / €650–780
$880–1,050 ➹ SK

A Corona ware bowl, by Molly Hancock, decorated with Cremorne pattern, c1930, 8in (20.5cm) diam.
£270–300 / €390–440
$420–480 ⊞ HEW

A tea service, by Raoul Lachenal, comprising 15 pieces, painted marks, French, c1930, teapot 6½in (16.5cm) high.
£190–220 / €260–310
$350–420 ➹ SK

▶ **A Radford jug,** decorated with Anemone pattern, 1930s, 5in (12.5cm) high.
£85–95 / €125–140
$165–185 ⊞ HOM

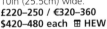

Two Sadler teapots, modelled as racing cars, with silver lustre, 1930s, 10in (25.5cm) wide.
£220–250 / €320–360
$420–480 each ⊞ HEW

> **For further information on**
> Ceramics see pages 81–142

A Weatherby Falcon ware jug, with hand-painted decoration, 1930s–40s, 7in (18cm) high.
£35–40 / €50–60
$65–75 ⊞ HO

Art Nouveau

A silver buckle, marked, c1895, 6in (15cm) wide.
£140–155 / €200–220
$270–300 ⊞ TDG

A silver tea service, by Lazarus Posen, comprising four pieces and a matching tray, chased with floral decoration, German, Frankfurt, early 20thC, tray 19½in (49.5cm) wide.
£460–550 / €650–780
$880–1,050 ⚒ Mal(O)

A silver rose bowl, by Elkington & Co, embossed with tendrils, Sheffield 1907, 6¼in (16cm) high.
£360–420 / €520–610
$690–810 ⚒ RTo

An Emile Gallé glass vase, decorated with acid-etched fuschias, raised signature, French, Nancy, 1908–14, 4½in (11.5cm) high.
£340–410 / €500–600
$650–780 ⚒ DORO

A Liberty-style pewter tankard, with stylized decoration, early 20thC, 9½in (24cm) high.
£90–105 / €130–150
$170–200 ⚒ BWL

A Royal Vienna ceramic vase, by Reishner, Stellmacher & Kessel, with enamelled floral decoration, marked, c1900, 7in (18cm) high.
£120–140 / €175–200
$230–270 ⚒ Hal

◀ **An Emile Gallé glass vase,**

A pewter vase, probably by Archibald Knox for Liberty & Co, with three handles, No. 0226, early 20thC, 6¼in (16cm) high.
£130–155 / €190–220
$250–300 ⚒ MAR

A Lötz iridescent glass vase, Austrian, 1900, 4in (10cm) high.
£270–300 / €390–440
$520–580 ⊞ MiW

◀ **A pair of Thomas Forester ceramic vases,** decorated with peacocks, c1910, 13in (33cm) high.
£630–700 / €900–1,000
$1,200–1,350 ⊞ HEW

A pair of WMF candelabra, German, c1910, 7in (18cm) high.
£175–195 / €250–280
$330–370 ⊞ WAC

Arts & Crafts

A silver and amethyst brooch, by Murrle Bennett, 1896–1916.
£400–480 / €580–700
$770–920 ⚒ TEN

A Newlyn copper inkstand, dated 1897, 8in (20.5cm) diam.
£540–600 / €780–870
$1,000–1,150 ⊞ WAC

An Arts & Crafts oxidized copper lantern, with a vaseline and cranberry glass shade, 11in (28cm) high.
£580–650 / €840–940
$1,100–1,250 ⊞ JeH

► **A copper jug,** c1900, 11in (28cm) high.
£100–110 / €145–160
$190–210 ⊞ HOM

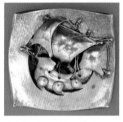

A Liberty & Co silver brooch, depicting a galleon in full sail, Birmingham 1903, 2¼in (5.5cm) square.
£420–500 / €610–730
$810–960 ⚒ G(L)

A Goberg metal chamberstick, c1905, 8in (20.5cm) high.
£145–165 / €210–240
$280–330 ⊞ TDG

A hammered-silver mustard pot, salt cellar and spoon, by A. E. Jones, Birmingham 1906, spoon Birmingham 1920, mustard pot 3in (7.5cm) high.
£450–500 / €650–730
$860–960 ⊞ DAD

◄ **A Liberty Tudric pewter biscuit barrel,** by Archibald Knox, c1910, 6in (15cm) high.
£500–550 / €720–800
$950–1,050 ⊞ WAC

◄ **A pair of polished steel and iron coal buckets,** c1910, 20in (51cm) high.
£145–165 / €210–240
$290–330 ⊞ JeH

► **A hammered silver vase,** by F. S., with three strap handles, London 1911, 9½oz.
£230–270 / €330–390
$440–420 ⚒ DMC

A steel coal bucket, with original liner, c1920, 19in (48.5cm) high.
£165–185 / €240–270
$320–360 ⊞ HOM

Art Pottery

An Aller Vale Pottery vase, decorated with an Isnik pattern, 1890s, 8in (20.5cm) high.
£50–60 / €75–85
$100–115 ⊞ DPC

A Burmantofts faïence jardinière, with tube-lined decoration, damaged, repaired, late 19thC, 46¾in (119cm) high.
£330–390 / €480–570
$630–750 ↗ MAR

A Burmantofts faïence vase, applied with a coiled dragon, restored, gilt impressed marks, late 19thC, 13½in (34.5cm) high.
£850–1,000 / €1,250–1,500
$1,600–1,900 ↗ WW

A Pilkington vase, early 18thC, 8in (20.5cm) high.
£150–170 / €220–250
$290–330 ⊞ JFME

A Pilkington's Royal Lancastrian vase, with two handles, impressed marks, 1924–29, 8in (20.5cm) high.
£60–70 / €85–100
$115–135 ↗ PFK

A pair of Brannam pottery candlesticks, slight damage, incised marks, dated 1901.
£300–360 / €440–520
$580–690 ↗ WL

For further information on **Ceramics** see pages 81–141

A Crown Dorset potpourri vase, decorated with windmills and a motto, c1910, 5in (12.5cm) high.
£35–40 / €50–60
$65–75 ⊞ DPC

▶ **A San Marti vase,** decorated with incised panels and stylized flowers, marked, French, c1930, 12¼in (31cm) high.
£220–260 / €290–340
$410–490 ↗ SK

▶ **A Ruskin Souffle vase,** marked, 1932, 9¼in (23.5cm) high.
£280–330 / €410–480
$540–640 ↗ L

Autographs

Queen Alexandra, a signed cabinet photograph by C. Merlin, dated 1893, 13 x 7in (33 x 18cm).
£520–580 / €750–840
$1,000–1,100 ⊞ CFSD

Roald Amundsen, a signed map of the southern oceans and Antarctica, 1912, 13¾ x 10¼in (35 x 26cm).
£820–980 / €1,200–1,400
$1,600–1,900 ⋗ BBA

LOCATE THE SOURCE
The source of each illustration in Miller's can be found by checking the code letters below each caption with the Key to Illustrations, pages 443–451.

◄ **Robert Baden-Powell,** a signed letter and photograph and an envelope, 1901, framed and glazed, 11¾ x 8in (30 x 20.5cm).
£150–180 / €220–260
$290–350 ⋗ SWO

Stanley Baldwin, a signed letter on 10 Downing Street headed paper, 1928, 9 x 7in (23 x 18cm).
£75–85 / €110–125
$145–165 ⊞ AEL

Ethel Barrymore, a signed cabinet photograph, by Sarony, New York, 1902, 6 x 4in (15 x 10cm).
£150–180 / €220–260
$290–350 ⋗ VS

HRH Prince Charles, Prince of Wales, a signed presentation photograph, 1984, mounted and framed, 5 x 4in (12.5 x 10cm).
£1,100–1,250
€1,600–1,800
$2,100–2,400 ⊞ CFSD

Sir Winston Churchill, a signed certificate of Naturalization to an Alien, 1911.
£250–300 / €360–430
$480–580 ⋗ LAY

◄ **Sir Winston Churchill,** a signed photograph, 1941, 5½ x 6¾in (14 x 17cm).
£1,900–2,250 / €2,750–3,250
$3,650–4,300 ⋗ S
This photograph was evidently taken on board the *Duke of York* during Churchill's Atlantic crossing in December 1941. It depicts Churchill with four other chief officials, including General Sir John Greer Dill, Admiral Sir Dudley Pound, Vice Air Chief Marshal Sir Wilfred Freeman and one other. They had embarked on 12 December, five days after the Japanese attack on Pearl Harbor. As a guest of President Roosevelt at the White House, Churchill discussed with the President the strategic implications of America's entry into the war, both then signed the declaration leading to the creation of the United Nations Organization and on 26 December, Churchill successfully addressed both Houses of Congress.

Warwick Davis, a signed photograph of Goblin Teller from *Harry Potter and the Philosopher's Stone*, 2000, 8 x 10in (20.5 x 25.5cm).
£35–40 / €50–60
$65–75 ⊞ RaA

Diana, Princess of Wales, a signed copy of *Majesty* magazine, Vol No. 9, 1989, 11¾ x 11½in (30 x 29cm), mounted, framed and glazed.
£3,000–3,500 / €4,350–5,100
$5,700–6,700 ⊞ FRa

Queen Elizabeth, the Queen Mother, a signed letter and a WWII Women's Land Army badge, 1948, 9 x 7in (23 x 18cm).
£60–70 / €85–100
$115–135 ⊞ HOM

Doris Day, a signed photograph, 1960s, 10 x 8in (25.5 x 20.5cm).
£35–40 / €50–60
$65–75 ⊞ SDP

HRH Prince Edward, Prince of Wales, a signed letter and envelope, 1918, 8 x 5in (20.5 x 12.5cm).
£850–950 / €1,250–1,400
$1,600–1,800 ⊞ AEL

Melvina Dean, a signed photograph, c1917, 10 x 8in (25.5 x 20.5cm).
£25–30 / €40–45
$50–55 ⊞ RaA
Melvina Dean was a survivor of the *Titanic* disaster.

Albert Einstein, a signed photograph, inscribed 'To Dr Albert Einstein, relativity and quanta are clues to a greater understanding of the laws which govern the universe', 1879–1955, 13 x 9½in (33 x 24cm), mounted framed and glazed.
£11,000–12,500 / €16,000–18,100
$21,100–24,000 ⊞ FRa
This is a rare and sought-after signature combined with a superb image of one of the of the greatest figures of the 20th century.

◄ **Ruth Ellis,** a signed letter, damaged, 1955, 8°.
£1,100–1,300 / €1,600–1,900
$2,100–2,500 ↗ DW
Ruth Ellis shot her lover David Blakely dead on 10 April 1955. She was arrested at the scene of the crime and taken straight to Holloway Prison. Her trial at the Old Bailey began on 20 June and a guilty verdict was returned two days later. She was executed on 13 July – the last woman to be hanged in England.

◄ **George VI,** a set of four Traveller's Ration Books, for His Majesty the King, Her Majesty the Queen, Her Royal Highness Princess Elizabeth and Her Royal Highness Princess Margaret, few coupons remaining, 1940, 5½ x 4½in (14 x 11.5cm).
£900–1,000
€1,300–1,450
$1,700–1,900 ✗ F&C

King George VI and Queen Elizabeth, a signed Christmas card, 1939–44, 6 x 7in (15 x 18cm).
£670–750 / €970–1,100
$1,300–1,450 ⊞ AEL

John F. Kennedy, a signed invitation to the concert in honour of President-Elect Kennedy and Vice President-Elect Johnson, 1961, 10 x 8in (25.5 x 20.5cm), framed and mounted with a photograph.
£3,000–3,500 / €4,350–5,100
$5,700–6,700 ⊞ FRa

Alfred Hitchcock, a photograph and signed self caricature, mid-20thC, photograph 11½ x 8in (29 x 20.5cm).
£670–750 / €970–1,100
$1,300–1,450 ⊞ TYA

James Earl Jones, a signed photograph of Darth Vader from *Star Wars,* 2001, 3¾ x 2½in (9.5 x 6.5cm).
£90–100 / €130–145
$170–190 ⊞ SSF

► **Madonna,** a signed photograph, 1994, 10 x 8in (25.5 x 20.5cm), framed and mounted.
£200–230 €290–330
$380–440 ⊞ IQ

Laurel & Hardy, a signed and inscribed photograph, 1930s, 4 x 6in (10 x 15cm).
£460–550 / €670–800
$880–1,050 ✗ VS

Pierre Auguste Renoir, a signed certificate of authenticity for one of his paintings, 1915, 11½ x 9in (29 x 23cm), mounted.
£6,700–7,500
€9,700–10,900
$12,900–14,400 ⊞ **FRa**

Louis Mounbatten, 1st Earl Mountbatten of Burma, a signed and inscribed photograph, slight damage, 1946, 12 x 8in (30.5 x 20.5cm).
£110–125 / €160–180
$210–240 ⊞ **CFSD**

Cecil John Rhodes, a signed letter, late 19thC, 8°.
£290–330 / €420–480
$560–630 ⊞ **CFSD**

Alistair Sim, an autograph, mounted with a photograph, c1950, 10 x 8in (25.5 x 20.5cm).
£75–85 / €110–125
$145–165 ⊞ **SDP**

Donald Sinden, a signed photograph, c1940, 5 x 4in (12.5 x 10cm).
£4–8 / €6–12
$8–15 ⊞ **S&D**

Peter Ustinov, a signed photograph, inscribed in German, 1955, 6 x 4in (15 x 10cm).
£35–40 / €50–60
$65–75 ⚒ **VS**

Queen Victoria, a signed letter, 1855, 8¾ x 7in (22 x 18cm), framed.
£100–120 / €145–175
$200–230 ⚒ **BR**

Queen Victoria, a signed leaf from *Our Life in the Highlands*, 1868.
£280–330 / €410–490
$540–650 ⚒ **CHTR**

◄ **Mary and Harold Wilson,** a signed Christmas card, c1970, 7 x 5in (18 x 12.5cm).
£55–65 / €80–95
$105–125
⊞ **AEL**

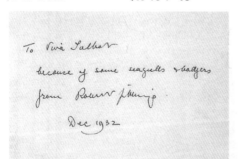

Hugh Walpole, a signed copy of *The Apple Trees: Four Reminiscences*, published by The Golden Cockerel Press, 1932, 8°, also signed and inscribed to Viva Talbot from the printer Robert Gibbings, No. 268 of 500.
£90–100 / €130–145
$170–190 ⚒ **BBA**

► **Orville Wright,** a signed and inscribed first edition of *The Wright Brothers*, by Fred Kelly, 1943, 9in (23cm) high.
£1,250–1,400
€1,800–2,050
$2,400–2,700
⊞ **IQ**

Automobilia

Over the past 20 years, the market for classic cars and automobilia has undergone considerable changes. 'It's currently at a fascinating point,' says Martyn Moore, editor-in-chief of *Classic Cars* magazine and the BBC *Roadshow* expert. 'The '80s boom, when people were speculating and paying record prices for cars at every level, was followed by the '90s bust, when the market crashed. Now prices are reaching higher levels again, but not for everything, only for good, prestigious cars. In the '80s a lot of cars sold that looked good on the surface but were disastrous underneath. Today, collectors are more informed and discerning; they are looking for quality, and tend to be buying for love rather than just investment. I think in many ways it's a much healthier market. It's much harder to sell a dodgy item just by papering over the cracks.'

One of the by-products of tumbling car prices in the '90s was a growth of interest in automobilia. 'When investing in cars became a bit scary, people began looking at smaller items,' explains Martyn. 'Automobilia used to be tacked on to car sales but suddenly we began to see specific auction houses and dealers devoted to automobilia and now we give it its own pages in our magazine.' Some collectors focus on specific subjects such as mascots, owner's club badges and material connected with racing (posters, programmes, badges etc) – currently a very sought-after subject. Advertising is another popular theme. 'Bibendum is a constant,' notes Martyn. 'Michelin have cashed in on the popularity of their famous figure, so you do get a lot of modern copies and replicas and you do have to be a bit careful. The older pieces make the best prices, for example artwork from the first part of the 20th century advertising bicycle tyres.'

Many collectors centre their automobilia collection around their classic car. 'I'm a case in point,' admits Martyn. 'First I bought a 1960s Jaguar, then I collected the original sales literature and handbook; I got the period Dinky car in the same colour, and I basically looked for any related material.' Equipping your vehicle in period style could range from buying an expensive auto part or mascot to an affordable piece of ephemera, such as a vintage tax disc from the year that your vehicle was first taxed. 'Classic cars are a passion,' concludes Martyn, 'and collecting automobilia is part of that.'

A Rolls Royce Spirit of Ecstasy chromium-plated car mascot, signed 'Charles Sykes', c1908, 5¼in (13.5cm) high, on an oak plinth.
£190–220 / €280–330
$360–420 ⚲ DW

▶ **A set of four graduated copper and steel petrol measures,** 1920s.
£165–185 / €240–270
$320–360 ⊞ JUN

A coloured lithograph print, by Gamy, entitled 'De Bazelaire dans le Tour de France', published by Mabileau & Co, Paris, 1912, 17¾ x 35½in (45 x 90cm).
£220–260 / €320–380
$420–500 ⚲ NSal

◀ **A poster,** 'Château de Saumur circuit automobile', by Léon Constan-Duval, printed by Imp Champenois, Paris, 1924, 41¼ x 29½in (105 x 75cm).
£250–300 / €360–430
$480–570 ⚲ VSP

A brass AA motorcycle badge, 1915, 5in (12.5cm) high.
£130–150 / €190–210
$250–280 ⊞ MURR
The first AA badge was introduced in 1906.

A silver-mounted and mahogany-veneered vanity case, by Keller, inlaid with marquetry, comprising powder compact, perfume flasks, mirror, notepad and clock, French, 1925–26, 9in (23cm) wide.
£1,650–1,850 / €2,400–2,700
$3,150–3,550 ⊞ AU

◄ **An Essex Terraplane Six radiator grille,** 1920s–30s, 34in (86.5cm) high.
£190–220 / €280–330
$370–440 ⋏ JAA
'The Power of a Plane – The Silence of a Glider' boasted a 1930s' advertisement for Terraplane cars. The name was chosen because as an aeroplane flew in the air and an aquaplane flew over water, so the Terraplane was designed to fly over land. The Essex brand was introduced in 1919 by the Hudson Motor Company (established 1909) based in Detroit, Michigan. Cars were aimed at the middle-class market and the name Essex was picked from an English map to give an image of tradition and quality.

A Price's Motor Lubricants enamel sign, 1930s, 36 x 42in (91.5 x 106.5cm).
£90–100 / €130–145
$170–190 ⋏ CGC

◄ **A Bugatti folder,** containing illustrated specification sheets for the Type 46 Sportsman saloon, Type 50 Supercharged Sports chassis, Type 51 Grand Prix model, Type 55 Standard De Luxe roadster and the Type 57 saloon, 1930s.
£210–250 / €300–360
$400–480 ⋏ DW

A chrome-plated presentation clock, barometer and thermometer, inscribed 'SS Jaguar from William Lyons', 1933, 6in (15cm) wide.
£1,150–1,300
€1,650–1,900
$2,200–2,500 ⊞ HOM

A carton of Britannia car bulbs, 1930s, 6¼in (16cm) wide.
£55–65 / €80–95
$105–125 ⋏ BBR

An aluminium Kewpie doll car mascot, 1930s, 5in (12.5cm) high.
£20–25 / €30–35
$40–45 ⊞ UD

► **A Jaguar SS chrome-plated brass car mascot,** by Desmo, c1937, 8in (20.5cm) wide.
£155–175
€220–250
$300–340 ⊞ ET

► **A London Transport Green Line Coach map,** 1938, 5¾ x 3in (14.5 x 7.5cm).
£2–6 / €3–9
$4–11 ⊞ RTT

A Wakefield Castrol Motor Oil enamel sign, 1940s, 14 x 16in (35.5 x 40.5cm).
£80–90 / €115–130
$155–175 ⚲ CGC

► **A Birch Bros Coaches timetable board,** with timetable for Luton, Hitchin and Bedford routes, 1930s, 12in (30.5cm) wide.
£85–95
€125–140
$165–185
⚲ WilP

► **A Johnston's map of the Yorkshire Dales,** c1950, 8 x 4in (20.5 x 10cm).
£1–5 / €2–7
$3–9 ⊞ JUN

Autocar magazine, June 1950, 11 x 9in (28 x 23cm).
£1–5 / €2–7
$3–9 ⊞ HOM

A Tokheim petrol pump, c1950s, 59in (150cm) high.
£90–100 / €130–145
$170–190 ⚲ JAA

► **A Mobiland Tractor Oil aluminium sign,** 1950s, 20in (51cm) wide.
£130–150 / €190–220
$250–280 ⊞ MURR

◄ **A Riley Brothers sweet tin,** 1950s, 6in (15cm) wide.
£6–10 / €9–15
$12–19 ⊞ JUN

A Super Shell glass petrol globe, 1950s, 18in (45.5cm) high.
£200–240 / €290–350
$380–450 ↗ BBR

A Mobil glass petrol globe, c1960, 17in (43cm) wide.
£220–250 / €320–360
$420–480 ⊞ JUN

A Redex dispenser, 1960s, 23in (58.5cm) high.
£105–120 / €150–175
$200–230 ⊞ JUN

A poster, advertising the 1000km-Rennen race at Nürburgring, 1967, 32¾ x 23¼in (83 x 59cm).
£50–60 / €75–85
$100–115 ↗ SAS

A poster, advertising the RAC European Grand Prix at Brand's Hatch, 1967, 30 x 20in (76 x 51cm).
£40–45 / €60–70
$75–85 ↗ SAS

◀ **A poster,** advertising the Woolmark British Grand Prix at Silverstone, 1971, 30 x 20½in (76 x 51cm).
£30–35 / €45–50
$55–65 ↗ SAS

▶ **A Centurion motorcycle helmet,** c1970.
£25–30
€40–45
$50–55 ⊞ JUN

Michelin

A Michelin Cycle Tyres poster, depicting the Bibendum figure riding a bicycle, 1920s, 40 x 29in (101.5 x 73.5cm), framed.
£760–850 / €1,100–1,250
$1,450–1,650 ⊞ JUN

A Michelin Bakelite ashtray, surmounted by the Bibendum figure, c1935, 5in (12.5cm) high.
£160–180 / €230–260
$310–350 ⊞ HEW

A Michelin moulded rubber Bibendum figure, c1950, 16in (40.5cm) high.
£180–200 / €260–290
$340–380 ⊞ JUN

A Michelin plastic Bibendum figure, c1970, 19in (48.5cm) high.
£55–65 / €80–95
$105–125 ⊞ FRD

Badges

A pilgrim's pewter badge, in the form of a heart, with pin, c1350, 1in (2.5cm) high.
£85–95 / €125–140
$165–185 ⊞ **MIL**
In the medieval period, pilgrimages were encouraged by the Church and were practised by every level of society. Traders at religious sites sold pilgrims' badges which were purchased as proof of visit and were believed to have spiritual powers and to bring good luck and protection to the wearer. Made of lead or pewter, many badges have survived and are often discovered by people using metal detectors.

A pilgrim's pewter badge, in the form of a beehive, with pin, 1325–50, 1in (2.5cm) high.
£85–95 / €125–140
$165–185 ⊞ **MIL**

A tin badge, 'Welcome Home Our Heroes', 1940s, 1½in (4cm) diam.
£15–20 / €22–29
$29–38 ⊞ **HUX**

A silver Tank Corps officer's badge, c1940, 2in (5cm) high.
£105–120 / €150–170
$200–230 ⊞ **ABCM**

A Sooty tin badge, c1960, 2in (5cm) diam.
£1–5 / €2–7
$3–9 ⊞ **UD**

Two ABC Cinemas Minors tin button badges, 1960–70, 1in (2.5cm) diam.
£1–5 / €2–7
$3–9 ⊞ **MRW**

A Butlin's enamelled badge, 1960s, 1½in (4cm) high.
£2–6 / €3–9
$4–11 ⊞ **TASV**

◀ **A badge,** depicting Andrew Logan, 1970s, 2¼in (5.5cm) diam.
£15–20 / €22–29
$29–38 ⊞ **LBe**
Andrew Logan is an artist and jewellery designer.

A Robertson's golly badge, McGolly, 1990s, 1in (2.5cm) high.
£35–40 / €50–60
$65–75 ⊞ **MRW**
The McGolly badge with a white sporran is rarer than the version with a black sporran.

Bicycles

A Raleigh poster, 'The All-Steel Bicycle', c1930, 20 x 14¾in (51 x 37.5cm).
£130–150 / €190–220
$250–290 ➹ VSP

A Bradbury Cycles enamel sign, slight damage, restored, 1890–1900, 18 x 12in (45.5 x 30.5cm).
£1,900–2,250 / €2,750–3,250
$3,650–4,300 ➹ BBR

A cast-iron bicycle stand, c1890, 20in (51cm) high.
£135–150 / €195–220
$260–290 ⊞ JUN

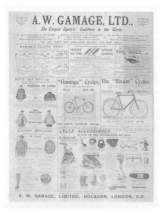

An A. W. Gamage poster, 'The Largest Cyclists' Outfitters in the World', c1900, 22½ x 17¾in (57 x 45cm), mounted, framed and glazed.
£45–50 / €65–75
$85–95 ➹ DW

A Premier brass acetylene bicycle lamp, c1910, 4in (10cm) high.
£25–30 / €40–45
$50–55 ⊞ JUN

J. A. Thundull, a *carte-de-visite* photograph of a man with a penny farthing bicycle, c1880, 4 x 2½in (10 x 6.5cm).
£80–90 / €115–130
$155–175 ➹ DW

◄ **A Fearnought Harmo bicycle bell,** 1930s, 3in (7.5cm) diam.
£15–20 / €22–29
$29–38 ⊞ JUN

► **A pair of leather cycling shoes,** 1950s.
£25–30 / €40–45
$50–55 ⊞ SPA

Books

The book section is divided into various categories including Arts & Design; Children's; Cookery; Modern First Editions; Natural History; Poetry; Travel & Topography. Within each section works are arranged in alphabetical order by author or, where this is not possible, by illustrator or publisher.

Generally speaking, first editions tend to be most prized by collectors. The opening pages of a book often have a 'first published' entry and will also list reprints and subsequent impressions. Reprints are usually of much less interest to collectors, as are Book Club editions, which are often worth very little.

It is not just the most famous books by celebrated authors that are desirable, as is illustrated in our Children's Books section. Philip Pullman became internationally renowned for the 'His Dark Materials' trilogy (published 1995–2000), a collection of which recently sold at auction for an impressive £3,900 / €5,700 / $7,500. Shown here is *Count Karlstein*, Pullman's first book for children, published in 1982 when the author was relatively unknown, and today highly collectable. Often it is the earliest books by well-known authors – printed in small runs before they and their works became famous – that are the most sought after. Sometimes, however, it can work the other way round. *William the Lawless* (1970) (see Children's Books) was the last in the magnificent William series begun by Richmal Crompton with *Just William* in 1922. Nearly five decades on and in the age of television, glam rock and space hoppers, William and his creator were both past their prime. The print run of this final book was small, making surviving examples very collectable.

Rarity is crucial to value, as is condition. Children's books often have a hard shelf life and, returning to William, there are certain volumes that are extremely difficult to find complete with dust jacket, the presence and condition of which is critical to the value of a book. Dust jackets only became commonly used in Britain and the USA from c1910. Early examples were extremely plain, gradually becoming more decorative as publishers recognized the potential of the jacket as a marketing tool. Dust jackets are prized both for their artwork and biographical information and can even have a value in their own right. Recently a dust jacket for *Casino Royale*, Ian Fleming's first and rarest James Bond novel, sold at auction, without its book, for £11,500 / €16,700 / $22,100. Jackets are sought after because if you reunite a book with its matching period cover its value can be hugely increased. Recent world record prices for James Bond first editions include £19,400 / €28,000 / $37,000 for *Dr No* and £22,700 / €33,000 / $44,000 for *From Russia with Love*, both presentation copies signed and inscribed by the author. (See Record Breakers, page 427.)

Art & Design

Ansel Adams, *Death Valley*, a book of photographs, published by 5 Associates, San Francisco, 1963, signed, 4°.
£110–130 / €160–190
$210–250 ⊁ JAA

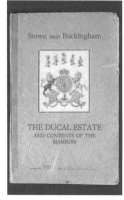

The Home Decorator and Color Guide, illustrated by Rockwell Kent, paint colour samples mounted on inside covers, slight damage, published by Sherwin-Williams Paints, Cleveland, 1939, 4°.
£85–95 / €125–140
$165–185 ⊁ BBA

◄ *The Ducal Estate and Contents of the Mansion*, auction catalogue of sale at Stowe House, 1921, 14¾ x 9¾in (37.5 x 25cm).
£150–180 / €220–260
$290–350 ⊁ DW

◄ **Roger Fry,** *Henri Matisse*, 1935, 4°, plates and illustrations, cloth-backed printed boards.
£65–75 / €95–105
$125–145 ✗ **BBA**

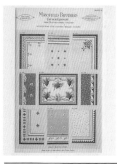

◄ **Mansfield Brothers,** *Tiles*, 28 lithographic plates of designs, c1905, 2°.
£290–340
€420–500
$560–650
✗ **DW**

Moore & Evans, a jewellery catalogue, c1920, 2°.
£45–50 / €65–75
$85–95 ✗ **JAA**

W. F. Stanley & Co, a catalogue of scientific instruments, c1920, 7in (18cm) high.
£45–50
€65–75
$85–95 ⊞ **HO**

Children's & Illustrated

Hans Christian Andersen, *Fairy Stories*, published by Strand Publishers, 1930s, 9 x 7in (23 x 18cm), a pop-up book.
£125–140 / €180–200
$240–270 ⊞ **NW**

► **Margaret Hamer Andrewes (Maggie Browne),** *The Book of Betty Barber*, illustrated by Arthur Rackham, published by Duckworth & Co, first edition, 1910, 4°.
£350–420 / €510–610
$670–810 ✗ **BBA**

Nicola Bayley (illustrator), *Puss in Boots*, published by Jonathan Cape, first edition, signed, 1976, 12 x 8in (30.5 x 20.5cm), pop-up book.
£65–75 / €95–105
$125–145 ⊞ **BIB**

Beacon reading cards, set of 30, 1930s, 8 x 5in (20.5 x 12.5cm).
£6–10 / €9–15
$12–19 ⊞ **RTT**

Charles H. Bennett and Robert B. Brough, *The Wonderful Drama of Punch and Judy and Their Little Dog Toby*, published by James Blackwood, c1860, 4°.
£370–440 / €540–640
$710–840 ✗ **BBA**

► **R. D. Blackmore,** *Lorna Doone*, illustrated by C. E. Brittan and C. E. Brock, published by Sampson Low, Marston & Co, 1920, 9 x 7in (23 x 18cm).
£45–50 / €65–75
$85–95 ⊞ **BAY**

Enid Blyton, *Go Ahead Secret Seven*, illustrated by Bruno Kay, published by Brockhampton Press, 1965, 7½ x 5in (19 x 12.5cm).
£10–15 / €15–22
$19–28 ⊞ **NW**

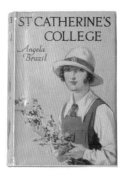

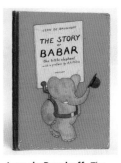

Jean de Brunhoff, *The Story of Babar,* published by Methuen & Co, first edition, 1934, 14 x 10½in (35.5 x 26.5cm).
£140–155 / €200–220
$270–300 ⊞ BIB

Michael Bond, *More About Paddington,* published by Collins, first edition, 1959, 8°.
£260–310 / €380–450
$500–600 ↗ BBA

Angela Brazil, *St Catherine's College,* illustrated by Frank Wiles, published by Blackie & Sons, first edition, 1929, 8 x 6in (20.5 x 15cm).
£125–140 / €175–200
$230–260 ⊞ NW

Elinor M. Brent-Dyer, *The Highland Twins at the Chalet School,* published by W. R. Chambers, first edition, 1942, 7½ x 5in (19 x 12.5cm).
£310–350 / €450–510
$600–670 ⊞ NW

◄ **Frances Hodgson Burnett,** *Little Lord Fauntleroy,* illustrated by Reginald B. Birch, published by Charles Scribner's Sons, New York, first edition, 1886, 4°.
£560–670 / €810–970
$1,100–1,300 ↗ BBA

▶ **Edgar Rice Burroughs,** *The Son of Tarzan,* published by Methuen & Co, 1939, 8 x 5in (20.5 x 12.5cm).
£35–40 / €50–60
$65–75 ⊞ BAY

Richmal Crompton, *William the Lawless*, illustrated by Henry Ford, published by George Newnes, 1970, 7 x 6in (18 x 15cm).
£840–1,000 / €1,200–1,450 $1,600–1,900 ⚒ CBP

Roald Dahl, *James and the Giant Peach*, illustrated by Quentin Blake, first illustrated edition, 1973, 9in (23cm) high.
£20–25 / €30–35 $40–45 ⊞ HOM

Dean & Sons, *Monster Book for Boys*, 1950s, 10¼ x 7¾in (26 x 19.5cm).
£6–10 / €9–15 $12–19 ⊞ RTT

Kathleen Hale, *Orlando the Marmalade Cat – A Camping Holiday*, published by Country Life, first edition, 1938, 2°.
£140–165 / €200–240 $270–320 ⚒ DW
Kathleen Hale used her own cat, Orlando, as the model for the central character in her books and based this particular story on her own camping holidays.

Walt Disney's Bambi, adapted from the novel by Felix Salten, published by Jonathan Cape, 1943, 7 x 5in (18 x 12.5cm).
£35–40 / €50–60 $65–75 ⊞ NW

Edmund Dulac (illustrator), *Sinbad the Sailor and Other Stories from the Arabian Nights*, published by Hodder & Stoughton, first edition, 1914, 11 x 8¾in (28 x 22cm).
£720–800 / €1,000–1,150 $1,400–1,550 ⊞ BI

Kenneth Grahame, *The Wind in the Willows*, frontispiece by Graham Robertson, published by Methuen & Co, first edition, 1908, 7½ x 5¼in (19 x 13.5cm).
£3,150–3,500 €4,550–5,100 $6,000–6,700 ⊞ BI

G. A. Henty, *By England's Aid or The Freeing of the Netherlands*, published by Blackie & Son, c1893, 8 x 5½in (20.5 x 14cm).
£65–75 / €95–105 $125–145 ⊞ BAY

Robin Jarvis, *The Dark Portal*, published by Purnell, 1989, first book of Deptford Mice trilogy, 8 x 5in (20.5 x 12.5cm).
£290–330 / €420–480 $560–630 ⊞ BIB

Captain W. E. Johns, *Biggles in Africa*, first edition, 1936, 8°.
£280–330 / €410–480 $540–640 ⚒ BBA

Captain W. E. Johns, *Biggles and the Poor Rich Boy*, illustrated by Leslie Stead, published by Brockhampton Press, first edition, 1961, 7½ x 5in (19 x 12.5cm).
£70–80 / €100–115 $135–155 ⊞ NW

Andrew Lang, *Violet Fairy Book*, illustrated by D. L. Gregory, published by Longman, sixth edition, 1966, 8½ x 6in (21.5 x 15cm).
£35–40 / €50–60 $65–75 ⊞ NW

Hugh Lofting, *Dr Dolittle and the Secret Lake,* published by Jonathan Cape, first edition, 1949, 8 x 6in (20.5 x 15cm).
£70–80 / €100–115
$135–155 ⊞ NW

Alexander MacDonald, *The Quest of the Black Opals,* illustrated by William Rainey, published by Blackie & Son, first edition, 1908, 7½ x 5½in (19 x 14cm).
£45–50 / €65–75
$85–95 ⊞ BAY

Kay Nielsen (illustrator), *East of the Sun and West of the Moon, Old Tales from the North,* first edition, 1914, 4°.
£520–620 / €750–900
$1,000–1,200 ↗ DW

Albert Bigelow Paine, *The Arkansaw Bear,* illustrated by Harvey Rowntree, first edition, 1911, 10in (25.5cm) high.
£165–185 / €240–270
$320–360 ⊞ HOM

David Pelham, *A Piece of Cake,* 1998, 6in (15cm) square, a pop-up book.
£15–20 / €22–29
$29–38 ⊞ LAS

Beatrix Potter, *The Tale of Benjamin Bunny,* published by F. Warne & Co, first edition, 1904, 16°.
£460–550 / €670–800
$880–1,050 ↗ DW

Philip Pullman, *Count Karlstein,* signed, first edition, 1982, 8°.
£700–840 / €1,000–1,200
$1,350–1,600 ↗ BBA

▶ **J. K. Rowling,** *Harry Potter and the Prisoner of Azkaban,* published by Bloomsbury, first edition, second issue, 1999, 8 x 5in (20.5 x 12.5cm).
£290–330 / €420–480
$560–630 ⊞ NW

M. Sterling & K. Neale, *My Picture and Easy Reading Book,* published by F. Warne & Co, revised edition, 1936, 9½in (24cm) high.
£55–65 / €80–95
$105–125 ⊞ HOM

Antoine de Saint-Exupéry, *The Little Prince,* first edition, 1944, 8°.
£470–560 / €680–810
$920–1,100 ↗ BBA

Dr Seuss, *Yertle the Turtle and Other Stories,* published by Random House, New York, 1958, 11 x 8in (28 x 20.5cm).
£270–300 / €390–440
$520–580 ⊞ NW

◀ **Robert Louis Stevenson,** *Kidnapped,* illustrated by Rowland Hilder, published by Oxford University Press, 1930, 9 x 7in (23 x 18cm).
£65–75 / €95–105
$125–145 ⊞ BAY

Louis Wain, *Days in Catland*, published by Raphael Tuck & Sons, Father Tuck's Panorama series, 1935, 10 x 11in (25.5 x 28cm).
£1,100–1,250 / €1,600–1,800
$2,100–2,400 ⊞ BIB

▶ **Alec Wilder,** *Lullabies and Night Songs*, illustrated by Maurice Sendak, published by The Bodley Head, first edition, 1969, 13 x 9¼in (33 x 23.5cm).
£45–50 / €65–75
$85–95 ⊞ BIB

Archibald Williams, *Petrol Peter*, illustrated by A. Wallis Mills, published by Methuen & Co, c1906, 10 x 9in (25.5 x 23cm).
£350–390 / €510–570
$670–750 ⊞ NW

Further reading
Miller's Collecting Modern Books, Miller's Publications, 2003

Cookery

Rev Charles David **Badham,** *Ancient and Modern Fish Tattle*, published by Parker, first edition, 1854, 8°.
£180–210 / €260–310
$340–400 ⚒ DW

Mrs Isabella Beeton, *Book of Household Management*, published by Ward Lock & Co, 1899, 8°.
£380–450 / €550–650
$730–860 ⚒ DW

▶ **Harry Craddock,** *The Savoy Cocktail Book*, published by Constable & Co, 1937, 7 x 5in (18 x 12.5cm).
£100–110 / €145–160
$190–210 ⊞ BIB

◀ **Hamlyn (publisher),** *The Hamlyn All Colour Cook Book*, 1970, 11½in (29cm) high.
£4–8 / €6–12
$8–15 ⊞ LBM

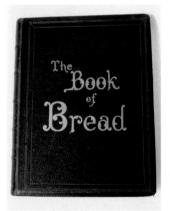

◀ **Owen Simmons,** *The Book of Bread*, published by Maclaren & Sons, 1900, 12in (30.5cm) high, edition of 350, with original photographs.
£105–120
€150–170
$200–220
⊞ B&R

May E. Southworth, *The Motorist's Luncheon Book*, 1923, 6¾ x 4½in (17 x 11.5cm).
£20–25 / €30–35
$40–50 ⊞ MSB

Amy Vanderbilt, *Complete Cookbook*, illustrated by Andrew Warhol, published by Doubleday & Co, New York, 1961, 8½ x 5½in (21.5 x 14cm).
£90–100 / €130–145
$170–190 ⊞ EMH

Modern First Editions

Julian Barnes, *Flaubert's Parrot*, published by Jonathan Cape, first edition, 1984, 9 x 6in (23 x 15cm).
£270–300 / €390–440
$520–580 ⊞ NW

H. E. Bates, *The Flying Goat*, published by Jonathan Cape, first edition, 1939, 8 x 5½in (20.5 x 14cm).
£220–250 / €320–360
$420–480 ⊞ NW

► **Thomas S. Blakeney,** *Sherlock Holmes Fact or Fiction?*, published by John Murray, first edition, 1936, 7 x 5in (18 x 12.5cm).
£220–250
€320–360
$420–480
⊞ NW

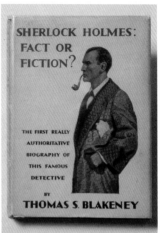

Vera Caspary, *Laura*, published by Eyre & Spottiswoode, first edition, 1944, 7½ x 5in (19 x 12.5cm).
£400–450 / €580–650
$770–860 ⊞ NW

Agatha Christie, *Death in the Clouds*, published by Collins Crime Club, first edition, 1935, 8 x 5in (20.5 x 12.5cm).
£5,400–6,000
€7,800–8,700
$10,400–11,500 ⊞ NW

Anthony Burgess, *Time for a Tiger*, published by William Heinemann, first edition, 1956, 7½ x 5in (19 x 12.5cm).
£540–600 / €780–870
$1,050–1,200 ⊞ NW

Malcolm Campbell, *Salute to the Gods,* published by Cassell & Co, first edition, 1934, 8 x 5½in (20.5 x 14cm).
£220–250 / €320–360
$420–480 ⊞ NW

Cross Reference
Comics & Annuals
see pages 150–154

◄ **Agatha Christie,** *At Bertram's Hotel*, published by Collins Crime Club, first edition, 1965, 8 x 5in (20.5 x 12.5cm).
£30–35 / €45–50
$55–65 ⊞ HOM

Bernard Cornwell, *Sharpe's Eagle*, first edition, 1981, 8°.
£210–250 / €300–360
$400–480 ⋏ BBA

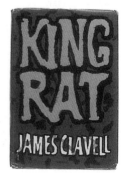

James Clavell, *King Rat*, first edition, 1963, 8°.
£45–50 / €65–75
$85–95 ⋏ BBA

Colin Dexter, *The Dead of Jericho*, signed by the author, published by Macmillan, first edition, 1981, 8°.
£330–390 / €480–570
$630–750 ➚ BBA

Sebastian Faulks, *Birdsong,* published by Hutchinson, first edition, 1993, 8°.
£300–360 / €440–520
$580–690 ➚ BBA

▶ **Ian Fleming,** *For Your Eyes Only,* published by Jonathan Cape, first edition, 1960, 8°.
£210–250
€300–360
$400–480
➚ DW

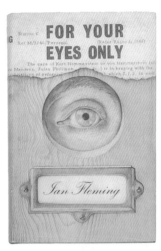

Dick Francis, *Flying Finish*, ink inscription, first edition, 1966, 8°.
£200–240 / €290–350
$380–450 ➚ BBA

Graham Greene, *A Burnt Out Case,* published by Heinemann, first edition, 1961, 8 x 5½in (20.5 x 14cm).
£720–800 / €1,000–1,150
$1,400–1,550 ⊞ BIB

Graham Greene, *The Comedians,* published by The Bodley Head, first edition, 1966, 8 x 5½in (20.5 x 14cm).
£50–60 / €75–85
$100–115 ⊞ BAY

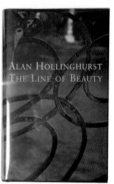

Alan Hollinghurst, *The Line of Beauty,* published by Picador, first edition, 2004, 9 x 5½in (23 x 14cm).
£220–250 / €320–360
$420–480 ⊞ BIB

Jack Higgins, *In The Hour Before Midnight*, first edition, 1969, 8°.
£105–120 / €150–180
$200–240 ➚ BBA

Ronald A. Knox, *Still Dead,* published by Hodder & Stoughton, first edition, 1934, 8 x 5¼in (20.5 x 13.5cm).
£810–900 / €1,150–1,300
$1,550–1,750 ⊞ BIB

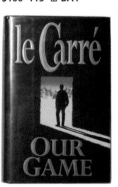

Le Carré, *Our Game,* published by Hodder & Stoughton, first edition, second issue, 1995, 9½ x 6½in (24 x 16.5cm).
£490–550 / €710–800
$940–1,050 ⊞ NW

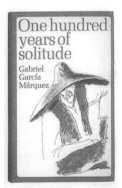

Gabriel García Márquez, *One Hundred Years of Solitude,* published by Jonathan Cape, first UK edition, 1970, 8°.
£210–250 / €300–360
$400–480 ➚ BBA

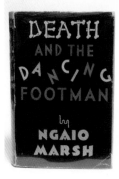

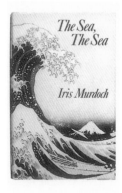

Ngaio Marsh, *Death and the Dancing Footman*, published by Collins Crime Club, first edition, 1942, 8 x 5½in (20.5 x 14cm).
£520–580 / €750–840 $1,000–1,100 ⊞ BIB

Nancy Mitford, *Don't Tell Alfred*, published by Hamish Hamilton, first edition, 1960, 7½ x 5in (19 x 12.5cm).
£25–30 / €40–45 $50–55 ⊞ BAY

Iris Murdoch, *The Flight from the Enchanter*, dust jacket illustrated by Edward Bawden, published by Chatto & Windus, first edition, 1956, 8°.
£490–580 / €710–840 $940–1,100 ⚹ BBA

Iris Murdoch, *The Sea, The Sea*, first edition, 1978, 8°.
£75–85 / €110–125 $145–165 ⚹ BBA

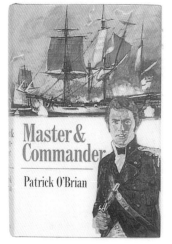

◀ **Patrick O'Brian,** *Master & Commander*, published by Collins, first edition, 1970, 8°.
£500–600 €730–870 $960–1,150 ⚹ DW

Patrick O'Brian, *The Nutmeg of Consolation*, first edition, 1991, 8°.
£125–150 / €185–220 $240–290 ⚹ BBA

Liam O'Flaherty, *The Puritan*, published by Jonathan Cape, first edition, 1932, 8 x 5in (20.5x 12.5cm).
£85–95 / €125–140 $165–185 ⊞ BIB

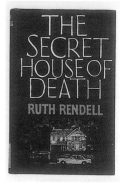

Frank O'Connor, *The Saint and Mary Kate*, published by Macmillan & Co, first edition, 1932, 8 x 5½in (20.5 x 14cm).
£290–330 / €420–480 $560–630 ⊞ NW

Ian Rankin, *Strip Jack*, published by Orion, first edition, 1992, 8°.
£490–580 / €710–840 $940–1,100 ⚹ BBA

Ruth Rendell, *The Secret House of Death*, published by John Long, first edition, 1968, 8°.
£470–560 / €680–810 $910–1,100 ⚹ BBA

Jean Rhys, *Voyage in the Dark*, first edition, 1934, 8°, signed.
£410–490 / €590–710 $790–940 ⚹ BBA

Siegfried Sassoon, *Memoirs of a Fox-Hunting Man*, illustrated by William Nicholson, published by Faber & Faber, 1929, 9in (23cm) high.
£45–50 / €65–75
$85–95 ⊞ HTE

Nevil Shute, *Trustee from the Toolroom*, published by Heinemann, 1960, 8 x 5½in (20.5 x 14cm).
£15–20 / €22–29
$29–38 ⊞ BAY

Freya Stark, *The Coast of Incense*, published by John Murray, first edition, 1953, 9in (23cm) high.
£40–45 / €60–70
$75–85 ⊞ HOM

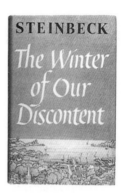

John Steinbeck, *The Winter of Our Discontent*, first edition, New York, 1961, 8°.
£110–130 / €160–190
$210–250 ⚲ BBA

William Trevor, *The Day We Got Drunk on Cake*, first edition, 1967, 8°.
£490–580 / €710–840
$940–1,100 ⚲ BBA

Edgar Wallace, *Four-Square Jane, Crime Series*, published by The Readers Library Publishing Co, first edition, 1929, 6½ x 4½in (16.5 x 11.5cm).
£55–65 / €80–95
$105–125 ⊞ NW

Edgar Wallace, *The Door with the Seven Locks*, published by Hodder & Stoughton, 1974, 8 x 5in (20.5 x 12.5cm).
£15–20 / €22–29
$29–38 ⊞ NW

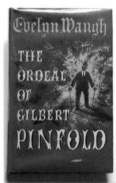

Evelyn Waugh, *The Ordeal of Gilbert Pinfold*, published by Chapman & Hall, first edition, 1957, 7½ x 5in (19 x 12.5cm).
£50–60 / €75–85
$100–115 ⊞ BAY

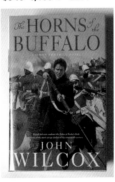

John Wilcox, *The Horns of the Buffalo*, published by Headline Book Publishing, first edition, signed, 2004, 10 x 6in (25.5 x 15cm).
£180–200 / €260–290
$350–390 ⊞ BIB

Henry Williamson, *The Innocent Moon*, published by Macdonald, first edition, 1961, 8 x 5½in (20.5 x 14cm).
£50–60 / €75–85
$100–115 ⊞ BAY

► **P. G. Wodehouse,** *Quick Service*, published by Herbert Jenkins, 1940, 7½ x 5in (19 x 12.5cm).
£155–175
€220–250
$300–340
⊞ NW

Natural History

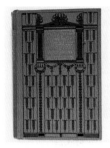

Robert Fulton, *The Illustrated Books of Pigeons With Standards for Judging,* edited by Lewis Wright, published by Cassell, Petter & Co, c1875, 4°, 50 plates after J. Ludlow, wood engravings, cloth.
£170–200 / €250–300
$330–390 ➢ DW

Henry Noel Humphreys, *The Butterfly Vivarium; or, Insect Home,* 1858, 8°.
£280–330 / €410–480
$540–640 ➢ BBA

▶ **Beverley R. Morris,** *British Game Birds and Wildfowl,* revised by W.B. Tegetmeier, published by John C. Nimmo, 1897, 8°, 2 vols.
£580–690 / €840–1,000
$1,100–1,300 ➢ RTo

◀ **Francis T. Buckland,** *Curiosities of Natural History,* published by Macmillan & Co, 1903–05, 4 vols, 8 x 5in (20.5 x 12.5cm).
£75–85 / €110–125
$145–165 ⊞ BIB

Lionel Edwards, *My Hunting Sketchbook,* 1928.
£300–360 / €440–520
$580–690 ➢ CHTR

BEE EATER.

Samuel John Galton, *The Natural History of Birds,* published by J. Johnson, 1791, 12°, 3 vols, each title page signed and dated 1813.
£490–580 / €710–840
$940–1,100 ➢ DW

TEN HAND-COLORED WOODCUTS
1958

Antonio Frasconi, *Birds From My Homeland,* with notes from W. H. Hudson's *Birds of La Plata,* New York, 1958, 4°, No. 173 of 200, signed and inscribed by the artist, on Japanese Hosho paper.
£350–420 / €510–610
$670–810 ➢ BBA

Captain M. H. Hayes, *Illustrated Horse Breaking,* illustrated by J. H. Oswald Brown, published by W. Thacker & Co, 1889, 8in (20.5cm) high.
£45–50 / €65–75
$85–95 ⊞ HTE

W. B. Tegetmeier, *The Poultry Book,* illustrated by Harrison Weir, published by Routledge, 1867, 8°.
£210–250 / €300–360
$400–480 ➢ DW

Louisa Anne Twamley, *The Romance of Nature,* first edition, 1836, 8°.
£250–300 / €360–430
$480–580 ➢ BBA

Poetry

Robert Browning, *The Pied Piper of Hamelin*, illustrated by Harry Quilter, 1898, 12°, printed on vellum, contemporary ink inscription.
£370–440 / €540–640
$710–840 ↗ BBA

◀ **Ted Hughes,** *Crow*, published by Faber & Faber, first edition, 1989, 9 x 5½in (23 x 14cm), inscribed by the author.
£360–400 / €520–580
$690–770 ⊞ NW

Christina Rossetti and Laurence Houseman, *Goblin Market*, published by Macmillan, 1893, 8°, with presentation copy stamp.
£250–300 / €370–440
$480–580 ↗ BBA

T. S. Eliot, *Collected Poems 1909–1935*, published by Faber & Faber, first edition, 1936, 9 x 6in (23 x 15cm).
£155–175 / €220–250
$300–340 ⊞ BIB

▶ **Henry Noel Humphreys (illustrator),** *The Poets' Pleasaunce*, by Eden Warwick, published by Longman & Co, 1847, 8°.
£130–155 / €190–220
$250–300 ↗ DW

Sir Walter Scott, *Scott's Poetical Works*, c1876, 6¾in (17cm high), with ivory-coated paper boards.
£135–150 / €195–220
$260–290 ⊞ TDG

Robert Herrick, *One Hundred and Eleven Poems*, illustrated by Sir William Russell Flint, published by Golden Cockerel Press, 1955, 4°, No. 16 of 500, signed by the author, sheepskin.
£280–330 / €410–480
$540–640 ↗ BBA

Alfred Lord Tennyson, *Idylls of the King*, illuminated manuscript possibly by Alberto Sangorski, 1870s, 2°.
£840–1,000
€1,200–1,450
$1,600–1,900 ↗ DW

Seamus Heaney, *Door Into the Dark*, published by Faber & Faber, first edition, 1969, 9 x 6in (23 x 15cm).
£400–450 / €580–650
$770–860 ⊞ BIB

William Morris, *The Defence of Guenevere*, illustrated by Jessie Marion King, published by John Lane, 1904, 7½ x 5½in (19 x 14cm).
£720–800 / €1,050–1,200
$1,400–1,550 ⊞ BI

Robert Eldridge Avis Wilmott, *English Sacred Poetry*, engravings by the Dalziel Bros after Holman Hunt and others, 1865, 9in (23cm) high.
£190–220 / €280–320
$360–400 ⊞ TDG

Travel

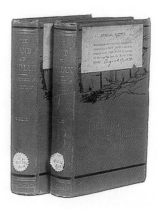

▶ **S. L. Bensusan,** *Morocco*, colour plates by A. S. Forrest, published by A. & C. Black, 1904, 4°, No. 247 of 250.
£320–380
€460–550
$610–730
🔨 **BBA**

W. H. Bartlett & Stirling J. Coyne, *The Scenery and Antiquities of Ireland*, c1840, 4°, 2 vols.
£500–600 / €730–870
$880–1,050 🔨 **DW**

▶ **Bruce Chatwin,** *In Patagonia*, published by Jonathan Cape, first edition, 1977, 8°, dust jacket.
£250–300 / €370–440
$480–580 🔨 **BBA**

Richard F. Burton, *The Land of Midian (Revisited)*, published by C. Kegan Paul, first edition, 1879, 8°, 2 vols.
£320–380 / €460–550
$610–730 🔨 **DW**

◀ **G. B. Depping,** *L'Angleterre*, 1824, 12°, 6 vols, 59 miniature maps by Perrot.
£630–750 / €920–1,100
$1,200–1,450 🔨 **DW**

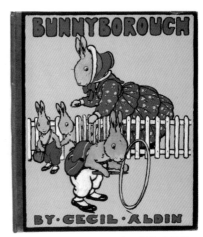

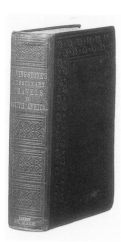

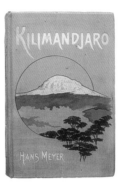

Dr Hans Meyer, *Der Kilimandjaro*, first edition, 1900, 4°, with two folding maps.
£580–690 / €840–1,000
$1,100–1,300 ⚒ BBA

Albert Millican, *Travels and Adventures of an Orchid Hunter*, published by Cassell & Co, first edition, 1891, 8°.
£400–480 / €580–700
$770–920 ⚒ BBA

William Libbey and Franklin E. Hoskins, *The Jordan Valley and Petra*, published by the Knickerbocker Press, first edition, 1905, 2 vols.
£420–500 / €610–730
$810–960 ⚒ BBA

David Livingstone, *Missionary Travels and Researches in South Africa*, first edition, second issue, 1857, 8°, one folding map.
£390–460 / €570–670
$750–880 ⚒ DW

John Rymill, *Southern Lights*, published by Chatto & Windus, first edition, 1938, 4°, signed and inscribed by the author, with three folding maps.
£580–690 / €840–1,000
$1,100–1,300 ⚒ BBA

Robert W. Shufeldt, *Reports of Explorations and Surveys*, first edition, Washington, 1872, 4°, inscribed, 20 folding maps.
£125–150 / €185–220
$240–290 ⚒ BBA

► Edward Money, *Twelve Months with the Bashi-Bazouks*, 1857, 8°.
£140–165 / €200–240
$270–320 ⚒ BBA

Major Serpa Pinto, *How I Crossed Africa*, 1881, 8°, 2 vols, with folding map.
£400–480 / €580–700
$770–920 ⚒ BBA

Theodor Wundt, *Wanderbilder aus den Dolomiten*, Stuttgart, 1894, 2°.
£640–760 / €930–1,100
$1,200–1,450 ⚒ BBA

N. P. Willis, *American Scenery*, 1840, 4°, 2 vols.
£470–560 / €680–810
$910–1,100 ⚒ DW

LOCATE THE SOURCE

The source of each illustration in Miller's can be found by checking the code letters below each caption with the Key to Illustrations, pages 443–451.

Bottles

A bellarmine, decorated with a moulded mask above a crest, German, c1700, 7½in (19cm) high.
£360–430 / €520–620 $690–830 ➤ Hal

A glass wine bottle, the seal inscribed 'EN', chipped, c1710, 4½in (11.5cm) high.
£1,200–1,400 €1,750–2,050 $2,300–2,700 ➤ S

▶ **A ceramic gin flask,** in the form of a boot, Scottish, c1840, 7in (18cm) high.
£180–200 €260–290 $340–380 ⊞ HOW

◀ **A stoneware ginger beer bottle,** with a transfer-printed label, 19thC, 7in (18cm) high.
£4–8 / €6–12 $8–15 ⊞ BoC

A Horace Elliott glazed bottle, in the form of a leather bottle, with scraffito decoration, painted mark, 1889, 7½in (19cm) high.
£420–500 / €610–730 $810–960 ➤ PF

A stoneware whisky flask, embossed with Masonic emblems, royal cypher and a shield impressed 'William Sim, Loch Side Aberdeen', Scottish, c1830, 9½in (24cm) high.
£200–240 / €290–350 $380–450 ➤ Bea

A stoneware flagon, inscribed 'Style, James & Co, Wine, Spirit, Ale and Porter Merchants, Dorchester 1833', 19in (48.5cm) high.
£65–75 / €95–105 $125–145 ➤ HYD

◀ **An Edwardian stoneware ginger beer flagon,** printed 'Dove, Phillips & Pett, Rochester', 17¼in (44cm) high.
£45–50 / €65–75 $85–95 ⊞ TASV

◄ **A glass soda syphon,** c1910, 12in (30.5cm) high.
£75–85 / €110–125
$145–165 ⊞ JAM

A Lewis & Towers Patent glass poison bottle, c1910, 5½in (14cm) high.
£3–7 / €4–10
$6–13 ⊞ OIA

◄ **A stoneware ginger beer flagon,** transfer-printed 'Biddle & Gingell, Clyde Place, Leyton', 1933, 10in (25.5cm) high.
£30–35 / €45–50
$55–65 ⊞ JUN

A stoneware sample bottle, transfer-printed 'A. W. Buchan & Co', Scottish, 1910–20, 7in (18cm) high.
£1,500–1,800
€2,200–2,600
$2,900–3,450 ⋏ BBR
This is an exceptionally rare ginger beer bottle.

► **A bottle of Charrington's Centenary Ale,** 1957, 8½in (21.5cm) high.
£25–30 / €40–45
$50–55 ⊞ HUX

A glass soda syphon, 1920–30, 12in (30.5cm) high.
£20–25 / €30–35
$40–50 ⊞ HO

Three glass milk bottles, advertising Crusha, Mars and Colegate, 1970s, 7¼in (18.5cm) high.
£1–5 / €2–7
$3–9 each ⊞ TWI
Glass milk bottles from between WWI and WWII were squat with wide necks and were closed with circular cardboard disks. Advertising and local place names on the bottle and the disc add interest for collectors. 'Milk's Gotta Lotta Bottle' boasted advertisers in the 1970s, when it became fashionable to use milk bottles to promote a wide range of different products. These colourful bottles are still very affordable.

A Coca Cola bottle, advertising Mickey's Toontown, Disneyland, California, 1993, 7in (18cm) high.
£2–6 / €3–9
$4–11 ⊞ HeA

A Becks beer bottle, label designed by Jeff Koons, 'Pam, Easy, Fun, Ethereal, The Fruitmarket Gallery, Edinburgh', 2000, 8½in (21.5cm) high.
£30–35 / €45–50
$55–65 ⊞ PLB

Boxes

A horn box, inscribed 'T. Jones', 1700, 3in (7.5cm) wide.
£70–80 / €100–115
$135–155 ⊞ MB

◀ **A partridge-wood tea caddy,** with boxwood stringing and a brass handle, the two inner compartments flanking a glass sugar bowl, c1815, 12in (30.5cm) wide.
£270–300 / €390–440
$520–580 ⊞ JTS

A Regency burr-maple workbox, with brass handles and a base drawer, 13in (33cm) wide.
£190–220 / €280–330
$360–430 ⚒ SWO

▶ **A Tunbridge ware box,** 1835, 4in (10cm) wide.
£70–80
€100–115
$135–155
⊞ MB

◀ **A maple and rosewood writing slope,** 19thC, 14in (35.5cm) wide.
£60–70
€85–100
$115–135
⚒ G(L)

A lacquered papier-mâché box, with painted floral decoration, Russian, c1850, 2½in (6.5cm) diam.
£60–70 / €85–100
$115–135 ⊞ MB

◀ **A Victorian burr-oak decanter box,** with Gothic brass mounts and lock, 8½in (21.5cm) wide.
£55–65 / €80–95
$105–125 ⚒ BWL

A tortoiseshell and ebonized *nécessaire,* the hinged cover with a mirror, fitted interior, 19thC, 5½in (14cm) high.
£290–330 / €420–480
$560–630 ⚒ GAK

▶ **A Tunbridge ware box,** the cover with a carved knob, 1860, 4in (10cm) wide.
£85–95
€125–140
$165–185 ⊞ MB

A papier-mâché spectacle case, inlaid with mother-of-pearl, 1860, 7in (18cm) wide.
£55–65 / €80–95
$105–125 ⊞ MB

A gilt-metal and glass casket, in the form of a Louis XV serpentine front commode, the hinged bevelled glass cover enclosing a buttoned silk interior, slight damage, French, 19thC 7¼in (18.5cm) wide.
£80–90 / €115–130
$155–175 ✂ Hal

A mahogany box, with mother-of-pearl inlay, c1870, 12in (30.5cm) wide.
£50–60 / €75–85
$100–115 ⊞ AL

A birchwood box, carved in the form of a miniature trunk, c1870, 3½in (9cm) wide.
£50–60 / €75–85
$100–115 ⊞ MB

A Mauchline ware box, depicting Osborne House, c1870, 3in (7.5cm) wide.
£50–60 / €75–85
$100–115 ⊞ MB

An oak cigar box, the cover mounted with a carved wood fox's head and a silver-plated horseshoe, whip and stirrups, late 19thC, 11¾in (30cm) wide.
£380–450 / €550–650
$730–860 ✂ SWO

A Gothic-style carved oak box, with brass fittings, late 19thC, 12in (30.5cm) wide.
£300–330 / €430–480
$570–630 ⊞ TDG

▶ **A lacquered box,** Japanese, 1890, 9in (23cm) wide.
£60–70 / €85–100
$115–135 ⊞ MB

A sycamore box, painted with an archer within a floral border, 1919, 3in (7.5cm) diam.
£100–120 / €145–175
$195–230 ⊞ MB

A walnut, ash, cedar and sycamore box, in the form of five stacked books, c1920, 5in (12.5cm) wide.
£100–120 / €145–175
$195–230 ⊞ WAA

A pine egg box, with original paint, c1920, 13in (33cm) wide.
£115–130 / €165–190
$220–250 ⊞ B&R

Breweriana

Breweriana – objects connected with spirits, wine, beer, breweries, pubs and bars – is collected across the world. When it comes to spirits, whisky tends to be the most popular. In 2002 a collector paid a record auction price of £20,150 / €29,200 / $39,000 for a 1926 bottle of Macallan single Highland malt.

Pub jugs, the ceramic water pitchers supplied to public houses and bars by distilleries to advertise their whisky brands, were introduced in Britain from the 19th century onwards, but in the USA they did not become commonplace until after WWII. Today in many areas US Federal laws have forbidden the distribution of free products to promote the consumption of liquor. In Britain, pub jugs were made by many leading potteries including Doulton, Wade and Shelley, and US manufacturers include Hall China. Early jugs are sought after, particularly those promoting smaller distilleries. Some collectors focus on works by a specific pottery (for example Doulton or Wade) while others concentrate on their favourite brand of whisky. Visual appeal is very important, as is condition.

Whisky crocks, the ceramic jugs or flasks used for bottling whisky (not water), often designed for export and frequently finely decorated with transfer printing are another popular area and rarities such as the Loffet's whisky jug shown below can fetch high sums.

Guinness is another drink that attracts a huge number of collectors, largely because of the brilliance of the campaigns launched by advertising agency S. H. Benson in the 1920s and '30s. They introduced the famous 'Guinness is Good for You' slogan along with a series of animal images including the Guinness toucan. Period posters by artist John Gilroy, who devised the Zookeeper series, are very collectable as are ceramics from the 1950s and '60s, although buyers should be aware of the large number of Carlton Ware fakes that were produced in the late 20th century, and be very cautious when buying, particularly over the internet.

While some breweriana collectors concentrate on a specific field, such as beer mats or bottle labels, others seek to preserve the whole traditional pub atmosphere by creating their own bar at home. This is a perfect way to use and display breweriana, hence the demand for items such as pub optics.

A set of three stoneware liquor barrels, moulded with Royal arms, lions, banners and foliage, one tap missing, 1814–37, 11½in (29cm) high.
**£330–390 / €480–570
$630–750** ⚘ G(L)

◀ **A Royal Doulton Loffet & Co ceramic whisky jug,** with transfer-printed decoration and original stopper, impressed mark, late 19thC, 7in (18cm) high.
**£610–730 / €880–1,050
$1,200–1,400** ⚘ BBR

An Andrew A. Watt & Co Tyrconnell Irish Whiskey poster, 1900–10, 26 x 36in (66 x 91.5cm).
**£220–250 / €320–360
$420–480** ⊞ RTT

▶ **A W. Wilders & Co Cream Gin poster,** slight damage and restoration, c1900, 24 x 19½in (61 x 49.5cm).
**£300–360
€440–520
$580–690**
⚘ DW

◀ **A Vieux Marc Clos Vougeot metal jotter pad,** French, 1905, 2¼in (5.5cm) wide.
**£70–80 / €100–115
$135–155** ⊞ HUX

A Dunville's Whisky glass jug, c1910, 4¾in (12cm) high.
£55–65 / €80–95
$105–125 ⊞ HUX

An Old Orkney Whisky advertising card, 1920s, 24 x 17in (61 x 43cm).
£135–150 / €195–220
$260–290 ⊞ Do

A Robertson, Sanderson Original Mountain Dew glass whisky dispenser, c1910, 19in (48.5cm) high.
£360–400 / €520–580
$690–770 ⊞ JUN

◄ **A Mitchells & Butlers Bally Boy Old Irish Whisky ceramic water jug,** 1920s, 8in (20.5cm) high.
£135–150
€195–220
$260–290
⊞ MURR

A Whitbread's Ales and Stout enamel sign, c1910, 36in (91.5cm) high.
£250–280 / €360–410
$480–540 ⊞ JUN

A Dunville's Whisky advertising card, 1920–30, 25 x 19½in (63.5 x 49.5cm), framed.
£110–130 / €160–190
$210–250 ⋟ BBR

A wooden bottle stopper, carved as a man's head and shoulders, Italian, c1920, 4in (10cm) high.
£8–12 / €12–18
$16–23 ⊞ Dall

◄ **Two chrome optics,** for Haig Whisky and Gordon's Gin, c1950, 6in (15cm) high.
£20–25 / €30–35
$40–50 ⊞ JUN

◀ **Four bowls measures,** advertising Bass and Worthington beers, 1950s, 2in (5cm) wide.
£10–15 / €15–22 $19–28 each ⊞ HUX

◀ **A Martell ceramic ashtray,** 1950s, 5in (12.5cm) square.
£6–10 / €9–15 $12–19 ⊞ HUX

▶ **A Long John Scotch Whisky ceramic ashtray,** 1960, 6in (15cm) diam.
£8–12 / €12–18 16–22 ⊞ HUX

A Glenfiddich Pure Malt Whisky ceramic jug, 1960s, 5½in (14cm) high.
£15–20 / €22–29 $29–38 ⊞ HUX

A plastic cocktail shaker, 1960s, 8in (20.5cm) high.
£10–15 / €15–22 $19–28 ⊞ RTT

A Martell Cognac plastic advertising figure, c1960, 7in (18cm) high.
£25–30 / €40–45 $50–55 ⊞ JUN

A ceramic whisky barrel, c1890, 19in (48.5cm) high.
£100–120 / €145–175 $195–230 ⊞ JUN

A Gilbey's Whisky plastic advertising figure, 1960s, 10½in (26.5cm) high.
£115–130 / €165–190 $220–250 ⊞ MURR

A Trumans plastic advertising figure, 1960s, 7½in (19cm) high.
£50–60 / €75–85 $100–115 ⊞ HUX

An Olympia Beer Thermo-Serv tankard, American, 1960s, 6¼in (16cm) high.
£8–12 / €12–18 $16–22 ⊞ RTT

Guinness

A Guinness Bull Dog Bottling composition advertising figure, with glass eyes, electrically operated, 1920–30, 26in (66cm) wide.
£340–400 / €490–580
$650–770 ⚒ BBR

A Guinness ceramic ashtray, by Arklow Pottery, 1930–40, 5½in (14cm) wide.
£25–30 / €40–45
$50–55 ⚒ BBR

Further reading

Miller's Bottles & Pot Lids: A Collector's Guide, Miller's Publications, 2002

◀ **A Guinness poster,** 'My Goodness Where's the Guinness', by Alfred Leete, printed by Sanders Phillips, 1945, 59¾ x 40¼in (152 x 102cm).
£150–180 / €220–260
$290–350 ⚒ ONS

A Guinness poster, 'My Goodness My Guinness', by John Gilroy, printed by John Waddington, 1936, 30 x 40¼in (76 x 102cm).
£280–330 / €400–480
$530–630 ⚒ ONS

A Guinness celluloid sign, 'Guinness for Strength', by John Gilroy, 1949–54, 10 x 12in (25.5 x 30.5cm).
£490–550 / €710–800
$940–1,050 ⊞ MURR

A set of six Guinness waistcoat buttons, 1952.
£70–80 / €100–115
$135–155 ⊞ JBB

A Carlton Ware Guinness advertising figure, in the form of a tortoise with a glass of Guinness on its back, 1950s, 3in (7.5cm) high.
£60–70 / €85–100
$115–135 ⚒ BBR

A Guinness pottery advertising figure, by Wiltshaw & Robinson Ltd, modelled as a toucan with a glass of Guinness, 'How Grand to be a Toucan Just think what Toucan do', printed mark, 1950s, 9in (23cm) high.
£200–240 / €290–340
$390–460 ⚒ SWO

A Guinness celluloid advertising sign, 'Its good to relax with a Guinness', 1950s–60s, 12 x 9in (30.5 x 23cm).
£180–200 / €260–290
$340–380 ⊞ MURR

Buttons

A shell and silver button, the cameo Roman head surrounded by a border set with paste stones, late 18thC, 1½in (4cm) diam.
£1,350–1,550 / €1,950–2,250
$2,600–3,000 ⊞ TB

A porcelain button, hand-painted with a bird, late 18thC, 1in (2.5cm) diam.
£550–620 / €800–900
$1,050–1,200 ⊞ TB

A brass and ivory button, painted with a lady, surrounded by a silver-plated brass border set with paste stones, late 19thC, 1¼in (3cm) diam.
£700–780 / €1,000–1,150
$1,350–1,500 ⊞ TB

A silver-plated livery button, c1880, 1in (2.5cm) diam.
£10–15 / €15–22
$19–28 ⊞ MRW

A metal button, with celluloid and glass decoration, 1880–90, 1¼in (3cm) diam.
£20–25 / €30–35
$40–45 ⊞ TB

A set of four Victorian metal and glass buttons, decorated with silver lustre, 1in (2.5cm) diam.
£5–9 / €8–13
$10–16 ⊞ EV

A stamped brass button, depicting two saddled horses, late 19thC, 1½in (4cm) diam.
£45–50 / €65–75
$90–100 ⊞ TB

An enamel and brass button, decorated with a rural landscape, French, 1880–90, 1¼in (3cm) diam.
£130–145 / €180–210
$250–280 ⊞ TB

▶ **A carved and pierced mother-of-pearl button,** depicting a lady and a house, late 19thC, 1in (2.5cm) diam.
£140–155 / €200–220
$270–300 ⊞ TB

A tinted mother-of-pearl button, inlaid with two birds in a nest, engraved and pigmented with gold, late 19thC, 1in (2.5cm) diam.
£140–155 / €200–220
$270–300 ⊞ TB

A carved and tinted mother-of-pearl button, commemorating the Eiffel Tower and the Paris Exhibition of 1889, engraved and pigmented with gold, c1889, 1½in (4cm) diam.
£700–780 / €1,000–1,150
$1,350–1,500 ⊞ TB

Two brass hunt buttons, c1890, 1in (2.5cm) diam.
£10–15 / €15–22
$19–28 ⊞ MRW

A set of six silver-plated trade buttons, Chinese, c1900, 1in (2.5cm) diam.
£25–30 / €40–45
$50–55 ⊞ JBB

A set of six blister pearl and enamelled-gold buttons, c1900, ½in (1cm) diam, in a fitted case.
£150–170 / €220–250
$290–330 ⊞ JBB

Two brass, fabric and metal buttons, each decorated with a stamped brass teddy bear, 1905–10, ¾in (2cm) diam.
£9–13 / €13–19
$18–25 ⊞ TB
These buttons were inspired by Theodore Roosevelt's refusal to shoot a bear cub while on a hunting expedition.

A set of six brass buttons, each depicting a car, c1920, 1½in (4cm) diam.
£25–30 / €40–45
$50–55 ⊞ JBB

A set of six silver buttons, French, c1900, ¾in (2cm) diam.
£85–95 / €125–140
$165–185 ⊞ JBB

► A fabric and paste button, c1950, 1in (2.5cm) diam.
£2–6 / €3–9
$4–11 ⊞ FMN

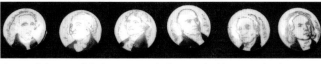

A set of six porcelain buttons, each decorated with a portrait of an American President, 1940–50, 1in (2.5cm) diam.
£45–50 / €65–75
$85–95 ⊞ JBB

Cameras

◄ **A Houghton Ensignette folding camera,** 1909–30, 4in (10cm) wide.
£50–60 / €75–85
$100–115 ⊞ HEG

A Kodak No. 2 folding pocket camera, c1900, 8in (20.5cm) wide.
£65–75 / €95–105
$125–145 ⊞ APC

► **A Pathé Baby 9.5mm cine camera,** with Camo motor winder, Hermagis f3.5/20mm lens and case, c1926, 4½in (11.5cm) high.
£60–70 / €85–100
$115–135 ⊞ CaH

◄ **A Zeiss Ikon Maximar A207/3 camera,** with Tessar f4.5/10.5cm lens, Compur shutter plate, darkslide and leather case, 1927–39,
5in (12.5cm) high.
£90–100 / €130–145
$170–190 ⊞ CaH

A Dr Nagel Vollenda 70/0 camera, German, c1930, 7in (18cm) high.
£40–45 / €60–70
$75–85 ⊞ ARP

A Purma Special camera, with gravity shutter, c1930,
6in (15cm) wide.
£35–40 / €50–60
$65–75 ⊞ ARP

A Fotofex Minifex 16mm sub-miniature camera, 1932,
3in (7.5cm) wide.
£450–500 / €650–730
$860–960 ⊞ APC

A Coronet Bakelite 3-D camera,
1930s, 7in (18cm) wide.
£70–80 / €100–115
$135–155 ⊞ JUN

A Houghton-Butcher Ensign Midget camera, c1934, 4in (10cm) wide.
£45–50 / €65–75
$85–95 ⊞ ARP

◄ **A Wirgin Wirginex Bakelite camera,** German, c1935,
4½in (11.5cm) high.
£135–150 / €195–220
$260–290 ⊞ ARP

An EKC Bullet camera, 1936,
4½in (11.5cm) wide, with box.
£30–35 / €45–50
$55–65 ⊞ APC

▶ An Ansco Readyset Royal camera,
1940, 8in (20.5cm) high, with box.
£50–60 / €75–85
$100–115 ⊞ APC

An Agfa Solinette folding camera,
with Solinar f3.5/35mm lens and
flashbulb, c1952, 5in (12.5cm) wide.
£40–45 / €60–70
$75–85 ⊞ ARP

▶ An Agilux Agiflash camera,
c1953, 7in (18cm) wide.
£30–35 / €45–50
$55–65 ⊞ ARP

A Eumig C16R cine camera, with
two extra lenses, c1957,
9in (23cm) high.
£220–250 / €320–360
$420–480 ⊞ ARP

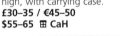

A Bell & Howell Autoload
8mm cine camera, with a
f1.8/9-29mm zoom reflex
manual and auto animation
facility, 1952–54, 9in (23cm)
high, with carrying case.
£30–35 / €45–50
$55–65 ⊞ CaH

A Mamiya Super 16 sub-miniature camera,
1950, 2½in (6.5cm) wide, with case.
£35–40 / €50–60
$65–75 ⊞ APC

A Haneel Trivision Stereo camera and
viewer, 1953, 6in (15cm) wide.
£135–150 / €195–220
$260–290 ⊞ APC

A Wirgin 35mm Stereo camera, German,
c1954, 7¾in (19.5cm) wide.
£110–125 / €160–180
$210–240 ⊞ ARP

A Rangefinder 35mm camera,
Russian, 1955–70, 5½in (14cm) wide.
£50–60 / €75–85
$100–115 ⊞ HEG

◀ A Kodak Retinette IIB
camera, with Reomar Ctd
f2.8/45 lens, Compur Rapid
shutter, selenium exposure
meter and case, 1958–59,
5in (12.5cm) wide.
£45–50 / €65–75
$85–95 ⊞ CaH

A Bell & Howell 16mm 613H silent film projector, 1950s, 18in (45.5cm) high.
£55–65 / €80–95
$105–125 ⊞ ARP

An Agfa Ambi Silette camera, with coupled rangefinder interchangeable lens, c1960, 5in (12.5cm) wide.
£70–80 / €100–115
$135–155 ⊞ ARP

A Leitz Leicina 8SV 8mm cine camera, c1964, 9in (23cm) long.
£45–50 / €65–75
$85–95 ⊞ ARP

A Paillard Bolex M8 8mm projector, with a sonorizer unit, c1955, 15in (38cm) wide.
£90–100 / €130–145
$170–190 ⊞ ARP

A Paillard Bolex B8L camera, with 12.5mm and 5.5mm Switar lenses, grip and case, c1960, 5in (12.5cm) high.
£55–65 / €80–95
$105–125 ⊞ ARP

▶ **A Canon 8mm Motor Zoom 8EEE cine camera,** with Canon C8 f1.7/10-40mm and f1.7/6.5-26mm zoom lenses, pistol grip, filter and case, c1965, 7in (18cm) long.
£50–60 / €75–85
$100–115 ⊞ CaH

A Zeiss Ikon Movinette 8B 8mm cine camera, c1959, 6in (15cm) wide.
£30–35 / €45–50
$55–65 ⊞ ARP

A Leitz Visoflex II housing and magnifier, 1960, 5in (12.5cm) high.
£90–100 / €130–145
$170–190 ⊞ APC

A Paillard Bolex 16mm H16 RXVS Triple Turret cine camera, with Pizar f1.5/25mm RX, Switar f1.8/16mm RX and Yvar f2.8/75mm AR lenses, turret handle, eyecup, eye-level focus, Octameter, rewind handle, filter holder, instructions, exposure table, and Bolex case, c1970, 11in (28cm) high.
£610–680 / €880–990
$1,150–1,300 ⊞ CaH

An Elmo Super 8 230SXL cine camera, with Elmo f1.2/10.5-26.5mm zoom lens, microphone, MC024 remote and cap, c1978, 9in (23cm) long.
£140–155 / €200–220
$270–300 ⊞ CaH

Ceramics
Animals

A Staffordshire caddy, in the form of an owl, 19thC, 8in (20.5cm) high.
£60–70 / €85–100
$115–135 ➢ WilP

A ceramic model of a cat, with treacle glaze, damaged, 19thC, 11¼in (28.5cm) high.
£160–190 / €230–270
$310–370 ➢ PFK

► **A Kutani model of a cat,** restored, Japanese, Meiji period, 1868–1912, 8in (20.5cm) wide.
£125–140
€180–200
$240–270 ➢ Hal`

◄ **An Ernst Bohne & Sons model of a hawk,** with glass eyes, damaged, impressed marks, c1890, 19¼in (49cm) high.
£220–260 / €320–380
$420–500 ➢ TEN

◄ **A ceramic inkwell and penstand,** in the form of four owls surrounding an owlet in a nest with pen holders in the form of branches, German, late 19thC, 5½in (14cm) wide.
£160–180
€230–260
$310–350
➢ HOLL

A Gallé faïence model of a cat, with glass eyes, damaged, signed, c1900, 12¾in (32.5cm) high.
£500–600 / €730–870
$960–1,150 ➢ SWO

A ceramic model of two budgerigars, by Rosa Neuwirth, probably produced by Ceramic Co-operative Factory, model No. 314/67, Austrian, Vienna, impressed marks, 1911–12, 8¼in (21cm) high.
£340–410 / €500–600
$650–780 ➢ DORO

A Royal Copenhagen model of a fawn, c1923, 3½in (9cm) high.
£90–100 / €130–145
$170–190 ⊞ PSA

A ceramic model of a pony, by Walter Bosse, restored, marked, 1924–37, 6in (15cm) high.
£310–370 / €450–540
$600–710 ↗ DORO

A Keramos model of an elephant, by Eduard Klablena, model No. 1169, restored, marked, Austrian, c1930, 9½in (24cm) high.
£340–410 / €500–600
$650–780 ↗ DORO

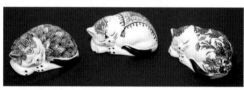

Three ceramic models of cats, by Piero Fornasetti, 1950s, 3½in (9cm) wide.
£65–75 / €95–105
$125–145 each ⊞ MARK

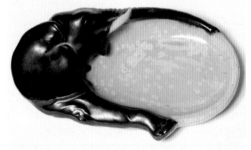

Two Jan Plitcha ceramic pigs, one decorated with a shamrock, the other with clover, c1930, 3in (7.5cm) long.
£45–50 / €65–75
$85–95 each ⊞ CCs

A ceramic model of the Pink Panther, marked '©UAC Geoffrey', 1980s, 4in (10cm) high.
£35–40 / €50–60
$65–75 ⊞ HYP

A Royal Crown Derby cat paperweight, c1990.
£320–380 / €460–550
$610–730 ↗ LT

A pottery elephant ashtray, c1950, 9in (23cm) wide.
£50–60 / €75–85
$100–115 ⊞ HEW

▶ **A Royal Albert model of Beatrix Potter's Benjamin Bunny,** entitled 'Benjamin Wakes Up', 1991–97, 4in (10cm) wide.
£30–35 / €45–50
$55–65 ⊞ BAC

A Winstanley pottery model of a cat, No.8, 2001.
£45–50 / €65–75
$85–95 ⊞ CP

Belleek

A Belleek pierced lattice dish, the rim applied with flowers, Irish, First Period, 1863–90, 4¾in (12cm) long.
£270–320 / €390–460
$520–610 ⚘ JBe

A Belleek cream jug, in the form of a shell with a coral handle, Irish, First Period, 1863–90.
£130–155 / €190–220
$250–300 ⚘ JAd

A Belleek Aberdeen jug, with flower-encrusted decoration, marked 'Co. Fermanagh Ireland', Irish, First Period, 1863–90, 9½in (24cm) high.
£300–360 / €440–520
$580–690 ⚘ DA

A Belleek part tea service, comprising nine pieces, relief-moulded with Grass pattern, marked, Irish, First Period, 1863–90, teapot 6in (15cm) high.
£300–360 / €440–520
$580–690 ⚘ Hal

A Belleek milk jug, with opalescent glaze, Irish, Second Period, 1891–1926, 6¼in (16cm) high.
£145–170 / €210–250
$280–330 ⚘ JAd

A Belleek Honeysuckle vase, decorated with Shamrock pattern, Irish, Second Period, 1891–1926, 7in (18cm) high.
£360–400 / €520–580
$690–770 ⊞ WAA

A Belleek plate, decorated with Mask pattern, Irish, Third Period, 1926–46, 6½in (16.5cm) diam.
£65–75 / €95–105
$125–145 ⊞ MLa

▶ **A pair of Belleek Ribbon vases,** decorated with applied flowers, Irish, c1950, 8in (20.5cm) high.
£100–115 / €145–165
$190–220 ⊞ DeA

A Belleek bust of Sorrow, Irish, Sixth Period, 1965–80, 11in (28cm) high.
£360–400 / €520–580
$690–770 ⊞ MLa

A Belleek model of an Irish Wolfhound, limited edition, Irish, c2000, 7in (18cm) high.
£270–300 / €390–450
$520–600 ⊞ DeA

Beswick

A Beswick model of a monkey, c1930, 7in (18cm) high.
£270–300 / €390–450
$520–600 ⊞ HEW

A Beswick teapot, in the form of a coach, c1930, 9in (23cm) wide.
£760–850 / €1,100–1,250
$1,450–1,650 ⊞ BEV

A Beswick model of a Wessex Saddleback pig, designed by Colin Melbourne, 'Merrywood Silver Wings 56th', No. 1511, 1957–69, 2¾in (7cm) high.
£210–250 / €300–360
$400–480 ✗ PFK

▶ **A Beswick model of a Lifeguard,** No. 1624, 1959–77, 9½in (24cm) high.
£480–570
€700–830
$920–1,100
✗ GIL

A Beswick model of Beatrix Potter's Anna Maria, by Albert Hallam, stamped mark, 1963–72, 3in (7.5cm) high.
£160–190 / €240–280
$300–360 ✗ PFK

A Beswick vase, decorated with an abstract pattern, 1950s, 10in (25.5cm) high.
£50–60 / €75–85
$100–115 ⊞ HOM

A Beswick model of a lion, by Graham Tongue, No. 2089, 1967–84, 5½in (14cm) high.
£45–50 / €65–75
$85–95 ✗ BBR

▶ **Two Beswick models of a lioness and a cub,** by Graham Tongue, No. 2098, 1967–84, lioness 5¾in (14.5cm) high.
£40–45 / €60–70
$75–85 ✗ BBR

A Beswick model of a polar bear, No. MN1533, 1960s, 5in (12.5cm) high.
£200–240 / €290–350
$380–450 ✗ Pott

A set of six Beswick Rupert Bear and Friends figures, 1980s, tallest 4in (10cm) high.
£660–790 / €960–1,150
$1,250–1,500 ✗ LT

Blue & White

Up until the late 18th, century ceramics were painted by hand – a process that was time-consuming and expensive and the cost of blue and white porcelain imported from China was prohibitive to all but the wealthy. The reduction of tax on tea in 1784, combined with the duties levied on silver to help pay for the war with France, increased demand for pottery teapots and tableware. There was a real gap in the market for affordable, attractive china, and this was filled by the development of transfer-printed decoration in the 1780s.

While several Staffordshire potteries experimented with this new technique, it was Josiah Spode who perfected the process. In transfer printing an engraver draws a design onto paper which is then traced and engraved in dots onto a copper plate. A mixture of ink and oils is applied to the copper plate, the excess is scraped off and the copper plate is then covered with a piece of strong tissue paper coated in a solution of soap and water. After pressing, the paper is removed and placed on the ceramic blank, which is then soaked in a tub of water, fired, glazed and refired. The result produced decorative, durable and economical ceramics, and transfer-printed pottery was eventually introduced throughout the house from bathroom to dining room.

Although a range of colours was eventually produced, blue and white is by far the most collected and commonly found colour combination, both because the Staffordshire potters were inspired by Chinese blue and white porcelain and because cobalt blue (which looks black until the final firing) was initially the only colour that remained stable in the kiln. The blues come in many different variations from deep cobalt to delicate sky blue.

Transfer-printed pottery was produced by many British manufacturers and while some enthusiasts collect by factory, others collect by pattern and shape. An infinite number of patterns were produced and until the passing of the Registration of Design Act in 1842 copyright laws were extremely vague. The same design might be copied by many different factories, and engravers used images from prints, drawings and every conceivable source, leading to an extremely rich output including architectural views, animal pictures and chinoiserie scenes. Although many famous designs, such as Willow Pattern and Spode's Italian, are still in production today, for many collectors the golden age is between 1780 and 1840. Condition and quality are always important. Ideally a piece will have a clear, crisp transfer, a good glaze and no damage to the body. Some imperfections – variations in colour or unevenly placed transfers – exist from the period of manufacture and will not necessarily affect the value of an item too much, particularly if it is a rare piece.

◄ **A Worcester pierced basket,** transfer-printed with Pinecone pattern, slight damage, hatched crescent mark, c1780, 8¾in (22cm) wide.
**£280–330 / €410–480
$540–640** ✕ DN

A Lowestoft mug, transfer-printed with butterflies and flower sprays, slight damage, 1770–80, 5½in (14cm) high.
**£160–190 / €240–280
$300–360** ✕ WW

► **A teapot,** transfer-printed with Conversation pattern, slight damage, 1790–1800, 4in (10cm) high.
**£120–140 / €170–200
$230–270** ✕ DN

A meat dish, transfer-printed with Piping Shepherd pattern, 19thC, 17¾in (45cm) wide.
£280–330 / €410–480
$540–640 ➹ HOLL

A Donovan dessert plate, probably by Davenport, transfer-printed with Fisherman pattern, slight damage, impressed mark, 1800–10, 8¼in (21cm) diam.
£140–165 / €200–240
$260–310 ➹ DN

A meat dish, attributed to Minton, transfer-printed with Beeston Castle, from the Monk's Rock series, slight damage, 1820–30, 20¾in (52.5cm) wide.
£200–240 / €290–350
$380–450 ➹ DN

A Staffordshire pearlware punchbowl, transfer-printed with a chinoiserie pattern, slight damage, c1800, 13½in (34.5cm) diam.
£65–75 / €95–105
$125–145 ➹ WL

▶ A Turner segmented dish, transfer-printed with a chinoiserie pattern, c1810, 9¼in (23.5cm) wide.
£110–130 / €160–190
$210–250 ➹ SWO

A dessert plate, transfer-printed with Classical Ruins pattern, with a basketweave rim, 1815–20, 8in (20.5cm) diam.
£45–50 / €65–75
$85–95 ➹ DN

A jug, transfer-printed with flowers and birds among fruit, slight damage, 1820–30, 9¼in (23.5cm) high.
£300–360 / €440–520
$580–690 ➹ DN

◀ A Wood & Challinor meat dish, transfer-printed with Pheasant pattern, printed marks, 1830–40, 21¾in (55.5cm) wide.
£300–360 / €440–520
$580–690 ➹ DN

A Swansea meat dish, transfer-printed with Long Bridge pattern, impressed mark, 1800–15, 17½in (44.5cm) wide.
£230–270 / €330–390
$440–520 ➹ DN

A drainer, transfer-printed with Endsleigh Cottage pattern, probably from the Passionflower Border series, slight damage, 1825–35, 6½in (16.5cm) square.
£190–220 / €280–320
$360–420 ➹ DN

A Wood & Sons jug, transfer-printed with Castles pattern, 1930s, 5in (12.5cm) high.
£50–60 / €75–85
$100–115 ⊞ HO

Burleigh Ware

Burleigh Ware was manufactured by the Staffordshire firm of Burgess & Leigh (established 1851). Among the most collectable Burleigh Ware pieces are flower jugs designed in the 1930s. Shapes were created by Earnest Tansley Bailey and decoration was produced by Art Director and watercolourist Harold Bennett. Harold Lowe developed the characteristic primrose glaze used for the body. Jugs were sold through smart department stores and many remained in production until the mid-1950s. However, it is the less successful designs that can today command the highest prices – for example, the Guardsman jug shown here, which was not popular in the '30s and only had a limited production run. This jug came in two versions, one of which included a sentry box. Many jugs were produced in different colourways and sizes and these variations can affect value. In terms of dinnerware, one of the most popular designs is Pan.

A Burleigh Ware jug, moulded with a highwayman, c1933, 8in (20.5cm) high.
£400–450 / €580–650
$770–860 ⊞ BEV

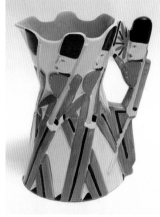

A Burleigh Ware jug, moulded with guardsmen, c1933, 8in (20.5cm) high.
£1,600–1,800 / €2,300–2,600
$3,050–3,450 ⊞ HOM

▶ **A Burleigh Ware jug,** moulded with a parrot, c1935, 8in (20.5cm) high.
£135–150 / €195–220
$260–290 ⊞ HEW

A Burleigh Ware jug, moulded with a pixie, 1930s, 5in (12.5cm) high.
£50–60 / €75–85
$100–115 ⊞ HOM

A Burleigh Ware jug, moulded with honeycomb and bees, c1933, 8in (20.5cm) high.
£990–1,100
€1,450–1,600
$1,900–2,100 ⊞ HOM

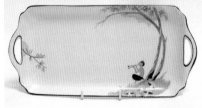

A Burleigh Ware dish, decorated with Pan pattern, 1930s, 11in (28cm) wide.
£25–30 / €40–45
$50–55 ⊞ HOM

▶ **A Burleigh Ware plate,** moulded with a gnome, c1935, 7in (18cm) high.
£55–65 / €80–95
$105–125 ⊞ HEW

Candle Extinguishers

▶ **A ceramic candle extinguisher,** in the form of French Cook, c1880, 3in (7.5cm) high.
£390–440 / €570–640
$750–840 ⊞ TH

A Staffordshire candle extinguisher, in the form of a Bluecoat schoolboy, c1880, 3½in (9cm) high.
£290–330 / €420–480
$560–630 ⊞ TH

A Berlin porcelain candle extinguisher, c1890, 3¼in (8.5cm) high.
£220–250 / €320–360
$420–480 ⊞ TH

A Royal Worcester candle extinguisher, in the form of a monk, 1913, 4¾in (12cm) high.
£95–110 / €140–165
$185–220 ↗ G(L)

A Royal Worcester candle extinguisher, 'Mandarin', 1919, 4in (10cm) high.
£360–400 / €520–580
$690–770 ⊞ TH

Carlton Ware

A Carlton Ware jam pot, in the form of a cottage, c1930, 5in (12.5cm) high.
£130–145 / €190–210
$250–280 ⊞ BEV

A Carlton Ware lustre biscuit barrel, decorated with fruit, 1930s, 6in (15cm) high.
£120–135 / €175–195
$230–260 ⊞ BEV

A Carlton Ware jam pot, 1930s, 3in (7.5cm) high.
£110–125 / €160–180
$210–240 ⊞ BEV

◀ A Carlton Ware ginger jar and cover, decorated in enamel and gilt with Persian pattern, marked, c1930, 10¼in (26cm) high.
£350–420 / €510–610
$670–810 ⋏ LAY

A Carlton Ware dish, c1938, 7in (18cm) wide.
£50–60 / €75–85
$100–115 ⊞ HEW

A Carlton Ware teapot, decorated with Wild Rose pattern, 1930s, 7in (18cm) wide.
£175–195 / €250–280
$330–370 ⊞ BEV

A Carlton Ware breakfast set, comprising teapot, cup, saucer and sugar bowl, 1950s.
£25–30 / €40–45
$50–55 ⋏ AMB

A Carlton Ware coffee can and saucer, with matching cream jug and sugar basin, c1930.
£65–75 / €95–105
$125–145 ⋏ WilP

A Carlton Ware vase, decorated in enamel and gilt with hollyhocks, printed mark, 1930s, 11in (28cm) high.
£380–450 / €550–650
$730–860 ⋏ Hal

A Carlton Ware money box, in the form of a pirate's head, 1970, 6in (15cm) high.
£40–45 / €60–70
$75–85 ⊞ FRD

Chinese Ceramics

Much of the Chinese porcelain illustrated below is cargo ware rescued from sunken ships. The Vung Tau cargo was excavated from the wreck of a Chinese junk which floundered off the coast of Vietnam, south of Vung Tau in 1690. Some 60 years later, in 1752 a Dutch export vessel sank in the South China Sea. An expedition led by Englishman Mike Hatcher in 1985 resulted in a haul of 18th-century Chinese porcelain that was sold at auction under the collective name of the Nanking cargo. The huge success of this sale encouraged the search for other vessels. In 1995, Christie's auctioned porcelain salvaged from the *Diana*, a trading ship lost in 1816 while working the India to China route. Some 24,000 objects were recovered but even this astonishing number was exceeded by the *Tek Sing* cargo, recovered in 1999. When she sank in the China seas in 1822, the *Tek Sing* (*True Star*) was carrying approximately 350,000 pieces of porcelain, making this by far the largest cargo of Chinese ceramics to be rescued from the sea and providing a fascinating insight into an early 19th-century shipment. With all the objects illustrated, condition is crucial to value and it is the pieces that have best survived centuries in the sea that command the highest prices.

Two miniature vases, from the Vung Tau cargo, c1690, 2¼in (5.5cm) diam.
£90–100 / €130–145
$170–190 each ⊞ RBA

A saucer, from the Vung Tau cargo, c1690, 5in (12.5cm) diam.
£80–90 / €115–130
$155–175 ⊞ RBA

A saucer, from the Vung Tau cargo, with floral decoration, c1690, 6in (15cm) diam.
£220–250 / €320–360
$420–480 ⊞ RBA

◀ **A cup and saucer,** from the Vung Tau cargo, painted with floral panels, c1690, saucer 5in (12.5cm) diam.
£350–400 / €510–580
$670–770 ⊞ RBA

A Chinese export plate, 1730–45, 11in (28cm) diam.
£75–85 / €110–125
$145–165 ⊞ McP
18th-century Chinese blue and white pottery is far more common than English delftware.

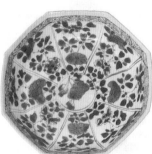

A plate, from the Nanking cargo, c1750, 9in (23cm) diam.
£400–450 / €580–650
$770–860 ⊞ RBA

A dish, decorated with waterlilies and pansies, 18thC, 14¼in (36cm) wide.
£20–25 / €30–35
$40–50 ↗ TRM(D)

◀ **A Chinese Imari tea cup and saucer,** from the Nanking cargo, decorated with chrysanthemums, c1750, saucer 5in (12.5cm) diam.
£180–200 / €260–290
$340–380 ⊞ RBA
The fact that the overglaze has remained in such good condition shows how well it must have been protected from the sea.

Two bowls, from the *Diana* cargo, 1817, 5½in (14cm) diam.
£60–70 / €85–100
$115–135 ⊞ RBA

A bowl, from the *Diana* cargo, with spiral lotus, 1817, 6in (15cm) diam.
£190–220 / €280–320
$360–410 ⊞ RBA

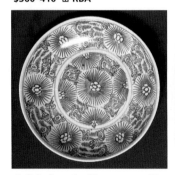

◀ **A figural group of a man and a woman,** from the *Diana* cargo, 1817, 2½in (6.5cm) high.
£105–120 / €150–170
$200–220 ⊞ RBA

A dish, from the *Diana* cargo, with starburst decoration, 1817, 11in (28cm) diam.
£190–220 / €280–320
$360–420 ⊞ RBA

A saucer, from the *Tek Sing* cargo, decorated with peonies and magnolias, 1822, 6in (15cm) diam.
£110–130 / €160–180
$210–240 ⊞ RBA

A bowl, from the *Tek Sing* cargo, with spiral lotus, 1822, 5in (12.5cm) diam.
£110–130 / €160–180
$210–240 ⊞ RBA

A fish paste bowl, from the *Tek Sing* cargo, the finial in the form of a fish, 1822, 6in (15cm) diam.
£720–800 / €1,000–1,150
$1,400–1,550 ⊞ RBA

A bowl, from the *Tek Sing* cargo, painted with a basket of flowers, 1822, 5in (12.5cm) diam.
£105–120 / €150–170
$200–220 ⊞ RBA

A bowl, from the *Tek Sing* cargo, c1822, 3¼in (8.5cm) diam.
£60–70 / €85–100
$115–135 ⊞ McP

Clarice Cliff

Although not as strong as it was five years ago, the market for Clarice Cliff is still underpinned by a solid fan base including the Clarice Cliff Collectors' Club and other private buyers. With high-quality works becoming increasingly hard to find (collectors tend to hang on to their treasures when prices are less buoyant), rarities that are fresh to the market can attract considerable interest. Recent events in the colourful world of Clarice Cliff include the heart-warming story of a lady who paid £1 / €1.50 / $2 for a fine Latonia Dhalia charger from a car boot sale

in Manchester. 'I spotted the dish sitting underneath an old teapot and was attracted by its bright colours,' she explained. It was sold at Christie's last year and fetched £1,920 / €2,800 / $3,700. Rarity and quality will always attract potential buyers, particularly when combined with an invitingly conservative estimate. In the same sale, an Orange Lucerne sandwich set, estimated at a modest £1,500–2,000 / €2,175–2,900 / $2,900–3,850, encouraged fierce bidding and an eventual hammer price of £9,000 / €13,000 / $17,300.

A Clarice Cliff cruet set, decorated with Crocus pattern, c1930, 3in (7.5cm) high.
£240–280 / €350–410 $460–540 ⚹ WilP

A Clarice Cliff Bizarre tea service, comprising 41 pieces, printed marks, c1930.
£950–1,100 / €1,400–1,650 $1,800–2,150 ⚹ WL

A Clarice Cliff Flora wall mask, c1930, 15in (38cm) wide.
£1,050–1,250 €1,500–1,800 $2,000–2,400 ⚹ LAY

◀ **A Clarice Cliff Bizarre Isis vase,** marked, restored, c1930, 9¾in (25cm) high.
£340–400 €490–580 $650–770 ⚹ SWO

◀ **A Clarice Cliff teapot,** in the form of a cockerel, damaged, c1930, 8in (20.5cm) high.
£100–120 / €145–175 $195–230 ⚹ G(L)

A Clarice Cliff plate, decorated with Rhodanthe pattern, c1934, 9in (23cm) diam.
£360–400 / €520–580 $690–770 ⊞ HEW

A Clarice Cliff part coffee service, decorated with Secrets pattern, printed marks, 1933–37.
£1,400–1,650 / €2,000–2,400 $2,700–3,200 ⚹ S(O)

A Clarice Cliff candlestick, decorated with Viscaria pattern, c1934, 10in (25.5cm) high.
£510–580 / €740–840 $980–1,100 ⊞ JFME

A Clarice Cliff bowl, decorated with Rhodanthe pattern, c1934, 9in (23cm) diam.
£360–400 / €520–580
$690–770 ⊞ HEW

A Clarice Cliff beaker, decorated with Feather and Leaves pattern, 1930s, 3in (7.5cm) high.
£240–270 / €350–390
$460–520 ⊞ JFME

A Clarice Cliff candlestick, decorated with Chintz pattern, 1930s, 3in (7.5cm) high.
£100–115 / €145–165
$190–220 ⊞ TAC

A Clarice Cliff plate, decorated with Capri pattern, c1935, 10in (25.5cm) diam.
£400–450 / €580–650
$770–860 ⊞ HEW

A Clarice Cliff Bon Jour tea service, comprising two cups, saucers, side plates, a teapot, milk jug and sugar bowl, decorated with Green Cowslip pattern, Bizarre backstamp, 1930s.
£1,100–1,300 / €1,600–1,900
$2,100–2,500 ⚶ G(L)

◀ **A Clarice Cliff Fantasque Bizarre biscuit barrel,** with a chrome-plated handle and cover, printed marks, 1930s, 6¼in (16cm) high.
£300–360 / €440–520
$580–690 ⚶ SWO

A Clarice Cliff sugar sifter, decorated with My Garden Sunrise pattern, 1930s, 5½in (14cm) high.
£300–360 / €440–520
$580–690 ⚶ G(L)

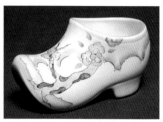

A Clarice Cliff sabot, decorated with Tiger Tree pattern, c1936, 6in (15cm) wide.
£360–400 / €520–580
$690–770 ⊞ JFME

A pair of Clarice Cliff jugs, 1930s, 6in (15cm) high.
£90–100 / €130–145
$170–190 ⊞ SAT

A Clarice Cliff tureen, decorated with Lodore pattern, 1930s, 8¼in (21cm) wide.
£70–80 / €100–115
$135–155 ⚶ WilP

A Clarice Cliff wall plaque, decorated with a swallow, c1947, 8in (20.5cm) wide.
£220–250 / €320–360
$420–480 ⊞ HEW

Susie Cooper

◄ **A Susie Cooper trio,** decorated with Asterisk pattern, c1930, cup 3in (7.5cm) diam.
£65–75 / €95–105
$125–145 ⊞ BEV

A Susie Cooper coffee service, comprising six coffee cans and saucers, a cream jug, a sugar basin and a coffee pot, decorated with Whispering Grass pattern, 1960s, coffee pot 9¼in (23.5cm) high.
£80–90 / €115–130
$155–175 ⋏ WilP

A Susie Cooper plate, c1930s, 6¾in (17cm) diam.
£15–20 / €22–29
$29–38 ⊞ FOX

A Susie Cooper Wedgwood cup and saucer, decorated with Camellia pattern, c1950, cup 2in (5cm) diam.
£25–30 / €40–45
$50–55 ⊞ BEV

► **A Susie Cooper plate,** decorated with Mariposa pattern, 1960s, 10in (25.5cm) diam.
£30–35 / €45–50
$55–65 ⊞ CHI

Cups, Saucers & Mugs

A Worcester coffee cup, painted with dragons, 18thC.
£100–120 / €145–175
$195–230 ⋏ HYD

A cabinet cup and saucer, with floral decoration, the gilt handle in the form of a wing, early 19thC.
£210–250 / €300–360
$400–480 ⋏ BWL

► **A pearlware pottery tyg,** inscribed 'Duke William Inn, Shelf', damaged, c1840.
£320–380 / €460–550
$610–730 ⋏ TEN

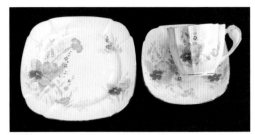

A Paragon trio, decorated with Spring Flowers
pattern, c1930.
£145–165 / €210–240
$280–320 ⊞ BEV

A Paragon trio, the cup with a flower handle, 1930s.
£155–175 / €220–250
$300–340 ⊞ SCH

A Royal Albert cup and saucer,
decorated with Masquerade
pattern, 1950s.
£15–20 / €22–29
$29–38 ⊞ CHI

A Franciscan tea cup and saucer,
decorated with Reflections
pattern, 1960s.
£10–15 / €15–22
$19–28 ⊞ CHI

**A Royal Albert tea cup and
saucer,** decorated with Chelsea Bird
pattern, 1970s.
£20–25 / €30–35
$40–50 ⊞ CHI

Delftware

Delftware is the name given to the tin-glazed earthenware made at Delft in Holland and in England, where it was introduced by immigrant Dutch craftsmen. The industry emerged in Delft in the mid-17th century when potters took over a number of breweries following a decline in the beer market. Designs were inspired by the Oriental pottery imported by the Dutch East India Company, hence the typical blue and white patterns. English delft items were produced in the areas of Bristol, London and Liverpool – ports were a favourite place for ceramic manufacture as clay could be shipped in and finished wares sent out.

English delftware peaked in popularity in the mid-18th century, after which the development of creamware and porcelain sent the industry into decline. The fragile nature of tin-glazed earthenware means that damage and chipping are extremely commonplace; depending on the desirability of the piece, however, this does not necessarily deter collectors.

A pair of Dutch Delft marriage plates, damaged, c1716, 8¾in (22cm) diam.
£220–260 / €320–380
$420–500 ↗ Oli

A pair of Dutch Delft vases and covers, painted with a man fishing by a riverbank, 18thC, 13¼in (33.5cm) high.
£300–360 / €440–520
$580–690 ↗ G(L)

▶ **A Dutch Delft bowl,** painted with trailing flowers and leaves, 18thC, 10¼in (26cm) diam.
£280–330 / €410–480
$540–640 ↗ WW

A Bristol delft plate, decorated with a quail, 18thC, 8½in (21.5cm) diam.
£120–140 / €170–200
$230–270 ↗ GIL

A Dutch Delft plate, painted with a deer and a rabbit, repaired, 1749, 8¾in (22cm) diam.
£220–260 / €320–380
$420–500 ↗ WW

▶ **A delft vase,** decorated with a bird and flowers, 18thC, 8½in (21.5cm) high.
£180–210 / €260–310
$340–400 ↗ G(L)

A Liverpool delft plate, painted with a bird and a hedge, slight damage, mid-18thC, 9in (23cm) diam.
£140–165 / €200–240
$270–320 ↗ SWO

Denby

A Denby Danesby ware vase, 1920s,
7in (18cm) high.
£45–50 / €65–75
$85–95 ⊞ HeA

A Denby model of a rabbit, 1930s,
11in (28cm) high.
£260–290 / €370–420
$500–550 ⊞ BEV

► **A Denby Ode platter,** c1963, 12in (30.5cm) wide.
£20–25
€30–35
$40–50 ⊞ CHI

◄ **A Denby Mayflower dinner plate, side plate, cup and saucer,** 1960s, plate 10in (25.5cm) diam.
£10–15 / €15–22
$19–28 each
⊞ CHI

◄ **A Denby Sonnet egg cup,** c1977.
£10–15 / €15–22
$19–28 ⊞ CHI

For further information on Egg Cups see page 103

A Denby Rondo tea cup and saucer, 1970s.
£15–20 / €22–29
$29–38 ⊞ CHI

A Denby Romany milk jug, 1970s,
4½in (11.5cm) high.
£6–10 / €9–15
$12–19 ⊞ CHI

Derby

Two Derby dishes and two plates,
with floral decoration, painted marks,
c1790, dishes 9in (23cm) diam.
£220–260 / €320–380
$420–500 ✦ SWO

A Royal Crown Derby *sucrier*,
painted in the Imari palette, pattern
No. 2451, printed mark, c1900,
5½in (14cm) wide.
£70–80 / €100–115
$135–155 ✦ GAK

A Royal Crown Derby basket and six dessert plates, hand-painted with
floral decoration, pattern No. 7241,
printed and impressed marks, 1905.
£120–140 / €170–200
$230–270 ✦ SWO

Doulton

Doulton & Watts was founded by John Doulton in 1815 in Lambeth, south London. The pottery produced salt-glazed stoneware bottles, flasks, storage jars, chimney pots and other utilitarian products. True success came after a series of cholera epidemics in the mid-19th century prompted a campaign to clean up London by building an efficient sewer system. Doulton's stoneware pipes and drainage accessories, used across London and subsequently all over the world, established the great prosperity of the company and laid a secure foundation for the development of Doulton's Art Pottery which was exhibited at the International Exhibition at South Kensington in 1871. Doulton forged close links with Lambeth School of Art which provided many famous decorators including brothers Arthur and George Tinworth and the sisters Florence and Hannah Barlow. 'Early Doulton pieces signed by the artist are going from strength to strength,' says auctioneer Clive Hillier from Louis Taylor. 'Even more run-of-the-mill stoneware has been keeping its value in what is generally a difficult market.'

Other Doulton successes from the Victorian and Edwardian periods include objects that appeal to more niche-based collectors such as inkwells and novelty paperweights. Doulton is certainly better known for its Pretty Lady figures. Initiated by modeller Charles Noke, the series took off in 1913, when the HN (for chief colourist Harry Nixon) numbering system was introduced, and figures have been produced ever since. 'Early and rare figures have been making good prices,' says Clive Hillier. 'The 1920s and '30s examples by designers such as Leslie Harradine, have real quality, tremendous energy of design and they're very popular. Prototype figures also appeal strongly to collectors, even when they are damaged.' For later and more run-of-the-mill Pretty Lady-style figures, condition is all-important and price levels have certainly dropped but, according to Hillier, this could change. 'The Doulton factory is set to close and will be relocated to Asia,' he explains. 'When Beswick closed their factory a couple of years ago, interest in Beswick rose and prices went up, and I predict that the same could happen with Doulton.'

A Doulton Lambeth jug,
c1880, 7in (18cm) high.
£85–95 / €125–140
$165–185 ⊞ SAT

A Doulton Impasto ware vase, decorated with flowers, impressed marks, dated 1886, 10½in (26.5cm) high.
£90–100 / €130–145
$170–190 ⋏ G(L)

◀ **A Royal Doulton Iris vase,** with gilt decoration, c1900, 6in (15cm) high.
£85–95 / €125–140
$165–185 ⊞ BET

A Doulton Lambeth jug,
incised with a crown, 'C.R.' and '1646', 1887, 11in (28cm) high.
£180–200 / €260–290
$340–380 ⊞ BS

▶ **A Doulton Lambeth Harvest ware jug,** with a silver rim, assay mark 1901, 12in (30.5cm) high.
£85–95 / €125–140
$165–185 ⋏ AMB

A pair of Doulton vases,
impressed marks, signed, late 19thC, 15½in (39.5cm) high.
£220–260 / €320–380
$420–500 ⋏ Hal

A Doulton Lambeth ring tray, by Harry Simeon, surmounted by a model of a bird, impressed mark, incised initials, 1920s, 5¾in (14.5cm) high.
£300–360 / €440–520
$580–690 ⚒ RTo

For further information on Jugs see page 115

▶ **A Royal Doulton jug,** entitled 'Treasure Island', No. 390 of 600, slight damage, c1934, 7½in (19cm) high.
£260–310 / €380–450
$500–600 ⚒ BWL

A Royal Doulton jug, by C.J. Noke, entitled 'The Shakespeare Jug', decorated with a continuous frieze of characters, No. 817 of 1,000, printed mark, c1933, 10¾in (27.5cm) high.
£620–740 / €900–1,050
$1,200–1,400 ⚒ S(O)

◀ **A Royal Doulton jug,** entitled 'Pied Piper' decorated with a relief-moulded scene, No. 312 of 600, signed 'Noke' and 'H. Fenton', c1934, 10¼in (26cm) high.
£720–860
€1,050–1,250
$1,400–1,650
⚒ LJ

A Royal Doulton teapot, decorated with Camelot pattern, 1960s, 7in (18cm) high.
£50–60 / €75–85
$100–115 ⊞ CHI

Doulton Character Jugs

A Royal Doulton Mephistopheles character jug, No. D5757, 1937–48, 7in (18cm) high.
**£470–560 €680–810
$950–1,100** ♙ MAR

A Royal Doulton Field Marshall Smuts character jug, No. D6198, 1946–48, 6½in (16.5cm) high.
**£450–540 / €650–780
$870–1,050** ♙ CHTR

A Royal Doulton John Peel character jug, by Henry Fenton, No. D5612, marked, 1936–60, 6½in (16.5cm) high.
**£40–45 / €60–70
$75–85** ♙ BBR

▶ **A Royal Doulton The Poacher character jug,** 1954, 4½in (11.5cm) high.
**£40–45 / €60–70
$75–85** ⊞ HEI

◀ **A Royal Doulton Thomas Jefferson character jug,** No. D6943, 1994, 6¾in (17cm) high.
**£180–210
€260–300
$340–400**
♙ Pott

Doulton Figures

A Royal Doulton flambé model of a cat, 1920–36, 3½in (9cm) wide.
**£410–490
€590–710
$790–940** ♙ LT

▶ **A Royal Doulton figure,** designed by Leslie Harradine, entitled 'Flower Seller's Children', No. HN1342, 1929–93, 8in (20.5cm) high.
**£180–210
€260–310
$340–400** ♙ DN

A Royal Doulton flambé model of a pig, slight damage, 1920–36, 5¼in (13.5cm) high.
**£680–800 / €990–1,150
$1,300–1,550** ♙ LT

▶ **A Royal Doulton model of a fox,** No. HN130, impressed date for 1930, 8½in (21.5cm) high.
**£160–190 / €240–280
$300–360** ♙ G(L)

A Royal Doulton figure, entitled 'Micawber', No. HN557, 1923–39, 7¼in (18.5cm) high.
**£160–190 / €220–260
$300–360** ♙ SWO

◄ A Royal Doulton figure, entitled 'Dulcinea', No. HN1419, 1930–38, 5½in (14cm) high.
£2,000–2,400
€2,900–3,450
$3,850–4,600
↗ LT

A Royal Doulton figure, entitled 'Janet', No. HN1537, 1932–95, 6½in (16.5cm) high.
£45–50 / €65–75
$85–95 ↗ AMB

A Royal Doulton figure, entitled 'Cobbler', No. HN1706, 1935–69, 8¼in (21cm) high.
£100–120 / €145–175
$195–230 ↗ BWL

A Royal Doulton figure, designed by C.J. Noke, entitled 'Calmet', No. HN1689, 1935–49, 6¾in (17cm) high.
£300–360 / €440–520
$580–690 ↗ SWO

A Royal Doulton figure, designed by Leslie Harradine, entitled 'Daffy Down Dilly', No. HN1712, 1935–75, 8¼in (21cm) high.
£25–30 / €40–45
$50–55 ↗ SJH

► A Royal Doulton model of a mallard drake, No. HN1198, damaged, 1937–52, 13in (33cm) high.
£580–690 / €830–1,000
$1,100–1,300 ↗ LT

◄ A Royal Doulton figure, entitled 'The Farmer's Boy', No. HN2520, marked, 1938–60, 8¼in (21cm) high.
£500–600
€730–870
$960–1,150
↗ TEN

► A Royal Doulton figure, entitled 'The Orange Lady', No. HN1953, marked, 1940–75, 8½in (21.5cm) high.
£70–80
€100–115
$135–155
↗ AMB

A Royal Doulton figure, entitled 'Roseanna', No. HN1926, 1940–59, 8in (20.5cm) high.
£70–80 / €100–115 $135–155 ⚡ CHTR

A Royal Doulton figure, entitled 'The Ermine Coat', No. HN1981, printed marks, 1945–67, 7½in (19cm) high.
£25–30 / €40–45 $50–55 ⚡ SJH

A Royal Doulton figure, entitled 'Bernice', No. HN2071, marked, 1951–53, 7¾in (19.5cm) high.
£560–670 / €810–970 $1,100–1,300 ⚡ LT

A Royal Doulton figure, entitled 'Princess Badoura', No. HN2081, 1952, 24in (61cm) high.
£4,500–5,400 €6,500–7,800 $8,600–10,400 ⚡ Pott

◄ **A Royal Doulton prototype figure of a girl and a crib,** marked, 1950s, 5in (12.5cm) high.
£1,900–2,250 €2,750–3,250 $3,650–4,300 ⚡ LT

A Royal Doulton figure, entitled 'In the Stocks', No. HN2163, 1955–59, 5¾in (14.5cm) high.
£350–420 / €510–610 $680–880 ⚡ LT

A Royal Doulton figure, entitled 'Jolly Sailor', No. HN2172, 1956–65, 6½in (16.5cm) high.
£390–460 / €570–670 $750–800 ⚡ LT

A Royal Doulton figure, entitled 'Mary, Countess of Howe', No. 842 of 5,000, No. HN3007, 1990, 9¼in (23.5cm) high, with original box and letter of authenticity.
£220–260 / €320–380 $420–500 ⚡ AMB

A Royal Doulton figure, entitled 'Sophia Charlotte, Lady Sheffield', No. 1373 of 5,000, No. HN3008, 1990, 10in (25.5cm) high, with box and certificate of authenticity.
£150–180 / €220–260 $290–340 ⚡ AMB

A Royal Doulton prototype figure of a woman brushing her hair, c1995, 8½in (21.5cm) high.
£1,050–1,250 €1,500–1,800 $2,000–2,400 ⚡ LT

A Royal Doulton figure, by Martyn Alcock, entitled 'Cruella de Vil', No. DM1, marked, 1997–2001, 6¼in (16cm) high.
£35–40 / €50–60 $65–75 ⚡ BBR

Egg Cups

A Minton egg cup, c1845, 2¼in (5.5cm) high.
£45–50 / €65–75
$85–95 ⊞ AMH

◄ **A Staffordshire egg cup,** with enamel and gilt decoration, c1880, 2½in (6.5cm) high.
£35–40 / €50–60
$65–75 ⊞ AMH

► **A Staffordshire egg cup,** c1880, 2¼in (5.5cm) high.
£35–40 / €50–60
$65–75 ⊞ AMH

► **A Powell, Bishop and Stonier egg cup,** with enamel and gilt decoration, c1881, 2in (5cm) high.
£75–85 / €110–125
$145–165 ⊞ AMH

An egg cup, c1980, 4in (10cm) high.
£1–5 / €2–7
$3–9 ⊞ POS

Fairings

A fairing, entitled 'Hark Jo Somebody's coming', 1850–1914, 4in (10cm) wide.
£180–200 / €260–290
$340–380 ⊞ DHJ

► **A fairing,** entitled 'Attack', incised numbers, jars restored, c1870, 2¾in (7cm) wide.
£70–80 / €100–115
$135–155 ⋏ SAS

► **A fairing,** entitled 'After You My Dear Alfonso', c1870, 4in (10cm) wide.
£310–350 / €450–510
$600–670 ⊞ Cas

A fairing, entitled 'Good Templars', c1870, 4in (10in) wide.
£155–175 / €220–250
$300–340 ⊞ Cas

A fairing, entitled ' The Landlord in Love', c1870, 4in (10cm) wide.
£450–500 / €650–730
$860–960 ⊞ Cas

A fairing, entitled 'Now Ma-am, Say When', c1870, 4in (10cm) wide.
£115–130 / €165–185
$220–250 ⊞ Cas

A fairing, entitled 'Return From the Bath', c1870, 4in (10cm) wide.
£310–350 / €450–510
$600–670 ⊞ Cas

◀ A fairing, by Conta & Boehme, entitled 'Tea Party', c1870, 4in (10cm) wide.
£135–150 / €195–220
$260–290 ⊞ Cas

A fairing, entitled 'Sarah's Young Man', c1870, 5½in (14cm) high.
£80–90 / €115–130
$155–175 ➤ SAS

A fairing, entitled 'The Wedding Night', c1870, 3½in (9cm) wide.
£125–140 / €180–200
$240–270 ⊞ Cas

A fairing, entitled 'Tug of War', restored, c1870, 5in (12.5cm) wide.
£75–90 / €110–130
$145–175 ➤ SAS

A fairing, by Conta & Boehme, entitled 'Which Is The Prettiest', c1870, 4in (10cm) wide.
£115–130 / €170–190
$220–250 ⊞ Cas

◀ A Victorian fairing box, in the form of figures on horseback, 7¼in (18.5cm) high.
£65–75 / €95–105
$125–145 ➤ SAS

A Victorian fairing inkwell and cover, in the form of a mother and child, restored, 7¼in (18.5cm) high.
£95–110 / €140–165
$185–220 ➤ SAS

Figures

A pottery figural group, entitled
'The Marriage Act Group', probably
19thC from an 18thC mould,
6½in (16.5cm) high.
£170–200 / €250–300
$330–390 ⚘ **BWL**

**A J.&T. Bevington
Parian figure of a girl,**
impressed marks, 1865,
12in (30.5cm) high.
£70–80 / €100–115
$135–155 ⚘ **GAK**

A pair of Moore Brothers figural dishes,
damaged, late 19thC, 8¾in (22cm) high.
£620–740 / €900–1,050
$1,200–1,400 ⚘ **LT**

▶ **A Vienna
Werkstätte-style
figure of
Pan,** damaged,
Continental,
c1910, 25¼in
(64cm) high.
£190–220
€280–330
$360–420
⚘ **SWO**

◀ **A Gmundner
Keramic figure
of a Madonna
and child,**
model No. 170,
impressed
'GK', German,
c1909, 8½in
(21.5cm) high.
£410–490
€600–720
$780–940
⚘ **DORO**

**A pair of glazed figures of a
huntress and her companion,**
slight damage, impressed numerals,
Continental, late 19thC,
19¾in (50cm) high.
£85–95 / €125–140
$165–185 ⚘ **DMC**

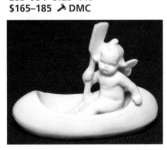

**A bisque figure of a cherub in a
canoe,** German, 1910–20,
3in (7.5cm) wide.
£70–80 / €100–115
$135–155 ⊞ **CCs**

▶ **A Katzhütte
porcelain figure
of a snake
dancer,** printed
marks, Austrian,
c1920, 6¾in
(17cm) high.
£155–185
€230–270
$300–360
⚘ **SWO**

A Goldscheider figure,
entitled 'Lady in the
Wind', model No. 493,
Austrian, 1925–30,
10¾in (27.5cm) high.
£620–720 / €900–1,050
$1,200–1,400 ⚘ **DORO**

A Royal Dux figure of a dancing couple, c1929, 16in (40.5cm) high.
£670–750 / €970–1,100
$1,300–1,450 ⊞ HEW

A Goldscheider figure, entitled 'Dancing Lady', marked '7855', Austrian, c1930, 14in (35.5cm) high.
£500–600 / €730–870
$960–1,150 ✣ BWL

A Katzhütte porcelain figure of a showgirl, Austrian, c1930, 12in (30.5cm) high.
£600–700 / €870–1,000
$1,200–1,350 ⊞ HEW

◄ **A porcelain figure of a lady,** Continental, c1930, 9in (23cm) high.
£135–150 / €195–220
$260–290 ⊞ HEW

A Katzhütte porcelain figure of a woman with a fawn Austrian, c1930, 14in (35.5cm) wide.
£580–650 / €840–940
$1,100–1,250 ⊞ HEW

► **A Crown Staffordshire figure of a boy,** 1930s, 7in (18cm) high.
£360–400
€520–580
$690–770
⊞ SCH

◄ **A Crown Staffordshire figural group of two children,** 1930s, 12in (30.5cm) wide.
£620–700 / €900–1,000
$1,200–1,350 ⊞ SCH

◄ **A Tintagel Pottery figure,** 1950s, 4in (10cm) high.
£25–30 / €40–45
$50–55 ⊞ DPC

► **A Bretby figure,** entitled 'Sarah Gamp', c1950, 9in (23cm) high.
£75–85 / €110–125
$145–165 ⊞ HeA

A Lladro figure, entitled 'Jester's Serenade', c1994, 14½in (37cm) high.
£360–420 / €520–610
$690–820 ✣ JAA

Goebel

In 1871, father and son Franz and William Goebel founded a company in Thuringia, Germany, producing slate pencils and marbles. Using the profits from this business they opened a porcelain factory in 1876, where production included tableware and figurines. Recognizing the importance of the American market, William sent his son Max to research and train in America. On his return, Max created new modern lines in the factory, forging bonds with contemporary artists and sculptors and, in the 1920s, introduced a range of finely potted earthenware that reflected the latest Art Deco styles. It was Max's son Franz, however, who discovered the company's most important designer when, in the early 1930s, he came across the drawings of academy-trained artist and Franciscan nun, Sister Maria Innocentia Hummel (1909–47). Convinced that in a time

of political turmoil the general public would respond to her gentle depictions of childhood, Franz Goebel obtained permission from Sister Hummel and the convent of Siessen to transform her illustrations into figures.

Launched in 1935, Hummel models were a huge success. Since then, over 500 figures have been designed; today models are still based upon Sister Hummel's drawings and approved by the artistic board set up at the Convent of Siessen. Figures are marked with 'M. I. Hummel'. Impressed numbers indicate mould or shape and an impressed date indicates the year that a mould was designed (not necessarily the year that the figure was made). The factory backstamp changed over the years. The early mark, used from 1935 to 1949, includes a crown, a V-shape and a bee motif was used from 1950 and the addition of the factory name Goebel indicates a date after 1964.

A pair of Goebel Shau part-biscuit glamour figures, 1950s, larger 4½in (11cm) high.
£180–210 / €260–300
$350–400 ⚡ LAY

A Goebel cardinal miniature jug, German, c1930, 1½in (4cm) high.
£45–50 / €65–75
$85–95 ⊞ BEV

A Goebel cockerel ashtray, c1930, 5in (12.5cm) wide.
£70–80 / €100–115
$135–155 ⊞ HEW

A Hummel figure of a girl with a basket, 'Meditation', No. 13/V TMK-6, initialled and dated 1980, 14in (35.5cm) high.
£230–270 / €330–390
$430–510 ⚡ JAA

A pair of Goebel bookends, in the form of a stylized cat and a dog, 1950s, 5in (12.5cm) high.
£60–70 / €85–100
$115–135 ⊞ HEI

A Goebel hot water plate and cup, in the form of chicks, 1970s, plate 8in (20.5cm) diam.
£40–45 / €60–70
$75–85 ⊞ LAS

Goss & Crested China

A model of a Welsh hat, with Llanwrtyd Wells crest, 1900–25, 2¼in (5.5cm) high.
£15–20 / €22–29
$29–38 ⊞ CCC

A model of a pig, with Salisbury crest, 1920–25, 4in (10cm) wide.
£25–30 / €40–45
$50–55 ⊞ JMC

A model of a post box, with Skegness crest, 1920s, 2½in (6.5cm) high.
£15–20 / €22–29
$29–38 ⊞ HeA

▶ **An Arcadian model of a caddy on a golf ball,** with Norwich crest, 1903–33, 3in (7.5cm) high.
£50–60 / €75–85
$100–115
⊞ JMC

An Arcadian model of a WWI Red Cross van, with Salisbury crest, c1916, 4in (10cm) wide.
£50–60 / €75–85
$100–115 ⊞ BtoB

An Arcadian pin dish, 1920s, 4in (10cm) wide.
£80–90 / €115–130
$155–175 ⊞ MURR

▶ **A Carlton model of an E.9. submarine,** with crest, 1914–18, 5¾in (14.5cm) wide.
£70–80
€100–115
$135–155
⊞ G&CC

Items in the Ceramics section have been arranged in date order within each sub-section.

◀ **A Carlton figure of a Yorkshireman,** with Scarborough crest, 1920s, 5in (12.5cm) high.
£40–45 / €60–70
$75–85 ⊞ HeA

A Corona model of a WWI war memorial, with Romsey crest, 1914–18, 6½in (16.5cm) high.
£135–150 / €195–220
$260–290 ⊞ G&CC

A Goss model of the Eddystone lighthouse, with Corfe Castle crest, 1920s, 5in (12.5cm) high.
£40–45 / €60–70
$75–85 ⊞ HeA

A Goss jam pot, decorated with strawberries and leaves, the cover with a knop in the form of a strawberry, c1890, 4in (10cm) high.
£85–95 / €125–140
$165–185 ⊞ HO

A Goss model of a font, late 19thC, 5¼in (13.5cm) high.
£180–210 / €250–300
$340–400 ⋗ G(L)

◄ **A Goss model of the Stratford-on-Avon church font,** entitled 'Model of font in which Shakespeare was Baptised', 1920s, 4in (10cm) diam.
£50–60 / €75–85
$100–115
⊞ HeA

◄ **A Goss vase,** with three handles and hospital crests, 1881–1929, 2¼in (5.5cm) high.
£75–85 / €110–125
$145–165 ⊞ G&CC

A Goss cabaret set, comprising 13 pieces, with Royal Crown and 1887 Jubilee patterns.
£165–195 / €240–280
$310–370 ⋗ DMC

► **A Goss milk jug,** with transfer-printed decoration of Plas Newydd, Llangollen and the Ladies of Llangollen to the reverse, c1890, 4¼in (11cm) high.
£140–160
€200–230
$270–310
⊞ CCC

A Goss pin tray, with Skegness crest, 1920s, 6in (15cm) wide.
£15–20 / €22–29
$29–38 ⊞ HeA

A Goss figure of a parson, 1920s–30s, 3½in (9cm) high.
£170–200 / €250–290
$330–380 ⏶ Pott

A Rita China model of the Folly, Pontypool, with crest, 1905–30, 3in (7.5cm) high.
£110–125 / €160–180
$210–240 ⊞ G&CC

▶ **A Shelley model of a horn gramophone,** 1903–23, 4in (10cm) high.
£40–45 / €60–70
$75–85 ⊞ G&CC

▶ **A Willow Art model of St Ann's Well, Great Malvern,** 1905–30, 4in (10cm) wide.
£135–150 / €195–220
$260–290 ⊞ G&CC

T. G. Green

◀ **A T. G. Green Flame trio,** 1930s.
£15–20
€22–29
$29–38 ⊞ RET

A T. G. Green Streamline castor sugar storage jar, 1930s, 6in (15cm) high.
£60–70 / €85–100
$115–135 ⊞ SCH

A T. G. Green Streamline hot water jug, 1930s, 5in (12.5cm) high.
£130–145 / €190–210
$250–280 ⊞ SCH

A set of two T. G. Green plates and two bowls, decorated with Seagull pattern, 1930s, plate 6½in (16.5cm) diam.
£35–40 / €50–60
$65–75 ⊞ CAL

A T. G. Green Hunt Club plate, mid-1950s, 7½in (19cm) diam.
£40–45 / €60–70
$75–85 ⊞ CAL

A T. G. Green Cornish Ware milk jug, c1940, 5in (12.5cm) high.
£90–100 / €130–145
$170–190 ⊞ CHI

A T. G. Green pot and cover, damaged, 1950s, 2½in (6.5cm) high.
£25–30 / €40–45
$50–55 ⊞ CAL

A T. G. Green platter, 1950s, 12in (30.5cm) wide.
£15–20 / €22–29
$29–38 ⊞ CAL

A T. & G. Green Oakville sugar bowl, 1950s, 4in (10cm) high.
£15–20 / €22–29
$29–38 ⊞ CAL

▶ **A set of four T. G. Green Polo Ware cups,** together with a sugar bowl and cream jug, 1950s, jug 3in (7.5cm) high.
£50–60 / €75–85
$100–115 ⊞ CAL

A T. G. Green Cornish Ware storage jar, 1960, 6in (15cm) high.
£25–30 / €40–45
$50–55 ⊞ CAL

A T. G. Green storage jar, 1980s, 7in (18cm) high.
£10–15 / €15–22
$19–28 ⊞ CAL

A T. G. Green Cornish Ware Millennium mug, with a Man-in-the-Moon handle, limited edition, 2000, 4in (10cm) high.
£30–35 / €45–50
$55–65 ⊞ CAL
This mug was a limited edition issue, only available to members of the Collectors' Club.

Honey Pots

A Belleek honey pot and cover, decorated with bees and grasses, Irish, First Period, 1863–90, 6in (15cm) high.
**£280–330 / €410–480
$540–630** ↗ HOLL

A Belleek-style honey pot, slight damage, Japanese, 1930s, 6in (15cm) high.
**£60–70 / €85–100
$115–135** ⊞ EHCS

A Marutomo Ware honey pot, with stamped marks, Japanese, 1930s, 4¼in (11cm) high.
**£65–75 / €95–105
$125–145** ⊞ EHCS

A Wadeheath honey pot, stamped mark, c1930, 3¾in (9.5cm) high.
**£30–35 / €45–50
$55–65** ⊞ EHCS

▶ **A Marutomo Ware honey pot,** stamped marks, Japanese, 1930s, 4¼in (11cm) high.
**£55–65 / €80–95
$105–125** ⊞ EHCS

A Clarice Cliff Bizarre honey pot and cover, decorated with Gayday pattern, 1930s, 3½in (9cm) high.
**£70–80 / €100–115
$135–155** ↗ SWO

◀ **A Carlton Ware lustre honey pot,** stamped marks, 1920s–30s, 4¼in (11cm) high.
**£100–120
€145–175
$195–230**
⊞ EHCS

A Carlton Ware lustre honeycomb box, stamped marks, 1920s–30s, 6¾in (17cm) square.
**£140–160 / €200–230
$270–310** ⊞ EHCS

A Wadeheath honey pot, stamped mark, c1930, 3¾in (9.5cm) high.
**£35–40 / €50–60
$65–75** ⊞ EHCS

A Wadeheath honey pot, stamped mark, c1930, 3¾in (9.5cm) high.
**£45–50 / €65–75
$85–95** ⊞ EHCS

A Marutomo Ware honey pot, stamped marks, Japanese, 1930s, 3¼in (8.5cm) high.
**£40–45 / €60–70
$75–85** ⊞ EHCS

◀ **A Royal Winton beehive honey pot,** stamped marks, 1930s, 3½in (9cm) high.
**£100–120 / €145–175
$195–230** ⊞ EHCS

A Crown Devon honey pot,
1940s, 5in (12.5cm) high.
£40–45 / €60–70
$75–85 ⊞ BAC

An Isle of Man Pottery honey pot, marked, 1960s–70s,
4¾in (12cm) high.
£65–75 / €95–105
$125–145 ⊞ EHCS

A honey pot, the cover with a knop in the form of a teddy bear,
1990s, 6in (15cm) high.
£1–5 / €2–7
$3–9 ⊞ BAC

Three Goebel honey pots, stamped marks,
German, 1960–90, largest 6in (15cm) high.
£85–95 / €125–140
$165–185 ⊞ EHCS

Two Goebel honey pots, stamped, German,
1979, larger 5¼in (13.5cm) high.
£60–70 / €85–100
$125–145 each ⊞ EHCS

Two Alexander Ceramics honey pots,
stamped marks, Welsh, 1990s,
5¼in (13.5cm) high.
£8–12 / €12–18
$16–23 each ⊞ EHCS

A Wedgwood jasper ware honey pot,
impressed marks, 1967,
4½in (11.5cm) high.
£400–450 / €580–650
$770–860 ⊞ EHCS

A Goebel honey pot,
stamped mark, German,
1979, 5in (12.5cm) high.
£40–45 / €60–70
$75–85 ⊞ EHCS

◄ **Two honey pots,**
impressed marks, Italian,
1990s, larger
5¼in (13.5cm) high.
£15–20 / €22–29
$29–38 each ⊞ EHCS

A Vicary Ware honey pot, the decoration highlighted with 22ct gold, No. 1/25, marked 'Silent Night', stamped marks, 2001, 5¼in (13.5cm) high.
£140–160 / €200–230
$270–310 ⊞ EHCS

Japanese Pottery & Porcelain

A pair of Satsuma buttons, c1910, 1in (2.5cm) diam.
£25–30 / €40–45
$50–55 each ⊞ JCH

A Satsuma vase, by Kinkozan, decorated in enamel with cartouches of fish, birds and flowers, impressed signature, Meiji period, 1868–1912, 4½in (11.5cm) high.
£1,000–1,200
€1,450–1,750
$1,950–2,300 ↗ DN(BR)

A saucer dish, painted and gilded in the Imari palette with a lady walking among peonies, impressed seal marks, signed, early 20thC, 13½in (34.5cm) diam.
£95–110 / €140–165
$180–210 ↗ PFK

A Noritake footed bowl, marked, 1920s, 5½in (14cm) diam.
£40–45 / €60–70
$75–85 ⊞ DgC

▶ **A Noritake box,** 1920s, 3in (7.5cm) wide.
£85–95 / €125–140
$165–185 ⊞ SAT

◀ **A plate,** decorated with a geisha girl, signed, c1930, 9in (23cm) diam.
£35–40 / €50–60
$65–75 ⊞ BAC

A lithophane geisha cup and saucer, 1930s–40s, saucer 2½in (6.5cm) diam.
£30–35 / €45–50
$55–65 ⊞ BAC
This cup contains a lithophane in its base – a thin, translucent porcelain plaque decorated with a recessed 3-D image that can be viewed by transmitted light, ie when the cup is raised. The process was patented in France in 1827 by Baron Paul de Bourgoing and lithophanes were produced by a wide range of Continental factories throughout the 19th century. One popular application was incorporating them into drinking vessels – from German beer steins to French demitasse sets. From the early 20th century, Japan produced decorated tea sets (called dragon ware) with lithophanes of geisha girls in the bases of the cups. These were popular tourist items with American GIs in the aftermath of WWII, but production tailed off in the 1950s.

A lemon squeezer, in the form of a clown, 1940s, 7in (18cm) high.
£140–160 / €200–230
$270–310 ⊞ SCH

A Napco vase, modelled as a female head, 1950s, 6in (15cm) high.
£55–65 / €80–95
$105–125 ⊞ TWI

Jugs

A slipware jug, damaged, 19thC, 8in (20.5cm) high.
£240–280 / €340–400
$460–540 ⚒ WW

A jug, probably Coalport, enamelled and gilded with sprays of flowers, marked with pattern No. 52, 6¼in (16cm) high.
£80–95 / €115–135
155–180 ⚒ PFK

◀ **A jug,** in the form of Mr Punch, his hat forming the cover, 19thC, 12in (30.5cm) high.
£200–230 / €290–330
$380–440 ⊞ TOP

◀ **An Ironstone jug,** printed and enamelled with bamboo and flowers, c1850, 6in (15cm) high.
£40–45
€60–70
$75–85 ⚒ G(L)

An East Moor Pottery puzzle jug, the pierced rim with three spouts, inscribed, losses, restored, dated 1837, 8¼in (21cm) high.
£130–155 / €190–220
$250–300 ⚒ BBR

A Staffordshire jug, attributed to Elsmore & Forster, printed and enamelled with Grimaldi, Harlequin and other similar figures, cock-fighting scenes and Mr Punch and his dog, damaged, 1855–70, 9¼in (23.5cm) high.
£320–380 / €460–550
$610–730 ⚒ DN

▶ **A stoneware jug,** the front moulded with a portrait, a coat-of-arms to the reverse, the handle moulded with medals, restored, 1861, 10¾in (27.5cm) high.
£35–40
€50–60
$65–75 ⚒ SAS

A Coalport jug, 1880–90, 3in (7.5cm) high.
£45–50 / €65–75
$85–95 ⊞ HER

Two Copeland milk jugs, c1910, larger 11in (28cm) high.
£135–150 / €195–220
$260–290 each ⊞ SMI

A Gray's Pottery Paris cream jug, with hand-painted floral decoration, c1930, 3in (7.5cm) high.
£80–90 / €115–130
$155–175 ⊞ BEV

Lustre Ware

A Sunderland lustre jug, transfer-printed with a view of the cast-iron bridge over the River Wear, slight damage, 19thC, 7¾in (19.5cm) high.
£50–60 / €75–85
$100–115 ⚹ CHTR

A Maling lustre plaque, inscribed 'Thou God See'st Me', early 19thC, 7in (18cm) diam.
£190–220 / €270–320
$360–420 ⚹ G(L)

A Sunderland lustre jug, decorated with a sailor's return and motto, early 19thC, 6in (15cm) high.
£260–310 / €380–450
$500–600 ⚹ G(L)

Sunderland lustre

Sunderland lustre is the name given to pottery that was produced in the Sunderland area of England in the first half of the 19th century. It is decorated with black transfer prints (some of which have been hand-coloured) and framed in pink lustre, often painted in a splashed, irregular style. Typical subjects include sailing vessels, maritime figures and the Iron Bridge over the River Wear. Plaques inscribed with religious mottos were also popular.

A Sunderland lustre fruit bowl, by Scott & Co, printed with *The Great Eastern* steamship, a view of the Sunderland Bridge and arms of the Crimea, impressed mark, c1850, 10½in (26.5cm) diam.
£180–210 / €260–300
$360–420 ⚹ G(L)

A lustre plate, decorated with a house and a garden, c1850, 7in (18cm) diam.
£10–15 / €15–22
$19–28 ⊞ NAW

▶ **A set of five graduated silver lustre jugs,** c1910, largest 6¼in (16cm) high.
£120–140 / €170–200
$230–270 ⚹ SWO

A Carlton Ware lustre powder box, 1920s, 5in (12.5cm) high.
£155–175 / €220–250
$300–340 ⊞ BEV

◀ **A lustre egg timer,** in the form of a windmill, German, c1930, 5in (12.5cm) high.
£55–65 / €80–95
$105–125 ⊞ BEV

▶ **A lustre egg timer,** in the form of a boy, German, c1930, 3in (7.5cm) high.
£45–50 / €65–75
$85–95 ⊞ BEV

Majolica

In the 19th century, love of opulent decoration combined with the fashion for elaborate meals with many courses stimulated a passion for majolica tableware – brightly coloured tin-glazed earthenware that came in the form of everything from oyster plates to dishes in the form of flowers. Herbert Minton launched his majolica range at the Great Exhibition of 1851, where it was a huge hit both with Queen Victoria and the general public. Other British manufacturers included George Jones and Wedgwood, while in France a host of different factories flourished supplying moulded tin-glazed plates and dishes in extravagant shapes and colours.

A majolica jug, in the form of a cockatoo, the handle in the form of bamboo, slight damage, 19thC, 10in (25.5cm) high.
£160–190 / €230–270
$300–360 ⚒ BWL

A pair of majolica vases, marked 'W.F. & S.', 19thC, 13in (33cm) high.
£55–65 / €80–95
$105–125 ⚒ WilP

▶ **A majolica cruet set,** with three bowls, damaged, 19thC, 7in (18cm) high.
£45–50 / €65–75
$85–95 ⚒ BWL

A Minton majolica jug, moulded with oak leaves and acorns, impressed date code for 1863, 7in (18cm) high.
£55–65 / €80–95
$105–125 ⚒ G(L)

A Karlsruhe majolica bowl, by Wilhelm Süs, in the form of a putto riding a swan, model No. 1167, impressed mark, inscribed 'Baden', German, 1910, 7¼in (18.5cm) wide.
£410–490 / €600–720
$790–940 ⚒ DORO

A pair of Minton majolica oyster plates, c1912, 9in (23cm) diam.
£130–145 / €190–210
$250–280 ⊞ DEB

A set of six majolica shell plates, 1930, 8in (20.5cm) wide.
£130–145 / €190–210
$250–280 ⊞ MLL

▶ **A majolica spill vase,** decorated with fish, slight damage, c1950, 4in (10cm) high.
£60–70 / €85–100
$115–135 ⚒ MUL

A Palissy-style majolica dish, by Geoffrey Luff, 2000, 17in (43cm) diam.
£1,800–2,000 / €2,600–2,900
$3,450–3,850 ⊞ BRT

Midwinter

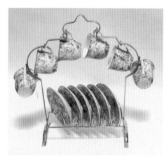

A Midwinter coffee service, decorated with Brama pattern, with original metal stand, 1930s, 14in (35.5cm) high.
£100–115 / €145–170
$200–220 ⊞ BEV

A Midwinter Fashion trio, designed by Jessie Tait, decorated with Zambesi pattern, 1956, plate 10in (25.5cm) diam.
£60–70 / €85–100
$115–135 ⊞ CHI

A Midwinter celery vase, designed by Jessie Tait, decorated with Savanna pattern, 1950s, 8in (20.5cm) high.
£120–135 / €175–195
$230–260 ⊞ BEV

A Midwinter bowl, designed by Jessie Tait, decorated with Savanna pattern, 1950s, 9in (23cm) wide.
£75–85 / €110–125
$145–165 ⊞ BEV

A Midwinter casserole dish and cover, decorated with Fleur pattern, c1970, 7in (18cm) diam.
£35–40 / €50–60
$65–75 ⊞ CHI

A Midwinter plate, designed by Jessie Tait, decorated with Blue Dahlia pattern, 1972–75, 7in (18cm) diam.
£8–12 / €12–18
$16–23 ⊞ CHI

◄ **A Midwinter cup and saucer,** designed by Eve Midwinter, decorated with Wild Strawberry pattern, 1970s.
£15–20 / €22–29
$29–38 ⊞ CHI

A Midwinter Stonehenge teapot, designed by Eve Midwinter, decorated with Autumn pattern, 1974–82, 7in (18cm) high.
£40–45 / €60–70
$75–85 ⊞ CHI

► **A Midwinter Stonehenge side plate,** designed by Eve Midwinter, decorated with Primula pattern, 1970s, 7in (18cm) diam.
£8–12 / €12–18
$16–23 ⊞ CHI

A Midwinter Stonehenge flan dish, decorated with Still Life pattern, c1982, 9in (23cm) diam.
£20–25 / €30–35
$40–50 ⊞ CHI

Moorcroft

A Moorcroft vase, decorated with Pansy pattern, impressed mark, signed, 1914, 3in (7.5cm) high.
£280–330 / €400–480
$540–630 ↗ Hal

A Moorcroft bowl, decorated with Pomegranate pattern, signed, c1920, 6½in (16.5cm) diam.
£450–540 / €650–780
$860–1,000 ↗ G(L)

◄ **Two Moorcroft vases,** by William Moorcroft, decorated with Wisteria pattern, signed, c1920, larger 12in (30.5cm) high.
£1,350–1,500 / €1,950–2,200
$2,600–2,900 ⊞ MPC

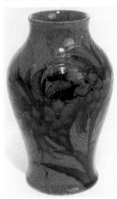

► **A Liberty & Co Moorcroft tazza,** decorated with Eventide pattern, on a pewter base, impressed mark, c1930, 8½in (21.5cm) high.
£900–1,000
€1,300–1,450
$1,700–1,900
↗ GAK

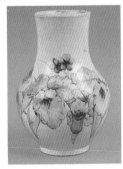

A Moorcroft vase, decorated with flowers, signed, 1930–40, 10in (25.5cm) high.
£400–480 / €580–700
$770–920 ↗ L

A Moorcroft vase, decorated with Cornflower pattern, damaged, painted signature and impressed marks, c1920, 7in (18cm) high.
£160–190 / €240–280
$310–360 ↗ G(L)

A Moorcroft vase, decorated with Orchid pattern, initialled, 1935–39, 3in (7.5cm) high.
£560–630 / €810–910
$1,050–1,200 ⊞ GOv

A Walter Moorcroft scent bottle, decorated with Anemone pattern, c1947, 6in (15cm) high.
£450–500 / €650–730
$860–960 ⊞ GOv

A Moorcroft vase, decorated with Butterfly pattern, 1996, 6¾in (17cm) high.
£90–100 / €130–145
$170–190 ↗ DN

Further reading

Miller's Twentieth-Century Ceramics,
Miller's Publications, 2005

A Moorcroft vase, decorated with Furzey Hill pattern, c1999, 10in (25.5cm) high.
£310–350 / €450–510
$600–670 ⊞ MPC

Nurseryware

A Staffordshire pearlware plate,
with transfer-printed decoration,
inscribed 'For A Good Girl', c1830,
6in (15cm) high.
£220–250 / €320–360
$420–480 ⊞ ReN

**A Royal Doulton Bunnykins
teapot,** signed 'Barbara Vernon',
c1930, 7in (18cm) wide.
£430–480 / €620–700
$830–920 ⊞ BEV

A porridge plate, transfer-printed
with the nursery rhyme, 'Little Miss
Muffet...', c1910, 9in (23cm) diam.
£135–150 / €195–220
$260–290 ⊞ SMI

A Grimwades platter, decorated
with The Imps pattern, c1930,
12in (30.5cm) diam.
£40–45 / €60–70
$75–85 ⊞ HEW

An Empire Porcelain Co bowl,
depicting Peter Pan, c1920,
6¼in (16cm) diam.
£60–70 / €85–110
$115–135 ⊞ c20th

A bowl, decorated with a pixie
pushing a wheelbarrow, late 1950s,
6½in (16.5cm) diam.
£4–8 / €6–12
$8–15 ⊞ LAS

◀ **A child's
tea service,**
decorated with
Noddy scenes,
1960s, teapot
3½in (9cm) high.
£50–60
€75–85
$100–115
⊞ BBe

A Gray's mug, decorated with a
Thelwell cartoon, 1960s,
4in (10cm) high.
£15–20 / €22–29
$29–38 ⊞ LAS

▶ **A mug,** decorated with Tom &
Jerry, 1970, 3½in (9cm) high.
£8–12 / €12–18
$16–23 ⊞ LAS

A mug, decorated with ducks,
1970s, 3in (7.5cm) high.
£4–8 / €6–12
$8–15 ⊞ LAS

Poole Pottery

A Carter Stabler & Adams vase, decorated with Grape pattern, slight damage, c1920, 7½in (19cm) high.
£60–70 / €85–100
$115–135 ⚒ LF

A Poole Pottery vase, the handles in the form of stylized doves, c1930, 10in (25.5cm) high.
£310–350 / €450–510
$600–670 ⊞ HEW

A Poole Pottery jar, with stylized floral decoration, 1930s, 12in (30.5cm) high.
£630–700 / €900–1,000
$1,200–1,350 ⊞ HEW

A Poole Pottery vase, designed by Truda Carter, decorated by Eileen Prangnell, impressed mark, initialled, incised '599', c1930s, 8in (20.5cm) high.
£280–330 / €410–480
$540–630 ⚒ RTo

A Poole Pottery dish, with three sections, decorated with fish and shellfish, c1950, 10in (25.5cm) wide.
£40–45 / €60–70
$75–85 ⊞ BAC

A Poole Pottery jardinière, 1950s, 9in (23cm) high.
£80–90 / €115–130
$155–175 ⊞ GRo

A Poole Pottery jar, painted with a bluebird and stylized flowers, 1930s, 4in (10cm) high.
£135–150 / €195–220
$260–290 ⊞ HEW

▶ **A Poole Pottery Delphis bowl,** 1960s, 10in (25.5cm) diam.
£160–185 / €230–270
$310–360 ⊞ CHI

A Poole Pottery Atlantis vase, by Guy Sydenham, impressed and incised marks, 1970s, 8in (20.5cm) diam.
£180–210 / €250–300
$340–400 ⚒ SWO

◀ **A Poole Pottery Scenic plate,** 1990s.
£35–40 / €50–60
$65–75 ⊞ CHI

A Poole Pottery breakfast cup and saucer, by Robert Jefferson, decorated with Bramble pattern, c1970, 3in (7.5cm) high.
£15–20 / €22–29
$29–38 ⊞ CHI

Portmeirion

A Portmeirion storage jar,
decorated with Talisman pattern,
c1962, 8in (20.5cm) high.
**£145–165 / €210–240
$280–320 ⊞ CHI**

A Portmeirion mug, decorated
with Totem pattern, c1963,
4½in (11.5cm) high.
**£35–40 / €50–60
$65–75 ⊞ CHI**

A Portmeirion tureen and cover,
in the form of a hen, c1963,
9in (23cm) wide.
**£50–60 / €75–85
$100–115 ⊞ CHI**

▶ **A Portmeirion jug,** decorated with
Dolphins pattern, c1965, 5in (12.5cm) high.
**£65–75 / €95–105
$125–145 ⊞ CHI**

**A Portmeirion coffee
pot,** decorated with
Jupiter pattern, c1964,
12in (30.5cm) high.
**£80–90 / €115–130
$155–175 ⊞ CHI**

A Portmeirion rolling pin, decorated with Sailing Ships
pattern, 1960s, 13in (33cm) long.
**£85–95 / €125–140
$165–185 ⊞ CHI**

**A Portmeirion coffee
pot,** decorated with
Magic City pattern, c1966,
12in (30.5cm) high.
**£75–85 / €110–125
$145–165 ⊞ CHI**

◀ **A Portmeirion Botanic
Garden storage jar,**
1980s, 9in (23cm) high.
**£50–60 / €75–85
$100–115 ⊞ CHI**

A Portmeirion tankard,
inscribed 'A Year to
Remember 1971', 1971,
4in (10cm) high.
**£25–30 / €40–45
$50–55 ⊞ CHI**

◀ **A Portmeirion coffee storage jar,** decorated with
Dolphins pattern, c1965, 7in (18cm) high.
**£70–80 / €100–115
$135–155 ⊞ CHI**

Pot Lids

'The Ornamental Garden', No. 121, 19thC, 3in (7.5cm) diam.
£400–480 / €580–700
$770–920 ⚲ SAS

'New York Exhibition', No. 154, with oak-leaf border, 1853, 4¾in (12cm) diam.
£400–480 / €580–700
$770–920 ⚲ BBR

'The Village Wakes', No. 232, restored, c1855, 3¾in (9.5cm) diam.
£580–690 / €840–1,000
$1,100–1,300 ⚲ SAS

'Tria Juncta In Uno', by Mayer, No. 2020,1850s, 4¼in (11cm) diam.
£200–240 / €290–350
$380–450 ⚲ BBR

'Yardley's Toothpaste', 1880–1900, 3¾in (9.5cm) diam.
£160–190 / €230–270
$300–360 ⚲ BBR

'Otto of Rose Cold Cream, S. Maw, Son & Sons', 1880–1900, 2¾in (7cm) diam.
£35–40 / €50–60
$65–75 ⚲ BBR

'Cold Cream of Roses, Sydney Huggett Dispensing Chemists, London', 1880–1900, 3in (7.5cm) diam.
£150–180 / €220–260
$290–350 ⚲ BBR

▶ 'Areca Nut and Cherry Toothpaste, Hempsted & Co Chemists, St Leonards', 1900–20, 3½in (9cm) diam.
£90–100 / €130–145
$170–190 ⚲ BBR

'Mrs Ellen Hale's Celebrated Heal-All Ointment', 1880–1900, 4in (10cm) diam.
£70–80 / €100–115
$135–155 ⚲ BBR

'Prepared White Gutta Percha, Messrs. Gabriel Dentists, London', 1870–1880, 2in (5cm) diam.
£35–40 / €50–60
$65–75 ⚲ BBR

Pot lid numbers

The numbers in the captions refer to the system used by A. Ball in his reference work *The Price Guide to Pot Lids*, Antique Collectors Club, 1980.

Quimper

◀ **A Quimper faïence dish,** from Alfred Beau's 'Botanique' series, painted with blackberry branches, slight damage, marked, c1885, 17¾in (45cm) wide.
£1,500–1,800
€2,200–2,600
$2,900–3,450 🔨 S

A pair of Quimper wall pockets, 20thC, 7in (18cm) high.
£55–65 / €80–95
$105–125 ⊞ SER

A Quimper bowl, c1940, 6in (15cm) diam.
£25–30 / €40–45
$50–55 ⊞ SER

A Quimper cup and saucer, by Paul Foullien, c1940.
£10–15 / €15–22
$19–28 ⊞ SER

A Quimper teapot stand, 1940s, 8½in (21.5cm) square.
£60–70 / €85–100
$115–135 ⊞ SER

A Quimper pot and cover, c1940, 2½in (6.5cm) wide.
£35–40 / €50–60
$65–75 ⊞ SER

A Quimper jug, by the Henriot factory, c1940, 8in (20.5cm) high.
£50–60 / €75–85
$100–115 ⊞ SER

A Quimper Le Treport bowl, c1950, 6½in (16.5cm) wide.
£20–25 / €30–35
$40–45 ⊞ SER

A Quimper Le Treport bowl, c1950, 6¼in (16cm) wide.
£25–30 / €40–45
$50–55 ⊞ SER

A pair of Quimper plates, late 20thC, 4½in (11.5cm) diam.
£20–25 / €30–35
$40–45 ⊞ SER

Charlotte & Frederick Rhead

A Charlotte Rhead Bursley ware dish, decorated with a seed poppy, printed mark, 1918–22, 11¾in (30cm) diam.
£240–280 / €350–410
$460–540 ✗ GAK

A pair of Frederick Rhead vases, decorated with Bagdad pattern, c1920, 6in (15cm) high.
£240–270 / €350–390
$460–520 ⊞ JFME

A Charlotte Rhead Bursley ware bowl, No. 1975, 1928, 9in (23cm) diam.
£220–250 / €320–360
$420–480 ⊞ HEW

A Charlotte Rhead Crown Ducal charger, printed mark, signed, c1930, 12½in (32cm) diam.
£200–240 / €290–350
$380–450 ✗ WW

A Charlotte Rhead Crown Ducal jug, c1930, 5in (12.5cm) high.
£195–220 / €280–320
$370–420 ⊞ HEW

A Charlotte Rhead Bursley ware dish, painted with flowers and berries, c1930, 10in (25.5cm) wide.
£130–155 / €185–220
$250–300 ✗ G(L)

A Charlotte Rhead Crown Ducal vase, with floral tube-lined decoration, c1930, 5¾in (14.5cm) high.
£65–75 / €95–105
$125–145 ✗ DA

Further reading
Miller's Ceramics of the '20s & '30s: A Collector's Guide, Miller's Publications, 1999

A Charlotte Rhead charger, with tube-lined decoration, No. 6016, c1930s, 12½in (32cm) high.
£190–220 / €280–330
$360–420 ✗ WilP

A Charlotte Rhead Bursley ware jar and cover, c1947, 7in (18cm) high.
£270–300 / €390–440
$520–580 ⊞ HEW

Royal Copenhagen

A Royal Copenhagen dinner service, comprising 90 pieces, with gilt decoration, slight damage, Danish, c1910.
£220–260 / €320–380
$430–510 ⋏ JAA

A Royal Copenhagen silver-mounted box and cover, the cover enamelled with a crab and applied with a band of seaweed, silver mounts by A. Michelsen, Copenhagen 1922, stamped mark, Danish, 6¼in (16cm) wide.
£680–800 / €990–1,150
$1,300–1,550 ⋏ LHA

A Royal Copenhagen vase, by Karri Christensen, Danish, c1967, 11in (28cm) high.
£95–110 / €140–160
$180–210 ⊞ FRD

Royal Winton

Established as a branch of Grimwades pottery in Stoke-on-Trent in 1885, Royal Winton produced their first lithographed chintz design, Marguerite, in 1928. Reputedly inspired by a needlepoint cushion worked by director Leonard Grimwade's wife, the floral pattern was a huge success. Royal Winton went on to produce some 65 different chintz designs and were at the height of their popularity during the interwar period. Decorations often reflected contemporary fabrics and, according to legend, Leonard Grimwade would pay his factory girls a shilling a time to be able to copy their pretty pinafores. 'Some chintz ware designs can be compared or even matched up with period Liberty prints,' says dealer Beverley.

Prices reflect shape, pattern and condition and for maximum value the transfer-printed pattern should be crisp and cleanly printed. Rare shapes such as breakfast sets and stacking teapots will command a premium and the ideal combination is a rare object with a desirable pattern. Royal Winton often stamped pattern names in the base of the object and sought-after patterns include Evesham, Julia, Sweet Pea, Welbeck, Somerset and Hazel. Teapots, coffee pots and larger ceramics are popular, while tableware such as sugar shakers, toast racks and cruet sets attract specialist collectors and can be costly. Cups, saucers and tea plates, however, are among the most affordable and plentiful shapes found today.

A Royal Winton chintz ware comport, decorated with Somerset pattern, c1930, 5in (12.5cm) high.
£110–125 / €160–180
$210–240 ⊞ BEV

A Royal Winton chintz ware Norman teapot, decorated with Welbeck pattern, c1930, 5in (12.5cm) high.
£200–230 / €290–330
$380–440 ⊞ BEV

A Royal Winton chintz ware bowl, decorated with Summertime pattern, c1930, 5in (12.5cm) wide.
£55–65 / €80–95
$105–125 ⊞ BEV

A Royal Winton vase, c1930,
5in (12.5cm) high.
£135–150 / €195–220
$260–290 ⊞ HEW

A Royal Winton chintz ware
toast rack, decorated with Spring
pattern, c1930, 5in (12.5cm) wide.
£80–90 / €115–130
$155–175 ⊞ BEV

Further reading

*Miller's Ceramics
Buyers Guide*, Miller's
Publications, 2000

A Royal Winton chintz ware
cruet set, decorated with Cottage
pattern, c1930, 5in (12.5cm) wide.
£130–145 / €190–210
$250–280 ⊞ BEV

A Royal Winton chintz ware coffee
cup, decorated with English Rose
pattern, c1930, 2in (5cm) diam.
£65–75 / €95–105
$125–145 ⊞ BEV

A Royal Winton chintz ware cheese
dish, decorated with Sweet Pea
pattern, c1930, 6in (15cm) wide.
£145–165 / €210–240
$280–320 ⊞ BEV

A Royal Winton chintz ware cake
stand, decorated with Hazel
pattern, c1930, 11in (28cm) wide.
£50–60 / €75–85
$100–115 ⊞ BEV

A Royal Winton chintz
ware bowl, with a handle,
decorated with Somerset
pattern, c1930,
12in (30.5cm) diam.
£250–280 / €360–410
$480–540 ⊞ BEV

▶ A Royal Winton
chintz ware sugar
shaker, decorated with
Somerset pattern, c1930,
6in (15cm) high.
£180–200 / €260–290
$340–380 ⊞ BEV

A Royal Winton chintz ware sweet dish, decorated with Richmond pattern, c1930, 6in (15cm) wide.
£100–115 / €145–165
$200–220 ⊞ BEV

A Royal Winton jug, decorated with a pixie, c1930, 10in (25.5cm) high.
£270–300 / €390–440
$520–580 ⊞ HEW

A Royal Winton lemon squeezer, c1930, 5in (12.5cm) wide.
£70–80 / €100–115
$135–155 ⊞ BEV

◀ **A Royal Winton vase,** decorated with Dovecote pattern, c1930, 6in (15cm) high.
£100–115 / €145–165
$200–220 ⊞ BEV

A Royal Winton toast rack, c1930, 5in (12.5cm) wide.
£35–40 / €50–60
$65–75 ⊞ BEV

A Royal Winton chintz ware teapot, decorated with Victoria Rose pattern, dated 1953, 5in (12.5cm) high.
£360–400 / €520–580
$690–770 ⊞ HOM

Rye Pottery

◀ **A Rye Pottery box and cover,** in the form of a boar, inscribed 'Wunt Ledrur', early 20thC, 4¾in (12cm) wide.
£50–60 / €75–85
$100–115 ➴ HOLL

A Rye Pottery jardinière, 1950s, 6in (15cm) high.
£85–95 / €125–140
$165–185 ⊞ EMH

A Rye Pottery plate, 1950s, 7¾in (19.5cm) diam.
£45–50 / €65–75
$85–95 ⊞ TAC

◀ **A Rye Pottery model of a chicken,** 1960s, 7¾in (19.5cm) high.
£15–20 / €22–29
$29–38 ⊞ HEI

Shelley

Shelley produced kitchenware as well as decorative ceramics and tableware in the 1920s and 1930s. The company was well known for jelly and blancmange moulds – a 1920s catalogue boasts 50 types of mould 'for every conceivable purpose.' Among the most desirable examples today are the novelty moulds that came in the form of swans, chickens, crayfish and even an armadillo.

Unlike many ceramic moulds, these were decoratively shaped on the outside as well as within so that cooks could see exactly how their creation would turn out. In the 1930s these moulds cost just a few shillings each, depending on size. Today they can fetch three-figure sums and are sought after by both Shelley collectors and kitchenware enthusiasts. Look out for the printed Shelley mark in greenish-black.

A set of Shelley jelly moulds, each in the form of a swan, c1920, largest 9in (23cm) wide.
£180–200 / €260–290
$340–380 ⊞ SMI

A Shelley shortbread mould, c1900, 8in (20.5cm) diam.
£40–45 / €60–70
$75–85 ⊞ B&R

◀ **A Shelley chintz ware trio,** decorated with Primrose pattern, c1930, cup 3in (7.5cm) high.
£80–90
€115–130
$155–175
⊞ HOM

A Shelley Harmony drip ware vase, c1930, 5in (12.5cm) high.
£80–90 / €115–130
$155–175 ⊞ HEW

A pair of Shelley vases, decorated with Tulip pattern, c1930, 8in (20.5cm) high.
£340–380 / €490–550
$650–730 ⊞ HEW

◀ **A Shelley cigarette box,** decorated with Melody pattern, the cover forming an ashtray, c1930, 5in (12.5cm) wide.
£120–135 / €175–195
$230–260 ⊞ BEV

◀ **A Shelley Harmony ginger jar,** 1930s, 5in (12.5cm) high.
£155–175 / €220–250
$300–340 ⊞ BEV

▶ **A Shelley coffee service,** comprising 15 pieces, slight damage, printed marks, 1930s.
£130–155 / €185–220
$250–300 ✦ SWO

Shorter

A Shorter honeycomb box, decorated with fruit and a bee, stamped and impressed marks, c1920, 4½in (11.5cm) square.
£75–85 / €110–125
$145–165 ⊞ EHCS

A Shorter jam pot, c1930, 4in (10cm) high.
£55–65 / €80–95
$105–125 ⊞ BEV

A Shorter Anemone butter dish, c1930, 6in (15cm) wide.
£110–125 / €160–180
$210–240 ⊞ HOM

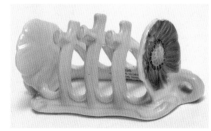

A Shorter wall plaque, in the form of two birds sitting on a branch, c1930, 11in (28cm) wide.
£100–115 / €145–165
$200–220 ⊞ BEV

A Shorter Anemone toast rack, 1930s, 6in (15cm) wide.
£80–90 / €115–130
$155–175 ⊞ HOM

Spode

Five Copeland Spode dessert plates, painted with vignettes of figures, slight wear, printed and impressed marks, late 19thC, 8in (20.5cm) diam.
£160–190 / €240–280
$300–360 ⋏ DN

A set of eight Spode New Stone plates, painted with Imari colours, impressed marks, 1805–20, 9½in (24cm) diam.
£160–190 / €240–280
$300–360 ⋏ G(L)

A pair of Spode spill vases, with hand-painted and gilt floral decoration, 19thC, 4¾in (12cm) high.
£280–330 / €400–480
$540–640 ⋏ JAd

▶ **A Spode Olympus vegetable dish and cover,** 1950s, 8in (20.5cm) diam.
£35–40
€50–60
$65–75 ⊞ CHI

A Spode Hamilton trio, 1960s, cup 3in (7.5cm) high.
£20–25 / €30–35
$40–45 ⊞ CHI

Staffordshire

A pair of Staffordshire spill vases, each with a deer and a fawn, slight damage, 19thC, 9¼in (23.5cm) high.
£280–330 / €410–480
$530–630 ⚲ WW

A pair of Staffordshire figures of musicians, seated on settees, slight damage, 19thC, 9in (23cm) wide.
£130–155 / €185–220
$250–300 ⚲ G(L)

A Staffordshire figure of Prince Albert, 19thC, 14½in (37cm) high.
£140–165 / €200–240
$270–320 ⚲ DMC

◀ **A pair of Staffordshire figures of the Prince and Princess of Wales on horseback,** 19thC, 10in (25.5cm) high.
£110–130
€160–190
$210–250 ⚲ DA

▶ **A Staffordshire spill vase,** with a sheep, damaged, 19thC, 6in (15cm) high.
£110–130
€160–190
$210–250 ⚲ BWL

A Staffordshire figure of St John, slight damage, early 19thC, 8½in (21.5cm) high.
£95–110 / €140–160
$180–210 ⚲ G(L)

A Staffordshire pearlware figure of Elijah and the Raven, slight damage, numbered '27', early 19thC, 9½in (24cm) high.
£130–155 / €185–220
$250–300 ⚲ DN

A Staffordshire model of a horse and a lion, c1850, 12in (30.5cm) high.
£490–550 / €710–800
$940–1,050 ⊞ HOW

▶ A Staffordshire figure of a sleeping huntsman, c1850, 9in (23cm) high.
£200–230 / €290–330
$400–440 ⊞ SER

▶ A pair of Staffordshire creamware models of lions, damaged and restored, c1850, 5½in (14cm) high.
£550–660 / €800–960
$1,050–1,250 ↗ TEN

A Staffordshire figure of Admiral Sir Deans Dundas, slight damage, 1854–56, 11½in (29cm) high.
£140–165 / €200–240
$270–320 ↗ DN

A Victorian Staffordshire figure of Wellington, 12½in (32cm) high.
£150–180 / €220–260
$290–350 ↗ G(L)

A Victorian Staffordshire figural group, of a young woman having her palm read, 13in (33cm) high.
£110–130 / €160–190
$210–250 ↗ JAd

▶ A Victorian Staffordshire model of a zebra, 6¼in (16cm) high.
£45–50
€65–75
$85–95 ↗ G(L)

◀ A Staffordshire tureen and cover, in the form of a hen in a basket, slight damage, 1850–80, 8¾in (22cm) wide.
£260–310
€380–450
$500–600 ↗ DN

A pair of Staffordshire models of cats, with gilt collars, late 19thC, 7¼in (18.5cm) high.
£180–210 / €250–300
$340–400 ↗ DMC

A Staffordshire figural group, of Darby and Joan, late 19thC, 11in (28cm) high.
£60–70 / €85–100
$115–135 ↗ DMC

Studio Pottery

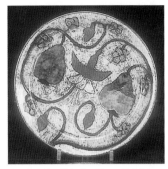

A ceramic dish, by Birger Kaipiainen (1915–88), signed 'Kaipiainen Arabia', Finnish, 8¼in (21cm) diam.
£380–450 / €550–660
$730–860 ⚲ BUK(F)

A Gustavsberg earthenware vase, by Berndt Friberg, signed, Swedish, 1942, 6¼in (16cm) high.
£750–900 / €1,100–1,300
$1,450–1,750 ⚲ BUK

A Chelsea Pottery vase, 1950, 8½in (21.5cm) high.
£50–60 / €75–85
$100–115 ⊞ DSG

An Aldermaston Pottery teapot, painted mark, c1966, 9½in (24cm) high.
£150–180 / €220–260
$290–350 ⚲ DN

A stoneware bowl, by Britt-Louise Sundell, 1960s, 5in (12.5cm) high.
£85–95 / €125–140
$165–185 ⊞ MARK

A Bitossi Pottery lampbase, by Aldo Mondi, Italian, c1960, 22in (56cm) high.
£55–65 / €80–95
$105–125 ⊞ FRD

A stoneware bowl, by David Leach, impressed mark, c1980, 8¼in (21cm) diam.
£340–400 / €490–580
$650–760 ⚲ Bea

A stoneware bowl, by David Leach (1911–2005), with an iron-flecked glaze, impressed seal, 8¼in (21cm) diam.
£340–400 / €490–580
$650–760 ⚲ Bea

◄ **A Briglin Pottery vase,** decorated with sunflowers, 1974, 8in (20.5cm) high.
£35–40 / €50–60
$65–75 ⊞ FRD

◄ **A stoneware bowl,** by David Leach, impressed mark, c1980, 6¾in (17cm) high.
£560–670
€810–970
$1,100–1,300
⚲ Bea

Teapots & Coffee Pots

◀ **A Stafford-shire agateware teapot and cover,** slight damage, mid-18thC, 5½in (14cm) high.
£580–690
€840–1,000
$1,100–1,300
⚲ WW

A Yorkshire Pottery bachelor's teapot, c1820, 2½in (6.5cm) high.
£155–175 / €220–250
$300–340 ⊞ ReN

A Cadogan teapot, possibly Swinton Pottery, 19thC, 7½in (19cm) high.
£60–70 / €85–100
$115–135 ⚲ DA
The Cadogan is a novelty teapot that is closed at the top and filled through a conical hole in the bottom. Cadogan teapots were first produced in Britain in the late 18th century at the Rockingham factory. The design was inspired by a Chinese peach-shaped wine pot and named after the Honourable Mrs Cadogan, who gave a Chinese wine pot, brought to England by her son, to Lady Rockingham.

An earthenware teapot, with a double spout, inscribed 'Mr & Mrs Taylor', 19thC, 10in (25.5cm) wide.
£200–240 / €290–350
$380–450 ⚲ TMA

A Dresden coffee pot and cover, German, 1895–1910, 9in (23cm) high.
£220–250 / €320–360
$420–480 ⊞ BEV

◀ **A Stafford-shire tea service,** decorated with Country Gardens pattern, c1930, teapot 6in (15cm) high.
£45–50 / €65–75
$85–95 ⊞ SAT

A Cottage ware tea service, comprising four pieces, c1930, largest 6in (15cm) high.
£130–145 / €190–210
$250–280 ⊞ HOM

A Windsor China coffee service, comprising 15 pieces, decorated with a chintz pattern, c1946, coffee pot 8in (20.5cm) high.
£110–125 / €160–180
$210–240 ⊞ DEB

A Crown Ducal teapot, decorated with an inscription and Allied flags, 1940s, 6in (15cm) high.
£125–140 / €180–200
$240–270 ⊞ JFME

A Denby Lucerne coffee pot, cup and saucer, c1965, coffee pot 7½in (19cm) high.
£40–45 / €60–70
$75–85 ⊞ CHI

A Barker Bros coffee service, decorated with Fiesta pattern, 1960s, coffee pot 9in (23cm) high.
£65–75 / €95–105
$125–145 ⊞ FRD

A Franciscan Pottery coffee pot, decorated with Reflections pattern, 1960s, 10in (25.5cm) high.
£45–50 / €65–75
$85–95 ⊞ CHI

A Royal Worcester coffee pot, decorated with Padua pattern, 1960s, 9in (23cm) high.
£80–90 / €115–130
$155–175 ⊞ CHI

A Rouen Pottery teapot, French, late 20thC, 12in (30.5cm) high.
£100–110 / €145–160
$190–210 ⊞ SER

► **A teapot,** by James Sadler, depicting a scene from *The Wind in the Willows,* 2002–03.
£15–20
€22–29
$29–38
⊞ KWCC

A Dennis Chinaworks Strawberry teapot, by Sally Tuffin, edition of 30, 2003, 5in (12.5cm) high.
£420–470 / €610–680
$810–900 ⊞ CBi

Tiles

A set of 35 Dutch Delft tiles, each decorated with flowers in a vase, 1650–1700, each tile 5¼in (13.5cm) square.
£400–480 / €580–700
$770–920 ⚲ SWO

A set of 12 tin-glazed tiles, some decorated with biblical scenes, some damaged, together with six matching part-tiles, 18thC, each tile 5¼in (13.5cm) square.
£450–540 / €650–780
$860–1,000 ⚲ LAY

▶ **A Liverpool delft tile,** depicting a coastal scene, c1770, 5in (12.5cm) square.
£55–65 / €80–95
$105–125 ⊞ JHo

◀ **Two Minton tiles,** each depicting a lady in 19thC costume, 19thC, 6in (15cm) square.
£55–65 / €80–95
$105–125 ⚲ AMB

A set of 30 Dutch Delft tiles, depicting children at play, 19thC, each tile 5¼in (13.5cm) square.
£170–200 / €250–290
$320–380 ⚲ SWO

◀ **A T. & R. Boote tile,** with embossed decoration, c1885, 6in (15cm) square.
£6–10 / €9–15
$12–19 ⊞ SAT

A Minton tile, the centre embossed with a rose, 1875–1910, 6in (15cm) square.
£6–10 / €9–15
$12–19 ⊞ SAT

A Victorian tile, with floral decoration, 6in (15cm) square.
£10–15 / €15–22
$19–28 ⊞ TASV

Two Minton tiles, each decorated with a bird, c1890, 6in (15cm) square.
£45–50 / €65–75
$85–95 each ⊞ OLA

A Sherwin & Colton tile, with floral decoration, c1890, 6in (15cm) square.
£6–10 / €9–15
$12–19 ⊞ SAT

An Edge Malkin & Co tile, depicting a lady and a gentleman playing croquet, c1893, 6in (15cm) square.
£90–100 / €130–145
$170–190 ⊞ ReN

A Minton butcher's tile, depicting a bull's head, late 19thC, 12in (30.5cm) square.
£270–300 / €390–440
$520–580 ⊞ SMI

A set of four William de Morgan India tiles, marked, c1896, 9in (23cm) square.
£2,300–2,750 / €3,350–4,000
$4,400–5,300 ✗ SWO
These tiles are from the P&O ship *India*, built at Greenock in 1896 by Caird & Co, one of 12 ships for which de Morgan supplied tiles. The architect T.E. Colcutt commissioned them on behalf of P&O and de Morgan supplied 88 of these 9in (23cm) tiles for the companionway frieze.

A set of six Wedgwood tiles, entitled 'The Months of the Year', comprising January, February, April, September, November and December, late 19thC, 8in (20.5cm) square.
£160–190 / €240–280
$310–360 ✗ HOLL

◄ **A set of three tiles,** with transfer-printed and painted songbirds, late 19thC, 6in (15cm) square, in oak frames.
£150–180 / €220–260
$290–350 ✗ PFK

A tile picture, possibly Dutch, depicting a flower-filled censer with Arabesque borders, late 19thC, 36in (91.5cm) wide.
£190–220 / €270–320
$360–420 ✗ HOLL

A set of three tiles, c1900, largest 6 x 2in (15 x 5cm).
£15–20 / €22–29
$29–38 ⊞ C&R

◄ **A Joost Thooft & Abel Labourghere Dutch Delft tile,** painted with a horse and trap, signed 'O. Eeselman', early 20thC, 10 x 8in (25.5 x 20.5cm).
£130–155 / €185–220
$250–300 ✗ G(L)

Troika

A Troika lamp base, decorated by Avril Bennett, 1960s, 17in (43cm) high.
£640–760 / €920–1,100 $1,250–1,450 ➢ MAR

A Troika vase, decorated by Penny Black, 1960s, 14¼in (36cm) high.
£290–340 / €420–490 $560–650 ➢ MAR

A Troika vase, 1960s, 5½in (14cm) high.
£650–780 / €960–1,150 $1,250–1,500 ➢ BWL

A Troika vase, decorated with incised geometric pattern, 1960s, 12½in (31.5cm) high.
£200–240 / €290–350 $380–450 ➢ L&E

A Troika cube vase, decorated with geometric patterns, marked 'Troika Cornwall SB', 1960s, 5¾in (14.5cm) high.
£240–280 / €350–410 $460–540 ➢ SPF

A Troika dish, with painted marks and artist's monogram, 1960s, 8in (20.5cm) square.
£300–360 / €440–520 $580–690 ➢ WW

◀ **A Troika cylinder vase,** with painted marks and artist's monogram, 1960s, 6in (15cm) high.
£100–120 / €145–175 $185–220 ➢ WW

A Troika vase, marked 'Troika' and 'LH', c1970, 9¾in (25cm) high.
£350–420 / €510–610 $670–810 ➢ HOLL

A Troika vase, decorated with applied geometric patterns, painted mark, c1970, 8in (20.5cm) high.
£280–330 / €410–480 $540–630 ➢ PF

◀ **A Troika slab vase,** with embossed decoration, c1970, 6¾in (17cm) high.
£450–540 / €650–780 $870–1,050 ➢ AH

Wade

A Wade Shamrock cottage, inscribed 'Windermere', 1956–61, 3in (7.5cm) wide.
£10–15 / €15–22
$19–28 ⊞ UD

A Wade Whimsies model of an Alsatian dog, 1957, 2in (5cm) wide.
£20–25 / €30–35
$40–45 ⊞ UD

A Wade Minikin model of a cow, 1957, 1in (2.5cm) high.
£10–15 / €15–22
$19–28 ⊞ UD

A Wade Disney model of Am, c1960, 2in (5cm) wide.
£30–35 / €45–50
$55–65 ⊞ UD

A Wade Disney Blow Up model of Thumper, 1961, 5¼in (13.5cm) high.
£130–155 / €185–220
$250–300 ⚒ BBR

► **A Wade Nursery Favourites figure of Humpty Dumpty,** 1972, 2½in (6.5cm) high.
£10–15 / €15–22
$19–28 ⊞ UD

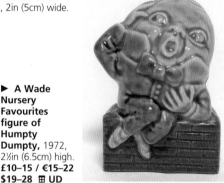

◄ **A Wade Whimsey-on-Wye model of The Manor,** Set Three, 1982–83, 3in (7.5cm) wide.
£10–15
€15–22
$19–28 ⊞ UD

► **A Wade Whimsey-on-Wye model of Dr Healer's House,** 1980–87, 2in (5cm) wide.
£3–7 / €4–10
$6–13 ⊞ UD

Wedgwood

◀ **Two Wedgwood caneware tureens and covers,** the larger with a cauliflower knop and moulded with a fruiting vine, slight damage, the other with a hare knop and game hanging from a grapevine, both with impressed marks, 19thC, larger 12¼in (31cm) wide.
£140–165 / €200–240
$270–320 ↗ WW

A Wedgwood part dessert service, comprising four tazze and 16 plates, decorated in the Imari palette, printed and painted marks, slight damage, late 19thC.
£440–520 / €640–750
$840–1,000 ↗ RTo

A Wedgwood jasper ware Stilton dish and cover, 19thC, 7½in (19cm) high.
£45–50 / €65–75
$85–95 ↗ WilP

A Wedgwood majolica jug, relief-decorated with panels of birds on branches, 19thC, 5in (12.5cm) high.
£80–90 / €115–130
$155–175 ↗ MAR

A Wedgwood lustre footed bowl, c1929, 8in (20.5cm) diam.
£720–800 / €1,000–1,150
$1,400–1,550 ⊞ HEW

A Wedgwood trio, decorated with Blue Gardenia pattern, c1959, cup 3in (7.5cm) high.
£45–50 / €65–75
$85–95 ⊞ CHI

A Wedgwood Age of Jazz boxed set, comprising two men with a drum, shape No. 435 and a man at a piano, shape No. 436, edition of 1,000, 1999, with box, 7 x 10in (18 x 25.5cm).
£90–100 / €130–145
$170–190 ⊞ HeA
This item is based on an original design by Clarice Cliff.

Worcester

A Royal Worcester vase, applied with three moulded tortoises, 19thC, 9in (23cm) diam.
£160–190 / €240–280
$310–360 ✗ BWL

A Royal Worcester jar, with cover, decorated with floral sprays, model No. 1720, printed mark and date code for 1897, 6½in (16.5cm) high.
£180–210 / €250–300
$340–400 ✗ PFK

A Royal Worcester bowl, entitled 'Harrington', decorated with a rural scene of a thatched cottage, signed 'R. Rushton', shape No. 2770, printed marks and date cipher, early 20thC, 8½in (21.5cm) diam.
£300–360 / €440–520
$580–690 ✗ GAK

A Royal Worcester miniature jug, painted with a pheasant, c1906, 5½in (14cm) high.
£130–155 / €185–220
$250–300 ✗ MAR

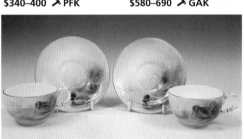

Two Royal Worcester cups and saucers, painted by James Stinton with mallard and woodcocks, slight damage, signed, c1912, saucer 4¾in (12cm) diam.
£250–300 / €370–440
$480–580 ✗ SWO

A Royal Worcester pot, hand-painted with flowers, code for 1913 and 1914 and flag mark for the onset of WWI, 4in (10cm) high.
£50–60 / €75–85
$100–115 ✗ AMB

A Royal Worcester vase, with two handles, decorated with a floral spray, signed 'W. Hale', shape No. 2337, printed and impressed marks, 1908, 12¼in (31cm) high.
£240–280 / €350–410
$460–540 ✗ SWO

A Royal Worcester bowl, painted by Ethel Spilsbury with flowers, slight damage, c1918, 8½in (21.5cm) diam.
£270–320 / €390–460
$520–610 ✗ MAR

A Royal Worcester jug, c1930, 3in (7.5cm) high.
£60–70 / €85–100
$115–135 ⊞ DEB

▶ **A Royal Worcester figure,** entitled 'Joan', modelled by Freda Doughty, printed marks and date code for 1932, 4½in (11.5cm) high.
£170–200 / €250–290
$320–380 ✗ DN

A matched pair of Royal Worcester side plates, by Freeman and Ayrton, painted with fruit, with gilded rims, dated 1935 and 1952, 6in (15cm) diam.
£360–430 / €520–620
$690–830 ⚲ AH

A Royal Worcester posy vase, by K. Blake, painted with autumn berries, leaves and flowers, signed, c1936, 3in (7.5cm) high.
£260–310 / €380–450
$500–600 ⚲ G(L)

◄ **A Royal Worcester miniature jug,** hand-painted with fruit, indistinct signature, printed mark and date code for 1955, 1¼in (3cm) high.
£110–130 / €160–190
$210–250 ⚲ PFK

A Royal Worcester figure, entitled 'Only Me', modelled by Freda Doughty, 1938–72, 5½in (14cm) high.
£160–190 / €240–280
$310–360 ⚲ PFK

► **A Royal Worcester figure,** entitled 'Little Jack Horner', c1950, 5in (12.5cm) high.
£340–380 / €490–550
$650–730 ⊞ WAC

A Royal Worcester potpourri jar and cover, painted and gilded with fruit, cover damaged and repaired, signed, printed mark, date mark for 1952, 6¼in (16cm) high.
£320–380 / €460–550
$610–730 ⚲ PF

A Royal Worcester model of a pair of coal tits, c1962, 5in (12.5cm) high.
£160–180 / €230–260
$310–350 ⊞ WAC

A Royal Worcester figure, entitled 'Fantails', c1962, 7in (18cm) high.
£170–190 / €250–280
$320–360 ⊞ WAC

► **A Royal Worcester figure of a monk,** 1969, 5in (12.5cm) high.
£80–90 / €115–130
$155–175 ⊞ WAC

► **A Royal Worcester model of Stroller and Marion Coakes,** by Doris Lindner, No. 624 of edition of 750, c1970, 10½in (26.5cm) high, with certificate.
£500–600
€730–870
$960–1,150
⚲ LT

Christmas

Father Christmas, also known as Santa Claus or St Nicholas, is a complex character who has evolved from ancient myth, Christian religion and modern invention. Part Bacchus figure, part Druid, Father Christmas made his first appearance in medieval mummers' plays. Christmas figures across Europe ranged from the elf Jultomten in Scandinavia, who delivered gifts in a sleigh drawn by goats, to the witch Befana in Italy, who visited children on her broomstick. It was partly to counter such pagan characters that the Catholic Church adopted St Nicholas, Bishop of Myra in Turkey during the 4th century, as patron saint of children and Christmas. His feast day was celebrated on 6 December and in Holland children left out their clogs filled with carrots and hay for St Nicholas's white horse. When Dutch settlers arrived in the Americas they introduced their tradition of St Nicholas visiting at Christmas. Dutch children abbreviated his name to Sinter Klass which was Americanized to Santa Claus. St Nicholas was also patron saint of a range of professions from pawnbrokers to thieves (from which we get the expression 'to nick').

In 1822, Clement Clarke Moore, an American professor of Divinity, wrote a Christmas poem, 'The Visit of St Nicholas'. It was Moore who gave St Nicholas his team of reindeer pulling a sleigh filled with toys – and who created what was to become Santa's standard cheerful, chubby appearance. In 1863, American artist Thomas Nast was commissioned to produce a Christmas picture

based on Moore's poem for *Harpers Weekly* magazine. Nast's Santa Claus illustrations, which ran for 23 years, transformed Father Christmas into a maker of toys, gave him his famous address at the North Pole, and truly popularized his 'Yo-ho-ho' image.

One vital element, however, was still to be fixed. In the 19th century, Santa Claus was portrayed in a range of different outfits. Thanks in part to the development of the colourful printed Christmas card (invented in Britain by Henry Cole in 1843), a scarlet suit trimmed with white fur gradually became the favourite choice. This was confirmed as the classic Santa Claus outfit by the creators of another famous red and white symbol. In 1931, Coca-Cola was looking to increase winter sales. Illustrator Haddon Sundblom created a series of Christmas advertisements featuring Santa Claus in the corporate colours of red and white. Gone was any image of the ascetic St Nicholas, who gave away his worldly goods to save the world from sin. Haddon's Santa Claus, modelled on his Michigan neighbour, a retired salesman, was a coke-drinking American. These hugely popular advertisements ran for some 35 years fuelling the myth that Coca-Cola had actually invented the red and white Santa. They did not, but in a world without television and where films were black and white, Coca-Cola's colourful posters and advertisements popularized the image of a twinkly-eyed jovial Santa with his white beard, pink cheeks and brilliant red and white suit.

◀ **A pen and ink Christmas Fraktur,** inscribed 'A Christmas present for my dear parents David and Sarah Parkman', with a hand-coloured rose flanked by two German verses, slight damage, American, dated 1831, in a bird's-eye maple frame, 17 x 14½in (43 x 37cm).
£300–360 / €440–520
$580–690 ≯ JDJ
Fraktur is an ornate style of written or printed German, but Pennsylvanian Germans used the term to describe birth and baptism certificates and other such documents, even if they did not contain Fraktur lettering.

A Rookwood Pottery Christmas teapot, by Amelia Browne Sprague, decorated with holly leaves and berries, slight damage, marked and numbered, American, Cincinnati, 1892, 6¼in (16cm) high.
£240–280 / €350–410
$460–540 ≯ SK

▶ **Two Christmas postcards,** depicting Father Christmas, one by Raphael Kirchner, slight damage, c1900, 6 x 4in (15 x 10cm).
£115–135 / €165–195
$220–260 ≯ JAA

An Aulsebrook's ceramic Christmas pudding bowl, c1910, 7in (18cm) diam.
£90–100
€130–145
$170–190 ⊞ SMI

A composite Christmas decoration, in the form of Father Christmas riding on a donkey, c1900, 5in (12.5cm) high.
£150–170 / €220–250
$290–330 ⊞ LEI

A Christmas card, depicting Father Christmas posting toys down a chimney, c1908, 5 x 3in (12.5 x 7.5cm).
£25–30 / €40–45
$50–55 ⊞ Qua

◀ **A Christmas sweet tin,** depicting Father Christmas and a lady, 1925, 6in (15cm) diam.
£35–40
€50–60
$65–75 ⊞ HUX

A Harvino Toffee Christmas tin, c1930, 5in (12.5cm) wide.
£25–30 / €40–45
$50–55 ⊞ MRW

▶ **A photographic Christmas card,** from Stanley Baldwin, 1937, 6 x 4in (15 x 10cm).
£40–45 / €60–70
$75–85 ⊞ AEL
Stanley Baldwin was Prime Minister three times in the 1920s and '30s.

▶ **An artificial Christmas tree shop display,** with decorations and cards, 1930s, 56in (142cm) high.
£350–420 / €510–610
$670–810 ⋌ BWL
Artificial Christmas trees first appeared in Germany in the 19th century. Metal frames were covered with goose and turkey feathers which were sometimes dyed green to imitate pine needles. The first plastic Christmas tree was produced by the Addis Company in America in the 1930s, using the same materials and machinery that produced their toilet brushes.

Lawson Wood, 'Be a Sport!', 'Come Along!', 'Merry Xmas!!', water-colour drawing, reverse titled and numbered A/590, dated 1937, 17½ x 13½in (44.5 x 34.5cm).
£1,500–1,800
€2,200–2,600
$2,900–3,450 ⋌ BBA
This drawing first appeared in the *Sketch* Christmas number 1937.

▶ **A Royal Doulton figure of a lady,** entitled 'Christmas Morn', No. HN 1992, 1947–96, 7in (18cm) high.
£55–65 / €80–95
$105–125 ⋌ AMB

A Fuller's Toffee Christmas tin, decorated with a Christmas scene, c1950, 7in (18cm) high.
£15–20 / €22–29
$29–38 ⊞ JUN

Film Fun **Christmas annual,** 1952, 11 x 8in (28 x 20.5cm).
£15–20 / €22–29
$29–38 ⊞ UD

◀ **A plastic Christmas brooch,** by ART, in the form of a boot, American, 1950s, 1½in (4cm) high.
£40–45
€60–70
$75–85 ⊞ DRE

A BEA advertising poster, 'Merry Christmas, Fly BEA in the New year', by Szomanski, c1955, 39¾ x 25in (101.5 x 63.5cm).
£180–210 / €260–300
$350–400 ➤ VSP

A pair of gilt and paste earrings and a brooch, in the form of Christmas trees, 1950s, brooch 2½in (6.5cm) high.
£70–80 / €100–115
$135–155 ⊞ DRE

▶ **A photographic Christmas card,** from Queen Elizabeth II and the Duke of Edinburgh, signed, c1980, 6 x 8in (15 x 20.5cm).
£760–850
€1,100–1,250
$1,450–1,650
⊞ AEL

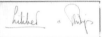

A Moorcroft vase, by Sally Tuffin, entitled 'Robin', printed and painted marks, 1988–91, 5½in (15cm) high.
£100–120 / €145–175
$195–230 ➤ WW

R.D. Wingfield, *Frost at Christmas,* first edition, 1989, 8°.
£320–380 / €460–550
$610–730 ➤ BBA

A Toby jug, by Kevin Francis, in the form of Father Christmas in a rocking chair, limited edition, c1990, 7in (18cm) high.
£80–90 / €115–130
$155–175 ➤ Pott

A Christmas card, from Sir Edward Heath, c1990, 10 x 8in (25.5 x 20.5cm).
£45–50 / €65–75
$85–95 ⊞ AEL
Sir Edward Heath was Prime Minister from 1970 to 1974.

◀ **A Royal Doulton Father Christmas character jug,** the handle modelled as a Christmas tree, No. D7123, limited edition, 1995, 8in (20.5cm) high.
£130–155
€190–220
$250–300
➤ Pott

Cigarette, Trading & Trade Cards

Liebig Extract of Meat Co, Japanese Festivals, set of six trade cards, 1907.
£10–15 / €15–22
$19–28 ⊞ LENA

Humpty-Dumpty Toy Savings Bank, lithographed trade card, slight damage, American, 1884.
£240–280 / €350–410
$460–540 ⚒ Bert

Uncle Sam Bank, lithographed trade card, American, 1886.
£450–540 / €650–780
$860–1,050 ⚒ Bert

John Player & Sons, Game Birds and Wild Fowl, set of 50 cigarette cards, 1927.
£60–70 / €85–100
$115–135 ⊞ JBa

W.D. & H.O. Wills, Flower Culture in Pots, set of 50 cigarette cards, 1925.
£15–20 / €22–29
$29–38 ⊞ MUR

John Player & Sons, Dandies, set of 50 cigarette cards, 1932.
£10–15 / €15–22
$19–28 ⊞ SOR

◄ **Lambert & Butler,** How Cars Work, set of 25 cigarette cards, 1931.
£50–60 / €75–85
$100–115 ⊞ MUR

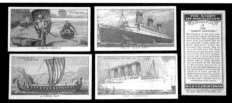

W.A. & A.C. Churchman, The Story of Navigation, set of 50 cigarette cards, 1936.
£15–20 / €22–29
$29–38 ⊞ LCC

John Player & Sons, Motor Cars, Series 2, set of 50 cigarette cards, 1937.
£40–45 / €60–70
$75–85 ⊞ SOR

◄ **W.D. & H.O. Wills,** Railway Equipment, set of 50 cigarette cards, 1938.
£15–20 / €22–29
$29–38 ⊞ SOR

▶ **John Player & Sons,** Animals of the Countryside, set of 50 cigarette cards, 1939.
£6–10 / €9–15
$12–19 ⊞ SOR

▶ **Liebig Extract of Meat Co,** Mountaineering, set of six trade cards, 1939, framed.
£50–60 / €75–85
$100–115 ⊞ JBa

John Player & Sons, Cycling, set of 50 cigarette cards, 1939.
£40–45 / €60–70
$75–85 ⊞ SOR

John Player & Sons, Animals of the Countryside, set of 50 cigarette cards, 1939.
£7–11 / €11–17
$13–20 ⊞ LCC

Godfrey Phillips Ltd, Beauties of To-Day, set of 36, 1940.
£35–40 / €50–60
$65–75 ⊞ LOC

Topps bubble gum, *Star Wars*, set of 66 trade cards, 1977.
£50–60 / €75–85
$100–115 ⊞ SSF

Topps bubble gum, *Star Wars* Series 3, set of 66 trade cards, 1977.
£90–100 / €130–145
$170–190 ⊞ OW

Carreras, Sport Fish, set of 50 cigarette cards, 1978.
£1–5 / €2–7
$3–9 ⊞ LCC

W.D. & H.O. Wills, World of Fire arms, set of 36 cigarette cards, 1982.
£5–9 / €8–13
$10–16 ⊞ LCC

John Player & Sons, Exploration of Space, set of 32 cigarette cards, 1983.
£3–7 / €4–10
$6–13 ⊞ LCC

Bassetts, *Dandy* and *Beano*, set of 48 trade cards, 1989.
£4–8 / €6–12
$8–15 ⊞ MUR

► **Walrus Cards,**
The Beatles, Let It Be series, set of 10 per album, late 1980s.
£6–10 / €9–15
$12–19 per set ⊞ SOR

► **Frameability,**
Fire Engines, set of 17 trade cards, 1996.
£1–5 / €2–7
$3–9 ⊞ MUR

► **Field Galleries,** Race Horses and Jockeys, Series 2, set of six trade cards, 1997.
£30–35 / €45–50
$55–65 ⊞ MUR

Buffy the Vampire Slayer, Series One, Inkworks trading cards, contains 36 packs of seven cards, unopened, 1998.
£180–200 / €260–290
$340–380 ⊞ SSF

▶ **Marlow Civil Engineering,** Clowns, set of 25 trade cards, 1990s.
£30–35 / €45–50
$55–65 ⊞ JBa

Star Trek Voyager, Species 8472 Ship profiles trading card, 1998.
£30–35 / €45–50
$55–65 ⊞ SSF

◀ **Alien Legacy,** set of 90 Inkworks trading cards, 1999.
£6–10 / €9–15
$12–19 ⊞ SSF

▶ **X-Men the Movie,** set of 72 Topps trading cards, 2000.
£6–10 / €9–15
$12–19 ⊞ SSF

Angel trade cards, Season 1, set of 90 trading cards, 2000.
£15–20 / €22–29
$29–38 ⊞ SSF

Buffy the Vampire Slayer, Season Four, set of 90 trading cards, 2000.
£10–15 / €15–22
$19–28 ⊞ SSF

For further information on Autographs see pages 43–46

◀ **Star Wars,** Topps autograph trading card, Jeremy Bullock as Boba Fett, 2001.
£70–80 / €100–115
$135–155 ⊞ SSF

Comics & Annuals

At the time of writing, the record price for a British comic is held by a *Dandy* No. 1, which was sold by Comic Book Postal Auctions for £20,350 / €29,500 / $39,000 (see *Miller's Collectables Price Guide 2005*). 'Only a handful of first issues still exist,' explains director Malcolm Phillips. 'This one was in excellent condition and still had its free gift (a tin whistle) – the only known example to survive! This combination made collectors really excited and we broke the world record.' According to Phillips, the market for British comics is robust and growing. 'Prices for rare items in top condition seem to know no bounds,' he notes. 'But the market is discerning. People understand about rarity and are looking for high-grade examples and strong, bright colours.' Classics such as *Beano* and *Dandy* (shown on page 152 is a *Dandy* No. 2 – again complete with free gift – that also made a record auction price), have been performing well. 'It's still a developing subject in Britain,' explains Phillips. 'In the USA comic collecting is far more established and prices tend to be better known and more specific. For example, there is a far bigger disparity in price in America when it comes to condition. A comic described as vg – very good – which effectively means in average condition, might be worth £52 / €65 / $100, but that same comic in fine condition could sell for ten times as much.'

With American Golden Age comics (produced up to 1954), early items in a high grade are hard to get hold of and command high prices. 'Comics with WWII propaganda covers are very sought after in the current market,' says Phillips. 'Prices for Silver Age comics (1955–70) continue to spiral. Modern movies and computer games have helped stimulate demand for Marvel characters such as X-Men and Spiderman and when the *Fantastic Four* film is released it will also generate new collectors.'

Comics and cartoons do not only grow in popularity, they can also wane. Carl Ronald Giles (1916–95) was one of Britain's best-loved cartoonists. He joined the *Daily Express* in 1943 and the famous Giles family first appeared on 5 August 1945. The first *Giles Annual* was published in 1946 and continued yearly, even after the artist's death. The most sought after annuals are the first ten, particularly the first five but, according to Phillips, prices have dropped. *Rupert,* another famous annual, has also experienced shifting fortunes. 'I sold a 1930s' *Rupert Annual* No. 1 this year complete with original case and dust jacket for £800 / €1,150 / $1,500. Five or six years ago I might have expected it to fetch twice as much,' says Phillips. Various factors explain this shift. As Phillips notes, the publication of facsimile editions of vintage *Rupert* annuals damaged the market for period originals, yet while earlier volumes might be suffering, *Rupert* annuals from the 1960s (complete with virgin and unpainted Magic Painting pages) can now make £200–250 / €290–360 / $380–480 each.

Collectors often return to the comics and annuals of their youth. Thirty- and forty-somethings are often big spenders in the comics field and, concludes Phillips, '1960s' comics and annuals are an increasingly strong area.'

◄ *All Star Comics*, No. 9, 1942.
£450–520 / €650–750
$860–1,000 ➤ JAA

► *The Amazing Spiderman* comic, No. 1, slight damage, 1963.
£1,450–1,700
€2,100–2,450
$2,750–3,250 ➤ JAA

◄ *Action Comics*, No. 165, published by DC Comics, The Man Who Conquered Spiderman, American, 1952.
£75–85 / €110–125
$145–165 ➤ CBP

◄ **Batman comic,**
No. 9, 1942.
£880–1,050
€1,300–1,550
$1,700–2,000 ⚡ JAA

► **Batman's Detective Comics,** No. 340, published by DC Comics, Batman and Batgirl, American, 1965.
£10–15 / €15–22
$19–28 ⊞ CoC

Amazing Fantasy comic,
No. 15, Enter Spider-Man, slight damage, 1962.
£550–660 / €800–960
$1,050–1,250 ⚡ CBP

The Beano comic, No. 4, slight damage, 1938.
£930–1,100
€1,350–1,600
$1,800–2,150 ⚡ CBP

The Beano comic, No. 5, slight damage, 1938.
£800–960 / €1,200–1,400
$1,550–1,850 ⚡ CBP

The Beano comic,
No. 100, 1940.
£220–260 / €320–380
$420–500 ⚡ CBP

The Beano comic, No. 3, slight damage, 1938.
£1,200–1,400
€1,750–2,050
$2,300–2,700 ⚡ CBP

The Beano comic, No. 125, Christmas number, slight damage, 1940.
£70–80 / €100–115
$135–155 ⚡ CBP

The Broons book,
hardback, slight damage, 1956.
£330–390 / €480–570
$630–750 ⚡ CBP

► **Buster,** No. 1, published by Fleetway Publications, 1960.
£70–80 / €100–115
$135–155 ⚡ VAU

Countdown, Nos. 1–17, the first six issues complete with their free gifts, published by Polystyle Publications, 1971.
£185–220 / €270–320 $360–420 ✗ **VAU**

The Dandy comic, No. 1, slight damage, 1937.
£7,200–8,600 / €10,400–12,500 $13,800–16,500 ✗ **CBP**

The Dandy comic, No. 2, with Jumping Frog free gift, 1937.
£3,750–4,500 / €5,400–6,500 $7,200–8,600 ✗ **CBP**
This was a record price for a Dandy comic No. 2.

The Dandy Monster Comic, No. 5, Korky leads the Bicycle Race, slight damage and restoration, 1943.
£2,750–3,300 €4,000–4,800 $5,300–6,300 ✗ **CBP**

The Dandy Monster Comic, Korky Warms Up the Sea, slight damage, 1950.
£195–230 / €280–330 $370–440 ✗ **CBP**

The Dandy book, 1976.
£1–5 / €2–7 $3–9 ⊞ **UD**

The Dr Who Annual, No. 1, 1965.
£10–15 / €15–22 $19–28 ⊞ **HeA**

◄ **The Eagle,** original full-colour artwork by William Stobbs, Cortez befriends Emperor Montezuma of Mexico, poster paint on board, 1950, 21 x 15in (53.5 x 38cm).
£115–135 / €165–195 $220–260 ✗ **CBP**
William Stobbs was born in 1914 and was Head of Design at the London College of Printing. He illustrated more than 100 books including 20 of his own and 'Cortez' was his only comic strip work.

Fantastic Four, No. 5, published by Marvel Comics Group, slight damage, 1962.
£60–70 / €85–100 $115–135 ✗ **VAU**

Giggle, No.1, published by Fleetway, 1967.
£35–40 / 50–60 $65–75 ✗ **VAU**

◄ **Giles Cartoons,** Series 6, published by the *Daily Express*, 1952.
£90–100 / €130–145 $170–190 ⊞ **NW**

► **Giles Cartoons,** Series 19, published by the *Daily Express*, 1965.
£10–15 / €15–22 $19–28 ⊞ **NW**

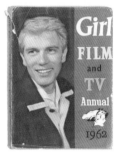

◀ **Giles Cartoons,** Series 25, published by the *Daily Express*, 1971.
£1–5 / €2–7
$3–9 ⊞ NW

Girl Film and TV Annual, published by Lomgrace Press, 1962.
£1–5 / €2–7
$3–9 ⊞ UD

The Goodies Annual, 1974.
£3–7 / €4–10
$6–13 ⊞ IQ

Jonny Quest Annual, published by Hanna-Barbera, 1966.
£6–10 / €9–15
$12–19 ⊞ UD

◀ **Mandy,** No. 1, published by D.C. Thomson, 1967.
£75–85 / €110–125
$145–165 ⚲ VAU

▶ **Mickey Mouse Weekly,** Vol 1, Nos. 1–3, No. 112, published by Willbank & Odhams, plus two loose issues, 1936–38.
£380–450 / €550–650
$730–860 ⚲ DW

Mickey Mouse Annual, 1947.
£40–45 / €60–70
$75–85 ⊞ UD

Mysteries Weird and Strange, No. 1, slight damage, 1953.
£40–45 / €60–70
$75–85 ⚲ CBP

Radio Fun, No. 2, Clarke Gable, slight damage, 1938.
£35–40 / €50–60
$65–75 ⚲ CBP

Ranger, Nos. 1–20, in a bound volume, published by Fleetway, 1965–66.
£290–340 / €420–490
$560–650 ⚲ VAU

The Rupert Book,
published by the *Daily Express*, slight damage and repair, 1941.
£140–165 / €200–230
$270–310 ⚲ DW

More Adventures of Rupert, published by the *Daily Express*, 1947.
£6–10 / €9–15
$12–19 ⊞ UD

Rupert Annual,
published by the *Daily Express*, 1949.
£135–150 / €195–220
$260–290 ⊞ UD

School Friend Annual, 1953.
£1–5 / €2–7
$3–9 ⊞ HeA

Tales from the Crypt,
No. 21, published by M.C. Gaines, 1950.
£1,700–2,000
€2,450–2,900
$3,250–3,850 ⚲ VAU
The publishers kept up to 12 copies of each issue and these are in excellent condition.

Victor, No. 1, published by D. C. Thomson, 1961.
£85–95 / €125–140
$165–185 ⚲ VAU

◀ **TV Tornado,**
Nos. 1, 2 and 3, No. 2 with *TV Tornado* Magic Cards free gift, published by City Magazines, 1967.
£100–120
€145–175
$195–230
⚲ VAU

▶ **TV 21 Century Annual,** published by Jarrod & Sons, 1966.
£4–8 / €6–12
$8–12 ⊞ UD

◀ **Witches Tales,**
No. 25, 1954.
£120–140 / €170–200
$230–270 ⚲ CBP

X-Men comic book, No. 1, slight damage, 1963.
£360–430 / €520–620
$690–820 ⚲ JAA

Items in the the Comics & Annuals section have been arranged in alphabetical order.

◀ **X-Men comic,**
No. 41, 1968.
£40–45 / €60–70
$75–85 ⚲ CBP

◀ **Young Marvelman Annual,** No. 1, published by L. Miller, slight damage, 1954.
£50–60 / €75–85
$100–115 ⚲ VAU

Commemorative Ware
Military & Naval

A character jug, in the form of the Duke of Wellington, c1850, 7in (18cm) high.
£310–350 / €450–510
$600–670 ⊞ SER

A Wilkinson Toby jug, designed by Sir Frances Carruthers Gould, in the form of Admiral David Beatty, inscribed 'Dread Nought', c1920, 10in (25.5cm) high.
£490–550 / €710–800
$940–1,050 ⊞ BRT

A ceramic plate, transfer-printed with a portrait of Robert Baden-Powell, 1899–1900, 9in (23cm) diam.
£75–85 / €110–125
$145–165 ⊞ BtoB

▶ **A pair of Gray's Pottery lustre tankards,** commemorating Navy Week, Plymouth, 1934, 4in (10cm) high.
£480–540 / €700–780
$920–1,050 ⊞ MMc

A Paragon Patriotic Series cup and saucer, inscribed 'There will always be an England', 1940s, saucer 4in (10cm) diam.
£165–185 / €240–270
$320–360 ⊞ WAA

◀ **A ceramic mug,** commemorating the Falklands campaign, decorated with a photograph of Admiral J. Woodward, edition of 500, 1982, 4in (10cm) high.
£10–15 / €15–22
$19–28 ⊞ IQ

A naval woolwork panel, depicting a crown, rose and flags, inset with a photograph, early 20thC, 14 x 19½in (35.5 x 49.5cm).
£150–180 / €220–260
$290–340 ⋊ G(L)

◀ **A Copeland trinket box,** decorated with a portrait of F.M. Earl Kitchener in a garland of oak leaves and flowers, 1914, 5in (12.5cm) wide.
£145–165 / €210–240
$280–320 ⊞ BtoB

A Royal Worcester mug, commemorating Victory in the Gulf, 1997, 3½in (9cm) high.
£15–20 / €22–29
$29–38 ⊞ H&G

Political

A **Paragon bowl,** decorated with a portrait of the Rt Hon Neville Chamberlain, 1938, 3½in (9cm) diam.
£75–85 / €110–125
$145–165 ⊞ BtoB

◀ A **plaster figure of Sir Winston Churchill,** c1942, 8in (20.5cm) high.
£170–190
€250–280
$320–360
⊞ H&G

▶ A **Royal Doulton Toby jug,** in the form of Sir Winston Churchill, 1940s, 8½in (21.5cm) high.
£100–115
€145–165
$200–220 ⊞ Tus

A **ceramic salt cellar,** in the form of a bust of Sir Winston Churchill, c1950, 3½in (9cm) high.
£55–65 / €80–95
$105–125 ⊞ H&G

A **set of cardboard coasters,** depicting Harold Wilson, 1960s, 3¾in (9.5cm) square.
£10–15 / €15–22
$19–28 ⊞ RTT

Items in the Commemorative Ware section have been arranged in date order within each sub-section.

A **Royal Doulton pin tray,** commemorating the election of Margaret Thatcher as first woman Prime Minister, 1979, 4in (10cm) diam.
£8–12 / €12–18
$16–23 ⊞ H&G

A **ceramic mug,** inscribed 'Support the Miners', 1984, 4in (10cm) high.
£35–40 / €50–60
$65–75 ⊞ H&G

A **Royal Crown Derby loving cup,** commemorating Margaret Thatcher's third term as Prime Minister, edition of 650, 1987, 3in (7.5cm) high.
£150–170 / €220–250
$270–300 ⊞ H&G

A **ceramic plate,** commemorating the 10th anniversary of the miners' strike of 1984–85, 1994, 10in (25.5cm) diam.
£50–60 / €75–85
$100–115 ⊞ H&G

Royalty

The first recorded Royal commemorative ceramic item was produced for Charles II and celebrated the restoration of the monarchy in 1660; however, it was not until the late 19th century and Queen Victoria's Golden Jubilee that Royal commemoratives were mass-produced and made available to everybody.

Commemoratives from the first part of the 19th century are comparatively rare and correspondingly costly. Queen Victoria acceded the throne in 1837 and married her cousin Prince Albert of Saxe-Coburg-Gotha in 1840. The marriage was happy and they went on to have nine children but, following Albert's death in 1861, the grief-stricken Queen went into mourning for over 25 years. The Golden Jubilee in 1887 marked her return to public life and was celebrated with a range of commemorative items. Ten years later, the Diamond Jubilee spawned even more souvenirs and established the tradition of marking royal events with mass-produced commemoratives.

Part of the fascination of these objects is that they record the changing fortunes of the monarchy. Vast numbers of commemoratives were released for the proposed coronation of Edward VIII in 1937 – they are not rare as people often imagine. When the king abdicated because of his love for Mrs Simpson, manufacturers swiftly adapted their designs and instead of bearing the head of Edward VIII, ceramics were typically decorated with portraits of George VI and Queen Elizabeth, sometimes including the two Princesses, stressing the stability of the monarchy and the importance of the family after a period of constitutional crisis.

Values of commemorative pieces depend largely on rarity and among the most unusual pieces are objects commemorating the wedding of Princess Elizabeth and Prince Philip in 1947. Rationing and emergency restrictions resulting from WWII prevented the production of all but a handful of commemoratives and even the Princess herself was only allotted 100 clothing coupons to produce her wedding dress. Quality of manufacture, the appeal of the monarch and charm of image are all important. Commemoratives depicting Princesses Margaret and Elizabeth as children are popular with collectors. In more recent and troubled times commemoratives have often reflected a less respectful attitude to the monarchy. Satirical pieces from the 1980s and mugs marking the numerous divorces as well as the marriages of Royal figures are now increasingly sought after.

A ceramic saucer, commemorating Princess Charlotte, 1817, 5½in (14cm) diam.
£100–120 / €145–175
$195–230 ⊞ H&G

LOCATE THE SOURCE
The source of each illustration in Miller's can be found by checking the code letters below each caption with the Key to Illustrations, pages 443–451.

A pair of pearlware nursery plates, each moulded with a portrait of Queen Caroline, 1821, 8¼in (21cm) diam.
£420–500 / €610–730
$810–960 ↗ G(L)

A ceramic plate, commemorating Queen Adelaide, 1830s, 7in (18cm) diam.
£340–380 / €490–550
$650–730 ⊞ BRT

◀ A Rutland plate, commemorating Queen Victoria's coronation, 1837, 7in (18cm) diam.
£260–290 / €380–420
$500–560 ⊞ WAA

A Sèvres vase, depicting Queen Victoria, French, 1851, 11in (28cm) high
£3,150–3,500
€4,550–5,100
$6,000–6,700 ⊞ H&G
This vase was exhibited by the French Government at the 1851 Great Exhibition at Crystal Palace.

◄ **A Sèvres plaque,** by J. Peyre, moulded with a portrait of Napoleon III, French, 1869, 9¼in (23.5cm) diam.
£175–210
€250–300
$340–400
🔨 JAA

► **A ceramic plate,** depicting King Edward VII and Queen Alexandra, 1885, 9in (23cm) wide.
£270–300
€390–440
$520–580
⊞ BRT

A Berlin two-handled vase, decorated with a portrait of Wilhelm I, German Emperor and King of Prussia, slight damage, sceptre mark, 1871–88, 20¾in (52.5cm) high.
£1,900–2,250
€2,750–3,250
$3,600–4,300 🔨 S(NY)

A ceramic Trade and Industry plate, commemorating Queen Victoria's Golden Jubilee, 1887, 11in (28cm) wide.
£85–95 / €125–165
$165–185 ⊞ BRT

A ceramic plate, commemorating Tsar Nicholas II and Empress Alexandra's visit to Paris, 1896, 8in (20.5cm) diam.
£290–330 / €420–480
$560–630 ⊞ BRT

A ceramic plate, commemorating Queen Victoria's Diamond Jubilee, transfer-printed with portraits depicting a young and old Victoria, 1897, 9in (23cm) diam.
£140–160 / €200–230
$270–310 ⊞ BRT

A Doulton Lambeth jug, commemorating Queen Victoria's Diamond Jubilee, 1897, 7in (18cm) high.
£100–120 / €145–175
$200–240 🔨 CHTR

A ceramic mug, commemorating Queen Victoria's Diamond Jubilee, inscribed 'All Honour to our Empress Queen', 1897, 3½in (9cm) high.
£145–165 / €210–240
$280–320 ⊞ BRT

A ceramic plate, commemorating Queen Victoria's Diamond Jubilee, 1897, 9½in (24cm) diam.
£90–100 / €130–145
$170–190 ⊞ BRT

A Royal Doulton vase, commemorating Queen Victoria's Diamond Jubilee, 1897, 7in (18cm) high.
**£140–160 / €200–230
$270–310** ⊞ H&G

◄ **An earthenware mug,** commemorating the death of King Edward VII, 1910, 4in (10cm) high.
**£85–95 / €125–140
$165–185** ⊞ H&G

A Copeland two-handled vase and cover, commemorating the Transvaal War, with a portrait of Queen Victoria, 1899–1900, 11in (28cm) high.
**£1,550–1,850
€2,250–2,700
$3,000–3,550** ⋌ LT

▶ **An Aynsley cup and saucer,** commemorating the coronation of King Edward VII, printed with portraits and flags, 1902.
**£65–75
€95–105
$125–145**
⋌ SAS

The Graphic, commemorating the coronation of King Edward VII, 1902, 16 x 12in (40.5 x 30.5cm).
**£35–40 / €50–60
$65–75** ⊞ J&S

A Cadbury's chocolate tin, commemorating the coronation of King Edward VII, with contents, 1902, 3½in (9cm) wide.
**£65–75 / €95–105
$125–145** ⊞ HUX

A Royal Crown Derby miniature loving cup, commemorating the coronation of George V, 1911, 1½in (4cm) high.
**£80–95 / €115–140
$155–185** ⋌ SAS

▶ **An earthenware beaker,** commemorating the coronation of George V, retailed by Collins Stores, Wisbech, 1911, 4in (10cm) high.
**£125–140 / €180–200
$240–270** ⊞ H&G

A lithophane cup and saucer, commemorating the coronation of George V, 1911, 3in (7.5cm) diam.
£90–100 / €130–145
$170–190 ⊞ BRT

Two ceramic mugs, one depicting Princess Elizabeth, the other Princess Margaret, 1930s, 2½in (6.5cm) diam.
£170–190 / €250–280
$320–360 ⊞ BRT

A Royal Doulton mug, commemorating the coronation of King Edward VIII, 1936–37, 3½in (9cm) high.
£45–50 / €65–75
$85–95 ⊞ H&G

Two bone china beakers, commemorating the coronation of King George VI and Queen Elizabeth, and the coronation of King Edward VIII, 1936–37, 3in (7.5cm) high.
£220–250 / €320–360
$420–480 each ⊞ H&G

A paper bag, commemorating King Edward VIII, c1937, 7in (18cm) square.
£4–8 / €6–12
$8–15 ⊞ UD

An earthenware egg cup, commemorating the coronation of King George VI, 1937, 2½in (6.5cm) high.
£25–30 / €40–45
$50–55 ⊞ H&G

A Cadbury's chocolate tin, commemorating the coronation of King George VI, with contents, 1937, 5½in (14cm) wide.
£55–65 / €80–95
$105–125 ⊞ HUX

A Hammersley mug, commemorating the coronation of Queen Elizabeth II, 1953, 3in (7.5cm) high.
£35–40 / €50–60
$65–75 ⊞ JMC

A Wemyss goblet, commemorating the 80th birthday of the Queen Mother and the Wemyss centenary, 1980, 8in (20.5cm) high.
£220–250 / €320–360
$420–480 ⊞ RdeR

A Boehm porcelain centrepiece, commemorating the marriage of the Prince of Wales and Lady Diana Spencer, in the form of the Prince Charles Rose and the Lady Diana Rose, 1981, 21in (53.5cm) wide.
£190–220 / €280–330
$360–430 ↗ Oli

◀ **A Doulton mug,** commemorating the marriage of the Prince of Wales and Lady Diana Spencer, edition of 5,000, 1981, 3in (7.5cm) high.
£40–45 / €60–70
$75–85 ⊞ WAA

A ceramic mug, commemorating the marriage of the Prince of Wales and Lady Diana Spencer, retailed by Debenhams, 1981, 3in (7.5cm) diam.
£30–35 / €45–50
$55–65 ⊞ H&G

A Coalport urn and cover, commemorating the 30th anniversary of the coronation of Queen Elizabeth II, No. 10 of 50, c1983, 9½in (24cm) high.
£140–165 / €200–240
$270–320 ⚲ DA

A J. & J. May ceramic mug, commemorating the death of the Duchess of Windsor, 1986, 3½in (9cm) high.
£65–75 / €95–105
$125–145 ⊞ H&G

A ceramic beaker, commemorating the 90th birthday of the Queen Mother, 1990, 5in (12.5cm) high.
£50–60 / €75–85
$100–115 ⊞ WAA

A Rye Pottery tankard, commemorating Queen Elizabeth II's Golden Jubilee, 2002, 4in (10cm) high.
£30–35 / €45–50
$55–65 ⊞ H&G

A Caverswall mug, commemorating Queen Elizabeth II's Golden Jubilee, edition of 2,000, 2002, 4in (10cm) high.
£20–25 / €30–35
$40–50 ⊞ H&G

A Royal Crown Derby loving cup, commemorating the birth of Prince Harry, edition of 750, 1984, 3in (7.5cm) high.
£150–175 / €220–250
$290–340 ⊞ H&G

A Royal Crown Derby loving cup, commemorating the marriage of Prince Andrew and Sarah Ferguson, 1986, 4in (10cm) high.
£110–125 / €160–180
$210–240 ⊞ H&G

▶ **A Chown China mug,** commemorating the 35th birthday of the Princess of Wales, edition of 70, 1996, 4in (10cm) high.
£80–90
€115–130
$155–175 ⊞ H&G

A Chown China loving cup, commemorating the death of Princess Margaret, 2002, 3in (7.5cm) diam.
£65–75 / €95–105
$125–145 ⊞ H&G

Corkscrews

A brass corkscrew, by Robert Jones & Son, with a turned bone handle, No. 423, dated 1840, 6¾in (17cm) long.
£1,000–1,200 / €1,450–1,750
$2,000–2,300 ⚒ DD
The 19th century was a golden age for English mechanical corkscrews. Over 300 different designs were patented and rarities from this period, such as this example by Robert Jones & Son, can fetch four-figure sums at auction. Record prices for corkscrews include £18,500 / €26,800 / $35,500 for an 18th-century silver pocket corkscrew sold at Christie's in 1997.

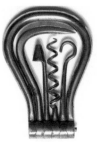

An Underwood-style brass corkscrew, with a turned bone handle, 19thC.
£185–220 / €270–320
$350–420 ⚒ DMC

A turned chestnut corkscrew, with dusting brush, c1850, 6in (15cm) long.
£15–20 / €22–29
$29–38 ⊞ CS

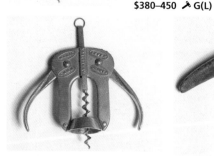

A steel folding four-tool bow corkscrew, c1850, 3in (7.5cm) long.
£45–50 / €65–75
$85–95 ⊞ CS

◀ **A bronze King's corkscrew,** by Joseph Rodgers & Sons, with a bone handle, brush missing, 19thC, 9in (23cm) extended.
£200–240 / €290–350
$380–450 ⚒ G(L)

A brass corkscrew, 'L'Excelsior Paris', by Armand Guichard, French, c1880, 7in (18cm) long.
£60–70 / €85–100
$115–135 ⊞ CS

A steel Magic Lever Cork Drawer corkscrew, c1920, 6in (15cm) long.
£35–40 / €50–60
$65–75 ⊞ CS

◀ **A steel corkscrew,** French, c1890, 6in (15cm) long.
£50–60 / €75–85
$100–115 ⊞ CS

A nickel corkscrew, with a stag horn handle and a cap lifter, American, 6in (15cm) long.
£50–60 / €75–85
$100–115 ⊞ CS

Cosmetics & Hairdressing

A pair of paste and tortoiseshell hair combs, late 19thC.
£220–260 / €320–380
$420–500 ⚖ G(L)

A silver-mounted toothbrush, Birmingham 1903, 3in (7.5cm) long.
£145–165 / €210–240
$280–320 ⊞ FOF

A petit point mirror case and mirror, with a press-stud fastener, early 20thC, 5in (12.5cm) wide.
£15–20 / €22–29
$29–38 ⊞ LBr

A set of silver dressing table accessories, comprising a glove stretcher, shoe horn and button hook, the handles in the form of leopards' heads, c1930, 7in (18cm) long.
£120–135 / €175–195
$230–260 ⊞ CoHA

▶ **A silver powder compact,** by Georg Jensen, signed, marked, Danish, 1940, 3¼in (8.5cm) diam.
£280–330 / €400–480
$540–640 ⚖ DORO

A Yardley's Lavender shaving stick, boxed, 1925–35, 3½in (9cm) high.
£15–20 / €22–29
$29–38 ⊞ HUX

A tin of Sun-Tan talcum powder, 1930s, 6in (15cm) high.
£10–15 / €15–22
$19–28 ⊞ HUX

A gilt-metal and petit point perfume holder, in the form of a handbag, 1950s, 3in (7.5cm) wide.
£30–35 / €45–50
$55–65 ⊞ LBr

A silver dressing table set, by William Comyns & Sons, comprising a mirror, box and covered dish, chased with putti, London 1909–13, mirror 11¼in (28.5cm) long.
£145–170 / €210–250
$280–330 ⚖ LHA

A Myatt lady's razor, cased, 1930s, ¾in (2cm) square.
£25–30 / €40–45
$60–70 ⊞ RTT

A gilt-metal and enamel powder compact, with floral decoration, 1950s, 2½in (6.5cm) diam.
£55–65 / €80–95
$105–125 ⊞ LBr

Costume & Textiles

The market for vintage fashion continues to flourish. In addition to specialist dealers, a number of high street department stores now have vintage sections. There is a growing number of vintage fashion fairs and internet businesses continue to expand. With the latter, however, when not buying from an established or recognized source, caution is advised in certain areas. For example, the high prices being paid for original punk material from the 1970s have stimulated a number of Vivienne Westwood and Malcolm McLaren fakes. 'It's not just the clothes they are copying, it's also the labels,' warns Stephen Phillips from Rellik, specialist in Westwood material. 'If you are not buying from a known dealer and if you don't have an airtight provenance, you have to be very careful.'

If you are buying to wear, it is always advisable to try clothes on in order to check both sizing and condition. Certain areas such as under arms, fastenings and hems are particularly prone to staining and damage. Some clothes are very fragile; for example a 1920s' beaded dress can be prohibitively expensive to restore. Cleaning of old fabrics should be undertaken with care. While some materials are very durable (1950s cottons for

example), others need more careful handling. For any collector a good dry-cleaner is essential. A good tip is to ask your nearest vintage clothes dealer which dry cleaner they use or, failing that, find one who specializes in theatrical costumes (ask your local theatre), since they will be used to dealing with more unusual fabrics and designs.

As in every other field, prices for vintage fashion can go up and down. Demand for certain designers can be stimulated by an exhibition or new book. Following a recent successful publication on Biba – one of London's most fashionable stores from the 1960s and 1970s – interest and prices for Biba material have risen considerably. High values tend to bring a wealth of material on to the market, so sometimes a boom period can be followed by levelling out or a drop in prices as supply outstrips demand. Typically, and not surprisingly, it is good pieces that are in the best condition that will keep their value. However, the joy of the vintage market is its variety. You may spend a three- or four-figure sum on a designer classic but just as much pleasure can be had out of a more affordable high street vintage frock, and both are equally true to their period.

Victorian & Edwardian

A Victorian lace and silk **bodice**, with a silk sash.
£70–80 / €100–115
$135–155 ⊞ VICT

▶ A Victorian silk taffeta day dress.
£400–450 / €590–650
$770–860 ⊞ Ech

▶ A Victorian satin wedding dress.
£580–650 / €840–940
$1,100–1,250 ⊞ Ech

A Victorian child's broderie anglaise dress.
£20–25 / €30–35
$40–50 ⊞ BaN

◀ **A lace bib,** with quilted decoration, c1890.
£15–20 / €22–29
$29–38 ⊞ JUC

◀ **A wool christening cape,** with embroidered decoration, c1900.
£45–50 / €65–75
$85–95 ⊞ BaN

A **Paisley shawl,** c1860, 128in (325cm) square.
£400–450 / €590–650
$770–860 ⊞ JPr

◀ **An Edwardian silk grosgrain and lace wedding dress.**
£160–180 / €230–260
$310–350 ⊞ DE

▶ **A broderie anglaise skirt and blouse,** c1900.
£280–320 / €410–460
$540–610 ⊞ VICT

A **late Victorian velvet and lace evening dress,** decorated with sequins.
£310–350 / €450–510
$600–670 ⊞ Ech

Twenties & Thirties

A child's wool coat, with brass buttons, c1920.
£35–40 / €50–60
$65–75 ⊞ BaN

A **chiffon evening dress,** decorated with beads and embroidery, 1920.
£400–450 / €580–650
$770–860 ⊞ Ech

▶ **A lamé cape,** with batwing sleeves, French, 1920s.
£270–300 €390–440
$520–580 ⊞ HSR

A silk crepe flapper dress, with hand-beaded decoration, 1920.
£160–180 / €230–260
$310–350 ⊞ LaF

Items in the Costume & Textiles section have been arranged in date order within each sub-section.

◄ **A net over-dress,** decorated with beads, 1920s.
£250–280 / €360–410
$480–540 ⊞ Ech

A beaded over-dress, decorated with roses, 1920s.
£540–600 / €780–870
$1,000–1,150 ⊞ Ech

A chiffon evening dress, decorated with glass beads, 1920s.
£580–650 / €840–940
$1,100–1,250 ⊞ Ech

◄ **A crepe evening dress,** decorated with beads and embroidery, 1920s.
£490–550 / €710–800
$940–1,050 ⊞ Ech

A silk organza dress, 1920s.
£200–230 / €290–330
$380–440 ⊞ TIN

A Paisley cape, with a fur collar, French, 1920s.
£200–230 / €290–330
$380–440 ⊞ Ech

A silk satin wedding dress, decorated with a flower, 1920s.
£130–145 / €190–210
$250–280 ⊞ Ech

◄ **A devoré evening coat dress,** 1920s.
£130–145 / €190–210
$250–280 ⊞ Ech

◀ **A silk housecoat,** with block-printed decoration, 1920s.
£75–85 / €110–125
$145–165 ⊞ Ech

A chiffon evening jacket, decorated with beads, 1920s.
£290–330 / €420–480
$560–630 ⊞ Ech

▶ **A silk shawl,** with embroidered decoration, 1920s, 60in (152.5cm) wide.
£250–280 / €360–410
$480–540 ⊞ Ech

A devoré evening coat, 1920s.
£340–380 / €490–550
$650–730 ⊞ Ech

A chiffon evening jacket, decorated with beads, 1920s.
£340–380 / €490–550
$650–730 ⊞ Ech

◀ **A devoré wrap-around coat dress,** 1920s.
£310–350 / €450–510
$600–670 ⊞ HSR

▶ **Four silk bow dress trims,** 1920s, 12in (30.5cm) wide.
£6–10 / €9–15
$12–19 each
⊞ DE

Thirties & Forties

A printed acetate dress
and cape, early 1930s.
£75–85 / €110–125
$145–165 ⊞ Ech

A rayon satin evening
dress, 1930.
£75–85 / €110–125
$145–165 ⊞ Ech

A rayon crepe dress,
with appliqué floral
decoration, c1930.
£80–90 / €115–130
$155–175 ⊞ Ech

A net dress, 1930s.
£75–85 / €110–125
$145–165 ⊞ DE

A velvet evening
jacket, 1930s.
£50–60 / €75–85
$100–115 ⊞ Ech

A slipper satin evening
dress, with embroidered
detail, 1930s.
£70–80 / €100–115
$135–155 ⊞ DE

A velvet evening
coat, 1930s.
£100–110 / €145–160
$190–210 ⊞ Ech

A printed silk kimono-
style dressing
gown, c1930.
£40–45 / €60–70
$75–85 ⊞ Ech

► A chiffon evening
jacket, decorated with
beads, 1930s.
£200–220 / €290–320
$380–420 ⊞ Ech

A sequined evening jacket, 1930s.
£175–195 / €250–280
$330–370 ⊞ Ech

A printed rayon satin housecoat, 1930–40.
£35–40 / €50–60
$65–75 ⊞ Ech

◀ A rayon satin evening dress, 1930–40.
£65–75 / €95–105
$125–145 ⊞ Ech

An embroidered cotton day dress, 1940.
£20–25 / €30–35
$40–50 ⊞ Ech

A rayon satin wedding dress, with lace trim and covered buttons, 1940.
£70–80 / €100–115
$135–155 ⊞ Ech

A Moygashel linen day dress, 1940s.
£20–25 / €30–35
$40–50 ⊞ Ech

◀ A Renee Meneely satin day dress, 1940–50.
£30–35 / €45–50
$55–65 ⊞ Ech

Fifties

A Ramar flocked velvet evening dress, retailed by Richards Shops, 1950.
£35–40 / €50–60
$65–75 ⊞ Ech

▶ A Hilderbrand taffeta evening dress, 1950s.
£25–30 / €40–45
$50–55 ⊞ Ech

A taffeta evening dress, 1950s.
£100–120 / €145–175
$195–230 ⊞ DRE

▶ A brocade ball gown, c1950.
£160–180 / €230–260
$310–350 ⊞ DE

◀ A wool cardigan, with heather embroidery, 1950.
£20–25 / €30–35
$40–50 ⊞ DE

A cotton dress, 1950s.
£55–65 / €80–95
$105–125 ⊞ HSR

▶ A Jenners of Edinburgh brocade ball gown, limited edition, 1950s.
£135–150 / €195–220
$260–290 ⊞ DE

A jersey and taffeta dress, 1950s.
£20–25 / €30–35
$40–50 ⊞ CCO

▶ An evening dress, 1950s.
£90–100 / €130–145
$170–190 ⊞ HIP

A California taffeta dress, 1950.
£20–25 / €30–35
$40–50 ⊞ Ech

◄ **A Clydesdale child's cotton dress,** 1950s.
£8–12 / €12–18
$16–23 ⊞ CCO

► **A sequined and hand-painted skirt,** Mexican, 1950s.
£120–135
€175–195
$230–260
⊞ SpM

A Dorland silk dress, 1950s.
£135–150 / €195–220
$260–290 ⊞ Ci

◄ **A cotton skirt,** printed with cats, American, 1950s.
£115–130
€165–190
$220–250
⊞ DRE

► **A papier-mâché and rabbit fur headdress,** in the form of a bear's head, 1950s.
£100–120
€145–175
$195–230
⊞ AUTO

An embroidered velvet housecoat, c1950.
£40–45 / €60–70
$75–85 ⊞ Ech

A ruched cotton swimsuit, French, 1950s.
£40–45 / €60–70
$75–85 ⊞ HSR

► **A pair of nylon and lace pants,** with original tag, 1950s.
£25–30
€40–45
$50–55 ⊞ SpM

Sixties

A chiffon cocktail dress, 1960.
£10–15 / €15–22
$19–28 ⊞ Ech

A Leshgold lace and velvet cocktail dress, 1960.
£30–35 / €45–50
$55–65 ⊞ Ech

▶ **A Jean Dessés taffeta bolero jacket and muff,** decorated with velvet and organza petals, 1960s.
£500–600
€730–870
$960–1,150
⚒ KTA

A pair of cotton wide-leg trousers, American, 1960s.
£60–70 / €85–100
$115–135 ⊞ DRE

A Peter Robinson crepe cocktail dress, 1960s.
£40–45 / €60–70
$75–85 ⊞ Ech

A Christian Dior silk and linen mix jacket, No. 5907, embroidered and beaded with trailing blooms, early 1960s.
£400–480 / €580–700
$770–920 ⚒ KTA

◀ **A shirt,** decorated with Noddy and Big-Ears, 1960s.
£55–65 / €80–95
$105–125 ⊞ LAS

A Dolly Rockers cotton mini dress, designed by Sambo, 1960s.
£35–40 / €50–60
$65–75 ⊞ DE

▶ **A woven paper Campbell's Pop-Art 'Souper' dress,** printed with Campbell's Soup motifs, with label, care instructions and reorder form, American, c1966.
£800–960 / €1,200–1,400
$1,550–1,850 ⚒ KTA

Seventies & Eighties

A Biba moss crepe dress, c1970.
£160–180 / €230–260
$310–350 ⊞ DE

A cotton halter-neck dress, c1970.
£35–40 / €50–60
$65–75 ⊞ DE

An Ossie Clark moss crepe evening dress, retailed by Radley, c1970.
£110–125 / €160–180
$210–240 ⊞ Ech

A Zandra Rhodes chiffon Knitted Circle kaftan robe, with printed decoration, balloon sleeves and a hood, labelled, early 1970s.
£900–1,000
€1,300–1,450
$1,750–1,950 ⚒ KTA

A Jean Patou silk scarf, decorated with perfume bottles, c1980.
£80–90 / €115–130
$155–175 ⊞ HIP

A Bill Gibb chiffon skirt, top, jacket and headband, the top inset with a satin plastron and glass buttons, the skirt in three tiers, the jacket with batwing sleeves, labelled, early 1970s.
£300–360 / €440–520
$580–690 ⚒ KTA

An Ossie Clark moss crepe Traffic Light Gown, with a tiered flamenco-style skirt and ruched panelled sleeves, labelled, early 1970s.
£500–600 / €730–870
$960–1,150 ⚒ KTA

A Burberry raincoat, 1970s.
£75–85 / €110–125
$145–165 ⊞ OH

A Pierre Cardin wool dress, with a patent leather belt carrier, French, c1980.
£900–1,050
€1,300–1,500
$1,750–2,000 ⚒ KTA

Hats

A C. A. Dunn & Co moleskin top hat, with a leather carrying case, c1900.
£90–100 / €130–145
$170–190 ✗ PFK

A Victorian velvet bonnet, decorated with feathers.
£55–65 / €80–95
$105–125 ⊞ Ech

An R. W. Forsyth silk top hat, 1900–20.
£120–140 / €175–200
$230–270 ⊞ MCa
Size is critical to the value of top hats. Those under size 7 are worth very little and hats measuring between 7½ and 8¼ are very sought after. A good-quality silk top hat in good condition can sell for as much as £1,500–2,000 / €2,200–2,900 / $2,900–3,850.

A cloche hat, French, c1920.
£50–60 / €75–85
$100–115 ⊞ DE

A cotton cloche hat, 1920.
£75–85 / €110–125
$145–165 ⊞ Ech

A velvet hat, with bird of paradise decoration, 1920s.
£155–175 / €220–250
$300–340 ⊞ Ech

A Louis Warburton straw hat, decorated with flowers, 1920s.
£130–145 / €190–210
$250–280 ⊞ Ech

A straw cloche hat, with velvet trim, 1920s.
£90–100 / €130–145
$170–190 ⊞ Ech

◄ A straw hat, with rope decoration, c1930.
£40–45 / €60–70
$75–85 ⊞ Ech

► A straw hat, with velvet trim and embroidered decoration, 1930s.
£40–45 / €60–70
$75–85 ⊞ Ech

A straw hat, decorated with flowers, 1930s.
£40–45 / €60–70
$75–85 ⊞ Ech

A straw hat, decorated with flowers, 1930s.
£50–60 / €75–85
$100–115 ⊞ Ech

A Hattie Carnegie silk velvet hat, American, 1940s.
£65–75 / €95–105
$125–145 ⊞ DRE
Hats by major designers are sought after.

A straw and net hat, 1940s.
£60–70 / €85–100
$115–135 ⊞ DRE

A Janet Allen velvet hat, decorated with ostrich feathers, 1940s.
£50–60 / €75–85
$100–115 ⊞ DRE

A Bee Jones net hat, decorated with flowers, American, 1940s–50s.
£25–30 / €40–45
$50–55 ⊞ DRE

A Michael Terry wool felt hat, decorated with sequins and a tassel, American, 1950s.
£45–50 / €65–75
$85–95 ⊞ DRE

A hat, decorated with pansies, 1950s.
£50–60 / €75–85
$100–115 ⊞ RER

A Henry Margu wool hat, decorated with feathers, 1950s.
£60–70 / €85–100
$115–135 ⊞ DRE

A straw boater, 1960s.
£40–45 / €60–70
$75–85 ⊞ OH

A straw pillbox hat, decorated with berries, 1960s.
£25–30 / €40–45
$50–55 ⊞ JUJ

Linen & Lace

A tambour work handkerchief, with Ayrshire embroidery, Irish, c1850, 13in (33cm) square.
£30–35 / €45–50
$55–65 ⊞ JPr
Tambour work is a surface embroidery of chain stitch worked on machine-made net. It became known as tambour work because the material was stretched between two hoops, resembling a drum or tambour.

A Victorian Maltese lace handkerchief, 11in (28cm) square.
£10–15 / €15–22
$19–28 ⊞ Ech

A Mountmellick white cotton 'jean' nightdress case, 1890–1910, 12 x 16in (30.5 x 40.5cm).
£60–70 / €85–100
$115–135 ⊞ HILL

A Honiton lace wedding handkerchief, c1860, 13in (33cm) square.
£60–70 / €85–100
$115–135 ⊞ JPr

▶ **A pair of Brussels lace cuffs,** c1870, 11in (28cm) wide.
£75–85 / €110–125
$145–165 ⊞ JPr

A Victorian Chantilly lace stole, slight damage, 64in (162.5cm) wide.
£45–50 / €65–75
$85–95 ⊞ VICT

▶ **A lace pincushion,** with a Turkish embroidery panel, late 19thC, 8in (20.5cm) square.
£50–60 / €75–85
$100–115 ⊞ JPr

A Honiton lace handkerchief, c1860, 13in (33cm) square.
£130–145 / €190–210
$250–280 ⊞ HL

A piece of Brussels Rosaline bobbin lace, late 19thC, 17in (43cm) wide.
£55–65 / €80–95
$105–125 ⊞ HL
Brussels Rosaline or Rose Point lace has extra petals added to the tiny needlepoint flowers to make them three dimensional. This lace was popular in the late 19th century.

A crochet collar, Irish, early 20thC, 22in (56cm) wide.
£40–45 / €60–70
$75–85 ⊞ DHa

A crochet collar, Irish, early 20thC, 17in (43cm) wide.
£30–35 / €45–50
$55–65 ⊞ DHa

A linen tablecloth, 1900–10, 42in (106.5cm) square.
£35–40 / €50–60
$65–75 ⊞ HILL

A linen and crochet tablecloth, 1910–20, 40in (101.5cm) square.
£40–45 / €60–70
$75–85 ⊞ HILL

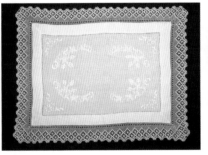

A linen and crochet tray cloth, with embroidered decoration, 1910–20, 25in (63.5cm) wide.
£20–25 / €30–35
$40–50 ⊞ DHa

A hand- and machine-worked linen mat, 1920s, 5in (12.5cm) wide.
£10–15 / €15–22
$19–28 ⊞ HILL

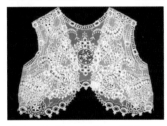

A chemical lace bolero, 1920s, 14in (35.5cm) long.
£40–45 / €60–70
$75–85 ⊞ DHa
Chemical lace is created by embroidering designs with machines on a background fabric which is then chemically removed, leaving the 'lacy' holes between the embroidery and giving the effect of 'lace'. This technique is over 100 years old and is commonly found in what today is called wedding lace.

▶ **A linen table cloth,** hand-embroidered with garden motifs, 1940s–50s, 48in (122cm) square.
£45–50 / €65–75
$85–95 ⊞ HILL

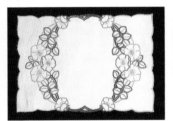

A linen tray cloth, with embroidered decoration, 1930s, 17½in (44.5cm) wide.
£8–12 / €12–18
$16–23 ⊞ HILL

A set of six linen coasters, hand-embroidered with cockerels, 1930s, 3in (7.5cm) diam.
£8–12 / €12–18
$16–23 ⊞ HILL

A linen tray cloth, embroidered with a dog, 1940s–50s, 21in (53.5cm) wide.
£6–10 / €9–15
$12–19 ⊞ HILL

Men's & Unisex Fashion

Vintage denim made record prices in the early 1990s, with collectors spending four- and even five-figure sums on rare jeans and jackets. Recognizing the profit to be made out of old denim, Levi Strauss & Co reintroduced their old designs; thanks to these 'new vintage lines' to some extent the bottom fell out of the antique denim market and prices dropped considerably. Today, however, according to specialists in the field, interest has revived and prices are once again rising. 'There is still a very dedicated following for vintage denim in the UK, the USA and across the world,' says dealer John Cornish. 'People want the original items and modern copies are never as good. Different dyes and fabrics mean that modern versions age in a different way – they lack the patina and quality of the real McCoy.'

Post-war American clothing is a growth area, particularly among men. Western shirts are currently fashionable, including examples by big name firms such as Blue Bell Wrangler. There is also a lot of interest in US Air Force material, particularly jackets from the 1960s (see Aeronautica section, pages 26–31). Flying jackets are often dated and labelled inside and zips are another means of identification. In the 1970s, aluminium zips were used, in the 1960s it was brass that was sometimes painted or blackened, and the zips were far chunkier. Hooded sweatshirts, 'hoodies', are very much a feature of modern fashion but there is also a market for vintage hoodies. Sweatshirts were developed in the USA for athletes in the 1920s and Champion Products USA were leading manufacturers of athletic wear. They developed a flocking process to put raised letters on clothing, pioneered reversible T-shirts and mesh fabric sportswear and in the 1930s introduced a 'sideline sweatshirt' with a zipper front and a hood for footballers waiting in the wings – allegedly the first hoodie. 'Classic hoodies are attracting collectors,' advises Cornish. 'Values reflect condition and quality, and team and college logos make for added interest.'

A Lee 101J denim jacket, with label, 1957.
£290–330 / €420–480
$560–630 ⊞ DeJ

A pair of Levi's 501 jeans, with copper rivets and offset belt loop, Levi's label missing, 1950s.
£400–450 / €580–650
$770–860 ⊞ DeJ

◄ **A Blue Bell Wrangler cotton shirt,** 1950s.
£100–120 / €145–170
$195–230 ⊞ DeJ

A Tootal rayon scarf,
1950s, 48in (122cm) long.
£8–12 / €12–18
$16–23 ⊞ CCO

► **A polyester jacket,** c1960.
£20–25 / €30–35
$40–50 ⊞ REPS

A USAF wool and viscose L-2B flying jacket, with badges, dated 1962.
£135–150 / €195–220
$260–290 ⊞ **DeJ**

A USMC jungle camouflage jacket, with anchor and globe stencil, 1969.
£50–60 / €75–85
$100–115 ⊞ **DeJ**

A pair of Malcolm McLaren and Vivienne Westwood bondage trousers, with Seditionaries label, c1977.
£670–750 / €970–1,100
$1,300–1,450 ⊞ **REK**
These trousers came with an outer black Seditionaries label on the left back side just beneath the waistband. Most pairs also had a white Seditionaries label on the inside.

A USAF wool and cotton N-3B flying jacket, by Alpha Industries Inc, with hood, dated 1966.
£100–110 / €145–160
$190–210 ⊞ **DeJ**

A pair of Levi's 501 Big E jeans, 1960s.
£310–350 / €450–510
$600–670 ⊞ **DeJ**

A Malcolm McLaren and Vivienne Westwood muslin Destroy top, featuring a swastika, an inverted image of the crucified Christ, a postage stamp with the Queen's severed head and the opening lyrics of 'Anarchy in the UK', c1977.
£580–650 / €850–940
$1,050–1,200 ⊞ **REK**

▶ **A Vivienne Westwood leather Time Machine Collection armour jacket,** 1988.
£750–900 / €1,100–1,300
$1,450–1,700 ↗ **KTA**

A Blue Bell Wrangler 8MJL denim jacket, slight damage, 1964–66.
£80–90 / €115–130
$155–175 ⊞ **DeJ**

A Hawaiian shirt, Hawaiian, 1970s.
£35–40 / €50–60
$65–75 ⊞ **SBT**

A Champion hooded sweatshirt, 1970s.
£120–140 / €175–200
$230–270 ⊞ **DeJ**

Shoes

A pair of Victorian leather
lace-up boots.
£65–75 / €95–105
$125–145 ⊞ Ech

A pair of embroidered silk shoes,
Chinese, early 20thC.
£65–75 / €95–105
$125–145 ⊞ JPr
Foot binding began in China in
the 10th century. In upper-class
society, girls between the ages
of three and eight had their feet
bandaged by their mothers.
The wrapping would be
tightened after each wash in the
hope of creating the ideal
'Golden Lotus', a foot measuring
only three inches. Lotus feet
were hugely prized and regarded
as sexually attractive – bandages
were traditionally only removed
for bathing or as part of the
love-making act. These feet were
shown off in tiny, beautifully
embroidered silk slippers.
A wealthy woman might have
several hundred pairs and a
husband would also display the
shoes to demonstrate the
smallness of his wife's feet.
The custom began to go out of
fashion in the 20th century and
was eventually banned by
Chairman Mao.

A pair of Victorian leather
lace-up boots.
£200–230 / €290–330
$380–440 ⊞ Ech

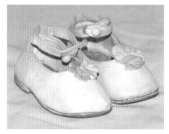

A child's pair of kid leather shoes,
decorated with silk rosettes, c1910.
£30–35 / €45–50
$55–65 ⊞ BaN

► A pair of W. Barratt & Co
evening shoes, 1920.
£75–85 / €110–125
$145–165 ⊞ Ech

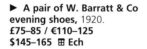

A pair of Mascott lamé
shoes, 1920s.
£75–85 / €110–125
$145–165 ⊞ TIN

► A pair of leather shoes,
with diamanté decoration, 1920s.
£40–45 / €60–70
$75–85 ⊞ CCO

An apprentice-piece leather
boot, late 19thC.
£165–185 / €240–270
$320–360 ⊞ NEW

A pair of leather boots, c1920.
£130–145 / €190–210
$250–280 ⊞ Ech

A pair of deerskin and leather
shoes, 1920s.
£75–85 / €110–125
$145–165 ⊞ Ech

A pair of canvas and leather
riding boots, c1930.
£310–350 / €450–500
$600–670 ⊞ MSh

A pair of Country Walker leather
shoes, 1940s, boxed.
£40–45 / €60–70
$75–85 ⊞ NFR

▶ A pair of suede and snakeskin
shoes, 1940s.
£75–85 / €110–125
$145–165 ⊞ HSR

A pair of snakeskin shoes, 1930s.
£45–50 / €65–75
$85–95 ⊞ L&L

A pair of carved and painted
wood shoes, Filipino, 1940s.
£110–125 / €160–180
$210–240 ⊞ SpM

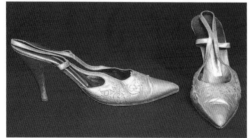

A pair of leather shoes, retailed by Russell &
Bromley, 1950s.
£20–25 / €30–35
$40–50 ⊞ CCO

A pair of SAKS Fifth Avenue shoes, American,1950s.
£75–85 / €110–125
$145–165 ⊞ Ci

◀ A pair of Sabrina
alligator skin shoes,
American, 1950s.
£65–75 / €95–105
$125–145 ⊞ DRE

▶ A pair of
Kerrybrooke cotton
shoes, American, 1950s.
£45–50 / €65–75
$85–95 ⊞ DRE

A pair of Davito printed silk shoes, 1950s.
£50–60 / €75–85
$100–115 ⊞ DRE

A pair of GM leather shoes, 1960s.
£35–40 / €50–60
$65–75 ⊞ TWI

A pair of leather lacrosse/hockey boots, 1950s.
£25–30 / €40–45
$50–55 ⊞ SA

A pair of Freeman Hardy & Willis platform sandals, 1970s.
£50–60 / €75–85
$100–115 ⊞ DE

For more Fifties collectables
see pages 208–209

A pair of Balenciaga shoes, 1960s.
£65–75 / €95–105
$125–145 ⊞ SBT

A pair of Di Renzo leather spat shoes, American, 1970s.
£45–50 / €65–75
$85–95 ⊞ TWI

A pair of Yves St Laurent canvas and rope espadrilles, 1970s.
£35–40 / €50–60
$65–75 ⊞ HIP

A pair of platform shoes, 1970s.
£55–65 / €80–95
$105–125 ⊞ HSR

A pair of Terry De Havilland shoes, 1970s.
£135–150 / €195–220
$260–290 ⊞ Ci

A pair of Chanel suede shoes, 1980.
£85–95 / €125–140
$165–185 ⊞ RER

A pair of Salvatore Ferragamo leather shoes, 1980s.
£50–60 / €75–85
$100–115 ⊞ SBT

Textiles

A tapestry fragment, late 17thC, 23in (58.5cm) wide.
£50–60 / €75–85
$100–115 ⊞ JPr

A beaded and petit point pole screen, c1850, 20 x 15in (51 x 38cm).
£165–185 / €240–270
$320–360 ⊞ JPr

A pair of beaded face fan banners, c1880, 10in (25.5cm) high.
£40–45 / €60–70
$75–85 ⊞ JPr

A sampler, worked with the alphabet and a verse, 18thC, 9½ x 7½in (24 x 19cm).
£75–85 / €110–125
$145–165 ⚲ WL

A woolwork sampler, by Richard Tattersall, worked with a motto and two lovers in a garden, dated 1853, framed, 24½in (62cm) square.
£300–360 / €440–520
$580–690 ⚲ DD

▶ **A Victorian plush velvet tablecloth,** 66in (167.5cm) square.
£55–65 / €80–95
$105–125 ⊞ Ech

A pair of beaded face fan banners, c1880, 10in (25.5cm) high.
£40–45 / €60–70
$75–85 ⊞ JPr

A needlework sampler, by Mary Anne Charles, worked with a bride and a groom in a landscape, 1861, 7½ x 9½in (19 x 24cm).
£110–130 / €160–190
$210–250 ⚲ WilP

A Victorian woolwork panel, worked with two yachts at sea, framed, 12 x 17½in (30.5 x 44.5cm).
£570–680 / €830–980
$1,100–1,300 ⚲ G(L)

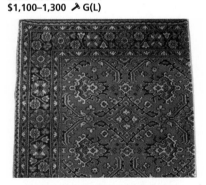

A Victorian walnut kettle stand, with a beadwork panel depicting birds under a hat.
£90–105 / €130–150
$170–200 ⚲ DA

A Victorian plush velvet tablecloth, 66in (167.5cm) square.
£40–45 / €60–70
$75–85 ⊞ Ech

A length of printed Toile de Jouy cotton, 1900, 62 x 110in (157.5 x 279.5cm).
£310–350 / €450–500
$600–670 ⊞ LGU

An Alpha Farnell plush tea cosy, in the form of a monkey, 1940, 10in (25.5cm) wide.
£90–100 / €130–145
$170–190 ⊞ BINC

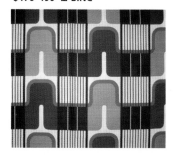

A late Victorian patchwork coverlet, 99¼ x 98½in (252 x 250cm).
£210–250 / €300–360
$400–480 ⚒ PFK

A length of Lyon silk, French, 1920s, 21 x 110in (53.5 x 279.5cm).
£450–500 / €650–720
$860–960 ⊞ LGU

A wool blanket, 1940s, 94 x 82in (239 x 208.5cm).
£10–15 / €15–22
$19–28 ⊞ JWK

◄ **A length of fabric,** 1970s, 780in (2000cm) long.
£6–10 / €9–15
$12–19 per metre ⊞ MARK

A patchwork coverlet, c1900, 89 x 84½in (226 x 214.5cm).
£100–120 / €145–175
$190–220 ⚒ PFK

A silk tea cosy, in the form of a pierrot, with a hand-painted face, 1920s, 14in (35.5cm) wide.
£135–150 / €200–220
$260–290 ⊞ LBe

A wool rug, 1940s, 68 x 54in (172.5 x 137cm).
£10–15 / €15–22
$19–28 ⊞ JWK

A length of fabric, mounted, 1970s, 40 x 23in (101.5 x 58.5cm).
£35–40 / €50–60
$65–75 ⊞ HSR

Dogs

People often theme their collections around a favourite animal and this year we devote a special section to dogs. Where cat enthusiasts are often comparatively indiscriminate, collecting anything and everything with a feline image, dog collectors tend to be more faithful, often focusing on a particular breed. This affects the current market for material such as birthday cards, which are generally more likely to feature kittens than puppies.

Used for hunting, protection and companionship, dogs have been portrayed in art and literature from the earliest times. In classical mythology, Cerberus the three-headed dog guarded the entrance to Hades, in Christian symbolism a dog represented St Roch (patron saint of the plague-stricken), and in some versions of the Old Testament a dog accompanied Tobias and the angel Raphael on their perilous journey – Toby the dog in Punch and Judy was named after this legend. In medieval art, dogs symbolized fidelity and were portrayed in effigy in funeral monuments, often lying under the feet of their masters.

From King Charles spaniels to the late Duke and Duchess of Windsor's pugs to the Queen's corgis, dogs have always been associated with royalty. It was Queen Victoria – a passionate animal enthusiast – who popularized the trend for keeping dogs as pets rather than just as working animals. Pet ownership flourished during her reign, a period that saw the rise of the great dog painters (most famously Sir Edwin Landseer, whose greyhound was called Brutus); the opening of Battersea Dogs' Home in 1860 and the launch in 1866 of the most famous dog show in the world by dog biscuit manufacturer Charles Cruft.

As dogs became regarded as members of the family, so they were increasingly represented in the fine and decorative arts and many of the objects in this section date from the Victorian and Edwardian periods. In the 20th century, famous dogs in film and literature include Bonzo – the highly collectable cartoon puppy created by George Studdy in 1922; Rin Tin Tin – film star dog of the 1920s and '30s; Pluto – created by Walt Disney in 1930; Eric Knight's Lassie who starred in a series of MGM adventure films; Dodie Smith's *101 Dalmations* – inspired by the writer's own Dalmation dogs; Walt Disney's *Lady and the Tramp* in 1955; Charles Schulz's Snoopy from the Peanuts cartoon strip launched in 1950 and Laika, the Russian dog who was sent into space on Sputnik II in 1957. However, perhaps the most reproduced dog in history is Nipper, the HMV dog, who has been used in the company's advertising from c1900.

◄ A pottery model of a bull mastiff, with a moulded collar and glass eyes, impressed 'L.L', Continental, 19thC, 31in (78.5cm) long. **£900–1,050 / €1,300–1,550 $1,700–2,000 ➚ AH**

A metal dog collar, German, 18thC, 21½in (54.5cm) long. **£250–280 €360–400 $480–540 ⊞ GGv**

A Georgian brass dog collar, engraved with crossed cutlasses and 'Crown, Garside, Murray St, Camden Square, N.W.', with brass lock engraved 'Charley', 7¼in (18.5cm) diam. **£750–900 / €1,100–1,300 $1,450–1,750 ➚ JNic**

A metal and micro-mosaic brooch, depicting a spaniel holding a duck, with wirework decoration, slight damage, 19thC. **£1,200–1,400 / €1,700–2,000 $2,300–2,700 ➚ CHTR**

A porcelain tobacco jar, in the form of a dog's head, Continental, 19thC, 5in (12.5cm) high. **£360–400 / €520–580 $690–770 ⊞ SRi**

A deer horn whistle, carved in the form of dog's head, 19thC, 4in (10cm) long.
£180–200 / €260–290
$340–380 ⊞ SEA

An ivory whistle, carved in the form of a dog's head, 19thC, 2in (5cm) long.
£140–165 / €200–240
$270–320 ➶ DA

A plaster model of a mastiff, with glass eyes, slight damage, 19thC, 21¼in (54cm) high.
£220–260 / €320–380
$420–500 ➶ SWO

A Meissen figural group of a lady and a dog, crossed swords mark, 19thC, 5½in (14cm) high.
£460–550 / €660–780
$880–1,050 ➶ G(L)

A Staffordshire jug, in the form of a begging dog, 19thC, 9½in (24cm) high.
£150–180 / €220–260
$290–350 ➶ BWL

A pair of Staffordshire quill holders, in the form of Dalmations, 19thC, 6in (15cm) high.
£320–380 / €460–550
$610–730 ➶ DMC

A Staffordshire pearlware figural group of a child, dog and snake, c1830, 6½in (16.5cm) high.
£320–380 / €460–550
$610–730 ➶ Hal
It has been suggested that this dog is Bagshaw, a Newfoundland who belonged to the Duke of Dudley c1831. The dog is the subject of a statue by M.C. Wyatt, (1777–1862), now in the Victoria & Albert Museum.

A Galena Pottery model of a King Charles spaniel, American, Illinois, 1843–85, 9¼in (23.5cm) high.
£810–970 / €1,200–1,450
$1,550–1,850 ➶ S(NY)

A pottery tobacco jar, in the form of a dog's head, c1840, 6½in (16.5cm) high.
£740–830 / €1,050–1,200
$1,400–1,600 ⊞ SRi

▶ **A Staffordshire model of a Dalmation,** c1850, 7¼in (18.5cm) high.
£220–260 / €320–380
$420–500 ➶ DN

A Victorian silver dish, by J. Aldwinkle & T. Slater, in the form of a Labrador's mask, London 1887, 4¼in (11cm) wide. 2.25oz.
£340–400 / €490–580
$650–770 ➹ WW

A Victorian carved ivory cane handle, in the form of a boxer's head, 2½in (6.5cm) wide.
£110–130 / €160–190
$210–250 ➹ SWO

A Victorian woolwork picture, depicting a lady and a spaniel, framed, 16 x 15in (40.5 x 38cm).
£120–140 / €170–200
$230–270 ➹ AH

A majolica desk stand, by T.C. Brown Westhead, Moore & Co, surmounted with a terrier's head, flanked by two inkwells and a pen tray, impressed motto, c1870, 11½in (29cm) wide.
£600–720 / €850–1,000
$1,150–1,350 ➹ G(L)

A ceramic fairing, entitled 'Now They'll Blame Me For This', c1870, 5½in (14cm) high.
£120–140 / €170–200
$230–270 ➹ SAS

A glass paperweight, with an itaglio of a dog, c1880, 2½in (6.5cm) diam.
£170–200 / €250–280
$330–380 ⊞ SRi

A spelter lead rack, in the form of a dog in a kennel, French, 1880, 12in (30.5cm) high.
£450–500 / €650–720
$850–960 ⊞ SRi

An ivory and malacca walking stick, the ivory handle carved in the form of a greyhound's head, with glass eyes, late 19thC, 35in (89cm) long.
£420–500 / €600–700
$800–960 ➹ DA

A carved ivory brooch, depicting a group of four hounds within vines, late 19thC.
£230–270 / €330–390
$440–520 ➹ Bea

◀ **A brass dog collar,** inscribed 'H. Rapsey, Wootton', late 19thC, 5in (12.5cm) diam.
£80–90
€115–130
$155–175
➹ WW

A brass-plated cloak fastener, in the form of Yorkshire terriers, late 19thC, 3½in (9cm) wide.
£160–180 / €230–260
$310–350 ⊞ SRi

◄ **A pair of Staffordshire models of poodles,** late 19thC, 9½in (24cm) high.
£200–240
€290–350
$380–450
⚹ BWL

A steel dog collar, with a brass name plate, late 19thC, 18in (45.5cm) long.
£360–400 / €520–580
$690–770 ⊞ SRi

A maplewood and silver snuff box, the cover with a silver sixpence painted with a dog, 1890, 4¾in (12cm) wide.
£270–300 / €390–440
$520–580 ⊞ SRi

A bronze and copper trinket box, in the form of a spaniel and puppies, signed 'T. Hingre', French, c1890, 4in (10cm) wide.
£580–650 / €840–940
$1,100–1,250 ⊞ SRi

A Black Forest hardwood nutcracker, carved in the form of a bloodhound, German, late 19thC, 6in (15cm) long.
£240–270 / €350–390
$460–520 ⊞ SRi

A cast-iron inkwell, in the form of a dog's head, German, 1890s, 4½in (11.5cm) high.
£520–580 / €750–840
$1,000–1,100 ⊞ SRi

◄ **A ceramic oil lamp,** in the form of dog's head, German, 1890s, 16½in (42cm) high.
£540–600 / €780–870
$1,000–1,100 ⊞ SRi

A London Dog Show silver medal, by A. Fenwick, depicting 11 breeds of dog, c1900, 3in (7.5cm) diam.
£220–250 / €320–360
$420–480 ⊞ TML

◄ **A ceramic nightlight,** in the form of a Yorkshire terrier's head, 1890–1900, 3½in (9cm) high.
£90–100 / €130–145
$170–190 ⚹ BBR

► **A meerschaum cigarette/cigar holder,** carved with pug dogs, with an amber mouthpiece, c1900, 4½in (11.5cm) long.
£100–120
€145–170
$195–230
⊞ SRi

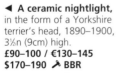

A brass paper clip, in the form of a boxer's head, 1900, 3in (7.5cm) long.
£160–180 / €230–260
$310–350 ⊞ SRi

A silver card case, decorated with a dog, German, 1900, 3½in (9cm) high.
£175–195 / €250–280
$340–380 ⊞ SRi

A bronze model of a dog, by Janos Istok, Hungarian, early 20thC, 10in (25.5cm) long.
£300–360 / €440–520
$580–690 ➤ G(L)

A Royal Dux model of a golden retriever, early 20thC, 16in (40.5cm) wide.
£420–500 / €610–720
$810–960 ➤ PBA

◄ A pottery match striker, impressed 'Bass Dog's Head, Guinness', and 'Read Bros, London', early 20thC, 4¼in(11cm) high.
£200–240 / €290–350
$390–460 ➤ BWL

► A watercolour illustration, by Cecil Charles Windsor Aldin, entitled 'Little Jack Horner, Sat in the Corner, Eating a Christmas Pie', signed, slight damage, c1904, 14½ x 9½in (37 x 24cm).
£500–600 / €730–870
$960–1,150 ➤ DW

A silver scent pomander, in the form of a dog's head, Birmingham 1905, 2in (5cm) high.
£260–310 / €380–450
$500–600 ➤ JBe

A set of five buttons, decorated with dogs, 1910, ½in (1.5cm) diam.
£210–240
€300–3550
$400–460 ⊞ SRi

► A Gotha model of a French bulldog, German, c1920, 8in (20.5cm) wide.
£360–400
€520–580
$690–770 ⊞ SRi

A MacDonalds Kilty Brand die-cut stone litho showcard, depicting a Scottie dog, 1910–20, 21½ x 17½in (54.5 x 44.5cm).
£45–50 / €65–75
$85–95 ➤ BBR

Two Bonzo frosted glass scent bottles, by Potter & Moore, with painted features, c1920, larger 3¼in (8.5cm) high.
£170–200 / €250–300
$330–390 ➤ SWO

A box of His Master's Voice gramophone needles, with Nipper the dog logo, c1920, 2in (5cm) wide.
£15–20 / €22–29
$29–38 ⊞ AAA

► A dog show bronze medal, by A. Rivet, French, c1920, 2in (5cm) diam.
£55–65
€80–95
$105–125
⊞ SRi

A brass and steel Pradel pocket knife, embossed with a dog, French, 1920s, 3½in (9cm) long.
£360–400 / €520–580
$690–770 ⊞ SRi

A display box of His Master's Voice Half Tone Needles, depicting Nipper the dog, 1920s, 10in (25.5cm) wide.
Box £30–35 / €45–50
$55–65
Tins £2–6 / €3–9
$4–11 each ⊞ MURR

A Melox Dog Foods enamel sign, depicting a terrier, damaged, 1920s, 14 x 10in (35.5 x 25.5cm).
£350–420 / €510–610
$670–810 ⋟ BBR

A Muller & Co model of a dachshund, 1920s, 15in (38cm) long.
£790–880 / €1,150–1,300
$1,500–1,700 ⊞ SRi

◀ A bronze model of a dog, on a marble base, French, 1920s, 3½in (9cm) high.
£130–145
€190–210
$250–280
⊞ SRi

A bronze plaque of an Afghan hound, by Domingells, signed, 1920s, 5½in (14cm) wide.
£270–300 / €390–440
$520–580 ⊞ SRi

▶ A Royal Worcester model of a Pekinese, c1930, 3in (7.5cm) long.
£140–160 / €200–230
$270–310 ⊞ WAC

An onyx and spelter mantle clock, the eight-day movement striking on a bell, the case surmounted with a huntress and hound, French, c1930, 15in (38cm) high.
£95–110 / €140–160
$185–210 ⋟ DA

A Goebel toothpick holder, in the form of a dog's head, c1930, 1½in (4cm) high.
£70–80 / €100–115
$135–155 ⊞ BEV

◀ A cold-painted bronze and ivory figural group of a boy and dog, in the manner of Preiss, on a later onyx desk stand, slight damage, c1930, 8¼in (21cm) high.
£420–500 / €610–730
$810–960 ⋟ CHTR

◀ **A paper and Bakelite box of handkerchiefs,** decorated with a dog's head, c1930, 6in (15cm) square.
£50–60 / €75–85
$100–115
⊞ BET

▶ **A bronze and brass clock,** decorated with a dog, on an onyx base, 1930, 11in (28cm) wide.
£360–400
€520–580
$690–770 ⊞ SRi

A Royal Copenhagen model of a dachshund, signed 'Jensen', stamped '856', c1930, 8in (20.5cm) high.
£160–190 / €230–270
$300–360 ⚏ BWL

A porcelain model of a dog, Continental, c1930, 9in (23cm) high.
£125–140 / €180–200
$240–270 ⊞ HEW

A Royal Worcester model of a dog, dated 1933, 3in (7.5cm) wide.
£135–150 / €195–220
$260–290 ⊞ WAC

Agatha Christie, *The Hound of Death,* published by Odhams Press, first edition, 1933, 8°.
£160–190 / €230–270
$300–360 ⚏ DW

A pair of brass and Bakelite bookends, c1935, 5in (12.5cm) wide.
£70–80 / €100–115
$135–155 ⊞ HOM

A Royal Dux model of a Pekinese, Czechoslovakian, c1935, 8in (20.5cm) wide.
£100–120 / €145–170
$195–230 ⊞ SRi

A frosted glass perfume bottle, in the form of a dog, 1930s, 3in (7.5cm) high.
£100–110 / €150–165
$190–210 ⊞ LBe

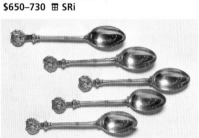

A silver-plated bronze car mascot, in the form of a dachshund, 1930s, 2½in (6.5cm) high.
£340–380 / €500–550
$650–730 ⊞ SRi

◀ **A Buchanan's Black & White Whisky ashtray,** depicting two dogs, 1930s, 6in (15cm) square.
£45–50 / €65–75
$85–95 ⊞ MURR

Five silver spoons, each terminal in the form of dog's head, Birmingham 1930s, 4½in (11.5cm) long.
£210–240 / €300–340
$400–450 ⊞ SRi

A **moulded glass inkwell,** in the form of a dog, possibly French, 1930s, 3½in (9cm) high.
£220–250 / €320–360
$420–480 ⊞ SRi

A **Poole Pottery tile,** depicting a terrier, after Cecil Aldin, stamped 'Carter', 1930s–50s, 6in (15cm) square.
£145–170 / €210–250
$280–330 ➚ HOLL

For more Ceramic animals see pages 81–82

A **Goebel cruet set,** in the form of poodles, c1950, 4in (10cm) high.
£80–90 / €115–130
$155–175 ⊞ BEV

▶ *Bonzo's Annual,* published by Dean & Sons, 1952, 10 x 8in (25.5 x 20.5cm).
£45–50 / €65–75
$85–95 ⊞ J&J

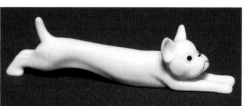

◀ **A Gotha porcelain knife rest,** German, 1930s, 5in (12.5cm) wide.
£50–60
€75–85
$100–115
⊞ SRi

A **Midwinter model of a dog,** c1940, 3in (7.5cm) wide.
£50–55 / €70–80
$95–105 ⊞ BEV

A **pen, ink and crayon illustration,** 'The vet says there's nothing radically wrong with us – we're just worried about Chiang Kai Shek', by Sir Osbert Lancaster, signed, stamped and inscribed, 1949, 9½ x 6¾in (24 x 17cm).
£180–210 / €250–300
$340–400 ➚ Bea

A **Royal Doulton model of a British bulldog,** factory marks, 1941–61, 4in (10cm) high.
£140–165 / €200–240
$270–320 ➚ DN

A **chrome car mascot,** in the form of a dog, American, 1940s, 5in (12.5cm) wide.
£180–200 / €260–290
$340–380 ⊞ HEW

A **Keele Street Pottery cream jug,** in the form of a basset hound, 1950s, 4½in (11.5cm) high.
£45–50 / €65–75
$85–95 ⊞ SRi

A metal waste paper basket, decorated with a poodle, American, 1950s, 12in (30.5cm) high.
£35–40 / €50–60
$65–75 ⊞ DRE

A silk moiré carry case, containing a metal purse decorated with dogs, 1950s, 3¾in (9.5cm) wide.
£70–80 / €100–115
$135–155 ⊞ SUW

◄ **A metal and mother-of-pearl powder compact,** inlaid with a springer spaniel, American, 1950s, 3in (7.5cm) square.
£75–85
€110–125
$145–165
⊞ SUW

A rubberoid money box, in the form of a dog, inscribed 'Hush Puppies' 1950s, 7½in (19cm) high.
£70–80 / €100–115
$135–155 ➤ BBR

Bengo Annual, by Tim, published by Cooper, 1963, 10 x 8in (25.5 x 20.5cm).
£4–8 / €6–12
$8–15 ⊞ J&J

► **A Royal Doulton model of a foxhound,** slight damage, c1960.
£280–330
€410–480
$540–640
➤ Pott

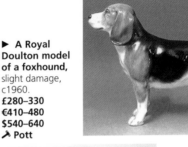

► **A Beswick model of a Dalmation,** No. MN961, 1960s, 6in (15cm) high.
£45–50 / €65–75
$85–95 ➤ Pott

◄ **A Pelham poodle string puppet,** 1960s, 10in (25.5cm) high.
£65–75
€95–105
$125–145
⊞ UD

► **A WMF pewter model of a pointer,** German, 1960s, 4½in (11.5cm) wide.
£270–300
€390–440
$520–580
⊞ SRi

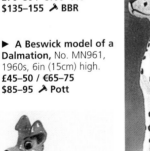

◄ **A Wade model of Tramp,** c1976, 6in (15cm) high.
£120–140 / €170–200
$230–270 ➤ GTH

An 18ct gold and diamond brooch, in the form of an English setter, with a ruby eye, London 1984.
£220–260 / €320–380
$420–500 ➤ DN

Dolls & Dolls' Houses
Dolls

A wax-headed doll, with glass eyes, human hair wig, cloth body and kid lower arms, 1830–60.
£210–240 / €310–350
$400–450 ⊞ SaB

A bisque doll, with painted features and jointed body, in a wicker basket, German, c1890, doll 2in (5cm) long.
£70–80 / €100–115
$135–155 ⊞ BGe

A Simon & Halbig bisque-headed doll, No. 949, with glass eyes, mohair wig, wooden ball-jointed body and original clothes, German, c1895, 19in (48.5cm) high.
£1,650–1,950
€2,400–2,850
$3,200–3,750 ⚒ THE

◄ **A Schönau & Hoffmeister Oriental bisque-headed doll,** with a composition body, 1900, 8in (20.5cm) high.
£310–350
€450–510
$600–670
⊞ BGe

◄ **A Kestner bisque-headed doll,** No. 1211, with glass eyes and original clothes, German, 1910, 12in (30.5cm) high.
£400–450 / €590–650
$770–860 ⊞ BGe

► **Two bisque dolls' house dolls,** with glass eyes and original clothes, German, c1900, 3½in (9cm) high.
£220–250 / €320–360
$420–480 each ⊞ BGe

◄ **Two Heubach Kopplesdorf bisque-headed dolls,** No. 250, with sleeping eyes and composition bodies, German, c1910, 9in (23cm) high.
£320–360
€460–520
$610–690 ⊞ BGe

A Gebrüder Kühnlenz bisque-headed doll, with sleeping glass eyes, original wig and clothes, German, c1910, 23in (58.5cm) high.
£430–480 / €620–700
$830–920 ⊞ BGe

An Armand Marseille bisque-headed Dream Baby doll, No. 351, with open mouth, glass eyes and original clothes, marked, German, c1910, 17in (43cm) high.
£195–220 / €280–320
$370–420 ⊞ BGe

◄ **A Kämmer & Reinhardt bisque doll,** No. 177X, with a flapper body, German, 1920, 14in (35.5cm) high.
£1,100–1,250 / €1,600–1,800
$2,100–2,400 ⊞ BGe
Kämmer & Reinhardt was founded in 1886 in Walterhausen, Germany, by designer and model-maker Ernst Kämmer and entrepreneur Franz Reinhardt. The company produced some of the most highly-prized and collectable German dolls. Character dolls were first registered in 1909. The first character doll was known as Kaiser Baby and was reputedly modelled on the Emperor's son who had polio as a child, leaving him with a crippled hand. This doll was given the mould number 100 and subsequent character dolls were numbered from 100. Some dolls in the 100 series are harder to find than others and values depend on rarity.

A Schoenhut wooden boy doll, No. 107, with painted hair and eyes, wooden spring-jointed body with toddler legs and original clothes, American, c1917, 11in (28cm) high.
£220–260 / €320–370
$420–500 ➚ THE

A bisque-headed Bye-Lo Baby doll, with glass eyes, celluloid hands and a muslin body, head German, c1923, head 13in (33cm) diam, with original box.
£260–310 / €310–450
$500–600 ➚ THE
The Bye-Lo Baby doll was designed by the American artist Grace Storey Putnam.

A Schönau & Hoffmeister bisque-headed Pouty Baby doll, with a cloth body, German, c1920, 12in (30.5cm) long.
£400–450 / €580–650
$770–860 ⊞ DOL

A Chad Valley felt Mabel Lucie Attwell Babina doll, with glass eyes and original clothes, 1920s, 17in (43cm) high.
£580–650 / €840–940
$1,100–1,250 ⊞ BGe

◄ **A ceramic half-doll,** with a painted bodice and taffeta and cloth dress, Continental, c1930, 3¼in (8.5cm) high).
£35–40 / €50–60
$65–75
➚ WEBB

A celluloid doll, with glass eyes, French, c1930, 23in (58.5cm) high.
£180–200 / €260–290
$340–380 ⊞ GLEN

A painted wood miniature doll, in a painted wood egg, c1930, 1in (2.5cm) high.
£30–35 / €45–50
$55–65 ⊞ UD

◄ **A paper Shirley Temple cut-out doll and clothes,** c1938, 14in (35.5cm) high.
£40–45 / €60–70
$75–85 ⊞ BGe

A celluloid doll,
Japanese, 1930s,
6in (15cm) high.
£20–25 / €30–35
$40–50 ⚡ **GAZE**

A Native American doll,
German, 1930s,
8in (20.5cm) high.
£45–50 / €65–75
$85–95 ⊞ **HeA**

**Two Dean's Rag Book
Company rag dolls,**
1940s, 14in (35.5cm) high.
£10–15 / €15–22
$19–28 each
⊞ **UD**

▶ **A pair
of souvenir
dolls,** Spanish,
c1950, 8in
(20.5cm) high.
£10–15
€15–22
$19–28 ⊞ **UD**

A composition doll,
1940s, 17in (43cm) high.
£70–80 / €100–115
$135–155 ⊞ **HeA**

Two celluloid dolls, Japanese, 1940s, 8in (20.5cm) high.
£25–30 / €40–45
$50–55 ⚡ **GAZE**

◀ **A Rosebud
Suck-a-Thumb
doll,** with
original clothes,
1950s, 6in
(15cm) high.
£50–60
€75–85
$100–115
⊞ **POLL**

**A British National Doll
Co plastic walker doll,**
with original wig, 1950s,
21in (53.5cm) high.
£150–170 / €220–250
$290–330 ⊞ **POLL**

A Pedigree walker doll,
with original wig, c1955,
16in (40.5cm) high.
£145–165 / €210–240
$280–310 ⊞ **POLL**

▶ **A Roddy hard
plastic baby
doll,** with tin
eyes, 1950s, 10in
(25.5cm) high.
£10–15 / €15–22
$19–28 ⚡ **GAZE**
From the late
1930s, British
doll makers
D.G. Todd and
J. Robinson
combined their
names and
faces to create
a range
of injection-
moulded
plastic dolls
called Roddy.

A Roddy plastic doll, 1950s, 6in (15cm) high.
£30–35 / €45–50
$55–65 ⊞ POLL

A Combex plastic Kewpie-style baby doll, 1950s, 7in (18cm) high.
£6–10 / €9–15
$12–19 ⊞ HeA

A plastic Kewpie doll, 1950s–60s, 4in (10cm) wide.
£4–8 / €6–12
$8–15 ⊞ HeA

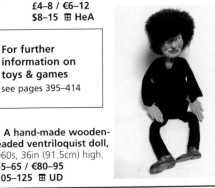

For further information on toys & games
see pages 395–414

▶ **A hand-made wooden-headed ventriloquist doll,** 1960s, 36in (91.5cm) high.
£55–65 / €80–95
$105–125 ⊞ UD

A Dam Things vinyl troll, with jointed limbs, c1960, 14in (35.5cm) high.
£20–25 / €30–35
$40–50 ⊞ UD

A Living Barbie gift set, with a range of sporting outfits, c1969, 12½ x 13½in (32 X 33.5cm).
£1,350–1,500
€1,950–2,200
$2,600–2,900 ⊞ T&D

A plastic Pippa Princess doll, 1960s, 6in (15cm) high.
£35–40 / €50–60
$65–75 ⊞ UD

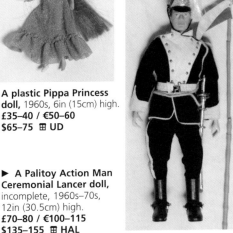

▶ **A Palitoy Action Man Ceremonial Lancer doll,** incomplete, 1960s–70s, 12in (30.5cm) high.
£70–80 / €100–115
$135–155 ⊞ HAL

A **Sindy doll,** with long hair, c1969, 12in (30.5cm) high.
£75–85 / €110–125
$145–165 ⊞ LAS

Sindy

Sindy, 'the doll you love to dress', was designed by Dennis Arkinstall and issued by the Pedigree Doll Co in 1962. Her first 'Weekender' outfit of jeans and a striped sweater was created by London designers Foale & Tuffin, and the doll's major selling point was her range of fashionable clothes. Her figure and hairstyle also changed throughout the 1960s and 1970s. Beginning with short hair, Sindy grew long hair c1968 and began to part it on the side. In about 1970 she developed a more flexible fully-jointed body and adopted a centre parting. In 1974, Sindy's face and body was slimmed down and that same year saw the launch of the ballet dancer 'Active Sindy' which was produced in various versions and was to prove a popular series. In 1978, Sindy was launched in the USA and distributed by Marx Toys, and from 1981 by Wesco.

In 1986 Pedigree again remodelled Sindy giving her smaller eyes and a slimmer face bringing to an end, for many enthusiasts, the golden age of Sindy. In 1987, Sindy was purchased by Hasbro and began to resemble Barbie, leading to litigation with Mattel and resulting in the removal of Sindy from American stores. Today the Sindy name is owned by Vivid Imaginations and the doll is only marketed in the UK.

Three Mego *The Waltons* dolls, 1970, 5in (12.5cm) high.
£15–20 / €22–29
$29–38 ⊞ UD

A **Palitoy vinyl Christopher doll,** with original clothes and a rocking horse chair, 1970, 5in (12.5cm) high.
£55–65 / €80–95
$105–125 ⊞ POLL

A **Palitoy Action Man Field Commander doll,** with field radio, 1970, 12in (30.5cm) high, with original box, free gift stars missing.
£100–120 / €145–175
$195–230 ⊞ HAL

Items in the Dolls & Dolls' Houses section have been arranged in date order within each sub-section.

A **Denys Fisher vinyl Katie Kiss doll,** 1974, 17in (43cm) high.
£15–20 / €22–29
$29–38 ⊞ UD

▶ A **Sasha vinyl Gregory doll,** c1970, 16in (40.5cm) high.
£180–200 / €260–290
$340–380 ⊞ UD

A **Palitoy Action Man Red Devil doll,** 1970s, 12in (30.5cm) high.
£25–30 / €40–45
$50–55 ⊞ HAL

A **Sasha baby doll,** with original clothes, 1970s, 11in (28cm) high.
£140–155 / €200–220
$270–300 ⊞ POLL

A Ljn Michael Jackson doll, 1984, 13in (33cm) high.
£20–25 / €30–35
$40–50 ⊞ IQ
Ljn was a Japanese toy company started as a subsidiary of Matsushita. It was acquired by Acclaim Entertainment and ventured into the video game market in the 1980s.

A Sasha doll, with original clothes, 1970s, 16in (40.5cm) high.
£90–100 / €130–145
$170–190 ✎ GAZE

A Matchbox Freddy Krueger *A Nightmare on Elm Street* **doll,** in original box, 1989, 21in (53.5cm) high.
£40–45 / €60–70
$75–85 ⊞ IQ

A Pedigree Sindy Holiday Girl doll, in original box, 1980s, 13in (33cm) high.
£70–80 / €100–115
$135–155 ✎ GAZE

Clothing, Furniture & Accessories

A ceramic toy teapot, with transfer-printed decoration, c1830, 3½in (9cm) diam.
£45–50 / €65–75
$85–95 ⊞ OD

▶ **A dolls' house metal companion set,** German, 1890, 3in (7.5cm) high.
£65–75
€95–105
$125–145
⊞ BGe

A dolls' house metal umbrella stand, German, 1890, 3in (7.5cm) high.
£75–85 / €110–125
$145–165 ⊞ BGe

A dolls' house tinplate clock, with a glass dome, 1890, 2½in (6.5cm) high.
£75–85 / €110–125
$145–165 ⊞ BGe

A dolls' house pine bureau bookcase, with two drawers, German, 1890, 6in (15cm) high.
£140–160 / €200–230
$270–310 ⊞ BGe

◀ **A dolls' house tin wash stand,** German, 1890–1900, 6in (15cm) high.
£85–95 / €125–140
$165–185 ⊞ BGe

A Victorian set of dolls' house dining chairs, with velvet upholstery, 4in (10cm) high.
£140–155 / €200–220
$270–300 ⊞ BGe

▶ A Victorian leather and pine doll's pram, with metal wheels, 20in (51cm) long.
£140–160
€200–230
$270–310
⊞ BGe

▶ A Victorian dolls' house stained pine davenport, 3½in (9cm) high.
£120–135
€175–195
$230–260
⊞ BGe

A Victorian dolls' house pine sideboard, 7in (18cm) high.
£120–135 / €175–195
$230–260 ⊞ BGe

A late Victorian wicker doll's pram, 19in (48.5cm) high.
£40–45 / €60–70
$75–85 ➹ GAZE

A dolls' house pine mirror-back sofa, 1900, 8in (20.5cm) high.
£270–300 / €390–440
$520–580 ⊞ BGe

A dolls' house metal and cloth screen, German, 1910, 4in (10cm) high.
£100–110 / €145–165
$190–210 ⊞ BGe

Three pieces of painted pine doll's furniture, c1910, table 16in (40.5cm) wide.
£135–150 / €195–220
$260–290 ⊞ JUN

◀ A doll's leather and pine chaise longue, 1910, 19in (48.5cm) long.
£170–190 / €250–280
$320–360 ⊞ BGe

▶ A doll's metal stove, with two pots, 1910–15, 4in (10cm) wide.
£55–65 / €80–95
$110–125 ⊞ MSB

A Kenton cast-iron Kent doll's gas range, with a set of cast-iron cookware, American, c1927, 10in (25.5cm) wide.
£310–370 / €450–540
$600–710 ➢ Bert

A dolls' house tin bathroom, German, c1920, 6in (15cm) high.
£220–250 / €320–360
$420–480 ⊞ BGe

A dolls' house metal cake stand, 1920, 3½in (9cm) high.
£85–95 / €125–140
$165–185 ⊞ BGe

◄ **A dolls' house pine hall stand,** with mirror, 1920, 7in (18cm) high.
£85–95 / €125–140
$165–185 ⊞ BGe

A dolls' house tin-plate range, c1900, 6in (15cm) wide.
£25–30 / €40–45
$50–55 ⊞ JUN

A dolls' house mahogany dresser, c1900, 8in (20.5cm) high.
£270–300 / €390–440
$520–580 ⊞ BGe

▶ **A dolls' house lead vacuum cleaner,** 1950s, 5in (12.5cm) high.
£15–20 / €22–29
$29–38 ⊞ UD

A doll's dress and bonnet, made with 19thC fabric, French, 1950s.
£310–350 / €450–510
$600–670 ⊞ JPr

◄ **A Barbie vinyl pillow,** c1961, 11in (28cm) diam.
£450–500 / €650–730
$860–960 ⊞ T&D
Rare Barbie items, such as this pillow, can command high prices.

▶ **A Barbie shower mitt and powdered soap sachets,** c1961, with box 7 x 5in (18 x 12.5cm).
£175–195 / €250–280
$330–370 ⊞ T&D

A set of doll's clothes, in a Harrod's Home Shopping Service box, 1967, 13 x 11in (33 x 28cm).
£25–30 / €40–45
$50–55 ⊞ UD

▶ **A Knickerbocker Holly Hobbie Dress Mates set,** 1970s, 12 x 8in (30.5 x 20.5cm).
£6–10 / €9–15
$12–19 ⊞ UD

▶ **A Pedigree Toys Sindy's Electronic Magic Cooker,** battery powered, 1980s, with box, 13in (33cm) high.
£10–15 / €15–22
$19–28 ⚒ GAZE

A Silver Cross doll's pram, with original canopy and bag, early 1970s, 28in (71cm) long.
£430–480 / €620–700
$830–920 ⊞ POLL

▶ **A dolls' house bronze model of an Egyptian,** by Neil Carter, 2001, 3in (7.5cm) high.
£70–80 / €100–115
$135–155 ⊞ CNM

Dolls' Houses

A Moritz Gottschalk wooden dolls' shop, German, 1900–10, 24in (61cm) wide.
£540–600 / €780–870
$1,000–1,150 ⊞ BGe

A hand-made wooden dolls' house, c1900, 24in (61cm) wide.
£110–125
€160–180
$210–240 ⊞ LIT

An Edwardian dolls' house, 32in (81.5cm) wide.
£750–900 / €1,100–1,300
$1,450–1,750 ⚒ HOK

▶ **A painted wood single-storey dolls' house,** dated 1923, 24in (61cm) wide.
£50–60
€75–85
$100–115
⚒ GAZE

A painted wood dolls' house, c1910, 25in (63.5cm) wide.
£150–180 / €220–260
$290–350 ⚒ G(L)

▶ **A painted wood dolls' house,** with a bisque doll, 1930s furniture, and Taylor & Barret vacuum cleaner, 1920, 36in (91.5cm) wide.
£360–430 / €520–620
$690–830 ⚒ BWL

◀ **A Lines Bros Tri-Ang wooden dolls' house,** 1920s, 28in (71cm) wide.
£450–500 / €650–730
$860–960 ⊞ HOB

◀ **A Tri-Ang mock-Tudor-style dolls' house,** c1938, 35in (89cm) wide.
£220–250
€320–360
$420–480
⊞ HOB

A wooden dolls' house, with stained-glass windows, fitted for electricity, 1930s, 31in (78.5cm) high.
£400–450 / €580–650
$770–860 ⊞ HOB

A wooden mock-Tudor-style dolls' house, 1950s, 33in (84cm) wide.
£60–70 / €85–100
$115–135 ⚒ GAZE

A Gee Bee Tudor Toys dolls' house, 1965, 25in (63.5cm) wide.
£35–40 / €50–60
$65–75 ⊞ LIT

Sylvanian Family houses

In the 1980s, toy production moved predominantly to the Far East and plastic became by far the most common material. Children's toys were increasingly influenced by television, and dolls' houses were no exception. Sylvanian Families were first introduced in Japan in 1985 by a company called Epoch. Later that year they were launched by Tomy in the USA, reaching the UK in 1987. These woodland creatures were a huge hit. They typify the '80s fashion among little girls for 'cute' toys such as *Care Bears* and *My Little Pony*. Many different Sylvanian houses were produced and they can still be found at boot sales. As the children of the '80s have grown up, so has adult interest in collecting Sylvanian Families

A Tri-Ang Crest Cottage dolls' house, 1960s, 22in (56cm) wide.
£45–50 / €65–75
$85–95 ⊞ LIT

A Sylvanian plastic house, with furniture, 1989, 14in (35.5cm) wide.
£45–50 / €65–75
$85–95 ⊞ LIT

◀ **A BBC Editoy plastic Pingu igloo house,** 1992, 8in (20.5cm) wide.
£6–10 / €9–15
$12–19 ⊞ LIT

Ephemera

A manuscript, detailing 296 veterinary remedies, c1800, 4°.
£400–480 / €580–700
$770–920 ⚒ F&C

A paper Valentine puzzle, unfolds to reveal 17 verses and watercolour illustrations, dated 1813.
£120–140 / €170–200
$230–270 ⚒ G(L)

A paper silhouette Valentine card, depicting an owl on an anchor, with a poem, c1830, 9 x 7½in (23 x 19cm).
£90–100 / €130–145
$170–190 ⚒ G(L)

A Victorian parchment warrant, with a Queen Victoria wax seal and original case with royal coat-of-arms, 11in (28cm) wide.
£200–230 / €290–330
$380–470 ⊞ FST

An Inland Revenue tax form, 1868, 11 x 8in (28 x 20.5in).
£6–10 / €9–15
$12–19 ⊞ J&S

A Victorian cut out and embossed greetings card, 4 x 10in (10 x 25.5cm).
£1–5 / €2–7
$3–9 ⊞ J&S

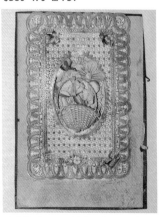

A foiled paper Valentine card, c1880, 7 x 5in (18 x 12.5cm).
£8–12 / €12–18
$16–23 ⊞ POS

A Saint Joseph Blanc fashion catalogue, French, Paris, 1883, 8 x 5in (20.5 x 12.5cm).
£15–20 / €22–29
$29–38 ⊞ J&S

A Challis Patent, for 'Means For Locking the Stretcher Bars of Folding Chairs, Settees and the Like', dated 1909, 10½ x 7½in (26.5 x 19cm) closed.
£15–20 / €22–29
$29–38 ⊞ ChC
James Challis of Hercules Works, Holloway, north London, applied for this patent in 1908 which was accepted in 1909. This patent highlights the huge increase in the design of folding furniture at the end of the 19th century and beginning of the 20th century.

A Women's Social and Political Union membership card, with ink inscriptions, damaged, early 20thC.
£70–80 / €100–115
$135–155 ↗ DNW

An indenture for a draper or milliner, 1913, 10 x 15in (25.5 x 38cm).
£25–30 / €40–45
$50–55 ⊞ J&S

A fashion plate, French, 1917, 14 x 11in (35.5 x 28cm).
£15–20 / €22–29
$29–38 ⊞ J&S

A Palais de la Nouveauté fashion trade catalogue, winter issue, 1924, 10 x 7½in (25.5 x 19cm).
£6–10 / €9–15
$12–19 ⊞ J&S

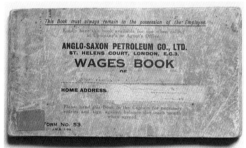

An Anglo-Saxon Petroleum Co wages pay book, 1935, 4 x 7in (10 x 18cm).
£6–10 / €9–15
$12–19 ⊞ J&S

◀ **A Ministry of Defence Mines and Booby Traps training booklet,** 1945, 7 x 5in (18 x 12.5cm).
£2–6 / €3–9
$4–11 ⊞ J&S

The Gale & Polden Training Series Intelligence and Liaison booklet, 1940s, 7 x 5in (18 x 12.5cm).
£2–6 / €3–9
$4–11 ⊞ J&S

A Weldons Knitted Toys pattern book, 1940s, 8 x 5in (20.5 x 12.5cm).
£1–5 / €2–7
$3–9 ⊞ MRW

A Ministry of Defence Home Guard Instruction booklet, No. 54, 1942, 5 x 4in (12.5 x 10cm).
£6–10 / €9–15
$12–19 ⊞ J&S

A Mabel Lucie Attwell Hankie Clock book, 1940s, 5 x 4in (12.5 x 10cm).
£50–55 / €70–80
$95–105 ⊞ MEM

▶ **A Riviera mail order catalogue,** winter 1960–61, 5½ x 9½in (14 x 24cm).
£4–8 / €6–12
$8–15 ⊞ RTT

Erotica

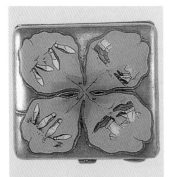

◄ **A silver cigarette case,** the cover enamelled with the four stages of courtship and a lucky four-leaf clover, German, c1900, 3¼in (8.5cm) square, 4.5oz.
£600–720
€850–1,050
$1,150–1,350
⚒ WW

A glamour postcard, by Gerbault, No. 6 of 36, French, c1910, 6 x 4in (15 x 10cm).
£15–20 / €22–29
$29–38 ⊞ S&D

A set of four fashion magazine advertisements, 1920s, 16½ x 11¾in (42 x 30cm).
£25–30 / €40–45
$50–55 ⚒ AMB

A Rosenthal painted porcelain figure of a swimmer, by Gerhard Schliepstein, marked, impressed No. 783, German, 1933–34, 13¼in (33.5cm) high.
£450–540 / €650–780
$860–1,000 ⚒ DORO

► **A Walton Films 8mm film,** entitled 'Nudist Paradise', c1960, 6in (15cm) square.
£15–20
€22–29
$29–38 ⊞ JUN

◄ **A painted metal bottle opener,** 1950s, 6¼in (16cm) high.
£6–10 / €9–15
$12–19 ⊞ RTT

A set of five cartoon lithographs, by Ronald Searle, No 28 of edtion of 70, signed and dated 1969, 19¼ x 25¼in (49 x 64cm).
£540–640 / €780–920
$1,000–1,200 ⚒ DD

◄ **A Rosenthal soap dish,** by Raymond Peynet, depicting a lady in a bath and a peeping Tom, German, 1960s, 4 x 5in (10 x 12.5cm).
£55–65 / €80–95
$105–125 ⊞ PrB

A Galerie Adrien Maeght poster, by Jean Tinguely, French, c1970, 28¼ x 20in (72 x 51cm).
£90–100 / €130–145
$170–190 ⚒ VSP

Fans

A pair of face screens, painted with Oriental scenes, c1820, 15in (38cm) high.
£490–550 / €710–800
$940–1,050 ⊞ HA

An ivory and vellum fan, with carved sticks, Continental, 19thC, 10in (25.5cm) long.
£340–400 / €490–580
$650–770 ⚲ RTo

A painted fabric fan, decorated with sequins, with wooden sticks, 1920s, 10in (25.5cm) long.
£25–30 / €40–45
$50–55 ⊞ CCO

A painted fan, with wooden sticks, European, c1950, 9in (23cm) high.
£15–20 / €22–29
$29–38 ⊞ DE

▶ **A Chinese export ivory fan,** pierced and carved with pagodas, figures and a shield, 19thC, 10½in (26.5cm) long.
£480–570
€700–830
$920–1,100
⚲ DN

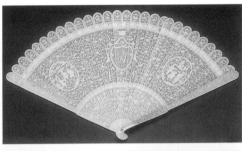

A Victorian painted fabric fan, with wooden sticks, 11in (28cm) long.
£30–35 / €45–50
$55–65 ⊞ CCO

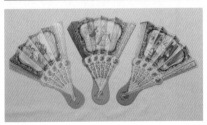

Three cardboard fans, advertising a Spanish restaurant, 1970s, 6in (15cm) high.
£1–5 / €2–7
$3–9 each ⊞ POS

LOCATE THE SOURCE
The source of each illustration in Miller's can be found by checking the code letters below each caption with the Key to Illustrations, pages 443–451.

A sample fan, advertising Westinghouse Mazda Lamps, c1916, 11½in (29cm) long.
£75–85 / €110–125
$145–165 ⚲ JAA

◀ **An ostrich feather fan,** 1920s, 25in (63.5cm) wide.
£40–45 / €60–70
$75–85 ⊞ Ech

A paper fan, advertising the Tokyo Commodity Exchange, with bamboo sticks, 1990s, 15in (38cm) high.
£1–5 / €2–7
$3–9 ⊞ POS

Fifties

Fifties' objects are included throughout this guide and the following items are only a small illustration of period styling. The post-war decorative arts have been performing well in the current marketplace. The clean and curvaceous lines of contemporary fifties' furnishing suit today's modern houses, apartments and loft conversions and demand remains strong for works by the great designers of the period such as Charles Eames, Arne Jacobsen and textile designer Lucienne Day. In the case of some furniture designers, such as Eames and Jacobsen, certain examples of their work are regarded as classics that have never gone out of production, but collectors still want a first edition or an original period piece.

However, the fifties were not just about fine design. The post-war period was a golden age of kitsch, and it was a decade that gave us colourful excesses such as brushed nylon, nodding poodles and long-necked pottery cats, all of which have their own collecting enthusiasts.

In recent times, fifties' fashion has undergone a revival and high street shops have been filled with so-called 'new vintage' circular skirts and prom dresses inspired by the fifties' models of the time.

A brass side lamp, French, c1950, 18in (45.5cm) high.
£250–290 / €360–400
$480–550 ⊞ BOOM

A Philips 141U Bakelite portable mains radio, 1950, 12in (30.5cm) wide.
£50–60 / €75–85
$100–115 ⊞ OTA

A brass plate, commemorating the Festival of Britain, 1951, 12in (30.5cm) diam.
£45–50 / €65–75
$85–95 ⊞ HUX

◀ **An Ultra R906 simulated crocodile skin battery/mains radio,** 1952, 15in (38cm) wide.
£90–100 / €130–145
$170–190 ⊞ GM

Design in the Festival, an illustrated review of British goods, published by the Council of Industrial Design, 1951, 11 x 8½in (28 x 21.5cm).
£20–25 / €30–35
$40–50 ⊞ HUX

A Venini glass handkerchief vase, marked, Italian, Murano, c1955, 6¼in (16cm) high.
£620–720 / €900–1,050
$1,200–1,400 ⋋ DORO

Two Shenango China glazed stoneware dinner plates, by Frank Lloyd Wright, from the dining area of the Price Tower, Bartlesville, Oklahoma, stamped, American, c1956, 9in (23cm) diam.
£550–650 / €800–940
$1,050–1,250 ⋋ S(NY)

A pair of pierced gilt-metal cufflinks, 1950s,
1in (2.5cm) wide.
£30–35 / €45–50
$55–65 ⊞ CAD

A Sherdley Conical glass,
by Alexander Hardie
Williamson, decorated
with Festival pattern, 1950s,
4½in (11.5cm) high.
£15–20 / €22–29
$29–38 ⊞ COO

A Gustavsberg vase,
decorated by Stig Lindberg
with a basket of flowers,
painted marks, Swedish, early
1950s, 10½in (26.5cm) high.
£220–260 / €320–380
$420–500 ⚒ SWO

▶ **A box of
Zeus Bakelite
cigarette
holders,**
American,
1950s, box 6in
(15cm) wide.
£50–60
€75–85
$100–115
⊞ SUW

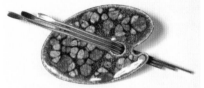

A Matisse enamel and copper brooch,
in the form of an artist's palette, 1950s,
4½in (11cm) wide.
£80–90 / €115–130
$155–175 ⊞ JUJ

A Bush Bakelite television, 1950s,
with 13in (33cm) screen.
£100–120 / €145–175
$190–230 ⚒ AMB

A Lucite handbag,
American, 1950s,
9in (23cm) wide.
£100–110 / €130–145
$190–210 ⊞ JUJ

A tin tray, by Piero Fornasetti, with enamel
decoration, 1950s, 10 x 23in (25.5 x 58.5cm).
£155–175 / €220–250
$300–330 ⊞ MARK

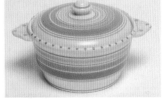

◀ **A ceramic sugar bowl,**
possibly Honiton Pottery,
1950s, 3in (7.5cm) high.
£15–20 / €22–29
$29–38 ⊞ BrL

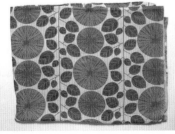

A length of fabric, Scandinavian, 1950s.
£15–20 / €22–29
$29–38 per metre ⊞ FRD

A brass ceiling light, with glass
shades, 1950s, 20in (51cm) wide.
£135–150 / €195–220
$260–290 ⊞ SOU

A Sherdley glass, by
Alexander Hardy
Williamson, late 1950s,
4½in (11.5cm) high.
£2–6 / €3–9
$4–11 ⊞ COO

A Majestic Pictures poster, *The Vampire Bat*, starring Lionel Atwill and Fay Wray, on japan paper, American, 1933, 41 x 27¼in (104 x 69cm).
£2,200–2,600
€3,200–3,800
$4,200–5,000 ➤ VSP

A film poster, *Son of Kong*, starring Robert Armstrong, American, 1933, 41 x 27¼in (104 x 69cm).
£11,600–13,900
€16,800–20,100
$22,300–26,700 ➤ VSP

A film poster, *The Silver Streak,* starring Sally Blane, on japan paper, American, 1934, 41 x 27¼in (104 x 69cm).
£970–1,150
€1,400–1,650
$1,850–2,200 ➤ VSP

A film synopsis of *The Arab,* controlled by J. D. Walker's World's Films, slight damage, c1915, 8°.
£170–200 / €250–290
$330–380 ➤ DW

A film poster, *La Cucaracha,* starring Steffi Duna, on japan paper, American, 1934, 41 x 27¼in (104 x 69cm).
£620–740 / €900–1,050
$1,200–1,400 ➤ VSP

A poster, by Joop Geesink, *Mannequin,* starring Joan Crawford and Spencer Tracy, on japan paper, Dutch, c1935, 33½ x 22in (85 x 56cm).
£370–440 / €540–640
$710–840 ➤ VSP

◀ **A Metro-Goldwyn-Mayer poster,** by J. Bénari, 'Stan Laurel', on japan paper, French, c1935, 30¼ x 22in (77 x 56cm).
£690–830 / €1,000–1,200
$1,300–1,550 ➤ VSP

▶ **Walt Disney,** *Snow White and the Seven Dwarfs,* published by Collins, 1938, damaged, 10 x 7½in (25.5 x 19cm).
£50–60 / €75–85
$100–115 ➤ VAU

A film poster, by Frans Mettes, *Jongens-stad,* starring Spencer Tracy and Mickey Rooney, on japan paper, Dutch, c1935, 34 x 18¾in (86.5x47.5cm).
£370–440 / €540–640
$710–840 ➤ VSP

A Metro-Goldwyn-Mayer poster, by J. Bénari, 'Oliver Hardy', on japan paper, French, c1935, 30¾ x 22¼in (78 x 56.5cm).
£690–830 / €1,000–1,200
$1,300–1,550 ➤ VSP

A film poster, *Robin Hood,* Dutch, c1938, 35¾ x 27½in (91 x 70cm).
£860–1,000
€1,250–1,500
$1,600–1,900 ➤ VSP

A Metro-Goldwyn-Mayer poster, by Roger Soubie, *Autant En Emporte Le Vent,* French, 1939, 62½ x 47in (159 x 119.5cm).
£830–1,000
€1,200–1,400
$1,600–1,900 ➤ DuM

A die-cut cardboard theatre display, *Tobacco Road,* starring Charley Grapewin, c1941, 36½ x 20in (92.5 x 51cm).
£45–50 / €65–75
$85–95 ➤ JAA

An autographed print, Bob Hope, c1949, 12 x 9in (30.5 x 23cm), with photobiography.
£50–60 / €75–85
$100–115 ➤ DuM

Sheet music, for *The Gold Diggers of Broadway,* 1930s, 12 x 10in (30.5 x 25.5cm).
£1–5 / €2–7
$3–9 ⊞ POS

▶ **A foyer card,** *Adventures of Captain Marvel,* Chapter 6 Lens of Death, c1941, 11 x 14in (28 x 35.5cm).
£45–50 / €65–75
$85–95 ➤ JAA

Sheet music, for 'Mickey Mouse Presents Who's Afraid of the Big Bad Wolf', published by Francis Day & Hunter, 1940s, 11 x 9in (28 x 23cm).
£6–10 / €9–15
$12–19 ⊞ CTO

◀ **A die-cut cardboard Temple Theatre display,** *Western Union,* starring Robert Young and Randolph Scott, c1941, 35 x 20in (89 x 51cm).
£60–70 / €85–100
$115–135 ➤ JAA

Sheet music, 'Shirley Temple Song Album No. 2', 1940s, 11 x 9in (28 x 23cm).
£6–10 / €9–15
$12–19 ⊞ UD

◀ **A set of three front-of-house cards,** *The Great Dictator,* 1940, cards 8 x 9½in (20.5 x 24cm).
£175–195 / €250–280
$330–370 ⊞ Lim

A film poster, by Joop van der Berg, *Wee Willie Winkie,* starring Shirley Temple and Victor McLagen, Dutch, c1940, 33¼ x 25¾in (84.5 x 65.5cm).
£540–640 / €780–930
$1,050–1,250 ➤ VSP

Sheet music, Walt Disney's 'Fun and Fancy Free', published by The Sun Music Publishing Co, c1950, 11 x 9in (28 x 23cm).
£6–10 / €9–15
$12–19 ⊞ CTO

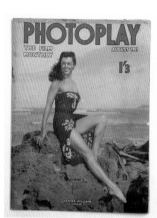

Photoplay, The Film Monthly magazine, featuring Esther Williams, 1951, 11 x 9in (28 x 23cm).
£1–5 / €2–7
$3–9 ⊞ HOM

▶ *Picturegoer* **magazine,** 1955, 11 x 9in (28 x 23cm).
£1–5 / €2–7
$3–9 ⊞ HOM

Roy Schatt, a silver print of Steve McQueen, stamped and numbered, signed in ink, 1956, 20 x 16in (51 x 40.5cm).
£960–1,150 / €1,400–1,650
$1,850–2,200 ⋗ S

A film poster, *Raiders of the Seven Seas,* starring Lon Chaney, c1953, 30 x 39¾in (76 x 101cm).
£45–50 / €65–75
$85–95 ⋗ ONS

A film poster, *The Wind Cannot Read,* starring Dirk Bogarde, c1958, 30 x 39¾in (76 x 101cm).
£40–45 / €60–70
$75–85 ⋗ ONS

Roy Schatt, a silver print of James Dean, signed in pencil, 1954, 20 x 16in (51 x 40.5cm).
£1,400–1,650 / €2,050–2,400
$2,700–3,200 ⋗ S

A film poster, *Stagecoach to Fury,* c1956, 30 x 40in (76 x 101.5cm).
£70–80 / €100–115
$135–155 ⋗ LAY

A film poster, *Sciarada,* starring Cary Grant and Audrey Hepburn, on linen, Italian, 1963, 78 x 55in (198 x 139.5cm).
£450–500 / €650–720
$860–960 ⊞ Lim

◀ **A film poster,** *The Birds,* c1963, 30 x 40in (76 x 101.5cm).
£200–240
€290–340
$380–450
⋗ LAY

A film poster, *Marilyn*, American, c1963, 41¼ x 27¼in (105 x 69cm).
£210–250 / €300–360
$400–480 ⚲ VSP

A film poster, *To Catch a Thief*, starring Cary Grant and Grace Kelly, American, 1965, 41¼ x 27in (105 x 68.5cm).
£660–790 / €960–1,150
$1,250–1,500 ⚲ VSP

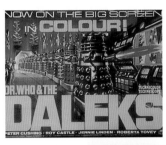

◄ A film poster, *Dr Who & the Daleks*, 1965, 30 x 40in (76 x 101.5cm).
£200–240
€290–340
$380–450
⚲ LAY

► A film poster, *The Impossible Years*, starring David Niven, c1968, 30 x 39¾in (76 x 101cm).
£20–25
€30–35
$40–50 ⚲ ONS

A film poster, *Vampire Circus*, 1972, 30 x 40in (76 x 101.5cm).
£70–80 / €100–115
$135–155 ⚲ VAU

A film poster, *Flesh Gordon*, starring Jason Williams, 1974, 30 x 40in (76 x 101.5cm).
£20–25 / €30–35
$40–50 ⚲ VAU

A film poster, for *Feast of Friends* and *Jimi Plays Berkeley*, 1975, 30¼ x 22½in (77 x 57cm).
£95–110 / €140–165
$180–210 ⚲ VSP

◄ A film poster, by Hibner, *The Man from Maisinicu*, Polish, 1970s, 32 x 23in (81.5 x 58.5cm).
£75–85 / €110–125
$145–165 ⊞ Lim

Further reading
Miller's Movie Collectibles, Miller's Publications, 2002

A Walt Disney Mickey Mouse jacket, 1980s.
£15–20 / €22–29
$29–38 ⊞ COB

A film poster, *An American Werewolf in London/Dracula*, 1981, 30 x 40in (76 x 101.5cm).
£20–25 / €30–35
$40–50 ⊞ CTO

A bag, used on the film set of *Golden Eye*, 1990s, 17in (43cm) wide.
£20–25 / €30–35
$40–50 ⊞ COB

Games

Although items in this section begin in the 19th century, the origins of many of the games illustrated are far older. Playing cards first came to Europe from the Middle East in the 14th century and early suit marks, Swords, Cups, Coins and Batons, were inspired by Islamic prototypes. It was the French who developed the use of Hearts, Diamonds, Spades and Clubs, and by the 16th century France was the leading exporter of playing cards in Europe.

Chess originated in India or China during the 6th century, deriving from a variety of different sources. The game spread through Arabia to Western Europe, where it became known as the Royal Game because of its popularity with the aristocracy and the intelligentsia. The first professional chess manuscripts were written in Spain in the 15th century and, up until the 17th century, Spain and Italy provided the leading chess Masters who were held in huge (and lucrative) esteem. Dominance passed to France in the 18th century and then to Britain by the mid-19th century, where Howard Staunton (1810–74) not only organized the world's first modern international chess championship, but also designed the chess pieces that were to become standard all over the world (see below). Benjamin Franklin popularized chess in North America with his pamphlet *The Morals of Chess* (1786) and the USA and Russia produced some of the most famous chess Masters of the 20th century.

As well as including competitive games, this section also features puzzles. The puzzle was invented in 1760 by London mapmaker John Spilsbury who stuck a map onto a mahogany board and cut round the countries. He called his creation a 'dissection'. Dissections were used as educational tools for children in the 19th century, but with the invention of the power-scroll saw – the jigsaw – in the 1870s, dissections could now be made more complex and more affordable and jigsaw puzzles became a popular pastime for adults as well as children. In the 1900s there was a high society puzzle craze in the USA and in the 1920s and '30s they were hugely popular in the UK. Many collectable puzzles come from this period and transport themes such as ocean liners and trains are favourite subjects today.

Whereas games such as chess, cards and puzzles go on forever and can be endlessly reprinted by manufacturers, other games last only for a brief period. The board games shown here have been inspired by everything from sport to current affairs to children's literature. The post-war period has seen many games based on favourite films or TV shows, typically devised to capitalize quickly on the success of a programme or movie rather than provide long-lasting playing pleasure. Values of such items depend on the popularity of the character or subject represented and the completeness and condition both of the contents and the box, which, since the game is often purchased for display rather than to play with, is particularly critical. Many traditional games, such as chess and cards, are now played on line. The dominance of computer and video games has affected demand for contemporary board games but has also given vintage examples even more nostalgic value.

A mahogany and boxwood chess and games board, 19thC, 18in (45.5cm) square.
£175–210 / €250–300 $340–400 ✗ BBA

A set of bone pachisi pawns, with stencilled decoration, together with three ivory scoring counters, Indian, 19thC, pawns 1½in (4cm) high.
£300–360 / €440–520 $580–690 ✗ BBA
Pachisi, the royal game of India, can be traced back to 500 BC. Legend has it that the game was played on palace grounds using slave girls as the various red, yellow, blue and green pawns.

An ivory chess set, 19thC, king 3½in (9cm) high.
£190–220 / €280–330 $360–420 ✗ DN

A Jaques Staunton boxwood and ebony chess set, white king stamped, king 2¾in (7cm) high, in a wooden box with hinged lid.
£300–360 / €440–520
$580–690 ➶ BBA
Ebony was used for the black pieces on the best quality chess sets and boxwood for the white pieces. In cheaper sets all the pieces were made from boxwood and were coloured accordingly.

A carved and stained ivory chess set, 19thC, king 7¾in (19.5cm) high, with a chess board.
£550–660 / €800–960
$1,050–1,250 ➶ CHTR

Two Nailsea glass marbles, mid-19thC, 1¼in (3cm) diam.
£20–25 / €30–35
$40–50 each ⊞ HUM

A paper on wood dissection, depicting a historical scene, early 19thC, 7in (18cm) wide.
£65–75 / €95–105
$125–145 ⊞ HUM

A silver chess prize, modelled as a chess piece, maker's mark 'RW', London 1848, 1¼in (3cm) high.
£550–660 / €800–960
$1,050–1,250 ➶ F&C
The first 'modern' chess tournament took place in London in 1849 at the Cigar Divan in the Strand.

◄ **A Victorian lacquered wood counter tray,** 3½in (9cm) diam.
£30–35 / €45–50
$55–65 ⊞ HUM

► **A Victorian Tartan ware marker,** 3in (7.5cm) wide.
£80–90 / €115–130
$155–175 ⊞ HTE

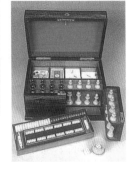

Two Victorian double-sided jigsaw puzzles, larger 7 x 12in (18 x 30.5cm).
£45–50 / €65–75
$85–95 ⊞ J&J

◄ **A Victorian coromandel games compendium,** containing a stained wood chess set, cribbage set, dominoes, dice, markers, draughts, playing cards, a dice shaker and two bezique markers, 12½in (32cm) wide.
£420–500 / €610–730
$810–960 ➶ TEN

A Victorian rosewood games compendium, with an ebonized chess set, leather chess boards, dominoes, dice and counters, 12½in (32cm) wide.
£650–780 / €940–1,100
$1,250–1,500 ⋏ TRM(D)

A mahogany patented game, the hinged board opening to form a deck with four numbered indentations, together with a set of 12 bone counters, 1862, board 23¼in (59cm) wide.
£250–300 / €360–430
$480–580 ⋏ BBA

A De La Rue & Co cardboard pocket chess and draught board, with a set of 32 printed chess pieces, c1870, 6in (15cm) high, in a cloth-covered slip-case.
£80–90 / €115–130
$155–175 ⋏ BBA

▶ **A miniature Tartan ware domino set,** inscribed 'Prince Charlie', c1870, 2½in (6.5cm) long.
£300–330 / €440–490
$580–640 ⊞ RdeR

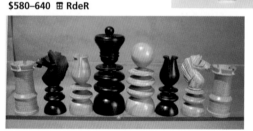

An ebony and boxwood chess set, c1870, king 3¼in (8.5cm) high.
£135–150 / €195–220
$260–290 ⊞ TMi

The Prince's Quest board game, with six wood and card markers, a shaker, and a bone dice, c1890, 18 x 28¼in (45.5 x 72cm), in original box, together with a copy of *Six Victorian & Edwardian Board Games*, 1995.
£125–150 / €180–210
$240–290 ⋏ BBA

The Prince's Quest is the first board game chosen by Olivia Bristol for her book *Six Victorian & Edwardian Board Games*, published by Michael O'Mara Books in 1995. She writes: 'The Prince's Quest reflects the increasing interest in children's stories at the end of the Victorian era. The Brothers Grimm, Hans Christian Andersen and other European fairy-story writers had their work translated and "sweetened" for bedtime reading to the children of upper and upper middle-class families. Several stories have been amalgamated to form this game, the most obvious being *Sleeping Beauty*. The board originally folded into three sections.'

▶ **A Something to Make construction game,** German, c1910, 7 x 10in (18 x 25.5cm).
£25–30 / €40–45
$50–55 ⊞ J&J

◀ **A Chad Valley board game,** Across Africa with Livingstone, 1910–20, 16in (40.5cm) square.
£30–35
€45–50
$55–65 ⊞ J&J

◀ **A Suffragette card game,** c1918, 4½ x 3½in (11.5 x 9cm).
£180–200
€260–290
$340–380
⊞ MURR

► A Gro-Quik wooden advertising jigsaw puzzle, with illustration by Lawson Wood, c1920, 9 x 7in (23 x 18cm).
£35–40
€50–60
$65–75 ⊞ J&J

A jigsaw, c1920, 7 x 6in (18 x 15cm).
£10–15 / €15–22
$19–28 ⊞ J&J

A Chad Valley game, Fun with the Pepper Family, c1920, 6 x 7in (15 x 18cm).
£15–20 / €22–29
$29–38 ⊞ J&J

► **A Victory wooden jigsaw puzzle,** Friendly Greetings Hunting Days, 1920s, 7 x 9in (18 x 23cm).
£40–45 / €60–70
$75–85 ⊞ J&J

A Frederick Warne Peter Rabbit race board game, with cast-metal figural counters of Squirrel Nutkin, Jeremy Fisher, Peter Rabbit and Jemima Puddleduck, c1925, board 29½in (75cm) extended.
£370–440 / €540–640
$710–840 ⚹ BBA

A Grays of Cambridge Catalin Silette chess set, c1925, king 2¾in (7cm) high, with a wooden box.
£175–210 / €250–300
$340–400 ⚹ BBA
The invention of Catalin revolutionized the manufacture of plastics during the 1920s and 1930s. Catalin, in fluid form, could easily be moulded, and colour added to the process to create swirling marble effects. Catalin was also used to a large extent in the production of radio sets.

A Chad Valley Blow Football game, 1920s, 6 x 11in (15 x 28cm).
£25–30 / €40–45
$50–55 ⊞ J&J

A Waddington's pack of playing cards, London & North Eastern Railway Beautiful Britain, advertising Royal Deeside, 1920s, 4½ x 2½in (11.5 x 6.5cm).
£30–35 / €45–50
$55–65 ⊞ MURR

A Lonsdale & Bartholomew Adventure around Sydney, board game, 1920s, board 10 x 20in (25.5 x 51cm).
£25–30 / €40–45
$50–55 ⊞ J&J

► **A London & North Eastern Railway wooden jigsaw,** 1920s, 12 x 9in (30.5 x 23cm).
£50–60 / €75–85
$100–115 ⊞ J&J

A Rippon Magic Blackboard game, American, 1920s, 11 x 19in (28 x 48.5cm).
£40–45 / €60–70
$75–85 ⊞ J&J

A Waddington's Geographical jigsaw puzzle, North America, No. 303, c1930, 21 x 15in (53.5 x 38cm), with box.
£15–20 / €22–29
$19–28 ⊞ J&J

An Osborne Famous Paintings jigsaw puzzle, Fair City by a Sapphire Sea, c1930, 12 x 9in (30.5 x 23cm), with box.
£15–20 / €22–29
$19–28 ⊞ J&J

A Hayter & Co Picture Book box of Victory jigsaw puzzles,
A Tale of Toyland, c1930, 11 x 9in (28 x 23cm).
£20–25 / €30–35
$40–50 ⊞ J&J

A Geographia game, Kwest, A Game of the Sea, 1930s, 15 x 24in (38 x 61cm).
£35–40 / €50–60
$65–75 ⊞ J&J

A wooden Solitaire game, with a drawer for the pieces, 1930s, 6in (15cm) diam.
£15–20 / €22–29
$19–28 ⊞ UD

A Spears game, The International Mail, 1930s, 10 x 14in (25.5 x 35.5cm), with box.
£15–20 / €22–29
$29–38 ⋌ GAZE

A Lumar jigsaw, depicting the Cunard White Star Line Queen Elizabeth, 1930s, 4 x 10in (10 x 25.5cm), with box.
£25–30 / €40–45
$50–55 ⊞ J&J

A pack of playing cards, advertising Bryant & May matches, 1930s, 3½ x 2½in (9 x 6.5cm).
£15–20 / €22–29
$19–28 ⊞ BOB

▶ **A pack of playing cards,** decorated with aeroplanes, 1930s, 3½in (9cm) high.
£10–15 / €15–22
$19–28 ⊞ HUX

A John Waddington game, Buccaneer, 1930s, 12in (30.5cm) wide.
£60–70 / €85–100
$115–135 ⋌ GAZE

A Schach Dame und Mühle Army field set, with embossed card chess counters and a folding board, German, c1942, 9in (23cm) wide.
£60–70 / €85–100
$115–135 ⚲ **BBA**

An aluminium chess set, the pieces made of turned aircraft parts, c1948, king 3¼in (8.5cm) high.
£420–500 / €610–730
$810–960 ⚲ **BBA**
Sets such as these were made from the surplus aluminium stocks left over from aircraft manufacture during WWII.

◄ **A pack of playing cards,** advertising Metrovick Lamps 1940s, 3¼in (8.5cm) high.
£10–15 / €15–22
$19–28 ⊞ **HUX**

A Waddington's jigsaw puzzle, *Alice in Wonderland*, c1950, 20in (51cm) diam, with box.
£20–25 / €30–35
$40–50 ⊞ **J&J**

◄ **A Chad Valley BBC *The Archers* game,** c1958, 19in (48.5cm) wide.
£30–35 / €45–50
$55–65 ⊞ **HUX**

A Berwick indoor football game, Shoot, c1950, 6 x 10in (15 x 25.5cm).
£10–15 / €15–22
$19–28 ⊞ **J&J**

A G. J. Hayter & Co Victory wooden jigsaw puzzle, The Indian Camp, 1950s, 8 x 12in (20.5 x 30.5cm).
£10–15 / €15–22
$19–28 ⊞ **J&J**

A Spears Bali card game, 1950s, 3 x 6in (7.5 x 15cm).
£6–10 / €9–15
$12–19 ⊞ **RTT**

◄ **A Chad Valley *Muffin the Mule* bagatelle game,** 1950s, 19¼ x 9in (49 x 23cm), with box.
£540–600 / €780–870
$1,000–1,150 ⊞ **MTMC**

► **A Chad Valley *Muffin the Mule* skittles game,** 1950s, 7 x 12¼in (18 x 31cm), with box.
£630–700
€900–1,000
$1,200–1,350
⊞ **MTMC**

◄ **A Waddington's *Thunderbirds* board game,** one alarm marker missing, 1966, 8¼ x 15¼in (21 x 38.5cm).
£25–30 / €40–45
$50–55 ✗ VAU

A Milton Bradley Co board game, James Bond Secret Agent 007 American, 1960s, 10 x 19in (25.5 x 48.5cm).
£35–40 / €50–60
$65–75 ✗ GAZE

◄ **A pack of Jet playing cards,** 1960s, 3½ x 2½in (9 x 6.5cm).
£6–10 / €9–15
$12–19 ⊞ RTT

◄ **A Paddington Bear plastic bagatelle game,** c1970, 16in (40.5cm) long.
£25–30 / €40–45
$50–55 ⊞ HarC

A Golden Wonder James Bond card game, *Licence to Kill*, 1960s, 5 x 4in (12.5 x 10cm).
£10–15 / €15–22
$19–28 ⊞ UD

A *Star Trek* jigsaw, No. 2, Command Team, 1972, 10 x 11in (25.5 x 28cm).
£15–20 / €22–29
$19–28 ✗ J&J

► **A Whitman jigsaw,** *Six Million Dollar Man,* 1976, 7 x 8in (18 x 20.5cm).
£4–8 / €6–12
$8–15 ⊞ HeA

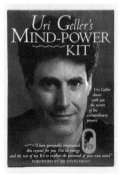

A Whitman jigsaw puzzle, *Dr Who,* 1977, 7 x 9in (18 x 23cm).
£4–8 / €6–12
$8–15 ⊞ HeA

A Walt Disney plastic bagatelle game, c1980, 17 x 9in (43 x 23cm).
£15–20 / €22–29
$19–28 ⊞ HarC

A Uri Geller's Mind Power kit, 1990s, 13in (33cm) high.
£15–20 / €22–29
$19–28 ⊞ IQ

Garden Collectables

A metal sheep bell, with a yew-wood yoke, c1880, 10in (25.5cm) wide.
£130–145 / €190–210 $250–280 ⊞ NEW

A ceramic bird feeder, 1880–90, 3½in (9cm) high.
£20–25 / €30–35 $40–50 ➢ BBR

A Victorian Coalbrookdale cast-iron garden seat, cast with Serpent and Grapes pattern and hound arm terminals, stamped No. 17597, registration mark, 61¾in (157cm) wide.
£650–780 / €940–1,100 $1,250–1,500 ➢ DN

Cast-iron garden furniture flourished in the 19th century. The most famous manufacturer was the Coalbrookdale Iron Co established in 1709 at Ironbridge in Shropshire. By the Victorian period the firm was well known for outdoor furniture, and their huge catalogue published in 1875 included 100 pages devoted to 'Garden and Park Embellishments'. Among their best-known products were garden seats and benches, the iron work often modelled on plants and flowers, hence the Convolvulus Seat and the Nasturtium Seat. A simple design such as Serpent and Grapes can sell for £600–800 / €870–1,150 / $1,150–2,200 at auction. Rarer patterns such as the Passion Flower seat will make considerably more. Some pieces are stamped with the company name – check for a design registration mark or number which indicates the year that a particular design was registered. Many copies of Coalbrookdale pieces have been produced and reproductions of Victorian designs are still being manufactured today. To distinguish if an object is made from modern aluminium rather than cast-iron, use a magnet – a magnet will not stick to aluminium.

▶ **A wire potato basket,** with a wooden handle, 1900, 16in (40.5cm) wide.
£65–75 €95–105 $125–145 ⊞ MLL

▶ **A Verwood pill,** early 20thC, 5in (12.5cm) high.
£180–200 €260–290 $340–380 ⊞ IW
A pill or owl was a container traditionally used by labourers and farm workers to carry cider or cold tea.

A J. Armitage stoneware urn, 1901–10, 20in (51cm) high.
£75–85 / €110–125
$145–165 ⊞ DEB

A metal cultivator, with a wooden handle, c1920, 13in (33cm) long.
£30–35 / €45–50
$55–65 ⊞ HOP

An iron hand-held cultivator, with a wooden handle, c1930, 15in (38cm) long.
£8–12 / €12–18
$16–23 ⊞ AL

A tin watering can, 1920s, 16in (40.5cm) high.
£50–60 / €75–85
$100–115 ⊞ YT

◄ A Cooper Stewart Rain King water sprinkler, c1930, 10in (25.5cm) wide.
£10–15 / €15–22
$19–28 ⊞ AL

► A wooden Sussex trug, c1938, 24in (61cm) wide.
£35–40 / €50–60
$65–75 ⊞ HOP

A metal and pine folding bench, c1940, 47in (119.5cm) wide.
£200–230 / €290–330
$390–440 ⊞ Lfo

A metal folding garden table, c1940, 35in (89cm) wide.
£125–140 / €180–200
$240–270 ⊞ Lfo

An iron edging tool, with a wooden handle, c1950, 35in (89cm) long.
£5–9 / €8–13
$10–16 ⊞ AL

English Garden Ornament
PAUL EDWARDS

◄ Paul Edwards, *English Garden Ornament*, published by G. Bell & Sons, London, 1965, 9 x 6in (23 x 15cm).
£15–20 / €22–29
$29–38 ⊞ BIB

► Tom Carter, *The Victorian Garden*, published by Bracken Books, 1988, 11 x 8in (28 x 20.5cm).
£20–25 / €30–35
$40–50 ⊞ BIB

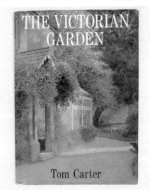

THE VICTORIAN GARDEN

Tom Carter

Glass

Items in the glass section are arranged in chronological order and this year we include a large number of pieces by 20th-century designers. This is one of the fastest growing areas among collectors with particular interest being focused on objects from the post-war period. One of the most collectable British glass factories in recent years has been Whitefriars, notably works by Geoffrey Baxter who, in the 1960s and '70s, produced a range of distinctively shaped and brilliantly coloured glass that captured the psychedelic mood of the moment. While standard Whitefriars pieces can still be picked up for a a small amount (see examples illustrated), more uncommon and large designs can now fetch four-figure sums. I know of two instances where collectors have paid over £5,000 / €7,300 / $9,600 for a particularly rare Whitefriars Banjo vase. These objects are now regarded as 20th-century design classics,' says glass dealer and collector Graham Cooley.

While Geoffrey Baxter is a well established name, he was not the only talented figure of the period. 'In the 1950s and 1960s the Royal College of Art in London was very strong in industrial design and produced a range of talented glass makers,' says Cooley. 'They created some fine work which until recently has been unappreciated. This means that, if you are lucky, you can still pick up good pieces cheaply in charity shops and boot fairs.' One of Cooley's favourite designers is Ronald Stennett-Willson, who worked in

Industrial Glass at the Royal College of Art before opening King's Lynn Glass in 1967 which went on to become a subsidiary of Wedgwood glass. Examples of his work, such as candlesticks, are notable for their elegant shape. Alexander Hardie Williamson (1907–94), however, was a specialist in surface pattern. Williamson had trained as a textile designer, and the patterned drinking glasses that he produced for Sherdley and Ravenhead from the 1950s were covered in largely abstract designs that reflected developments in contemporary fabrics.

Other names to look out for include Domhnall O'Broin (b1934) who worked for Caithness Glass in the early 1960s, Michael Harris (1933–94), another RCA graduate who went on to found Mdina Glass and Isle of Wight Glass, and Frank Thrower (1932–87) who worked for different companies including Dartington. 'One of the best ways to find out about these designers is to look at journals from the period such as *Glass Trade Review*, the *Pottery Gazette*, *Ideal Home* magazine and the *Studio Year Book*. Adverts and articles will show you the leading designers of the day and provide information about dates, designs and original prices.' Cooley concludes 'They are invaluable research tools and if you can be at the head of the queue when it comes to identifying works by top designers of the past, that is the best way to pick up a bargain and to find their best pieces.'

A glass carafe, moulded with vertical ribs, slight damage, Dutch, late 17thC, 9¾in (25cm) high.
£2,250–2,700
€3,250–3,900
$4,300–5,200 ⚹ S

◀ **A Beilby glass goblet,** the bucket bowl painted in opaque white enamel with a vine, the reverse with a butterfly, on a double-series opaque-twist stem and folded foot, stem and foot replaced, gilding rubbed, c1765, 7¾in (19.5cm) high.
£900–1,050
€1,300–1,500
$1,750–2,000 ⚹ S

▶ **A Bristol glass decanter,** 'Rum', early 19thC, 11¾in (30cm) high.
£220–260 / €320–380
$420–500 ⚹ WilP

A pair of Bristol glasses, with trumpet bowls, early 19thC, 4½in (11.5cm) high.
£55–65 / €80–95
$105–125 ↗ SJH

A Bristol glass cream jug, 19thC, 3in (7.5cm) high.
£65–75 / €95–105
$125–145 ↗ BWL

A cut-panel and etched glass stein, engraved 'Curhaus in Steben', German, 19thC, 8½in (21.5cm) high.
£90–105 / €130–150
$170–200 ↗ JAA

A glass goblet, with a bucket bowl and coloured rim, 19thC, 5in (12.5cm) high.
£160–190 / €230–270
$310–370 ↗ WW

◄ **A silver-mounted glass cruet bottle,** by Nathaniel Mills, Birmingham 1832, 6in (15cm) high.
£60–70 / €85–100
$115–135 ⊞ WAC

A gilt-brass mounted glass vase, with wheel-engraved floral decoration and an alabaster base, mid-19thC, 25in (63.5cm) high.
£220–260 / €310–370
$420–500 ↗ G(L)

► **A pair of glass candlesticks,** c1850, 10in (25.5cm) high.
£110–125 / €160–180
$210–240 ⊞ GLAS

A set of three Victorian cranberry glass bells, largest 12in (30.5cm) high.
£300–360 / €440–520
$580–690 ↗ G(L)

Three Stourbridge-style vaseline glass vases, with opaline decoration, mid-19thC, 3in (7.5cm) high.
£60–70 / €85–100
$115–135 ↗ PFK

A Victorian glass wasp bottle, 9½in (24cm) high.
£35–40 / €50–60
$65–75 ⊞ WiB

A Bohemian wine glass, with engraved decoration, c1870, 6¾in (17cm) high.
£190–220 / €280–320
$360–420 ⊞ GLAS

A cranberry glass goblet, c1880, 6in (15cm) diam.
£190–220 / €280–320
$360–420 ⊞ GLAS

A Stourbridge glass frigger, in the form of a walking cane, c1890, 44in (112cm) high.
£135–150
€195–220
$260–290
⊞ GLAS

◄ **A Victorian glass hyacinth vase,** 8in (20.5cm) high.
£25–30 / €40–45
$50–55 ⊞ SAT

► **A cranberry glass covered dish,** c1880, 6in (15cm) diam.
£85–95 / €125–140
$165–185 ⊞ WAC

◄ **A cranberry glass custard cup,** c1890, 2in (5cm) high.
£35–40
€50–60
$65–75
⊞ WAC

◄ **A mercury glass goblet,** c1890, 5½in (14cm) high.
£50–60 / €75–85
$100–115 ⊞ OD

Mercury glass, also known as silvered glass, was produced by pouring a solution of silver nitrate inside a double-walled glass vessel through a hole in the base, which was then sealed with a glass disk. The silvering process was patented in 1849 by F. Hale Thompson of London, and patented again in 1855 by William Leighton of the New England Glass Company in America. Sometimes the seal or the area near the seal bears the mark of the manufacturer. This type of glass, which was popular in the second half of the 19th century, was also produced in France and Belgium.

A pair of mercury glass candlesticks, c1890, 9in (23cm) high.
£90–100 / €130–145
$170–190 ⊞ OD

◀ **A glass bowl,** with hand-painted decoration, c1890, 4in (10cm) high.
£165–185 / €240–270
$320–360 ⊞ MGA

▶ **A crystoleum,** by Arthur Elsley, depicting children playing in a garden, late 19thC, 8 x 10½in (20.5 x 26.5cm).
£160–190 / €230–270
$310–360 ⋋ GAK

A glass night light, decorated with cameos of Queen Victoria, slight damage, marked, c1896, 3¾in (9.5cm) high.
£100–120 / €145–170
$195–230 ⋋ BBR

A Bohemian glass pickle jar and cover, with engraved decoration, late 19thC, 7in (18cm) high.
£120–140 / €170–200
$230–270 ⋋ G(L)

A Moser cut-glass vase, Czechoslovakian, c1900, 7in (18cm) high.
£250–280 / €360–400
$480–540 ⊞ MiW

A glass hyacinth vase, c1900, 6¼in (16cm) high.
£50–55 / €70–80
$95–105 ⊞ GAU

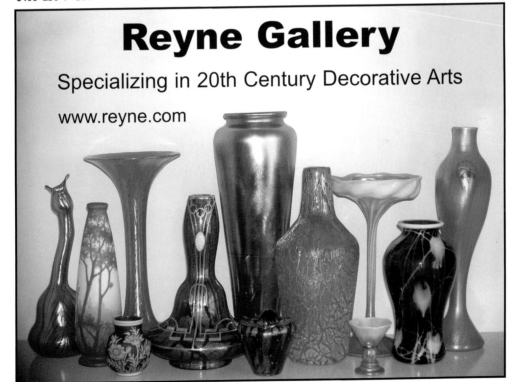

A **Tiffany Favrille glass spice dish,** inscribed 'L.C.T.', American, c1900, 2¾in (7cm) diam.
£100–120 / €145–170
$195–230 ⚘ JAA

A **pair of Bohemian glass vases,** with enamel decoration, c1900, 14¼in (36cm) high.
£490–570 / €710–830
$950–1,100 ⚘ SK

◄ A **Löetz iridescent glass dish,** c1900, 8in (20.5cm) diam.
£160–180 / €230–260
$310–350 ⊞ MiW

A **Webb vaseline glass footed bowl,** c1900, 6in (15cm) high.
£340–380 / €490–550
$650–730 ⊞ MiW
Vaseline glass was produced using uranium which gives a yellow/green colour.

A **Löetz iridescent glass jug,** c1900, 5in (12.5cm) high.
£250–280 / €360–400
$480–540 ⊞ MiW

A **Webb vaseline and cranberry glass vase,** 1900, 5½in (14cm) high.
£340–380 / €490–550
$650–730 ⊞ MiW

A **glass night light,** on a metal base, 1900–10, 3½in (9cm) high.
£60–70 / €85–100
$115–135 ⚘ BBR

A **glass night light,** embossed 'Crystal Palace Lamp Made in Austria', slight damage, 1910, 3½in (9cm) high.
£45–50 / €65–75
$85–95 ⚘ BBR

A **Legras & Cie glass vase,** with acid-etched and painted decoration, signed, French, Paris, 1900–14, 3in (7.5cm) high.
£310–370 / €450–540
$600–710 ⚘ DORO

A **Steuben Gold Aurene footed bowl,** American, c1910, 6½in (16.5cm) diam.
£250–300 / €360–430
$480–570 ⚘ JAA

◄ An **Edwardian souvenir glass bell,** filled with sand from Alum Bay, Isle of Wight, 4in (10cm) high.
£35–40 / €50–60
$65–75 ⊞ HUM

A **glass vase,** German, early 20thC, 6½in (16.5cm) high.
£130–145 / €190–210
$250–280 ⊞ MGA

A pair of cranberry and emerald glass wine glasses, German, early 20thC, 7¼in (18.5cm) high.
£360–420 / €520–610
$690–820 ↗ JAA

▶ **A set of five jadeite glass sundae dishes,** c1920, 3in (7.5cm) high.
£30–35 / €45–50
$55–65 ↗ JAA

A John Walsh Walsh cut-glass jar and cover, designed by William Clyne Farquharson, 1930s, 5½in (14cm) high.
£70–80 / €100–115
$135–155 ⊞ COO

A pair of James A. Jobling glass candlesticks, 1930s, 4½in (11.5cm) high.
£50–60 / €75–85
$100–115 ↗ HOLL

A set of six glass wine goblets, by John Walsh Walsh, signed, c1920, 6in (15cm) high.
£200–230 / €290–330
$380–440 ⊞ GGD

A pressed glass bowl, c1930, 16in (40.5cm) wide.
£50–60 / €75–85
$100–115 ⊞ HEW

▶ **A glass bowl,** with a chrome rim, c1930, 8in (20.5cm) diam.
£45–50 / €65–75
$85–95 ⊞ HEW

A Schott & Genossen glass tea service, by Wilhelm Wagenfeld, comprising 24 pieces, marked, German, 1931, teapot 5½in (14cm) high.
£120–140 / €170–200
$230–270 ↗ SK

A Carnival glass bonbon dish, c1920, 7in (18cm) wide.
£50–60 / €75–85
$100–115 ⊞ HEW

A cameo glass three-handled bowl, signed 'Richard', Austrian, 1925, 6in (15cm) high.
£720–800 / €1,000–1,150
$1,400–1,550 ⊞ MiW

A James Powell & Sons Whitefriars glass bowl, by William Butler, 1930s, 7½in (19cm) diam.
£140–160 / €200–230
$270–310 ⊞ TCG

A Whitefriars glass vase,
with trailing decoration,
c1938, 10in (25.5cm) high.
£200–220 / €290–320
$380–420 ⊞ HEW

**A James Powell & Sons
Whitefriars glass vase,**
1930s, 7in (18cm) diam.
£45–50 / €65–75
$85–95 ⊞ TCG

A Nazeing glass vase,
1930s, 8in (20.5cm) high.
£100–120 / €145–175
$195–230 ⊞ TCG

A Monart glass vase,
with Mica inclusions,
1930s, 9in (23cm) high.
£220–250 / €320–360
$420–480 ⊞ SAAC

**A uranium pressed glass sugar
bowl,** 1930s, 5in (12.5cm) diam.
£8–12 / €12–18
$16–23 ⊞ GRo

**A Monart glass powder bowl and
cover,** 1930s, 5in (12.5cm) high.
£200–230 / €290–330
$380–440 ⊞ RW

A Monart glass basket, 1930s,
9in (23cm) high.
£70–80 / €100–115
$135–155 ⊞ TCG

▶ **A set of six Lalique glass dishes,**
French, 1930s, 7½in (19cm) diam.
£400–450 / €580–650
$770–860 ⊞ MiW

**A pair of Lalique glass Chêne
candlesticks,** with frosted decoration,
French, 1945–47, 6in (15cm) high.
£480–530 / €700–770
$920–1,050 ⊞ GGD

A Lalique glass vase, 'Ferrières',
French, 1930s, 7in (18cm) high.
£720–800 / €1,000–1,150
$1,400–1,550 ⊞ MiW

◀ **A Vasart glass vase,** 1946–64,
3½in (9cm) high.
£25–30 / €40–45
$50–55 ⊞ TCG

A set of 12 Lalique glass plates, decorated with stylized leaves, inscribed mark, French, c1950, 8½in (21.5cm) diam.
£150–180 / €220–260
$290–340 ✗ JAA

A Lalique frosted glass bowl, applied with two birds, engraved mark, French, c1946, 12¼in (31cm) wide.
£600–720 / €870–1,000
$1,150–1,350 ✗ S(O)

A glass ashtray, applied with a polar bear, c1950, 9in (23cm) wide.
£90–100 / €130–145
$170–190 ⊞ HEW

A cut-glass vase, c1950, 9in (23cm) high.
£70–80 / €100–115
$135–155 ⊞ HEW

◄ **A Wuidart glass ice cream bowl,** 1954, 4in (10cm) diam.
£10–15 / €15–22
$19–28 ⊞ COO

A Sherdley Conical glass, by Alexander Hardie Williamson, decorated with Skylon pattern, early 1950s, 4½in (11.5cm) high.
£15–20 / €22–29
$29–38 ⊞ COO
The Alexander Hardie Williamson glasses in this section were manufactured by Sherdley then Ravenhead after they took over Sherdley in 1964.

A Sherdley Conical glass, by Alexander Hardie Williamson, decorated with Festival pattern, early 1950s, 4½in (11.5cm) high.
£15–20 / €22–29
$29–38 ⊞ COO

► **An Orrefors glass vase,** 1950s, 7in (18cm) high.
£75–85 / €110–125
$145–165 ⊞ MCC

A Nazeing glass vase, 1950s, 8in (20.5cm) high.
£70–80 / €100–115
$135–155 ⊞ TCG

► **A Monart glass vase,** 1950s, 8in (20.5cm) high.
£290–330 / €420–480
$560–630 ⊞ RW

A glass vase, c1950, 11in (28cm) high.
£15–20 / €22–29
$29–38 ⊞ DEB

A cut-glass vase, Czechoslovakian, 1950s, 7in (18cm) high.
£100–120 / €145–170
$195–230 ⊞ COO

A Sherdley Cocktail Party shot glass, by Alexander Hardie Williamson, late 1950s, 3in (7.5cm) high.
£4–8 / €6–12
$8–15 ⊞ COO

▶ **A Sherdley Slim Jim glass,** by Alexander Hardie Williamson, decorated with Chinese Lantern pattern, late 1950s, 5½in (14cm) high.
£10–15 / €15–22
$19–28 ⊞ COO

A Sherdley Conical glass, by Alexander Hardie Williamson, late 1950s, 4½in (11.5cm) high.
£4–8 / €6–12
$8–15 ⊞ COO

A Sherdley Conical glass, by Alexander Hardie Williamson, decorated with Clematis pattern, late 1950s, 4½in (11.5cm) high.
£10–15 / €15–22
$19–28 ⊞ COO

A Strömbergshyttan glass vase, with engraved decoration, Swedish, 1950s, 9in (23cm) high.
£45–50 / €65–75
$85–95 ⊞ MARK

A Holmegaard Orchid glass vase, by Per Lütken, 1961, 6in (15cm) high.
£85–95 / €125–140
$165–185 ⊞ FRD

A Murano glass bowl, c1960, 12in (30.5cm) wide.
£30–35 / €45–50
$55–65 ⊞ FRD

▶ **A set of Holmegaard Gul glass vases,** by Otto Brauer, Danish, 1960, largest 20in (51cm) high.
£100–120 / €145–170
$195–230 largest vase ⊞ FRD

A Whitefriars glass vase, by Geoffrey Baxter, 1961, 9in (23cm) high.
£50–55 / €70–80
$95–105 ⊞ COO

A Whitefriars glass vase, by Geoffrey Baxter, 1961, 9½in (24cm) high.
£50–55 / €70–80 $95–105 ⊞ COO

A Whitefriars glass vase, by Geoffrey Baxter, 1961, 9in (23cm) high.
£75–85 / €110–125 $145–165 ⊞ COO

A Whitefriars glass Soda vase, by Geoffrey Baxter, 1961, 6in (15cm) high.
£45–50 / €65–75 $85–95 ⊞ COO

A Whitefriars glass Optic vase, by Geoffrey Baxter, 1962, 6½in (16.5cm) high.
£35–40 / €50–60 $65–75 ⊞ COO

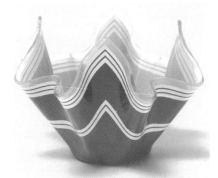

A Chance Glass Handkerchief vase, 1962, 6in (15cm) high.
£15–20 / €22–29 $29–38 ⊞ COO

A Whitefriars glass Optic Cannon Ball vase, 1962, 5in (12.5cm) high.
£40–45 / €60–70 $75–85 ⊞ COO

A Riihimaki glass Presto vase, by Tamara Aladin, Finnish, 1966, 8in (20.5cm) high.
£55–65 / €80–95 $105–125 ⊞ FRD

◀ **A Wedgwood glass Brancaster candle holder,** by Ronald Stennett-Willson, 1967–69, 8in (20.5cm) high.
£40–45 / €60–70 $75–85 ⊞ COO

> **Cross Reference**
> Sixties & Seventies
> see pages 350–352

▶ **A Wedgwood glass Brancaster candle holder,** by Ronald Stennett-Willson, 1967–69, 5in (12.5cm) high.
£25–30 / €40–45 $50–55 ⊞ COO

A Whitefriars glass Guitar vase, by Geoffrey Baxter, No. 9675, 1967, 7¼in (18.5cm) high.
£160–190 / €230–270 $310–370 ⚒ G(L)

A Wedgwood glass Sandringham candle holder, by Ronald Stennett-Willson, 1967–69, 7in (18cm) high.
£40–45 / €60–70
$75–85 ⊞ COO

A Whitefriars glass vase, designed by Geoffrey Baxter, 1969, 7in (18cm) high.
£95–110 / €140–160
$180–210 ⊞ COO

A Wedgwood glass Sheringham candle holder, by Ronald Stennett-Willson, 1967–69, 6in (15cm) high.
£30–35 / €45–50
$55–65 ⊞ COO

▶ **A Whitefriars glass Bark vase,** designed by Geoffrey Baxter, from the Textured range, 1969, 7½in (19cm) high.
£30–35 / €45–50
$55–65 ⊞ COO

A Holmegaard glass Carnaby vase, by Per Lütken, Danish, 1969, 9in (23cm) high.
£180–200 / €260–290
$340–380 ⊞ FRD

◀ **A Dartington glass vase,** designed by Frank Thrower, 1969, 5½in (14cm) high.
£25–30 / €40–45
$50–55 ⊞ COO

A Wedgwood glass candle holder, by Ronald Stennett-Willson, 1967–69, 4in (10cm) high.
£40–45 / €60–70
$75–85 ⊞ COO

A Dartington glass carafe, designed by Frank Thrower, 1969, 6in (15cm) high.
£85–100 / €125–145
$165–190 ⊞ COO

An Alsterfors glass vase, by P. Strom, signed, Swedish, 1958, 9in (23cm) high.
£75–85 / €110–125
$145–165 ⊞ FRD

A Thomas Webb glass bowl, designed by David Hammond, 1969, 5in (12.5cm) high.
£40–45 / €60–70
$75–85 ⊞ COO
This bowl was designed for Coventry Cathedral.

A Whitefriars cut-glass vase, designed by Geoffrey Baxter, 1960s, 5in (12.5cm) high.
£30–35 / €45–50
$55–65 ⊞ COO

◀ A textured **A textured glass ashtray,** 1960s, 5in (12.5cm) diam. **£6–10 / €9–15 $12–19** ⊞ MARK

A Ravenhead Slim Jim glass, designed by Alexander Hardie Williamson, decorated with Royalty pattern, 1960s, 6in (15cm) high. **£6–10 / €9–15 $12–19** ⊞ COO

A Riihimaki glass vase, Finnish, 1970–72, 7½in (19cm) high. **£30–35 / €45–50 $55–65** ⊞ COO

A Whitefriars glass vase, designed by Geoffrey Baxter, from the Textured range, 1972, 6in (15cm) high. **£40–45 / €60–70 $75–85** ⊞ COO

A Riihimaki glass vase, 1970–74, 10in (25.5cm) high. **£40–45 / €60–70 $75–85** ⊞ COO

A Lundberg Studios glass Blue Flower and Vine vase, American, Davenport, Ca, 1979, 10in (25.5cm) high. **£200–240 / €290–340 $400–480** ↗ DuM

A Whitefriars lead crystal Glacier decanter, designed by Geoffrey Baxter, 1974, 14in (35.5cm) high. **£40–45 / €60–70 $75–85** ⊞ COO

▶ **A Mdina glass bottle,** Maltese, 1970s, 9in (23cm) high. **£40–45 / €60–70 $75–85** ⊞ COO

A Mdina glass vase, Maltese, 1970s, 7in (18cm) high. **£75–85 / €110–125 $145–165** ⊞ COO

▶ **A Mdina glass vase,** Maltese, 1970s, 5½in (14cm) high. **£50–55 / €65–75 $85–95** ⊞ COO

A Caithness glass vase,
Scottish, 1970s,
8in (20.5cm) high.
£30–35 / €45–50
$55–65 ⊞ COO

A Mdina stemmed glass, Maltese, 1970s,
7in (18cm) high.
£30–35 / €45–50
$55–65 ⊞ COO

A Lalique frosted glass vase, by Marie Claude Lalique, 'Tarpon', decorated with fish swimming among seaweed, signed and numbered, French, 1970s,
6in (15cm) high.
£400–450 / €580–650
$770–860 ⊞ GGD

An Isle of Wight glass bowl, 1970s,
3½in (9cm) high.
£25–30 / €40–45
$50–55 ⊞ COO

A Wedgwood glass candle holder, designed by Frank Thrower, 1982,
8in (20.5cm) high.
£30–35 / €45–50
$55–65 ⊞ COO

◄ **An Isle of Wight glass vase,** 1980s,
8½in (21.5cm).
£1–5 / €2–7
$3–9 ⊞ MARK

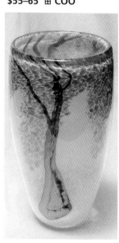

A Caithness glass vase,
Scottish, 1970s,
5in (12.5cm) high.
£30–35 / €45–50
$55–65 ⊞ COO

A Memphis glass Alioth vase, by Ettore Sottsass, manufactured by Toso Vetri d'Arte, Italian, Milan, designed 1983,
18in (45.5cm) high.
£370–440 / €540–640
$700–840 ➚ S(NY)

A Siddy Langley glass vase, 2001–02,
10½in (26.5cm) high.
£135–150 / €195–220
$260–290 ⊞ RW

A Siddy Langley glass vase, 2001–02,
8in (20.5cm) high.
£85–95 / €125–140
$165–185 ⊞ RW

◄ **A Jonathan Harris Studio cameo glass Tulip vase,** decorated with enamels and sterling silver leaf, edition of 50, 2003, 7½in (19cm) high.
£280–310 / €400–450
$540–600 ⊞ JHS
The decoration on this vase was achieved by hand carving through the layers of enamel and silver leaf.

Paperweights & Dumps

A glass dump, 19thC,
5½in (14cm) high.
£60–70 / €85–100
$115–135 ➚ AMB

A Victorian lead glass faceted paperweight, slight damage,
2½in (7cm) high.
£20–25 / €30–35
$40–50 ➚ FHF

A Paul Ysart glass paperweight, with a flower on a muslin ground and an H cane, signed, c1970, 2¾in 7cm) diam.
£490–550 / €710–800
$940–1,050 ⊞ SWB
Paul Ysart personally signed his weights for family and friends only.

A Whitefriars faceted millefiori glass paperweight, with 'monk' signature cane and date, 1971, 3in (7.5cm) diam.
£100–120 / €145–175
$195–230 ➚ PFK

▶ **A Jonathan Harris Studio glass Wilderness paperweight,** decorated with 24ct gold, 2001–02, 3½in (9cm) diam.
£50–55
€65–75
$85–95 ⊞ RW

▶ **A Caithness Glass Calla Lily paperweight,** designed by Gordon Hendry, edition of 500, 2004, 4in (10cm) high.
£100–120 / €145–170
$195–230 ⊞ Cai

Gramophones

A cylinder musical box, playing eight airs, with lever wind mechanism, in a rosewood case with boxwood stringing, the top inlaid with a bird, Swiss, 19thC, 19½in (50cm) wide.
£320–380 / €460–550 $610–730 ⚲ **G(L)**

An Edison phonograph, with two cylinder records, in an oak case inscribed 'Edison Home Phonograph', early 20thC, 18in (45.5cm) wide.
£500–600 / €730–870 $960–1,150 ⚲ **LHA**

A Symphonion disc musical box, with 20 discs, in walnut case, early 20thC, 17¾in (45cm) wide.
£500–600 / €730–870 $960–1,150 ⚲ **WilP**

◀ **A Neophone gramophone,** with a painted horn, early 20thC, 13in (33cm) wide.
£270–320 / €390–460 $520–610 ⚲ **BWL**

A Victrola Model W-XIV phonograph, in an oak cabinet, American, early 20thC, 47in (119.5cm) high.
£190–220 / €280–330 $370–430 ⚲ **JAA**

A phonograph cylinder, plays an opera, c1910, in a box, 5in (12.5cm) high.
£10–15 / €15–22 $19–28 ⊞ **CBGR**

A Claritone tin speaker, c1920, 18in (45.5cm) high.
£135–150 / €195–220 $260–290 ⊞ **JUN**

A Decca Trench portable gramophone, c1924, 12in (30.5cm) square.
£90–100 / €130–145 $170–190 ⊞ **OIA**

An HMV Model 156 gramophone, c1926, in a mahogany cabinet, 37in (94cm) high.
£270–300 / €390–430
$520–580 ⊞ GM

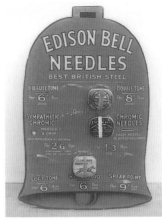

A quantity of Edison Bell gramophone needles tins, on a showcard, 1920s, 8in (20.5cm) wide.
£180–210 / €260–300
$340–400 ⊞ MURR

An His Favourite Song gramophone needles tin, 1920s, 2in (5cm) wide.
£100–110 / €145–160
$190–210 ⊞ HUX

Two Sem Nadeln gramophone needles tins, 1930s, 2in (5cm) wide.
£55–65 / €80–95
$105–125 each ⊞ HUX

A Peacock gramophone needles tin, 1930, 3in (7.5cm) wide.
£65–75 / €95–105
$125–145 ⊞ HUX

Four Sem gramophone needles tins, 1930s, 2in (5cm) wide.
£70–80 / €100–115
$135–155 each ⊞ HUX

A Pye record player, 1950, 14in (35.5cm) wide.
£70–80 / €100–115
$135–155 ⊞ CBGR

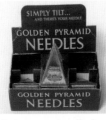

A shop counter display box of Golden Pyramid radiogram needles, contains three packs, 1950, 5½in (14cm) wide.
£100–120 / €145–170
$195–230 ⊞ HUX

Handbags

A beaded drawstring bag,
19thC, 9in (23cm) long.
£70–80 / €100–115
$135–155 ⊞ HTE

◀ **A beaded drawstring bag,** 1880s, 9in (23cm) long.
£130–145
€190–210
$250–280
⊞ Ech
Price ranges for beaded bags depend on condition and the quality and fineness of the beading.

A needlepoint handbag, with a German silver clasp and chain, c1900, 15in (38cm) long.
£40–45 / €60–70
$75–85 ⋀ DuM

◀ **A needlepoint and petit point handbag,** with a gold and semi-precious stone frame, early 20thC, 8in (20.5cm) wide.
£50–60 / €75–85
$100–115 ⊞ JPr

▶ **A celluloid, rhinestone and moire silk evening purse,** French, 1925–35, 5½in (14cm) wide.
£145–165
€210–240
$280–320
⊞ SUW

A beaded purse, c1920, 11in (28cm) long.
£260–290 / €380–420
$500–560 ⊞ JPr

A beaded evening bag, with metal clasp, 1920, 8in (20.5cm) wide.
£175–195 / €250–280
$340–380 ⊞ Ech

◀ **A Whiting Davis mesh handbag,** with original box, 1920–30.
£65–75
€95–105
$125–145
⋀ DuM

▶ **A beaded clutch bag,** with mirror, French, 1920s, 7½in (19cm) wide.
£20–25
€30–35
$40–50 ⊞ JUJ

A beaded evening bag, with plastic clasp, 1920s, 9in (23cm) long.
£155–175 / €220–250
$300–340 ⊞ Ech

A beaded evening bag, with enamel clasp, 1920s, 9in (23cm) long.
£130–145 / €190–210
$250–280 ⊞ Ech

A calf and snakeskin clutch bag, c1930, 11in (28cm) wide.
£85–95 / €125–140
$165–185 ⊞ MCa

A crocodile-skin handbag, 1930s, 11in (28cm) wide.
£110–125 / €160–180
$210–240 ⊞ MCa

A crocodile-skin handbag, silk-lined, with matching mirror and purse, 1930s, 9in (23cm) wide.
£160–180 / €230–260
$300–350 ⊞ MCa

A satin handbag, c1945, 7in (18cm) high.
£70–80 / €100–115
$135–155 ⊞ HOM

▶ **A crocodile-skin handbag,** c1950, 10in (25.5cm) wide.
£65–75 / €95–105
$125–145 ⊞ HIP

A lizard-skin handbag, American, 1950s, 10in (25.5cm) wide.
£45–50 / €65–75
$85–95 ⊞ DRE

A Lucite and gilt-metal handbag, with lace inserts, 1950s, 10in (25.5cm) high.
£175–195 / €250–280
$340–380 ⊞ SpM

▶ **A crocodile-skin shoulder bag,** 1960s, 12in (30.5cm) wide.
£175–195 / €250–280
$340–380 ⊞ LBe

◀ **A crocodile-skin handbag,** with a gilt frame and suede lining, c1960, 10in (25.5cm) wide.
£60–70
€85–100
$115–135
⊞ SBL

▶ **A leather satchel,** 1960, 16in (40.5cm) wide.
£10–15 / €15–22
$19–38 ⊞ JUN

◀ **A Hermès leather handbag,** with a canvas handle, 1960s, 11in (28cm) wide.
£220–250
€320–360
$420–480
⊞ HIP

Jewellery
Bracelets

A Victorian gold hinged bangle, set with rubies and diamonds.
£160–190 / €230–270
$310–360 ➶ WW

A Victorian hinged bangle, set with diamonds and seed pearls.
£250–300 / €360–430
$480–580 ➶ TEN

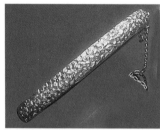

A gold bangle, chased with flowers, c1880, in a fitted case.
£200–240 / €290–350
$390–460 ➶ TEN

A Victorian hinged bangle, set with graduated half pearls.
£350–420 / €510–610
$670–810 ➶ WW

A gold bangle, engraved with foliate decoration, c1890.
£70–80 / €100–115
$135–155 ➶ TEN

An 18ct gold hinged bangle, set with a sapphire, opals and diamonds, with rope twist, beaded and enamel decoration, 1891, 2½in (6.5cm) diam.
£300–360 / €440–520
$580–690 ➶ SWO

▶ **An Edwardian 15ct gold bracelet,** set with peridots and mabé pearls, 6¼in (16cm) long.
£480–570 / €700–830
$920–1,100 ➶ TEN

A gold sovereign bracelet, with a yellow-metal clasp, coins dated 1896–1914.
£320–380 / €460–550
$610–730 ➶ PFK

A Sorrento ware bracelet, 1900, 3in (7.5cm) diam.
£25–30 / €40–45
$50–55 ⊞ MB
Sorrento ware is a form of wood mosaic similar to Tunbridge ware, but using dyed as opposed to natural-coloured woods.

◀ **A yellow metal bracelet,** the filigree decoration set with glass rhinestones, Czechoslovakian, 1950s, 2½in (6.5cm) wide.
£45–50 / €65–75
$85–95 ⊞ SUW

A cocktail bracelet, by Hobé, decorated with Swarowski crystals and poured glass stones, American, 1950s, 1½in (4cm) wide.
£115–130 / €165–190
$220–250 ⊞ LaF

Brooches

Brooches, or pins as they are known in the US, have been enjoying a revival thanks to the recent fashion for fifties-style tailored jackets and tweed suits that has created a demand for brooches to decorate the lapels. Modern costume jewellery designers have been echoing designs from the post-war period when large paste brooches came into vogue, and interest in vintage costume pieces has also expanded.

Although we prize brooches for their decorative quality, originally they were practical pieces of jewellery that evolved from the fibula – a two-sided safety pin-style brooch dating from about 800 BC that was used to fasten cloaks and other garments. The brooches in this section date from the 19th century, but many were influenced by ancient prototypes.

Inspired by classical examples and stimulated by excavations of great Roman sites, cameos were a 19th-century favourite. The fashion started in the early 1800s when Emperor Napoleon gave his wife Josephine a magnificent parure containing 82 antique cameos surrounded by pearls. Where the French court led, everybody else followed, and cameos remained in fashion throughout the 19th century, and the cameo brooch – worn as a shawl clasp or perhaps pinned to a velvet ribbon choker – was a typical Victorian accessory. They were produced in every material from finely carved precious and semi-precious stones to shell cameos that were manufactured in Italy, France and England. They were carved from ivory, jet, coral and lava stone and moulded both in

ceramics and vulcanite – a rubber substitute that provided a cheap alternative to jet. Values today depend on materials, appeal of subject matter and quality – look for a sharp, well-defined image.

Queen Victoria's passion for all things Scottish stimulated the fashion for Scottish pebble jewellery, made from multi-coloured agates and hardstones and typically set in silver. Despite their Scottish origins, these pieces were often made in Birmingham, a main centre for mass-produced jewellery. Shapes were inspired by ancient British and Irish fibulae and cloak pins. Celtic art and archaeology was also an important influence with the new generation of Arts and Crafts designers that emerged in the later part of the century. In 1899, Arthur Lazenby Liberty called his new range of jewellery 'Cymric', alluding to the Celtic shapes and images that had inspired the pioneering Art Nouveau designs.

In terms of size, Victorian brooches ranged from the large designs that suited the cloaks and crinolines of the high Victorian period to the smaller pins and bar brooches that set off the more delicate, high-necked fashions of the turn of the century. Pearls, tiny diamonds and moonstones provided light colours, and novelty designs (insects, animals, sporting themes) were popular, along with moons, stars and sentimental symbols. In the late 1850s, the international price of silver fell after the discovery of the Comstock Lode – the richest known deposit in the USA. A consequence of this was the mass production of cheap silver jewellery, such as name brooches.

A Victorian paste brooch, in the form of a ribbon and drop, 2in (5cm) long.
£150–180 / €220–260
$290–350 ⚲ G(L)

A Victorian pearl and ruby brooch, in the form of a stylized flowerhead.
£220–260 / €320–380
$420–500 ⚲ HYD

A Victorian gold and shell cameo brooch, carved with the bust of a lady, with original fitted case.
£750–900 / €1,100–1,300
$1,450–1,750 ⚲ JBE

A Victorian gold brooch, set with rhodolite garnet and yellow quartz, the reverse with a crystal compartment.
£140–165 / €200–230
$270–310 ↗ LHA

An ivory brooch, carved with the head of a bacchante, c1860.
£250–300 / €360–430
$480–580 ↗ TEN

An amethyst and seed pearl brooch, c1890.
£110–130 / €160–190
$210–250 ↗ TEN

A shell cameo brooch, depicting The Last Supper, on an 18ct gold chain, c1860.
£130–155 / €190–220
$250–300 ↗ DuM

An enamel brooch, set with half pearls and a diamond in a scroll mount, the reverse with a locket, c1860.
£320–380 / €460–550
$610–730 ↗ TEN

A moonstone brooch, in the form of a star, c1890.
£360–430 / €520–620
$690–830 ↗ TEN

◀ **A ruby and half pearl brooch,** in the form of a bee, c1890.
£120–140 / €175–200
$230–270 ↗ TEN

▶ **A late Victorian citrine brooch,** in a 15ct gold Etruscan-style mount.
£160–190 / €230–270
$310–360 ↗ HAM

A Mauchline ware brooch, decorated with a view of Alloway Kirk, 1860–80, 2in (5cm) wide.
£200–230 / €290–330
$380–440 ⊞ GAU

A smoky quartz and enamel brooch, with goldwork decoration, c1870.
£360–430 / €520–620
$690–830 ↗ HAM

A ruby and diamond brooch, in the form of entwined hearts, c1890.
£380–450 / €550–650
$730–860 ↗ TEN

A diamond and pearl brooch, in the form of a bee, c1890.
£500–600 / €730–870
$960–1,150 ↗ TEN

A diamond, ruby and seed pearl brooch,
late 19thC.
£90–100 / €130–145
$170–190 ⚷ CHTR

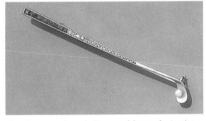

A diamond brooch, in the form of a Scottish
terrier with red gem eyes, c1900.
£400–480 / €580–700
$770–920 ⚷ TEN

A ruby, pearl and diamond brooch, in the
form of a golf club, c1910.
£200–240 / €290–350
$380–460 ⚷ TEN

A silver and pebble brooch, the
central cairngorm surrounded by
agates and heliotropes, Scottish,
late 19thC.
£110–130 / €160–190
$210–250 ⚷ PFK

**A Keswick School of
Industrial Arts copper
brooch,** hand-engraved,
c1900, 2½in (6.5cm) long.
£70–80 / €100–115
$135–155 ⊞ TDG

**A silver and granite
brooch,** inscribed 'Jersey',
c1900, 1½in (4cm) long.
£70–80 / €100–115
$135–155 ⊞ Aur

**An enamel and half pearl
regimental brooch,** the intertwined
swags beneath an enamelled crown,
c1910, with original fitted case.
£180–210 / €260–300
$350–400 ⚷ HAM

Further reading

Miller's Antiques Checklist: Jewellery,
Miller's Publications, 2001

▶ **An 18ct gold brooch,** by John Hislop,
with vine leaf decoration, the reverse with a
locket, signed, New Zealand, early 20thC,
with original fitted box.
£210–250 / €300–360
$400–480 ⚷ WEBB

**An Edwardian ruby and
half pearl brooch.**
£180–210 / €260–300
$350–400 ⚷ TEN

▶ **A silver brooch,** with
floral decoration, maker's
mark 'AB' over 'AR',
c1925, 1½in (4cm) long.
£270–320 / €400–480
$540–640 ⚷ DORO

A silver brooch, by Hubert Landa, c1930,
1¾in (4.5cm) wide.
£410–490 / €600–710
$790–940 ⚷ DORO

A **sterling silver brooch,** by Georg Jensen, in the form of a stylized bird, hallmarked, c1940, 3¾in (9.5cm) wide.
£145–170 / €210–250
$280–330 ⚒ JAA

▶ A **gold, tourmaline and diamond brooch,** in the form of a stylized flower, c1950.
£260–310 / €380–450
$500–600 ⚒ TEN

An **18ct gold brooch,** set with rubies and diamonds, 1950s.
£400–480 / €580–700
$770–920 ⚒ FHF

◀ A **gilt-metal brooch,** in the form of a lion's head set with glass stones, 1960s, 4in (10cm) wide.
£90–100 / €130–145
$170–190 ⊞ DRE

A **paste brooch,** in the form of a lizard, c1960, 4in (10cm) wide.
£40–45 / €60–70
$75–85 ⊞ JBB

A **silver and enamel brooch,** by Georg Jensen, import mark for London 1963, 2¾in (7cm) wide.
£150–180 / €220–260
$290–350 ⚒ FHF

A **silver brooch,** by Georg Jensen, in the form of a deer, London 1960, 1¾in (4.5cm) wide.
£140–165 / €200–230
$270–310 ⚒ FHF

A **resin brooch,** in the form of a 1920s' flapper, 1980s, 4in (10cm) long.
£55–65 / €80–95
$105–125 ⊞ LBe

Buckles

An **enamel buckle,** Czechoslovakian, c1900, 4in (10cm) wide.
£45–50 / €65–75
$85–95 ⊞ JBB

▶ A **pair of plated cut-steel shoe buckles,** early 19thC, 3in (7.5cm) wide.
£85–95 / €125–140
$165–185 ⊞ HUM

▶ A **cloisonné buckle,** signed, Japanese, 1930s, 3½in (9cm) diam.
£70–80 / €100–115
$135–155 ⊞ SUW

◀ A **metal buckle,** set with emerald green stones, c1935, 1½in (4cm) diam.
£25–30
€40–45
$50–55 ⊞ EV

Earrings

A pair of Victorian gold earrings, each set with garnets and a white stone.
£300–360 / €440–520
$580–690 ✒ WW

◀ A pair of enamelled gold earrings, with lapis drops, Italian, 19thC, 2¼in (5.5cm) long.
£175–210
€250–300
$340–400
✒ JAA

A pair of peridot and pearl earrings, c1900.
£150–180 / €220–260
$290–350 ✒ TEN

A pair of silver and *faux* coral earrings, 1940s–50s, 1½in (4cm) long.
£80–90 / €115–130
$155–175 ⊞ SUW

A pair of ruby and diamond earrings, in the form of flowers, 1950s.
£440–520 / €640–750
$840–1,000 ✒ DN

A pair of Matisse copper and enamel earrings, 1950s–60s, 1¼in (3cm) long.
£35–40 / €50–60
$65–75 ⊞ JUJ

Hatpins

Hatpins were an essential part of an Edwardian lady's wardrobe. Large picture hats, the fashion of the day, were secured with a pair of extremely sharp hatpins measuring up to 12in (30.5cm) long. Hatpins with uncovered ends were banned from omnibuses, and various patents were taken out for point protectors. Pins came in many different designs and materials, and prominent makers included silversmith Charles Horner. Values depend on maker, medium and style, and matching pairs are worth more than single hatpins.

A celluloid hatpin, decorated with gilt beads, 1930, 4in (10cm) long.
£6–10 / €9–15
$12–19 ⊞ JBB

A silver and amethyst hatpin, by Charles Horner, Chester 1913, 7in (18cm) long.
£90–100 / €130–145
$170–190 ⊞ JBB

▶ A brass and *faux* pearl hatpin, 1930s, 4in (10cm) long.
£6–10 / €9–15
$12–19 ⊞ JBB

Men's Accessories

Men's jewellery was influenced by changing trends in male fashion. Tie pins or stick pins came into vogue in the 18th century, reflecting the development of the cravat which had replaced the falling collar. Early models tend to be shorter than 19th-century examples and can be distinguished by a zigzagging pin that was designed to catch in the material. Pins were produced in precious stones and in a huge variety of forms from mourning pins to sporting subjects. These were widely worn throughout the Victorian and Edwardian periods and were also popular in the 1920s and 1930s, when styles reflected the Art Deco movement. With growing informality in the post WWII period, tie pins and, as far as many were concerned, ties themselves fell increasingly from popularity, and many of the more valuable pins were broken up so that their stones could be reset.

Although 'sleeve buttons' were used from the 17th century, cufflinks as we know them did not emerge until the 19th century with the evolution of the French cuff, and the development of cheaper production methods to provide affordable jewellery to an expanding middle class. Victorian designs tend to be comparatively restrained, but by the 1900s styles had become more varied and opulent. Edward VII and subsequently his grandson Edward VIII, both fashion leaders and dandies, helped popularize this form of male jewellery and cufflinks were produced in every style and for every level of the market. Some cufflinks will be marked with the name of the maker but, unless it is a piece of jewellery of significance, value will depend above all on medium and shape. Not just the front but also the back of cufflinks came in different designs. Some are linked by chains or loops, while others have a baton designed for pushing through the cuff with one hand. When buying, the condition of both sides should be checked.

A silver Lodge medallion, the centre engraved 'No. 4 Loyal Lodge of Good Fellows 1817', the reverse with the Prince of Wales feathers and 'Thomas Crumpton P. G. September 24th 1817', early 19thC.
£80–90 / €115–130
$155–175 ↗ WL

A Victorian gold stick pin, in the form of a coiled snake, with box.
£210–250
€300–360
$400–480
↗ WW

A gold and reverse intaglio crystal stick pin, depicting a racehorse with a jockey up, within a rope edge border, the reverse inscribed 'Heaume, Paris, le 4 Mai 1890'.
£360–430 / €520–620
$690–830 ↗ BUDD

An 18ct gold double snake ring, set with two diamonds, c1900.
£240–280 / €350–410
$460–540 G(L)

A pair of rose gold marquise cufflinks, Birmingham 1900.
£75–85 / €110–125
$145–165 ⊞ Aur

A pair of metal snap cufflinks, 1925–30, ½in (1cm) diam.
£30–35 / €45–50
$55–65 ⊞ CUF

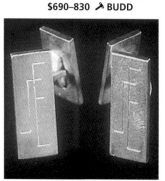

◄ **A pair of metal cufflinks,** monogrammed 'S.E.', stamped marks, 1943, 1in (2.5cm) long.
£540–640 / €780–930
$1,050–1,250 ↗ S

Necklaces & Pendants

A bronze heraldic pendant, decorated with an enamelled owl, 13thC, 1¾in (4.5cm) high.
£175–195 / €250–280
$330–370 ⊞ MIL

A Regency paste pendant, with three drops, marked, French.
£310–370 / €450–540
$600–710 ✦ WW

A paste necklace, one stone having a pendant attachment, 19thC, 15in (38cm) long.
£550–660 / €800–960
$1,050–1,250 ✦ G(L)

Paste

The 18th century saw a fashion for paste – glass that simulates diamonds and other precious stones. Paste was not only worn by the middle classes who could not afford real jewels, it was also worn by the rich. Many ladies preferred to wear paste and leave their valuables at home when travelling as it was a risky business – highwaymen (the muggers of their day) were prevalent. In the 1670s, London glassmaker George Ravenscroft developed lead glass, a material soft enough for cutting but with a diamond-like brilliance, that was perfect for even the smartest jewellery. The Parisian jeweller Georges Frederic Stras (1701–73) was appointed official jeweller to the King of France. His lead glass creations were worn by the most elegant ladies at court, such as Royal mistress Madame du Barry. He became so famous that even today 'Stras' is a synonym for paste. Early paste (both clear and coloured) is high in quality and very collectable.

A Victorian locket, the front decorated with an enamel star set with a diamond, the reverse with enamel Greek key design and woven hair panel, the interior with two woven hair panels.
£450– 540 / €650–780
$860–1,000 ✦ WL

▶ **A late Victorian peridot and pearl pendant,** with two drops and a chain.
£350–420 / €510–610
$670–810 ✦ MAL

A silver and gold locket and chain, the locket with a gold floral motif and border, 19thC.
£300–360 / €440–520
$580–690 ✦ WEBB

◀ **A diamond and sapphire pendant,** c1900.
£270–320 / €390–460
$520–610 ✦ WW

An opal, peridot and ruby pendant, with a chain, c1900.
£300–360 / €440–520
$580–690 ✦ TEN

An Edwardian opal and pearl pendant, the trefoil mount set with an opal, the knife-edge bars terminating with a seed pearl, suspending an opal drop, the chain with an opal-set clasp.
£480–570 / €700–830
$920–1,100 ✦ TEN

An Edwardian 15ct gold pendant, set with two peridots and half pearls.
£340–400 / €490–580
$650–770 ✎ AMB

An Edwardian 18ct gold cross pendant, set with citrines, 3¼in (8.5cm) long.
£340–400 / €490–580
$650–770 ✎ FHF

An Edwardian 9ct gold pendant, set with an amethyst and seed pearls, with a 9ct gold belcher chain.
£170–200 / €250–290
$330–380 ✎ FHF

Charles Horner

In the late 19th century there was a reaction both to the ostentation of much fine jewellery and the poor quality of cheap products. Arts and Crafts designers cultivated simpler styles, handmade by individual craftsmen, often using comparatively inexpensive materials such as silver, enamel and semi-precious stones. These one-off, avant-garde pieces were imitated in machine-made, hand-finished affordable jewellery by larger more commerical firms such as Murrle Bennett (1884–1914) and Halifax jewellers and silversmiths Charles Horner (1869–1984). Established by the eponymous Charles Horner (1837–96) and continued by his sons, this company made its fortune with the invention and patenting in the 1880s of an indestructable silver thimble with an inner core of steel, named the Dorcas after a Jerusalem seamstress in the New Testament. From the turn of the century, Charles Horner became well-known for his mass-produced but nevertheless good-quality modern jewellery which followed contemporary fashions in Arts and Crafts, Art Nouveau and Art Deco styles. The pendants illustrated on this page are typical of their period and examples by Horner are sought after.

An Edwardian 15ct gold necklace, with an amethyst and seed pearl drop.
£260–310 / €380–450
$500–600 ✎ WW

A silver and enamel pendant, by Kolo Moser, decorated with a mouse, Austrian, 1904–05, 1¼in (3cm) wide.
£200–240 / €290–350
$390–460 ✎ DORO

A silver and enamel pendant, by Charles Horner, with a freshwater pearl drop, 1911, 1½in (4cm) long.
£220–260 / €320–380
$420–500 ✎ WW

▶ **A silver-gilt pendant,** by H. T. & Co, set with a cairngorm in a cast laurel surround, maker's mark, London 1919.
£80–90 / €115–130
$155–175 ✎ PFK

An Edwardian peridot and seed pearl necklace, the two half pearl line connections terminating with a peridot, on a two-colour chain.
£400–480 / €580–700
$770–920 ✎ WW

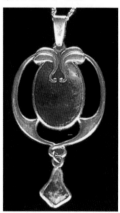

A silver and enamel pendant, by Charles Horner, with an enamel drop, Chester 1910, with a curb chain.
£170–200 / €250–290
$330–380 ✎ DN

A silver dollar pendant, American, 1923.
£20–25 / €30–35
$40–50 ♪ DuM

A glass bead and sequin choker, on a velvet band, 1920s, band 1½in (4cm) wide.
£40–45 / €60–70
$75–85 ⊞ JUJ

A silver and enamel necklace, 1930s, pendant 2½in (6.5cm) diam.
£250–280 / €360–410
$480–540 ⊞ SUW

A gilt-metal, glass and rhinestone cross pendant, by Joseff of Hollywood, 1940s, 4in (10cm) long.
£240–270 / €350–390
$460–520 ⊞ JUJ

Joseff of Hollywood

America led the way in costume jewellery. Hollywood had a major influence on the demand for twinkling and extravagant accessories and the company that provided the jewellery for over 3,000 movies from the 1930s to the 1960s was Joseff of Hollywood. Founded by Eugene Joseff (1905–48), the firm created everything from the crown worn by Shirley Temple in *The Little Princess* (1939) to the gilded asps sported by Elizabeth Taylor in *Cleopatra* (1963). Stars such as Marlene Dietrich and Marilyn Monroe took to wearing the jewellery off, as well as on, the silver screen. In 1937 Joseff created a successful retail line, sold through department stores, that was inspired by his film creations and is extremely collectable today. Brass pieces were given a matt gold finish – know as Russian gold – which was devised to minimise the glare from studio lights and also created an antique look. Designs were always dramatic and often representational: favourite subjects included bees, bulldogs, snakes and, as here, suns. Joseff's pieces are marked on the back with the company name.

A Russian gold-plated copper and rhinestone necklace, by Joseff of Hollywood, 1940s, drop 4in (10cm) long.
£280–320 / €410–460
$540–610 ⊞ JUJ

A Robertson's Golly pendant, with a leather case, 1960s, 1½in (4cm) long.
£15–20 / €22–29
$29–38 ⊞ UD

A silver torque necklace and earrings set, by David Anderson, the necklace and earrings with suspended wooden beads, Norwegian, 1975.
£540–600 / €780–870
$1,050–1,100 ⊞ BOOM

◄ **A glass bead choker,** by Sphinx, the pendant decorated with paste stones, 1970s, pendant 2in (5cm) wide.
£50–60 / €75–85
$100–1115 ⊞ SBL

► **A silver pendant and chain,** by Georg Jensen, No. 1989, London 1999.
£85–95 / €125–140
$165–185 ♪ FHF

Jewellery Sets

◄ An Edwardian 9ct gold, peridot and half-pearl pendant and earrings set, on a curb chain, stamped mark.
£170–200
€250–290
$330–380 ➤ DN

A gilt-metal and enamel brooch and earrings set, by David Andersen, marked, Norwegian, 1950s.
£40–45 / €60–70
$75–85 ➤ PFK

► A gilt and glass necklace and bracelet set, by Alice Caviness, set with rhinestones, 1950s, bracelet 1¼in (4cm) wide.
£200–230
€290–330
$380–470
⊞ JUJ

A chrome and plastic bracelet and necklace set, 1940s, bracelet 3in (7.5cm) wide.
£270–320 / €390–460
$420–610 ⊞ SUW

► A Matisse copper and enamel bracelet and earrings set, 1960s, bracelet 1½in (4cm) wide.
£95–110 / €140–160
$180–210 ⊞ JUJ

Rings

An early Victorian gold ring, set with a garnet and seed pearls.
£210–250 / €300–360
$400–480 ➤ WW

► A Victorian 18ct gold ring, set with a diamond within a horseshoe.
£160–190 / €230–280
$310–360 ➤ Bea

A Victorian 18ct gold and enamel mourning ring, set with a diamond, London 1885.
£120–140 / €175–200
$230–270 ➤ WW

A ruby and diamond ring, c1900.
£600–720 / €870–1,050
$1,150–1,400 ➤ TEN

An 18ct gold ring, set with emeralds and diamonds, Birmingham 1900.
£180–210 / €260–300
$350–400 ➤ WW

► A silver and gold ring, set with a sapphire and rose diamonds, one diamond missing, early 20thC.
£180–210 / €260–300
$350–400 ➤ DN

An Art Deco gold plaque ring, set with diamonds and black onyx.
£400–480 / €580–700
$770–920 ➤ WW

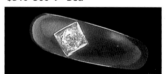

Kitchenware

A wood and brass service bell, early 20thC,
8in (20.5cm) wide.
£35–40 / €50–60
$65–75 ⊞ FST

A Household Wants Indicator,
by Charles Letts & Co, listing Almonds
to Wines, early 20thC,
13 x 11in (33 x 28cm).
£85–95 / €125–140
$165–185 ⚒ Hal

**A wooden Norwegian
Self-Acting Cooking
Apparatus and Simple
Refrigerator,** c1900,
14in (35.5cm) wide.
£70–80 / €100–115
$135–155 ⊞ SA

► **A metal
ice box,** with
adjustable shelves,
c1900, 47in
(119.5cm) high.
**£150–180
€200–240
$280–330 ⚒ JAA**

**A cardboard box of Columbia
Wax Works birthday candles,**
American, 1900–25, 1¼in (3cm) wide.
£10–15 / €15–22
$19–28 ⊞ MSB

An oak kitchen cabinet,
c1930, 30in (76cm) wide.
£220–250 / €320–360
$420–480 ⊞ B&R

A cardboard box of pie dish collars, 1930s,
7⅜in (19.5cm) wide.
£40–45 / €60–70
$75–85 ⊞ MSB

◄ **A Kelvinator oak
five-door fridge,** 1930s,
55in (139.5cm) wide.
**£2,900–3,300
€4,200–4,800
$5,600–6,300 ⊞ DRU**

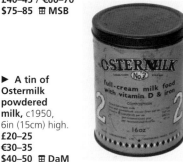

► **A tin of
Ostermilk
powdered
milk,** c1950,
6in (15cm) high.
**£20–25
€30–35
$40–50 ⊞ DaM**

► **A packet of Bird's
Blancmange Powder,**
1970s, 5in (12.5cm) wide.
£4–8 / €6–12
$8–15 ⊞ DaM

Ceramics

◀ **A Shropshire pottery barm pot,** early 19thC, 7in (18cm) high.
£100–120
€145–175
$195–230 ⊞ IW

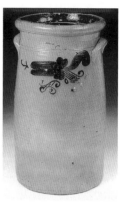

A ceramic quart mug, inscribed 'Imperial Measure', c1860, 6in (15cm) high.
£135–150 / €195–220
$260–290 ⊞ OD

A Cedar Falls stoneware churn, probably by Martin White, slight damage, impressed mark, American, Iowa, c1865, 17¼in (44cm) high.
£1,500–1,750
€2,200–2,550
$2,850–3,400 ⚶ JAA

◀ **A Wetheriggs-style pottery salt kit,** with slip-trailed decoration, slight damage, late 19thC, 10in (25.5cm) high.
£70–80 / €100–115
$135–155 ⚶ PFK

A Kent's ceramic egg beater and batter mixer, c1880, 7in (18cm) high.
£310–350 / €450–510
$600–670 ⊞ SMI
It is rare to find this beater complete with its original whisk.

▶ **A yellow ware custard cup,** American, 1880–1900, 4½in (11.5cm) diam.
£7–11 / €11–17
$13–20 ⊞ MSB

A ceramic storage jar, inscribed 'Rice', Scottish, c1890, 8½in (21.5cm) high.
£50–60 / €75–85
$100–115 ⊞ B&R

A Farnham Pottery jug, c1900, 8in (20.5cm) high.
£60–70 / €85–100
$115–135 ⊞ IW

▶ **Three pottery storage jars,** inscribed 'Icings', 'Currants' and 'Almonds', marked 'AS', c1900, largest 7½in (19cm) high.
£320–380
€460–550
$610–730 ⚶ PFK

A Thomas Farar ceramic Isobel rolling pin, with wooden handles, c1910, 21in (53.5cm) wide.
£135–150 / €195–220
$260–290 ⊞ B&R

A Doulton Lambeth stoneware Improved Bread Pan, c1910, 15in (38cm) diam.
£100–120 / €145–175 $195–230 ⊞ Cot

A set of three Maling Cakeoma for Cakes ceramic storage jars, inscribed 'Currants', 'Salt' and 'Tapioca', c1910, largest 6in (15cm) high.
£65–75 / €95–105 $125–145 ⊞ SMI

A Burslem ceramic plate, advertising Harris's Sausages, c1910, 10in (25.5cm) diam.
£90–100 / €130–145 $170–190 ⊞ SMI

A Gourmet & Co ceramic Eddystone milk boiler, c1910, 7in (18cm) high.
£180–200 / €260–290 $340–380 ⊞ SMI

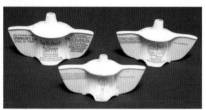

A set of three Grimwades ceramic The Blériot pie dividers, c1910, 5in (12.5cm) wide.
£270–300 / €390–440 $520–580 each ⊞ SMI

▶ **A Grimwades ceramic Combined Cream Skimmer and Spout Cover,** c1910, 6in (15cm) high.
£135–150 / €195–220 $260–290 ⊞ SMI

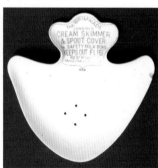

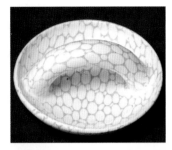

◀ **A Maling ceramic cabbage press,** c1920, 5in (12.5cm) diam.
£50–60 / €75–85
$100–115 ⊞ **B&R**

▶ **A Cakeoma for Cakes ceramic bowl,** c1920, 12in (30.5cm) diam.
£70–80 / €100–115
$135–155 ⊞ **B&R**

A Sadler ceramic Kleen Ware rolling pin, 1940s, 17in (43cm) long.
£50–60 / €75–85
$100–115 ⊞ **SCH**

▶ **A Sadler ceramic Kleen Ware storage jar,** inscribed 'Barley', 1940s, 17in (43cm) long.
£40–45 / €60–70
$75–85 ⊞ **SCH**

A Nutbrown ceramic pie funnel, slight damage, 1950, 3½in (9cm) high.
£35–40 / €50–60
$65–75 ⊞ **BS**

Copper

A copper straining spoon, with mahogany handle, 19thC, 23in (58.5cm) long.
£230–270 / €330–390
$440–520 ⊞ **BS**

A copper grain scoop, with turned wooden handle, 19thC, 16in (40.5cm) long.
£45–50 / €65–75
$85–95 ⊞ **OD**

A copper pan, with steel and wood handle, repaired, c1800, 35in (89cm) long.
£130–145 / €190–210
$250–280 ⊞ **HOM**

▶ **A copper strainer,** c1900, 20in (51cm) long.
£75–85 / €110–125
$145–165 ⊞ **BS**

A Victorian copper fish kettle, 18in (45.5cm) wide.
£110–130 / €160–190
$210–250 ➚ **PBA**

A Victorian copper sugar sieve, c1890, 14in (35.5cm) diam.
£120–135 / €175–195
$230–260 ⊞ **HOM**

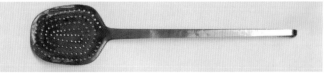

Dairying

Dairying antiques are among the most attractive and collectable items of kitchenware. They reflect the enormous amount of labour required to produce milk, cream, cheese and butter, and objects from ceramic milk pans to wooden butter stamps were often appealingly decorated in order to publicize the dairy. 'Waste not, want not' was a favourite Victorian motto, and dairying equipment was made to last. From the late 19th century, householders used tin and brass milk cans. Often inscribed with the name of the owner, these would have been left outside the door to be refilled.

The milkman, who travelled by horse-drawn milk float, would fill the cans from his churn with a milk measure containing a gill, half a gill or the exact amount required. Glass milk bottles did not become commonplace until after WWI.

Butter was purchased in a butter crock that, once used, could be returned to the dairy for refilling. Decoration affects value and those pieces with appealing images, attractive typography or information of local historical interest will carry a premium.

A Yorkshire iron-glazed pottery butter pot, mid-19thC,
10in (25.5cm) diam.
£80–90 / €115–130
$155–175 ⊞ IW

A brass and steel milk can,
inscribed 'Mrs Astley', c1900,
10in (25.5cm) high.
£70–80 / €100–115
$135–155 ⊞ SMI

A Pond & Son steel and brass milk bucket, c1900, 14in (35.5cm) wide.
£80–90 / €115–130
$155–175 ⊞ B&R

◀ **A wooden butter stamp,** c1920, 5in (12.5cm) diam.
£150–175 / €220–250
$290–340 ⊞ SMI
Butter-making involved a wealth of equipment and accessories, from churns in which butter was made, to wooden scales on which it was weighed. Sycamore was the preferred wood for use in the dairy because it did not absorb smells or affect the taste of the milk. The finished butter was then stamped. Sycamore butter stamps, often carved with plants or animals, were used for decoration and sometimes served as the trademark of the dairy.

A sycamore butter hand, c1920,
6in (15cm) diam.
£8–12 / €12–18
$16–23 ⊞ AL

A ceramic butter cooler, inscribed 'Milk' and 'Butter', c1920,
8in (20.5cm) diam.
£110–130 / €160–190
$210–250 ⊞ SMI

An Iceberg butter box and butter safe, with original paint, 1920s,
14in (35.5cm) wide.
£130–145 / €190–210
$250–280 ⊞ B&R

Enamel

A set of five graduated enamel storage jars, c1920, largest 7in (18cm) high.
£135–150 / €195–220
$260–290 ⊞ B&R

An enamel storage jar, inscribed 'Salt', 1920s, 6in (15cm) high.
£25–30 / €40–45
$50–55 ⊞ AL

An enamel jug and cover, 1920s, 6½in (16.5cm) high.
£30–35 / €45–50
$55–65 ⊞ AL

A Taylor enamel and glass meat thermometer, c1930, 6in (15cm) high.
£65–75
€95–105
$125–145 ⊞ Cot

► An enamel tray, commemorating the coronation of Queen Elizabeth II, 1953, 12in (30.5cm) wide.
£25–30
€40–45
$50–55 ⊞ Cot

A set of three enamel storage jars, 1920s, 9in (23cm) high.
£35–40 / €50–60
$65–75 each ⊞ B&R

A set of three enamel storage jars, French, 1920s, 6½in (16.5cm) high.
£125–140 / €180–200
$240–270 ⊞ AL

Enamelware was mass produced from the Victorian period until WWII. It was made from sheets of metal and coated with powdered glass that was fused to the metal in a hot oven. It became a kitchen favourite because it was durable, affordable and easy to clean. France specialized in brightly decorated, stencilled pieces and sets of storage jars decorated with Art Deco-style designs are sought after. This set includes a canister for chicory – a coffee substitute that first became popular in France during the Napoleonic wars when, due to military blockades, coffee was hard to obtain.

◄ An enamel cake tin, c1930, 10in (25.5cm) wide.
£45–50 / €65–75
$85–95 ⊞ B&R

An enamel measuring jug, 1950s, 6¼in (16cm) high.
£6–10 / €9–15
$12–19 ⊞ WeA

Homepride

The Spillers Homepride men were invented in 1964 and first starred on flour bags and in TV commercials in 1965. Fred, whose job it was to sort out the lumps, was the leader of the flour graders, hence the famous slogan 'graded grains make finer flour'. The smiling bowler-hatted figures were an instant hit and in 1969 Homepride launched Fred as a plastic flour-sifter. The figures were manufactured by Airfix and cost three shillings and sixpence with tokens collected from the flour bags. Over 500,000 figures were produced, followed by a range of other items from spice racks to thermometers.

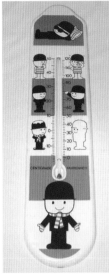

A Spillers Homepride plastic thermometer, 1979, 18in (45.5cm) high.
£50–60 / €75–85
$100–115 ⊞ MMa

Two Spillers Homepride plastic flour sifters, 1970s, 8½in (21.5cm) high.
£1–5 / €2–7
$3–9 each ⊞ MMa

A Spillers Homepride plastic salt and pepper pot set, 1970s, 3in (7.5cm) high.
£10–15 / €15–22
$19–28 ⊞ MMa

▶ A Spillers Homepride plastic and wood spice rack, 1970s, 14in (35.5cm) wide.
£25–30 / €40–45
$50–55 ⊞ MMa

A Spillers Homepride plastic Fred figure, the face is a mixing bowl, the hat is a sieve, with two biscuit cutters, rolling pin and measuring spoons missing, 1970s, 14½in (36cm) high.
£15–20 / €22–29
$29–38 ⊞ MMa

A Spillers Homepride ceramic mustard pot, 1970s, 5in (12.5cm) high.
£50–60 / €75–85
$100–115 ⊞ MMa

A Spillers Homepride ceramic pie funnel, 1970s, 4in (10cm) high.
£25–30 / €40–35
$50–55 ⊞ MMa

Metalware

A cast-iron pestle and mortar, 17thC, mortar 6¼in (16cm) high.
£100–120 / €145–170
$200–230 ↗ WW

A Kenrick & Sons cast-iron coffee grinder, 19thC, 5in (12.5cm) high.
£300–340 / €440–490
$580–650 ⊞ BS
Archibald Kenrick established an iron foundry in West Bromwich in the Midlands c1791. The firm was known for manufacturing high-quality domestic metalware, including designs by Sir Christopher Dresser. In 1815, Kenrick patented a new box-type cast-iron coffee grinder. Coffee beans were poured in to the copper or brass hopper, the iron and lignum vitae handle was turned and ground coffee fell into the drawer below. The lugs enabled the grinder to be mounted on a shelf or table. Kenrick's design came in various sizes, from No. 000 – the smallest, which ground enough coffee for a single cup, to No. 5 – the largest model. Look out for an impressed number on the grinder. Many other makers copied this model, the manufacturer's name often appearing on the brass plate on the front. Period coffee grinders are collectable and value depends on size and design, with rare variants being particularly sought after.

▶ A cast-iron Ezy raisin seeder, American, 19thC, 6in (15cm) high.
£310–350 / €450–510
$600–670 ⊞ BS

A wrought-iron game crown, early 19thC, 12in (30.5cm) high.
£400–450 / €580–650
$770–860 ⊞ WeA

A cast-iron mincer, c1890, 18in (45.5cm) wide.
£75–85 / €110–125
$145–165 ⊞ DaM

A spice tin, nutmeg grater missing, c1890, 7in (18cm) diam.
£50–60 / €75–85
$100–115 ⊞ AL

A metal meat cleaver, with a wooden handle and brass finial, 19thC, 21¾in (55.5cm) long.
£180–200 / €260–290
$340–380 ⊞ WeA

An iron fish slice, c1870, 21in (53.5cm) long.
£40–45 / €60–70
$75–85 ⊞ Cot

A cast-iron chestnut shovel, c1890, 20in (51cm) long.
£35–40 / €50–60
$65–75 ⊞ DaM

A cast-iron cauldron, late 19thC, 15in (38cm) wide.
£65–75 / €95–105
$125–145 ⊞ DEB

A tin bread pan, American, 1890–1910,
11¾in (30cm) wide.
£35–40 / €50–60
$65–75 ⊞ MSB

▶ A tin nutmeg
grater, with a
wooden handle,
1900, 5¼in
(13.5cm) wide.
£55–65 / €80–95
$105–125
⊞ WeA

A tin baking pan,
American, c1900,
9¼in (23.5cm) wide.
£80–90 / €115–130
$155–175 ⊞ MSB

A tin biscuit pricker,
c1900, 3in (7.5cm) diam.
£40–45 / €60–70
$75–85 ⊞ BS

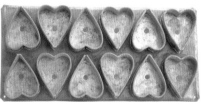

A tin baking pan, American, c1900, 13½in (34.5cm) wide.
£115–130 / €165–190
$220–250 ⊞ MSB

A metal baking pan, American, early 20thC,
8in (20.5cm) wide.
£35–40 / €50–60
$65–75 ⊞ MSB

A tin apple roaster, French, c1920, 14in (35.5cm) wide.
£40–45 / €60–70
$75–85 ⊞ B&R

◄ **A metal whisk,** c1920, 12in (30.5cm) long.
£25–30 / €40–45
$50–55 ⊞ Cot

► **A spring-loaded metal whisk,** with a wooden handle, c1920, 11in (28cm) long.
£20–25 / €30–35
$40–50 ⊞ Cot

A metal picnic kettle and stand, 1920, 9½in (24cm) high.
£35–40 / €50–60
$65–70 ⊞ AL

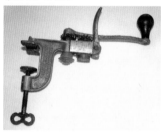

A metal apple peeler and tin opener, with a clamp, 1920s, 9½in (24cm) wide.
£50–60 / €75–85
$100–115 ⊞ WeA

A tin cake icer, 1920s, 7in (18cm) long.
£50–60 / €75–85
$100–115 ⊞ BS

A galvanized-steel Hovis bread tin, 1930, 6in (15cm) wide.
£15–20 / €22–29
$29–38 ⊞ DaM

An aluminium Zanzibar coffee maker, Italian, 1950s, 9in (23cm) high, with box.
£8–12 / €12–18
$16–23 ⊞ DaM

◄ **An aluminium Juistractor,** 1935, 2in (5cm) high.
£20–25 / €30–35
$40–50 ⊞ BS

A Lincoln Ware chrome mini kitchen, for coffee, sugar, flour, tea and bread, American, 1950s, 12in (30.5cm) high.
£95–110 / €140–160
$180–210 ⊞ TWI

► **An aluminium apple slicer,** 1950s, 7in (18cm) wide, with box.
£25–30 / €40–45
$50–55 ⊞ DaM

A Pifco chrome-plated battery-operated drink mixer, 1950s, 6in (15cm) high, with box.
£25–30 / €40–45
$50–55 ⊞ DaM

Moulds

With the rise of the middle classes in the 19th century, eating habits became increasingly elaborate. Meals had more courses and food was required to be decorative. Sweet jellies, savoury mousses, towering blancmanges and ornamental ice creams were favourite centrepieces, providing the perfect opportunity for cooks to demonstrate their skills and for the master and the mistress of the house to show off their wealth and sophistication. Food moulds were an essential part of the 19th-century *batterie de cuisine*. They were produced in every material from copper to earthenware, in every size and shape and, because of their decorative qualities, are popular with collectors today. 'Some people will buy two or three moulds to decorate a country dresser, others just collect moulds,' explains kitchenware dealer Skip Smithson. 'Enthusiasts often concentrate on a specific medium such as copper or ceramic, and may focus on examples by a particular pottery or moulds in a particular range of shapes.'

Although we tend to associate jelly with a dessert course, many moulds were designed for savoury foods. Ring moulds were used for rice and pureed vegetables and fish moulds were produced in every size from small tin minnows to huge party-sized salmon. 'Different materials were used for different foods,' says Annie Marchant from Wenderton Antiques. 'Double-sided tin moulds were used for chocolate and pewter was used for ice cream.'

Some moulds (including ceramic examples) were comparatively plain on the outside and have to be displayed on their sides to reveal the inner patterns of animals or plants. Others are as decorative on the outside as they are on the inside, although this could create a challenge for the cook. 'You have to remember that the mould has to be turned upside down to be filled, so you need to be able to stand it on a table,' says Skip. Ceramic moulds sometimes have little peg feet on the top but these are frequently found damaged or missing. Many castellated copper moulds come with flattened crenulations so that they could be easily upended. If the design was raised (such as the copper and tin wheat sheaf example shown on page 264), the mould might come with a simple tin stand. 'People don't know what these are,' says Skip, 'so they often get thrown away.'

The mid-19th to the early 20th century was the golden age of the jelly mould. Although handsome and very collectable ceramic moulds were produced in the 1920s, as the 20th century progressed pressed glass and aluminium became common materials. However, these were superseded by plastic as jelly was relegated to the children's tea table.

A Benham & Froud copper jelly mould, 19thC, 7in (18cm) high.
£500–550 / €720–800
$960–1,100 ⊞ BS

For further information on **Moulds** see page 129

▶ A Benham & Froud copper jelly mould, 19thC, 7in (18cm) high.
£210–240
€300–350
$400–460 ⊞ BS

◀ A copper entrée mould, in the form of a butterfly, 19thC, 2½in (6.5cm) wide.
£50–60
€75–85
$100–115 ⊞ BS

A copper entrée mould, with golf clubs pattern, 19thC, 2¼in (5.5cm) wide.
£65–75 / €95–105
$125–145 ⊞ BS

A steel and copper jelly mould,
19thC, 6in (15cm) wide.
£200–230 / €290–330
$380–430 ⊞ BS

A Burslem ceramic jelly mould,
advertising Mrs Olive's plum
pudding, c1880, 7in (18cm) wide.
£135–150 / €195–220
$260–290 ⊞ SMI

A tin chocolate mould, in the form
of a boot, c1900, 7in (18cm) high.
£110–125 / €160–180
$210–240 ⊞ YT

A tin chocolate mould, in the form
of a duck, Continental, c1920,
3in (7.5cm) wide.
£25–30 / €40–45
$50–55 ⊞ B&R

**A Benham & Froud pewter three-
piece ice cream mould,** 19thC,
7in (18cm) high.
£145–165 / €210–240
$280–320 ⊞ BS
Ice cream moulds were made
from pewter and can be
distinguished from jelly moulds
by the fact that they have close-
fitting lids so that the mould can
be placed in an ice box.

**A Grimwades ceramic The
Paragon blancmange and jelly
mould,** c1910, 7in (18cm) wide.
£135–150 / €195–220
$260–290 ⊞ SMI

A Shelley ceramic jelly mould,
in the form of a rabbit, c1920,
10in (25.5cm) wide.
£220–250 / €320–360
$420–480 ⊞ SMI

A Wedgwood ceramic jelly mould,
impressed with a sheep and lamb,
c1880, 4in (10cm) wide.
£135–150 / €195–220
$260–290 ⊞ SMI

A ceramic cheese mould, French,
c1900, 8in (20.5cm) wide.
£20–25 / €30–35
$40–50 ⊞ B&R

A ceramic jelly mould, impressed
with an elephant, c1910,
6in (15cm) wide.
£115–130 / €165–190
$220–250 ⊞ SMI

**A Brown & Polson ceramic
shortbread mould,** advertising
Raisley raising powder, c1920,
8in (20.5cm) diam.
£65–75 / €95–105
$125–145 ⊞ B&R

◀ **A tin chocolate mould,** in the form of a pig, Continental, c1920, 6in (15cm) wide.
£30–35 / €45–50
$55–65 ⊞ B&R

A stoneware jelly mould, impressed with an elephant, c1920, 9in (23cm) wide.
£70–80 / €100–115
$135–155 ⊞ SMI

A Brown & Polson earthenware blancmange mould, inscribed with a recipe, 1920s, 7in (18cm) high.
£120–135 / €175–195
$230–260 ⊞ BS

◀ **A wooden shortbread mould,** c1930, 5½in (14cm) diam.
£8–12 / €12–18
$16–23 ⊞ AL

▶ **A glass jelly mould,** in the form of a rabbit, 1930–50, 8in (20.5cm) wide.
£30–35 / €45–50
$55–65 ⊞ DaM

A plastic jelly mould, in the form of a racing car, 1940s, 5¼in (13.5cm) wide.
£1–5 / €2–7
$3–9 ⊞ TWI

Plastic

A Bandaware plastic picnic set, comprising seven pieces, 1940s, plate 6¼in (16cm) diam.
£8–12 / €12–18
$16–23 ⊞ TWI

An Embee plastic cheese dish, 1950s, 8¼in (21cm) wide.
£15–20 / €22–29
$29–38 ⊞ TWI

An Embee plastic butter dish, 1950s, 5in (12.5cm) diam.
£10–15 / €15–22
$19–29 ⊞ TWI

▶ **A plastic and chrome biscuit barrel,** 1950s, 7in (18cm) high.
£30–35
€45–50
$55–65 ⊞ AL

▶ **A set of six T. G. Green plastic napkin rings,** 1950s, 2in (5cm) diam.
£40–45
€60–70
$75–85 ⊞ SCH

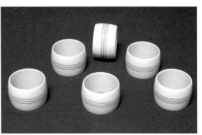

A Ritter plastic and metal Schneidboy universal mincer, c1960, 6in (15cm) wide, with box.
£25–30 / €40–45
$50–55 ⊞ DaM

A plastic egg stand, 1970s, 9½in (24cm) wide.
£8–12 / €12–18
$16–23 ⊞ TWI

Two acrylic honey pots, one with a spoon the other with a drizzler, 1990s, larger 5¾in (14.5cm) high.
£4–8 / €6–12
$8–15 each ⊞ EHCS

◄ **A Tupperware plastic egg separator,** 1970s, 2¼in (5.5cm) high.
£1–5 / €2–7
$3–9 ⊞ TWI

Tupperware – light, unbreakable polythene kitchenware – was invented by US plastics chemist Earl S. Tupper who launched his new product on the market in 1946. He was particularly proud of the patented airtight seal (inspired by the lids of paint cans), but Tupperware sold poorly in shops until the company introduced home demonstrations in 1948. Employee Brownie Wise came up with the idea of the Tupperware party, and a marketing legend was born. Tupperware parties were a success across the world. For the company these parties offered direct access to the housewife, for women they provided not just Tupperware, but social entertainment and a job that could be combined with family life. Vintage Tupperware – particularly the more colourful items from the 1950s through to the 1970s – is collected today, but values remain low.

Washing & Cleaning

Irons

The iron was first recorded in the 17th century. In the 18th century the box iron, which had a hollow body for a slug of heated metal, was developed. Ember irons held burning charcoal and sad irons were set by the fire so that the whole iron could heat up – they usually came in pairs so that one could be warmed while the other was in use. The Victorians developed irons powered by gas and methylated spirits and 1880 saw the invention of the electric iron. Early cordless models which had to be placed on an electrically heated pad were soon followed by a model that could be plugged into the light socket. By the early 20th century, Hotpoint (so named because their iron had as much heat in its tip as in its centre) was selling a large number of electric irons in the USA. With the introduction in 1927 of an adjustable automatic thermostat the electric iron became a standard domestic appliance.

A Victorian cast-iron and wood wall clothes rack, 20in (51cm) high.
£95–110 / €140–160
$185–210 ⊞ FST

A Victorian box iron, with a wooden handle, surmounted with a cockerel, 8in (20.5cm) wide.
£35–40 / €50–60
$65–75 ⊞ HOM

A papier-mâché dustpan and brush, c1880, brush 12in (30.5cm) long.
£60–70 / €85–100
$115–135 ⊞ WAC

A Dowsing's cast-iron electric iron, with a wooden handle, 1880–90, 10in (25.5cm) wide.
£60–70 / €85–100
$115–135 ⊞ GAC

Wood

A Victorian oak rolling pin, 24in (61cm) wide.
£20–25 / €30–35
$40–50 ⊞ Cot

An oak wall tidy, early 19thC.
£360–400 / €520–580
$690–770 ⊞ SEA

A boxwood slicer, 1880, 9¾in (25cm) long.
£55–65 / €80–95
$105–125 ⊞ WeA

A sycamore bread board,
carved with flowers, c1890,
14in (35.5cm) diam.
£135–150 / €195–220
$260–290 ⊞ B&R

▶ **A fruitwood bowl,** with carved
decoration, c1900,
12in (30.5cm) diam.
£20–25 / €30–35
$40–50 ⊞ MLL

A sycamore bread board, carved
with the motto 'We Eat To Live
Not Live To Eat', c1900,
12in (30.5cm) diam.
£70–80 / €100–115
$135–155 ⊞ B&R

Bread boards

A handmade bread board
was a popular wedding
gift in the Victorian and
Edwardian periods.
Borders were often inscribed
with religious or moral
mottos and were carved with
flowers and ears of corn – a
reference to the bread and a
symbol of fertility. In order
to preserve the decoration,
people would often turn the
boards over and cut on the
plain underside. Values of
bread boards depend on
decoration and condition
– avoid boards with a dry
white appearance as these
will have been immersed in
water for a long period of
time and are prone to
warping. Stains can be
cleaned by rubbing boards
gently with an abrasive
powder and then polishing
with beeswax.

A mahogany knife tray, c1915, 16in (40.5cm) wide.
£65–75 / €95–105
$125–145 ⊞ OD

▶ **A wooden egg stand,** c1920, 37in (94cm) high.
£310–350 / €450–510
$600–670 ⊞ B&R

A boxwood salt box,
c1920, 8in (20.5cm) high.
£45–50 / €65–75
$85–95 ⊞ Cot

Lighting

A wrought-iron rush light holder, on a wooden base, c1770, 40in (101.5cm) high.
£1,750–1,950
€2,550–2,850
$3,350–3,750 ⊞ SEA
A rush light, formed by soaking a rush in kitchen fat, was the cheapest form of lighting and also had the advantage of being exempt from the candle tax. Imposed in 1709, the tax prohibited the manufacture of candles without a licence and was not repealed until 1831. These holders were such mundane and simple items that few were preserved, hence their value in the current market.

► **A late Victorian vaseline glass oil lamp,** with a later shade, 11½in (29cm) high.
£350–420 / €490–590
$560–670 ↗ SWO

A wrought-iron double-valve cruzie lamp, French, c1780, 13in (33cm) high.
£155–175 / €220–250
$300–340 ⊞ SEA
A cruzie lamp consisted of a simple iron bowl containing oil and a floating wick of moss or wool. It was in use from the Iron Age until the early 20th century. The cruzie lamp was introduced to North America by European settlers where it became known as the Betty or Phoebe lamp.

An iron wax jack, Scandinavian, c1840, 8in (20.5cm) high.
£400–450 / €580–650
$770–860 ⊞ NEW

A Victorian brass oil lamp, with twin duplex burner and glass shade, 12¼in (31cm) high.
£170–200 / €250–290
$330–380 ↗ WilP

Oil lamps

In 1850 James Young, a Scotsman, patented a refining process for producing paraffin. The fuel burned efficiently without danger of spontaneous combustion and its discovery led to the mass production of oil lamps. Many different designs were mass produced and lamps were imported to Britain from Germany and the USA. On 19th- and early 20th-century examples the brass tends to be weighty while glass shades are often light and finely made, hence the reason that many original shades were broken. Good oil lamps are often marked on the burner and the discovery of a maker's name can be a sign of quality. When buying, the vendor should state if the oil lamp is all original or a marriage between an early base and a later shade. Ask for a demonstration of how the lamp works and be aware of modern reproductions – the brass tends to be lighter and brighter than that of an original lamp.

An ormolu figural table candelabra, 19thC, 15in (38cm) high.
£180–210 / €250–300
$340–400 ↗ L&E

An engineer's metal lamp, 19thC, 9in (23cm) high.
£45–50 / €65–75
$85–95 ⊞ FST

A pair of brass and mahogany candlesticks, 19thC, 13in (33cm) high.
£220–260 / €320–380
$420–500 ⚲ BWL

▶ A brass gas pole lamp, with an etched cranberry glass shade, converted for electricity, c1900, 29in (73.5cm) high.
£180–200 / €260–290
$340–380 ⊞ JeH

◀ An etched glass shade, French, c1900, 12in (30.5cm) wide.
£75–85
€110–125
$145–165
⊞ SOU

A copper chamberstick, c1900, 6in (15cm) high.
£55–65 / €80–95
$105–125 ⊞ WAC

A brass hall lantern, with a satin glass shade, c1900, 13in (33cm) high.
£135–150 / €195–220
$260–290 ⊞ EAL

A vaseline glass shade, 1900, 5in (12.5cm) high.
£180–200 / €260–290
$340–380 ⊞ MiW

◀ An engineer's metal lamp, early 20thC, 4in (10cm) high.
£45–50 / €65–75
$85–95 ⊞ FST

A gold Aurene glass shade, early 20thC, 6½in (16.5cm) diam.
£100–120 / €145–175
$195–230 ⚲ JAA

◀ A pair of silver candlesticks, London 1905, 10¼in (26cm) high.
£240–280 / €350–410
$460–540 ⚲ AMB

A pair of W. I. Broadway & Co silver candlesticks, Birmingham 1901, 8in (20.5cm) high.
£130–150 / €185–220
$250–290 ⚲ G(L)

◀ An opaque glass ceiling light, c1910, 14in (35.5cm) diam.
£100–120 / €145–175
$195–230 ⊞ SOU

A banker's brass lamp, with a glass shade, c1910, 19in (48.5cm) high.
£160–180 / €230–260
$310–350 ⊞ EAL

A metal and slag glass lamp, probably by Bradley & Hubbard, c1915, 21in (53.5cm) high.
£240–280 / €350–410
$460–550 ⋟ JAA

A pair of brass wall lights, with glass flambeau shades, c1920, 16in (40.5cm) high.
£195–220 / €280–320
$370–420 ⊞ EAL

An Oldham Bakelite and brass battery-operated Toucan lamp, c1920, 10in (25.5cm) high
£45–50 / €65–75
$85–95 ⊞ FST

An aluminium street lamp, c1920, shade 14in (35.5cm) wide.
£80–90 / €115–130
$155–175 ⊞ SOU

A battery-operated wooden lamp, c1930, 4in (10cm) high.
£20–25 / €30–35
$40–50 ⊞ FST

A plastic lamp, c1930, 11in (28cm) high.
£270–300 / €390–440
$520–580 ⊞ TOL

A brass hall lantern, with a glass shade, c1930, 15in (38cm) high.
£70–80 / €100–115
$135–155 ⊞ EAL

A chrome table lamp, the glass shade decorated with roses, c1930, 18in (45.5cm) high.
£400–450 / €580–650
$770–860 ⊞ TOL

A Ruskin lustre table lamp, marked, c1930, 9in (23cm) high.
£200–240 / €290–350
$380–450 ⋟ L

◀ **A chrome table lamp,** the glass shade decorated with roses, c1930, 18in (45.5cm) high.
£400–450 / €580–650
$770–860 ⊞ TOL

A brass lamp, c1930, 6in (15cm) high.
£25–30 / €40–45
$50–55 ⊞ HO

A Light Corporation oxidized brass table lamp, American, New York, c1930, 14in (35.5cm) high.
£135–150 / €195–220 $260–290 ⊞ EAL

An oxidized brass desk lamp, American, 1930s, 18in (45.5cm) wide.
£135–150 / €195–220 $260–290 ⊞ SOU

An enamel oil lamp, with a glass shade, 1930s, 5in (12.5cm) high.
£8–12 / €12–18 $16–23 ⊞ JWK

◀ **A metal lamp,** c1940, 12in (30.5cm) high.
£70–80 €100–115 $135–155 ⊞ SOU

▶ **A metal cycle lamp,** 1939–44, 5in (12.5cm) high.
£10–15 / €15–22 $19–28 ⊞ FST

An enamelled desk lamp, French, c1950, 13¾in (35cm) high.
£200–230 / €290–330 $380–430 ⊞ BOOM

An aluminium desk lamp, 1960, 25in (63.5cm) high.
£220–250 / €320–360 $420–480 ⊞ SOU

A Phillips plastic shade, early 1960s, 10in (25.5cm) high.
£85–95 / €125–140 $165–185 ⊞ SOU

A pair of Sputnik-style chrome ceiling lights, French, c1970, 30in (76cm) high.
£670–750 / €970–1,100 $1,300–1,450 ⊞ BOOM

A Habitat rise and fall lamp, early 1970s, 16in (40.5cm) diam.
£65–75 / €95–105 $125–145 ⊞ SOU

▶ **A Guzzini enamel and chrome Harmony lamp,** with a plastic shade, 1974, 18in (45.5cm) diam.
£195–220 €280–320 $370–420 ⊞ FRD

A metal standard lamp, Italian, 1970s, 62in (157.5cm) high.
£70–80 / €100–115 $135–155 ⊞ SOU

Luggage

As travel improved in the 19th century with the development of the railways and shipping routes, there was an increasing need for luggage of different types. Fitted trunks served as portable wardrobes, and metal cases and hat boxes were a favourite with those embarking for tropical climates, providing added protection against insects. For those travelling light, there was a range of smaller bags such as the Gladstone and the portmanteau, all paving the way for the suitcase which, by the 1900s, had become a standard portable favourite. Demand expanded further with the advent of the motorcar. Luxury manufacturers catered to the needs of wealthy tourists, providing trunks, fitted dressing cases and picnic sets.

On the Continent, Hermès (who started as saddle makers) and Gucci provided high-quality luggage to an international clientele, but perhaps the most famous name in vintage luggage is Louis Vuitton. The company was founded in Paris in 1854 and supplied travel goods to European royalty and the wealthy across the world. In 1890, Vuitton developed a five-tumbler lock that enabled each client to have an exclusive combination and 1896 saw the introduction of the famous LV monogram canvas.

The market is currently strong for good-quality luggage. Designer names such as Louis Vuitton command a hefty premium; materials are important (crocodile-skin bags are sought after) and, as ever, condition is crucial to the value.

A brass-bound trunk, with painted floral decoration, late 17thC, 30in (76cm) wide.
£400–480 / €580–700
$770–920 ✗ G(L)

A leather and brass-studded trunk, lined with New England Bible Society papers, c1790, 21in (53.5cm) wide.
£110–125 / €160–180
$210–240 ⊞ DEB

A leather and brass-bound trunk, 19thC, 30in (76cm) wide.
£70–80 / €100–115
$135–155 ✗ CHTR

◀ **A leather top hat box,** with brass fittings and silk lining, c1870, 13in (33cm) wide.
£160–180 / €230–260
$310–350 ⊞ HA

A crocodile-skin jewellery box, relined with suede, 1890–1900, 11in (28cm) wide.
£200–230 / €290–330
$380–440 ⊞ MCa

A Louis Vuitton leather case, French, c1900, 26in (66cm) wide.
£540–600 / €780–870
$1,050–1,200 ⊞ MINN

A Louis Vuitton leather and canvas suitcase, French, c1900, 24in (61cm) wide.
£520–620 / €100–115
$1,000–1,200 ✗ DuM

▶ **A leather suitcase,** c1900, 31in (78.5cm) wide.
£270–300 / €400–440
$520–580 ⊞ JUN

A barrister's wig tin, 1900, 9in (23cm) diam.
£80–90 / €115–130
$155–175 ⊞ MB

▶ A fabric-covered suitcase, with leather trim and White Star Line labels, c1950, 30in (76cm) wide.
£60–70
€85–100
$115–135 ⊞ DEB

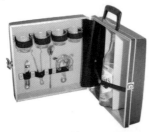

▶ An Adidas plastic sports bag, 1980s, 18in (45.5cm) wide.
£15–20
€22–29
$29–38 ⊞ TWI

A Coracle picnic set, with contents, 1920s, 17in (43cm) wide.
£270–300 / €400–440
$520–580 ⊞ JUN

◀ A brass-bound leather writing case, c1940, 12in (30.5cm) wide.
£120–135 / €175–195
$230–260 ⊞ HA

◀ A Fliteline drinks case, 1970s, 13in (33cm) high.
£50–60
€75–85
$100–115
⊞ PPH

◀ **A leather double bucket hat box,** c1910, 15in (38cm) high.
£250–280 / €360–410
$480–540 ⊞ MINN

◀ A leather case, with brass fittings, c1910, 27in (68.5cm) wide.
£85–95 / €125–140
$165–185 ⊞ HO

A crocodile-skin suitcase, with brass fittings and original keys, 1920s, 18in (45.5cm) wide.
£350–390 / €510–570
$670–750 ⊞ HIP

Medals & Badges

A silver medal, by J. Smeltzing, depicting the beheading of the Duke of Monmouth, 1685.
£1,100–1,250
€1,600–1,800
$2,100–2,400 ⊞ TML

A medal, containing paper tokens commemorating British battle victories in Portugal, Spain and France, decorated in relief with the Duke of Wellington, early 19thC.
£260–310 / €380–450
$500–600 ↗ CHTR

A medal, commemorating the Manchester Art Treasures Exhibition, 1857, 3in (7.5cm) diam, with box.
£70–80 / €100–115
$135–155 ⊞ MB

A bronze medal, commemorating the voyage of HMS *Challenger*, depicting Neptune and Britannia, 1872–76, 3in (7.5cm) diam.
£380–450 / €550–650
$730–860 ↗ DNW
The *Challenger* Expedition of 1872 to 1876 was the first oceanographic research cruise. HMS *Challenger* was loaned by the Royal Navy and modified for the task – gaining two laboratories, one for chemistry and one for natural sciences. She left Plymouth on 7 December 1872 under the command of Captain G. S. Nares, with 20 naval officers, 200 crew and a team of six scientists led by Dr Wyville Thomson. During the 80,000-mile, three-and-a-half year cruise of the world's oceans the scientific team gathered data on the weather and examined the oceans and ocean floor. Discoveries included the driving force of the oceanic currents, 4,714 new species of marine life and a new understanding of oceanic topography. HMS *Challenger* returned to Spithead, near Portsmouth on 24 May 1876.

A silver medal, awarded to Peter F. Morris by the New York Life Saving Benevolent Association, American, 1884, 2in (5cm) diam, with a plastic case.
£230–270 / €330–390
$440–520 ↗ DNW
Susanna Schmidt of 116 East 80th Street, New York, had been bathing at the foot of East 89th Street and was drowning when Peter Morris jumped in and rescued her. In August 1883, Morris had also rescued a man from drowning in the same place. He was awarded the Association's silver medal and the sum of £13 / €19 / $25.

▶ **A silvered-bronze Cherry medal,** with brooch bar, 1900–04,
£210–250 / €300–360
$400–480 ↗ DNW
Captain George Cherry RN was such an unpopular captain with his crew that they commissioned the Cherry medal (supplied by Gamages) to commemorate having survived service with such an unpleasant officer.

A silver medal, commemorating the 25th wedding anniversary of the Emperor Mutsuhito and his Empress, Japanese, 1894.
£500–600 / €730–870
$960–1,150 ↗ DNW
Instituted by Imperial Edict, dated 6 March 1894, this medal was awarded in gold to Imperial princes and princesses and in silver to others of noble blood or high rank who were called upon to attend the ceremonies.

A bronze plaque, by F. C. V. de Vernon, commemorating the constuction of the Paris Metro, decorated with figures and a train, 1912, 3½in (9cm) wide.
£140–165 / €200–240
$270–320 ✦ DNW

A silvered-bronze badge, commemorating the Marine Airship, German, 1920–22, 2½in (6.5cm) wide.
£550–660 / €800–960
$1,050–1,250 ✦ DNW

A silver medal, by Wyon, for the Humane Society of Massachusetts, awarded to Norman S. Powers for bravery in saving life, with brooch bar, American, 1901, 1½in (4cm) diam.
£150–180 / €220–260
$290–350 ✦ DNW
The Humane Society of Massachusetts was instituted in 1785 and incorporated in 1791, making it one of the oldest life-saving societies in the world.

An RAF Barrington Kennett silver trophy medal, by Boucher, with two bars 'Athletics Junior 1933' and 'Athletics Junior 1932', London 1932, 1½in (4cm) diam.
£240–280 / €350–410
$460–540 ✦ DNW

▶ **A silver presentation medal,** awarded to M. Rahim Bakhsh, Head Driver, Government House, Peshawar, with claw and swivel ring suspension, Indian, 1932, 2in (5cm) diam.
£210–250 / €300–360
$400–480 ✦ DNW

A silver cricket medal, by Phillips, for the Special Boat Service inter-port cricket match, 1934, 1¼in (3cm) diam.
£45–50 / €65–75
$85–95 ⊞ FOF

▶ **A 9ct gold badge,** by J. R. Gaunt & Son, for the Queen's Institute of District Nursing, awarded to Mercy Wilmshurst, General Superintendent, Birmingham 1935, 2¼in (5.5cm) high, with neck ribbon and case.
£240–290 / €350–420
$460–550 ✦ DNW

A bronze medal, for the Carnegie
Hero Fund, awarded to L. Brown
Jnr, American, 1955,
3in (7.5cm) diam, with case.
£250–300 / €360–430
$480–580 ➚ **DNW**

A sterling silver medal, by the
Pobjoy Mint, commemorating
Concorde's first passenger flight
from London to Bahrain, 1976,
with case and certificate.
£50–60 / €75–85
$100–115 ➚ **GTH**

**A silver and silver-gilt Order of
the Sea Eagle, Namibia, badge,**
by Spink, with enamel decoration,
London 1995.
£90–100 / €130–145
$170–190 ➚ **DNW**

Masonic

The Order of Freemasons is the largest secret
society in the world, with most members
living in the USA and UK. The order evolved
from the guilds of stonemasons and cathedral
builders of the Middle Ages who, when major
ecclesiastical building declined with the
Reformation, began to accept honorary
members from other professions. In 1717,
the first Grand Lodge was founded in
London, ancestor of all subsequent lodges
across the world. In the USA, the first regular
lodge was founded in Boston in 1733.

Masonic jewels, badges and watches appear
regularly in the marketplace. While some
rarities command high sums, much of the
memorabilia remains very affordable.

Typically, objects are decorated with a range
of Masonic symbols that carry multi-layered
meanings and draw on both Christian and
esoteric imagery. The compass and square –
architects' tools representing the origins of the
society – symbolize God as architect of the
universe and man's ability to scan the workings
of creation. Solomon's Seal – the pentagram
or five-pointed star, the six-pointed star,
the all-seeing eye, the sun and the moon are
all used by the Masons as well as many other
sects and religions. The twin columns Jachin
and Boaz derive from Solomon's temple and
the ⊓ emblem is known as the triple Tau,
symbolizing the temple of Jerusalem, the Key
to the treasure and the 'precious thing' itself.

A Masonic silver jewel,
for the Harmony &
Industry Lodge, No. 381,
1825, 4in (10cm) high.
£20–25 / €30–35
$40–50 ⊞ **WAC**

**A Masonic gilt-bronze
badge,** by Evans, with a
six-pointed star engraved
'Concord, Beauty, Truth,
Wisdom, Peace, Strength',
1840, 2¾in (7cm) high.
£135–150 / €195–220
$260–290 ⊞ **TML**

A Masonic silver jewel,
for the Institution for Girls,
inscribed 'Steward', 1935,
4in (10cm) high.
£15–20 / €22–29
$29–38 ⊞ **WAC**

**A Masonic R.M.I.B.
jewel,** with bar 'Steward
1943', 4in (10cm) high.
£10–15 / €15–22
$19–28 ⊞ **WAC**

Military

A group of five medals, awarded to Chief Boatswain W. Jones, Royal Navy: India General Service Medal with one bar; Egypt & Sudan; Queen's South Africa; Royal Navy Long Service & Good Conduct; Khedive's Star, 19thC.
£750–900 / €1,100–1,300
$1,450–1,750 ⏶ DNW
This is a rare combination of medals.

▶ A group of three medals, awarded to Inspector of Shipwrights J. F. James, HM Dockyards: Egypt & Sudan with one bar; Imperial Service Medal; Khedive's Star, 19thC.
£650–780 / €960–1,150
$1,250–1,500 ⏶ DNW
This a rare and early example of a civilian dockyard shipwright receiving a medal for his presence aboard a Royal Navy ship during a Fleet gunnery action. The medal roll states that his Egypt Medal and Khedive's Star were sent to the superintendent of Malta Dockyard for presentation.

A pair of medals, awarded to Colour Sergeant Henry Bowers, 64th Foot/1st North Staffs Regiment: India General Service Medal with one bar; Indian Mutiny with one bar, 19thC.
£820–980 / €1,200–1,400
$1,600–1,900 ⏶ BBA

A Victoria medal, awarded to Sergeant E. Still, 4th Rifle Brigade, with two bars, Samana 1891 and Burmah 1889–92.
£320–380 / €460–550
$610–730 ⏶ AMB

▶ A group of three medals, awarded to Private W. Baylis, including South Africa with four bars, 1901.
£200–240 / €290–350
$380–450 ⏶ MAL

An East and West Africa medal, awarded to Private J. Grant, 1892, with four bars 1892, 1893–4, 1897–98 and Sierra Leone 1898–99.
£380–450 / €550–650
$730–860 ⏶ WAL

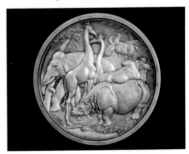

A group of five medals, awarded to J. A. Taylor, comprising Africa General Service medal, with one bar; 1914 Star; British War & Victory medals; Long Service medal.
£350–420 / €510–610
$670–810 G(L)

An Iron Cross, first class, German, 1914.
£115–135 / €165–195
$220–260 BBA

A silver and enamel Indian Order of Merit medal, awarded to Subadar Jehanded Khan, 40th Pathans, third class, Reward of Valor, ribbon missing.
£500–600 / €730–870
$960–1,150 DNW
Subadar Jehanded Khan was killed in action in the battle of Wieltje, about one mile northeast of Ypres, on 26 April 1915. This medal appears to be an unusual instance of a piece of obsolete insignia being used out of necessity, due to shortage of stock, for presentation to his next of kin in India. The contemporary engraving was probably undertaken regimentally prior to a presentation at the regiment's headquarters at Sialkot. It is well known that there was a severe shortage of insignia during the first couple of years of war, hence the unusual badges made by J. W. Benson in London.

A group of four miniature medals, comprising Military Cross; 1914 Star; British War medal; Victory medal.
£55–65 / €80–95
$105–125 Tus

A silver, gold and enamel Legion of Honor Nile Temple medal, awarded to Robert. M. Watkins, American, 1937.
£65–75 / €95–105
$125–145 BBA

A Hong Kong Royal Naval Dockyard Police Long Service bronze medal, first issue.
£290–340 / €420–500
$550–650 WAL

A Campaign Services medal, with Palestine bar, 1939, 4in (10cm) high.
£40–45 / €60–70
$75–85 ABCM

◀ **A group of four medals,** awarded to Pilot Officer David Cooper Leary, including a Distinguished Flying Cross medal.
£1,400–1,650
€2,000–2,400
$2,700–3,200 E

Militaria

Twelve straw, hay, cord and horsehair
incendiary quoits, German, c1625.
£2,400–2,850 / €3,500–4,150
$4,600–5,500 ➶ S(O)
Incendiary quoits of this type would have
been commonly included in the ordnance
of castles throughout the broad sphere
of the Holy Roman Empire. Very few
have survived.

A wooden tipstaff, late 18thC, 9in (23cm) long.
£90–100 / €130–145
$170–190 ⊞ MB

▶ A military drum, decorated
with the royal coat-of-arms, 3rd
Battalion Grenadier Guards,
damaged, 19thC, 15in (38cm) high.
£35–40 / €50–60
$65–75 ➶ GH

A Hackney Special Police Constable wooden truncheon,
19thC, 17in (43cm) long.
£100–120 / €145–170
$195–230 ⊞ MB

A pair of Hyatt metal Chungi jail
maximum security handcuffs, 19thC.
£270–300 / €390–440
$520–580 ⊞ ET

A pen and pencil map of
the Battle of Waterloo,
by Sir John Morillyon
Wilson, sketched on site,
slight damage and repair,
1815, 17¼ x 13in
(44 x 33cm), framed.
£330–390 / €480–570
$630–750 ➶ DNW

A pencil drawing of Napoleon I
on his deathbed, attributed to
Captain Ward at St Helena, slight
damage and repair, 1821,
4½ x 7¾in (11.5 x 20cm).
£380–450 / €550–650
$730–860 ➶ DW

▶ A set of
19 watercolour
drawings
of military
costumes, in a
morocco album,
French, 1827,
drawings 8½ x 6in
(21.5 x 15cm).
£380–450
€550–650
$730–860 ➶ DW

▶ A ceramic jug, possibly
Chamberlain's Worcester,
inscribed 'Success to the
Manchester Cavalry', and
'In Defence of King &
Country', c1830,
8¾in (22cm) high.
£340–400 / €490–580
$650–770 ➶ SWO

A wooden truncheon, with painted
decoration, c1850, 18in (45.5cm) long.
£65–75 / €95–105
$125–145 ⊞ MDL

A brass cavalry trumpet, 17th Lancers, 4th trumpet, inscribed 'Carried by Trumpeter M. Lanfried 25th October 1854', with mouthpiece, some damage, 19in (48.5cm) long.
£1,900–2,250 / €2,750–3,250
$3,650–4,300 ➶ WAL
Memorabilia associated with famous battles carries a premium. Lanfried was one of the 17th Lancers who rode in the ill-fated Charge of the Light Brigade which took place on 25 October 1854, during the Battle of Balaclava in the Crimean War. A famous symbol of reckless bravery, the charge was celebrated in Tennyson's eponymous poem and, in the 20th century, inspired two films and even an Iron Maiden song. Charge of the Light Brigade material is very sought after, hence the value of this item, which is not the most famous trumpet from the battle. The copper bugle which actually sounded the charge was blown by trumpeter Billy Britain, who died from his wounds despite being nursed by Florence Nightingale. Billy's bugle was sold by Sotheby's in 1964 and purchased by actor Laurence Harvey, who later presented it to the Queen's Royal Lancers Museum, where it remains today.

▶ A British Cavalry painted brass marching compass, with a leather case, c1890, 2¼in (5.5cm) diam.
£125–140
€180–200
$240–270
⊞ FOF

A Securem leather, brass and rubber tent pole strap, c1905, 5in (12.5cm) long.
£100–110 / €145–160
$190–210 ⊞ ChC
The Securem tent pole strap was designed and patented to provide hanging hooks around a tent pole. It is illustrated in the Army & Navy catalogue of 1907 with the description 'This strap, lined with corrugated rubber, adheres closely to the pole, and so does not slip when articles are hung on it, the hooks being short and strong do not bend. Besides serving military purposes, it will be found useful in bathing and cricket tents.'

◀ A ceramic plate, with transfer-printed decoration, French, 1914, 8in (20.5cm) diam.
£150–170
€220–250
$290–330
⊞ BRT

◀ A leather and brass barrack strap, with six hooks, early 20thC, 30in (76cm) long.
£60–70 / €85–100
$115–135 ⊞ ChC

A George Proctor & Co ceramic cup and saucer, inscribed 'Hands Off', 1914, cup 3in (7.5cm) high.
£65–75 / €95–105
$125–145 ⊞ BtoB

▶ A hand-embroidered lace-trimmed Royal Engineers sweetheart gift, 1914–18, 12in (30.5cm) square.
£15–20 / €22–29
$29–38 ⊞ Tus

▶ A spongeware ceramic bowl, inscribed 'It's a Long Way to Tipperary', 1914–18, 6in (15cm) diam.
£90–100 / €130–145
$170–190 ⊞ OD

A hand-embroidered memorial picture, entitled 'Victory for the Allies', with a photograph, 1914–18, 21 x 24in (53.5 x 61cm).
£100–120 / €145–170
$195–230 ⊞ SER

A brass Princess Mary tin, containing a bullet pencil and card from Princess Mary, photograph of Princess Mary missing, 1915, 5in (12.5cm) wide.
£50–60 / €75–85
$100–115 ⊞ Tus
In the autumn of 1914, Princess Mary, the only daughter of King George V and Queen Mary, conceived the idea of sending a Christmas gift to all service personnel away from home. She helped form an appeal committee which raised funds for the project. The gift was a brass box containing cigarettes, a pipe and tobacco, a lighter and a card from Princess Mary. The lid of the box was embossed with her profile. The gift was later modified to contain candy for nurses, non-smokers and the Indian troops whose religion forbade smoking.

A nickel hunter-cased British Army compass, by C. Haseler & Son, dated 1916, 1¾in (4.5cm) diam.
£75–85 / €110–125
$145–165 ⊞ FOF

A poster, by Ferdinand Warren, 'Buy War Bonds', printed by the US Government Printing Office, American, 1942, 45 x 32½in (114.5 x 82.5cm).
£80–90 / $115–130
$155–175 ⚒ DW

A Free French poster, declaring General de Gaulle's leadership of French West Africa and taking command of the sea, land and air forces, 1939–44, glazed.
£115–135 / €165–195
$220–260 ⚒ DW

◄ **A cast-aluminium Air Raid Warden sign,** 1939–44, 11in (28cm) wide.
£20–25 / €30–35
$40–50 ⊞ FST

A pair of submariner binoculars, with rubber protectors, 1939–44.
£1,000–1,200
€1,450–1,750
$1,950–2,300 ⚒ SPF

► **Sir Winston Churchill,** *The Eve of Action,* published by W. & G. Baird Ltd, first edition, 1944, 4°, a report of Churchill's speech delivered 22 February 1944 to the House of Commons.
£580–690
€840–1,000
$1,100–1,300 ⚒ BBA

A list of the 1939–45 British Commonwealth and Empire war dead at the Kiel War Cemetery, a printed pamphlet, 1957, 10 x 8in (25.5 x 20.5cm).
£10–15 / €15–22
$19–28 ⊞ J&S

Armour & Uniform

A metal gauntlet,
German, 1530–40.
£570–680 / €830–990
$1,100–1,300 ↗ WEBB

A metal gorget, northern
European, 1650–1700,
14in (35.5cm) long.
£1,200–1,400
€1,700–2,000
$2,300–2,700 ↗ S(O)

**A Victorian National Fire
Brigades Association
brass helmet,**
10¼in (26cm) high.
£270–320 / €390–460
$520–610 ↗ DN(BR)

**A Victorian 2nd Life
Guards officer's gilt,
enamel, silver, horse
hair and silver-plate
helmet,** some repair.
£620–740 / €900–1,050
$1,200–1,400 ↗ WAL

◀ **A leather and brass
military headdress,**
German/Prussian, c1880,
10½in (26.5cm) high.
£310–370 / €450–540
$600–710 ↗ DuM

**A Victorian Royal
Artillery officer's full
dress pouch,** embroidered
with a gilt cannon
and mounts.
£160–190 / €230–270
$310–360 ↗ WAL

▶ **A Sherwood Rangers
Yeomanry sealskin full
dress busby,** decorated
with gold cord and thread
lace, with brass chin chain
and egret and vulture
feather plume, 1890–1914,
with a cloth drawstring
carrying bag and tin.
£350–420 / €510–610
$670–810 ↗ DNW

A 15thC-style kettle hat, German, c1900, 9in (23cm) high.
£1,200–1,400 / €1,700–2,000
$2,300–2,700 ↗ S(O)

A fireman captain's tin and aluminium helmet, American, c1900, 14in (35.5cm) wide.
£80–95 / €115–135
$150–180 ⚒ DuM

An Alexandra, Princess of Wales's Own Volunteer Battalions cloth and leather forage cap, Yorkshire Regiment, with white metal Royal Arms buttons and cap badge, retailed by Hobson & Sons, 1904.
£80–90 / €115–130
$155–175 ⚒ DNW

A piper's silver arm plate presentation shield, decorated with a set of bagpipes and inscribed 'Comunn. Phiobairean. Lunnain', with presentation inscription to the reverse, slight damage, Scottish, dated January 1910, 4½in (11.5cm) wide.
£60–70 / €85–100
$115–135 ⚒ WAL

A Canadian Royal Air Force Flight Officer's uniform, with brass RAF crown and buttons, labelled 'D. J. Lewis', together with two photographs of Lewis and letters dated 1966–70 describing the uniform and Lewis's military service.
£1,650–1,950 / €2,400–2,850
$3,150–3,750 ⚒ JDJ

> **Cross Reference**
> Aeronautica see pages 26–31

A West Yorkshire Regiment officer's cloth helmet, with a gilt-metal plate, chin chain and spike, together with a hinged metal box with a brass plate inscribed 'Major J.B.G. Tottie, 4th Bn. West Yorkshire Regiment', 1914–18, box 9¾in (25cm) high.
£400–480 / €580–700
$770–920 ⚒ AH

A Military Veteran's uniform blouse, Austrian, c1918.
£110–130 / €160–190
$210–250 ⚒ DORO

A Servant of the City of Vienna's cloth uniform jacket, lowest rank, the front with two rows of buttons and sleeve buttons, Austrian, c1918.
£125–140 / €180–200
$240–270 ⚒ DORO

A silver-plated plaid brooch, c1950, 4½in (11.5cm) wide.
£90–100 / €130–145
$170–190 ⊞ Q&C

A set of ten Royal Engineers brass buttons, 1950s, largest 1in (2.5cm) diam.
£4–8 / €6–12
$8–15 ⊞ Tus

Edged Weapons

A sabre, with a wood and silver wire hilt, steel guard, steel blade with decoration and presentation inscription, steel scabbard, slight damage, 18thC, 27in (68.5cm) long.
£420–500 / €610–730
$810–960 ⚔ **F&C**

A Bavarian cavalry officer's sword, with an iron semi-basket guard and etched blade, c1826, blade 36in (91.5cm) long.
£250–280 / €360–410
$480–540 ⊞ **FAC**

An iron semi-bowl NCO's sword, with a sharkskin grip, twisted wire missing, Swiss, c1842, blade 32½in (82.5cm) long.
£200–230 / €290–330
$400–450 ⊞ **FAC**

A replica bowie knife, the chequered horn grip with a vacant silver escutcheon, the pommel decorated with horses' heads in relief, the silver-mounted leather sheath with traces of gilt tooling, stamped marks, American, c1920, blade 10½in (26.5cm) long.
£430–510 / €620–740
$830–980 ⚔ **WAL**

A trench knife, German, c1915, 7in (18cm) long.
£70–80 / €100–115
$135–155 ⊞ **FST**

The distinctively-shaped bowie knife is part of US history and is named after Colonel Jim Bowie (1796–1836). The original knife was made for Bowie by Arkansas blacksmith James Black in December 1830, following a design by Bowie's brother Rezin. Bowie was returning to Texas with his knife when he was attacked by three hired assassins. He killed them all with his new weapon. One was nearly decapitated, the second disembowelled, the third had his skull split open, and the fame of the Bowie knife spread far and wide. Bowie was killed at the Battle of the Alamo five years later, alongside Davy Crockett. Though Bowie's original knife disappeared, Black established a successful business selling bowie knives from his Arkansas shop and added several modifications to the first design. The traditional bowie is a sheath knife with a 12in (30.5cm) blade, 2in (5cm) wide and ¼in (1cm) thick. A soft metal inlay on the back of the blade was designed to catch an opponent's blade, the curved clip point was sharpened to provide backslash ability and a brass quillon protected the hand. Many variations of this knife have been produced and today 'bowie knife' is almost a generic term for any large sheath knife. Collecting bowie knives is a popular hobby in the USA and there are a number of bowie knife shows. Modern bladesmiths have developed their own new designs and techniques as well as recreating the work of the historic knife-makers. Related bodies include the American Bladesmith Society, established to promote the craft and educate the collector.

Firearms

◄ **A powder horn,** American, early 19thC, 15in (38cm) long.
£100–120
€145–175
$200–240
⚒ DuM

A percussion pistol, the mahogany stock with brass fittings, with an engraved crown and 'W.R.', early 19thC, 8¾in (22cm) long.
£290–340 / €420–490
$560–650 ⚒ JBe

◄ **A brass-mounted flintlock pistol,** decorated with figures, animals and floral motifs, western European, 19thC, barrel 9½in (24cm) long.
£520–620 / €750–900
$1,000–1,200 ⚒ G(L)

◄ **A percussion cap pistol,** with brass-scrolled walnut stock and turned barrel, 19thC, 7in (18cm) long.
£220–260
€320–380
$420–500 ⚒ G(L)

An embossed copper powder flask, with entwined ropework decoration, 1860s, 8in (20.5cm) high.
£40–45 / €60–70
$75–85 ⚒ WAL

A bronze shot mould, with spaces for six moulds, late 19thC, 19¼in (49cm) long.
£80–90 / €115–130
$155–175 ⚒ SWO

▶ **A .177 Webley Mark I air pistol,** early 20thC, with box, cleaning brush, spare wallets and .22 Special Pellets.
£160–190
€230–270
$310–360
⚒ WAL

A .22 Webley Service Mark II air rifle, with a walnut stock, rearsight missing, with an adapted webbing case, dated 1943, with an original Webley pellet tin and targets.
£250–300 / €360–430
$480–580 ⚒ WAL

Money Boxes

A Derbyshire salt-glazed money box, c1850, 7in (18cm) high.
£80–90 / €115–130
$155–175 ⊞ IW

▶ **A cast-iron mechanical money box,** in the form of a clown with a dog jumping through a hoop, trap missing, American, c1880, 8in (20.5cm) high.
£360–400 / €520–580
$690–770 ⊞ HAL

A cast-iron mechanical money box, by J. & E. Stevens Co, the building opening to reveal a teller, damaged, American, 1870–80, 4½in (11.5cm) wide.
£490–570 / €710–830
$940–1,100 ↗ SK(B)

◀ **A boxwood money box,** in the form of a rook chess piece, c1880, 3¼in (8.5cm) high.
£50–60 / €75–85
$100–115 ↗ BBA

A mahogany money box, in the form of a bank, late 19thC, 12in (30.5cm) high.
£220–260 / €320–380
$420–500 ↗ BWL

◀ **A cast-iron mechanical money box,** in the form of a lighthouse, c1890, 10½in (26.5cm) high.
£400–470 / €580–680
$760–910 ↗ SK(B)

Money Boxes

Known as money banks in the USA, money boxes have been produced since ancient times when coins were hidden in sealed pottery jars which could be buried in the gound. Ceramics remained a favourite material, but money boxes were also produced from wood and metal. The 19th century saw the development of the cast-iron money box. This was a favourite material in the USA where mechanical and still (non-animated) banks of great ingenuity were made from the 1870s to the 1920s. Leading manufacturers included J. & E. Stevens Co of Cromwell, Connecticut and the Shepard Hardware Co. The design of the first mechanical bank is credited to John Hall of Watertown, Massachusetts. It was called Hall's Excelsior and was manufactured in large numbers by J. & E. Stevens, and is still quite easy to find today. In the UK, cast-iron money banks were made by John Harper & Co, with bank buildings being a popular design for still banks.

A cast-iron mechanical money box, by J. & E. Stevens Co, in the form of a man aiming his rifle at an apple on a boy's head, marked 'patented June 23 1896', American, 6½in (16.5cm) high.
£400–470 / €580–680
$760–910 ⚒ SK(B)

A cast-iron money box, modelled with a beehive and bears, 19thC, 7in (18cm) high.
£90–100 / €130–145
$170–190 ⊞ HAL

A tinplate money box, in the form of a building, Austrian, late 19thC, 6in (15cm) high.
£50–60 / €75–85
$100–115 ⊞ HAL

A Halifax pottery money box, inscribed 'Harold Dean', c1900, 5in (12.5cm) high.
£135–150 / €195–220
$260–290 ⊞ IW

A Yorkshire pottery glazed money box, c1900, 5in (12.5cm) high.
£70–80 / €100–115
$135–155 ⊞ IW

An A1 Biscuit Company biscuit tin money box, in the form of a Victorian post box, late 19thC, 6in (15cm) high.
£30–35 / €45–50
$55–65 ⊞ HAL

A Bristol glazed stoneware money box, inscribed 'Alice Pearce', late 19thC, 6in (15cm) high.
£50–60 / €75–85
$100–115 ⊞ IW

◀ A cast-iron mechanical money box, by J. & E. Stevens Co, in the form of an eagle and eaglets, marked 1883, American, c1900, 5¼in (13.5cm) high.
£270–320
€390–460
$520–610
⚒ SK(B)

A cast-iron mechanical money box, 1910, 7in (18cm) high.
£100–120 / €145–175
$195–230 ⊞ JUN

◀ A Shenandoah pottery money box, inscribed 'Andrew Bell Thompson', and dated 1910, 7½in (19cm) high.
£310–370 / €450–540
$600–710 ⚒ DuM

▶ A cast-iron money box, commemorating the coronation of George V, 1911, 7in (18cm) high.
£70–80 / €100–115
$135–155 ⊞ HAL

◀ **A cast-iron mechanical money box,** by John Harper & Co, inscribed 'Dinah', 1911–25, 6½in (16.5cm) high.
£260–300
€370–440
$500–580
⚒ SK(B)

A tin and cardboard money box, German, c1930, 9in (23cm) high.
£2–6 / €3–9
$4–11 ⊞ HAL

A tinplate money box, 'Poor Weary Willie', 1930s, 5in (12.5cm) high.
£70–80 / €100–115
$135–155 ⊞ HAL

A Yorkshire Penny Bank chrome money box, 1930s, 3½in (9cm) diam, with box.
£30–35 / €45–50
$55–65 ⊞ HAL

A biscuit tin money box, in the form of a Georgian post box, 1930s, 8in (20.5cm) high.
£60–70 / €85–100
$115–135 ⊞ HAL

A silver-plated money box, in the form of a champagne bottle in a cooler, German, 1930s, 5in (12.5cm) high.
£50–60 / €75–85
$100–115 ⊞ HAL

◀ **A Walt Disney tinplate money box,** in the form of a post box, depicting Mickey, Minnie and baby Mouse, 1935, 6in (15cm) high.
£80–90 / €115–130
$155–175 ⊞ HUX

A tinplate money box, by Chad Valley, in the form of a telephone box, 1950s, 6in (15cm) high.
£45–50 / €65–75
$85–95 ⊞ JUN

An Airways tin money box, by Chad Valley, early 1960s, 4½in (11.5cm) high.
£6–10 / €9–15
$12–19 ⊞ RTT

▶ **A die-cast Spinaround 'Plan-It' money box,** in the form of the solar system, c1962, 8½in (21.5cm) diam.
£115–135 / €165–195
$220–260 ⚒ Bert

Musical Instruments

A Regency carved giltwood harp, by Sebastian Erard, in need of restoration, 67in (170cm) high.
£310–370 / €450–540
$600–710 ⚒ BWL

A lap organ, by Busson, c1880, 19in (48.5cm) wide, with case.
£100–120 / €145–175
$195–230 ⚒ GH

▶ **A violin,** labelled 'Carrodus Violin No. 191 Anno 1889', with two bows and a case, French, length of back 14¼in (36cm).
£320–380 / €460–550
$610–730 ⚒ GH

A cello, labelled 'Samuel Gilkes London 18..', 19thC, length of back 29¼in (74.5cm), with case.
£620–740 / €900–1,050
$1,200–1,400 ⚒ GH

A violin, c1890, length of back 14¼in (36cm).
£230–270 / €330–390
$440–520 ⚒ GH

A cello, French, late 19thC, length of back 27¼in (69cm).
£400–480 / €580–700
$770–920 ⚒ GH

A rosewood guitar, with mother-of-pearl inlay, 19thC, 39in (99cm) long, with case.
£400–480 / €580–700
$770–920 ⚒ GH

A violin, labelled 'Secchi Luthier 19 Bvld Beaumarchais, Paris, Année 1896', French, length of back 14¼in (36cm).
£580– 690 / €840–1,000
$1,100–1,300 ⚒ GH

▶ **A pierced ebony concertina,** by Lachenal & Co, c1900, 7in (18cm) diam, with case.
£750–900 / €1,100–1,300
$1,450–1,750 ⚒ GH

A nickel-mounted violin bow, stamped 'Dodd', the ebony frog inlaid with nickel rings enclosing pearl eyes, the ebony adjuster with two silver bands, frog replaced, c1900, 29in (73.5cm) long.
£100–120 / €145–175
$195–230 ⚒ GH

A mahogany concertina,
by Wheatstone & Co, No.
24339, with brass reeds
and bone buttons, 1908,
7in (18cm) diam, with case.
£120–140 / €175–200
$230–270 ⚒ GH

◀ **A silver-plated 200 tenor saxophone,** by Beuscher
Elkhart Ind, No. 168711, 1914, 32in (81.5cm) high.
£65–75 / €95–105
$125–145 ⚒ GH

A Neopolitan mandolin, by Walter Taylor, Liverpool, with
a fluted back, labelled, early 20thC, 24in (61cm) long.
£110–130 / €160–190
$210–250 ⚒ GH

▶ **An ebony
concertina,**
damaged,
Continental,
c1920, 9in
(23cm) diam.
£120–140
€175–200
$230–270
⚒ GH

A ukulele, decorated with chevron banding and inlay,
1930s, 25in (63.5cm) long, with case.
£260–310 / €380–450
$500–600 ⚒ GH

A Starline trumpet, by
Rudall Carte & Co, 1940s,
19in (48.5cm) long,
with case.
£35–40 / €50–60
$65–75 ⚒ GH

A satinwood banjolele,
decorated with chevron
inlay, branded 'British
Make', c1940, 23in
(58.5cm) long, with case.
£100–120 / €145–175
$190–230 ⚒ GH

**A silver-plated baritone
prototype horn,** by F.
Besson, 1940s, 27in
(68.5cm) long, with case.
£60–70 / €85–100
$115–135 ⚒ GH

**A Gretsch Synchromatic
acoustic guitar,** 1950s.
£1,350–1,500
€1,950–2,200
$2,600–2,900 ⊞ VRG

◀ **A tinplate toy flute,**
1950s, 13in (33cm) long.
£10–15 / €15–22
$19–28 ⊞ JUN

◄ **William C. Retford,** *Bows and Bow Makers,* published by *The Strad* magazine, first edition, 1964, 10 x 7in (25.5 x 18cm), signed.
£45–50 / €65–75
$85–95 ⚒ **GH**

A Hofner Senator semi-acoustic guitar, No. 1256, with Gibson pickup, c1960, 41in (104cm) long, with a soft case.
£180–210 / €260–300
$350–400 ⚒ **GH**

A Gibson LG1 acoustic guitar, 1962.
£1,100–1,300
€1,600–1,900
$2,100–2,500 ⊞ **VRG**

► **A Hofner President acoustic guitar,** the neck inlaid with rosewood and mother-of-pearl, with pickup, early 1960s.
£340–400 / €490–580
$650–770 ⚒ **BWL**

A Howard Roberts Epiphone acoustic guitar, 1964.
£1,300–1,500
€1,900–2,200
$2,500–2,900 ⊞ **VRG**

A Martin 0-18 acoustic guitar, 1965.
£2,000–2,350
€2,900–3,400
$3,850–4,500 ⊞ **VRG**

A Gibson FJN acoustic guitar, 1965.
£1,200–1,400
€1,750–2,050
$2,300–2,700 ⊞ **VRG**

A Gibson SG Junior electric bass guitar, 1966.
£1,550–1,750
€2,250–2,550
$3,000–3,350 ⊞ **VRG**

A Fender Jaguar electric guitar, 1967.
£2,000–2,250
€2,900–3,250
$3,850–4,300 ⊞ **VRG**

A Gibson Hummingbird
acoustic guitar, 1967.
£2,250–2,500
€3,250–3,650
$4,300–4,800 ⊞ VRG

A Guild SF4 electric
guitar, 1967.
£1,300–1,500
€1,900–2,200
$2,500–2,900 ⊞ VRG

A Gretsch Tennessee
electric guitar, 1968.
£1,800–2,000
€2,600–2,900
$3,450–3,850 ⊞ VRG

A Gibson ES-330 electric
bass guitar, 1968.
£2,500–2,800
€3,650–4,050
$4,800–5,400 ⊞ VRG

A Hofner President
semi-acoustic
guitar, 1960s.
£360–430 / €520–620
$690–830 ⋏ GH

A Hofner Violin electric
guitar, 1960s.
£1,300–1,500
€1,900–2,200
$2,500–2,900 ⊞ VRG

A Hohner Professional
L90 electric guitar, 1970.
£160–190 / €230–270
$310–360 ⋏ GH

A Gibson Thunderbird
bass guitar, 1977.
£2,800–3,200
€4,050–4,650
$5,400–6,100 ⊞ VRG

◀ **A Hohner melodeon,** with a
pokerwork floral case, c1990,
11in (28cm) wide, with case.
£90–100 / €130–145
$170–180 ⋏ GH

▶ **A brass pocket cornet,** by Bessons
& Co, 1990s, 8in (20.5cm) wide.
£40–45 / €60–70
$75–85 ⋏ GH

Natural History

A peronopsis interstrictus multiblock, from Utah, American, Cambrian period, 520 million years old, 5in (12.5cm) wide.
£20–25 / €30–35
$40–50 ⊞ FOSS

An araucaria pine cone, Jurassic period, 135 million years old, 3½in (9cm) high.
£950–1,100 / €1,400–1,600
$1,800–2,100 ⚒ S(S)

An antrimpos shrimp plaque, Solnhofen Formation, German, Jurassic period, 135 million years old, 13in (33cm) wide.
£950–1,100 / €1,400–1,600
$1,800–2,100 ⚒ S(S)

A dragonfly plaque, Solnhofen Formation, German, Jurassic period, 135 million years old, 14½in (37cm) wide.
£840–1,000 / €1,200–1,450
$1,600–1,900 ⚒ S(S)

An iguanodon dorsal vertebra, from the Isle of Wight, 120 million years old, 20in (51cm) wide.
£4,000–4,500 / €5,800–6,500
$7,700–8,600 ⊞ FOSS

A dromaesaur deinonychus tooth, from Montana, American, Cretaceous period, 100 million years old, 1in (2.5cm) long.
£90–100 / €130–145
$170–180 ⊞ FOSS

A saurornitholestes tooth, Cretaceous period, 100 million years old, ½in (1.5cm) long.
£80–90 / €115–130
$155–175 ⊞ FOSS

An ankylosaur edmontonia rugosidens tooth, from Montana, American, Cretaceous period, 100 million years old, ½in (1.5cm) long.
£95–110 / €140–160
$180–210 ⊞ FOSS

A pair of sauropod eggs, possibly therizinosaurus cheloniformis, Chinese, 64 million years old, 7in (18cm) diam.
£310–350 / €450–510
$600–670 ⊞ Cas

A diplocynodon hantoniensis alligator jaw, from the Isle of Wight, Oligocene period, 40 million years old, 3in (7.5cm) long.
£50–55 / €70–80
$95–105 ⊞ FOSS

An oreodont skull, from Wyoming, American, Oligocene period, 40 million years old, 5in (12.5cm) wide.
£135–150 / €195–220
$260–290 ⊞ FOSS

A pectin scallop shell plaque, from Marseille, French, Miocene/Oligocene period, 25 million years old, 18in (45.5cm) wide.
£960–1,150 / €1,400–1,600
$1,850–2,200 ⚲ S(S)

► **A bison horn,** found in the UK, 20 thousand years old, 15in (38cm) long.
£110–125
€160–180
$210–240
⊞ FOSS

◄ **A hyena femur,** from Abingdon, Pleistocene period, 20 thousand years old, 9in (23cm) long.
£45–50 / €65–75
$85–95 ⊞ FOSS

◄ **A piece of juvenile amber,** from Madagascar, enclosing multiple insects, 20 thousand years old, 4in (10cm) wide.
£25–30 / €40–45
$50–55 ⊞ FOSS

A quern stone, Neolithic Period, 2000 BC, 6in (15cm) wide.
£30–35 / €45–50
$55–65 ⊞ HO
Quern stones were used for grinding grain to make flour, as well as for crushing seeds, spices and other similar materials. They have been manufactured from a wide range of stones including sandstone, quartzite and limestone, although igneous rocks such as basalt were the most efficient type of stone – querns were replaced by millstones.

Eleazar Albin, *A Natural History of Spiders and Other Curious Insects,* 1736, first edition, 4°, with 52 hand-coloured plates, slight damage.
£470–560 / €680–810
$900–1,050 ⚲ BBA

Rev Francis Orpen Morris, *A Natural History of British Moths,* 1872, 8°, 4 vols, with 132 hand-coloured plates, slight damage.
£400–480 / €580–700
$770–920 ⚲ BBA

Cross Reference
Books see pages 53–66

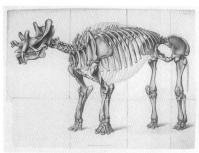

Othniel Charles Marsh, *Dinocerata: A Monograph of an Extinct Order of Gigantic Mammals,* Washington, 56 lithographed plates, slight damage, 1886, 4°.
£190–220 / €280–320
$360–420 ⚲ BBA

A set of six silver and glass menu holders, by William Comyns, enclosing specimen butterflies, three with a Patent Butterfly tablet beneath by Edwards & Sons, London 1906, 2½in (6.5cm) wide, in a fitted case.
£1,650–1,950 / €2,400–2,850
$3,150–3,750 ⚲ DN

Newspapers & Magazines

The *Salisbury Journal*, 1771,
18 x 12in (45.5 x 30.5cm).
£20–25 / €30–35
$40–50 ⊞ COB

The Times, 1822,
24 x 16in (61 x 40.5cm).
£15–20 / €22–29
$29–38 ⊞ J&S

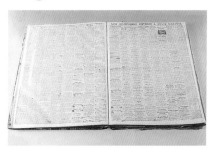

New Hampshire's Patriot & State Gazette,
a bound run from 1849 to 1853, slight
damage, American, 26 x 22in (66 x 56cm).
£130–155 / €190–220
$250–300 ⋏ JAA

Le Moniteur De La Mode
magazine, French, 1897,
16 x 12in (40.5 x 30.5cm).
£6–10 / €9–15
$12–19 ⊞ J&S

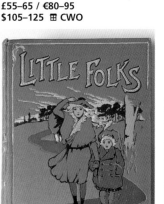

The *Illustrated London News*, 'Slaves for
Sale: A Scene in New Orleans', illustration,
1861, 6½ x 8in (16.5 x 20.5cm).
£55–65 / €80–95
$105–125 ⊞ CWO

The *Illustrated Sporting
and Dramatic News*, 1885,
17 x 12in (43 x 30.5cm).
£10–15 / €15–22
$19–28 ⊞ J&S

◀ *Little Folks* **magazine,** leather
bound, published by Cassell & Co,
1899, 10 x 8in (25.5 x 20.5cm).
£55–65 / €80–95
$105–125 ⊞ BIB

◀ *The Morning Post*, reporting
the departing of Queen Victoria's
body from the Isle of Wight, 1901,
26 x 21in (66 x 53.5cm).
£6–10 / €9–15
$12–19 ⊞ J&S

The *Illustrated London News*,
1907, 16 x 12in (40.5 x 30.5cm).
£6–10 / €9–15
$12–19 ⊞ J&S

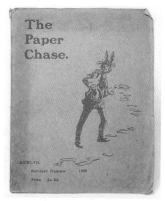

The Paper Chase, two issues, illustrated by Elizabeth Stanhope Forbes and others, printed by the Newlyn Press, 2°,1908–09.
£450–540 / €650–780
$860–1,050 ⚲ LAY

Punch magazine, November 1912, 11 x 9in (28 x 23cm).
£1–5 / €2–7
$3–9 ⊞ HOM

The **Daily Mirror,** October 1914, 12 x 9in (28 x 23cm).
£2–6 / €3–9
$4–11 ⊞ J&S

Boy's Own Paper, 1919, 11¼ x 8½in (28.5 x 21.5cm).
£1–5 / €2–7
$3–9 ⊞ RTT

Le Petit Echo de la Mode **magazine,** French, 1922, 16 x 12in (40.5 x 30.5cm).
£1–5 / €2–7
$3–9 ⊞ J&S

The *Union Jack* **magazine,** No. 451, Against Fearful Odds, 1920s, 11 x 7in (28 x 18cm).
£10–15 / €15–22
$19–28 ⊞ ADD

Paris Mode **magazine,** French, 1933, 13 x 10in (33 x 25.5cm).
£6–10 / €9–15
$12–19 ⊞ J&S

Paris **magazine,** 1938, 10¾ x 7¼in (27.5 x 18.5cm).
£3–7 / €4–10
$6–13 ⊞ RTT

Radio Times **magazine,** World Cup edition, 1966, 12 x 10in (30.5 x 25.5cm).
£15–20 / €22–29
$29–38 ⊞ J&S

Paper Money

A Christchurch & Wimborne Bank £1 note, 1825.
£30–35 / €45–50
$55–65 ⊞ NAR

A Saffron Walden Bank £1 note, No. 11809, depicting Brittania, for Jas Searle Jnr.
£280–330 / €410–480
$540–630 ⚹ SWO

A Tweed Bank £5 note, 1840.
£90–100 / €130–145
$170–190 ⊞ NAR

A United States of America $1 and $5 note, 1862 and 1863.
£310–370 / €450–540
$600–720 ⚹ JAA

An Essex Bank £5 note, No. 73108, depicting wheat sheaves, for Sparrow Tuffnell & Co, 1891.
£450–540 / €650–780
$860–1,000 ⚹ SWO

A Cuba Treasury 100 peso note, 1891.
£270–300 / €390–440
$520–580 ⊞ NAR

▶ **A Wisbech & Lincolnshire Bank, £10 note**, 1892.
£45–50 / €65–75
$85–95 ⊞ NAR

A Cape of Good Hope Bank £10 note, 1900.
£590–650 / €850–950
$1,100–1,250
⊞ NAR

▶ **A siege of O'okiep £5 note**, 1902.
£2,250–2,500
€3,250–3,600
$4,300–4,800
⊞ NAR

A National Bank of Scotland
£1 note, 1920.
£90–100 / €130–145
$170–180 ⊞ NAR

A Government of India 10
rupees note, 1920.
£60–70 / €85–100
$115–135 ⊞ NAR

A Reichsbank 1 million
marks note, 1923.
£1–5 / €2–7
$3–9 ⊞ NAR

► A Provincial Bank of
Ireland £10 note, 1931.
£1,000–1,200
€1,450–1,750
$1,950–2,300 ⊞ NAR

◄ An Isle of
Man Barclays
Bank £1 note, No.
13436, depicting
ships and a
harbour, 1935.
£400–480
€580–700
$770–920
⚲ SWO

A Palestine Currency Board
1 palestine pound note, 1939.
£520–620 / €750–900
$1,000–1,200 ⚲ DN

◄ An Onchan
Internment
Camp 5 shilling
note, Isle of
Man, 1940.
£310–350
€450–510
$600–670 ⊞ WP

► A Commercial
Bank of Scotland
£1 note, 1940.
£25–30 / €40–45
$50–55 ⊞ NAR

◄ A Central
Bank of Ireland
10 shilling
note, 1943.
£30–35
€45–50
$55–65 ⊞ WP

A Bank of England £5 note,
signed by K. O. Peppiatt, 1945.
£80–90 / €115–130
$155–175 ⚹ AMB

A Bank of England £1 note,
signed by Beale, 1949–55.
£4–8 / €6–12
$8–15 ⊞ NAR

A British Armed Forces two
shillings and six pence voucher,
2nd series, 1950–60.
£5–9 / €8–13
$10–16 ⊞ NAR

A Belfast Banking Company
£20 note, 1965.
£60–70 / €85–100
$115–135 ⊞ WP

A British Linen Bank £1 note, 1967.
£6–10 / €9–15
$12–19 ⊞ NAR

An East African Currency Board
100 shilling note, 1960.
£310–350 / €450–510
$600–670 ⊞ NAR

▶ A Bank of
England £5
note, signed by
J. B. Page, 1971.
£6–10 / €9–15
$12–19 ⊞ NAR

▶ A Government
of Seychelles
50 rupees
note, 1973.
£220–250
€320–360
$420–480
⊞ NAR

A Central Bank of Ireland £20 note, 1976.
£70–80 / €100–115
$135–155 ⊞ NAR

A Bank of England £50 note, signed by G. Gill, 1988.
£70–80 / €100–115
$135–155 ⊞ NAR

Photography

A pair of cabinet cards, depicting the wreck of the *Gypsy* on the river Avon, mid-19thC, 4¼ x 6½in (11 x 16.5cm).
£35–40 / €50–60
$65–75 ⊞ J&S

A Victorian *carte de visite* **photograph,** depicting a tram in the old market in Bristol, 2½ x 4in (6.5 x 10cm).
£10–15 / €15–22
$19–28 ⊞ J&S

A cabinet photograph, depicting the Countess Kleinmichel and Frau von Gortschasoff, 1874, 4½ x 7in (11.5 x 18cm).
£55–65 / €80–95
$105–125 ⊞ AEL

A half-plate ambrotype, of a woman wearing a mantilla, in a leather and wood case, signed 'Ambrotype by Chace & Hawes Cutting's Pat July 4 and 11 1854'.
£140–165 / €200–240
$270–320 ⋟ JDJ

A Victorian *carte de visite* **photograph,** depicting a horse-drawn cart, 2½ x 4in (6.5 x 10cm).
£4–8 / €6–12
$8–15 ⊞ J&S

Cartes de Visite

Cartes de visite were very popular from 1860 to 1905. These visiting card size photographs, originally developed in France, were cut and pasted onto special cards that had been printed on the back with the photographer's name and address. Such cards were widely collected in the Victorian period, when 'cartomania' became a craze. In addition to family pictures, enthusiasts could purchase pictures of celebrities (such as the Royal Family) which they would keep in albums with tooled covers and colour stencilled pages. So many *cartes de visite* were produced that they remain a very affordable way to collect vintage photography.

Cabinet prints, so-called because they could be displayed on a shelf or cabinet, were also turned out in large numbers towards the end of the 19th century. They were considerably larger than *cartes de visite* (about 4 x 5½in / 10 x 14cm) and were also mounted on card.

A late Victorian cabinet photograph, depicting two children, 6½ x 4¼in (16.5 x 11cm).
£2–6 / €3–9
$4–11 ⊞ J&S

◄ **Burton Brothers,** an albumen print of George Sound, New Zealand, c1890, 5½ x 7¾in (14 x 19.5cm).
£25–30 / €40–45
$50–55 ⋟ WEBB

A press photograph, depicting Winston Churchill presenting a prize cheque to John Alcock and Arthur Brown at the Savoy Hotel, 1919, 6 x 8in (15 x 20.5cm).
£100–120 / €145–170
$200–230 ⋟ DW
Captain John Alcock and Lieutenant Arthur Whitten Brown completed the first non-stop crossing of the Atlantic. They set off from St Johns, Newfoundland on 14 June 1919 and on 16th June they crash-landed in a bog near Clifden in County Galway, Ireland after a flight of 1,890 miles.

◀ **A photograph,** depicting Major Greig and Prince Albert in flying kit, c1920, 6 x 8in (15 x 20.5cm).
£90–100
€130–145
$170–190 ⊞ AEL

Cross Reference
Autographs see
pages 43–46

▶ **A photograph,** depicting a WWII Wren, 1940s, 8 x 6in (20.5 x 15cm).
£55–65 / €80–95
$105–125 ⊞ HOM

A photograph, depicting Lady Cambridge, 1923, 7½ x 5½in (19 x 14cm).
£90–100 / €130–145
$170–190 ⊞ AEL

Gylula Halász Brassï, a silver print of Ambroise Vollard with his cat, signed, 1932, printed later, 16 x 12in (40.5 x 30.5cm), framed and glazed.
£480–570 / €700–830
$920–1,100 ⋏ S

◀ **A photograph,** depicting motor racing at Goodwood, 1952, framed and glazed, 11¾ x 19¼in (30 x 49cm).
£50–60 / €75–85
$100–115
⋏ AMB

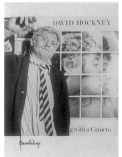

▶ **Harry Callahan,** a dye transfer print, signed, matted, 1970s, 14 x 17in (35.5 x 43cm).
£540–640
€780–920
$1,050–1,250
⋏ S

Norman Parkinson, a silver print of David Hockney, signed, 1983, framed and glazed, (50.5 x 40.5cm).
£540–640 / €780–920
$1,050–1,250 ⋏ S

Harold Chapman, 12 mounted gelatin prints of 1960s photographs, depicting Les Halles, Paris, signed, 1985, 4°.
£160–190 / €230–270
$310–360 ⋏ DW

Frames & Albums

An ivory-mounted photograph album, with carved decoration, late 19thC, 9in (23cm) wide.
£280–330 / €410–480
$540–630 ⋏ G(L)

A Tunbridge ware photograph frame, 13¼ x 10¼in (33.5 x 26cm).
£450–540 / €650–780
$860–1,000 ⋏ TEN

A Victorian carved mahogany photograph frame, 11 x 5in (28 x 12.5cm).
£50–60 / €75–85
$100–115 ⊞ AMR

Postcards

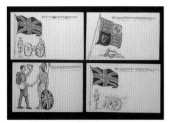

Four Boer War postcards, c1900, 4 x 6in (10 x 15cm).
£8–12 / €12–18
$16–23 each ⊞ S&D

A souvenir postcard, Helgoland, German, c1900, 4 x 6in (10 x 15cm).
£15–20 / €22–29
$29–38 ⊞ S&D

A souvenir postcard, by Florence Robinson, published by Tuck & Sons, New York, from the Views of US Cities series, No. 5068, 1900–05.
£4–8 / €6–12
$8–15 ⊞ JMC

A photographic postcard, depicting the typhoid outbreak in Lincoln, c1905.
£50–60 / €75–85
$100–115 ⚒ VS

Four postcards, by Zabier Sager, depicting flags of the world, French, 1900, 4 x 6in (10 x 15cm).
£8–12 / €12–18
$16–23 each ⊞ S&D

A silver-backed postcard, 'Daisy', 1906, 4 x 6in (10 x 15cm).
£1–5 / €2–7
$3–9 ⊞ POS

A set of four political postcards, depicting Billy Possum, American, c1908.
£45–50 / €65–75
$90–100 ⚒ JAA
President Roosevelt's association with the teddy bear had proven so popular with the voting public that when his chosen successor, William Henry Taft, was campaigning for the presidency in 1908, the Republican Party created the figure of Billy Possum to represent their candidate. The character appeared in various media, including postcards. The example bottom right entitled 'Goodbye Teddy' depicts Teddy Bear (Roosevelt) shaking hands with Billy Possum (Taft), as the latter heads off to the the White House in the distance. Taft became the 27th President of the United States (1909–13).

A Language of Vegetables postcard, inscribed 'An acquired taste. Wait! Love Will Come', 1907, 4 x 6in (10 x 15cm).
£1–5 / €2–7
$3–9 ⊞ POS

◄ **Two photographic postcards,** depicting UMC ammunition and firearms tents, American, c1908.
£130–155 / €190–220
$250–300 ⚒ JAA

A photographic postcard, depicting Lord George Sangers at Newport Pagnell, Buckinghamshire, c1908.
£15–20 / €22–29
$29–38 ✗ **DAL**

Three glamour postcards, by A. Jarach, French, 1908–10, 6 x 4in (15 x 10cm).
£15–20 / €22–29
$29–38 each ⊞ **S&D**

A postcard, inscribed 'Wishing you a most Happy New Year, c1910, 6 x 4in (15 x 10cm).
£1–5 / €2–7
$3–9 ⊞ **POS**

A silk Royal Flying Corps postcard, 1914, 3½ x 5½in (9 x 14cm).
£25–30 / €40–45
$50–55 ⊞ **J&S**

In the Edwardian period picture postcards were a favourite means of communication, and photographic cards were used as form of reportage for disasters such as shipwrecks and train crashes. Postcards were also an Edwardian collectable – there were specialist magazines and clubs, and there was a postcard album in almost every drawing room.

A Chocolat Lombart advertising postcard, c1909, 4 x 6in (10 x 15cm).
£4–8 / €6–12
$8–15 ⊞ **S&D**

A wooden revolving postcard stand, with a cast-iron base, c1910, 38in (96.5cm) high.
£220–250 / €320–360
$420–480 ⊞ **JUN**

▶ **A Tobacco advertising postcard,** inscribed 'To Wish You A Lifetime Fragrant With Joys', c1930, 3½ x 5½in (9 x 14cm).
£1–5 / €2–7
$3–9 ⊞ **POS**

A souvenir postcard, depicting the Russian Monument, Tientsin, China, German postmark, 1908, 3½ x 5½in (9 x 14cm).
£25–30 / €40–45
$50–55 ⊞ **J&S**

A Fry's Milk Chocolate advertising postcard, inscribed 'No Better Food', c1910.
£10–15 / €15–22
$19–28 ✗ **DAL**

A postcard, commemorating King George V, Queen Mary and their children, 1910, 6 x 4in (15x 10cm).
£10–15 / €15–22
$19–28 ⊞ **S&D**

A Good Luck postcard, published by Raphael Tuck & Sons, entitled 'Good Luck', c1930, 4 x 6in (10 x 15cm).
£1–5 / €2–7
$3–9 ⊞ POS

▶ **A set of 23 photo-graphic postcards,** depicting New York World Fair views, American, c1939.
£35–40 / €50–60
$65–75 ⊅ JAA

A Mabel Lucie Attwell postcard, 'Somehow whenever I walk this way, I finks – well p'raps you'll write to-day', published by Valentine, c1930.
£8–12 / €12–18
$16–23 ⊞ JMC

A Mabel Lucie Attwell postcard, 'I'm thanking my lucky old star things aint no wurser than wot they are!', c1950.
£6–10 / €9–15
$12–19 ⊞ JMC

A postcard, inscribed 'Clock for sale by a gentleman, with a richly coloured dial', 1930s, 3½ x 5½in (9 x 14cm).
£1–5 / €2–7
$3–9 ⊞ POS

◀ **A Luftwaffe photographic postcard,** of Major Harald von Hirchfield, German, 1942, 6 x 4in (15 x 10cm).
£25–30 / €40–45
$50–55 ⊞ S&D

A Donald McGill postcard, 'My purse is getting thinner, but you can see I am not', from the X L series, c1936.
£1–5 / €2–7
$3–9 ⊞ JMC
Donald McGill (1875–1962) was the king of the saucy seaside picture. His earliest cards were printed in Germany in 1905 and, in a career that spanned over 50 years, he produced more than 3,000 designs which were reproduced on countless cards. In 1939 alone, 1,000,000 McGill postcards were sold by a single shop in Blackpool. In real terms a vintage McGill card can cost little more today than it did at the time.

Posters

An American Line poster, by Hans Bohrdt, on cardboard, printed by Mühlmeister & Johler, Hamburg, c1905, 24 x 18in (61 x 45.5cm).
£220–260 / €330–390 $420–500 ↗ VSP

A recruitment poster, by W. A. Fry, 'There's Room for You Enlist To-Day', No. 122, printed by Wm Strain & Sons, 1914–18, 30 x 20in (76 x 51cm).
£120–140 / €175–200 $230–270 ↗ ONS

A recruitment poster, 'Who's Absent? is it you?', No. 125, printed by Andrew Read Co, 1914–18, 30 x 20in (76 x 51cm).
£120–140 / €175–200 $230–270 ↗ ONS

A recruitment poster, by Bernard Partridge, 'Take up the Sword of Justice', No. 111, printed by David Allen & Sons, 1915, 30 x 20in (76 x 51cm).
£50–60 / €75–85 $200–115 ↗ ONS

◀ **A Barnum & Bailey Circus poster,** on canvas, 1916, 31 x 39in (78.5 x 99cm).
£930–1,100 €1,350–1,600 $1,800–2,150 ↗ DuM

▶ **A White Star poster,** by T. J. Bond, 'Easter Cruise', printed by David Allen & Sons, 1931, 40 x 25in (101.5 x 63.5cm).
£125–140 / €180–210 $240–270 ↗ VSP

A Turmac cigarettes poster, c1920, 34¾ x 23¾in (88.5 x 60.5cm).
£180–210 / €260–310 $350–400 ↗ VSP

A promotional poster, by Alfons Walde, 'Come For Winter Sports to Austria', on japan paper, printed by Waldheim Eberle, c1930, 37½ x 25½in (95.5 x 65cm).
£620–720 / €900–1,050 $1,200–1,400 ↗ VSP

A Ministry of Defence poster, by Noke, 'The Enemy is Always Listening', printed by James Halworth, 1940s, 23 x 18in (58.5 x 45.5cm).
£200–220 / €290–320 $380–420 ⊞ HOM

▶ **A poster,** by John Gilroy, 'Still More Bones Wanted for Salvage', 1940s, 29 x 20in (73.5 x 51cm).
£165–185 / €240–270 $320–360 ⊞ IQ

▶ **An Aer Lingus poster,** by Melai, 'Dublin', printed by Chromoworks, 1952, (101.5 x 63.5cm).
£140–170 / €210–250 $270–320 ↗ VSP

A Yasuda Fire and Marine Insurance poster, by Seiji Togo, 1953, 20 x 14¼in (51 x 36cm).
£210–250 / €310–370 $400–480 ⚹ VSP

A poster, by Kai Rich, 'Zoo', printed by Egmont H. Petersen, c1955, 33½ x 24½in (85 x 62cm).
£330–390 / €480–570 $630–750 ⚹ VSP

A promotional poster, by Dick Effers, 'Holland Festival', printed by De Jong & Co, 1958, 39¾ x 24½in (100.5 x 62cm).
£260–310 / €380–450 $500–600 ⚹ VSP

A du Maurier cigarettes poster, 1950s, 15 x 10in (38 x 25.5cm).
£50–55 / €70–80 $95–105 ⊞ Do

A promotional poster, by Ben Shahn, 'Ben Shahn January 18 to February 12', printed by Sherwood Press Inc, American, c1960, 28¼ x 22in (72 x 56cm).
£70–80 / €100–120 $135–155 ⚹ VSP

A promotional poster, by René Gruau, 'Relax...Compagnie Maritime des Chargeurs Reunis', on linen, c1960, 38½ x 24¾in (98 x 63cm).
£180–210 / €260–310 $350–400 ⚹ VSP

A Sabena poster, by G. vanden Eynde, 'The Netherlands', printed by Jean de Vos, Belgian, c1960, 39½ x 25½in (100.5 x 65cm).
£180–210 / €260–310 $350–400 ⚹ VSP

A Lincoln Center Festival poster, by Frank Stella, American, 1967, 44¾ x 29½in (113.5 x 75cm).
£180–210 / €260–310 $350–400 ⚹ VSP

A promotional poster, by Kunert, 'Haus der Kunst Montemartre', printed by Paul Fröschl Siebdruck, German, 1968, 33 x 23½in (84 x 59.5cm).
£55–65 / €80–95 $105–125 ⚹ VSP

A Louisiana Museum of Modern Art poster, 'Louisiana – Miró', by Joan Miró, printed by Arte Adrien Maeght, 1975, 26 x 19½in (66 x 49.5cm).
£165–195 / €240–280 $320–370 ⚹ VSP

A Hayward Gallery poster, by David Hockney, 'David Hockney paints the stage', 1985, 55 x 38in (139.5 x 96.5cm), framed.
£120–140 / €170–200 $230–270 ⚹ SK

A promotional poster, 'Issey Miyake Bodyworks', by Tadanori Yokoo, printed in Japan, 1985, 30¼ x 20in (77 x 51cm).
£110–130 / €165–195 $210–250 ⚹ VSP

Puppets

Pelham Puppets was founded by Bob Pelham in 1947 after his wartime service. The earliest puppets came in a brown box complete with a flying pig logo – a reference to a comment from Bob Pelham's father who, although he'd helped finance the set up of the business, said that 'Pigs will fly before Bob makes a success of it.' By 1950, however, over 40,000 puppets had been sold and Bob had started the popular Pelpup club, in order to encourage children to become involved in puppetry.

Pelham Puppets flourished in the 1950s and '60s but by the late '70s business was in decline and the original company closed down in the '90s. Boxes are a useful tool for dating puppets. A brown cardboard box was used until 1956 when it was replaced by a solid yellow cardboard box. Examples from the 1950s feature an illustration of the Mad Hatter on the side, but in 1962 the artwork changed and it became a picture of a snake charmer. A cellophane window was added to the yellow box in 1970 and this enabled the puppet to be seen from the outside.

A Pelham wood and felt string puppet, c1950, 10in (25.5cm) high.
£30–35 / €45–50
$55–65 ⊞ UD

A Pelham Torchie the Battery Boy string puppet, strings missing, c1950, 12in (30.5cm) high.
£80–90 / €115–130
$155–175 ⊞ J&J

A Chad Valley Andy Pandy glove puppet, 1950s, 9in (23cm) high.
£15–20 / €22–29
$29–38 ⊞ LAS

A Pelham Skeleton string puppet, 1950s, with box.
£30–35 / €45–50
$55–65 ⋏ LAY

Cross Reference
Toys & Games
see pages 395–414

A pair of Noddy glove puppets, Noddy and Big Ears, with moulded plastic faces, 1950s, 12in (30.5cm) high.
£35–40 / €50–60
$65–75 ⊞ BBe

A Mickey Mouse glove puppet, with a rubber head, 1950s, 9in (23cm) high.
£10–15 / €15–22
$19–28 ⊞ LAS

A Pelham Minstrel Patrick string puppet, c1960, 12in (30.5cm) high, with box.
£45–50 / €65–75
$85–95 ⊞ J&J

◄ **A Pelham Florence string puppet,** 1960s, 12in (30.5cm) high, with box.
£90–105 / €130–150
$170–195 ✂ GAZE

A Pelham Dougal string puppet, 1960s, 11in (28cm) long, with box.
£90–105 / €130–150
$170–195 ✂ GAZE

A Pelham Father Bear string puppet, 1963, 12in (30.5cm) high.
£135–150 / €195–220
$260–290 ⊞ J&J

A Pelham Schoolmaster string puppet, c1970, 12in (30.5cm) high, with box.
£60–70 / €85–100
$115–135 ⊞ UD

◄ **A Pelham Frog string puppet,** c1970, 12in (30.5cm) high.
£30–35
€45–50
$55–65 ⊞ J&J

A Pelham Jumpette string puppet, 1970s, 9in (23cm) high.
£25–30 / €40–45
$50–55 ⊞ LAS

A Pelham Dopey shop display string puppet, 1970s, 24in (61cm) high.
£270–300 / €390–440
$520–580 ⊞ ARo

Quilts

The practice of quilting fabric for warmth and protection dates from ancient times. Quilted garments have been found in Egyptian tombs and the oldest known bed quilt is a Sicilian example depicting the legend of Tristram and Isolde, sewn in the late 14th century.

Quilting was taken to the New World by European settlers and the earliest surviving American quilts date from the late 1700s. Quilting began as a necessity as fabric was hard to make, expensive to import, and therefore endlessly recycled, but by the mid-19th century it had emerged as a favourite American art form. While many quilts were certainly pieced together from the rag bag, others were made from material specially acquired for the purpose.

There are three main methods by which quilts are produced: quilting alone, piecing or patchwork in which scraps of material (usually geometric shapes) are sewn together, and appliqué quilts, in which fabric cut-outs are sewn onto a textile base. This technique was often reserved for so-called best quilts, designed for display or competition rather than daily use. From these basic techniques a huge range of designs emerged.

Patterns evolved from many sources:

they developed in specific communities such as the Amish; they reflected rural life (for example Log Cabin and Wild Goose Chase); they commemorated public events from war to politics and private anniversaries such as the birth of a baby for which a crib quilt would be made, to death which was commemorated by mourning or widow quilts. Quilts literally record the history of the countries, communities and the individuals, predominantly women, who made them. Although many quilts were produced by a single person, quilt making was also an important social occasion as women joined together in quilting bees. Initially, quilts were hand-sewn and patterns were passed on by example and word-of-mouth. The 1850s saw the development of the sewing machine and by the late 19th century printed quilt patterns led to more standardized names and designs.

Quilts are assessed by technique, pattern, age, rarity and condition. Provenance can also be a factor. Some quilts are signed and dated, others will have been passed down through families and any oral or written history should be preserved. Values reflect the craftsmanship of a quilt and its artistry, and in the best quilts these two factors are perfectly combined.

◀ **A Broderie Perse centre medallion appliqué quilt,** American, possibly South Carolina, early 19thC.
**£3,000–3,400 / €4,400–4,950
$5,900–6,500 ⊞ LFNY**

A floral chintz Whole Cloth quilt, with original glaze, American, New England, early 19thC.
**£460–520 / $670–750
$880–1,000 ⊞ LFNY**

> **Cross Reference**
> Costume & Textiles
> see pages 164–184

▶ **A Sawtooth Triangle pieced quilt,** American, c1845, 88in (223.5cm) square.
**£880–980 / €1,250–1,400
$1,700–1,900 ⊞ HERR**

A Quaker quilt, with a central star, American, Pennsylvania, c1860, 90in (228.5cm) square.
**£3000–3,300 / €4,350–4,800
$5,700–6,300 ⊞ HERR**

A Durham cotton patchwork quilt, 1860–80, 100in (254cm) square.
£540–600 / €780–870
$1,000–1,150 ⊞ JPr

A Victorian silk Log Cabin quilt, 68in (172.5cm) square.
£200–220 / €290–320
$380–420 ⋌ Ech
Log Cabin quilts became popular in the 1860s during the premiership of Abraham Lincoln, and celebrated the President's humble birth in an Illinois log cabin in 1809. There are numerous variations on the style, but the basic block is a red square surrounded by rectangular strips, symbolizing the fire in the cabin's hearth, surrounded by the logs from which the cabin was built.

A patchwork quilt, American, mid-20thC, 80 x 68in (203 x 172.5cm).
£35–40 / €50–60
$75–85 ⋌ DuM

A Chips and Whetstones pieced quilt, with satellite twelve-point stars, American, mid-Atlantic region, c1860.
£1,250–1,450 / €1,800–2,100
$2,400–2,800 ⊞ LFNY
This pattern is also known as the Mariner's Compass pattern.

A Wild Goose Chase pieced quilt, with a double sawtooth border, American, New York State, 1870–80, 102 x 104in (259 x 264cm).
£165–195 / €240–280
$320–380 ⋌ JDJ

A Patriotic Star of Bethlehem cotton quilt, with 'Pray for Peace', American, Mid-West, c1940.
£700–780 / €1,000–1,150
$1,350–1,500 ⊞ LFNY

▶ **A pieced and appliqué cotton quilt,** depicting the White House, American, 1950–60.
£1,000–1,150 / €1,450–1,650
$1,900–2,200 ⊞ LFNY

A cotton quilt, with an appliqué eagle and a strawberry border, American, probably Pennsylvania, 1870–80, 86 x 84in (218.5 x 213.5cm).
£500–560 / €730–810
$960–1,100 ⋌ S(NY)

An Amish Hired Hands-Sho-Fly pieced cotton quilt, American, Ohio, 1920–30, 72 x 43in (183 x 109cm).
£65–75 / €95–105
$125–145 ⋌ JDJ

A Dresden Plate variation patchwork quilt, American, c1930, 83 x 68in (211 x 173cm).
£90–100 / €130–145
$175–195 ⋌ DuM

Radios, TVs & Tape Recorders

Many early crystal radio sets were built at home by amateur enthusiasts, hence the expression 'ham radio'. They were typically equipped with a single pair of headphones, so could only be used by one person at a time – not that there was initially much to listen to. Britain's first sustained and regular broadcasting service was started by the Marconi station in February 1922 and consisted of just one half-hour programme every Tuesday evening. However, November that year saw the launch of the British Broadcasting Service (the first day's programming consisting of two news bulletins and a weather report) and it wasn't long before radio became central to people's lives and living rooms.

From the 1930s, wirelesses reflected the Art Deco fashions of the day, with streamlined shapes and geometric fretwork patterns. Bakelite radios are often more sought after than wooden-cased models. Brown and black are the most frequently found Bakelite colours and brighter, coloured plastics can command a premium. Valve radios can be repaired, but their cases can be much harder to restore, particularly plastic examples. Therefore, in terms of value, the cabinet tends to be more important than the contents and, if a 1930s' Bakelite radio has a damaged case, its worth can be halved. Shape is another important factor. One of the most famous radios of the 1930s was the circular Ekco radio, created specifically for Bakelite, by architect Wells Coates in 1932, and today regarded as an Art Deco design classic. Size also matters, and table-top radios are more popular than the larger radiograms that take up considerable space and are more difficult to store.

Although traditional valve radios predominated in the immediate post-war period, in 1947 three American research scientists, William Shockley, John Bardeen and Walter Brattain, working at Bell Laboratories, New Jersey invented the transistor. The 1950s saw the development of the transistor radio both in America and Japan and Sony produced the first pocket-sized transistor set (model TR55) in 1955. From the late 1950s onwards, the radio was no longer just a household item but a personal accessory that you could take with you wherever you went, paving the way for the Sony Walkman of the 1970s and the modern iPod. Early transistor radios are collectable. To identify pre-1963 models, look out for what are known as CD (Civil Defence) marks on the dial. These two triangles were designed to show the emergency frequency to tune into in case of a nuclear attack.

An A. W. Gamage crystal set radio, in a mahogany case, with BBC approved label, early 20thC, 8in (20.5cm) wide.
£380–450 / €550–650
$730–860 ↗ G(L)

▶ **A Philips 634A cabinet radio,** in a walnut-veneered case, 1932, 19in (48.5cm) high.
£360–400 / €520–580
$690–770 ⊞ OTA

◀ **An Ekco RS2 'Odeon' radio,** in a Bakelite case, 1931, 14in (35.5cm) wide.
£270–300 / €390–440
$420–580 ⊞ LFi

A Philips 930A radio, in an Arbolite case, 1932, 18in (45.5cm) high.
£400–450 / €580–650
$770–860 ⊞ OTA

◄ **A Pye Superhit radio,** in a walnut case, 1934, 18in (45.5cm) wide.
£40–45 / €60–70
$75–85 ⊞ GM

A Kolster Brandes 433 two-valve radio, 1935, 14in (35.5cm) wide.
£70–80 / €100–115
$135–155 ⊞ GM

A Monarch three-valve tabletop Superhetrodine radio, in a burr-walnut case, with a square tuning dial and stepped top, c1935, 13in (33cm) wide.
£80–90 / €115–130
$155–175 ⊞ LFi

◄ **A Ferranti 837 radio,** in a Bakelite case, 1937, 18in (45.5cm) high.
£220–250 / €320–360
$420–480 ⊞ OTA

A Philips 218B battery-operated radio, in a Bakelite case, 1939, 19in (48.5cm) wide.
£90–100 / €130–145
$170–190 ⊞ GM

► **An Ekco U49 radio,** in a Bakelite case, 1930s, 23in (58.5cm) wide.
£70–80
€100–115
$135–155
⊞ JUN

◄ **An Addison 2 radio,** in a Catalin case, knobs replaced, Canadian, 1940, 10¼in (26cm) wide.
£660–790
€960–1,150
$1,250–1,500
⚹ S(P)

► **An Ekco AD75 radio,** in a Bakelite case, 1945, 14in (35.5cm) wide.
£540–600
€780–870
$1,000–1,150
⊞ OTA

A Fada 711 radio, in a Catalin case, American, 1946, 9¾in (25cm) wide.
£420–500 / €600–720
$790–960 ⚒ S(P)

An Addison radio, in a Bakelite case, c1950.
£140–165 / €210–250
$270–320 ⚒ S(P)

A Kolster Brandes FB10 radio, in a Bakelite case, 1952, 10in (25.5cm) wide.
£90–100 / €130–145
$170–190 ⊞ OTA

An Elpreq table-top radio, 1954, 12in (30.5cm) wide.
£25–30 / €40–45
$50–55 ⊞ GM

A Bush PB22 radio, in a walnut-veneered case, 1950, 23in (58.5cm) wide.
£50–60 / €75–85
$100–115 ⊞ GM

A Cossor Melody Maker 501 radio, in a Bakelite case, 1953, 16in (40.5cm) wide.
£45–50 / €65–75
$85–95 ⊞ GM

A GEC 5445 radio, 1954, 30in (76cm) wide.
£50–60 / €75–85
$100–115 ⊞ GM

◄ **An Ekco TS88 television,** in a mahogany case, 1946, 15in (38cm) wide.
£90–105 / €130–150
$170–195 ⚒ G(L)

An Ultra T491 radio, in a Bakelite case, 1949, 16in (40.5cm) wide.
£135–150 / €195–220
$260–290 ⊞ OTA

A Philco radio, in a plastic case, American, 1950s, 10in (25.5cm) wide.
£35–40 / €50–60
$65–75 ⊞ LFi

A Murphy A192 five-valve radio, in a Bakelite case, 1953, 15in (38cm) wide.
£45–50 / €65–75
$85–95 ⊞ OIA

A Philips Stella radio, in a Bakelite case, c1958, 12in (30.5cm) wide.
£55–60 / €80–95
$105–125 ⊞ OIA

A Bush DAC 70C radio, in a Bakelite and chrome case, 1959, 13in (33cm) wide.
£35–40 / €50–60
$65–75 ⊞ GM

A Walt Disney Concept 2000 Mickey Mouse radio, in a plastic case, c1960, 8¼in (21cm) wide.
£250–290 / €360–420
$480–560 ⚲ S(P)

◄ **A Leak Variscope Stereo 20 amplifier and preamplifier,** restored, filter added, 1962, 11in (28cm) wide.
£310–350 / €450–510
$600–670 ⊞ GM

An aluminium drive-in-movie speaker, c1960, 36in (91.5cm) high.
£200–230 / €290–330
$380–440 ⊞ AME

A Bang & Olufsen Beolit 600 radio, c1970, 12in (30.5cm) wide.
£25–30 / €40–45
$50–55 ⊞ OTA

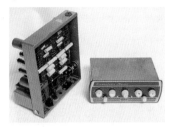

A Sinclair microvision MTV1B portable television, 1970s, 3in (7.5cm) wide, with original case.
£45–50 / €65–75
$85–95 ⊞ OTA

A Panasonic radio, 1970s, 4in (10cm) diam.
£35–40 / €50–60
$65–75 ⊞ FRD

A Weltron 2001 8-track radio cassette player, with 30 tapes, 1970s, 10½in (26.5cm) wide.
£35–40 / €50–60
$65–75 ⚲ G(L)

A Daniel Weil PVC radio bag, 1980s, 10¾in (27.5cm) high.
£80–90 / €115–130
$155–175 ⚲ WW

A Tradepower Adam and Eve plastic and chrome radio, 1980s, 7in (19cm) high.
£70–80 / €100–115
$135–155 ⊞ TWI

► **A Vanity Fair Michael Jackson plastic cassette player,** 1984, 7in (18cm) wide.
£45–50 / €65–75
$85–95 ⊞ IQ

Railwayana

The market for railwayana is small but extremely dedicated and enthusiasts are prepared to pay high prices for the right objects. Material connected with short-lived Victorian lines or stations is very sought after, such as the Sirhowy lamp shown below. The Sirhowy railway was 15 miles long and only operated for 16 years before amalgamating with the London & North Western Railway in 1876. This is possibly the only known lamp pertaining to the company, hence its high price range.

Among the most sought-after examples of railwayana are locomotive plates. These fall into three main types: worksplates recording the date and place of manufacture of the individual locomotive; numberplates and nameplates. Nameplates (a British speciality) are the most collectable of all railway-related objects. As shown here, good examples regularly attract substantial five-figure sums and record-breaking prices include just under £35,000 / €50,800 / $67,200 paid for a Duchess of Devonshire nameplate in 1999.

◀ **A station clock,** with fusee movement, the dial inscribed 'John Harrison, Liverpool', in a mahogany case, 19thC, 15¾in (40cm) diam.
£500–600 / €730–870 $960–1,150 🔨 **L&E**

A Great Western Railway cast-iron plaque, 19thC, 8in (20.5cm) wide.
£180–210 / €260–300 $350–400 🔨 **PFK**

Cross Reference
Trains see pages 409–414

A London & North Western Railway crest, on a mahogany plaque, 1890, 14in (35.5cm) wide.
£180–200 / €260–290 $340–380 ⊞ **MB**

A London & North Western Railway Sirhowy hand lamp, with a brass and ceramic burner, stamped marks, 1860–76.
£3,300–3,950 €4,800–5,700 $6,300–7,600 🔨 **SRA**

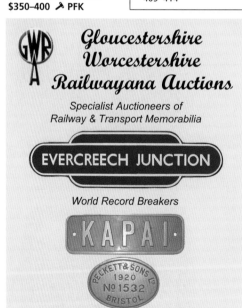

A mahogany Up Line signal box, with buttons inscribed 'Clearing Point Fouled' and 'Train at Signal', early 20thC, 12in (30.5cm) high.
£100–120 / €145–170 $195–230 🔨 **CAu**

A South Eastern & Chatham Railway poster, 'Calais – Douvres, Boulogne – Folkestone', on linen, printed by McCorquodale & Co, 1901, 40 x 25in (101.5 x 63.5cm).
£370–440 / €540–640 $710–840 🔨 **VSP**

A souvenir, commemorating the opening of the Axminster & Lyme Regis Light Railway, 1903, 21¾ x 16¾in (55.5 x 42.5cm), framed.
£50–60 / €75–85
$100–115 ↗ GTH

> **Cross Reference**
> Books see
> pages 53–66

A Great Western Railway plaque, decorated with a painted shield, early 20thC, 4½in (11.5cm) diam.
£90–105 / €130–150
$170–200 ↗ CAu

Ernest Nister, *The Train Scrap Book,* 1910, 10 x 12in (25.5 x 30.5cm).
£120–135 / €175–195
$230–260 ⊞ J&J

◄ *My Engine Book,* published by Humphrey Milford, 1920, 8 x 6in (20.5 x 15cm).
£10–15 / €15–22
$19–28 ⊞ J&J

A Southern Railway cast-brass nameplate, 'Robert Blake', first carried by the Maunsell Class E855 4–6–0, face restored, 1928, 53½in (136cm) wide.
£15,000–18,000 / €21,800–26,100
$28,800–34,000 ↗ SRA

A South African Railways brass plum bob, c1930, 5in (12.5cm) high.
£35–40 / €50–60
$65–75 ⊞ FST

A silver punch bowl, by Hamilton & Inches, engraved 'Highland Railway Company', Edinburgh 1909, 35½oz.
£400–480 / €580–700
$770–920 ↗ GIL

A London & North Eastern Railway cast-iron worksplate, '2242 Darlington Works 1918', face repainted, c1918, 9in (23cm) wide.
£550–660 / €800–960
$1,050–1,250 ↗ SRA

A London & North Eastern Railway cast-brass nameplate, 'The Oakley', carried by Hunt class D49/2 4–4–0, built at Darlington, repainted, 1934, 33½in (85cm) wide.
£21,400–25,700 / €31,000–37,000
$41,000–49,000 ≯ SRA

A North British Locomotive Company nameplate, 'London Scottish', with regimental crest, carried by 'Royal Scot', on an associated oak board, c1937, 49¾in (126.5cm) wide.
£26,000–31,000 / €38,000–45,000
$50,000–60,000 ≯ TEN

A station clock, inscribed 'Gents of Leicester', 1950s, 28in (71cm) diam.
£540–600 / €780–870
$1,000–1,150 ⊞ JUN

A London & North Eastern Railway cast-brass nameplate, 'Loch Long', carried by K4 class 2–6–0 3441, built at Darlington, c1937, 43in (109cm) wide.
£20,200–24,200 / €29,300–35,000
$39,000–46,000 ≯ SRA

A London Midland & Scottish Railway porcelain coffee pot and cover, slight damage, marked, 1937, 5½in (14cm) high.
£100–120 / €145–170
$195–230 ≯ SRA

Model Train Cut Out book, c1950, 7 x 11in (18 x 28cm).
£20–25 / €30–35
$40–50 ⊞ J&J

▶ **A British Railways and London Transport Festival of Britain souvenir map,** 1951, 17¼ x 22in (44 x 56cm), mounted, framed and glazed.
£40–45 / €60–70
$75–85 ≯ PFK

A cast-brass worksplate, 'Greenwood & Batley Limited No. 1746, Built 1941 Leeds', 9½in (24cm) wide.
£350–420 / €510–610
$670–800 ≯ SRA

A London & North Eastern Railway brass worksplate, 'No. 1944, Darlington 1944', carried by A2/1 class 4–6–2, the reverse stamped '509', 13in (33cm) wide.
£10,000–12,000 / €14,500–17,400
$19,200–23,000 ≯ SRA

A chromed-brass worksplate, 'The English Electric Co. Ltd, Vulcan Works, Newton-le-Willows, England No. 3394/D860 1963', carried by D6916, 1963, 10¾in (27.5cm) wide.
£320–380 / €460–550
$610–730 ≯ SRA

A British Railways cast-iron coach plate, 'BR, Derby, Lot No 30775, 1968', 7in (18cm) wide.
£10–15 / €15–22
$19–28 ⊞ HeA

Rock & Pop

A concert poster, 'Legendary B.B. King', c1960, 30¾ x 19¾in (78 x 50cm).
£95–110 / €140–165
$180–210 ✗ VSP

A Benny Goodman autograph, on a first day of issue American music stamp, c1964, 16in (40.5cm) high, framed.
£80–95 / €115–135
$150–180 ✗ DuM

A Vox musical instrument poster, featuring The Animals, 1965, 31 x 24in (78.5 x 61cm).
£50–60 / €75–85
$100–115 ⊞ CTO

A Ricky-Tock Club poster, advertising Graham Bond, The Gass and Geno & The Ram Jam, 1966, 30 x 20in (76 x 51cm).
£70–80 / €100–115
$135–155 ⊞ BRIG

A concert poster, by Edward D. Byrd, advertising The Rolling Stones, printed by Tea Lautrec Litho, 1969, 21¾ x 14in (55.5 x 35.5cm).
£90–105 / €130–155
$170–200 ✗ VSP

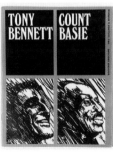

A concert programme, for Tony Bennett and Count Basie, c1969, 10 x 8in (25.5 x 20.5cm).
£15–20 / €22–29
$29–38 ⊞ CTO

Terry O'Neill, a silver print of Rod Stewart, signed in ink, 1974, 16 x 20in (40.5 x 51cm), framed.
£540–640 / €780–920
$1,050–1,250 ↗ S

◀ **A poster,** advertising *Pink Floyd* the film, Australian release, 1973, 30 x 13in (76 x 33cm).
£80–90 / €115–130
$155–175 ⊞ IQ

A Morrisey concert programme and ticket, for the 'Kill Uncle' tour, 1991, 13 x 10in (33 x 25.5cm).
£15–20 / €22–29
$29–38 ⊞ CTO

The Beatles

▶ **Six Yellow Submarine bubble gum cards,** by Anglo Confectionery, c1968.
£1–5 / €2–7
$3–9 each ⊞ CTO

A sachet of hair gel, featuring The Beatles, c1965, 2in (5cm) wide.
£6–10 / €9–15
$12–19 ⊞ UD

The Beatles, a postcard, 1960s, 5¾ x 4in (14.5 x 10cm).
£6–10 / €9–15
$12–19 ⊞ RTT

A Corgi model of a Yellow Submarine, 1968, 5in (12.5cm) wide.
£50–60 / €75–85
$100–115 ↗ GAZE

The Beatles, a poster, printed by Permild & Rosengreen, Danish, 1968, 24½ x 29in (62 x 73.5cm) wide.
£95–110 / €140–165
$175–200 ↗ VSP

▶ **A Prince William Pottery mug,** promoting The Cavern, Liverpool, decorated with a band resembling the Beatles, 1960s, 4in (10cm) high.
£75–85 / €115–130
$140–160 ⊞ IQ

An autograph book, containing a page signed by all four Beatles, also contains Mickey Dolenz, The Hideaways and Adriatis People, 12° 1960s.
£500–600 / €730–870
$960–1,150 ↗ LAY

Johnny Cash

Following the death of the country music legend Johnny Cash (1932–2003), Sotheby's in New York hosted a three-day auction of property from his estate and that of his late wife, June Carter Cash. The sale, which included over 650 items, attracted more than 1,000 bidders and raised a total of nearly £2,083,000 / €3,021,000 / $4,000,000. The most expensive lot was a 1986 Grammy Award which made $187,200 / €141,400 / £97,500 – almost 27 times the $7,000 / €5,200 / $3,600 estimate. Many other objects far exceeded their guide price.

A 14ct gold foxtail-link identification bracelet, engraved 'Johnny', the reverse engraved 'Thanks, Alex', stamped marks, 1972, 7¾in (19.5cm) long.
£2,000–2,400 / €2,900–3,500
$3,900–4,650 ✦ S(NY)

A Dobro maple six-string guitar, c1930, with case.
£4,700–5,600
€6,800–8,100
$9,000–10,800 ✦ S(NY)

A photograph of Johnny Cash and Johnny Horton, colour tinted and matted, 1950s, 13½ x 10½in (34.5 x 26.5cm).
£370–440 / €540–650
$720–860 ✦ S(NY)
Johnny Horton had several top ten songs in the late 1950s with Columbia Records. Johnny Cash and Johnny Horton became great friends. They went fishing together and performed together several times. Tragically, in November 1960, Horton was killed in an automobile accident in Milano, Texas following an appearance at the Skyline Club in Austin. Earlier in the year, he had a premonition that he would die in an alcohol-related accident, which he did.

Jim Marshall, a photograph of Johnny Cash and Waylon Jennings, signed by photographer, dated 1974, 8¼ x 12½in (21 x 32cm).
£1,100–1,300 / €1,600–1,900
$2,150–2,600 ✦ S(NY)

◀ **A Martin D76 acoustic guitar,** Bicentennial model, with mahogany neck, ebony fingerboard and bridge, three-piece Indian rosewood back, pegs possibly replaced, 1976, with strap, case and key.
£26,300–31,500
€38,000–45,700
$50,500–60,500 ✦ S(NY)
The D76 is a limited edition of 1,976 guitars produced in 1976 to commemorate the American bicentenary.

A concert poster, advertising four concerts at the Ice Hall in Prague, Czechoslovakia, 1978, 22¾ x 31½in (58 x 80cm).
£1,700–2,050 / €2,450–2,950
$3,300–3,950 ✦ S(NY)

A Manuel three-piece gabardine suit, comprising waistcoat and trousers, with hand-embroidered decoration, with label, 1970s.
£5,600–6,700
€8,100–9,700
$10,800–12,900 ➶ S(NY)
This suit was one of the first to be designed by Manuel after he left Nudie's Rodeo Tailors. Cash wore it on stage on numerous occasions in the late 1970s and 1980s, including a 1980 television memorial tribute to Mother Maybelle Carter.

A photograph of Johnny Cash and June Carter Cash in concert, 1970s, 10 x 13in (25.5 x 33cm), framed.
£990–1,150 / €1,450–1,650
$1,900–2,250 ➶ S(NY)

A passport, issued to Johnny Cash, with photograph and various immigration stamps and visas, signed, 1983, 3½ x 5in (9 x 12.5cm) folded.
£2,500–2,950 / €3,600–4,250
$4,800–5,700 ➶ S(NY)
The black and white photograph of Cash is actually a miniature of the publicity photograph for his film *The Baron and the Kid.*

◄ **A leather cowboy hat,** worn by Johnny Cash, Argentinian, dated 1983.
£1,550–1,850
€2,250–2,700
$3,000–3,600
➶ S(NY)

Jukeboxes

A Wurlitzer 500A jukebox, plays 24 records, serial No. 657262, with a 5–10–25 cent sliding coin deposit, 1938–39, 35in (89cm) wide.
£1,350–1,600
€1,950–2,300
$2,600–3,100 ➶ LHA

A Mills Constellation 951 jukebox, with 40 selections, plays 75rpm records, 1950, 34in (86.5cm) wide.
£900–1,000
€1,300–1,450
$1,750–1,950 ⊞ WAm

LOCATE THE SOURCE

The source of each illustration in Miller's can be found by checking the code letters below each caption with the Key to Illustrations, pages 443–451.

A Seeburg HF 100G Select-O-Matic jukebox, with 100 selections, restored, 1953, 34in (86.5cm) wide.
£4,500–5,000
€6,500–7,300
$8,600–9,600 ⊞ WAm

A Wurlitzer 1900 Centennial jukebox, with 104 selections, 1956, 36in (91.5cm) wide.
£5,000–5,600
€7,300–8,100
$9,600–10,800 ⊞ WAm

◄ **A Wurlitzer Lyric jukebox,** with 100 selections, plays 45rpm records, 1964, 31in (78.5cm) wide.
£900–1,000
€1,300–1,450
$1,750–1,950 ⊞ WAm

A Wurlitzer wall-mounted jukebox, 1956, 11in (28cm) wide.
£220–250 / €320–360
$420–480 ⊞ MARK

A Rock-Ola 1475 Tempo 1 jukebox, 1959, 31in (78.5cm) wide.
£4,250–4,750
€6,200–6,900
$8,200–9,100 ⊞ WAm

◄ **A Wurlitzer One More Time Elvis Presley jukebox,** endorsed by Elvis Presley Enterprises, limited edition, No. 630 of 730, plays 100 compact discs, 2004, 38in (96.5cm) high, with printed certificate of authenticity.
£10,500–12,000
€15,200–17,400
$20,000–23,000 ⊞ AME

Records

Chet Atkins, 'Teensville', LP record, by RCA, 1960.
£15–20 / €22–29
$29–38 ⊞ CTO

Syd Barrett, 'Barrett', LP record, by Harvest Records, 1970.
£15–20 / €22–29
$29–38 ⊞ CTO

► **'The Beat Merchants 1963–64',** compilation LP record, by United Artists, 1976.
£15–20
€22–29
$29–38 ⊞ CTO

'Brasamba', featuring Bud Shank, Clare Fischer and Joe Pass, LP record, by Fontana, 1963.
£10–15 / €15–22
$19–28 ⊞ CTO

James Brown, 'Body Heat', LP record, by Polydor, 1976.
£10–15 / €15–22
$19–28 ⊞ CTO

Johnny Cash, 'The Songs That Made Him Famous', LP record, by Sun, c1958.
£380–450 / €550–650
$720–860 ⚹ S(NY)
Johnny Cash's second Sun album was released in November 1958, after he had already released his first album with his new label, Columbia. Eleven of the 12 tracks (everything except for a cover of Hank Williams' 'I Cant Help It') hit the top ten of the country music charts, and there were four number ones. Included in the track list are several icons, such as, 'I Walk The Line' and 'Big River'. This particular LP was Johnny Cash's personal copy and was sold at the Johnny Cash sale at Sotheby's, New York.

Lyn Collins, 'Think (About It)', LP record, by Mojo, 1972.
£10–15 / €15–22
$19–28 ⊞ CTO

Sam Cooke, 'My Kind of Blues', LP record, by RCA, 1961.
£15–20 / €22–29
$29–38 ⊞ CTO

Fire, 'The Magic Shoemaker', LP record, by PYE Records, 1970.
£270–300 / €390–430
$520–580 ⊞ BNO

'The Jetsons', soundtrack LP record, by Hanna Barbera, 1966.
£10–15 / €15–22
$19–28 ⊞ CTO

◀ **The Who,** 'My Generation', LP record, by Brunswick, 1965.
£50–60 / €75–85
$100–115 ⊞ CTO

▶ **Bobby Womack,** 'Across 110th Street', soundtrack LP record, by United Artists, 1972.
£15–20 / €22–29
$29–38 ⊞ CTO

The Spotnicks, 'Out-A Space', LP record, by Oriole, 1962.
£20–25 / €30–35
$40–50 ⊞ CTO

Scent Bottles

Scent bottle collecting has grown in popularity in recent years with the development of collectors' clubs, specialist dealers and dedicated auctions. Up until the late 19th century, ladies and gentlemen would decant oils and flower waters – purchased from a perfumer or homemade – into their own personal bottles. These came in every size from large dressing table flacons, to small portable flasks that could be slipped into a handbag, or even worn suspended from a chatelaine or finger ring. The 20th century saw the development of the commercial industry as we know it today with branded perfumes sold in specifically designed bottles and boxes, a complete 'presentation' created to market a named fragrance. Chanel No. 5, launched in 1921, was the first scent to bear the name of a designer, and bottles became ever more inventive as the fashion industry competed with long-established traditional perfume makers such as Guerlain.

Both non-commercial and commercial bottles have their devoted collectors and, in each field, condition is crucial to value. Check for chips and other damage and ensure that stoppers are original. With commercial perfume bottles, the more complete the presentation the better. Bottles still with their boxes will command a premium, and any remaining perfume should not be decanted. Bottles by major glassmakers such as Baccarat and Lalique are highly sought after.

A Rockingham ceramic scent bottle, with floral encrusted decoration, 19thC, 4in (10cm) high.
£130–155 / €190–220
$250–300 ✗ CHTR

A Victorian silver-gilt and glass double-ended scent bottle, decorated with coral, London 1866.
£800–960 / €1,150–1,400
$1,550–1,850 ✗ LAY

◀ **A Victorian porcelain scent bottle,** with hand-painted floral decoration, 11in (28cm) high.
£320–380 / €460–550
$610–730 ✗ DA

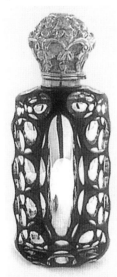

◀ **A Victorian mercury glass scent bottle,** with a hinged cover and a glass stopper, 4½in (11.5cm) high.
£550–660 / €800–960
$1,050–1,250 ✗ WW
Mercury glass (also called Varnish or silvered glass) is double-walled glass with a layer of silver nitrate or mercury trapped in the cavity between. This thin layer produces a rich silver tone similar to silver plate. The first patent for silvered glass was taken out in 1849 by Hale Thomson and Edward Varnish and they staged a major display at The Great Exhibition at Crystal Palace, London in 1851. Thomson and Varnish were retailers and dealers in glass only and did not manufacture the wares themselves. Some of the finer glasswares were made at James Powell's Whitefriars glassworks. The more expensive objects were 'flashed' or cased in coloured glass and cut through to the silvering beneath.

A silver-gilt and glass double-ended scent bottle, initialled 'S.O.N', with stamped lozenge, c1870, 3½in (9cm) long.
£550–660 / €800–960
$1,050–1,250 ✗ WW

A Victorian silver-gilt and glass scent bottle and vinaigrette, by Sampson Mordan & Co.
£440–520 / €640–750
$840–1,000 ⚲ SPF

A Roger & Gallet scent bottle _étui_, with one glass scent bottle and one wooden scent bottle, French, Paris, 1889, larger 3½in (9cm) high.
£80–95 / €120–140
$155–180 ⚲ DORO

◀ **A Guerlain Jicky glass scent bottle,** in original box, c1890, 3 x 4in (7.5 x 10cm).
£70–80 / €100–115
$135–155 ⊞ LBr

A Bohemian glass scent bottle, late 19thC, 4¾in (12cm) high.
£170–200 / €240–290
$330–380 ⚲ SWO

A painted alabaster scent bottle, in the form of a pear, c1890, 3¼in (8.5cm) high.
£160–180 / €230–260
$310–350 ⊞ VK

A silver scent bottle, by Sampson Mordan & Co, London 1891, 2in (5cm) high.
£220–260 / €320–380
$420–500 ⚲ SWO

A silver-mounted porcelain scent bottle, by Locke & Co, applied with trailing flowers, impressed mark, Birmingham 1899, 5½in (13.5cm) high.
£300–360 / €440–520
$580–690 ⚲ L

A Grossmith & Sons Shem-el-Nessim Scent of Araby glass scent bottle, London, 1900–10, 3¾in (9.5cm) high.
£35–40 / €50–60
$65–75 ⚲ BBR

An Eau de Coty glass scent bottle, 1905, 2¼in (5.5cm) high.
£20–25 / €30–35
$40–50 ⊞ LBr

A miniature scent bottle, by Royal Worcester, the white metal cover in the form of a bird's head, c1911, 1½in (4cm) long.
£210–250 / €300–360
$400–480 ⚲ BWL

A glass scent bottle, by Steuben, c1920, 4½in (11.5cm) high.
£145–170 / €210–250
$280–330 ⚲ JAA

A Corday Joyeux Moi glass perfume bottle, c1920, 3½in (9cm) high.
£20–25 / €30–35
$40–50 ⚲ **DuM**

A perfume casket, containing two glass bottles, 'Lily of the Valley' and 'White Rose', 1920s.
£50–60 / €75–85
$100–115 ⚲ **BBR**

An amethyst glass perfume bottle, the stopper in the form of a moon, 1920s, 5in (12.5cm) high.
£40–45 / €60–70
$75–85 ⊞ **TASV**

A glass scent bottle, in the form of a kneeling woman, French, 1920–30, 5in (12.5cm) high.
£190–220 / €280–320
$360–420 ⊞ **LBe**

A silver-mounted glass scent bottle, marked 'HP & S', London 1923, 3½in (9cm) high.
£60–70 / €85–100
$115–135 ⊞ **WAC**

A glass scent bottle, with Art Nouveau-style trailing decoration, French, 1920s, 3½in (9cm) high.
£115–130 / €165–190
$220–250 ⊞ **LBe**

A glass scent bottle, by Viard, French, 1920s, 3½in (9cm) high.
£360–400 / €520–580
$690–770 ⊞ **LBe**
Although their names were not well known by the French general public, Clovis Viard (1857–1927) and his son Julien (1883–1938) produced some of the most handsome and innovative glass bottle designs of the interwar years and today their works are very collectable.

A maplewood model of a top hat, containing four sample scent bottles, 1930s, 5in (12.5cm) high.
£210–240 / €300–350
$400–460 ⊞ **LaF**

A Nina Ricci L'Air du Temps glass scent bottle, by Marc Lalique, the stopper in the form of two doves, 1950s, 4in (10cm) high, with box.
£270–300 / €390–440
$520–580 ⊞ **LaF**

▶ **A Paco Rabanne La Nuit shop display scent bottle,** 1980, 15in (38cm) high.
£25–30 / €40–45
$50–55 ⊞ **LaF**

A yellow metal perfume bottle, decorated with paste stones, 1930s, 1in (2.5cm) high.
£40–45 / €60–70
$70–85 ⊞ **LBe**

Science & Technology

A cast-iron and brass belt-driven mechanical bellows, c1800, 28in (71cm) long.
£400–450 / €580–650
$770–860 ⊞ **FST**

A brass circumferentor, by Adams, with a silvered compass and brass telescope, 19thC, 2¾in (7cm) diam.
£250–300 / €360–430
$480–580 ⚒ **LAY**

▶ **A mahogany pocket compass,** early 19thC, 3½in (9cm) wide.
£110–125 / €160–180
$210–240 ⊞ **HUM**

A Victorian boxwood specimen box, 1½in (4cm) diam.
£45–50 / €65–75
$85–95 ⊞ **FOF**

▶ **A terrestrial globe,** by A. N. Lebèque et Cie, Belgian, 19thC, 25in (63.5cm) high.
£430–500 / €620–730
$830–960 ⊞ **DEB**

▶ **A pair of Georgian guinea weights,** full and half guinea.
£50–60
€75–85
$100–115
⊞ **FOF**

A brass dumpy level, by Louis Paschal Casella, No. 7, engraved mark, 19thC, 9in (23cm) long, with mahogany case and wooden tripod.
£60–70 / €85–100
$115–135 ⚒ **PFK**

A Victorian mahogany and brass wrap reel, by John Nesbitt, with striking dial, 27in (86.5cm) wide.
£160–190 / €230–270
$310–360 ⚒ **Mal(O)**

A planimeter, by J. Halden & Co, in a fitted case, c1870, 8¾in (22cm) long.
£175–195 / €250–280
$330–370 ⊞ **FOF**

A Victorian thread counter,
¼in (1cm) diam.
£40–45 / €60–70
$75–85 ⊞ FOF

A Victorian painted metal and brass barograph, by Negretti & Zambra, 9½in (24cm) wide.
£240–290 / €350–420
$460–550 ↗ S(O)

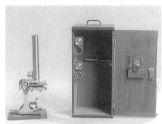

A brass monocular microscope, with rack-and-pinion focus, adjustable stage, two lenses, slides and other accessories, 19thC, 15½in (39.5cm) high, with a mahogany case.
£170–200 / €250–290
$330–380 ↗ PFK

◄ **A brass and mahogany three-draw telescope,** by T. Harris & Sons, late 19thC, lens 1½in (4cm) diam, with cover.
£85–95 / €125–140
$165–190 ↗ G(L)

► **A Victorian mahogany and brass pocket compass,** case, 2in (5cm) square.
£90–100 / €130–145
$170–190 ↗ HOLL

A pair of opera glasses, with enamel decoration, French, 19thC, 4½in (11.5cm) wide.
£90–105 / €130–150
$170–200 ⚶ DA

Opera glasses

The telescope was invented in the early 1600s and by the 18th century optical devices were being produced for many different purposes. The popularity of theatre and opera lead to the creation of decorative glasses. In the 18th century the monocular, or spyglass, predominated, followed in the 19th century by the paired monocular which evolved into opera glasses as we know them today, and was developed in Paris in the 1820s. The difference between opera glasses and binoculars is both strength and decoration. Opera glasses rarely magnify more than four times but binoculars can magnify eight times and more. Binoculars are designed to be practical and durable, whereas opera glasses were a fashion accessory and could be beautifully decorated. Prices depend on materials and condition. The presence of an original case enhances interest and also suggests that the instrument has been well looked after. The maker is also important. Paris produced some of the finest manufacturers and Lemaire is a well-known name. Look out for the Lemaire symbol which is in the form of a bee with outstretched wings.

A pair of opera glasses, with enamel decoration and mother-of-pearl eyepieces, impressed 'Maurice Faraggi', late 19thC, 4in (10cm) wide.
£75–85 / €110–125
$145–165 ⚶ SWO

A pair of leather and metal folding opera glasses, by Lemaire, French, c1880, 5in (12.5cm) wide.
£75–85 / €110–125
$145–165 ⊞ ARP

A lacquered-brass monocular microscope, with rack-and-pinion focus, concave mirror, brass fittings, late 19thC, 16½in (42cm) high.
£280–330 / €410–480
$540–630 ⚶ G(L)

An anodized metal prismatic marching compass, by Joseph Hicks, with paper dial and transit lock, c1890, 2¾in (7cm) diam, with leather case.
£165–185 / €240–270
$320–360 ⊞ FOF

A Watkins Bee Exposure Meter, c1900, 2in (5cm) diam.
£15–20 / €22–29
$29–38 ⊞ ARP

A pair of prismatic binoculars, by Atchison, c1900.
£60–70 / €85–100
$115–135 ⊞ ARP

A volt regulator, by A. H. Baird, Scottish, c1900, 22in (56cm) wide.
£220–250 / €320–360
$420–480 ⊞ JUN

A Wynne's Infallible Exposure Meter, c1900, 2in (5cm) diam.
£15–20 / €22–29
$29–38 ⊞ ARP

A brass-plated adjustable magnifying glass, c1900, 9in (23cm) high.
£90–100 / €130–145
$170–190 ⚲ **DuM**

A National Cash Register nickel-plated brass till, c1900, 18in (45.5cm) wide.
£360–400 / €520–580
$690–770 ⊞ **JUN**

◄ **A National Cash Register brass till,** c1900, 19in (48.5cm) wide.
£450–500 / €650–730
$860–960 ⊞ **JUN**

A National Cash Register brass till, c1900, 11in (28cm) wide.
£450–500 / €650–730
$860–960 ⊞ **JUN**

◄ **A brass championship leek gauge,** with engraved scale, early 20thC, scale to 6½in (16.5cm).
£30–35 / €45–50
$55–65 ⊞ **FOF**

An Addometer calculator, by Taylors, early 20thC, 11½in (29cm) long.
£50–60 / €75–85
$100–115 ⊞ **FST**

Cash registers

The cash register was an American invention. Typically, traders kept their money in pouches, cash boxes or a safe and, although this protected it from customers, employees had ready access to the takings. In 1879 – tired of staff pilfering from his Empire Saloon in Dayton, Ohio – owner James Ritty and his brother John patented a machine with a dial that would list transactions mechanically. They added a cash drawer with a bell and, when the keys were struck they pierced holes in a roll of paper, providing a register of every transaction. 'The Incorruptible Cashier', as the Ritty brothers called it, was not an immediate success since shopkeepers had to count the holes to record purchases (a tedious process). In 1884, the business was sold to local trader J. H. Patterson. He changed the name of the company to National Cash Register and added several modifications including pop-up metal numbers (replacing the dial) and an internal adding machine that kept an easy-to-read running total of the day's transactions. Thus the cash register assumed its familiar shape. Patterson, a brilliant salesman, began by making only a handful of tills a week, but by 1897 nearly 100 different models were available. By 1920, the company had sold one million models worldwide, exporting cash registers adjusted to the currencies of Europe, the Americas and Japan. The earliest models were made of wood, but soon they were covered with elaborately moulded metal (brass or nickel) which provided added protection and made registers a decorative centrepiece in the shop. A marble drawer top added to the weight and classical designs were popular. Values today depend on decoration and the more ornamental examples command higher prices. When buying, ring up every key to check that the indications are present and in working order. Ensure that models with a printer will take modern paper – and remember, tills are very heavy.

A brass yard measure, by Thomas Cheshire, Liverpool, with box, early 20thC, 18in (45.5cm) wide.
£100–120 / €145–170
$200–230 ⚲ **DA**

► **A pair of folding opera glasses,** by Mappin & Webb, c1903, 5in (12.5cm) wide.
£40–45 / €60–70
$75–85 ⊞ **ARP**

A pair of silver dividers, by Harper & Tunstall, c1920, 7½in (19cm) long, with original wooden case.
£120–135 / €175–195
$230–260 ⊞ FOF

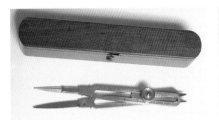

A Salter baby scale, with original basket, 1920s, 23in (58.5cm) wide.
£55–65 / €80–95
$105–125 ⊞ FST

A National Cash Register chrome-plated till, 1920s, 16in (40.5cm) wide.
£220–250 / €320–360
$420–480 ⊞ JUN

▶ **A chrome and glass desk barometer,** by Zeiss Ikon, German, 1930s, 6in (15cm) high.
£280–320
€400–460
$540–620
⊞ RTW

An ivorine weather forecasting device, by Negretti & Zambra, patent No. 6276/15, 1930s–40s, 2in (5cm) diam, with original box.
£55–65 / €80–95
$105–125 ⋗ DA

▶ **A metal electric fan,** by Cinni, Indian, c1960, 17in (43cm) high.
£80–90 / €115–130
$155–175 ⊞ SOU

Medical

A maiolica wet drug jar, painted with scrolling foliage, foot repaired, Italian, 18thC, 8¼in (21cm) high.
£220–260 / €320–380
$420–500 ⋟ DN

A Georgian ivory tongue depressor, 7in (18cm) long.
£20–25 / €30–35
$40–50 ⊞ FOF

A brass suppository mould, 19thC, 3½in (9cm) wide.
£15–20 / €22–29
$29–39 ⊞ FST

A pair of glass pharmacy jars, inscribed 'Rhubarb' and 'Sulphur', with printed decoration and gilded covers, 19thC, 33in (84cm) high.
£95–110 / €140–160
$185–210 ⋟ G(L)

A metal veterinary fleam, with a brass guard and seven blades, early 19thC, 3in (7.5cm) long.
£85–95 / €125–140
$165–185 ⊞ HUM

A tortoiseshell pocket fleam, by Stodart, c1810, 3½in (9cm) long, with original leather case.
£175–195 / €250–280
$340–380 ⊞ FOF

A syringe, by John Weiss & Son, in fitted case, 1834, 10¾in (27.5cm) long.
£200–230 / €290–330
$380–440 ⊞ FOF

A metal trocar, by John Weiss & Son, with an ebony handle, c1840, 4½in (11.5cm) long.
£70–80 / €100–115
$135–155 ⊞ FOF
A trocar is a sharp steel spike usually with an ebony or ivory handle. It was used to punch a hole through the chest or abdomen in order to introduce a cannula (silver tube) for draining fluid.

▶ **A set of 12 metal ophthalmic instruments,** by John Weiss & Son, in a leather-covered case, c1840, 4½ x 6¼in (11.5 x 16cm).
£330–370 / €480–540
$640–710 ⊞ FOF

A metal enema set, by S. Maw & Son and Thompson, c1850, in a mahogany box, 10½in (26.5cm) wide.
£220–250 / €320–360
$420–480 ⊞ AnB

A set of metal **Superior Surgeons' knives,** by George Turton & Sons, c1860, tin 7¼in (18.5cm) wide.
£175–195 / €250–280
$340–380 ⊞ FOF

A set of Victorian tortoiseshell ophthalmic testing lenses,
6in (15cm) wide.
£65–75 / €95–105
$125–145 ⊞ HUM

A set of **Victorian tortoiseshell ophthalmic testing lenses,**
6in (15cm) wide.
£135–150 / €195–220
$260–290 ⊞ HUM

A **porcelain medicine spoon,** c1870, 3¼in (8.5cm) long.
£65–75 / €95–105
$125–145 ⊞ FOF

▶ A **brass-mounted tourniquet,** by John Weiss & Son, c1900, screw 3½in (9cm) long.
£50–60 / €75–85
$100–115 ⚒ BWL

A **Victorian glass sputum bottle,** with brass top and base, 4¼in (11cm) high.
£135–150 / €195–220
$260–290 ⊞ FOF
Sputum bottles were carried in the pocket, providing a portable version of the spittoon.

A **British Military issue hernia bistoury,** by R. C. Nag & Co, with a bone handle, c1900, 8½in (21.5cm) long.
£110–125 / €1160–180
$210–240 ⊞ FOF
A bistoury is a knife used for the dissection of internal organs.
On hernia bistouries, only ½–1in (1–2cm) of the blade was sharpened.

▶ A **gold-plated ophthalmic speculum,** early 20thC, 2½in (6.5cm) long.
£35–40 / €50–60
$65–75 ⊞ FOF

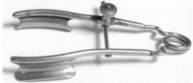

A **hand-blown and hand-painted glass eye,** by G. Taylor, c1900, in original box.
£70–80 / €100–115
$135–155 ⊞ FOF

A **plaster and glass teaching model of an eyeball,** early 20thC, 5in (12.5cm) wide.
£180–200 / €260–290
$340–380 ⊞ HUM

A set of **Streamline Hydrometers,** by Towers, in a fitted case, early 20thC, 9in (23cm) wide.
£50–60 / €75–85
$100–115 ⊞ FST

An **auriscope,** by Bruntons, c1905, in original velvet-lined case, 4in (10cm) square.
£60–70 / €85–100
$115–135 ⊞ WAC

◀ A white metal nasal speculum, early 20thC, 2¾in (7cm) long.
£35–40 / €50–60
$65–75 ⊞ FOF

▶ A set of minor surgical instruments, by Down Brothers, c1925, in a folding leather case, 7in (18cm) wide.
£150–170 / €220–250
$290–330 ⊞ WAC

M. D. Muller, The Household Medical Adviser, published by the Werner Co, c1910, 9½ x 7in (24 x 18cm).
£35–40 / €50–60
$65–75 ⊞ BAY

A painted plaster teaching model of the renal system, by Adam Rouilly & Co, 1925, 15in (38cm) high.
£135–150 / €195–220
$260–290 ⊞ HUM

◀ A stainless steel medical needle, c1930, 6in (15cm) long, with case.
£10–15 / €15–22
$19–28 ⊞ FST

▶ Two stainless steel dental mirrors, with interchangeable mirrors, 1930s, 7in (18cm) long.
£60–70 / €85–100
$115–135 ⊞ FST

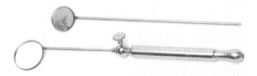

▶ A stainless steel ear syringe, by Arnold & Son, 1930s, 7in (18cm) long.
£10–15 / €15–22
$19–28 ⊞ FST

◀ A Bakelite pill box, 1940s–50s, 2½in (6.5cm) high.
£6–10 / €9–15
$12–19 ⊞ RTT

A glass eyebath, 1930s, 2½in (6.5cm) high.
£6–10 / €9–15
$12–19 ⊞ TASV

A brass denture mould, 1930s, 4in (10cm) wide.
£10–15 / €15–22
$19–28 ⊞ FST

▶ A glass eyebath, embossed 'Optrex Safe Guards Sight', 1970s, 2in (5cm) wide.
£1–5 / €2–7
$3–9 ⊞ TAC

Scripophily

A Kent Fire Insurance Office £50 share certificate, printed with a vignette of a prancing horse, on vellum, 1802.
£420–500 / €600–720
$800–960 ⚒ BBA

An Australian Cordillera Copper and Gold Mining Company certificate for 10 shares of £1, signed by members of the committee, dated 1852.
£175–195 / €250–280
$340–380 ⊞ GKR

An American Express Company share certificate, No. 642, decorated with a vignette of a dog, a dockside and a wagon, signed, revenue stamp, cancellation stamp, American, 1866.
£230–270 / €330–390
$440–520 ⚒ BBA

Valuing Scripophily

The value of scripophily items is determined by several factors:
- Condition
- Age – pre-1850 pieces are considered early
- Rarity
- Signatures – the autograph of a well-known figure will increase the value of the bond
- Visual appeal – many bonds were attractively coloured and engraved
- Historical interest – bonds cover a remarkable and international range of subjects from the California gold rush to the development of the railways in China

A Republica del Peru 7% government loan certificate for 100 soles, dated 1871.
£125–150 / €180–210
$240–280 ⊞ GKR

A Woodruff Sleeping & Parlor Coach bond, uncancelled, with coupons, American, 1888.
£80–90 €115–130
$155–175 ⊞ GKR

▶ An Imperial Chinese Government £100 bond, No. 107308, issued by J. P. Morgan and American Banks, with a vignette of a train, coupons, 1911.
£65–75 / €95–105
$125–145 ⚒ BBA

A Chinese Imperial Government £50 bond, with coupons, 1898.
£470–560 / €680–810
$900–1,050 ⚒ BBA

A British South Africa Company specimen certificate for 25 shares of £1, No. D0000, with vignettes and underprint by Bradbury, Wilkinson & Co, 1980s.
£175–195 / €250–280
$340–380 ⊞ GKR

▶ A Chinese Government £1,000 bond, with coupons, 1912.
£560–670 / €810–970
$1,100–1,3000 ⚒ BBA

Sewing

The majority of sewing tools that appear on the market date from the 19th century. Many originally came from fitted needlework boxes, others were sold individually. Sewing accessories were popular commemorative items and tourist souvenirs; examples include Mauchline ware pieces decorated with pictures of local towns and famous views. Styles range from simple, hand-crafted pieces, such as the Honiton wooden bobbin shown on page 338, to more sophisticated, professionally made creations. The most decorative and elaborate tools were made in Paris in the 19th century, such as the mother-of-pearl needle case illustrated below, and these are now identified by the term Palais Royal.

A silver-gilt bodkin holder, with filigree decoration, 19thC, 4in (10cm) long.
£130–150 / €185–210
$250–290 ⚲ WW

A collection of pincushions, in the form of hearts, butterflies, bellows and others, framed and glazed, 19thC, 15in (38cm) wide.
£360–430 / €520–620
$690–830 ⚲ BWL

A mahogany-veneered pincushion, with boxwood-strung and kingwood-crossbanded decoration, with one pin drawer and three dummy drawers, early 19thC, 5in (12.5cm) wide.
£145–165 / €210–240
$280–320 ⊞ GGD

◄ **A Tunbridge ware thimble holder,** with painted decoration, c1820, 2½in (6.5cm) long.
£155–175 / €220–250
$290–330 ⊞ AMH

► **An ivory pincushion,** in the form of a basket with a handle, inscribed 'Love the Giver', c1820, 2in (5cm) high.
£220–250 / €320–360
$420–480 ⊞ RdeR

A Palais Royal mother-of-pearl needle case, decorated in enamel with a pansy, French, c1820, 3in (7.5cm) long.
£180–200 / €260–290
$340–380 ⊞ RdeR

A Tunbridge ware emery cushion, with painted decoration, c1820, 1in (2.5cm) long.
£130–145 / €190–210
$250–280 ⊞ AMH

An ivory pincushion, inscribed 'A present from Oxford', c1820, 1½in (4cm) diam.
£50–60 / €75–85
$100–115 ⊞ RdeR

An ivory thimble, carved with oak leaves, French, c1830, 1in (2.5cm) high.
£90–100 / €130–145
$170–190 ⊞ RdeR

A **rosewood pincushion,** in the form of a teapot, with a painted Tunbridge ware handle, c1845, 1¾in (4.5cm) high.
£175–195 / €250–280
$340–380 ⊞ AMH

◀ **A set of R. Hemming & Son needles,** in a morocco portfolio, c1850, 9in (23cm) high.
£100–120 / €145–170
$200–230 ⚒ KTA

A **boullework sewing basket,** with a double tambour top and gilt-metal mounts, 1850–90, 11in (28cm) high.
£320–380 / €460–550
$610–730 ⚒ G(L)

A **wooden Honiton lace bobbin,** dated 1852, 4½in (11.5cm) long.
£55–65 / €80–95
$105–125 ⊞ HL

A **Victorian wooden Honiton lace bobbin,** 4½in (11.5cm) long.
£85–95 / €125–140
$165–185 ⊞ HL

A **Mauchline ware pincushion,** decorated with a scene of Fenton, c1860, 2in (5cm) wide.
£85–95 / €125–140
$165–185 ⊞ GAU

▶ **A stick ware thimble holder,** c1860, 2in (5cm) long.
£190–220
€280–320
$360–420
⊞ AMH

A **leather needle case,** containing four white metal needle holders, c1880, 3½in (9cm) wide.
£55–65 / €80–95
$105–125 ⊞ HUM

A **Tartan ware sewing *nécessaire*,** c1880, 3½in (9cm) wide.
£90–100 / €130–145
$170–190 ⊞ HUM

A **Tartan ware needle case,** inscribed 'McDonald', c1870, 2½in (6.5cm) high.
£135–150 / €195–220
$260–290 ⊞ RdeR

▶ **A silver thimble,** by Henry Griffiths & Son, decorated with ivy leaves, Chester 1892, 1in (2.5cm) high.
£50–55 / €70–80
$95–105 ⊞ CoHA

A **metal tape measure,** with embroidered decoration, early 20thC, 1½in (4cm) diam.
£15–20 / €22–29
$29–38 ⊞ LBr

Shipping

Shipping

◄ **A scrimshaw walrus tusk,** depicting a European sailor and a native girl on a beach, the reverse inscribed '18.08S, 178.25E', 19thC, 6in (15cm) long.
£540–640
€780–920
$1,050–1,250
🔨 **Bea**

A pair of Chinese Export porcelain plates, decorated with warships under sail, one entitled 'Sovereign of the Sea', the other 'La Themis', each inscribed 'To Lord Nelson', c1825, 10in (25.5cm) diam.
£60–70 / €85–100
$115–135 🔨 **SAS**

A bosun's silver whistle, by Hilliard & Thomason, engraved with wrigglework and foliate decoration, Birmingham 1891, 4¼in (11cm) long.
£280–330 / €410–480
$540–630 🔨 **G(L)**

A ceramic plate, with transfer-printed decoration of a sailor, entitled 'The Handy Man', 1899, 9in (23cm) diam.
£85–95 / €125–140
$165–185 ⊞ **BtoB**

A gilt-brass snuff box, by P. Wyon, the cover decorated with a bust of Admiral Lord Nelson within a Greek key border, inscribed 'Admiral Lord Nelson Born 29 Sepr. 1758', the reverse inscribed 'Conqueror at Aboukir 1 Augt. 1798, Copenhagen 2 April 1801, Trafalgar 21 Octr. 1805, where he gloriously fell', c1805, 3in (7.5cm) diam.
£650–750 / €940–1,100
$1,250–1,450 ⊞ **TML**

A Royal National Life Boat Institution brass aneroid barometer, by Dollond, late 19thC, 6in (15cm) diam.
£540–600 / €780–870
$1,000–1,150 ⊞ **RTW**

◄ **A mahogany ship's wheel,** with brass trim, c1900, 48in (122cm) diam.
£400–450 / €580–650
$770–860 ⊞ **JUN**

A gilt-brass and glass seal, with a profile of Admiral Lord Nelson, c1810, 12½in (32cm) high.
£300–330 / €450–500
$560–620 ⊞ **TML**

A turban shell, engraved with SS *Great Britain* and motifs, probably by C. H. Wood, c1843, 4½in (11.5cm) wide.
£430–480 / €620–700
$830–920 ⊞ **TML**
The steamship SS *Great Britain* was the brainchild of Isambard Kingdom Brunel and was launched on 19 July 1843 at Bristol, in the presence of Prince Albert.
C. H. Wood of Poplar, London, was a carver of shell and horn who came to public attention at the time of the Great Exhibition in London in 1851. Wood presented Queen Victoria with a similar shell on which was engraved the Royal arms, the Prince of Wales feathers, and the steamships *Great Britain* and *Great Western*. 'Executed with a common penknife' is an inscription frequently found on Wood's shells, and he is known to have sold his work to passengers aboard the two steamships.

LIEUT. E. J. SMITH, R.N.R.

◀ **Edward John Smith,** *Ocean Ferry Log,* for the White Star Line steamship *Majestic,* published by the Ocean Publishing Company, 12°, including illustrations, diary pages and autographs with the Captain's dated signature, 'Edw. J. Smith, 5th Sept. 1900', slight damage.
£980–1,150 / €1,400–1,650
$1,900–2,200 ↗ DW

Smith joined White Star Line in 1880, gaining his first command in 1887 and going on to captain the first *Republic,* the *Coptic, Majestic, Baltic, Adriatic* and *Olympic.* After he became Commodore of the White Star fleet in 1904, it became routine for Smith to command the line's newest ships on their maiden voyages. It was therefore no surprise that Smith took *Titanic* on her maiden voyage in April 1912. After the collision with the iceberg, Smith was last seen in the bridge area having given the final order to abandon ship. His fate remains a mystery as his body was never found. The value of this log lies in its association with the *Titanic.*

Regelmässige Dampfschiffverbindung zwischen **ROTTERDAM** und **BERGEN**
INGERID und **OLAF KYRRE**
D. BERGER & SONN, Rotterdam.

A Holland-Norwegen poster, printed by S. Lankhout & Co, Dutch, c1900, 29½ x 20in (75 x 51cm).
£530–630 / €770–910
$1,000–1,200 ↗ VSP

A Copeland Spode breakfast cup and saucer, inscribed 'The Royal Yacht', printed marks, 1905.
£260–310 / €390–470
$490–580 ↗ SAS

◀ **James Tait,** *Tait's Seamanship,* an educational booklet for Board of Trade examinations, published by James Brown & Son, Glasgow, 1910, 7 x 5in (18 x 12.5cm).
£6–10 / €9–15
£12–19 ⊞ J&S

The *Motor Ship and Motor Boat* **magazine,** July 1913, 11 x 8in (28 x 20.5cm).
£10–15 / €15–22
$19–28 ⊞ HOM

▶ **A postcard,** depicting the *Titanic,* published by State, captioned with details of the liner, dated December 6, 1911.
£90–100 / €130–145
$170–190 ↗ LAY

◀ **A poster,** entitled 'Titanic Disaster', for Frederick Best & Sons, Northam, Southampton, slight damage, April 1912, 17½ x 11in (44.5 x 28cm), together with a letter of provenance from Frederick Best's grandson.
£1,100–1,300 / €1,600–1,900
$2,100–2,500 ↗ DW

This poster 'Begs to call the attention of his many Patrons and others, that all takings in this shop, and the rounds by his sons, on Saturday Next, April 27th, will be handed over to the Mayor's Fund in aid of Widows, Orphans & Dependents of the Crew who lost their lives in the *Titanic* Disaster. Trusting you will all endeavour to swell the takings as large as possible, by so doing you will be helping many in their sad and sudden bereavement.' This is a rare and possibly unique survival of an emotive piece of post-*Titanic* ephemera. Hundreds of men from Northam and other areas of Southampton lost their lives when the *Titanic* went down, and the fate of all the missing passengers and crew was still not fully known when this poster was produced in the week after the disaster. The *Titanic's* captain, Edward J. Smith, whose body was never found, lived with his family on Winn Road, Portswood, Southampton.

A German submarine part, 1918,
5in (12.5cm) diam.
£75–85 / €115–130
$140–160 ⊞ COB

◀ **A White Star Line poster,** 'The World's Largest Liner', depicting the *Majestic*, c1920, 38½ x 24in (98 x 61cm).
£380–450
€550–650
$730–860
⚒ CHTR

A brass marine barometer, by Negretti & Zambra, London, c1920, 9in (23cm) diam.
£310–350 / €450–510
$600–670 ⊞ RTW

Negretti & Zambra was founded in 1850 by Henri Negretti (1817–79) and Joseph Warren Zambra (d1877). The firm, which remained in family hands until well into the 20th century, produced scientific instruments of all kinds – a 1930s' engineering instruments catalogue describes the company as 'Manufacturers to the British and Foreign Governments', and lists awards and gold medals received from the Great Exhibition of 1851 onwards. In the mid-19th century the company also produced stereoscopic photographs, and eventually became one of Britain's largest photographic publishers.

The Motorboat Manual, published by Temple Press, 1921, 8 x 5in (20.5 x 12.5cm).
£15–20 / €22–30
$28–38 ⊞ COB

A woolwork picture, depicting two two-masted sailing ships, c1925, 17¾in (45cm) diam.
£300–360 / €440–520
$580–690 ⚒ RTo

▶ **An East Asiatic Co Passenger Service poster,** by Erlinger, printed by Dansk Papirvarevabrik, Danish, c1930, 39½ x 24¼in (100.5 x 61.5cm).
£990–1,150
€1,450–1,650
$1,900–2,200 ⚒ VSP

◀ **A pewter tankard,** inscribed 'RMS *Atlantis*', c1930, 3½in (9cm) high.
£25–30
€40–45
$50–55 ⊞ OLD

A **George VI Royal Yacht cap band,** 1½in (4cm) wide.
£15–20 / €22–29
$29–38 ⊞ J&S

A **German Navy range finder,** by Carl Zeiss, model EM1 MR36, c1939, 32in (81.5cm) wide.
£310–350 / €450–510
$600–670 ⊞ OLD

A **Cunard Line tin,** by Edward Sharp & Sons, depicting RMS *Queen Elizabeth*, 1930s, 9in (23cm) wide.
£50–60 / €75–85
$100–115 ⊞ MB

Two ceramic White Star Line dishes, by Stony & Co, Liverpool, with transfer-printed decoration, 1930s, 8in (20.5cm) wide.
£350–420 / €510–610
$670–810 ➤ CHTR

A **marine barometer,** by Short & Mason for Tycos of Rochester, New York, in a mahogany stand, American, 1930s, 14in (35.5cm) wide.
£70–80 / €100–115
$135–155 ⊞ RTW

A **German Navy U-boat oak dinghy paddle,** c1940, 60in (152.5cm) long.
£45–50 / €70–80
$85–95 ⊞ OLD

A **Sirius brass gimbal ship's compass,** by E. Esdaile & Sons, Sydney, No. 2402, Australian, dated 1945, 9in (23cm) diam.
£60–70 / €85–100
$115–135 ➤ DA

A **scale model of *Equity*,** by Brooke Marine, Lowestoft, made for the Scottish Cooperative Society, 1947, in a display cabinet.
£120–140 / €175–200
$230–270 ➤ WilP

A **brass ashtray,** applied with a shipping company pennant, c1950, 5in (12.5cm) diam.
£15–20 / €22–30
$28–38 ⊞ OLD

A **Canadian Pacific liner passenger list,** 1957, 8in (20.5cm) high.
£10–15 / €15–22
$19–28 ⊞ MRW

A **silver-plated badge,** engraved 'M.S. *Oranje*', 1950s, 1¼in (3cm) diam.
£10–15 / €15–22
$19–28 ⊞ COB

A **brass and wood star globe,** by Kelwin Hughes, in a fitted box, c1975, 10in (25.5cm) wide.
£580–650 / €840–940
$1,100–1,250 ⊞ OLD

Silver & Metalware

A bronze cauldron,
with two handles,
on three legs, late 17thC,
9¾in (25cm) high.
£150–180 / €220–260
$290–350 ⚒ **WW**

**A Victorian painted
spelter watch holder,**
in the form of a parrot,
6in (15cm) high.
£185–220 / €270–320
$360–420 ⚒ **SWO**

A cast-iron bell, with leaf
decoration, dated 1839,
26in (66cm) high.
£540–600 / €780–870
$1,000–1,150 ⊞ **ET**

A pewter pepper pot,
c1850, 4¾in (12cm) high.
£45–50 / €65–75
$85–95 ⊞ **MFB**

A copper stomach warmer, late 19thC,
10in (25.5cm) diam.
£130–145 / €190–210
$250–280 ⊞ **BS**

◀ **A miniature penknife
and corkscrew,** in the
form of a bottle, with
mother-of-pearl-handle,
20thC, 2in (5cm) long.
£25–30 / €40–45
$50–55 ⊞ **TOP**

A copper shovel, c1920, 22in (56cm) long.
£4–8 / €6–12
$8–15 ⊞ **AL**

A brass Sonnette Keyway Panel, 1920s–30s,
7½in (19cm) wide.
£75–85 / €110–125
$145–165 ⊞ **BS**
This device was used by ironmongers for
cutting keys.

Brass

A brass and iron carriage handle, 18thC, 4in (10cm) wide.
£85–95 / €125–140
$165–185 ⊞ DRU

► Three brass pepper pots and a sifter, 1780–90, largest 6in (15cm) high.
£450–500
€650–730
$860–960 each
⊞ SEA

A brass jardinière, with embossed and engraved decoration, zinc liner and lion-mask handles, on paw feet, Dutch, early 19thC, 16½in (42cm) wide.
£280–330 / €410–480
$540–630 ⟋ WW

► A pair of Victorian brass candlesticks, in the manner of Dr Christopher Dresser, marked, 10in (25.5cm) high.
£200–240 / €290–350
$380–460 ⟋ MAL

◄ A brass and cut-steel fender, on three stylized paw feet, 19thC, 46in (117cm) wide.
£80–90
€115–130
$155–175
⟋ WW

► A brass padlock, with key, c1900, 4in (10cm) high.
£60–70 / €85–100
$115–135 ⊞ BS

◄ A pair of brass and copper mantelpiece ornaments, in the form of ladies' button boots, c1900, 4in (10cm) high.
£80–90 / €115–130
$155–175 ⊞ BS

A brass reception bell, c1890, 4in (10cm) diam.
£45–50 / €65–75
$85–95 ⊞ AL

An Acme brass whistle, 1930s–50s, 2in (5cm) long.
£15–20 / €22–29
$29–38 ⊞ HOM

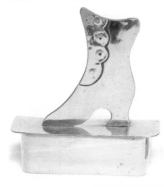

► An Acme City Range brass whistle, 1930s–40s, 3in (7.5cm) long.
£15–20 / €22–29
$29–38 ⊞ HOM

Silver

◀ **A silver pepper pot,** in the form of a swan, Dutch, 19thC, 3¼in (8.5cm) long.
£200–240
€290–350
$390–460
✗ SWO

A silver folding fork, with a mother-of-pearl handle, c1800, 6in (15cm) long.
£95–110 / €140–160
$180–210 ⊞ CoHA

▶ **A coffee pot and cover,** by Joseph and John Angell, cast with floral sprays, London 1848, 9in (23cm) high, 31oz.
£320–380 / €460–550
$610–730 ✗ WL

A silver folding fork, with a mother-of-pearl handle, Sheffield 1878, 4in (10cm) long.
£70–80 / €100–115
$135–155 ⊞ CoHA

A pair of silver grape scissors, by George Adams, London 1868, 7in (18cm) long.
£430–480 / €620–700
$830–920 ⊞ CoHA

A silver button hook, by Adie and Lovekin, c1880, 7in (18cm) long.
£115–130 / €165–190
$220–250 ⊞ CoHA

A Victorian silver butter knife, with a mother-of-pearl handle, 7¼in (18.5cm) long.
£15–20 / €22–29
$29–38 ⊞ TASV

◀ **A set of six silver caddy spoons,** in a fitted case, London 1889.
£260–310 / €380–450
$500–600 ✗ LT

A silver pin tray, by Cornelius Saunders and Frank Shepherd, in the form of a laughing cavalier, London 1888, 1½oz.
£110–130 / €160–190
$210–250 ✗ WW

▶ **A silver stirrup cup,** by Neresheime of Hannau, in the form of a fox's head, engraved with hunting scenes, German, c1895, 5½in (14cm) high, 5oz.
£320–380 / €460–550
$610–730 ✗ WW

A silver napkin ring, by W. M. Williams, Birmingham 1900, 2in (5cm) diam.
£40–50 / €65–75
$85–95 ⊞ WAC

A silver spoon, engraved 'Children's Home Boise, Idaho', c1900, 5½in (14cm) long.
£80–95 / €115–135
$150–180 ✗ JAA

A silver spoon, the handle in the form of a man, marked 'Sterling', c1900, 5in (15cm) long.
£175–210 / €115–135
$340–400 ✗ JAA

A silver toast rack, Birmingham 1900, 3in (7.5cm) wide.
£80–90 / €115–130
$155–175 ⊞ FOX

A pair of silver bonbon dishes, Birmingham 1901, 5in (12.5cm) wide, 2oz.
£80–95 / €115–135
$340–400 ✗ WW

A pair of silver sugar tongs, Birmingham 1901, 2½in (6.5cm) long.
£20–25 / €30–35
$40–50 ⊞ FOX

A silver-mounted cut-glass claret jug, Sheffield 1902.
£140–165 / €200–240
$270–320 ✗ JAd

An Edwardian silver stationery box, 7½in (19cm) wide.
£350–420 / €500–600
$670–800 ✗ LT

A silver glass holder, by A. Clark, with a cranberry glass liner, Birmingham 1902, 2½in (6.5cm) high.
£95–110 / €140–160
$180–210 ⊞ CoHA

A silver bread fork, 1903, 7½in (19cm) long.
£50–60 / €75–85
$100–115 ⊞ FOX

A silver toast rack, by T. H. Hazlewood & Co, Birmingham 1903, 3in (7.5cm) wide.
£55–65 / €80–95
$105–125 ⊞ CoHA

A silver fruit dish, with fretwork decoration, retailed by Z. Barraclough & Sons, London 1904, 15oz.
£120–140 / €175–200
$230–270 ✗ DD

A silver bread basket, with pierced and engraved decoration, London 1904, 8½in (21.5cm) wide.
£180–210 / €260–300
$350–400 ✗ Mal(O)

A silver taper stick, 1905, 11in (28cm) long.
£80–90 / €115–130
$155–175 ⊞ HO

A silver three-piece condiment set, with Copeland Spode liners, Birmingham 1906 and 1911,
£220–260 / €320–370
$420–500 ➢ SPF

A silver-mounted glass claret jug, with engraved decoration, Continental, import marks for Sheffield 1911, 8in (20.5cm) high.
£330–390 / €480–560
$630–750 ➢ Mal(O)

A silver trinket box and cover, with three legs, Birmingham 1919, 3in (7.5cm) diam.
£190–220 / €280–320
$360–420 ⊞ BrL

▶ A silver box and cover, in the form of a horseshoe, set with Connemara marble, Chester 1920, 2in (5cm) wide.
£140–165
€200–240
$270–320
➢ JBe

▶ A silver three-piece cruet set, by Walker & Hall, Sheffield 1920, pepper 3¼in (8.5cm) high.
£145–165 / €210–240
$280–320 ⊞ FOX

A silver-mounted glass sugar shaker, by H. & O., Birmingham 1921, 5½in (14cm) high.
£60–70 / €85–100
$115–135 ⊞ WAC

A silver napkin ring, Birmingham 1923, 2in (5cm) diam.
£25–30 / €40–45
$50–55 ⊞ CoHA

◀ A silver serving slice, by Georg Jensen, designed by Gail Spence, 1925, 9in (23cm) long.
£200–240 / €290–350
$380–460 ➢ G(L)

A pair of silver pepper mills, by L. A. Crichton, in the form of churns, 1926–27, 3in (7.5cm) high.
£150–180 / €220–260
$290–350 ➢ WW

A silver napkin ring, by H. G. & S., Birmingham 1929, 1¾in (4.5cm) diam.
£30–35 / €45–50
$55–65 ⊞ WAC

A set of silver coffee spoons, by Hukin & Heath, with enamel terminals, Birmingham 1934.
£60–70 / €85–100
$115–135 ➢ DN

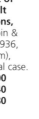

◀ **A set of silver-gilt teaspoons,** by Mappin & Webb, 1936, 4in (10cm), in original case.
£270–300
€390–440
$520–580
⊞ **TDG**

A silver basket, with pierced decoration, 1938, 11½in (29cm) wide.
£300–340 / €440–490
$580–650 ⊞ **FOX**

A silver miniature tea and coffee service, by J. L. C., comprising five pieces, with ivorine handles, London 1938, coffee pot 2in (5cm) high.
£300–360 / €440–520
$580–690 ⚷ **G(L)**

▶ **A silver mustard pot,** by Mappin & Webb, Birmingham 1939, 2½in (6.5cm) high.
£70–80
€100–115
$135–155
⊞ **BrL**

A silver toast rack, by H. A., Sheffield 1942, 3½in (9cm) wide.
£50–60 / €75–85
$100–115 ⊞ **WAC**

A silver teapot, by Raymond Semple, with a wooden cover and handle, 1968, 6in (15cm) high, 23½oz.
£300–330 / €430–480
$580–640 ⚷ **L**

A silver and parcel-gilt box, by Theo Fennell, in the form of a briefcase, London 1989, 2in (5cm) wide.
£230–270 / €330–390
$440–520 ⚷ **DN**

Silver Plate

A pair of silver-plated toast racks, in the form of stirrups, 19thC, 4¾in (12cm) high.
£55–65 / €80–950
$105–125 ⚷ **SWO**

A silver-plated spoon warmer, c1850, 4in (10cm) high.
£70–80 / €100–115
$135–155 ⊞ **HO**

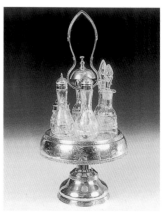

A Victorian silver-plated castor, with a servant's bell, 18in (45.5cm) high.
£80–95 / €115–135
$150–180 ⚷ **JAA**

A Victorian silver-plated coffee pot, embossed with floral decoration, 10in (25.5cm) high.
£20–25 / €30–35
$40–50 ➔ GAK

Items in the Silver & Metalware section have been arranged in date order within each sub-section.

▶ **An Art Deco silver-plated bread fork,** 5in (12.5cm) long.
£25–30 / €40–45
$50–55 ⊞ TOP

A silver-plated dish, by Elkington & Co, presented by Beckenham Cricket Club, c1879, 4in (10cm) diam.
£70–80 / €85–100
$115–135 ⊞ CoHA

▶ **A silver-plated cruet set,** 1950s, 3½in (9cm) high.
£20–25 / €30–35
$40–50 ⊞ RTT

Steel

◀ **A steel safe key,** 19thC, 4in (10cm) long.
£60–70
€85–100
$115–135 ⊞ BS

A steel Insurance two-lever padlock, 1930s, 3½in (9cm) high.
£50–60 / €75–85
$100–115 ⊞ BS

◀ **Two stainless steel Campden Range coffee pots and a sugar bowl,** by Robert Welsh for Old Hall, 1958, 7in (18cm) high.
£50–60 / €75–85
$100–115 ⊞ BS

Stainless Steel

Stainless steel is an alloy of chromium and iron, remarkable for its resistance to heat and corrosion. Discovered in 1913 by metallurgist Harry Brearly, head of a research laboratory run by the steel firms of John Brown and Thomas Firth & Sons, this tough, magnetic and rust-proof material was initially intended for naval guns. However, the Navy were not enthusiastic and Brearly turned his attention to the kitchen. The first stainless steel knife blades were forged in 1914, and soon cutlery was being made entirely from this new metal. In 1928, the firm of J. & J. Wiggin at Bloxwich, West Midlands, made a simple four-section toast rack, said to be the first piece of stainless steel tableware. This was followed in 1930 by the first stainless steel teapot. Products were originally stamped 'Olde Hall', but between 1933 and 1935 the trade mark 'Ye Olde Hall' was used. It wasn't until 1959 that the final 'e' was dropped, to reflect the crisp and contemporary image that came into vogue after WWII.

Having trained as a silversmith at the Royal College of Art, Robert Welch (1929–2000) was appointed consultant designer by J. & J. Wiggin in 1955. In his first tableware range entitled 'Campden', stainless steel coffee pots came with teak handles to protect fingers. The Campden range won a Design Centre Award in 1958. Robert Welch's designs are sought after by collectors.

Sixties & Seventies

A Desimone Pottery jug,
Italian, 1962,
11in (28cm) high.
£95–110 / €140–160
$180–210 ⊞ FRD

**A Royal Copenhagen
faïence vase,** by Nils
Thorssen, 1967,
8in (20.5cm) high.
£55–65 / €80–95
$105–125 ⊞ FRD

A length of fabric,
by Anne Ogle for Heal's,
decorated with Sonatina
pattern, 1967,
39½in (100.5cm) long.
£35–40 / €50–60
$65–75 ⊞ FRD

**A Wedgwood glass
Brancaster candle
holder,** by Ronald
Stennett-Willson, 1967–69,
8in (20.5cm) high.
£40–45 / €60–70
$75–85 ⊞ COO

◄ **A plastic Clam ashtray,** by Alan Fletcher
for Mebel, 1968, 6in (15cm) diam.
£15–20 / €22–29
$29–38 ⊞ FRD
British designer Alan Fletcher (b1931)
created the plastic Clam ashtray for the
Italian firm Mebel in the late 1960s.
The ashtray was produced in various
colours so that the individual parts could
be mixed and matched. This design was
subsequently manufactured by Habitat.

A roll of wallpaper,
1960s, 20½in (52cm) wide.
£35–40 / €50–60
$65–75 ⊞ TWI

**A set of chrome modular
candlesticks,** designed by
Nagel, West German, 1960s,
12in (30.5cm) high.
£75–85 / €110–125
$145–165 ⊞ FRD
The modular candlestick
pieces stack together to
form a larger candlestick
or sculpture.

A ceramic vase,
West German, 1960s,
11in (28cm) high.
£20–25 / €30–35
$40–50 ⊞ LUNA

► **A pair of glass door knobs,** by Seguso, Italian,
1960s, 7in (18cm) wide.
£580–650 / €840–940
$1,100–1,250 ⊞ EMH

◄ **A Kosta glass vase,**
by Vicke Lindstrand,
1960s, 9in (23cm) high.
£670–750 / €970–1,050
$1,300–1,450 ⊞ EMH

A synthetic fabric day dress, 1960s.
£55–65 / €80–95
$105–125 ⊞ HSR

A plastic clock, by Ruhla, German, c1970, 4in (10cm) wide.
£20–25 / €30–35
$40–50 ⊞ FRD

◄ **A ceramic vase,** West German, 1960s, 9in (23cm) high.
£20–25 / €30–35
$40–50 ⊞ LUNA

A leather-covered plywood desk chair, with aluminium frame and stand, c1970.
£160–190 / €230–270
$310–370 ➹ SWO

◄ **A Hornsea Muramic wall plaque,** 1971–72, 7½in (19cm) square.
£90–100 / €130–145
$170–190 ⊞ EMH

► **A Spectrum fabric panel,** by Vernor Panton for Mira X, 1972, 39½in (100.5cm) square.
£670–750 / €970–1,050
$1,300–1,450 ⊞ MARK

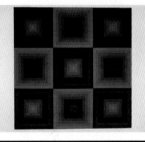

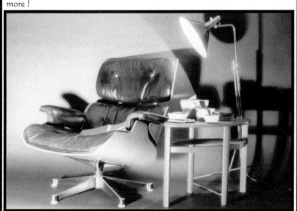

◀ **A length of fabric,** by Jyoti Bhomik for Heal's, c1974, 78¾in (200cm) long.
£20–25 / €30–35
$40–50 ⊞ FRD

▶ **A Whitefriars glass vase,** by Geoffrey Baxter, 1974, 8in (20.5cm) high.
£65–75 / €95–105
$125–145 ⊞ COO

A Whitefriars glass Banjo vase, by Geoffrey Baxter, 1970s, 12¾in (32.5cm) high.
£560–670 / €810–970
$1,100–1,300 ⋗ LT

A roll of wallpaper, decorated with Rupert the Bear, 1970s, 20in (51cm) wide.
£15–20 / €22–29
$29–38 ⊞ UD

A Midwinter Stonehenge bowl, by Eve Midwinter, decorated with Summer pattern, 1970s, 6in (15cm) diam.
£10–15 / €15–22
$19–28 ⊞ CHI

A rosewood and chrome magazine rack, possibly by Merrow Associates, 1970s, 21¾in (55.5cm) wide.
£200–240 / €290–350
$380–450 ⋗ SWO

A Caithness glass vase, 1970s, 7in (18cm) high.
£10–15 / €15–22
$19–28 ⊞ COO

A plastic vacuum jug, by Erik Magnussen for Stelton, Danish, 1970s, 11¾in (30cm) high.
£35–40 / €50–60
$65–75 ⊞ TWI
The classic vacuum jug with the unique rocker stopper was introduced in 1977 and is still made today. It was awarded the ID prize by the Danish Society of Industrial Design in 1977.

Smoking

A pearlware pipe, the bowl moulded in the form of a Turk's head, decorated with enamels, early 19thC, 12in (30.5cm) long.
£420–500 / €610–720
$810–960 ⚲ DN

A meerschaum pipe, moulded in the form of a hand holding a bowl, with silver-gilt mounts, the hinged cover inscribed 'In Fumo Vivimus', maker's mark possibly 'E.W.', London 1819, 4½in (11cm) high, with cover.
£150–180 / €220–260
$290–350 ⚲ DD

Pipes

Long, twisted-stem ceramic pipes were produced in Staffordshire in the 18th and 19th centuries. In theory these novelty designs also had the practical advantage of cooling down the tobacco smoke. Clay, which was cheap and a good insulator, was a favourite medium for pipes resulting in the wealth of clay pipe stems and bowls that can still be found when digging the garden. Produced in Britain as a result of the introduction of tobacco in the 16th century, these can be dated by the shape of the bowl. The 19th century saw the fashion for novelty designs, known as 'fancy clays', which came in the form of everything from famous buildings to contemporary celebrities. Meerschaum pipes were another Victorian favourite. Meerschaum (German for 'sea foam') was a form of magnesium silicate originally found on the shores of the Black Sea. According to enthusiasts it is an ideal material for smokers, because the taste of tobacco comes out fully in the first draw. Manufactured in Germany, Austria and Eastern Europe, meerschaum pipes were elaborately carved and waxed which improved the surface colour. Meerschaum pipes were also tinted with other materials ranging from nut oil to smoke itself. Value depends on the quality of the carving and the subject matter.

A silver-plated purse and cigar case, with engraved decoration, the cover inset with a vignette of a Rhenish view on a mother-of-pearl ground, marked '186', Continental, possibly Russian, c1850.
£80–90 / €115–130
$155–175 ⚲ PFK

Cross Reference
Silver & Metalware
see pages 343–349

◄ **A pressed horn vesta case,** 1870, 2½in (6.5cm) wide.
£80–90 / €115–130
$155–175 ⊞ MB

A brass tobacco box, with a penny slot, c1870, 9in (23cm) wide.
£340–380 / €490–550
$650–730 ⊞ JUN

► **A nickel-plated brass vesta case,** commemorating the Golden Jubilee of Queen Victoria, 1887, 2½in (6.5cm) wide.
£60–70 / €85–100
$115–135 ⊞ MB

A silver-mounted cloven hoof double snuff box, by Fergusson & McBean, set with citrines, Scottish, Edinburgh 1889, 1½in (4cm) wide.
£280–330 / €410–480
$540–630 ⚲ WW

A brass vesta case, in the form of Ally Sloper's head, late 19thC, 2in (5cm) high.
£110–125 / €160–180
$210–240 ⊞ HUM
Ally Sloper was a character from a popular British comic paper called *Ally Sloper's Half Holiday* (1884–1920). The hero was an unemployed man who would 'slope off' in order to avoid the rent collector.

A silver-mounted tortoiseshell cigarette case, by Saunders & Shepherd, inscribed 'Cigarettes', Chester 1893, 5in (12.5cm) wide.
£230–270 / €330–390
$440–520 ♪ G(L)

▶ **A box of Bryant & May Superior Candle Wax Vestas,** 1898–1908, 3½in (9cm) wide.
£40–45 / €60–70
$75–85 ⊞ MURR

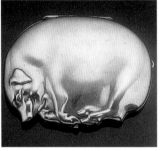

A silver cigarette case, in the form of a sleeping pig, the thumbpiece set with a sapphire, gilt interior, German, 1900–20, 4in (10cm) wide, 2½oz.
£520–620 / €750–900
$1,000–1,200 ♪ WW

An Edwardian vesta case, in the form of a champagne bottle, 3in (7.5cm) high.
£100–120 / €145–170
$195–230 ⊞ HUM

Further reading

Miller's Smoking Accessories: A Collector's Guide, Miller's Publications, 2000

A silver-mounted ivory cigar cutter, carved with a dragon, Birmingham 1905, 6½in (16.5cm) long.
£160–190 / €230–280
$310–360 ♪ WW

▶ **An I. Rutter & Co Mitcham Golden Virginia Cigarettes packet,** c1910, 1½in (4cm) wide.
£30–35 / €45–50
$55–65 ⊞ CPCC

A meerschaum pipe, the bowl carved in the form of a lion's head, with an amber mouthpiece, late 19thC, 6in (15cm) long, with a leather case.
£110–130 / €160–190
$210–250 ♪ DN(BR)

A brass tobacco tin, inscribed 'Edgar Colburn, New Year's Gift', c1900, 3in (7.5cm) wide.
£50–60 / €75–85
$100–115 ⊞ MB

An Edwardian meerschaum pipe, carved in the form of a head, 6in (15cm) long.
£75–85 / €110–125
$145–165 ⊞ HUM

A Hadges Nessim Egyptian Cigarettes tin, 1910, 3¼in (8.5cm) wide.
£50–55 / €70–80
$95–105 ⊞ HUX

A carved oak smoker's cabinet, c1915, 18in (45.5cm) high.
£100–120 / €145–170
$195–230 ⊞ OD

A Salmon & Gluckstein Homespun Cigarettes packet, 1918, 1¾in (4.5cm) wide.
£35–40 / €50–60
$65–75 ⊞ CPCC

A silver cigarette holder, Birmingham 1922, 3in (7.5cm) long.
£20–25 / €30–35
$40–50 ⊞ HO

A silver cigarette case, moulded and gilded with a sailing ship, Continental, possibly French, c1920, 3½in (9cm) wide.
£400–450 / €580–650
$770–860 ⊞ AU

A tobacco leaf cigar holder, c1920, 9in (23cm) high.
£40–45 / €60–70
$75–85 ➢ DuM

An Abdulla Special Egyptian Cigarettes tin, 1925, 3½in (9cm) wide.
£25–30 / €40–45
$50–55 ⊞ HUX

A W. D. & H. O. Wills Bulwark Cut Plug Tobacco tin, c1930, 7in (18cm) wide.
£20–25 / €30–35
$40–50 ⊞ JUN

A wooden ashtray holder, in the form of a man, 1920s, 35in (89cm) high.
£155–175 / €220–250
$300–340 ⊞ HEW

A Wills's Gold Flake Cigarettes tin tray, 1930, 16in (40cm) wide.
£90–100 / €130–145
$170–190 ⊞ HUX

A Richard Lloyd & Sons Sultan Cigarettes packet, c1930, 1½in (4cm) wide.
£25–30 / €40–45
$50–55 ⊞ CPCC

► A wooden cigarette box, in the form of a barrel, 1930s, 4in (10cm) diam.
£10–15
€15–22
$19–28 ⊞ OD

A J. Wix & Sons Mek-Bul Turkish Blend Cigarettes
packet, c1930, 2¼in (5.5cm) wide.
£20–25 / €30–35
$40–50 ⊞ CPCC

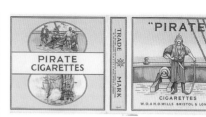

A W. D. & H. O. Wills Pirate Cigarettes packet,
c1935, 3¼in (8.5cm) wide.
£15–20 / €22–29
$29–38 ⊞ CPCC

A sycamore cigarette dispenser,
in the form of a dog kennel, with
inlaid and painted decoration,
1930s, 4in (10cm) high.
£40–45 / €60–70
$75–85 ⊞ MB

A silver-plated lighter,
by Dunhill, 1940s,
4in (10cm) high.
£310–350 / €450–510
$600–670 ⊞ OH

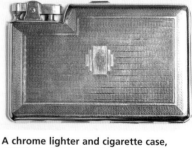

A Carlton Ware Rouge Royale lighter, in the
form of Aladdin's lamp, 1948, 8in (20.5cm) wide.
£65–75 / €95–105
$125–145 ⊞ WAC

▶ An enamel and
chrome lighter, 1950s,
3in (7.5cm) high.
£30–35 / €45–50
$55–65 ⊞ SUW

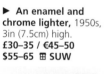

A chrome lighter and cigarette case,
c1950, 5in (12.5cm) wide.
£15–20 / €22–29
$29–38 ⊞ JUN

An Anstie's Gold Flake
Cigarettes tin sleeve,
1950s, 2¾in (7cm) high.
£20–25 / €30–35
$40–50 ⊞ HUX

A chrome table lighter, inscribed 'Allan
Clarke (Caravans) Ltd, Blackburn', 1950s,
4in (10cm) diam.
£20–25 / €30–35
$40–50 ⊞ SUW

◀ A ceramic ashtray, advertising 'Diplomat the
sporting cigarette', 1960, 4½in (11.5cm) diam.
£2–6 / €3–9
$4–11 ⊞ HUX

Sport

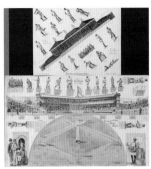

A feather shuttlecock,
Indian, c1850,
5in (12.5cm) high.
£100–120 / €145–175
$190–230 ⊞ MSh

A pair of snow shoes, North American
Indian, 1890s, 36in (91.5cm) long.
£360–400 / €520–580
$690–770 ⊞ MSh

A baseball game, an uncut
lithographed colour supplement
published in The *Press*, Philadephia,
3 May, 1896, by Forbes Lith. Co,
Boston and New York, together
with another baseball supplement
from The *Boston Sunday Globe*,
19 April 1896, American,
16¾in (42.5cm) wide.
£360–430 / €520–620
$690–830 ⋌ SK(B)

◄ **A billiards cue,** in a wooden
case, c1900, 62in (157.5cm) long.
£180–200 / €270–300
$330–370 ⊞ SA

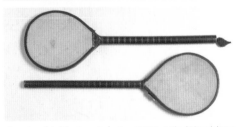

A pair of table tennis bats, c1900, 17in (43cm) long.
£30–35 / €45–50
$55–65 ⊞ SPA

**An Edwardian painted tin
rowing club megaphone,**
18in (45.5cm) long.
£135–150 / €195–220
$260–290 ⊞ HUM

**A Goodall copper and
nickel hunting horn,**
by Henry Keat, 1910–20,
10in (25.5cm) long.
£220–260 / €320–380
$420–500 ⋌ GTH

A set of four silver place card holders, by Stewart & Fanshaw, moulded to depict a cricket ball, rugby ball, football and and tennis ball engraved 'Spalding', London 1912, each 1¾in (4.5cm) diam.
£1,500–1,800 / €2,200–2,600
$2,900–3,450 ⚲ TEN

A Doulton Lambeth silver-mounted stoneware tyg, by Ethel Beard, applied with three panels depicting sporting figures within stylized flowers and scrolls, impressed marks, c1921, 6in (15cm) high.
£360–430 / €520–620
$690–830 ⚲ Bea

A wooden hurling stick, with a metal repair, Irish, c1920, 37in (94cm) long.
£10–15 / €15–22
$19–28 ⊞ AL

Two ash snooker cue rests, with brass fittings, c1930, 57in (145cm) long.
£20–25 / €30–35
$40–50 each ⊞ SA

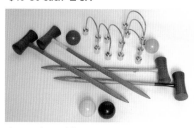

A wooden table croquet set, c1930, 12in (30.5cm) long.
£70–80 / €100–115
$135–155 ⊞ SA

An enamel souvenir medallion, from the Berlin Olympics, 1936, 3in (7.5cm) wide.
£25–30 / €40–45
$50–55 ⊞ Tus

A silver-mounted lignum vitae bowls ball, dated 1937, 5in (12.5cm) diam.
£45–50 / €65–75
$85–95 ⊞ MINN

> Items in the Sport section have been arranged in subject order.

A cast bronze figure of an ice hockey player, entitled 'Joe Brown 1956', signed and dated, 12½in (32cm) wide.
£590–700 / €860–1,000
$1,150–1,350 ⚲ JAA

A sporting cap, 1963–64.
£50–60 / €75–85
$100–115 ⊞ SA
Age can be critical to the value of sporting caps. A rugby cap embroidered with the dates 1872, 1823 and 1875 recently appeared at auction in the UK. Since the Rugby Football Union was only founded in 1871, this made it one of the earliest caps known, and it eventually sold for £4,000 / €5,800 / $7,700.

A signed colour photograph of Muhammad Ali, taken at the Liston fight, signed 'Muhammad Ali, aka Cassius Clay', 25½ x 21¾in (65 x 55.5cm), framed, with certificate of authenticity.
£300–360 / €440–520
$580–690 ⚲ BUDD

Cricket

◀ **A Doulton Lambeth lemonade jug,** the six panels decorated with raised cricketing figures and silver highlighting, two smaller vignettes, ball, bat and boater handle, stamped marks, slight damage, 1881, 9½in (24cm) high.
£1,500–1,800 / €2,200–2,600
$2,900–3,450 ⚒ VS
From about 1880 to 1914, Doulton's Lambeth factory produced a range of jugs and mugs decorated with sporting reliefs. Originally designed by John Broad, these complex motifs were cast in separate moulds before being applied to the vessel. Subjects ranged from bicycling to running, and today cricketing and golfing examples can command high prices. Later versions came with an Art Nouveau border.

A Doulton Lambeth two-handled loving cup, with raised figures of a batsman and a bowler in arched panels, with ball, bat and boater handles, slight damage, impressed marks and initials to base, 1883, 6½in (16.5cm) high.
£900–1,050 / €1,300–1,500
$1,750–2,000 ⚒ VS

A Staffordshire mug, decorated with raised cricketing figures, slight damage, 1880s, 3in (7.5cm) high.
£210–250 / €300–360
$400–480 ⚒ VS

A sepia photograph of the Clifton College First XI, including W. H. Brain, c1890, 12 x 14in (30.5 x 35.5cm).
£35–40 / €50–60
$55–65 ⚒ VS
William Henry Brain (1870–1934) played for Oxford University and Gloucestershire.

A silver and enamel fob, by Robinson Brothers, depicting a wicket keeper, Birmingham 1889, 1¾in (4.5cm) high.
£220–250 / €320–360
$420–480 ⊞ BEX

◀ **A Victorian photograph of a ladies' cricket team,** 9 x 12in (23 x 30.5cm).
£10–15
€15–22
$19–28 ⊞ J&S

Wisden's Cricketers' Almanack, edited by Sydney H. Pardon, slight damage, 1900, 6 x 4in (15 x 10cm).
£95–110 / €140–160
$180–210 ⚒ VS

A Doulton Lambeth stoneware jug, No. 325, decorated with portraits of W. G. Grace, George Giffin and Ranji, stamped marks, 1890s, 7¼in (18.5cm) high.
£920–1,100
€1,350–1,600
$1,750–2,100 ⚒ VS

▶ **A Doulton Lambeth jug,** decorated with three panels of cricketers, c1900, 5½in (14cm) high.
£300–360
€440–520
$580–690 ⚒ SPF

A Roedean School presentation prize cricket ball, 1926.
£40–45 / €60–70
$75–85 ⊞ SA

C. V. Grimmett, *'Flicker' No. 6, Over Spin Delivery and Finger Spin,* c1920, 3in (7.5cm) high.
£45–50 / €65–75
$85–95 ⊞ SA

A pair of leather wicket-keeping gloves, c1920.
£45–50 / €65–75
$85–95 ⊞ SA

An Australian Cricket Tour souvenir brochure, for Don Bradman's first UK tour, 8 x 5in (20.5 x 12.5cm).
£45–50 / €65–75
$85–95 ⋌ VS

The Cricketer magazine, August 1939, 11 x 9in (28 x 23cm).
£1–5 / €2–7
$3–9 ⊞ HOM

A willow cricket bat, c1930, 33in (84cm) long.
£55–65 / €80–95
$105–125 ⊞ MSh

A Nicolls miniature cricket bat, with facsimile signatures of the MCC 1956–57 team to South Africa, 11in (28cm) long.
£35–40 / €50–60
$65–75 ⋌ VS

A two-handled mug, by J. H. W., decorated with a vignette of Hedley Verity, his cricketing records to the reverse, restoration and repair, 1930s, 5in (12.5cm) high.
£140–165 / €200–230
$270–310 ⋌ VS

A Lancaster & Sandland mug, decorated with a vignette of Maurice Tate, 1950s, 4in (10cm) high.
£55–65 / €80–95
$105–125 ⋌ VS

◀ *The Cricketer* **Spring Annual,** 1961, 9 x 7in (23 x 18cm).
£1–5 / €2–7
$3–9 ⊞ HOM

A Berry wooden cricket bat, signed by 14 members of the 1964 tourists and 12 members of the Leicestershire squad, 1964, 33in (84cm) long.
£145–170 / €210–250
$280–330 ⋌ VS

Fishing

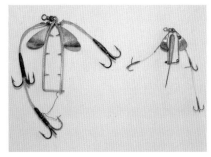

Two Hardy Crocodile dead bait mounts,
early 19thC, largest 2½in (6.5cm) long.
£10–15 / €15–22
$19–28 ⊞ OTB

**A Victorian Bowness & Bowness
brass reel,** 2½in (6.5cm) diam.
£130–145 / €190–210
$250–280 ⊞ SA

◀ **An iron fish spear head,**
French, 19thC, 11in (28cm) high.
£85–95 / €125–140
$165–185 ⊞ Cot

▶ **A Victorian beech and bamboo folding trout
net,** with brass fittings, 52in (132cm) long.
£80–90 / €115–130
$155–175 ⊞ MINN

A Victorian brass extending salmon gaff,
16in (40.5cm) long.
£60–70 / €85–100
$115–135 ⊞ MINN

A wooden roach pole, with brass fittings, c1880,
47in (119.5cm) long.
£55–65 / €80–95
$105–125 ⊞ SA

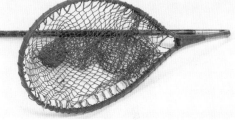

▶ **A brass
fishing reel,**
c1890, 4in
(10cm) diam.
£70–80
€100–115
$135–155
⊞ SA

◀ **A Farlow's brass
salmon fly reel,** with
patent drag control and
engraved backplate, late
19thC, 4in (10cm) diam.
£80–90 / €115–130
$155–175 ⊞ OTB

A tinplate bait carrier, late 19thC, 6in (15cm) high.
£40–45 / €60–70
$75–85 ⊞ HUM

A Jardine-style brass and ebonite trout fly reel, with a perforated brass face, c1900, 3in (7.5cm) diam.
£45–50 / €65–75
$85–95 ⊞ OTB

A Josephson's Hollow Fin Quill Devon, retailed by Hardy's, 1906–11, 2in (5cm) long, on original card.
£60–70 / €85–100
$115–135 ⊞ OTB

Cased fish

A D. Salter brass, ebonite and silver reel, c1910, 3¼in (8.5cm) diam.
£240–270 / €350–390
$460–520 ⊞ SA

▶ **A painted wood fish lure,** American, 1920, 7in (18cm) long.
£75–85 / €110–125
$145–165 ⊞ SA

A stuffed and mounted pike, by P. Spicer & Sons, caught by J. E. Swift at Compton Verney, in a glazed case, 1920, pike 28lbs.
£1,500–1,800 / €2,200–2,600
$2,900–3,450 ⋋ L&E

Cased fish provide an enduring way for a fisherman to prove the size of his catch and today this is one of the most popular forms of taxidermy. The most famous name in fish taxidermy was J. C. Cooper of London who, from the 1830s until the firm closed in the 1950s, was the leading specialist in the field. Cooper's fish, often in bowfronted cases with a gold trim, still command a premium at auction today. Another company of note was Spicer of Leamington Spa. Established in 1798 by Thomas Spicer, a saddler and harness maker, the firm became known as Peter Spicer & Sons from 1904. Active until the 1960s, they were very successful taxidermists and also produced cases of exceptional quality with finely painted backdrops shown off by glass side panels that gave the scene a 3-D effect. In addition to a label, a signed and dated pebble was often included in the groundwork of a Spicer case.

Companion to Alfred Ronald's Fly Fisher's Entomology, 6th edition, the parchment leaf fly wallet with details of flies for each month of the trout season, canvas binding later, some flies missing, c1925, 6½ x 4in (16.5 x 10cm).
£30–35 / €45–50
$55–65 ⊞ OTB

A stuffed and mounted roach, by P. J. Horton, Paddington, inscribed 'Taken by R. French at Reading, Nov 1st 1928 Wgt. 1lb 13.5oz, in a bowfronted case, 19in (48.5cm) wide.
£320–380 / €460–550
$610–730 ⋋ SWO

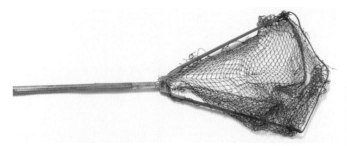

◄ **A wooden folding landing net,** with brass fittings and fish measuring gauge, 1920s, 55in (139.5cm) long.
£50–60 / €75–85
$100–115 ⊞ SA

A metal and brass fly-tying vice, with brass locking clamp and sliding bar jaw tightener, c1920, 13in (33cm) long.
£45–50 / €65–75
$85–95 ⊞ OTB

A wooden Nottingham reel, with brass fittings, c1920, 4½in (11.5cm) diam.
£35–40 / €50–60
$65–75 ⊞ OTB

► **A Hardy Silex No. 2 alloy casting reel,** with smooth foot, three crew drum latch and manual braking, c1920, 3¾in (9.5cm) diam.
£135–150
€195–220
$260–290
⊞ OTB

A turned mahogany trout priest, 1920s, 10½in (26.5cm) long.
£25–30 / €40–45
$50–55 ⊞ MINN

◄ **A wood and brass fishing reel,** 1920–30, 5in (12.5cm) diam.
£35–40
€50–60
$65–75 ⊞ SA

► **A leather cast case,** with gold embossing, the parchment leaves containing a selection of trout flies and gut, c1930, 5½in (14cm) wide.
£15–20 / €22–29
$29–38 ⊞ OTB

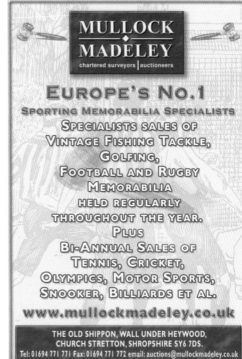

A Farlow's stainless steel trout priest, engraved 'Cairnton Killer', c1930, 5¼in (13.5cm) long.
£45–50 / €65–75
$85–95 ⊞ OTB

▶ **An Alex Martin celluloid dry fly box,** with eight compartments and a selection of flies, c1930, 6in (15cm) wide.
£15–20 / €22–29
$29–38 ⊞ OTB

A Hardy Silex No. 2 Spinning reel, with rim brake, ventilated spool and ivorine handles, 1930, 6in (15cm) diam.
£100–120 / €145–175
$195–230 ⌁ GTH

A Malloch alloy side casting reel, with black lead finish, fitted with Malloch & Gibb's patent lever for rotation of the drum, c1935, 4in (10cm) diam.
£45–50 / €65–75
$85–95 ⊞ OTB

A poster, 'Come to Austria for Fishing', c1935, 37½ x 24¾in (95.5 x 63cm).
£180–210 / €260–300
$350–400 ⌁ VSP

A metal line dryer with 3in brass crank handle reel, 1930s, 17½in (44.5cm) long.
£55–65 / €80–95
$105–125 ⊞ MINN

A Hardy mother-of-pearl and brass Devon Minnow, engraved with the maker's details, 1930s, 3in (7.5cm) long.
£80–90 / €115–130
$155–175 ⊞ OTB

A selection of rod spears, 1930s, largest 3in (7.5cm) long.
£4–8 / €6–12
$8–15 each ⊞ OTB

LOCATE THE SOURCE

The source of each illustration in Miller's can be found by checking the code letters below each caption with the Key to Illustrations, pages 443–451.

▶ **A Helical Reel Co metal fixed spool salmon reel,** with half bale arm and string-pull bag, 1940, 8in (20.5cm) high.
£85–95 / €125–140
$165–185 ⌁ GTH

◀ **A Hardy Elarex chromed freshwater multiplying reel,** with diagnostic slotted-brass cylinder, c1940, 2¾in (7cm) wide, with case.
£90–100 / €130–145
$170–190 ⊞ OTB

▶ **A Hardy Hardex No. 2 fixed spool reel,** with half bale arm, c1940, with case, 5in (12.5cm) square.
£35–40 / €50–60
$65–75 ⊞ OTB

A Heaton metal reel, c1950, 3¼in (8.5cm) diam.
£40–45 / €60–70
$75–85 ⊞ AL

A Mitchell Pêche enamel and tin sign, 'Moulinets en vente ici', French, c1955, 20 x 27in (51 x 68.5cm), in a wooden frame.
£25–30 / €40–45
$50–55 ⊀ MUL

A Hardy chrome and steel twig cutter/fly retriever, with threaded rod butt attachment, c1940, 3in (7.5cm) high.
£25–30 / €40–45
$50–55 ⊞ OTB

▶ **A stuffed and mounted trout,** inscribed 'Trout caught by Mrs E. M. Moore, River Wye, Rayadar. Aug.19th 1956. Weight 4lbs', in an ebonized case, 24¾in (63cm) wide.
£90–100 / €130–145
$170–190 ⊀ DN

A Mitchell Albatros Service enamel and tin advertising sign, c1957, in a wooden frame, 17 x 22in (43 x 56cm).
£65–75 / €95–105
$125–145 ⊀ MUL

A Hardy St George fly reel, with smoke agate line guide, right hand wind, two-screw latch, rim tension regulator and alloy foot, 1950s, 3in (7.5cm) diam, with original box.
£260–310 / €380–450
$500–600 ⊀ MUL

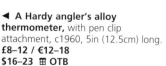

◀ **A Hardy angler's alloy thermometer,** with pen clip attachment, c1960, 5in (12.5cm) long.
£8–12 / €12–18
$16–23 ⊞ OTB

A brass spring scale, c1970, 7in (18cm) long.
£5–9 / €8–13
$10–16 ⊞ AL

Football

Football as we know it today started in the Victorian period. The Football Association (the ruling body for British soccer) was founded in 1863, and the term 'soccer' actually derived from a corruption of the second syllable of the word 'association'. The Football League was established in England in 1888. The first league championship was fought by 12 clubs and won by Preston North End. A second division was introduced in 1892, followed by a third division in 1920. Britain was largely responsible for exporting football around the world. FIFA (Federation Internationale de Football Association) was founded in 1904 and the first World Cup was staged in Uruguay in 1930 and won by the host team.

Because football was fundamentally a working-class game that could be played without a range of costly equipment (unlike golf, for example), the collecting of football memorabilia did not start seriously until the late 20th century. The market increased in the 1990s and, since then, demand and prices have continued to improve. Among the most popular items are programmes, particularly pieces pre-dating WWII. Examples from the 1940s and '50s are also desirable but, from c1960 onwards, with the exception of certain key games, programmes have survived in their thousands and most will be worth comparatively little. Condition is an important factor and if a programme has been damaged or written on, values will be affected. With more modern collectables, shirts are a popular area. These fall into different categories including replica shirts issued by the club for supporters, shirts worn by players, and shirts belonging to and signed by players. The last two categories are the most sought after. Although every club has its supporters, the big name teams still tend to command the highest prices, most notably Manchester United, because its fan base extends across the world.

A wooden souvenir pencil box, the lid depicting the International England v Scotland match at Crystal Palace, c1890, 10in (25.5cm) long.
£310–350 / €450–510
$600–670 ⊞ MURR

A Colman's Mustard enamelled metal vesta, inscribed 'English Cup to celebrate Bradford City's Victory, Manchester, April 1911', slight damage, 2in (5cm) high.
£300–360 / €440–520
$580–690 ↗ BUDD

An FA Cup Final programme, Preston North End v Sunderland, 1 May 1931.
£150–180 / €220–260
$290–350 ↗ BUDD

An FA Cup Final programme, Huddersfield Town v Preston North End, 30 April 1938.
£380–450 / €550–650
$730–860 ↗ BUDD

An FA Cup Final programme, Portsmouth v Wolverhampton Wanderers, 29 April 1939.
£320–380 / €460–550
$610–730 ↗ BUDD

Prices

The price ranges quoted in this book reflect the average price a purchaser might expect to pay for a similar item. The price will vary according to the condition, rarity, size, popularity, provenance, colour and restoration of the item, and this must be taken into account when assessing values. Don't forget that if you are selling it is quite likely that you will be offered less than the price range.

A leather lace-up football, c1950.
£50–60 / €75–85
$100–115 ⊞ PEZ

◄ **A 9ct gold and enamel Football League War Cup winner's medal,** enamelled with an English rose and the initials 'FL', inscribed 'The Football League, 1939–40, won by West Ham United FC at Wembley, A. C. Davis, Director'.
£550–660 / €800–960
$1,050–1,250 ⋏ BUDD
During WWII, a number of 'cup finals' were played. The first of these was the encounter between West Ham United and Blackburn Rovers at Wembley in 1939–40. A crowd of 42,399 watched the Hammers win 1–0. Albert (Bert) C. Davis was a famous Director of West Ham United. An engineer by profession, he had a long association with the Hammers – he was Director in two spells from 1900 to 1906 and 1923 to 1949.

A Scottish Football League No. 7 representative jersey, with an embroidered badge inscribed 'SFL v IFL, 1951–52', with a letter of authenticity.
£200–240 / €290–350
$390–460 ⋏ BUDD

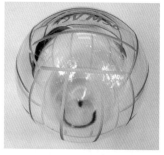

A World Cup commemorative glass football, etched '19VM58', Brazil v Sweden 1958, Swedish, in (7.5cm) diam.
£80–90 €115–130
$155–175 ⋏ SWO

> Items in the Sport section have been arranged in date order within each sub-section.

A tin cigarette dispenser, modelled as a football, inscribed 'Olympia', 1950s, 5in (12.5cm) diam.
£50–60 / €75–85
$100–115 ⊞ MSh

► **A World Cup poster,** by H. Meisse, 'Moch ein Tor!', published by Josef Deschler, German, Munich, 1963, 34½ x 24⅛in (87.5 x 62cm), framed.
£200–240 / €290–350
$390–460 ⋏ BUDD

◄ **Two Tottenham Hotspur official programmes,** 1961, 8in (20.5cm) high.
£2–6 / €3–9
$4–11 ⊞ MRW

A Northern Ireland international cap, inscribed 'E, S, W', 1963–64.
£750–900 / €1,100–1,300
$1,450–1,750 ⋏ BUDD
This cap was awarded to Arsenal's Bill McCullough for his appearances in the three home international matches of season 1963–64. This series began well with a 2–1 win over Scotland in Belfast but there followed a heavy 8–3 defeat at Wembley. Irish fortunes were revived with a 3–2 win over the Welsh in Swansea.

A film poster, 'Goal!', the World Cup 1966', published by Stafford & Co, 30 x 40in (76 x 101.5cm).
£150–180 / €220–260
$290–350 ✗ BUDD

▶ An FA Cup Final programme, Chelsea v Tottenham Hotspur, 1967, 9in (23cm) high.
£1–5 / €2–7
$3–9 ⊞ MRW

A Manchester United League Champions pennant, 1967, 10 x 8in (25.5 x 20.5cm).
£10–15 / €15–22
$19–28 ⊞ EE

◀ Five plastic Robertson's Golly footballers, 1960s, largest 3¼in (8.5cm) high.
£6–10 / €9–15
$12–19
⊞ TASV

A Northern Ireland goalkeeper's jersey, signed by Pat Jennings, with an embroidered badge, c1973.
£160–190 / €230–270
$310–360 ✗ BUDD

A leather football, signed by the Bobby Robson England squad, 1989–90.
£50–60 / €75–85
$100–115 ✗ BUDD

A Manchester United David Beckham No. 7 jersey, the sleeves with FA Premier League champions flashes, the reverse inscribed 'Beckham', 1997–98.
£600–720 / €870–1,050
$1,150–1,350 ✗ BUDD

A pair of David Seaman's goalkeeping gloves, signed, c2002, together with three photographs, two signed.
£100–120 / €145–175
$195–230 ✗ BUDD

◀ A Holsten Tottenham Hotspur replica shirt, signed by the team, c2001.
£200–220 / €290–320
$380–420 ⊞ SSL

Golf

An F. & A. Carrick steel and hickory rut iron, c1870, 37in (94cm) long.
£900–1,000
€1,300–1,450
$1,700–1,900 ⊞ SHER

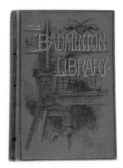

Horace G. Hutchinson, *The Badminton Library, Golf,* published by Longman Green & Co, 1890, 8in (20.5cm) high.
£90–100 / €130–145
$170–190 ⊞ SHER

▶ **A Carlton Ware ceramic match striker,** decorated with a golfing scene, c1890, 3in (7.5cm) diam.
£220–250
€320–360
$420–480 ⊞ MSh

◀ **A Gutty Ocobo golf ball,** c1895.
£180–200
€260–290
$340–380 ⊞ SHER

An Anderson's wooden golf club, with sockhead and greenheart shaft, 1892, 41in (104cm) long.
£180–200 / €260–290
$340–380 ⊞ SHER

A rut niblick, made for Willie Park, possibly by Nicholls of Leven, stamp to head, regripped, c1895.
£240–280 / €350–410
$460–540 ⋩ BUDD

A silver-plated inkstand, in the form of two golf ball inkwells and two crossed golf clubs, c1900, 8in (20.5cm) wide.
£310–350 / €450–510
$600–670 ⊞ MSh

◀ **A silver spirit flask,** by H. Mathews, decorated with a golfer, Chester 1904, 5in (12.5cm) high, 4oz.
£560–670 / €810–970
$1,100–1,300 ⋩ WW

▶ **A Standard Golf Co hickory and aluminium Mills G-plex 2½ model golf club,** c1905, 37in (94cm) long.
£270–300 / €390–440
$520–580 ⊞ SHER

An Expert Patent wood and canvas golf caddie, probably by Bussy & Co, c1905, 35½in (90cm) long.
£480–570 / €700–830
$920–1,100 ⋩ SWO

A Standard Golf Co patent Mills RL 1½ Standard the Duplex Model golf club, No. 45220, stamped, c1910, 36in (91.5cm) long.
£250–300 / €360–430
$480–580 ✦ BUDD

▶ **A silver-plated desk stand,** by Walker & Hall, the cut-glass inkwell flanked by golfing figures, c1910, 10in (25.5cm) wide.
£220–260
€320–380
$420–500 ✦ G(L)

◀ **A Robert Sinclair tobacco tin,** depicting a Gleneagles golfing scene, c1910, 6in (15cm) wide.
£70–80
€100–115
$135–155
⊞ SHER

A linen poster, depicting a golfer making notes, printed by Stetson Shoe Co, American, c1910, 24¾ x 17⅛in (63 x 43.5cm).
£100–120 / €145–175
$195–230 ✦ VSP

▶ **A Royal Doulton ceramic plate,** decorated with a golfing scene, c1910, 8½in (21.5cm) diam.
£210–240
€300–350
$400–460
⊞ MSh

A Noritake ceramic jar and cover, decorated with a golfer, Japanese, c1920, 7in (18cm) high.
£180–200 / €260–290
$340–380 ⊞ SHER

An F. H. Ayres Truput Shenectady-style putter, c1910, 34in (86.5cm) long.
£195–220 / €280–320
$370–420 ⊞ MSh

A set of miniature golf clubs, with a golf bag, c1910, 10in (25.5cm) long.
£270–300 / €390–440
$520–580 ⊞ SHER

A Leven hickory and persimmon practice driver, with distance gauge and reset button, c1920, 44in (112cm) long.
£270–300 / €390–440
$520–580 ⊞ SHER

◀ **A cut-glass water jug,** in the form of a golf ball, c1920, 6in (15cm) diam.
£180–200
€260–290
$340–380
⊞ SHER

◀ **A Cochranes steel and hickory Mammoth Niblick golf club,** c1920, 39in (99cm) long.
£450–500 / €650–730
$860–960 ⊞ SHER

▶ **A Royal Doulton ceramic milk jug,** decorated with golfers and inscribed 'Every Dog has his Day, Every Man has his Hour', c1920, 6in (15cm) high.
£270–300 / €390–440
$520–580 ⊞ SHER

A bronze golf plaque, 1920,
9in (23cm) diam.
**£180–200 €260–290
$340–380 ⊞ SHER**

◄ **Abe Mitchell,**
Essentials of Golf,
published by
Hodder &
Stoughton, 1927,
9in (23cm) high.
**£160–180
€230–260
$310–350
⊞ MSh**

**A silver course record
trophy,** the tripod base
forming a golf ball holder,
Birmingham 1928,
4in (10cm) high.
**£250–300 / €360–430
$480–580 ⚒ BUDD**

◄ **A leather golf bag,**
1930s, 36in (91.5cm) high.
**£100–120 / €145–175
$195–230 ⊞ MSh**

**A silver-plated golfing
trophy,** in the form of a
golfer, American, c1939,
6½in (16.5cm) high.
**£130–155 / €190–220
$250–300 ⚒ G(L)**

A silver caddy spoon,
the handle in the form of
a lady golfer, American,
1920s, 6in (15cm) long.
**£90–100 / €130–145
$170–190 ⊞ SHER**

For more silver
see pages 345–349

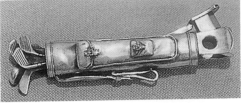

**A silver-plated cigar
cutter,** in the form of a
set of golf clubs, c1940,
6in (15cm) long.
**£180–210 / €260–300
$350–400 ⚒ DuM**

► **A Doulton Golfer
character jug,** by David
B. Briggs, edition of
1,000, marked, 1987,
7½in (19cm) high.
**£45–50 / €70–80
$85–95 ⚒ BBR**

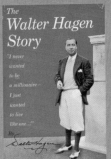

Horses

A cloisonné-mounted saddle and stirrups, slight damage, Chinese, 19thC, saddle 9¾in (25cm) high.
£1,050–1,250 / €1,500–1,800
$2,000–2,400 ↗ S(O)

A silver-mounted saddle and stirrups, with niello decoration, Caucasian, 19thC, 13¾in (35cm) high.
£1,200–1,400 / €1,750–2,050
$2,300–2,700 ↗ S(O)

A Victorian clay pipe, the bowl decorated with portraits of Fred Archer and Charlie Wood, inscribed 'Success', 5½in (14cm) long.
£50–60 / €75–85
$100–115 ↗ BUDD

A leather riding crop, with an antler handle and engraved silver band, c1880, 23in (58.5cm) long.
£50–60 / €75–85
$100–115 ⊞ GBr

A silver trophy, by Tiffany & Co, inscribed 'The Bennett School Horse Show 1924', 7½in (19cm) high, 43oz.
£130–155 / €190–220
$250–300 ↗ LHA

A wooden polo stick, 1930–50, 55in (139.5cm) long.
£15–20 / €22–29
$29–38 ⊞ SA

A photograph, of the Maharajah of Jahore on horseback, with a signed and dated inscription, 1928, 11½ x 9½in (29 x 24cm).
£80–90 / €115–130
$155–175 ↗ DW

A racing plate, inscribed 'Watling Street, Winner of the Derby 1942, Bred by Lord Derby, Trained by W. Earl, Ridden by H. Wragg', framed, 10in (25.5cm) square.
£400–480 / €580–700
$770–920 ↗ BUDD

◀ **A silk commemorative scarf,** depicting Nimbus, winner of the Derby, 1949.
£200–240 / €290–350
$390–460 ↗ BUDD

A silver flagon, inscribed 'The Bass Clubmen's Stakes, Haydock Park, 7th June 1975', London mark, 12½in (31cm) high.
£320–380 / €460–550
$610–730 ↗ SWO

Rugby

A photogravure picture, entitled 'A Rugby Match', after W. B. Woollen, published by Mawson, Swan & Morgan, 1896, 17½ x 29in (44.5 x 73.5cm), framed.
£250–300 / €360–440
$480–580 ⚲ BUDD

A set of six metal travelling cups, the leather case in the form of a rugby ball, c1920, 4½in (11.5cm) high.
£60–70 / €85–100
$115–135 ⊞ SA

A leather rugby ball, c1930.
£50–60 / €75–85
$100–115 ⊞ SA

An Arthur Wood Sporting Series ceramic mug, with two vignettes, each depicting a game of rugby, 1930s, 5in (12.5cm) high.
£35–40 / €50–60
$65–75 ⚲ VS

A wooden rugby trophy, inscribed 'Bombay Gymkhana Seven-a-Side Tournament', Indian, 1944, 4in (10cm) wide.
£45–50 / €65–75
$85–95 ⊞ PEZ

A pair of leather rugby boots, c1950.
£50–60 / €75–85
$100–115 ⊞ SA

A tobacco pouch, in the form of a rugby ball, c1950, 6in (15cm) wide.
£30–35 / €45–50
$55–65 ⊞ SA

A leather rugby cap, c1950.
£25–30 / €40–45
$50–55 ⊞ SA

A Sportsman Gin showcard, depicting a rugby player, 1950s, 11 x 7½in (28 x 19cm).
£60–70 / €85–100
$115–135 ⚲ VS

A Wigan Warriors RLFC 2000 Super League Grand Final kit, worn by Jason Robinson, comprising No. 5 shirt inscribed 'Tetley's Bitter Super League Grand Final 2000', the reverse with 'Robinson' signed by the Wigan team, together with shorts, socks, boots, boot bag and a letter of authenticity.
£1,000–1,200 / €1,450–1,750
$1,950–2,300 ⚲ BUDD

Shooting

A wooden powder flask, c1880, 6in (15cm) high.
£65–75 / €95–105
$125–145 ⊞ SA

▶ A copper and brass powder flask, c1890, 4in (10cm) high.
£65–75
€95–105
$125–145
⊞ SA

A brass cartridge loading device, c1900, 6in (15cm) long.
£65–75 / €95–105
$125–145 ⊞ SA

▶ A cast-iron clay pigeon trap, entitled 'The Taunton Trap', c1910, 32in (81.5cm) wide.
£70–80 / €100–115
$135–155 ⊞ JUN

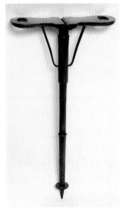

◀ An Edwardian rattan, bamboo and brass tripod shooting stick, 18in (45.5cm) high.
£220–250
€320–360
$420–480
⊞ MINN

An Edwardian mahogany shooting stick, 35in (89cm) high.
£90–100 / €130–145
$170–190 ⊞ MINN

▶ A wood and aluminium shooting stick, c1930, 35in (89cm) high.
£30–35 / €45–50
$55–65 ⊞ JUN

A leather cartridge bag, 1950s, 11in (28cm) wide.
£55–65 / €80–95
$105–125 ⊞ MINN

Tennis

The game of lawn tennis is descended from 'real tennis' an indoor sport first played in medieval France, where it was known as *Jeu de Paume* (palm game). The ball, made from sheepskin, and later from cloth, was originally struck with the bare hand – rackets were not used until the 15th century. Since the indoor court was bigger than a modern outdoor court, real tennis was the preserve of royalty and the super-rich. Henry VIII created one at Hampton Court which is still in use today, and in 1789, when Louis XVI locked the Third Estate out of their usual meeting place, the self-created 'National Assembly of France' repaired to the King's tennis courts at Versailles. It was there that they swore the famous 'Tennis Court Oath', vowing never to disperse until France had a constitution.

It was another revolution, this time a technological one, that facilitated the emergence of lawn tennis the following century. Thanks to developments in rubber there was a new type of tennis ball, and with the invention of the lawn mower a smooth lawn was possible. The man generally credited with inventing lawn tennis is Major Walter Wingfield who, in 1873, published a book of rules for 'Sphairistike or Lawn Tennis' and marketed kits for his new outdoor game. It was an instant success with both sexes, although women's long skirts and large hats meant that they were restricted to serving underarm. In 1875 the All-England Croquet Club at Wimbledon decided to set one of its lawns aside for tennis, and 1877 saw the first Wimbledon Tennis Championship.

Early rackets were made of wood, typically ash. The head of the racket varied in size and shape, and to make it easier to grip the wooden handle came in a number of different styles, such as fishtail, which had grooves in the wood to prevent the hand from getting too sweaty. Leather-wrapped handles were not introduced until c1930.

Sometimes rackets have a maker's name, but others are unmarked or might bear the name of the racket design rather than the manufacturer. It is important to learn to identify rackets by style and shape. One tip is to look at the wedge, the central piece of wood linking the head of the racket and the handle. On early examples (see the fishtail racket below) this has a convex curve, which was later replaced by a concave wedge that followed the downward curve of the frame.

With later 20th-century rackets, look out for examples endorsed by individual players, either with a printed signature or a portrait photo decal. These rackets can be worth four to five times more than identical rackets without endorsement.

A Tunnycliffe ceramic match holder, decorated with a tennis scene, c1880, 4in (10cm) diam.
£650–780 / €940–1,100
$1,250–1,500 ⊞ MSh

A brass and oak paper clip, in the form of two crossed tennis rackets and three tennis balls, 1890s, 5in (12.5cm) square.
£150–180 / €220–260
$290–350 ⊞ MSh

A Victorian brass table gong, in the form of two tennis rackets, net and striker, on an oak base, 15in (38cm) high.
£400–480 / €580–700
$770–920 ⚒ Mal(O)

◄ **A George Bussey & Co fishtail tennis racket,** 'The Diamond', with a grooved handle, c1900.
£760–850 / €1,100–1,250
$1,450–1,650 ⊞ MSh

A Feltham tennis racket, stamped 'The Alexandria' and '1602', with a convex wedge handle, damaged, early 20thC, 26½in (67.5cm) long.
£300–360 / €440–520
$580–690 ⚒ G(L)

A George Bussey & Co wooden tennis racket, 'Wimbledon Hexagon', c1910, 27in (68.5cm) long.
£135–150 / €195–220
$260–290 ⊞ MSh

A mahogany tennis racket press, c1910, 15in (38cm) long.
£180–200 / €260–290
$350–380 ⊞ MSh

Two Dayton tennis rackets, with wire stringing, American, c1920, 27in (68.5cm) long.
£80–90 / €115–130
$155–175 each ⊞ MINN

An embossed metal sign, 'The Slazenger Lawn Tennis Ball', 1920s, 7½ x 11½in (19 x 29cm).
£90–100 / €130–145
$170–190 ⚒ PF

◀ **A wooden tennis racket and frame,** c1930, 27in (68.5cm) long.
£270–300
€390–440
$520–580 ⊞ SA

▶ **A silver spoon,** by Martin, Hall and Co, in the form of a tennis racket, Sheffield 1931, 5¼in (13.5cm) long.
£610–680 / €880–990
$1,150–1,300 ⊞ BEX

A Keilers Polar Mint sweet tin, c1930, 7in (18cm) diam.
£35–40 / €50–60
$65–75 ⊞ JUN

◀ **A poster,** 'Erdal schoenwit', c1935, 34 x 24in (86.5 x 61cm).
£85–95
€120–135
$160–180
⚒ VSP

A tin of Dunlop tennis balls, c1960, 8in (20.5cm) high.
£50–60 / €75–85
$100–115 ⊞ MSh

▶ **An Imperial wooden tennis racket,** c1950, 27in (68.5cm) long.
£40–45 / €60–70
$75–85 ⊞ MSh

Teddy Bears & Soft Toys

'Compared to other fields, the collectors' market for vintage teddy bears is comparatively new. It has only been developed in the last 25 years and it is still settling down,' says Christie's toy and teddy bear expert, Daniel Agnew. In the 1980s and early '90s high prices were being paid across the board for bears of every period. Today, however, collectors appear more selective. 'Good things will still make high prices but at the lower end of the market, values have dropped,' says Agnew. 'Pre-WWI material is at a premium as there is less of it available and demand remains strong. Interest in post-WWII bears, however, has lessened. A few years ago, when they were commanding very high prices, people started to sell their family toys. Suddenly there were more objects available and as such prices have become more affordable.'

Another factor of this developing market is that purchasers have become more informed. 'Once upon a time, collectors were only prepared to pay large amounts of money for Steiff bears, but now there is serious interest in other makers,' says Agnew. 'One of the by-products of WWI in the UK was that people no longer wanted to buy German toys. This encouraged the manufacture of British bears. Many toy firms expanded their lines and new companies started up. Some wonderful bears were produced in Britain in the 1920s and '30s and they are attracting increasing attention.'

The high prices paid for bears have also encouraged enthusiasts to explore other areas. Over the past few years Agnew, an arctophile (bear collector) himself, has been turning his attention to soft toys. 'Because it is a less popular field, you can pick up really good, rare items for a fraction of the price you would pay for a bear of similar quality and vintage,' he enthuses. Here again, although Steiff is one of the leading names in the field, there were many other interesting makers active both in Europe and the USA in the interwar years. Soft toys are often inspired by pets, farm and zoo animals (elephants are one of the most sought-after subjects with collectors today) and, from the 1920s, films, comic strips and eventually television characters. Good pre-WWII soft toys tend to command the highest prices. The past 20 years have seen the production of a host of interesting soft toys from dinosaurs to African wildlife and, as far as many children are concerned, the traditional teddy has been relegated to the bottom of the toy box. Adult collectors often return to the favourite toys of their youth, so perhaps in the future, when today's children grow up, soft toys will provide an even more serious contender to the collectable teddy bear.

◀ **A Steiff teddy bear,** with ear button, c1907, 13in (33cm) high.
£540–600 / €780–870
$1,050–1,150 ⊞ WAC

A papier-mâché clockwork bear, with wooden feet, German, c1900, 6in (15cm) high.
£350–420 / €510–610
$670–810 ⋏ LAY

▶ **A Steiff felt elephant on wheels,** c1910, 11in (28cm) high.
£800–900 / €1,150–1,300
$1,550–1,750 ⊞ BBe

A William Terry mohair teddy bear, c1918, 18in (45.5cm) high.
£630–700 / €900–1,000
$1,200–1,350 ⊞ BBe

A teddy bear, possibly by Schuco, early 1920s,
£175–195 / €250–280 $330–370 ⊞ BINC

A Chiltern teddy bear, 1920s–30s,
15in (38cm) high.
£230–260 / €330–380 $440–500 ⊞ BINC

A Chad Valley teddy bear, c1930,
19in (48.5cm) high.
£540–600 / €780–870 $1,050–1,150 ⊞ BBe

A Merrythought teddy bear, with ear button and label, c1930,
18in (45.5cm) high.
£360–400 / €520–580 $690–770 ⊞ BBe

◀ **A Chiltern mohair teddy bear,** c1930,
16in (40.5cm) high.
£200–230 / €290–330 $380–440 ⊞ BBe

▶ **A Chad Valley Hygienic Toys teddy bear,** with ear button, feet pads replaced, 1930s,
16in (40.5cm) high.
£310–350 / €450–510 $600–670 ⊞ WAC

A Topsy Turvey bear/doll, 1930s,
12in (30.5cm) high.
£175–195 / €250–280 $330–370 ⊞ BBe

A Chad Valley silk plush elephant on wheels, button and label,
1930s, 8in (20.5cm) high.
£450–500 / €650–730 $860–960 ⊞ BBe

▶ **A Chad Valley dog,** with ear button,
1930s, 13in (33cm) high.
£175–195 €250–280 $330–370 ⊞ BBe

A Farnell teddy bear,
1930s, 15in (38cm) high.
£360–400 / €520–580 $690–770 ⊞ BBe

A Merrythought silk teddy bear, 1930s,
18in (45.5cm) high.
£310–350 / €450–510 $600–670 ⊞ BBe

A Dean's teddy bear,
1930s, 11in (28cm) high.
£360–400 / €520–580 $690–770 ⊞ BBe

◀ **A teddy bear,**
commemorating the Olympic Games, with a sash inscribed 'Berlin', German, 1930s,
15in (38cm) high.
£50–60 / €75–85 $100–115 ⊞ UD

A Farnell mohair monkey, with felt paws and label, 1930s, 14in (35.5cm) high.
£100–120 / €145–175
$195–230 ⊞ BBe

▶ **A Chad Valley bear,** c1940, 12in (30.5cm) high.
£125–140
€180–200
$240–270
⊞ WAC

A Dean's mohair teddy bear, 1930s, 14in (35.5cm) high.
£65–75 / €95–105
$125–145 ⊞ BBe

▶ **A Chad Valley mohair teddy bear,** with two labels, 1940s, 18in (45.5cm) high.
£310–350 / €450–510
$600–670 ⊞ BBe

A Pinter bear, riding a tricycle, French, 1940s–50s, 6½in (16.5cm) high.
£220–250 / €320–360
$420–480 ⊞ BINC

An Erris Toys mohair teddy bear, Irish, c1950, 12in (30.5cm) high.
£120–135 / €175–195
$230–260 ⊞ BBe

A Chiltern Hugmee teddy bear, c1950, 16in (40.5cm) high.
£270–300 / €390–440 $520–580 ⊞ BBe

A Pedigree teddy bear, c1950, 26in (66cm) high.
£240–270 / €350–390 $460–520 ⊞ BBe

A Chiltern Hugmee panda, 1950, 18in (45.5cm) high.
£450–500 / €650–730 $860–960 ⊞ BBe

A Chad Valley teddy bear, with card label and growler, 1950s, 24in (61cm) high.
£310–350 / €450–510 $600–670 ⊞ BBe

◀ **A Sooty teddy bear,** 1950s, 9in (23cm) high.
£30–35 €45–50 $55–65 ⊞ HYP

A Chad Valley Toffee teddy bear, from *Listen with Mother*, scarf missing, 1950s, 11in (28cm) high.
£210–240 / €300–350 $400–460 ⊞ BINC

▶ **A Tara teddy bear,** Irish, 1950s, 21in (53.5cm) high.
£270–300 €390–440 $520–580 ⊞ BINC

▶ **A set of two Dean's polar bears,** 'Ivy' and 'Brumas', with labels, 1950s, 18in (45.5cm) high.
£310–350 / €450–510 $600–670 ⊞ BBe
These polar bears were made to commemorate the birth of London Zoo's first polar bear cub, Brumas, born in 1949.

◀ **A Pedigree teddy bear,** with label and growler, 1950s, 16in (40.5cm) high.
£100–120 / €145–175 $195–230 ⊞ BBe

◀ **A Steiff bear,** 1950s, 15in (38cm) high.
£360–400 / €520–580 $690–770 ⊞ WAC

▶ **A Farnell Toffee teddy bear,** 1950s, 11in (28cm) high.
£450–500 / €650–730 $860–960 ⊞ BBe

An Ealon Toys musical bear, 1950s, 15in (38cm) high.
£180–200 / €260–290 $340–380 ⊞ BBe

A Merrythought Noddy muff, 1950s, 14in (35.5cm) high.
£180–200 / €260–290 $340–380 ⊞ BBe

An Invicta bear, early 1950s, 28in (71cm) high.
£320–360 / €460–520 $610–690 ⊞ BBe
Founded in 1935 by two ex-Farnell employees, Invicta ceased trading in the early 1950s.

A Merrythought silk plush Cheeky teddy bear, with label, late 1950s, 14in (35.5cm) high.
£270–300 / €390–440 $520–580 ⊞ BBe

A plastic and plush Noddy doll, 1950s, 12in (30.5cm) high.
£25–30 / €40–45 $50–55 ⊞ BBe

◄ **A Steiff velveteen Grissy donkey,** 1960, 6in (15cm) wide.
£55–65 €80–95 $105–125 ⊞ NAW

A Pedigree Jerry toy, c1960, 9in (23cm) high.
£20–25 / €30–35 $35–45 ⊞ HeA
Tom and Jerry first appeared in 1940 in a short film entitled *Puss Gets the Boot*, created for MGM by Bill Hanna and Joe Barbera. The cat was initially called Jasper, and the mouse had no name, but the characters and the format of chasing, escaping, extreme violence and remarkable humour was established. The names Tom and Jerry were literally picked out of a hat containing various suggestions from MGM staff. The series of films produced at MGM from 1940 to 1957 were hugely successful and won seven Academy Awards.

A Steiff Zotty teddy bear, with ear button and tag, c1960, 12in (30.5cm) high.
£540–600 / €780–870 $1,000–1,150 ⊞ BBe

A Schuco miniature teddy bear, c1960, 4in (10cm) high.
£95–110 / €140–160 $180–210 ⊞ WAC

◀ **A cloth golly,** c1960, 14in (35.5cm) high.
£25–30 / €40–45
$40–55 ⊞ UD

For more gollies
see pages 11–25

▶ **A cloth golly,** 1960s, 11in (28cm) high.
£25–30 / €40–45
$40–55 ⊞ LAS

A Gabrielle Designs Paddington Bear, with original clothing and Wellington boots, with label, 1972, 20in (50cm) high.
£75–90 / €110–130
$145–175 ⋏ GAZE

A Fisher Price Fozzy Bear, 1976, 14in (35.5cm) high.
£15–20 / €22–29
$29–38 ⊞ LAS

A Gabrielle Designs Aunt Lucy Bear, with original clothes and accessories, 1978, 18in (45.5cm) high.
£85–100 / €125–145
$165–190 ⋏ GAZE

A Wendy Boston Basil Brush, 1970s, 16in (40.5cm) high.
£55–65 / €80–95
$105–125 ⊞ POLL

A Merrythought monkey, 1980, 17in (43cm) high.
£45–50 / €65–75
$85–95 ⊞ POLL

A McDonald's cloth Grimace, 1980s, 12in (30.5cm) high.
£60–70 / €85–100
$115–135 ⊞ McD

◀ **A Steiff Polly Parrot,** with button and flag, 1980s, 12in (30.5cm) high.
£85–95 / €125–140
$165–185 ⊞ BBe

▶ **An Applause teddy bear,** by Robert Raikes, 1985, 11in (28cm) high.
£145–165 / €210–240
$280–320 ⊞ UD

A Miss Piggy soft toy, 1998, 47in (119.5cm) high.
£30–35 / €45–50
$55–65 ⊞ LAS

A Merrythought Jack-in-the-Box, 1990s, 11in (28cm) high.
£100–110 / €145–160
$190–210 ⊞ WAC

Telephones

A brass skeleton desk telephone, with hand-crank generator, No. 16, with two internal bells, c1900, 12in (30.5cm) high.
£280–330 / €410–480
$540–630 ⚷ G(L)

► A brass bell box for a 232 telephone, 1930s, 7in (18cm) long.
£60–70
€85–100
$115–135
⊞ TASV

► A Kellogg oak telephone, with original mechanism, American, c1900, 19in (48.5cm) high.
£85–100 / €120–145
$170–200 ⚷ JAA

A Bakelite telephone, with original chrome dial and braid lead, fully converted, 1920s, 7in (18cm) wide.
£160–180 / €230–260
$310–350 ⊞ TASV

► A Bakelite and nickel-plated telephone, Continental, c1925, 9in (23cm) high.
£35–45 / €50–60
$65–75 ⚷ JAA

◄ A Sterling Telephone & Electric Co walnut telephone, 1930s.
£35–45 / €50–60
$65–75 ⚷ AMB

◄ A Bakelite telephone, 1940s, 9in (23cm) wide.
£190–220
€280–320
$360–420
⊞ SAT

A Bakelite 323 telephone and bell set, 1940s, 9in (23cm) wide.
£175–195 / €250–280
$330–370 ⊞ CAB
This Bakelite 232 telephone and bell set was introduced in 1937 and produced until the late 1950s. Although black was the most common colour, the 232 telephone, complete with cheese drawer for a telephone exchange card, was also produced in ivory and more rarely in Chinese red and jade green. These coloured versions are sought after. Beware of modern reproductions and black telephones that have been sprayed a different colour.

A Bakelite 232 telephone, 1950s, 9in (23cm) wide.
£720–800 / €1,000–1,150
$1,400–1,550 ⊞ CAB

A 706L telephone, fully converted, 1960s, 5in (12.5cm) wide.
£50–60 / €75–85
$100–115 ⊞ TASV

An Ericsson telephone, 1950s, 6in (15cm) high.
£70–80 / €100–115
$135–155 ⊞ TL

A Trimphone, fully converted, 1970s, 8in (20.5cm) long.
£50–60 / €75–85
$100–115 ⊞ TASV

▶ **A plastic telephone,** in the form of R2D2, c1990, 11in (28cm) high.
£65–75
€95–105
$125–145
⊞ LUNA

A *Star Trek* telephone, in the form of the USS Enterprise, c1998, 8in (20.5cm) high.
£70–80 / €100–115
$135–155 ⊞ LUNA

Theatre

A silver pass, for the Cock Pit, London, c1765, 1½in (4cm) high.
£670–750 / €970–1,100 $1,300–1,450 ⊞ TML

A silver pass, for Dublin Private Theatre, by Mossop, c1780, 1½in (4cm) high.
£290–330 / €420–480 $560–630 ⊞ TML

A silver pass, for the King's Theatre and Opera House, Haymarket, pierced for suspension, last three lines later, possibly a reissue, 1784, 2in (5cm) high.
£850–950 / €1,250–1,400 $1,600–1,800 ⊞ TML

A silver pass, for the Halifax Theatre, c1789, 1¾in (4.5cm) diam.
£670–750 / €970–1,100 $1,300–1,450 ⊞ TML
The Theatre Royal in Halifax was erected in 1789 and each of the 12 sponsors was given a silver pass bearing the words 'Halifax Theatre'. These passes allowed unlimited admission to all performances at the theatre.

An ink and wash drawing of six miniature portraits of actors, by Robert Cruikshank, signed, 19thC, 48.5 x 9½in (19 x 24cm).
£410–490 / €590–710 $780–940 ✗ BBA
Robert Cruikshank (1786–1856), trained under his artist father Isaac Cruikshank. He served in the Merchant Navy during the Napoleonic wars before setting himself up as a painter of miniatures in London in 1814. Between 1816 and 1825 he rivalled his brother George Cruikshank (1792–1878) as illustrator and caricaturist of fashion, military life and the stage.

A theatre flyer, advertising *Tippoo Saib's Two Sons* and *Bagshot-Heath Camp*, Mr Astley's Saloon and New Amphitheatre, Westminster Bridge, the reverse with two songs, c1800, 19¾ x 7¼in (50 x 18.5cm).
£110–130 / €160–190 $210–250 ✗ BBA

A bronze medal, by I. Warwick, depicting John Philip Kemble, the reverse inscribed 'The Last of all the Romans. Fare Thee Well', 1817, 1½in (4cm) diam.
£65–75 / €95–105 $125–145 ⊞ TML
The legend on the reverse is taken from *Coriolanus,* John Kemble's last performance at Covent Garden. This medal was worn by the Committee at the public dinner given to Kemble on his retirement from the stage.

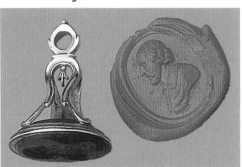

◄ **A glass seal,** moulded with the head of William Shakespeare, with gold bezel, c1830, 1in (2.5cm) high.
£175–195 / €250–280 $330–370 ⊞ TML

A theatrical print, depicting Mr Macready as Rob Roy Macgregor, published by A. Park, signed 'W. I. Langdon', 1837, 10½ x 8¼in (26.5 x 21cm).
£200–220 / €290–320
$380–420 ➢ BBA
British actor William Macready (1793–1873) was one of the most famous tragedians of his generation. He was also known for his rivalry with other actors, which itself culminated in a famous tragedy. In the spring of 1849, Macready and American actor Edwin Forrest both appeared in simultaneous productions of *Macbeth* in New York. Whipped up by the press and anti-British sentiment, their professional competitiveness escalated into a nationalist and class war with Forrest, who was performing at the Bowery, standing for working-class America, while Macready, at the Astoria Palace Opera house, came to epitomize upper-class British-influenced elitism. Macready's performances were disrupted by Forrest's predominantly working-class supporters. He wanted to finish the engagement early but was persuaded by his wealthy American patrons not to withdraw. On the night of 10 May 1849, a mob of 20,000 men descended on the Opera House in protest during Macready's performance. A full-scale street riot erupted outside the theatre and as the violence peaked police fired directly into the crowd, killing at least 22 people and wounding more than 150. The rioters did not disperse until cannons were brought in. This was the bloodiest event in the history of the New York theatre.

▶ **A theatre programme,** for *The Mighty Dollar*, Gaiety Theatre, 1880, 9½ x 7in (24 x 18cm).
£20–25 / €30–35
$40–50 ⊞ c20th

◀ **A theatre programme,** for *The Mikado*, Savoy Theatre, 1885, 9 x 5½in (23 x 14cm).
£25–30 / €40–45
$50–55 ⊞ c20th

The Playgoer and Society magazine, 1911, 10 x 8in (25.5 x 20.5cm).
£2–6 / €3–9
$4–11 ⊞ J&S

A spelter inkwell, in the form of Dan Leno dressed as a pantomime dame in *Bluebeard*, 1883, 4¾in (12cm) high.
£135–150 / €195–220
$260–290 ⊞ c20th

◀ **A theatre programme,** for the D'Oyly Carte Opera Company, Crystal Palace Theatre, 1907, 9¾ x 4¼in (25 x 11cm).
£35–40 / €50–60
$65–75 ⊞ c20th
The D'Oyly Carte Company produced programmes for all their performances with the respective theatres printing their details on the programme covers.

A Walther & Sohne glass flower bowl, with a figure of Peter Pan, German, 1934, 9¾in (25cm) high.
£220–250 / €320–360
$420–480 ⊞ c20th

◀ **A chrome and wood Peter Pan lamp base,** 1930s, 9½in (24cm) high.
£100–120 / €145–170
$195–230 ⊞ c20th

A Parrott Ware cruet set, decorated with characters from Gilbert and Sullivan's operettas, 1930s, 6in (15cm) wide.
£35–40 / €50–60
$65–75 ⊞ c20th

A theatre programme, for *Apple Sauce!*, London Palladium, 1941, 8¾in x 5½in (22 14cm).
£6–10 / €9–15
$12–19 ⊞ c20th

A theatre programme, for Théâtre de l'Etoile, Paris, starring Edith Piaf, 1947, 6 x 4¾in (15 x 12cm).
£25–30 / €40–45
$50–55 ⊞ c20th

A theatre poster, advertising *Tough at the Top*, Adelphi Theatre, 1949, 20 x 11¾in (51 x 30cm).
£60–70 / €100–115
$135–155 ⊞ c20th

A theatre programme, for a variety performance starring Judy Garland, London Palladium, 1951, 8¼ x 5¼in (21 x 13.5cm).
£10–15 / €15–22
$19–28 ⊞ c20th
This was Judy Garland's first British appearance.

A theatre programme, for The Hippodrome Hulme, Manchester, 1955, 9 x 5in (23 x 12.5cm).
£1–5 / €2–7
$3–9 ⊞ HOM

◀ **A theatre programme,** for *Jack and the Beanstalk*, Theatre Royal, Windsor, 1959, 9 x 7in (23 x 18cm).
£1–5 / €2–7
$3–9 ⊞ HOM

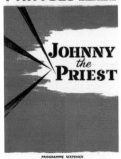

A theatre programme, for *Johnny The Priest*, Princes Theatre, 1960, 9 x 6¼in (23 x 16cm).
£25–30 / €40–452
$50–55 ⊞ c20th

A concert programme, for Anna Russell, Royal Festival Hall, 1960, 9½ x 7in (24 x 18cm).
£1–5 / €2–7
$3–9 ⊞ c20th

A theatre programme, for The Cambridge Footlights, starring John Cleese, at Cambridge Circus, 1963, 8¼ x 5½in (21 x 14cm).
£10–15 / €15–22
$19–28 ⊞ c20th

A theatre programme, by John Lennon, for 'Night of 100 Stars' charity event, London Palladium, 1964, 11¾ x 9½in (30 x 24cm).
£90–100 / €130–145
$170–190 ⊞ c20th

A theatre programme, for *Funny Girl*, starring Barbra Streisand, Prince of Wales Theatre, 1966, 11¾ x 9½in (30 x 24cm).
£90–100 / €130–145
$170–190 ⊞ c20th

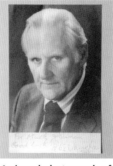

A Variety Show programme, featuring Max Bygraves, London Palladium, 1969, 9 x 6in (23 x 15cm).
£1–5 / €2–7
$3–9 ⊞ HOM

A theatre poster, advertising *Belle Starr*, starring Betty Grable, Palace Theatre, 1969, 20 x 11¾in (51 x 30cm).
£100–120 / €145–175
$195–230 ⊞ c20th

◄ **A theatre programme,** for the Royal Shakespeare Company tour of Japan, with Judi Dench, 1972, 9¾ x 9½in (25 x 24cm).
£25–30 / €40–45
$50–55 ⊞ c20th

A theatre programme, for 'A Night with Dame Edna', Piccadilly Theatre, 1979, 11¾ x 8¼in (30 x 21cm).
£6–10 / €9–15
$12–19 ⊞ c20th

A theatre poster, advertising *They're Playing Our Song*, Shaftsbury Theatre, 1981, 19¾ x 11¾in (51 x 30cm).
£3–7 / €4–10
$6–13 ⊞ c20th

A signed photograph of Peter Vaughan, 1980s, 6 x 4in (15 x 10cm).
£1–5 / €2–7
$3–9 ⊞ S&D

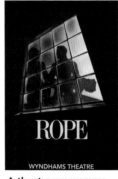

A theatre programme, for *Rope*, starring Anthony Head, Wyndhams Theatre, 1993, 9½ x 6¾in (24 x 17cm).
£2–6 / €3–9
$4–11 ⊞ c20th

A theatre programme, for *The Wizard of Oz*, Barbican Theatre, 1985, 11¾ x 8in (30 x 20.5cm).
£6–10 / €9–15
$12–19 ⊞ c20th

► **A theatre programme,** for *The Rocky Horror Show*, Piccadilly Theatre, 1990, 11¾ x 8¾in (30 x 22cm).
£1–5 / €2–7
$3–9 ⊞ c20th

Tools

Antique tool enthusiasts fall into two major categories: those who buy to use and those who purchase for collection and display. 'Vintage tools were far better made than today's mass-produced items,' explains David Stanley, whose auction house has specialized in antique woodworking tools for nearly 25 years. 'These objects were created for daily use and were built to last. They are heavier than modern alternatives and feel more comfortable in the hand. The wood, steel and other materials used tend to be higher in quality. The objects that people buy to use are often chisels and planes – the sort of tools that are still employed today by joiners, furniture makers and carpenters, who like working with the vintage, higher-quality equipment.'

However, the highest prices tend to be reserved for the older and rarer tools from the 18th and 19th centuries that are purchased as historical artefacts. 'The Americans are among the strongest collectors in this field, particularly for antique British tools,' says Stanley. 'While France produced good tools in the 17th century, from the mid-18th century up until the mid-20th century Britain manufactured some of the best tools in the world, particularly in the Sheffield area. America made good tools in the 19th century, but they tended to be plain, purely functional items. British tools were often more decorative as well as being useful, which is why people like them today.'

Decoration is one factor that affects value, another is the name. 'An 18th-century wooden plane by a major maker might sell for three- or four-figure sums. An identical-looking, unmarked plane might be worth as little as £10 / €15 / $19,' says Stanley. 'A good name is very important.'

Planes, one of the most collected tools, are also very popular in the USA. Some enthusiasts focus solely on this area, sometimes concentrating on either wood or metal examples. There has been much research into makers, and tools should always be checked for a mark or initials. However, many will be unmarked and even without a known manufacturer, a rare and high-quality tool will be desirable.

As in other fields, the best antique pieces are becoming harder to find. 'Ten years ago, we would get a lot of items brought in simply by people clearing out their garden sheds and removing grandad's old tools,' says Stanley. 'Today, items are much harder to find and you have to look further afield. Some good material has been coming from Germany, Holland and France.'

Whether buying for use or display, all collectors are, to some extent, attracted by nostalgia. 'Once upon a time, every village or town would have had a blacksmith, a cooper, a wheelwright and a host of other wood and metal workers. Many of these professions have all but disappeared, but by preserving vintage tools you are also saving a little bit of our craft history,' concludes Stanley.

◄ **A Bigorne anvil,** French, 17thC, 16in (40.5cm) high.
£1,900–2,250
€2,750–3,250
$3,650–4,300
⚒ **DStA**

A pair of brass dividers, with wheel device markings, Dutch, 17thC, 3½in (9cm) long.
£110–130 / €160–190
$210–250 ⚒ **DStA**

An iron and wood armourer's saw, with primitive decoration, German, dated 1660, 18in (45.5cm) long.
£3,500–4,200 / €5,100–6,100
$6,700–8,100 ⚒ **DStA**

A metal jeweller's piercing saw, with a turned fruitwood handle, French, 18thC, 9in (23cm) long.
£540–640 / €780–930
$1,050–1,250 ⚒ DStA

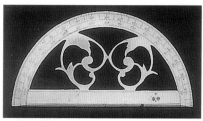

A brass protractor, French, 18thC, 4in (10cm) wide.
£180–210 / €260–300
$350–400 ⚒ DStA

A metal and wood jeweller's piercing saw, by Thewlis & Co, 18thC, 8½in (21.5cm) long.
£135–150 / €195–220
$260–290 ⊞ WO

A wooden moulding plane, by John Rogers, 18thC, 9½in (24cm) wide.
£50–55 / €70–80
$95–105 ⊞ WO

A metal mast-maker's blocking axe, with a wooden handle, European, 18thC, 12in (30.5cm) long.
£180–210 / €260–300
$350–400 ⚒ DStA

◄ **A goldsmith's bronze hammer head,** engraved with serpents, French, 18thC, 2½in (6.5cm) long.
£250–300 / €360–440
$480–580 ⚒ DStA

A pair of steel wine cooper's nips, one brass cap missing, impressed 'IW' mark, 18thC, 5in (12.5cm) long.
£45–50 / €76–75
$85–95 ⚒ DStA

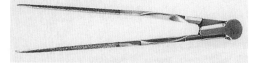

A pair of brass and steel double-hinge dividers, 18thC, 11in (28cm) long.
£160–190 / €230–280
$310–360 ⚒ DStA

A metal goosewing side axe, with a wooden handle, Austrian, 18thC, blade 12in (30.5cm) long.
£100–120 / €145–170
$200–230 ⚒ DStA

A pair of iron cooper's compasses, with moulded decoration, French, 18thC, 31in (78.5cm) long.
£140–165 / €200–240
$270–320 ⚒ DStA

▶ **A pair of iron cooper's compasses,** with fleur-de-Lys decoration, French, 18thC, 21in (53.5cm) long.
£45–50 / €65–75
$85–95 ⚒ DStA

A hand-forged metal bench vice, with swivel action and adjustment screw, 18thC, 4in (10cm) wide.
£210–250 / €300–360
$400–480 ≯ DStA

An iron plane, c1700, 4¾in (12cm) long.
£420–500 / €610–730
$810–960 ≯ DStA

A wooden moulding plane, by R. Elmore, 1713–15, 11in (28cm) wide.
£1,350–1,500 / €1,950–2,150
$2,600–2,900 ⊞ WO

A Georgian fruitwood and brass sash window dowelling box, 10in (25.5cm) wide.
£480–570 / €700–830
$920–1,050 ≯ DStA

▶ **B. & T. Langley,** *The Builder's Jewel: or the Youth's Instructor and Workman's Remembrancer Explaining Short and Easy Rules,* 1763, 5½in (14cm) high, 200 illustrations on 100 copper plates, bound in leather.
£150–180 / €220–260
$290–350 ≯ DStA

A brass hammer head, with engraved decoration, French, 1771, head 3in (7.5cm) long.
£1,050–1,250 / €1,550–1,800
$2,000–2,400 ≯ DStA

A metal cobbler's hammer, marked 'Esereux', French, 19thC, head 4in (10cm) wide.
£40–45 / €60–70
$75–85 ≯ DStA

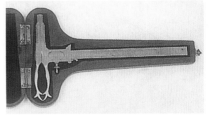

A metal engineer's calliper, French, 19thC, (25cm) long, in a fitted walnut case.
£145–170 / €210–250
$280–330 ≯ DStA

An iron block plane, with brass lever, 19thC, 5in (12.5cm) long.
£250–300 / €360–440
$480–580 ≯ DStA

A cast-iron cartridge crimper, 19thC, 10in (25.5cm) high.
£25–30 / €40–45
$50–55 ⊞ FST

◀ **A pair of brass and steel scissors,** 19thC, 7in (15cm) long.
£60–70 / €85–100
$115–135 ⊞ BS

A metal wheelwright's bruzz, by William Swift, with a wooden handle, 19thC, 13in (33cm) long.
£25–30 / €40–45
$50–55 ⊞ WO
A bruzz is a corner chisel.

A metal lock mortice chisel, with a wooden handle, 19thC, 21in (53.5cm) long.
£25–30 / €40–45
$50–55 ⊞ WO

A pair of steel cloth-cutting shears, 19thC, 5in (12.5cm) long.
£60–70 / €85–100
$115–135 ⊞ BS

A cast-iron jeweller's roller, 19thC, 14in (35.5cm) high.
£115–130 / €165–190
$220–250 ⊞ FST

An oak and boxwood bevel, 19thC, 26in (66cm) long.
£35–40 / €50–60
$65–75 ⊞ WO

> **Cross Reference**
> Science & Technology
> see pages 328–338

A metal jeweller's hammer, with a figured rosewood handle, marked 'L. Dupré', French, 19thC, head 2in (5cm) wide.
£65–75 / €95–105
$125–145 ➤ DStA

◀ A cormier-wood pistol router, by Aux Mines de Suisse, French, 19thC, 8in (20.5cm) long.
£240–280 / €350–410
$460–540 ➤ DStA
Cormier (*Sorbus domestica*) is a fine-grained wood of high density which was grown in France. Although rarely employed nowadays for making tools, it is still used in carving, wood turning, marquetry, rifle butts and musical instruments. In the UK it is known as the 'service', or 'whitty pear' tree, but is not commonly grown.

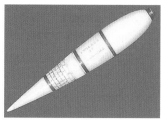

An ivory multiple tool, comprising a nutmeg grater, pencil, various blades and cutter, engraved with a calendar, stamped 'I. Wilkes', 19thC, 4½in (11.5cm) long.
£280–330 / €410–480
$540–630 ➤ BWL

▶ A metal bark spud, with a wooden handle, 19thC, 9in (23cm) long.
£10–15 / €15–22
$19–22 ⊞ WO
For many centuries, bark was used to tan leather. 'Bark peelers' cut down trees, peeled off the bark using a bark spud, and carried it to the tannery.

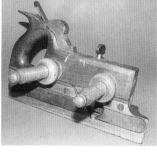

A brass-mounted beech and boxwood plough plane, by Alex Mathieson & Son, impressed marks, 19thC, 10¾in (27.5cm) long.
£80–90 / €115–130
$155–175 ➤ PFK

A cast-iron shoe stretcher, 19thC, 17in (43cm) long.
£25–30 / €40–45
$50–55 ⊞ FST

◀ A jeweller's miniature steelyard, Continental, c1800, 4in (10cm) long.
£220–250
€320–360
$420–480 ⊞ WO

A rosewood and metal smoother plane, by H. Slater, 19thC, 7½in (19cm) long.
£125–140 / €180–200
$240–270 ⊞ WO

◀ A brass gauge, by Shaw, with a protractor arc, 1825–40, 10in (25.5cm) long.
£200–240
€290–350
$390–460
➶ DStA

A brass gunner's calliper, by Gilbert, with steel tips, stamped 'East India Co', 19thC.
£1,700–2,000 / €2,450–2,900
$3,250–3,800 ➶ DStA

A drawknife, by Gilpin, c1850, 8in (20.5cm) wide.
£20–25 / €30–35
$40–50 ⊞ WO

A mahogany and satinwood-inlaid cabinetmaker's tool chest, by Phillip Walker, with two banks of 20 drawers and dummy drawers, c1850, 44in (112cm) wide.
£1,800–2,150
€2,600–3,100
$3,450–4,100 ➶ DStA

A steel mitre plane, by Spiers, c1850, 10½in (26.5cm) long.
£950–1,050 / €1,400–1,650
$1,800–2,150 ➶ DStA

A Victorian metal billhook, by Palmer, with a wooden handle, 7in (18cm) long.
£30–35 / €45–50
$55–65 ⊞ WO

A brass drawing set, comprising seven pieces including an ivory sector by Wellington, in a shagreen case, signed 'Edwin Downton', 1860, 7in (18cm) high.
£260–310 / €380–450
$500–600 ➶ DStA

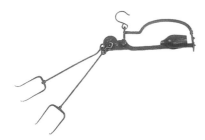

◀ A steelyard, marked 'Avery', c1900, 12in (30.5cm) long.
£260–310
€380–450
$500–600
✈ DStA
This tool was used for weighing bread.

A pair of elm and leather bellows, c1900, 20in (51cm) long.
£55–65 / €80–95
$105–125 ⊞ NEW

A pair of steel tailor's scissors, by J. Wiss & Sons, American, c1900, 14in (35.5cm) long.
£70–80 / €100–115
$135–155 ⊞ BS

A pine cigar mould, Dutch, c1900, 22in (56cm) long.
£10–15 / €15–22
$19–28 ⊞ Byl

A GPO telephone engineer's tool, early 20thC, 6in (15cm) long.
£35–40 / €50–60
$65–75 ⊞ BS
This pre-WWII tool would have been used to remove the covers from subscribers' meters in the telephone exchange.

A steel shoulder plane, early 20thC, 10in (25.5cm) long.
£90–100 / €130–145
$170–190 ⊞ WO

◀ A steel furrier's knife and comb, early 20thC, comb 6in (15cm) long.
£15–20 / €22–29
$29–38 ⊞ FST

A wooden miniature bow saw, by Maples, early 20thC, 16in (40.5cm) wide.
£35–40 / €50–60
$65–75 ⊞ FST

A wooden hat stretcher, by Stow & Huggins, c1915, 8in (20.5cm) wide.
£85–95 / €125–140
$165–185 ⊞ FST

A cast-iron jeweller's ring reducer, c1930, 10in (25.5cm) high.
£90–100 / €130–145
$170–190 ⊞ FST

A metal King Dick wrench, No. 0, 1930, 3in (7.5cm) long.
£10–15 / €15–22
$19–28 ⊞ WO

Toys

◀ **A Pratt & Letchworth metal two-horse dray,** with removable slats and side panels, repainted, c1893, 17in (43cm) long.
£400–480 / €580–700
$770–920 ✗ Bert

A Meccano Windmill Set, c1913, in original box, 9in (23cm) wide.
£1,250–1,500 / €1,800–2,150
$2,400–2,900 ✗ VEC

Meccano

Meccano was a metal construction system made of simple, unpainted steel strips patented by Frank Hornby, a Liverpool clerk, in 1901. Nickel-plated Meccano was introduced in 1908 and in 1926 the first sets were produced in red and green. The interwar years were a golden age for Meccano, and during the 1930s the range was extended to include car and aeroplane construction outfits. Frank Hornby's company became one of Britain's most important toy manufacturers, creating Hornby trains, Dinky toys and a wide range of other products from chemistry sets to radio receivers. Meccano remained popular in the 1950s, but demand began to tail off in the '60s and production at the famous Binns Road factory ceased in 1979. Early Meccano construction outfits, which came in attractive, well illustrated cardboard boxes, are very sought after. The windmill set shown here is possibly unique, and, until it appeared at auction, was an unrecorded model. The Meccano radio receiving set is another great rarity, dating from the earliest years of radio. It very seldom appears on the market today.

A Meccano No. 1 Radio Receiving Set, on an oak base, with spare crystals, original box and booklet and a pair of contemporary BBC/Ericsson headphones, c1922, 10in (25.5cm) wide.
£6,200–7,400 / €9,000–10,700
$11,900–14,200 ✗ VEC

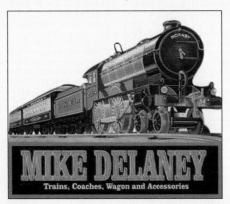

◀ **A Schoenhut wooden Felix the Cat toy,** by Pat Sullivan, with leather ears and painted features, restrung, American, 1924, 8in (20.5cm) high.
£160–190 / €230–270
$310–360 ⚲ **JDJ**
America's most famous cartoon creature before Mickey Mouse, Felix the Cat was created by animator Otto Messner for film maker Pat Sullivan and first appeared in the short film *Feline Follies* in 1919. With further films and a syndicated cartoon strip (1923–43), Felix became an international star to rival Charlie Chaplin and Buster Keaton. Felix inspired a wealth of merchandise and this is an early example. The tail served as a tripod so that the cat could stand, illustrating the words of his signature tune 'Felix keeps on walking . . . with his hands behind him.'

A Wilfar Mystic Designer set, 1930s, with box, 8 x 10in (20.5 x 25.5cm).
£35–40 / €50–60
$65–75 ⊞ Dob

A set of turned wood indoor skittles, 1950s, 13in (33cm) high.
£15–20 / €22–29
$29–38 ⊞ UD

A bus conductor's outfit, on original card, 1950s, 18in (45.5cm) high.
£40–45 / €60–70
$75–85 ⊞ JUN

A pack of six Art School Crayons, 1950s, 4 x 2in (10 x 5cm).
£1–5 / €2–7
$3–9 ⊞ RTT

◀ **A Chad Valley Muffin the Mule embroidery set,** 1950s, 10½ x 12½in (26.5 x 32cm).
£360–400 / €520–580
$690–770 ⊞ MTMC
Muffin the Mule was one of Britain's earliest children's television stars. The puppet first appeared on the BBC show *For the Children* in 1946, dancing on Annette Mills' piano as she played and sang. By 1950, there was a range of spin-offs including books, records of the much-loved 'We Want Muffin' theme tune and other objects. Annette Mills died in 1955, bringing Muffin's career to an end. Muffin material is very sought after by collectors and the character is set for a television revival.

A Marx Toys battery-operated plastic Hovercraft, 1960s, 10in (25.5cm) wide.
£45–50 / €65–75
$85–95 ⊞ HAL

A Bendy toys rubber Noddy and car, 1960s, 10in (25.5cm) wide.
£40–45 / €60–70
$75–85 ⊞ LAS

A My Little Pony Drink and Wet Baby Rainfeather, 1989, 3in (7.5cm) high.
£1–5 / €2–7
$3–9 ⊞ RAND

Cars & Vehicles

An Arcade cast-iron Chevrolet Coupé, with nickel wheels and silver-trimmed radiator, American, c1928, 8in (20.5cm) long.
£1,000–1,200 / €1,450–1,750
$1,900–2,300 ⚲ Bert

An Arcade cast-iron Dodge Coupe Taxi, slight damage, spare wheel embossed '1922', 8½in (21.5cm) long.
£800–950 / €1,200–1,400
$1,500–1,800 ⚲ Bert

A Fox diecast Toonerville trolley, with plastic wheels, 1923, 3¼in (8.5cm) wide.
£120–140 / €175–200
$230–270 ⚲ Bert

◀ **A C. I. Hubley No. 5 Boattail Racer,** with a hinged hood, American, 1920s–30s, 9¼in (23.5cm) long.
£370–440
€540–640
$710–840 ⚲ JDJ

An Arcade cast-iron Ford Sedan, with a nickel grill, roof inscribed 'Century of Progress–1933', American, 1934, 6½in (16.5cm) long.
£430–500 / €620–730
$820–960 ⚲ Bert

An Arcade cast-iron Greyhound Lines Tandem Bus, the roof inscribed 'Great Lakes Exposition 1936', American, 10¾in (27.5cm) long.
£680–810 / €990–1,150
$1,300–1,550 ⚲ Bert

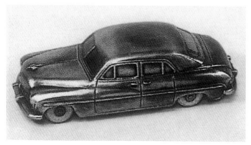

A National Products diecast Mercury Sedan, with rubber tyres and tin hubs, marked 'Authentic Scale Model Mercury', 1949, 6½in (16.5cm) long.
£100–120 / €145–175
$195–230 ⚲ Bert

A National Products diecast Nash Sedan, with rubber tyres and tin hubs, marked '1949 Nash Airflyte', 1950, 6½in (16.5cm) long.
£115–135 / €165–195
$220–260 ✹ Bert

A Master Caster diecast advertising Hudson Royal Sedan, marked 'L. C. Driesbach – Schuylkill Haven, Penna', manufacturer's marks, 1954, 7½in (19cm) long.
£350–420 / €510–610
$670–810 ✹ Bert

A Mettoy cast-metal Mechanical Tractor and Plough, 1950s–60s, with box.
£300–360 / €440–520
$580–690 ✹ GAZE

A Märklin Volkswagen van, No. 8033, c1960.
£2,300–2,750 / €3,350–4,000
$4,400–5,300 ✹ VEC

A Victory VIP Raceways Electric Racing Car set, 1961, 18 x 19in (45.5 x 48.5cm), with box.
£155–175 / €220–250
$300–340 ⊞ GTM

A Tri-Ang Spot-On presentation pack, with four sports cars, 1960s, 8 x 7in (20.5 x 18cm), with original box.
£450–500 / €650–730
$860–960 ⊞ HAL

A Tri-Ang Spot-On Meadows Frisky, No. 119, worn, 1960s, 3in (7.5cm) long, with box.
£20–25 / €30–35
$40–50 ✹ GAZE

A Politoys diecast Alfa Romeo, Italian, 1960s, 4in (10cm) long, with original box.
£50–60 / €75–85
$100–115 ⊞ HAL

A Budgie Models Routemaster Bus, No. 236, made for H. Seener Ltd, 1960s, 4½in (11.5cm) long, with box.
£6–10 / €9–15
$12–19 ✹ GAZE

A Budgie Models Royal Navy Scammell Scarab, No. 702, 1960s, 6in (15cm) long.
£20–25 / €30–35
$40–50 ✹ GAZE

▶ **A Muldenkipper Mercedes Benz friction toy,** early 1970s, 7in (18cm) long, with box.
£30–35 / €45–50
$55–65 ⊞ CBB

Corgi

Corgi Toys were produced by Mettoy Playcraft from 1956. Made in Swansea, south Wales, they were named after a Welsh dog (the favourite breed of the royal family) and the name was short and snappy like that of their established rival, Dinky. The diecast vehicles were of a very high standard and came with many attractive features: plastic windows (Dinky cars had open windows) and, from 1959, spring suspension and detailed plastic interiors. The early 1960s saw the introduction of 'jewelled' headlights and opening doors and boots, and this focus on moving parts and innovatory features made

Corgi the natural choice to produce *James Bond*'s gadget-packed Aston Martin DB5. This went on to be one of the most popular toys ever made, with sales of nearly three million. A host of other film- and television-related toys followed in the 1960s, such as the Batmobile, the *Man from U.N.C.L.E.* car, the *Avengers* Bentley and Lotus Elan, the Green Hornet's Black Beauty, the *Chitty Chitty Bang Bang* car and many others, including further Bond cars. In 1970, Corgi introduced their Whizwheels line to compete with Mattel's hugely successful Hotwheels series.

▶ **A Corgi Toys Euclid TC12 Twin Crawler Tractor,** No. 1103, tracks worn, 1950s, 5in (12.5cm) long, with box.
£70–80 / €100–115
$135–155 ⊞ HAL

◀ **A Corgi Toys Wall's Refrigerator Comma Van,** No. 435, 1950s, 5in (12.5cm) long.
£45–50 / €65–75
$85–95 ⋟ GAZE

A Corgi Toys Batmobile, No. 267, with Batman and Robin figures, c1966, 4½in (11.5cm) long, with box.
£250–300 / €360–430
$480–580 ⋟ WAL

A Corgi Toys James Bond Aston Martin DB5, No. 261, 1965–69, 4in (10cm) long, with box.
£190–220 / €280–320
$360–420 ⋟ GAZE

A Corgi Toys The Green Hornet Black Beauty, No. 268, c1967, 5in (12.5cm) long, with box.
£190–220 / €280–320
$360–420 ⋟ WAL

A Corgi Toys Chipperfields Circus Mobile Booking Office,
No. 426, slight wear, 1960s, 3½in (9cm) long, with box.
£105–120 / €150–175
$200–230 ⊞ HAL
If in mint condition the value of this model would rise to
£200–220 / €290–320 / $380–420.

A Corgi Toys James Bond Citroën 2CV, c1981, 4in (10cm) long, with box.
£40–45 / €60–70
$75–85 ⊞ IQ

Dinky

A Dinky Toys Pullmore Car Transporter, No. 982,
1955–61, 10in (25.5cm) long.
£65–75 / €95–105
$125–145 ⋟ GAZE

A Dinky Toys Castrol Tanker,
No. 441, c1950, 5in (12.5cm) long.
£60–70 / €85–100
$115–135 ⊞ HAL

A Dinky Toys Ford Fordor Sedan,
No. 170, 1950s, 4in (10cm) long.
£200–220 / €290–320
$380–420 ⊞ HAL

A Dinky Supertoys Turntable Fire
Escape, No. 956, with optional
fire station personnel No. 008,
1950s–60s, 8in (20.5cm)
long, with box.
£200–240 / €290–350
$390–460 ⋟ WAL

A Dinky Toys Guy Warrior Flat
Truck, No. 432, 1950s,
5in (12.5cm) long, with box.
£70–80 / €100–115
$135–155 ⋟ GAZE

A Dinky Toys police
box, 1960s,
2½in (6.5cm) high.
£15–20 / €22–29
$29–38 ⊞ HeA

A Dinky Toys Farm
Equipment Gift Set,
No. 398, minor wear,
early 1960s, with box,
10 x 12in (25.5 x 30.5cm).
£480–570 / €700–830
$920–1,100 ⋟ WAL

▶ A Dinky Toys
Speedwheels
Ford Capri,
No. 165, 1970s,
4in (10cm) long,
with box.
£50–60 / €75–85
$100–115
⊞ HAL

Matchbox

A Matchbox Marshall Horse Box,
No. 35, slight damage, 1957,
2in (5cm) long, with box.
£60–70 / €85–100
$115–135 ⚲ SAS

A Matchbox Cement Mixer, No. 3,
1950s, 2½in (6.5cm) wide.
£20–25 / €30–35
$40–50 ⊞ HAL

**A Matchbox Collector's Catalogue
1969,** 5in (12.5cm) wide.
£6–10 / €9–15
$12–19 ⊞ HAL

A Matchbox Service Station,
1960s, with box 11in (28cm) wide.
£45–50 / €65–75
$85–95 ⚲ GAZE

A Matchbox Major M-1 BP Tanker ,
1960s, 4in (10cm) long, with box.
£35–40 / €50–60
$65–75 ⊞ HAL

**A Matchbox Superfast Beach
Buggy,** No. 30, c1970,
2½in (6.5cm) long, with box.
£4–8 / €6–12
$8–15 ⊞ HAL

**A Matchbox Superfast Wheel
Tipper,** No. 518, c1970,
3in (7.5cm) long, with box.
£9–13 / €13–19
$18–25 ⊞ HAL

**A Matchbox Super Kings DAF
Building Transporter K-13,** 1970s,
6in (15cm) long, with box.
£15–20 / €22–29
$29–38 ⊞ HAL

A Matchbox ERF Cement Lorry,
No. 26, 1950s, 2in (5cm) long.
£20–25 / €30–35
$40–50 ⊞ HAL

A Matchbox ERF Road Tanker,
No. 11, slight damage to box,
1950s, 2in (5cm) long.
£30–35 / €45–50
$55–65 ⊞ HAL

**A Matchbox King Size Hatra
Tractor Shovel K-3,** 1960s,
5in (12.5cm) long, with box.
£35–40 / €50–60
$65–75 ⊞ HAL

**A Matchbox *Thunderbirds* Lady
Penelope's Rolls Royce FAB 1,**
1992, 3in (7.5cm) long, on card.
£4–8 / €6–12
$8–15 ⊞ IQ

Model Soldiers & Figures

A Britains Mounted 1st Dragoons
The Royals set, 1920s, in original
Whisstock box, 18in (45.5cm) wide.
£40–45 / €60–70
$75–85 ⚔ WAL

A Krausner hollow-cast Austro-
Hungarian Band, German, c1900,
2½in (6.5cm) high, in a wooden box.
£2,250–2,500 / €3,250–3,650
$4,300–4,800 ⊞ SAND

▶ A Britains Band of the 1st Life
Guards, No. 101, 1930s, with box,
12 x 18in (30.5 x 45.5cm).
£80–90 / €115–130
$155–175 ⚔ WAL

A Britains set of Bodyguard of the Emperor of
Abyssinia, No. 1424, late 1930s, in original box
14in (35.5cm) wide.
£110–130 / €160–190
$210–250 ⚔ WAL

A set of six lead racehorses, 1960s, horses
3in (7.5cm) high.
£35–40 / €50–60
$65–75 ⚔ GAZE

A Britains Swoppets
War of the Roses plastic
Knight, sword and visor
missing, 1960s,
4in (10cm) high.
£20–25 / €30–35
$40–50 ⊞ HAL

A Britains Deetail plastic
and metal figure of a
Native American on
horseback, 1970s–80s,
3in (7.5cm) high.
£1–5 / €2–7
$3–9 ⊞ HAL

▶ A Britains
Military
Vehicles US
Jeep, No. 9786,
1974, in box,
6in (15cm) wide.
£40–45 / €60–70
$75–85 ⊞ CBB

Ride-on Vehicles

A Keystone pressed steel Ride Em Locomotive, with electric headlight, c1933, 24½in (62cm) long.
£340–400 / €490–580
$650–770 ♪ **Bert**

A Buddy L pressed steel International Deluxe Ride Em Stake Truck, seat and pull-handle, slight damage, 1930s, 25in (63.5cm) long.
£680–810 / €990–1,150
£1,300–1,550 ♪ **Bert**

A wooden push-along truck, with two-handled steering, 1940s, 42in (106.5cm) long.
£20–25 / €30–35
$40–50 ♪ **GAZE**

A Tri-Ang tinplate ride-on lorry, c1960, 24in (61cm) long.
£130–145 / €190–210
$250–280 ⊞ **JUN**

A Tri-Ang tinplate LBL-type Edwardian motor car, 1960s, 32in (81.5cm) long.
£60–70 / €85–1100
$115–135 ♪ **GAZE**

Rocking Horses

A carved wood fairground galloper, built onto a tricycle, 1905, 59in (150cm) long.
£1,700–1,900
€2,450–2,750
$3,250–3,650 ⊞ **JUN**

A Mobo painted tinplate rocking horse, 1950s, 31in (78.5cm) long.
£10–15 / €15–22
$19–28 ♪ **GAZE**

◄ **A Mobo tinplate walking horse,** 1950s, 27in (68.5cm) long.
£35–40 / €50–60
$65–75 ♪ **GAZE**

Science Fiction & Television

A Louis Marx lithographed tinplate clockwork Rex Mars Rocket Fighter Ship, cockpit cover replaced, 1930s, 11½in (29cm) long, with box.
£740–880 / €1,100–1,300
$1,400–1,650 ✦ Bert

A Marx Toys lithographed tinplate *Flash Gordon* **Ray Pistol,** with click sound, 1950s, 10in (25.5cm) wide, with box.
£400–480 / €580–700
$770–920 ✦ Bert

▶ **A Palitoy Genuine battery-powered Dan Dare plastic Cosmic Ray Gun,** with morse code and identification sheet, 1950s, 5in (12.5cm) wide, with box.
£380–450 / €550–650
$730–860 ✦ WAL

Four Chad Valley *Thunderbirds* **Give-A-Show projector slides,** 1966, on original card, 11½ x 12½in (29 x 32cm).
£25–30 / €40–45
$50–55 ✦ VAU

A Cragston tinplate battery-operated talking robot, Japanese, c1950, 12in (30.5cm) high.
£240–280 / €350–410
$460–540 ✦ AMB

A tinplate friction-driven Jet Car, Japanese, 1960s, 7in (18cm) long.
£20–25 / €30–35
$40–50 ⊞ RTT

The LONE RANGER Rides Again!

A Yonezawa tinplate friction-powered lithographed X-27 Explorer, Japanese, 1950s, 8¾in (22cm) high.
£1,250–1,500 / €1,800–2,150
$2,400–2,900 ✦ SWO

Twelve *Batman* **plastic flicker rings,** depicting Batman, Robin and other associated characters, 1966.
£90–100 / €130–145
$170–190 ✦ VAU

A Horihawa Toys Tokyo tinplate battery-operated Rotate-o-Matic Super Astronaut, with gun sounds, rotating body and flashing light, Japanese, early 1970s, 9½in (24cm) high, with original box.
£120–140 / €175–200
$230–270 ✦ WAL

◀ **A Louis Marx** *Lone Ranger* **Tribal Powwow set,** 1973, with box, 12 x 15in (30.5 x 38cm).
£15–20 / €22–29
$29–38 ⊞ HeA

An Airfix Micronauts Force Commander magnetic assembly kit, rocket launcher missing, 1977, 6½in (16.5cm) high, with box.
£20–25 / €30–35
$40–50 🏹 VAU

A tinplate battery-operated Apollo 11 Eagle Lunar Module, Japanese, 1970s, 10in (25.5cm) high.
175–195 / €250–280
$330–370 ⊞ GTM

A Palitoy BBC battery-operated Talking Dalek, 1975, 7½in (19cm) high.
£120–135 / €175–195
$230–260 ⊞ GTM

Two *Star Fleet* model kits, Japanese, 1982, boxed, 4 x 6in (10 x 15cm).
£35–40 / €50–60
$65–75 each ⊞ OW

A Hasbro Transformers Deception Thrust model, American, 1985, with box, 7 x 8in (18 x 20.5cm).
£180–200 / €260–290
$340–380 ⊞ OW

◄ A *Dr Who* Viewmaster 3-D reel picture reel, 1980, on card, 10in (25.5cm) high.
£10–15
€15–22
$19–28 ⊞ HeA

A Mattel *Masters of the Universe* Rokkon Comet Warrior, American, 1985, 6in (15cm) high, on card.
£30–35 / €45–50
$55–65 ⊞ STa

A Hasbro World Wrestling Federation plastic Marty Janetty figure, American, 1990, 5in (12.5cm) high.
£25–30 / €40–45
$50–55 ⊞ STa

◀ Two Matchbox *Thunderbirds* figures, Brains and Parker, 1993, on card 8 x 5in (20.5 x 12.5cm).
£10–15 / €15–22
$19–28 each ⊞ LAS

◀ A *Space Precinct* Lieutenant Brogan action figure, 1994, 13in (33cm) high, boxed.
£10–15 / €15–22
$19–28 ⊞ CTO

A Playmates *Star Trek Voyager* Reginald Barclay figure, edition of 3,000, 1996, on card 10 x 8in (25.5 x 20.5cm).
£140–160 / €200–230
$270–310 ⊞ OW

A Hasbro Signature Series *Planet of the Apes* Gorilla Soldier figure, 1999, 12in (30.5cm) high, with box.
£25–30 / €40–45
$50–55 ⊞ SSF

A Playmates *Star Trek* Space Talk series Captain Jean Luc Picard talking figure, 1995, 7in (18cm) high, on card.
£30–35 / €45–50
$55–65 ⊞ SSF

◀ A *Thunderbirds* Captain Alan talking figure, 1999, 12in (30.5cm) high.
£8–12 / €12–18
$16–23 ⊞ LAS

Star Wars

◀ A Kenner *Star Wars* Boba Fett action figure 1979, on card, 9 x 6in (23 x 15cm).
£630–750
€910–1,100
$1,200–1,450
⋗ VAU

A Kenner *Star Wars* Greedo action figure, 1979, on card, 9 x 6in (23 x 15cm).
£155–185 / €220–270
$300–360 ⋗ VAU

A Palitoy *Star Wars The Empire Strikes Back* At-At All-Terrain Transport model, 1980, boxed. 9 x 23in (23 x 58.5cm).
£270–300 / €390–440
$520–580 ⊞ OW

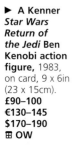

▶ A Kenner *Star Wars Return of the Jedi* Ben Kenobi action figure, 1983, on card, 9 x 6in (23 x 15cm).
£90–100
€130–145
$170–190
⊞ OW

▶ Two Kenner Star Wars Collector Series figures, Han Solo and Tauntaun, 1997, boxed, 18in (45.5cm) square.
£130–150 / €190–220
$250–290 ⊞ OW

Tinplate & Clockwork

Tinplate toys emerged in the 1800s and provided an affordable and colourful alternative to wooden toys as they could be made more quickly and in far greater numbers. Germany had the most sophisticated toy industry in Europe and became a leading producer with major companies that included Märklin (est. 1859), Bing (est. c1879) and Lehmann (est. 1881). America's toy industry developed in the 19th century, when one of the best known tinplate toy makers was George Brown & Co (est. 1856), who was the first to incorporate a clockwork mechanism into American toys. Other important US manufacturers were Louis Marx (est. 1896) and Ferdinand Strauss (est. c1914). Typical tinplate subjects included figures and vehicles, the horse-drawn favourite of the Victorian period gradually giving way in the 1900s to automobiles, aeroplanes, submarines and even airships, reflecting new developments in transport. Automative toys are very popular with collectors today and can command high prices, particularly the larger models. These would have been expensive at the time, which was why the 1900s also saw a proliferation of penny toys – often cheaper,

smaller versions of full-size toys (usually 2–4in / 5–10cm in length), which were designed for the pocket-money market.

Popular entertainment was a major influence on tinplate toys in the 1920s and '30s, which reflected film (particularly Disney productions), favourite radio programmes and contemporary music. The jazz musicians shown below, for example, are very sought after by collectors of African-American memorabilia today.

In the post-war period Japan became a leading producer of tinplate toys. Since costs were cheaper in the Far East, many American companies commissioned manufacture in Japan. A huge number of toys were made purely for export to the USA and reflected contemporary American culture and taste. Often however, toys were marked 'Foreign', rather than 'Made in Japan', so as not to stir up wartime resentments. Beginning with clockwork and friction models, the Japanese were among the first to use batteries for activating toys in the mid-1950s. With all the toys shown here condition is critical. Prices reflect maker, subject and, as ever, the presence of packaging adds historical interest and financial value.

A cast-iron acrobats and bells toy, the figures dance and ring the bells when the wheeled base is pulled along, slight damage, c1900, 6in (15cm) long.
£480–570 / €700–830
$920–1,100 ⇗ Bert

◄ **A tinplate clockwork Royal state coach and horses,** early 1900s, 6in (15cm) long.
£120–140
€175–200
$230–270
⇗ WAL

▶ **A Lehmann's tinplate clockwork Heavy Swell toy,** German, c1903, 9in (23cm) high.
£2,200–2,500 / €3,200–3,650
$4,200–4,800 ⊞ HAL

A Unique Art tinplate clockwork Hott 'n Tott toy, American, 1921, 8in (20.5cm) high.
£250–300 / €360–440
$480–580 ⇗ JDJ

◀ **A tinplate clockwork Prussian soldier,** German, 1920s, 11in (28cm) long.
£210–250
€300–360
$400–480 ⚡ JDJ

A Louis Marx tinplate clockwork Harold Lloyd Walker, American, 1929, 10½in (26.5cm) high, with box.
£250–300 / €360–440
$480–580 ⚡ Bert

▶ **A Louis Marx tinplate clockwork Charlie McCarthy and Mortimer Snerd private car,** the characters with spinning-head action, American, 1939, 16in (40.5cm) long.
£590–700 / €860–1,000
$1,150–1,350 ⚡ JDJ

A Louis Marx tinplate clockwork Jazzbo Jim, the banjo player dancing on the rooftop, American, 1930s, 10in (25.5cm) high, with box.
£560–670 / €810–970
$1,100–1,300 ⚡ JDJ

A Wells tinplate clockwork Mickey Mouse hand car, 1930s, 8in (20.5cm) long.
£85–95 / €125–140
$165–185 ⚡ GAZE

A tinplate clockwork hopping hare, 1930s, 5in (12.5cm) high.
£50–60 / €75–85
$100–115 ⚡ AMB

A P. P. tinplate clockwork table tennis game, 1950s, 9in (23cm) wide.
£35–40 / €50–60
$65–75 ⚡ GAZE

A lithographed tinplate Joe Palooka lunch box, slight damage, 1948, 6¼in (16cm) wide.
£170–200 / €250–290
$330–380 ⚡ Bert
In 1920 Hammond Edward 'Ham' Fisher, a young American sports journalist, interviewed a personable but not very bright boxer. This gave him the inspiration for a daily comic strip. It took ten years before he could sell the idea to the newspapers, but April 1930 saw the launch of Joe Palooka, the humorous story of a boxer, which was to become one of the most successful sports comic strips of all time.

A Louis Marx lithographed tinplate Popeye handcar, with rubber figures of Popeye and Olive Oyl, slight damage, American, 1950s, 7½in (19cm), with box.
£290–340 / €420–490
$560–650 ⚡ Bert

> **For further information** on cars & vehicles see pages 397–398

A Tri-Ang tinplate transport van, No. 200, 1950s, 18in (45.5cm) long.
£25–30 / €40–45
$50–55 ⚡ GAZE

A tinplate Baby-Pop gun, c1960, 4in (10cm) long.
£15–20 / €22–29
$29–38 ⊞ JUN

Items in the Toys section have been arranged in date order within each sub-section.

A Hubley tinplate battery-operated Mr Magoo, American, 1961, 9in (23cm) long, with box.
£270–300 / €390–440
$520–580 ⊞ IQ

A tinplate Rainbow Signs & Posters truck, 1960s, 10in (25.5cm) long.
£90–100 / €130–145
$170–190 ⊞ JUN

A tinplate battery-operated Ford tractor, possibly by Lincoln, Japanese, 1960s, 17in (43cm) long.
£220–250 / €320–360
$420–480 ⊞ HAL

A tinplate Military Police motorcycle, Japanese, 1960s, 4in (10cm) wide.
£15–20 / €22–29
$29–38 ⊞ UD

A T. M. Modern Toys battery-operated tinplate Mickey Mouse on a hand car, bump-and-go action, Mickey with a rubber head, Japanese, 1960s, 8in (20.5cm) long, with box.
£85–95 / €125–140
$165–185 ⚒ WAL

A Marusan Toys tinplate battery-powered flock-covered Smoky Bear Pioneer, with walking, smoking action, Japanese, 1960s, 9in (23cm) high.
£120–140 / €175–200
$230–270 ⚒ WAL

A T. M. Modern Toys tinplate battery-operated Super Eagle machine gun, 1960s, 24in (61cm) long.
£60–70 / €85–100
$115–135 ⊞ HAL

Trains

◀ **A Bassett-Lowke third/brake coach,** finished in GWR livery, slight damage, 1921.
£60–70 / €85–100
$115–135 ⚘ LAY

A Hornby No. 2 gauge 0 special Pullman brake end coach, 'Montana', 1937–38, 14in (35.5cm) long, with box.
£360–400 / €520–580
$690–770 ⊞ MDe

▶ **A Hornby No. 4E electric locomotive and tender,** No. 900, 'Eton', c1938, 15½in (39.5cm) long, with box.
£1,800–2,000 / €2,700–3,000
$3,350–3,750 ⊞ MDe
This Southern Schools class locomotive is the ultimate in Hornby locos. A clockwork version would be worth £800–1,200 / €1,150–1,750 / $1,550–2,300.

◀ **A Hornby No. 2 gauge 0 corridor coach,** c1938, 13in (33cm) long, with box.
£270–300 / €390–440
$520–580 ⊞ MDe

A Hornby Cadbury's Chocolates wagon, 1930s, 5in (12.5cm) long, with original box.
£400–480 / €580–700
$770–920 ⚘ VEC

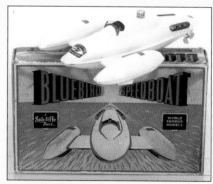

A Hornby Royal Daylight petrol tank wagon, 1930s, 4in (10cm) long, with associated box.
£120–145 / €175–210
$230–270 ⚡ VEC

A Hornby tinplate station, ramps missing, 1940s, 17in (43cm) wide.
£20–25 / €30–35
$40–50 ⊞ HAL

◀ **A Hornby gauge 0 double-arm signal,** 1940s, 9in (23cm) high.
£20–25 / €30–35
$40–50 ⊞ HAL

A Hornby Dublo D1 break van, c1950, 4in (10cm) long, with box.
£8–12 / €12–18
$16–23 ⊞ HAL

A Hornby Dublo coal wagon, 1954, 4in (10cm) long, with box.
£8–12 / €12–18
$15–22 ⊞ GTM

A Hornby Dublo British Rail First Class coach, 1950s, 10in (255.5cm) long, with box.
£30–35 / €45–50
$55–65 ⊞ HAL

A Hornby Dublo three-rail locomotive and tender, 'Duchess of Montrose', 1950s, 9in (23cm) long.
£90–100 / €130–145
$170–190 ⊞ HAL

A Bassett-Lowke wooden single road gauge 0 engine shed, with two hinged doors, tinplate advertisements, 19in (48.5cm) wide, together with a Hornby No. 3 tinplate station, 1950s.
£160–190 / €230–270
$310–360 ⚡ WAL

Two Bassett-Lowke gauge 0 LMS wagons, 12-ton box van, RN 91375, and 13-ton open wagon, RN 36271, each with metal-spoked wheels and original boxes, 1950s, 5in (12.5cm) long.
£70–80 / €100–115
$135–155 ⚡ WAL

A Tri-Ang Railways gauge 00 Southern EMU two car set, late 1950s, with box, 12 x 16in (30.5 x 40.5cm).
£120–140 / €175–200
$230–270 ⚡ WAL

A Hornby Dublo rail-cleaning wagon, two rail, 1960s, 4in (10cm) long, with original box.
£170–200 / €250–290
$330–380 ⚡ WAL

A T. & M. tinplate battery-operated 4–8–2 locomotive, 'Piston Silver Mountain', No. 4067, Japanese, dated 1969, 15in (38cm) long.
£25–30 / €40–45
$50–55 ⚡ AMB

A Hornby Dublo three-rail 0–6–2 N2 tank locomotive, WBR, RN 69567, 1960s, 6in (15cm) long, with original box and instructions.
£70–80 / €100–115
$135–155 ⚘ WAL

A Tri-Ang Electric Model Railway set, T43, 1960s, with box, 16 x 12in (40.5 x 30.5cm).
£200–240 / €290–350
$390–460 ⚘ GAZE

A Tri-Ang Hornby Electric train set, 'The Blue Pullman', 1960s, with box, 15in (38cm) wide.
£75–85 / €110–125
$145–165 ⊞ WOS

A Wrenn Southern Electric Pullman motor coach two car set, 'The Brighton Belle', 1970s, 10in (25.5cm) long, with box.
£120–140 / €175–200
$230–270 ⚘ GAZE

◄ **A Meccano model tank locomotive,** 'Countess', 1970s, 25in (63.5cm) long.
£75–85
€110–125
$145–165
⚘ GAZE

A Hornby Minitrix N-gauge locomotive, N205, c1980, 3in (7.5cm) long, with box.
£45–50 / €65–75
$85–95 ⊞ WOS

A Hornby gauge 0 4–6–2 LMS class 7P locomotive, 'The Princess Royal', 1980s, 14in (35.5cm) long, with box.
£40–45 / €60–70
$75–85 ⊞ GTM

A Wrenn gauge 00 locomotive and tender, 'Bullied Pacific', RN 21C155, with tender 'Fighter Pilot', 1980s, with instructions and original box.
£300–360 / €440–520
$580–690 ⚘ WAL

Treen

A pair of Drummond Tartan ware napkin rings, 19thC, 2in (5cm) diam.
£45–50 / €65–75
$85–95 ⊞ HTE

A Tunbridge ware calling card case, c1845, 4¼in (11cm) wide.
£360–400 / €520–580
$690–770 ⊞ AMH

A sycamore love spoon, c1850, 15in (38cm) long.
£850–950
€1,250–1,400
$1,600–1,800
⊞ NEW

◀ **A carved bog oak box and cover,** Irish, c1860, 2½in (6.5cm) diam.
£155–175 / €220–250
$300–340 ⊞ STA

▶ **A Mauchline ware match holder,** probably sycamore, decorated with a view of Belfast, 1860–80, 10½in (26.5cm) high.
£80–90 / €115–130
$155–175 ⊞ GAU

A Victorian yew-wood truncheon, 10in (25.5cm) long.
£60–70 / €85–100
$115–135 ⊞ MB

A Victorian Tunbridge ware extending book rack, decorated with a ruin and a castle, 13in (33cm) closed.
£140–165 / €200–230
$270–310 ⋌ CHTR

◀ **A Boxwood bottle box,** c1880, 7in (18cm) high.
£60–70 / €85–100
$115–135 ⊞ MB

▶ **A Tartan ware glove stretcher,** inscribed 'Prince Charlie', c1870, 5in (12.5cm) long.
£200–230 / €290–330
$380–440 ⊞ RdeR

A Mauchline ware box and cover, decorated with playing cards and fans, c1900, 3½in (9cm) diam.
£70–80 / €100–115
$135–155 ⊞ GAU

◀ **A carved wood apple,** containing a miniature table and tea set, 1950s, 5in (12.5cm) diam.
£6–10 / €9–15
$12–19 ⊞ UD

Walking Sticks

Walking sticks have been collected since the Victorian period, when gentlemen would take pride in having a range of different sticks such as a Malacca cane for daytime in town, an ebonized model for the evening and a sturdy wooden stick for country use. Canes with ornate handles in fine quality materials such as ivory can command high prices. Novelty designs such as defence canes, sword sticks, drinking canes (containing a flask or corkscrew) and doctors' sticks (concealing medical instruments) are also popular. Sticks were made for both town and country use and for every level of society, so styles, materials and prices vary accordingly. When buying, ensure that the handle is original to the stick – marriages are not unknown and some curved umbrella handles have been converted into canes. Sticks in perfect condition will command the highest prices, although since these were practical items some signs of wear are not uncommon, particularly on the ferule – the metal tip of the stick – and can be a reassuring sign that the object is original.

A wooden walking stick, the handle carved in the form of a smiling gentleman in a wig, traces of painted decoration, possibly American, 18thC, 35½in (90cm) long.
£250–300 / €360–430
$480–580 ➤ SWO

A metal-mounted stained bamboo swagger stick, the ivory handle carved in the form of a man's head, 19thC, 35in (89cm) long.
£150–180 / €220–260
$290–350 ➤ G(L)

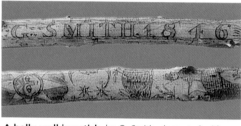

A holly walking stick, by G. Smith, decorated with rural scenes, dated 1846, 37¾in (96cm) long.
£420–500 / €610–730
$810–960 ➤ DD

A wooden defence cane, the handle carved in the form of a duck's head, c1860, 35in (89cm) long.
£310–350 / €450–510
$600–670 ⊞ GBr

A silver-mounted ebonized cane, the ivory handle carved in the form of a bulldog's head, with glass eyes, c1880, 35in (89cm) long.
£280–320 / €410–460
$540–610 ⊞ GBr

A specimen wood cane, c1880, 34in (86.5cm) long.
£100–120 / €145–175
$195–230 ⊞ GBr

An ebonized cane, the antler handle carved in the form of a lion's head, c1880, 36in (91.5cm) long.
£210–240 / €300–350
$400–460 ⊞ GBr

A silver-mounted ebonized cane, the handle carved in the form of a dog's head, c1880, 35in (89cm) long.
£270–300 / €390–440
$520–580 ⊞ GBr

An ebony and ivory cane, the handle in the form of a bird's head, c1890, 35in (89cm) long.
£175–195 / €250–280 $330–370 ⊞ GBr

A partridge-wood cane, with a gilt and porcelain handle, c1890, 34in (86.5cm) long.
£120–135 / €175–195 $230–260 ⊞ GBr

A white-metal-mounted whalebone walking stick, with a marine ivory handle, late 19thC, 33½in (85cm) long.
£350–420 / €510–610 $670–810 ⚒ SWO

A silver-mounted whangee bamboo cane, with an antler handle, c1890, 34in (86.5cm) long.
£35–40 / €50–60 $65–75 ⊞ GBr

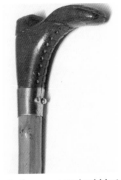

A wooden cane, the walnut handle carved as a monkey's head with a jockey cap, c1890, 35in (89cm) long.
£240–270 / €350–390 $460–520 ⊞ GBr

A silver-mounted cobbler's cane, the handle carved in the form of a boot, c1890, 36in (91.5cm) long.
£145–165 / €210–240 $280–310 ⊞ GBr

An ebonized cane, with a silver handle, c1890, 36in (91.5cm) long.
£240–270 / €350–390 $460–520 ⊞ GBr

A lead-weighted plaited-leather defence cane, c1900, 36in (91.5cm) long.
£85–95 / €125–140 $165–185 ⊞ GBr

A carved and painted wood stick or crook, the horn ferrule carved with four foxhounds, the handle carved with a fox, early 20thC, 51½in (131cm) long.
£300–360 / €440–520 $580–690 ⚒ PFK

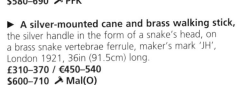

► **A silver-mounted cane and brass walking stick,** the silver handle in the form of a snake's head, on a brass snake vertebrae ferrule, maker's mark 'JH', London 1921, 36in (91.5cm) long.
£310–370 / €450–540 $600–710 ⚒ Mal(O)

A wooden cane, the handle carved in the form of a bird's head, Pitcairn Islands, c1930, 35in (89cm) long.
£85–95 / €125–140 $165–185 ⊞ GBr

Watches & Clocks

A Doulton 'Big Ben' porcelain mantel clock, with enamel dial, the case decorated with gilt and painted flowers, slight damage and losses, 19thC, 20in (51cm) high.
£270–320 / €390–460 $520–610 ✣ Mal(O)

A gold and enamel fob watch, with enamel dial and verge movement, the front with an oval reserve and pearl border, slight damage to enamel, Swiss, 19thC, 1¼in (3cm) diam, on a Georgian gold and pearl mourning brooch fob.
£250–300 / €360–440 $480–580 ✣ F&C

A Victorian ebonized mantel clock, the twin-train movement striking on a gong, the case inset with floral painted ceramic panels, 19¼in (49cm) high.
£240–280 / €350–410 $460–540 ✣ SWO

A spelter mantel timepiece, by Ansonia Clock Co, in the form of a horseshoe surmounted by a spread eagle, the rear strut cast as a horse's leg, American, c1878, 7in (18cm) high.
£90–100 / €130–145 $170–190 ✣ ROSc

A rosewood and mahogany Dreadnaught mantel timepiece, by Jerome & Co, with painted dial and 30-hour movement, slight damage, American, c1880, 14¼in (36cm) high.
£65–75 / €95–105 $125–145 ✣ ROSc

▶ **A gilt-brass carriage clock,** with enamel dial and platform lever escapement, French, c1900, 4½in (11.5cm) high.
£60–70 / €85–100 $115–135 ✣ Hal

A Royal Worcester ceramic Renaissance mantel clock, No. 1201, c1890, 10¾in (27.5cm) high.
£420–500 / €610–730 $810–960 ✣ MAR

A Black Forest oak wall clock, carved with game, the twin movement striking on a bell, German, late 19thC, 37in (94cm) high.
£280–330 / €410–480 $540–630 ✣ SWO

▶ **An oak station clock,** by Clare & Sons, with enamel dial and fusee movement, c1900, 17¼in (44cm) diam.
£280–330 / €410–480 $540–630 ✣ WilP

A silver-cased boudoir clock, London 1891, 6in (15cm) high.
£180–210 / €260–300 $350–400 ✣ AMB

An inlaid mahogany mantel timepiece, French, early 20thC, 11in (28cm) high.
£360–430 / €520–620
$690–830 ⚲ G(L)

An Edwardian inlaid mahogany mantel clock, with enamel dial and eight-day movement, 9¼in (23.5cm) high.
£55–65 / €80–95
$105–125 ⚲ FHF

An Edwardian walnut bracket clock, with gilt-metal inlay and eight-day movement, French, 11in (28cm) high.
£150–180 / €220–260
$290–350 ⚲ AMB

A white metal digital jump hour/wandering minute pocket watch, by Anton Schild, with pallet-type lever escapement, Swiss, c1910, 2in (5cm) diam.
£155–175 / €220–250
$300–340 ⊞ FOF

A wooden mantel clock, with Swiss movement, c1910, 12in (30.5cm) wide.
£145–165 / €210–240
$280–310 ⊞ SAT

A Rolex 18ct gold and diamond wristwatch, No. 580681, with silvered dial, signed, Swiss, London import mark for 1913.
£260–310 / €380–450
$500–600 ⚲ DN(HAM)

A Rolex silver wristwatch, No. 3985322, with silvered dial and enamelled bezel, Swiss, import marks for London 1914.
£160–190 / €230–270
$310–360 ⚲ DN

◀ **A Moeris 19ct gold wrist watch,** with enamel dial, c1920.
£200–220
€290–320
$380–420
⊞ WAC

A Bulova gold wrist-watch, 1930s, with box.
£160–180 / €230–260
$310–350 ⊞ TIC

An S. Smith & Sons Motor Accessories nickel panel/car clock, with enamel dial and eight-day movement, c1930, 2in (5cm) diam.
£175–195 / €250–280
$330–370 ⊞ FOF

◀ **A Rolex steel wristwatch,** No. 24545, 2755, signed, Swiss, c1930.
£190–220 / €280–320
$360–420 ⚲ DN(HAM)

An Eterna diver's-style steel wristwatch, Argentinian, c1940, 1½in (4cm) diam.
£360–400 / €520–580
$690–770 ⊞ HARP

An inlaid walnut mantel clock,
with a striking movement, 1930s,
17¼in (44cm) wide.
£35–40 / €50–60
$65–75 ⚲ AMB

A Galli enamelled alarm clock, with eight-
day movement, Swiss, Zurich, 1930s,
4in (10cm) wide.
£165–185 / €230–270
$310–360 ⊞ SUW

**A paste bracelet wrist-
watch,** with a 'jewelled'
hinged cover, 1940s.
£80–90 / €115–130
$155–175 ⊞ DRE

**A white metal and
diamond wristwatch,**
No. L.4840, with silvered dial,
Swiss movement, c1950.
£50–60 / €75–85
$100–115 ⚲ DN

**A white metal Mickey
Mouse wristwatch,** c1950.
£90–100 / €130–145
$170–190 ⊞ UD

**A Longines 14ct white
gold wristwatch,**
the dial set with 12
diamonds, Swiss, 1950.
£420–470 / €610–680
$810–900 ⊞ WAC

**A Rolex 9ct gold
wristwatch,** No. 13874
422278, with silvered dial,
case, movement and dial
signed, maker's mark
'ALD', hallmarked
Birmingham 1952, Swiss,
1½in (3.5cm) diam.
£600–720 / €870–1,050
$1,150–1,350 ⚲ TEN

**A Rolex Tudor Oyster
wristwatch,** with
presentation inscription
'Knights of Columbus',
Swiss, 1959.
£260–310 / €380–450
$500–600 ⚲ BBA

**A Longines 18ct gold
Coronation wristwatch,**
the double serpentine link
bracelet with crown
shoulders, hallmarked
London 1953, Swiss.
£180–200 / €260–290
$340–380 ⚲ DN(HAM)

**A Timex stainless steel
Cinderalla wrist-
watch,** 1950s.
£65–75 / €95–105
$125–145 ⊞ UD

**An Omega Sea Master
automatic wristwatch,**
Swiss, 1950s.
£130–145 / €190–210
$250–280 ⊞ TIC

A Jaeger LeCoultre Bumper stainless steel
automatic wristwatch, with a reserve indicator, c1960.
£650–730 / €940–1,050
$1,250–1,400 ⊞ WAC

A Rolex Oysterdate
stainless steel
wristwatch, Swiss, 1965.
£450–500 / €650–730
$860–960 ⊞ Bns

◄ A Bulova Accutron
18ct gold Tuning Fork
wristwatch, No. 1-
820578 M9, the brushed
gilt dial with day and date
aperture, with associated
18ct gold bracelet, c1975,
1½in (3.5cm) wide.
£270–320 / €390–460
$520–610 ➹ TEN

A Rolex 9ct gold
wristwatch, with silvered
dial, the case with a milled
coin edge, Swiss, 1965.
£630–700 / €910–1,000
$1,200–1,350 ⊞ Bns

A Romer Rockshell Mark
IV steel wristwatch,
c1972, 1½in (4cm) diam.
£250–280 / €360–410
$480–540 ⊞ HARP

An Omega gold-plated
wristwatch, with date
aperture, Swiss, 1970s.
£220–250 / €320–360
$420–480 ⊞ WAC

An Omega De Ville
quartz wristwatch,
Swiss, 1970s.
£150–170 / €220–250
$290–330 ⊞ TIC

A Breitling steel
chronograph wristwatch,
1970s, 1½in (4cm) diam.
£450–500 / €650–730
$860–960 ⊞ HARP

◄ An Omega Seamaster
F300HZ steel electronic
chronometer, Swiss,
1970s, 1½in (4cm) diam.
£310–350 / €450–510
$600–670 ⊞ HARP

► A Heuer Autavia steel
driver's automatic
chronograph wristwatch,
with two subsidiary dials
and date aperture, on a Tag
Heuer bracelet, 1970s.
£630–700 / €900–1,000
$1,200–1,350 ⊞ Bns

A Swatch Pop Orb
wristwatch, by Vivienne
Westwood, 1993,
with original plastic case
and cardboard box.
£130–155 / €190–220
$250–300 ➹ DN

A Swatch Irony Scuba
wristwatch, c1995,
with original cardboard
and Perspex case.
£50–60 / €75–85
$100–115 ➹ DN

Writing

This section includes seals, which have been used on documents for centuries. Before the advent of envelopes, letters had to be folded and sealed with wax or a thin wafer or sticker. Seals were used both to close and authenticate documents and, as the examples shown here demonstrate, were often decorated with the initials, crest or shield of their owners. Long-handled seals were used on the desk; smaller, portable seals could be hung from a watch chain or chatelaine, or worn as a ring. Seals were made from a wide range of materials, and value today depends largely on design and medium.

Writing was not restricted to the well-born with coats-of-arms. With the increase of literacy in the 19th century and the introduction of the penny post in 1840, letter writing became popular with all classes and the manufacture of writing equipment flourished. Inkwells were created for every level of society and appear in a huge range of designs and media. The salt-glazed pottery figural inkwell shown on page 423 might originally have been aimed at the lower end of the market (intended to amuse clerks rather than their masters). Nevertheless, today such items are very sought after and collecting inks is one of the most popular specialist areas among vintage bottle enthusiasts. Many pottery and glass ink bottles were simply thrown away after use,

hence the rarity of the designs shown on these pages.

Until the second half of the 19th century, ink could be very poor in quality. Nibs clogged up, hence the need for a bristle pen-wiper, such as the example illustrated on page 423. As ink improved so did writing equipment. Numerous patents were taken out for reservoir pens in the 19th century, culminating in 1883, when the American firm Waterman developed a feed system which introduced a regular supply of ink to the nib. This date is considered to be the birth of the fountain pen.

Maker, rarity, condition and originality are all critical to the value of fountain pens. Vintage examples should be checked for a maker's name and any relevant marks or numbers. Damage considerably reduces the value of a pen and, in addition to defects caused by wear, some plastics used in the manufacture of pens were unstable and can fade or discolour. As with other collectables, pens are best stored away from bright light and excessive fluctuations of temperature. When buying a pen, it should be carefully examined for defects and any replacement parts. There are three principal parts of the pen to check: the main body of the pen and the filling system, the cap (including clip or clip ring) and the nib unit. Although pens that do not function are significantly less valuable than working examples, most pens can be restored.

A cut-steel double-ended seal, engraved with armorials of the first Earl of Godolphin, early 18thC.
£500–600 / €730–870
$960–1,150 ⚷ DN

▶ **A slate paperweight,** decorated with a micro-mosaic of classical ruins within a malachite border, 19thC, 4½in (11.5cm) wide.
£460–550 / €670–800
$880–1,050 ⚷ G(L)

A porcelain inkwell, modelled as a buckled shoe, slight damage, early 19thC, 5½in (14cm) wide.
£40–45 / €60–70
$75–85 ⚷ SJH

A gold-mounted ivory desk seal, the cornelian matrix engraved with a coat-of-arms, 19thC, 3¼in (8.5cm) high.
£200–240 / €290–350
$380–460 ⚷ G(L)

A Tunbridge ware inkstand, by T. Barton, with two cut-glass bottles and two lidded compartments, paper maker's label, 19thC.
£520–620 / €750–900
$1,000–1,200 ⚒ LAY

◄ A brass-bound oak stationery box, the hinged top enclosing a fitted interior, the fall-front with a fold-out writing surface, drawers, pen tray, stationery compartment and ink pot, 19thC, 16½in (42cm) wide.
£300–360 / €440–520
$580–690 ⚒ E

A chrome and leather travelling double inkwell, French, 19thC, 4in (10cm) wide.
£95–110 / €140–160
$180–210 ⊞ PPL

A ceramic inkwell, by Perry & Co, modelled as a dolphin, printed marks, 19thC, 4½in (11.5cm) high.
£80–90 / €115–130
$155–175 ⚒ BBR

A salt-glazed pottery inkwell, modelled as the head of an ugly woman, her mouth forming the inkwell, flanked by a quill hole to each shoulder, 19thC, 2¾in (7cm) wide.
£520–620 / €750–900
$1,000–1,200 ⚒ BBR

A marble and *pietra dura* inkstand, inlaid with flower sprays, the glass inkwell with a brass lid, Italian, 19thC, 12½in (32cm) wide.
£320–380 / €460–550
$610–730 ⚒ DN

A Dieppe work carved ivory letter opener, c1840, 5in (12.5cm) long.
£90–100 / €130–145
$170–190 ⊞ HUM

A silver pen and pencil set, by Sampson Mordan, modelled as a pair of miniature pistols, 1840, in a leather case.
£680–810 / €990–1,150
$1,300–1,550 ⚒ L

A Victorian brass paper clip and pen wiper, modelled as a boar's head, 5in (12.5cm) wide.
£195–220 / €280–320
$370–420 ⊞ HUM

▶ A carved ivory and white metal desk seal, probably Palais Royale, the matrix engraved with a coat-of-arms, French, c1850, 4in (10cm) high.
£700–840 / €1,000–1,200
$1,350–1,600 ⚒ G(L)

A brass inkstand, in the form of a construction site, c1870, 12½in (32cm) wide.
£1,550–1,850 / €2,250–2,700
$3,000–3,550 ⚒ S(O)

◀ **A Victorian brass inkwell,** the cover surmounted by an eagle, the body with pierced foliate and mask decoration, liner damaged, 8½in (21.5cm) high.
£170–200 / €250–290
$330–380 ⚒ DA

A Tunbridge ware letter opener, 1880, 8in (20.5cm) long.
£25–30 / €40–45
$50–55 ⊞ MB

A late Victorian white metal-mounted ivory paper knife, the terminal by Ferguson & McBean, Scottish, Inverness, 14½in (37cm) long.
£180–210 / €260–300
$350–400 ⚒ WW

A silver-mounted simulated tortoiseshell wooden letter clasp, the clip decorated with two cherubs among scrolling foliage, 1891, 7in (18cm) wide.
£280–330 / €410–480
$540–630 ⚒ SWO

▶ **An oak and brass Post Office letterbox,** c1895, 16in (40.5cm) high.
£540–600 / €780–870
$1,000–1,150 ⊞ NAW

A Mabie Todd & Bard silver-overlaid fountain pen, engraved 'Nellie', American, 1890–1906, with a presentation case.
£700–840 / €1,000–1,200
$1,350–1,600 ⚒ BBA

A silver pen stand, by Sampson Mordan, in the form of an umbrella stand, with integral pen wipe, 1900, 4in (10cm) high.
£180–210 / €260–300
$350–400 ⚒ SWO

A silver-mounted hard rubber fountain pen, hallmarked 1906, 5½in (14cm) long.
£180–210 / €260–300
$350–400 ⚒ G(L)

◀ **A set of cast-iron postal scales and weights,** early 20thC, 13in (33cm) wide.
£60–70 / €85–100
$115–135 ⊞ FST

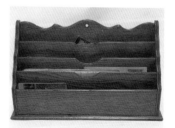

An Edwardian oak stationery rack, 13in (33cm) wide.
£50–60 / €75–85
$100–115 ⊞ MB

A Mabie Todd & Co Swan hard rubber half-overlaid gold fountain pen, American, 1908–15, with presentation case, instructions and accessories.
£80–90 / €115–130
$155–175 ⚷ BBA

A Simplo hard rubber safety fountain pen, German, 1913–15.
£55–65 / €80–95
$105–125 ⚷ BBA

A Mabie Todd & Co Swan 192/92 celluloid fountain pen, with moiré decoration, slight damage, American, late 1920s.
£55–65 / €80–95
$105–125 ⚷ BBA

A Montblanc 30 Masterpiece celluloid fountain pen, German, 1935–46.
£270–320 / €390–460
$520–610 ⚷ BBA

A Parker Senior Maxima vacuumatic fountain pen, 1930s, 4¾in (12cm) long.
£140–165 / €200–230
$270–310 ⚷ G(L)

A Waterman 100 Year pen, with amber ends, 1940s, 5in (12.5cm) long.
£110–130 / €160–190
$210–250 ⊞ PPL

A Parker Lucky Curve button-fill fountain pen, 1950s, 5¼in (13.5cm) long.
£75–85 / €110–125
$145–165 ⚷ G(L)

A De La Rue Onoto 9ct gold fountain pen, London 1912.
£640–760 / €930–1,100
$1,250–1,450 ⚷ BBA

A Waterman 52 Cardinal hard rubber fountain pen, American, 1923–27.
£80–90 / €115–130
$155–175 ⚷ BBA

A De La Rue Onoto Magna celluloid fountain pen, with hallmarked gold band, Scottish, 1935.
£210–250 / €300–360
$400–480 ⚷ BBA

A Parker Senior Maxima vacuumatic fountain pen, 1930s, 4¾in (12cm) long.
£100–120 / €145–175
$195–230 ⚷ G(L)

A Montblanc Masterpiece 146 celluloid fountain pen, turning knob replaced, German, c1949.
£320–380 / €460–550
$610–730 ⚷ BBA
This is an unusual variation with narrow green marbled stripes interspersed with opaque celluloid running the length of the pen. The celluloid on later pens has broader stripes that show the striations in the pattern more clearly.

A Montblanc Masterpiece 149 9ct gold fountain pen, the cap engraved with a crest, damaged, German, hallmarked London 1972.
£820–980 / €1,200–1,400
$1,600–1,900 ⚷ BBA

Pocket Money Collectables

A rolled fossilized dinosaur bone, from Sandown, Isle of Wight, Cretaceous period, 120 million years old, 2in (5cm) wide.
£1–5 / €2–7
$3–9 ⊞ FOSS

▶ A postcard, by Ernest Nister, depicting two children playing draughts, c1900, 4 x 6in (10 x 15cm).
£1–5 / €2–7
$3–9 ⊞ POS

◀ A selection of buttons, decorated with velvet, pearls, celluloid and diamanté, Austrian, 1890–1920, largest ½in (1cm) diam.
£1–5 / €2–7
$3–9 each ⊞ EV

A hand-worked linen napkin, c1900, 6in (15cm) square.
£1–5 / €2–7
$3–9 ⊞ HILL

A stoneware ginger beer bottle, transfer-printed 'Beesley & Co, Oxford', c1915, 8in (20.5cm) high.
£5–9 / €8–13
$10–16 ⊞ OIA

▶ A Spillers Homepride plastic salt and pepper pot, 1970s, 4¼in (11cm) high.
£6–10 / €9–15
$12–19 ⊞ MMa

A fashion magazine, La Mode Française, 1934, 16 x 10in (40.5 x 25.5cm).
£1–5 / €2–7
$3–9 ⊞ J&S

▶ A pressed glass vase, 1970s, 6in (15cm) high.
£1–5 / €2–7
$3–9 ⊞ BAC

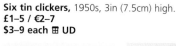

Six tin clickers, 1950s, 3in (7.5cm) high.
£1–5 / €2–7
$3–9 each ⊞ UD

A plastic Rubik's cube, 1970s, 2in (5cm) diam.
£1–5 / €2–7
$3–9 ⊞ FRD

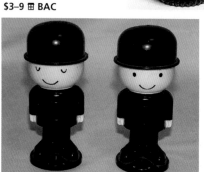

Giles Cartoons, 43rd Series, published by Express Publications, 1989, 8 x 10in (20.5 x 25.5cm).
£1–5 / €2–7
$3–9 ⊞ NW

Collectables of the Future

A Tiger Woods Collector Series 2 tin, depicting Tiger Woods winning the 129th Open Championship at St Andrews, 2000, 9in (23cm) wide.
£35–40 / €50–60
$65–75 ⊞ SHER
Tiger Woods is one of the world's best known sportsmen and material connected with him already attracts collectors.

Andrea Levy, *Small Island*, published by Headline Book Publishing, first edition, 2004, 8 x 5in (20.5 x 12.5cm).
£50–60 / €75–85
$100–115 ⊞ BIB
Small Island won the Whitbread book Awards in 2004 – first editions are already sought after by collectors and have risen in value.

A Lulu Guinness Florist Basket silk handbag, designed 1992, 11½in (29cm) high.
£270–310 / €390–450
$520–600 ⊞ LULU
Lulu Guinness is perhaps Britain's most famous handbag designer and this is her signature design.

Two bone china mugs, by Charlotte Firmin, commemorating the wedding of Prince Charles and Camilla Parker-Bowles, with hand-painted enamel decoration, 2005, 4in (10cm) high.
£10–15 / €15–22
$19–28 each ⊞ CFCC
These hand-painted mugs were produced before the delay was announced to the Royal Wedding. Artist Charlotte Firmin simply crossed out the first date and added the new one, providing a reflection of the confusion surrounding the marriage and an interesting piece of Royal memorabilia.

◀ **A Coca Cola Sunshine Collection painted glass bottle,** designed by Trevor Nelson, retailed by Harvey Nichols, limited edition, 2005, 8¼in (21cm) high.
£2–6 / €3–9
$4–11 ⊞ MMa
This limited edition Sunshine Collection Coca Cola bottle was retailed by Harvey Nichols. Fifteen celebrities from the worlds of fashion, music, television and sport submitted designs for these white bottles and four were put into production, including this example by Radio One's Trevor Nelson. Coca Cola memorabilia is a well-established collectable and unusual bottle variations are sought after.

Six rubber, plastic and fabric charity wristbands, 2005.
£1–5 / €2–7
$3–9 each ⊞ MMa
Charity wristbands have become a favourite accessory and are sported by film stars such as Nicole Kidman. Certain more desirable examples were being sold on eBay as soon as stocks ran out in the shops.

Record Breakers

A silver-gilt Golf Open Championship medal, won by Mungo Park in 1874, the display case with a plaque inscribed 'Mungo Park Medal, presented by A.M.B. Park-May, 1959', with related correspondence regarding the medal's endowment to Grim's Dyke Golf Club by the Park family in 1959.
World Record Price
£48,000 / €69,000
$92,000 ➚ BUDD

A Carpenter 'Tally Ho' cast-iron toy coach and four horses, with a driver and six passengers, patented 1880, 27½in (70cm) long.
World Record Price
£47,000 / €68,000
$90,000 ➚ JDJ
Toy catalogues from 1892 reveal that, in today's values, this coach originally sold for £10.50 / €15 / $20.50.

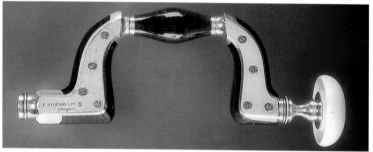

A silver-plated figured Brazilian rosewood brace, by E. Simpson & Co, Glasgow, the ivory screw cap with the coat-of-arms of the Sheffield Cutlers Company, late 19thC.
World Record Price
£12,500 / €17,500
$24,000 ➚ DStA

A Gaumont nitrate newsreel 'RMS Titanic', April 2 1912.
£16,000 / €23,200
$30,700 ➚ HAld
At over 12 minutes playing time, this is believed to be the longest unedited and unaltered *Titanic* newsreel so far discovered. It made a world record price for *Titanic* newsreel footage.

A Pendelphin Old Meg wall plaque, c1953, 4in (10cm) high.
World Record Price
£4,000 / €5,800
$7,600 ➚ ASHB

A Burleigh Ware charger, by Charlotte Rhead, c1930, 14in (35.5cm) diam.
£3,100 / €4,400
$5,900 ➚ AH

A Union Jack flag, from Changi Prison Camp, with signatures of camp prisoners, together with the signature of Lady Edwina Mountbatten, with service records and associated documentation, 1940s, 143¾ x 70in (365 x 178cm).
£17,000 / €24,600
$32,000 ➚ LJ
Before WWII, this flag was flown over the Palace of the Sultan of Johore. After the attack on Pearl Harbour the flag was taken by retreating Australian Army Captain Ken Parsons, to keep it out of enemy hands. In February 1942 Captain Parsons, along with 130,000 Allied troops, was captured by the Japanese following the fall of Singapore. With the help of fellow officers, Parsons ensured that the flag was hidden from the Japanese for the following three and a half years, until they were liberated at the infamous Changi Prison in August 1945.

Directory of Specialists

If you require a valuation for an item it is advisable to check whether the dealer or specialist will carry out this service, and whether there is a charge. Please mention Miller's when making an enquiry. Having found a specialist who will carry out your valuation, it is best to send a description and photograph of the item to them, together with a stamped addressed envelope for the reply. A valuation by telephone is not possible. Most dealers are only too happy to help you with your enquiry, however, they are very busy people and consideration of the above points would be welcomed.

U.S.A.

20th Century Vintage Telephones, 2780 Northbrook Place, Boulder, Colorado 80304 Tel: 303 442 3304

Antique Arcade, 1823 El Camino Real, Redwood City, CA 94061
Tel: 650 368 8267

Antique Associates at West Townsend, PO Box 129W, 473 Main Street, West Townsend, MA 01474
Tel: 978 597 8084 drh@aaawt.com

Antiques & Art, 116 State Street, Portsmouth, NH 03802 Tel: 603 431 3931

Sara Bernstein Antique Dolls & Bears, Englishtown, New Jersey 07726
Tel: 732 536 4101
santiqbebe@aol.com
www.sarabernsteindolls.com
Dolls and Teddy bears.

Bertoia Auctions, 2141 DeMarco Drive, Vineland, New Jersey 08360
Tel: 856 692 1881
bill@bertoiaauctions.com
www.bertoiaauctions.com
Mechanical bank and toy auctions.

Bloomington Auction Gallery, 300 East Grove St, Bloomington, Illinois 61701
Tel: 309 828 5533 joyluke@verizon.net
www.joyluke.com

Marilynn and Sheila Brass, PO Box 380503, Cambridge, MA 02238-0503
Tel: 617 491 6064
shelmardesign1@aol.com
Kitchenware.

The Calico Teddy Tel: 410 366 7011
CalicTeddy@aol.com
www.calicoteddy.com
Antique Teddy bears.

Henry T. Callan, 162 Quaker Meeting House Road, East Sandwich, MA 02537-1312 Tel: 508 888 5372

Copake Auction, Inc., 266 RT. 7A, Copake, NY 12516 Tel: 518 329 1142
info@copakeauction.com
www.copakeauction.com
Americana, antique & classic bicycles and textiles auctions.

The Dunlop Collection, P.O. Box 6269, Statesville, NC 28687 Tel: 704 871 2626 or Toll Free telephone (800) 227 1996
Paperweights.

Faganarms, Box 425, Fraser MI, 48026
Tel: 586 465 4637
info@faganarms.com
www.faganarms.com

M. Finkel & Daughter, 936 Pine Street, Philadelphia, Pennsylvania 19107-6128
Tel: 215 627 7797
mailbox@finkelantiques.com
www.finkelantiques.com
America's leading antique sampler and needlework dealer.

Laura Fisher Antique Quilts & Americana, 1050 Second Avenue, Gallery #84, New York, NY 10022
Tel: 212 838 2596
laurafisher@netlink1.net
www.laurafisherquilts.com

Goodfaith Antiques and Fine Art By appointment Tel: 518 854 7844
ntk@goodfaithantiques.com
www.goodfaithantiques.com
Paintings, porcelain, furniture, silver, glass Broad range of antiques, art, vintage collectibles.

Karen Michelle Guido, Karen Michelle Antique Tiles, PMB 243, 1835 US 1 South #119, St Augustine, FL 32084
Tel: 904 471 3226
karen@antiquetiles.com
www.antiquetiles.com
Antique and collectible tiles.

Hall's Nostalgia, 389 Chatham Street, Lynn, MA 01902 Tel: 781 595 7757

Harbor Bazaar, 5590 Main, Lexington, MI 48450 bazaar@tias.com
www.tias.com/stores/bazaar/
Antiques and collectibles.

The Herrs Antiques, 2363 Henbird Lane, Lancaster, PA 17601
Tel: 717 569 2268 trishherr@aol.com
donmherr@aol.com

Hunt Auctions, 75 E. Uwchlan Avenue, Suite 130, Exton, Pennsylvania 19341
Tel: 610 524 0822

info@huntauctions.com
www.huntauctions.com
Historical baseball and football memorabilia auctions.

Hurst Gallery, 53 Mt. Auburn Street, Cambridge, MA 02138
Tel: 617 491 6888
manager@hurstgallery.com
www.hurstgallery.com
Antiquities, Asian, African, Oceanic, Pre-Columbian and American Indian art and artifacts.

Randy Inman Auctions Inc., PO Box 726, Waterville, Maine 04903-0726
Tel: 207 872 6900
inman@inmanauctions.com
www.inmanauctions.com
Auctions specialising in advertising, coin-op, gambling devices, automata, soda pop, Coca Cola, breweriana, robots and space toys, C.I. and tin toys, Disneyana, mechanical music, mechanical and still banks, quality antiques.

J's Collectables, 5827 Encinita Avenue, Temple City, CA 91780
Tel: 818 451 0010

Jackson's International Auctioneers & Appraisers of Fine Art & Antiques, 2229 Lincoln Street, Cedar Falls, IA 50613 Tel: 319 277 2256/ 800 665 6743
sandim@jacksonsauctions.com
www.jacksonsauction.com
Antiques and collectibles auctions.

JMW Gallery, 144 Lincoln Street, Boston, MA 02111 Tel: 617 338 9097
www.jmwgallery.com
American Arts & Crafts, Decorative Arts, American Art Pottery, Mission furniture, lighting, color block prints, metalwork.

Jo Campbell, Jo's Antiques, Rt. 1, Box 2390, Mount Pleasant, Texas
Tel: 903 572 3173

James D Julia, Inc., P O Box 830, Rte.201 Skowhegan Road, Fairfield, ME 04937 Tel: 207 453 7125
www.juliaauctions.com
Americana, firearms, lamps and glass, advertising, toys and dolls auctions.

Lamps: By The Book, Inc., 514 14th West Palm Beach, Florida 33401 Tel: 561 659 1723 booklamps@msn.com www.lampsbythebook.com *Gift lamps. Also buy leather bound books.*

Joyce M. Leiby, PO Box 6048, Lancaster, PA 17607 Tel: 717 898 9113 joyclei@aol.com

Malchione Antiques & Sporting Collectibles, 110 Bancroft Road, Kennett Square, PA 19348 Tel: 610 444 3509

Millicent Safro, Tender Buttons, 143 E.62nd Street, New York, NY10021 Tel: 212 758 7004 *Author of BUTTONS.*

Old Timers, Box 392, Camp Hill, PA 17001-0392 Tel: 717 761 1908

Olde Port Bookshop, 18 State Street, Newburyport, Massachusetts 01950 Tel: 978 462 0100 Oldeport@ttlc.net

Olde Scissors Factory Antiques, 107 Avenue L, Matamoras, PA 18336 Tel: 570 491 2707 toyfolks@warwick.net

Rambling Rose Antiques, Marcy & Bob Schmidt, Frederick, MD Tel: 301 473 7010

Reyne Gallery www.reyne.com *20thc decorative arts.*

Right to the Moon Alice, Alice and Ron Lindholm, 240 Cooks Fall Road, Cooks Fall, NY 12776 Tel: 607 498 5750

Riverbank Antiques, Wells Union, Route 1, PO Box 3009, Wells, ME 04090 Tel: 207 646 6314

Mike Roberts, 4416 Foxfire Way, Fort Worth, Texas 76133 Tel: 817 294 2133

R. O. Schmitt Fine Art, Box 1941, Salem, New Hampshire 03079 Tel: 603 893 5915 bob@roschmittfinearts.com www.antiqueclockauction.com *Specialist antique clock auctions.*

Skinner Inc., 357 Main Street, Bolton, MA 01740 Tel: 978 779 6241 www.skinnerinc.com *Antiques, fine art and collectibles auctions.*

Skinner Inc., The Heritage On The Garden, 63 Park Plaza, Boston, MA 02116 Tel: 617 350 5400 www.skinnerinc.com *Antiques, fine art and collectibles auctions.*

Sloan's & Kenyon, 4605 Bradley Boulevard, Bethesda, Maryland 20815 Tel: 301 634 2330 info@sloansandkenyon.com www.sloansandkenyon.com *Art, antiques and collectibles auctions.*

Art Smith Antiques at Wells Union, Route 1, 1755 Post Road, Wells, ME 04090 Tel: 207 646 6996

Toy's N Such Toy's - Antiques & Collectables, 437 Dawson Street, Sault, Sainte Marie, MI 49783-2119 Tel: 906 635 0356

TreasureQuest Auction Galleries, Inc., 2690 S.E.Willoughby Blvd, Stuart, Florida 34994 Tel: 772 781 8600 customerservice@TQAG.com/TIM@TQAG.com www.TQAG.com *Toys, dolls, bears and collectibles auctions.*

Triple "L" Sports, P O Box 281, Winthrop, Maine 04364 Tel: 207 377 5787 lllsport@att.net *Winchester collectibles, fishing, hunting, trapping, knives, primitives, baseball, football, golf, tennis, memorabilia and advertising.*

The Unique One, 2802 Centre Street, Pennsauken, NJ 08109 Tel: 609 663 2554

VintagePostcards.com, 60-C Skiff Street, Suite 116, Hamden, CT 06517 Tel: 203 248 6621 quality@VintagePostcards.com www.VintagePostcards.com

Yanni's Antiques, 538 San Anselmo Avenue, San Anselmo, CA 94960 Tel: 415 459 2996

UK & REPUBLIC OF IRELAND

BEDFORDSHIRE

Sheffield Railwayana Auctions, 4 The Glebe, Clapham, Bedford, MK41 6GA Tel: 01234 325341 www.sheffieldrailwayana.co.uk *Railwayana, posters and models auctions.*

BERKSHIRE

Briggs, 54 Lupin Ride, Kings Copse, Crowthorne, RG45 6UR Tel: 01344 466022 enquiries@usebriggs.com www.usebriggs.com *Rock & pop memorabilia.*

Special Auction Services, Kennetholme, Midgham, Reading, RG7 5UX Tel: 0118 971 2949 www.invaluable.com/sas/

Commemoratives, pot lids & Prattware, Fairings, Goss & Crested, Baxter & Le Blond prints. Also toys for the collector.

BUCKINGHAMSHIRE

Yesterday Child Tel: 01908 583403 djbarrington@btinternet.com *Antique dolls and dolls house miniatures.*

CAMBRIDGESHIRE

Willingham Auctions, 25 High Street, Willingham, CB4 5ES Tel: 01954 261252 info@willinghamauctions.com www.willinghamauctions.com *Ceramics and collectable auctions.*

CHESHIRE

The Antique Garden, Grosvenor Garden Centre, Wrexham Road, Belgrave, Chester, CH4 9EB Tel: 01244 629191/07976 539 990 antigard@btopenworld.com www.antique-garden.co.uk *Original antique garden tools and accessories.*

Collector's Corner, PO Box 8, Congleton, CW12 4GD Tel: 01260 270429 dave.popcorner@ukonline.co.uk *Beatles and pop memorabilia.*

On The Air, The Vintage Technology Centre, The Highway, Hawarden, (Nr Chester), Deeside, CH5 3DN Tel: 01244 530300 or 07778 767734 www.vintageradio.co.uk *Vintage radios.*

Specialist Glass Fairs Ltd Tel: 01260 271975/01260 298042 info@glassfairs.co.uk www.glassfairs.co.uk *'National Glass Collectors Fair' (Est. 1991). Bi-annual event held in May & November. For more details visit www.glassfairs.co.uk or telephone 01260 271975.*

Sweetbriar Gallery Paperweights Ltd., 56 Watergate Street, Chester, CH1 2LA Tel: 01244 329249 sales@sweetbriar.co.uk www.sweetbriar.co.uk www.sweetbriarartglass.co.uk *Paperweights.*

Charles Tomlinson, Chester Tel: 01244 318395 charlestomlinson@tiscali.co.uk *Scientific instruments.*

CLEVELAND

Vectis Auctions Ltd, Fleck Way, Thornaby, Stockton-on-Tees, TS17 9JZ Tel: 01642 750616 admin@vectis.co.uk www.vectis.co.uk *Toy auctions.*

DORSET

Books Afloat, 66 Park Street, Weymouth, DT4 7DE Tel: 01305 779774
Books on all subjects, liner and naval memorabilia, shipping company china, ships bells, old postcards, models, paintings.

Murrays' Antiques & Collectables
Tel: 01202 823870
Shipping, motoring, railway, cycling items always required. Also advertising related items, eg showcards, enamel signs, tins & packaging and general quality collectables. Anything old and interesting. No valuations given.

Old Button Shop Antiques, Lytchett Minster, Poole, BH16 6JF
Tel: 01202 622169
info@oldbuttonshop.fsnet.co.uk
Buttons & collectables.

Onslow's Auctions Ltd, Patrick Bogue, The Coach House, Manor Road, Stourpaine, Dorset DT8 8TQ
Tel/Fax: 01258 488838
19th & 20th century posters, railwayana, motoring, aviation, Titanic and ocean liner collectors' items. Sales held twice a year, usually April and October.

Mark Terry, Madeira Cottage, 49 East Street, Chickerell, DT3 4DS
Tel: 01305 778 214 or 07913 630459
jackie.terry3@btinternet.com
Vintage fishing tackle collector.

ESSEX

20th Century Marks, Whitegates, Rectory Road, Little Burstead, Near Billericay, CM12 9TR
Tel: 01268 411 000 or 07831 778992
info@20thcenturymarks.co.uk
www.20thcenturymarks.co.uk
Original 20th century design.

Collect It!, 1–4 Eaglegate, East Hill, Colchester, CO1 2PR Tel: 01206 851117
sales@collectit.co.uk www.collectit.co.uk
Magazine for collectors.

Gazzas Pinballs Tel: 07753 949887
garypound@go.com
www.gazzaspinballs.co.uk
Pinball machines and one arm Bandits for sale or hire - short or long term for any event. All arcade machines bought, sold and repaired.

Haddon Rocking Horses Ltd, 5 Telford Road, Clacton on Sea, CO15 4LP Tel: 01255 424745
millers@haddonrockinghorses.co.uk
www.haddonrockinghorses.co.uk
Rocking horses.

FLINTSHIRE

Old Bears 4 U, 45 Chester Close, Shotton, Deeside, CH5 1AX
Tel: 01244 830066
info@oldbears4u.co.uk
www.oldbears4u.co.uk
Buying, selling, repairing & cleaning old bears.

GLOUCESTERSHIRE

Cottage Collectibles, Long Street Antiques, 14 Long Street, Tetbury, G18 8AQ Tel: 01666 500850/ 07967 713512
sheila@cottagecollectibles.co.uk
Open Mon–Sat 10.00am–5.00pm, Sun 12.00pm–4.00pm & by appointment. English & continental country antiques & kitchenalia. For enquiries please call 07967 713512.

Gloucester Toy Mart, Ground Floor, Antique Centre, Severn Road, Old Docks, Gloucester, GL1 2LE
Tel: 07973 768452
Buying and selling obsolete toys and collectables.

Grimes House Antiques, High Street, Moreton-in-Marsh, GL56 0AT
Tel: 01608 651029
grimes_house@cix.co.uk
www.grimeshouse.co.uk
www.cranberryglass.co.uk
Cranberry glass.

GWRA Auctions Tel: 01684 773487 or 01386 760109 admin@gwra.co.uk
www.gwra.co.uk
Specialist auctioneers of railway & transport memorabilia.

Specialised Postcard Auctions, 25 Gloucester Street, Cirencester, GL7 2DJ Tel: 01285 659057
Sales of early postcards and ephemera.

Telephone Lines Ltd, 304 High Street, Cheltenham, GL50 3JF
Tel: 01242 583699
info@telephonelines.net
www.telephonelines.net
Antique telephones.

GREATER MANCHESTER

Ivory restoration Tel: 0161 794 5381 or 07832 356105
Darren@ivoryrestoration.com
www.ivoryrestoration.com
Ivory repair and restoration specialist.

HAMPSHIRE

Jim Bullock Militaria, PO Box 217, Romsey, SO51 5XL Tel: 01794 516455
jim@jimbullockmilitaria.com
www.jimbullockmilitaria.com
War medals, decorations and militaria.

Classic Amusements Tel: 01425 472164
pennyslot@aol.com
www.classicamusements.net
Vintage slot machines.

Cobwebs, 78 Northam Road, Southampton, SO14 0PB
Tel: 023 8022 7458
www.cobwebs.uk.com
Ocean liner memorabilia. Also naval and aviation items.

Goss & Crested China Club & Museum, incorporating Milestone Publications, 62 Murray Road, Horndean, PO8 9JL
Tel: (023) 9259 7440
info@gosschinaclub.demon.co.uk
www.gosscrestedchina.co.uk
Goss & crested china.

HERTFORDSHIRE

The Collector, 20 Granville Road, Barnet, EN5 4DS Tel: 020 8441 2015
collector@globalnet.co.uk
Contemporary collectables including Royal Doulton, Beswick, Worcester, Lladro, Border Fine Art, Wedgwood, Coalport, Lilliput Lane, David Winter, etc. By appointment only.

ISLE OF WIGHT

Nostalgia Toy Museum, High Street, Godshill, Ventnor, PO38 3HZ
Tel: 01983 522148
toyman@nostalgiatoys.com
www.nostalgiatoys.com
Diecast toys specialist and museum.

KENT

Chris Baker Gramophones, All Our Yesterdays, 3 Cattle Market, Sandwich, CT13 9AE Tel: 01304 614756
cbgramophones@aol.com
www.chrisbakergramophones.com
Specialist dealer in gramophones and phonographs.

Candlestick & Bakelite, PO Box 308, Orpington, BR5 1TB
Tel: 020 8467 3743
candlestick.bakelite@mac.com
www.candlestickandbakelite.co.uk
Telephones from the 1920s to 70s.

Dragonlee Collectables Tel: 01622 729502
Noritake. Can be seen at Memories, Rochester High Street Tel: 01634 811044.

Heggie, Stuart Tel: 01227 471162 or 0783 3593344
Vintage cameras, optical toys and photographic images.

Lambert & Foster, 102 High Street, Tenterden, TN30 6HT
Tel: 01580 762083
saleroom@lambertandfoster.co.uk

www.salesroom@lambertandfoster.co.uk
Regular monthly sales held Tenterden Antique Auction Rooms.

The Old Tackle Box, PO Box 55,
High Street, Cranbrook, TN17 3ZU
Tel: 01580 713979 or 07729 278 293
tackle.box@virgin.net
Old fishing tackle.

The Neville Pundole Gallery, 8A & 9
The Friars, Canterbury, CT1 2AS
Tel: 01227 453471
neville@pundole.co.uk
www.pundole.co.uk
Moorcroft and contemporary pottery and glass.

Serendipity, 125 High Street, Deal,
CT14 6BB Tel: 01304 369165/01304
366536 dipityantiques@aol.com
Staffordshire pottery.

Toymart.com Ltd, Bilting Farm Business
Centre, Bilting, Ashford, TN25 4HF
Tel: 01233 811 866
collections@toymart.com
www.toymart.com
Monthly toy auctions.

Wenderton Antiques
Tel: 01227 720295 (by appt only)
Country antiques including kitchen, laundry and dairy.

Woodville Antiques, The Street,
Hamstreet, Ashford, TN26 2HG
Tel: 01233 732981
woodvilleantiques@yahoo.co.uk
Tools.

Wot a Racket, 250 Shepherds Lane,
Dartford, DA1 2PN Tel: 01322 220619
wot-a-racket@talk21.com

LANCASHIRE
Tony Croston, by private appointment
only, Lytham St Anne's-on-Sea
Tel: 07771 726726
tony.croston@talk21.com
www.tonycrostonantiques.com
Specialist in Art Deco bronzes by Chiparus, Zach, Lorenzl and Preiss.

Decades, 20 Lord St West, Blackburn,
BB2 1JX Tel: 01254 693320
Original Victorian to 1970s clothing, accessories, jewellery, decorative textiles, and more.

Tracks, PO Box 117, Chorley, PR6 0UU
Tel: 01257 269726
sales@tracks.co.uk www.tracks.co.uk
Beatles and pop memorabilia.

LEICESTERSHIRE
Pooks Books, Fowke Street, Rothley,
LE7 7PJ Tel: 0116 237 6222

pooks.motorbooks@virgin.net
Motoring books and automobilia.

David Stanley Auctions, Stordon Grange,
Osgathorpe, LE12 9SR Tel: 01530 222320
tools@davidstanley.com
www.davidstanley.com
Antique tools.

LINCOLNSHIRE
Junktion, The Old Railway Station,
New Bolingbroke, Boston, PE22 7LB
Tel: 01205 480068/480087
or 07836 345491
junktionantiques@hotmail.com
Advertising and packaging, automobilia, slot machines, pedal cars.

Skip & Janie Smithson Antiques
Tel: 01754 810265 or 07831 399180
smithsonantiques@hotmail.com
Kitchenware.

Garth Vincent, The Old Manor House,
Allington, Nr Grantham, NG32 2DH
Tel: 01400 281358 or 07785 352151
garthvincent@aol.com www.guns.uk.com
Antique arms, armour and medals.

LONDON
Apsley Science & Technology Fairs
Tel: 0796 8753218 www.apsleyfairs.com
The International Antique Scientific & Medical Instrument Fairs, April 23rd & October 29th 2006 at The Thistle Hotel, Bryantson St, Marble Arch, London, W1A 4UR.

Bloomsbury, Bloomsbury House,
24 Maddox Street, W1S 1PP
Tel: 020 7495 9494
info@bloomsburyauctions.com
www.bloomsburyauctions.com
Books, manuscripts, art, prints, collectables auctions.

Chelsea Military Antiques,
F4 Antiquarius, 131/141 Kings Road,
Chelsea, SW3 4PW Tel: 020 7352 0308
richard@chelseamilitaria.com
British campaign medals, 19th & 20thc allied & axis militaria.

Comic Book Postal Auctions Ltd,
40–42 Osnaburgh Street, NW1 3ND
Tel: 020 7424 0007
comicbook@compalcomics.com
www.compalcomics.com
Comic book auctions.

Dix-Noonan-Webb, 16 Bolton Street,
Piccadilly, W1J 8BQ Tel: 020 7016 1700
coins@dnw.co.uk medals@dnw.co.uk
www.dnw.co.uk
Auctioneers and valuers of orders, decorations and medals, coins, tokens and banknotes.

GB Military Antiques, 17–18 The Mall,
359 Upper Street, Islington, N1 0PD
Tel: 020 7354 7334
info@gbmilitaria.com www.gbmilitaria.com
Military antiques.

Michael German Antiques Ltd,
38B Kensington Church Street, W8 4BX
Tel: 020 7937 2771/020 7937 1776
info@antiquecanes.com
info@antiqueweapons.com
www.antiquecanes.com
Walking canes, arms and armour.

Lucias Red Roses, Admiral Vernon
Antique Markets, 67 & 68 Portobello
Road, Shops 57 & 58, W11
Tel: 01793 790 607 or 07778 803 876
sallie_ead@lycos.com
www.vintagemodes.co.uk
19th & 20thc fashion, accessories and textiles.

Lucias Red Roses, Gray's Antique
Markets, 1–7 Davies Mews, W1
Tel: 0207 409 0400 sallie_ead@lycos.com
www.vintagemodes.co.uk
19th & 20thc fashion, accessories and textiles.

Timothy Millett Ltd, Historic Medals
and Works of Art, PO Box 20851,
SE22 0YN Tel: 020 8693 1111
or 07778 637 898
tim@timothymillett.demon.co.uk
Medals and works of art.

Colin Narbeth & Son Ltd, 20 Cecil
Court, Leicester Square, WC2N 4HE
Tel: 020 7379 6975
Colin.Narbeth@btinternet.com
www.colin-narbeth.com
Old paper money.

Hilary Proctor, Vintage Modes,
Shop 6 Admiral Vernon Antiques
Market, 141–151 Portobello Road,
W11 2DY Tel: 07956 876428
hproctor@antiquehandbags.fsnet.co.uk

Spink & Son Ltd, 69 Southampton
Road, Bloomsbury, WC1B 4ET
Tel: 020 7563 4000 info@spink.com
www.spink.com
Auctioneers and dealers in coins, stamps, banknotes, medals and militaria.

Tablewhere Ltd, 4 Queens Parade Close,
N11 3FY Tel UK local rate:
0845 130 6111 or 020 8361 6111
kitson@tablewhere.co.uk
www.tablewhere.co.uk
Tableware matching specialists.

Twinkled, 1st Floor, Old Petrol Station,
11–17 Stockwell Street, Greenwich,
SE10 9JN Tel: 020 8269 0864

info@twinkled.net www.twinkled.net
*Purveyors of fine homeware from the
50s, 60s & 70s. Open Thurs–Tues
11am–5.30pm.*

Twinkled, 2nd Floor, 61a Faraday Way
(off Westfield St), Westminster Ind
Estate, SE18 5TR Tel: 07940 471569
info@twinkled.net www.twinkled.net
*Furniture and other items from the 50s,
60s & 70s. By appointment only.*

Vault Auctions Ltd, PO Box 257,
South Norwood, SE25 6JN
Tel: 01342 300 900
contact@vaultauctions.com
www.vaultauctions.com
*Vintage American and British comics,
related artwork, toys & memorabilia
auctions.*

June Victor, Vintage Modes, S041–43,
Alfies Antique Market, 13–25 Church
Street, NW8 8DT Tel: 020 7723 6066
or 07740704723

Vintage & Rare Guitars (London),
6 Denmark Street, WC2H 8LX
Tel: 020 7240 7500
enquiries@vintageandrareguitars.com
www.vintageandrareguitars.com

Vintage Modes, Grays Antique Markets,
1–7 Davies Mews, W1
Tel: 020 7409 0400
www.vintagemodes.co.uk
Vintage fashion.

Nigel Williams Rare Books, 25 Cecil
Court, WC2N 4EZ Tel: 020 7836 7757
nigel@nigelwilliams.com
www.nigelwilliams.com
*Books - first editions, illustrated,
childrens and detective.*

www.c20th.com Tel: 07775 704052
simon@c20th.com www.c20th.com
Theatre memorabilia bought and sold.

NORFOLK
Cat Pottery, 1 Grammar School Road,
North Walsham, NR28 9JH
Tel: 01692 402962
Winstanley cats.

NORTHAMPTONSHIRE
The Old Brigade, 10A Harborough
Road, Kingsthorpe, Northampton,
NN2 7AZ Tel: 01604 719389
theoldbrigade@btconnect.com
stewart@theoldbrigade.co.uk
www.theoldbrigade.co.uk
Military antiques.

NOTTINGHAMSHIRE
Michael D Long Ltd, 96–98 Derby
Road, Nottingham, NG1 5FB
Tel: 0115 941 3307

sales@michaeldlong.com
www.michaeldlong.com
Militaria and arms & armour.

Millennium Collectables Ltd, P.O. Box
146, Newark, NG24 2WR
Tel: 01636 703075
mail@millenniumcollectables.co.uk
www.millenniumcollectables.co.uk
*Limited edition Royal Doulton &
Coalport advertising icon figures.*

T. Vennett-Smith, 11 Nottingham Road,
Gotham, NG11 0HE Tel: 0115 983 0541
info@vennett-smith.com
www.vennett-smith.com
*Ephemera and sporting memorabilia
auctions.*

OXFORDSHIRE
Alvin's Vintage Games & Toys
Tel: 01865 772409
alvin@vintage-games.co.uk
http://www.vintage-games.co.uk
Pelham puppets.

Avrick Antiques Tel: 01295 738 318
avrick_antiques@tiscali.co.uk
www.avrick-antiques.co.uk
Antique firearms and edged weapons.

Mike Delaney Tel: 01993 840064 or
07979 910760
mike@vintagehornby.co.uk
www.vintagehornby.co.uk
*Vintage Hornby "0" gauge & other toy
trains.*

Julian Eade Tel: 01865 300349 or
07973 542971
*Doulton Lambeth stoneware and
signed Burslem wares.*

Stone Gallery, 93 The High Street,
Burford, OX18 4QA
Tel: 01993 823302
mail@stonegallery.co.uk
www.stonegallery.co.uk
*Specialist dealers in antique and
modern paperweights, gold and silver
designer jewellery and enamel boxes.*

Teddy Bears of Witney, 99 High Street,
Witney, OX28 6HY Tel: 01993 706616
www.teddybears.co.uk
Teddy bears.

REPUBLIC OF IRELAND
George Stacpoole, Main Street, Adare,
Co. Limerick Tel: 00353 (0)6139 6409
stacpoole@iol.ie
www.georgestacpooleantiques.com
*Furniture, pottery, ceramics, silver and
prints.*

SCOTLAND
Rhod McEwan - Golf Books,
Glengarden, Ballater, Aberdeenshire,

AB35 5UB Tel: 013397 55429
www.rhodmcewan.com
Rare and out-of-print golfing books.

SHROPSHIRE
Mullock & Madeley, The Old Shippon,
Wall-under-Heywood, Nr Church
Stretton, SY6 7DS Tel: 01694 771771
or 01584 841 428
auctions@mullockmadeley.co.uk
www.mullockmadeley.co.uk
Sporting auctions.

SOMERSET
Philip Knighton, 1c South Street,
Wellington, TA21 8NR
Tel: 01823 661618
philip.knighton@btopenworld.com
*Wireless, gramophones and all valve
equipment.*

London Cigarette Card Co Ltd,
Sutton Road, Somerton, TA11 6QP
Tel: 01458 273452
cards@londoncigcard.co.uk
www.londoncigcard.co.uk
Cigarette and trade cards.

Vintage & Rare Guitars (Bath) Ltd,
7–8 Saville Row, Bath, BA1 2QP
Tel: 01225 330 888
enquiries@vintageandrareguitars.com
www.vintageandrareguitars.com

STAFFORDSHIRE
Gordon Litherland, 25 Stapenhill Road,
Burton on Trent, DE15 9AE
Tel: 01283 567213 or 07952 118987
gordon@jmp2000.com
*Bottles, breweriana and pub jugs,
advertising ephemera and
commemoratives.*

The Potteries Antique Centre,
271 Waterloo Road, Cobridge,
Stoke on Trent, ST6 3HR
Tel: 01782 201455
sales@potteriesantiquecentre.com
www.potteriesantiquecentre.com
Collectable ceramics.

SUFFOLK
Jamie Cross, PO Box 73,
Newmarket, CB8 8RY
jamiecross@aol.com
www.thirdreichmedals.com
*We buy and sell, value for probate and
insurance British, German and foreign
war medals, badges and decorations.*

W. L. Hoad, 9 St. Peter's Road,
Kirkley, Lowestoft, NR33 0LH
Tel: 01502 587758
William@whoad.fsnet.co.uk
www.cigarettecardsplus.com
Cigarette cards.

Suffolk Sci-Fi and Fantasy,
17 Norwich Road, Ipswich, IP1 2ET
Tel: 01473 400655 or 07885 298361
symon@suffolksci-fi.com
www.suffolksci-fi.com
Science fiction.

SURREY
British Notes, PO Box 257, Sutton,
SM3 9WW Tel: 020 8641 3224
pamwestbritnotes@aol.com
www.britishnotes.co.uk
Banking collectables.

Connoisseur Policies Tel: 0870 241 0142
information@connoisseurpolicies.com
www.connoisseurpolicies.com
Insurance.

The Gooday Gallery, 14 Richmond Hill,
Richmond, TW10 6QX
Tel: 020 8940 8652 or 077101 24540
goodaygallery@aol.com
*Arts & Crafts, Art Deco, Art Nouveau,
Tribal, 1950s and 60s.*

Howard Hope, 19 Weston Park,
Thames Ditton, KT7 0HW
Tel: 020 8398 7130
howard_hope@yahoo.co.uk
www.gramophones.uk.com
*Specialising for 30 years in
gramophones, phonographs, anything
related to the history of recorded
sound and other mechanical/musical
items. Dealing by correspondence only,
please no visits - call first. Colour
pictures of any item in stock can be
sent on request by email. Exporting
worldwide. Shipping quotations given
for any machine.*

EAST SUSSEX
High Street Retro, 39 High Street,
Old Town, Hastings, TN34 3ER
Tel: 01424 460068

Tony Horsley, PO Box 3127, Brighton,
BN1 5SS Tel: 01273 550770
*Candle extinguishers, Royal Worcester
and other porcelain.*

Soldiers of Rye, Mint Arcade,
71 The Mint, Rye, TN31 7EW
Tel: 01797 225952
rameses@supanet.com
chris@johnbartholomewcards.co.uk
www.rameses.supanet.com
*Military badges, cigarette cards, prints,
medals, collectors figurines.*

Twinkled, High St Antiques Centre,
39 High Street, Hastings, TN34 3ER
Tel: 01424 460068
info@twinkled.net
limehouseblues47@aol.com
www.twinkled.net

*Purveyors of fine homeware from the
50s, 60s & 70s. Open Thurs–Tues
11am–5.30pm.*

Wallis & Wallis, West Street Auction
Galleries, Lewes, BN7 2NJ
Tel: 01273 480208
auctions@wallisandwallis.co.uk
grb@wallisandwallis.co.uk
www.wallisandwallis.co.uk
*Specialist auctioneers of militaria, arms,
armour, coins and medals. Also die-cast
and tinplate toys, Teddy bears, dolls,
model railways, toy soldiers and models.*

WEST SUSSEX
Rupert Toovey & Co Ltd, Spring
Gardens, Washington, RH20 3BS
Tel: 01903 891955
auctions@rupert-toovey.com
www.rupert-toovey.com
*Monthly specialist auctions of antiques,
fine art and collectors' items. Regular
specialist auctions of collectors' toys &
dolls and antiquarian & collectors' books.*

WALES
Jen Jones, Pontbrendu, Llanybydder,
Ceredigion, SA40 9UJ Tel: 01570 480610
quilts@jen-jones.com www.jen-jones.com
*Quilt expert dealing mainly in Welsh
quilts and blankets. Between 200 and
300 quilts in stock with a comparable
number of blankets. Looking to buy as
well as sell.*

WARWICKSHIRE
Chinasearch, PO Box 1202, Kenilworth,
CV8 2WW Tel: 01926 512402
info@chinasearch.co.uk
www.chinasearch.co.uk
*Discontinued dinner, tea and
collectable ware bought and sold.*

Collector Bits Tel: 02476 746981 or
07796 398 303 collectorbits@aol.com
www.collectorbits.com
*Specialists in pottery, glass and
ceramics, including Dennis Chinaworks,
Okra Studio glass, Roger Cockram
ceramics, Peter McDougall paperweights.*

WEST MIDLANDS
Fragile Design, 8 The Custard Factory,
Digbeth, Birmingham, B9 4AA
Tel: 0121 693 1001
info@fragiledesign.com
www.fragiledesign.com
Dealers of original 20th century design.

WILTSHIRE
Dominic Winter Book Auctions,
The Old School, Maxwell Street,
Swindon, SN1 5DR Tel: 01793 611340
info@dominicwinter.co.uk
www.dominicwinter.co.uk

*Auctions of antiquarian and general
printed books & maps, sports books
and memorabilia, art reference &
pictures, photography & ephemera
(including toys, games and other
collectables).*

YORKSHIRE
Echoes, 650a Halifax Road, Eastwood,
Todmorden, OL14 6DW
Tel: 01706 817505
*Antique costume, textiles including
linen, lace and jewellery.*

Gerard Haley, Hippins Farm, Black
Shawhead, Nr Hebden Bridge, HX7 7JG
Tel: 01422 842484
gedhaley@yahoo.co.uk
Toy soldiers.

John & Simon Haley, 89 Northgate,
Halifax, HX1 1XF Tel: 01422 822148/
360434 toysandbanks@aol.com
Old toys and money boxes.

Briar's C20th Decorative Arts, Skipton
Antiques & Collectors Centre, The Old
Foundry, Cavendish Street, Skipton,
BD23 2AB Tel: 01756 798641
bsdecoarts@aol.com
*Art Deco ceramics and furniture,
specialising in Charlotte Rhead pottery.*

EAST YORKSHIRE
The Crested China Co, Highfield,
Windmill Hill, Driffield, YO25 5YP
Tel: 0870 300 1 300
dt@thecrestedchinacompany.com
www.thecrestedchinacompany.com
Goss and Crested china.

DJ Auctions Ltd, 66 Scarborough Road,
Driffield, YO25 5DS Tel: 01377 272201
info@dj-auctions.co.uk
www.dj-auctions.co.uk
Specialist toy auctioneers.

SOUTH YORKSHIRE
BBR, Elsecar Heritage Centre, Elsecar,
Nr Barnsley, S74 8HJ Tel: 01226 745156
sales@onlinebbr.com www.onlinebbr.com
*Advertising, breweriana, pot lids, bottles,
Cornishware, Doulton and Beswick.*

WEST YORKSHIRE
The Camera House, 65 Oakworth Hall,
Oakworth, Keighley, BD22 7HZ
Tel: 01535 642333
colin@the-camera-house.co.uk
www.the-camera-house.co.uk
*Cameras & photographic equipment
from 1850. Cash purchases, sales and
repairs. National and international mail
order a speciality. Valuations for
probate & insurance. Online catalogue.
Please ring or email before visiting.
Prop. C Cox.*

Directory of Collectors' Clubs

With new Collectors' Clubs emerging every day this directory is by no means complete. If you wish to be included in next year's directory or if you have a change of details, please inform us by May 2006.

A.C.O.G.B (Autograph Club of Great Britain) SAE to Mr R. Gregson, 47 Webb Crescent, Dawley, Telford, Shropshire, TF4 3DS gregson@blueyonder.co.uk www.acogb.co.uk

Alice in Wonderland Collectors Network Joel Birenbaum, 2765 Shellingham Drive, Lisle, IL 60532-4245, U.S.A.

American Barb Wire Collector's Society John Mantz, 1023 Baldwin Road, Bakersfield, CA 93304-4203, U.S.A.

American Business Card Club UK Robin Cleeter, 38 Abbotsbury Road, Morden, Surrey, SM4 5LQ

American Business Card Club US Avery N. Pitzak, PO Box 460297, Aurora, CO 80046-0297, U.S.A.

American Credit Card Collectors Society Bill Wieland, President, PO Box 2465, MI 48640, U.S.A. acccs1@charter.net www.creditcollectibles.com

American Fish Decoy Collectors Association PO Box 252, Boulder Junction, WI 54512, U.S.A.

American Hatpin Society Virginia Woodbury, 20 Montecillo Drive, Rolling Hills Estates, CA 90274, U.S.A. www.americanhatpinsociety.com

American Lock Collectors Association 36076 Grennada, Livonia, MI 48154, U.S.A.

American Matchcover Collecting Club PO Box 18481, Asheville, NC 28814, U.S.A.

American Society of Camera Collectors, Inc. Sam Rosenfeld, 6570 Kelvin Ave, Canoga Park, CA 91306-4021, U.S.A.

American Toy Emergency Vehicle (ATEV) Club Jeff Hawkins, President, 11415 Colfax Road, Glen Allen, Virginia 23060, U.S.A.

The Antiquarian Horological Society Wendy Barr, Secretary, New House, High Street, Ticehurst, East Sussex, TN5 7AL Tel: 01580 200 155 secretary@ahsoc.demon.co.uk www.ahsoc.demon.co.uk

Antique Bottles & Collectibles Club Willy Young, PO Box 1061, Verdi, NV 89439, U.S.A.

Antique Comb Collectors Club International Jen Cruse, European Coordinator, 14 Hall Drive, London, SE26 6XB jen.cruse@eggconnect.net

Antique Comb Collectors Club International (US) Linda Shapiro, 8712 Pleasant View Road, Bangor, PA 18013, U.S.A.

Antique Fan Collectors' Association PO Box 5473, Sarasota, FL 34277-5473, U.S.A. Tel: 941 955 8232 membership@fancollectors.org www.fancollectors.org

Antique Wireless Association (AWA) Box E, Breesport, New York 14816, U.S.A.

Association for British Brewery Collectables 28 Parklands, Kidsgrove, Stoke-on-Trent, Staffordshire ST7 4US Tel: 01782 761048 michael.peterson@ntlworld.com

Association of Coffee Mill Enthusiasts John White, 5941 Wilkerson Road, Rex, GA 30273, U.S.A. Tel: 770 474 0509

Avon Magpies Club Mrs W. A. Fowler, Le Bourg, St Quentin les Chardonnets, 61800 Orne, Normandie, France Tel: (0)2 33 96 36 29

B.E.A.R. Collector's Club Linda Hartzfeld, 16901 Covello Street, Van Nuys, California 91406, U.S.A.

Badge Collectors' Circle c/o Frank Setchfield, 57 Middleton Place, Loughborough, Leicestershire, LE11 2BY www.badgecollectorscircle.co.uk

Barbie Collectors Club of Great Britain Elizabeth Lee, 17 Rosemont Road, Acton, London, W3 9LU

Barbie Lover's Club Amy Reed, 399 Winfield Road, Rochester, New York 14622, U.S.A.

Battery-Operated Toy Collectors of America Jack Smith, 410 Linden, PO Box 676, Tolono, IL 61880, U.S.A.

The Bead Society of Great Britain Carole Morris (Dr), 1 Casburn Lane, Burwell, Cambridge, CB5 0ED Tel: 01638 742024 www.beadsociety.freeserve.co.uk

Bearly Ours Teddy Club Linda Harris, 54 Berkinshaw Crescent, Don Mills, Ontario M3B 2T2, Canada

The Beatrix Potter Society UK Registered Charity No. 281198, c/o Membership Secretary, 9 Broadfields, Harpenden, Hertfordshire, AL5 2HJ info@beatrixpottersociety.org.uk www.beatrixpottersociety.org.uk

Beer Can Collectors of America Don Hicks, 747 Merus Court, Fenton, MO 63026-2092, U.S.A.

Belleek Collectors Group (UK) The Hon Chairman, Mr D. A. Reynolds, 7 Highfield Estate, Wilmslow, Cheshire, SK9 2JR chairman@belleek.org.uk www.belleek.org.uk

Betty Boop Fan Club Kim Gordon, PO Box 42, Moorhead, MN 56561, U.S.A.

Black Memorabilia Collectors Association Sharon Hart, 2482 Devoe Terrace, Bronx, NY 10468, U.S.A.

Blue & White Pottery Club Howard Gardner, 224 12th Street N.W., Cedar Rapids, Iowa 52405, U.S.A. Tel: 319 362 8116

British Art Medal Society Philip Attwood, c/o Dept of Coins and Medals, The British Museum, London, WC1B 3DG Tel: 020 7323 8260 pattwood@thebritishmuseum.ac.uk www.bams.org.uk/

British Banking History Society Membership: Mr P.M Lord, 14 Garsdale Road, Newsome, Huddersfield, HD4 6QZ

The British Beermat Collectors' Society Hon Sec, 69 Dunnington Avenue, Kidderminster, Worcestershire, DY10 2YT www.britishbeermats.org.uk

British Button Society Membership Secretary Mrs June Baron, Jersey Cottage, Parklands Road, Bower Ashton, Bristol, Gloucestershire, BS3 2JR

The British Compact Collectors' Society SAE to: PO Box 131, Woking, Surrey, GU24 9YR www.thebccs.org.uk

British Diecast Model Collectors Association PO Box 11, Norwich, Norfolk, NR7 0SP www.swapmeet.freeserve.co.uk

British Doll Collectors' Club Mrs Frances Baird, Publisher & Editor, The Anchorage, Wrotham Road, Culverstone, Meopham, Gravesend, Kent, DA13 0QW www.britishdollcollectors.com

British Equine Collectors Forum (Model Horses) SAE to Membership Secretary Miss Helen Cooke, 24 Coleridge Close, Bletchley, Milton Keynes, Buckinghamshire, MK3 5AF www.worldofpaul.com/becf

British Iron Collectors Julia Morgan, 87 Wellsway Road, Bath, Somerset, BA2 4RU

The British Model Soldier Society Honorable Secretary, 44 Danemead, Hoddesdon, Hertfordshire, EN11 9LU

British Novelty Salt & Pepper Collectors Club Ray Dodd (Secretary), Coleshill, Clayton Road, Mold, Flintshire, CH7 1SX www.bnspcc.com

The British Smurf Collectors Club The Club Secretary, PO Box 5737, Swanage, Dorset, BH19 3ZX www.globalserve.net/~astro1/bscc/register.htn

Brooklands Automobilia & Regalia Collectors' Club, The (B.A.R.C.C.) Hon. Sec. G. G. Weiner, 4–4a Chapel Terrace Mews, Kemp Town, Brighton, East Sussex, BN2 1HU Tel: 01273 622722 www.barcc.co.uk www.brmmbrmm.com/barcc www.brooklands-automobilia-regalia-collectors-club.co.uk

Bubble Gum Charm Collectors Maureen McCaffrey, 24 Seafoam Street, Staten Island, NY 10306, U.S.A.

The Burleigh Ware International Collectors Circle Tel: 01664 454570

Butter Pat Collectors' Notebook 5955 S.W. 179th Ave, Beaverton, OR 97007, U.S.A.

Butter Pats International Collectors Club Alice Black, 38 Acton Street, Maynard, MA 01754, U.S.A.

The Buttonhook Society (US contact) c/o Priscilla Stoffel, White Marsh, Box 287, MD 21162-0287, U.S.A. Tel: 410 256 5541 buttonhooksociety@tiscali.co.uk www.thebuttonhooksociety.com

The Buttonhook Society c/o Paul Moorehead, Chairman, 2 Romney Place, Maidstone, Kent, ME15 6LE Tel: 01622 752949 buttonhooksociety@tiscali.co.uk www.thebuttonhooksociety.com

Caithness Glass Paperweight Collectors' Society Mrs Caroline Clark, The Caithness Glass Compay Limited, Inveralmond, Perth, Scotland, PH1 3TZ Tel: 01738 492335 collector@caithnessglass.co.uk www.caithnessglass.co.uk

Campbell Soup Collectors International Association Betty Campbell Madden, President, 305 East Main Street, Ligonier, PA 15658, U.S.A.

Cane Collectors Club of America 2 Horizon Road, Suite G18, Fort Lee, NJ 07024, U.S.A.

Carlton Ware Collectors International Carlton Factory Shop, Carlton Works, Copeland Street, Stoke on Trent, Staffordshire, ST4 1PU Tel: 01782 410504

Carnival Glass Society (UK) PO Box 14, Hayes, Middlesex, UB3 5NU www.carnivalglasssociety.co.uk

The Cartophilic Society of Great Britain Ltd, Membership Secretary, Alan Stevens, 63 Ferndale Road, Church Crookham, Fleet, Hampshire, GU52 6LN www.csgb.co.uk

Cash Register Collectors Club Mike Hennessey, PO Box 20534, Dayton, OH 45420-0534, U.S.A. Tel: 937 433 3529 www.crcci.org

Cat Collectables 297 Alcester Road, Hollywood, Birmingham, West Midlands, B47 5HJ Tel: 01564 826277 cat.collectables@btinternet.com www.cat-collectables.co.uk

Charlotte Rhead Newsletter c/o 49 Honeybourne Road, Halesowen, West Midlands, B63 3ET Tel: 0121 560 7386

Cigarette Case Collectors' Club Colin Grey, 19 Woodhurst North, Raymead Road, Maidenhead, Berkshire, SL6 8PH Tel: 01628 781800

Cigarette Pack Collectors Association Richard Elliot, 61 Searle St, Georgetown, MA 01833, U.S.A.

Cigarette Packet Collectors Club of GB Barry Russell, Talisker, Vines Cross Road, Horam, Heathfield, East Sussex, TN21 0HF Tel: 01435 812453 www.cigarettpacket.com

Clarice Cliff Collectors' Club Fantasque House, Tennis Drive, The Park, Nottingham, NG7 1AE www.claricecliff.com

The Coca-Cola Club Membership Director, 4780 Ashford-Dunwoody Road Suite. A, Atlanta, Georgia 30338, U.S.A. www.cocacolaclub.org

The Coleco Collectors Club Ann Wilhite, 610 W 17th Freemont, NE 68025, U.S.A.

The Comic Journal C.J. Publications, c/o 6 Rotherham Road, Catcliffe, Rotherham, South Yorkshire, S60 5SW

Commemorative Collectors' Society and Commemoratives Museum c/o Steven Jackson, Lumless House, 77 Gainsborough Road, Winthorpe, Newark, Nottinghamshire, NG24 2NR Tel: 01636 671377 commemorativecollectorssociety@hotmail.com

Compact Collectors Club International Roselyn Gerson, PO Box 40, Lynbrook, NY 11563, U.S.A.

Cook Book Collectors Club Barbara Gelink, 4756 Terrace Drive, San Diego, CA 92116-2514, U.S.A. Tel: 619 281 8962 cookwithbabs@home.com

Cookie Cutters Collectors Club Ruth Capper, 1167 Teal Road S. W., Dellroy, OH 44620-9704, U.S.A.

Corgi Collector Club c/o Corgi Classics Ltd, Meridian East, Meridian Business Park, Leicester, LE19 1RL Tel: 0870 607 1204 susie@collectorsclubs.org.uk

Cornish Collectors Club PO Box 58, Buxton, Derbyshire, SK17 0FH

The Costume Society St Paul's House, Warwick Lane, London, EC4P 4BN www.costumesociety.org.uk

Cream Separator Association Dr. Paul Dettloff, Sec., Rt. 3, Box 189, Arcadia, WI 54612, U.S.A. Tel: 608 323 7470

The Crested Circle 42 Douglas Road, Tolworth, Surbiton, Surrey, KT6 7SA

Crunch Club (Breakfast Cereal Collectables) John Cahill, 9 Weald Rise, Tilehurst, Reading, Berkshire, RG30 6XB

The Dean's Collectors Club Euro Collectibles, PO Box 370565, 49 NE 39th Street, Miami FL33 137, U.S.A. US toll free 1 800 309 8336 www.deansbears.com

The Dean's Collectors Club Pontypool, Gwent, NP4 6YY Tel: 01495 764881 www.deansbears.com

Devon Pottery Collectors Group Mrs Joyce Stonelake, 19 St Margarets Avenue, Torquay, Devon, TQ1 4LW Virginia.Brisco@care4free.net

Die Cast Car Collectors Club c/o Jay Olins (Chairman), PO Box 67226, Los Angeles, California 90067-0266, U.S.A. Tel: 310 629 7113 jay@diecast.org www.diecast.org

Dinky Toy Club of America c/o Jerry Fralick, 6030 Day Break Circle, Suite A 150, PBM/132, Clarksville, Maryland 21029, U.S.A. www.dinkytoyclub.net

Doll House & Miniature Collectors PO Box 159, Bethlehem, CT 06751-0159, U.S.A.

Egg Cup Collectors' Club of GB Sue Wright, Subs Secretary, PO Box 39, Llandysul, Wales, SA44 5ZD suewright@suecol.freeserve.co.uk www.eggcupworld.co.uk

Eggcup Collectors' Corner Dr. Joan M. George, 67 Stevens Ave, Old Bridge, NJ 08857, U.S.A. drjgeorge@nac.net

The English Playing Card Society John Sings, Secretary, PO Box 29, North Walsham, Norfolk, NR28 9NQ Tel: 01692 650496

Ephemera Society of America, Inc. PO Box 95, Cazenovia, NY 13035-0095, U.S.A. Tel: 315 655 9139 info@ephemerasociety.org www.ephemerasociety.org

The Ephemera Society Membership Secretary, PO Box 112, Northwood, Middlesex, HA6 2WT Tel: 01923 829 079

The European Honeypot Collectors' Society John Doyle, The Honeypot, 18 Victoria Road, Chislehurst, Kent, BR7 6DF Tel: 020 8289 7725 johnhoneypot@hotmail.com www.geocities.com/tehcsuk

The Fairing Collectors Society Stuart Piepenstock Tel: 01895 824830

The Family Circle of Pen Delfin Susan Beard, 230 Spring Street N.W., Suite 1238, Atlanta, Georgia 30303, U.S.A.

Fan Circle International Sec: Mrs Joan Milligan, Cronk-y-Voddy, Rectory Road, Coltishall, Norwich, Norfolk, NR12 7HF

Festival of Britain Society c/o Martin Packer, 41 Lyall Gardens, Birmingham, West Midlands, B45 9YW Tel: 0121 453 8245 martin@packer34.freeserve.co.uk www.packer34.freeserve.co.uk

Fieldings Crown Devon Collectors' Club PO Box 462, Manvers, Rotherham, S63 7WT Tel: 01709 874433 fcdcc@tiscali.co.uk www.fieldingscrowndevclub.com

Friends of Blue Ceramic Society Terry Sheppard, 45a Church Road, Bexley Heath, Kent, DA7 4DD www.fob.org.uk

Friends of Broadfield House Glass Museum June Wilson, Broadfield House Glass Museum, Compton Drive, Kingswinford, West Midlands, DY6 9NS

Fruit Jar & Bottle Club Midwest Antiques, Norman & Junne Barnett, PO Box 38, Flat Rock, IN 47234, U.S.A. Tel: 812 587 5560

The Furniture History Society c/o Dr. Brian Austen, 1 Mercedes Cottages, St. John's Road, Haywards Heath, West Sussex, RH16 4EH Tel: 01444 413845 furniturehistorysociety@hotmail.com www.furniturehistorysociety.com

The Glass Gallery L.H. Selman Ltd., 123 Locust Street, Santa Cruz, CA 95060-3907, U.S.A. Tel: 831 427 1177 www.glassgallery.com

The Glove Collector Club Joe Phillips, 14057 Rolling Hills Lane, Dallas, TX 75240, U.S.A.

Golly Collectors' Club Keith Wilkinson, 18 Hinton Street, Fairfield, Liverpool, Merseyside, L6 3AR

Goss Collectors' Club (est 1970) Brian Waller, 35 Felstead Way, Luton, LU2 7LH Tel: 01582 732063 commercialofficer@gosscollectorsclub.org

Griswold & Cast Iron Cookware Association David G. Smith, P.O. Drawer B, Perrysburg, NY 14129-0301, U.S.A. Tel: 716 532 5154 DGSpanman@aol.com www.C1web.com/panman

Hagen-Renaker Collectors Club (UK) Chris and Derek Evans, 97 Campbell Road, Burton, Christchurch, Dorset, BH23 7LY www.priorycollectables.co.uk

The Hagen-Renaker Collectors Club Jenny Palmer, 3651 Polish Line Road, Cheboygan, Mitchigan 49721, U.S.A.

Happy Pig Collectors Club Gene Holt, PO Box 17, Oneida, IL 61467-0017, U.S.A.

The Hat Pin Society of Great Britain PO Box 110, Cheadle, Cheshire, SK8 1GG www.hatpinsociety.org.uk

Historical Model Railway Society 59 Woodberry Way, London, E4 7DY

Honiton Pottery Collectors' Society Ian McLellan (Chairman), 51 Cherryfields, Gillingham, Dorset, SP8 4TJ Tel: 01747 835299 jandimclellan@btinternet.com www.hpcs.info

Hornby Collectors Club PO Box 25, Melton Mowbray, Leicestershire LE13 1ZG Tel: 0870 062 4001 alexmckenzie@collectorsclubs.org.uk

The Hornby Railway Collectors' Association David Embling, 77 Station Road, Rayleigh, Essex, SS6 8AR Tel: 01268 775072 www.hrca.net

Hornsea Pottery Collectors' and Research Society c/o Mr Peter Tennant, 128 Devonshire Street, Keighley, West Yorkshire, BD21 2QJ hornsea@pdtennant.fsnet.co.uk www.hornseacollector.co.uk

The Indian Military Historical Society Secretary/Editor, A N McClenaghan, 33 High Street, Tilbrook, Huntingdon, Cambridgeshire, PE28 0JP

Inn Sign Society Chairman, Mr R. P. Gatrell, Flat 19, Stamford Grange, Dunham Road, Altrincham, Cheshire, WA14 4AN

Inner-Seal Collectors Club (National Biscuit Co and Nabisco Memorabilia) Charlie Brown, 6609 Billtown Road, Louisville, KY 40299, U.S.A.

International Association of Calculator Collectors PO Box 345, Tustin, CA 92781-0345, U.S.A.

International Bank Note Society c/o Milan Alusic, PO Box 1642, Racine, WI 53401, U.S.A.

International Bond & Share Society, American Branch Ted Robinson, Vice President, PO Box 814, Richboro, PA, U.S.A. Tel: 215 357 6820 fandr@voicenet.com

International Bond and Share Society c/o Peter Duppa-Miller, Beechcroft, Combe Hay, Bath, Somerset, BA2 7EG

International Perfume Bottle Association Details from Lynda Brine, Assembly Antique Centre, 6 Saville Row, Bath, Somerset, BA1 2QP Tel: 01225 448488 lyndabrine@yahoo.co.uk www.scentbottlesandsmalls.co.uk

International Perfume Bottle Association c/o Membership Secretary, 295 E. Swedesford Road, PMB 185, Wayne, PA 19087, U.S.A. paradise@sunset.net www.perfumebottles.org

International Philatelic Golf Society Ron Spiers (Secretary), 8025 Saddle Run, Powell, OH 43065, U.S.A.

International Philatelic Golf Society UK Secretary, Dr Eiron B.E. Morgan, 50 Pine Valley, Cwmavon, Port Talbot, Wales, SA12 9NF

International Playing Card Society PR Officer Yasha Beresiner, 43 Templars Crescent, London, N3 3QR

The International Society of Antique Scale Collectors (ISASC) Membership Chairman, Steve Beare, 7 E. Brookland Ave, Wilmington, DE 19805, U.S.A.

The International Society of Meccanomen Adrian Williams, Bell House, 72a Old High Street, Headington, Oxford OX3 9HW Tel: 01865 741 057 corvus@tinyworld.co.uk www.internationalmeccanomen.org.uk

International Swizzle Stick Collectors Association Ray P. Hoare, PO Box 1117, Bellingham, WA 98227-1117, U.S.A. veray.issca@shaw.com

James Bond Collectors Club PO Box 1570, Christchurch, Dorset, BH23 4XS Tel: 0870 4423007 www.bondbooks.biz

James Sadler International Collectors Club Customer Services, Churchill China PLC, High Street, Tunstall, Stoke on Trent, Staffordshire, ST6 5NZ Tel: 01782 577566 diningin@churchillchina.plc.uk www.james-sadler.co.uk

Jonathan Harris Studio Glass Ltd Woodland House, 24 Peregrine Way, Apley Castle, Telford, Shropshire, TF1 6TH Tel: 01952 246381/588441 jonathan@jhstudioglass.com www.jhstudioglass.com

Just Golly! Collectors Club SAE to Mrs A. K. Morris, 9 Wilmar Way, Seal, Sevenoaks, Kent, TN15 0DN www.gollycorner.co.uk

Kewpie Traveler Rose Morgan, PO Box 4032, Portland, OR 97208-4032, U.S.A. origppress@aol.com

King George VI Collectors' Society (Philately) Secretary, 17 Balcaskie Road, Eltham, London, SE9 1HQ www.kg6.info

Kitchen Antiques & Collectibles News Dana & Darlene Demore, 4645 Laurel Ridge Dr., Harrisburg, PA 17119, U.S.A.

The Lace Guild Charity Reg No 274397, The Hollies, 53 Audnam, Stourbridge, West Midlands, DY8 4AE Tel: 01384 390739 hollies@laceguild.org www.laceguild.org

Legend Products International Collector's Club Sheila Cochrane (Owner and club founder), 1 Garden Villas, Wrexham Road, Cefn Y Bedd, Flintshire, LL12 9UT Tel: 01978 760800 sheila@legend-lane.demon.co.uk www.legendproducts.co.uk

Lilliput Lane Collectors' Club PO Box 498, Itasca, IL 60143-0498, U.S.A.

Limoges Porcelain Collectors Club The Tannery, Park Stile, Haydon Bridge, Hexham, NE47 6BP Tel: 01434 684444 www.limogesboxoffice.co.uk

Lock & Key Collectors' Club Mr Richard Phillips, Merlewood, The Loan, West Linton, Peebleshire, Scotland, EH46 7HE rphillips52@btinternet.com

The Maling Collectors' Society Sec David Holmes, PO Box 1762, North Shields, NE30 4YJ www.maling-pottery.org.uk

Marble Collectors' Society of America MCSA PO Box 222, Trumball, CT 06611, U.S.A.

Matchbox International Collectors Association (MICA) of North America c/o Stewart Orr and Kevin McGimpsey, PO Box 28072, Waterloo, Ontario N2L 6J8, Canada

The Matchbox Toys International Collectors' Association Editor Kevin McGimpsey, PO Box 120, Deeside, Flintshire, CH5 3HE Tel: 01244 539414 kevin@matchboxclub.com www.matchboxclub.com

Mauchline Ware Collectors Club Secretary Mrs Christabelle Davey, PO Box 158, Leeds, LS16 5WZ davedavey@talk21.com www.mauchlineware.com

Memories UK, Mabel Lucie Attwell Club Abbey Antiques, 63 Great Whyte, Ramsey, Nr Huntingdon, Cambridgeshire, PE26 1HL www.mabellucieatwellclub.com

Menucard Collectors' Society PO Box 192, Sevenoaks, Kent, TN13 9BD www.menucards.org

Merrythought International Collector's Club Club Sec Peter Andrews, Ironbridge, Telford, Shropshire, TF8 7NJ Tel: 01952 433116 contact@merrythought.co.uk www.merrythought.co.uk

Merrythought International Collector's Club PO Box 577, Oakdale, California 95361, U.S.A.

Milk Bottle News Paul & Lisa Luke, 60 Rose Valley Crescent, Stanford-le-Hope, Essex, SS17 8EF www.milkbottlenews.org.uk

Moorcroft Collectors' Club W. Moorcroft PLC, Sandbach Road, Burslem, Stoke-on-Trent, Staffordshire, ST6 2DQ www.moorcroft.com

Muffin the Mule Collectors' Club 12 Woodland Close, Woodford Green, Essex, IG8 0QH Tel: 020 8504 4943 www.Muffin-the-Mule.com

Keith Murray Collectors Club (Patron Constance Murray), Fantasque House, Tennis Drive, The Park, Nottingham, NG7 1AE www.keithmurray.co.uk

Musical Box Society of Great Britain PO Box 373, Welwyn, AL6 0WY mail@mbsgb.org.uk www.mbsgb.org.uk

National Association of Avon Collectors Connie Clark, President, PO Box 7006, Kansas City, MO 64113, U.S.A.

National Button Society Lois Pool, Secretary, 2733 Juno Pl., Apt 4, Akron, Ohio 44333-4137, U.S.A.

National Doll & Teddy Bear Collector Rose Morgan, PO Box 4032, Portland, OR 97208-4032, U.S.A. origppress@aol.com

National Fishing Lure Collectors Club Secretary-Treasurer, NFLCC, 197 Scottsdale Circle, Reeds Springs, MO 65737, U.S.A.

National Toothpick Holder Collectors' Society PO Box 852, Archer City, TX 76351, U.S.A. www.nthcs.org

New Baxter Society Membership Secretary, 205 Marshalswick Lane, St Albans, Hertfordshire, AL1 4XA

NFFC - The Club for Disneyana Enthusiasts PO Box 19212, Irvine, CA 92623-9212, U.S.A. Tel: 714 731 4705 www.nffc.org

Nutcracker Collectors' Club Susan Otto, 12204 Fox Run Drive, Chesterland, OH 44026, U.S.A. Tel: 440 729 2686 nutsue@adelphia.net

Observer's Pocket Series Collectors Society (OPSCS) Alan Sledger, Secretary, 10 Villiers Road, Kenilworth, Warwickshire, CV8 2JB Tel: 01926 857047

The Official Betty Boop Fan Club Ms Bobbie West, 10550 Western Avenue #133, Stanton, CA 90680-6909, U.S.A. BBOOPFANS@aol.com

The Official International Wade Ceramics Collectors Club Royal Victoria Pottery, Westport Road, Burslem, Stoke on Trent, Staffordshire, ST6 4AG www.wade.co.uk

Official Popeye Fan Club 1001 State St, Chester, IL 62233, U.S.A.

Old Appliance Club PO Box 65, Ventura, CA 93002, U.S.A.

Old Bottle Club of Great Britain Alan Blakeman, c/o BBR, Elsecar Heritage Centre, Nr Barnsley, Yorkshire, S74 8HJ Tel: 01226 745156 sales@onlinebbr.com www.onlinebbr.com

The Old Hall Stainless Steel Tableware Collectors Club Nigel Wiggin, Sandford House, Levedale, Stafford, ST18 9AH Tel: 01785 780376 oht@gnwiggin.freeserve.co.uk www.oldhallclub.co.uk

The Old Lawnmower Club c/o Milton Keynes Museum, McConnell Drive, Wolverton, Milton Keynes, Buckinghamshire, MK12 5EL Tel: 01327 830675 enquiry@oldlawnmowerclub.co.uk www.oldlawnmowerclub.co.uk

On the Lighter Side (OTLS) PO Box 1733, Quitman, TX 75783-1733, U.S.A. Tel: 903 763 2795 info@otls.com,www.otls.com

Ophthalmic Antiques International Collectors' Club c/o Mrs H D Robin FBDO, 16 Sandy Lodge Road, Rickmansworth, WD3 1LJ Tel: 01923 773562 heatherd1230@hotmail.com www.oaicclub.org

Orders & Medals Research Society OMRS PO Box 1904, Southam, CV47 2ZX Tel: 01295 690009 generalsecretary@omrs.org www.omrs.org.uk

Paperweight Collectors Circle PO Box 941, Comberton, Cambridgeshire, CB3 7GQ

Peanuts Collector Club, Inc. 539 Sudden Valley, Bellingham, WA 98229-4811, U.S.A.

Pedal Car Collectors' Club (P.C.C.C.) Secretary A. P. Gayler, 4/4a Chapel Terrace Mews, Kemp Town, Brighton, East Sussex, BN2 1HU Tel: 01273 622722 www.brmmbrmm.com/pedalcars

Pelham Puppets Collectors Club Sue Valentine, 46 The Grove, Bedford, Buckinghamshire, MK40 3JN

Pen Delfin Family Circle Pendelfin Studios Ltd, Townley Street, Briercliffe Business Centre, Burnley, Lancashire, BB10 2HG Tel: 01282 432301 boswell@pendelfin.co.uk www.pendelfin.co.uk

The Pewter Society Llananant Farm, Penallt, Monmouth, NP25 4AP secretary@pewtersociety.org www.pewtersociety.org

The Photographic Collector's Club of Great Britain Membership Office, The Photographic Collector's Club International Ltd., 5 Buntingford Road, Puckeridge, Ware, Hertfordshire, SG11 1RT Tel: 01920 821611 info@pccgb.org www.pccgb.org

Pilkington's Lancastrian Pottery Society Wendy Stock, Sullom Side, Barnacre, Garstang, Preston, Lancashire, PR3 1GH www.pilkpotsoc.freeserve.co.uk/index.htm

Pillsbury InFoLine Donna L. McDaniel, 4224 Independence Dr., Flint, MI 48506, U.S.A. Tel: 810 736 7433 Cookbknut@aol.com/Cookbknut@comcast.net http://groups.yahoo.com/group/InFoLine/

The Pipe Club of London www.pcol.freewire.co.uk

Poole Pottery Collectors Club Poole Pottery Limited, Sopers Lane, Poole, Dorset, BH17 7PP Tel: 01202 666200 sales@poolepottery.co.uk www.poolepottery.co.uk

Postcard Club of Great Britain c/o Mrs D. Brennan, 34 Harper House, St James Crescent, London, SW9 7LW

The Pot Lid Circle c/o Ian Johnson, Collins House, 32/38 Station Road, Gerrards Cross, Buckinghamshire, SL9 8EL Tel: 01753 279001 ian.johnson@bpcollins.co.uk

Potteries of Rye Society Membership Secretary, Barry Buckton, 2 Redyear Cottages, Kennington Road, Ashford, Kent, TN24 0TF www.potteries-of-rye-society.co.uk

Radford Collectors' Club 27 Forest Mead, Denmead, Waterlooville, Hampshire, PO7 6UN www.radfordcollect.com

Railwayana Collectors Journal 7 Ascot Road, Moseley, Birmingham, West Midlands, B13 9EN

Road Map Collectors Association PO Box 158, Channelview, TX 77530-0158, U.S.A.

Robert Harrop Collectors Club Robert Harrop Designs Ltd, Coalport House, Lamledge Lane, Shifnal, Shropshire, TF11 8SD www.robertharrop.com

Royal Doulton International Collectors' Club Royal Doulton, Sir Henry Doulton House, Forge Lane, Stoke-on-Trent, Staffordshire, ST1 5NN www.icc@royal-doulton.com

The Royal Numismatic Society Hon Sec Andrew Meadows, c/o Department of Coins and Medals, The British Museum, London, WC1B 3DG Tel: 020 7323 8577 rns@dircon.co.uk www.rns.dircon.co.uk

The Russian Doll Collectors' Club Gardener's Cottage, Hatchlands, East Clandon, Surrey, GU4 7RT www.russiandolls.co.uk

Scientific Instrument Society Registered Charity No 326733, 31 High Street, Stanford in the Vale, Faringdon, Oxon, SN7 8LH Tel: 01367 710223 www.sis.org.uk

The Shelley Group (for collectors of Shelley and Wileman wares) Ruskin, 47 St Andrew's Drive, Perton, Staffordshire, WV6 7YL www.shelley.co.uk

Silver Spoon Club of Great Britain 26 Burlington Arcade, Mayfair, London, W1J 0PU Tel: 020 7491 1720 silverspoonclub@bexfield.co.uk

Snowdome Collectors Club PO Box 53262, Washington, DC 20009, U.S.A.

Snuff Bottle Society 14 Rossiters Quay, Christchurch, Dorset, BH23 1DZ Tel: 01202 469050 snuffbottles@onetel.com

The Soviet Collectors Club PO Box 56, Saltburn by the Sea, TS12 1YD collect@sovietclub.com www.sovietclub.com

Spoon Collectors Club, UK David Cross, General Secretary, 72 Edinburgh Road, Newmarket, Suffolk, CB8 0DQ Tel: 01638 665457 david@ukspoons.fsnet.co.uk

Steiff Club - North America Rebekah Kaufman, Steiff North America, Inc., 425 Paramount Drive, Raynham, MA 02767, U.S.A. www.steiffusa.com

The SylvaC Collectors Circle 174 Portsmouth Road, Horndean, Waterlooville, Hampshire, PO8 9HP www.sylvacclub.com

TEAMS Club - The official club for Brooke Bond Card Collectors PO Box 1, Market Harborough, Leicestershire, LE16 9HT Tel: 01858 466 441 sales@teamsclub.co.uk www.teamsclub.co.uk

Telecommunications Heritage Group PO Box 561, South Croydon, Surrey, CR2 6YL www.thg.org.uk

The Thimble Society c/o Bridget McConnel, Admiral Vernon Arcade, 107 Portobello Road, London, W11 2QB Open Sat only www.thimblesociety.co.uk

Tin Container Collectors Association P.O. Box 440101, Aurora, CO 80044, U.S.A.

Toaster Collector Association PO Box 485, Redding Ridge, CT 06876, U.S.A.

Tobacco Jar Society Colin Grey, 19 Woodhurst North, Raymead Road, Maidenhead, Berkshire, SL6 8PH Tel: 01628 781800

The Tool and Trades History Society The Membership Secretary, Church Farm, 48 Calne Road, Lyneham, Chippenham, Wiltshire, SN15 4PN Tel: 01249 891586 Taths@aol.com

Totally Teapots, The Novelty Teapot Collectors Club Vince McDonald, Euxton, Chorley, Lancashire, PR7 6EY Tel: 01257 450366 vince@totallyteapots.com www.totallyteapots.com

Toy Story Collectors' Club Paul Cross, 20 Thurstons Barton, Whitehall, Bristol, Gloucestershire, BS5 7BQ

Trade Card Collector's Association PO Box 284, Marlton, NJ 08053, U.S.A.

Train Collectors Society James Day, Membership Secretary, PO Box 20340, London, NW11 6ZE Tel: 020 8209 1589 www.traincollectors.org.uk

The Transport Ticket Society Membership Secretary, David Randell, Oaktree Lodge, 221A Botley Road, Burridge, Hampshire, SO31 1BJ

Treasury of Christmas Ornaments Collectors' Club PO Box 277, Itasca, IL 60143-0277, U.S.A.

Trix Twin Railway Collectors' Association c/o Mr C B Arnold, 6 Ribble Avenue, Oadby, Leicester, LE2 4NZ

UK 1/6th Collectors Club Adrian Pitman, 1 St Cadocs Rise, Barry, Vale of Glamorgan, South Wales, CF63 2FG www.onesixthcollectors.co.uk

UK Football Programme Collectors Club 46 Milton Road, Kirkcaldy, Scotland, KY1 1TL Tel: 01592 268718 progm@hotmail.com www.pmfc.co.uk

UK Headscarf Collectors Society 19 Poulton Old Road, Blackpool, Lancashire, FY3 7LD

UK McDonald's & Fast Food Collectors Club c/o Lawrence Yap, 110 Tithelands, Harlow, Essex, CM19 5ND

UK Sucrologists Club The Membership Secretary, 14 Marisfield Place, Selsey, West Sussex PO20 0PD

United Kingdom Spoon Collectors Club David Cross, General Secretary, 72 Edinburgh Road, Newmarket, Suffolk, CB8 0DQ

Universal Autograph Collectors Club Michael Hecht, President, UACC, PO Box 6181, Washington, DC 20044-6181, U.S.A. www.uacc.org

The Victorian Military Society PO Box 5837, Newbury, Berkshire, RG14 3FJ Tel: 01635 48628 vmsdan@msn.com www.vms.org.uk

Vintage Fashion & Costume Jewelry Club PO Box 265, Glen Oaks, NY 11004, U.S.A.

Vintage Model Yacht Group Alistair Roach, Windy Corner, Evercreech, Shepton Mallett, Somerset, BA4 6AG

Wade Attic Carole Murdock, 8199 Pierson Ct, Arvada, CO 80005, U.S.A. carole@wadeattic.com www.wadeattic.com

The Washington Historical Autograph and Certificate Organization - Whaco! PO Box 2428, Springfield, VA 22152-2428, U.S.A.

The Writing Equipment Society c/o Sec Mr John S. Daniels, 33 Glanville Road, Hadleigh, Ipswich, Suffolk, IP7 5SQ www.wesonline.org.uk

Zippo Click Collectors Club Zippo Manufacturing Company, 33 Barbour Street, Bradford, PA 16701, U.S.A. Tel: 814 368 2725 kjones@zippo.com www.zippo.com www.zippoclick.com

Directory of Markets & Centres

U.S.A.

Alhambra Antiques Center, 3640 Coral Way,
Coral Cables, Florida Tel: 305 446 1688
*4 antiques dealers that sell high quality decorative pieces
from Europe.*

Antique Center I, II, III at Historic Savage Mill,
Savage, Maryland Tel: 410 880 0918 or 301 369 4650
antiquec@aol.com
*225 plus select quality dealers representing 15 states.
Open every day plus 3 evenings - Sun through Wed
9.30am–6pm, Thurs, Fri and Sat 9.30am–9pm. Closed
Christmas, Easter and Thanksgiving days. Open New
Year's Day 12 noon–5pm.*

Antique Village, North of Richmond, Virginia,
on Historic US 301, 4 miles North of 1-295
Tel: 804 746 8914
*Mon, Tues, Thurs, Fri 10am–5pm, Sat 10am–6pm, Sun
12 noon–6pm, closed Wed. 50 dealers specialising in Art
Pottery, country & primitives, Civil War artifacts, paper
memorabilia, African art, toys, advertising, occupied
Japan, tobacco tins, glassware, china, holiday
collectibles, jewellery, postcards.*

Antiques at Colony Mill Marketplace, 222 West Street,
Keene, New Hampshire 03431
Tel: 603 358 6343
*Open Mon–Sat 10am–9pm, Sun 11am–6pm. Over 200
booths. Period to country furniture, paintings and prints,
Art Pottery, glass, china, silver, jewellery, toys, dolls,
quilts, etc.*

Fern Eldridge & Friends, 800 First NH Turnpike (Rte. 4),
Northwood, New Hampshire 03261
Tel: 603 942 5602/8131
FernEldridgeAndFriends@NHantiqueAlley.com
*30 dealers on 2 levels. Shipping available in USA.
Open 10am–5pm daily. Closed major holidays,
please call ahead.*

Goodlettsville Antique Mall, 213 N. Main St,
Germantown, Tennessee Tel: 615 859 7002

The Hayloft Antique Center, 1190 First NH Turnpike
(Rte. 4), Northwood, New Hampshire 03261
Tel: 603 942 5153
TheHayloftAntiqueCenter@NHantiqueAlley.com
*Over 150 dealers offering estate jewelry, sterling silver,
rare books, glass, porcelain, pottery, art, primitives,
furniture, toys, ephemera, linens, military, sporting
collectibles and much more. Open 10am–5pm daily.
Closed major holidays, please call ahead.*

Hermitage Antique Mall, 4144-B Lebanon Road,
Hermitage, Tennessee Tel: 615 883 5789

Madison Antique Mall, 320 Gallatin Rd, S. Nashville,
Tennessee Tel: 615 865 4677
18th and 19thc English antiques and objets d'art.

Michiana Antique Mall, 2423 S. 11th Street,
Niles, Michigan 49120
www.michianaantiquemall.com
Open 7 days a week 10am–6pm.

Morningside Antiques, 6443 Biscayne Blvd., Miami,
Florida Tel: 305 751 2828
*The city's newest antiques market specialising in English,
French and American furniture and collectibles in a mall
setting with many different vendors.*

Nashville Wedgewood Station Antique Mall,
657 Wedgewood Ave., Nashville, Tennessee
Tel: 615 259 0939

Parker-French Antique Center, 1182 First NH Turnpike
(Rt. 4), Northwood, New Hampshire 03261
Tel: 603 942 8852
ParkerFrenchAntiqueCenter@NHantiqueAlley.com
*135 antique dealers all on one level offering a good mix
of sterling silver, jewelry, glassware, pottery, early
primitives. No crafts, reproductions or new items.
Open 10am–5pm daily. Closed major holidays,
please call ahead.*

Quechee Gorge Antiques & Collectibles Center,
Located in Quechee Gorge Village
Tel: 1 800 438 5565
*450 dealers. Open all year, 7 days a week. Depression
glass, ephemera, tools, toys, collectibles, Deco,
primitives, prints, silver and fine china.*

Showcase Antique Center, PO Box 1122,
Sturbridge MA 01566 Tel: 508 347 7190
www.showcaseantiques.com
*Open Mon, Wed, Thurs, 10am–5pm, Fri, Sat 10am–5pm,
Sun 12 noon–5pm, closed Tues. 170 dealers.*

DERBYSHIRE

Alfreton Antique Centre, 11 King Street, Alfreton,
DE55 7AF Tel: 01773 520781
*30 dealers on 2 floors. Antiques, collectables, furniture,
books, militaria, postcards, silverware. Open 7 days
Mon–Sat 10am–4.30pm, Sundays 11am–4.30pm.
Customer car park.*

Chappells Antiques Centre - Bakewell, King Street,
Bakewell, DE45 1DZ Tel: 01629 812496
ask@chappellsantiquescentre.com
www.chappellsantiquescentre.com
*30 established dealers inc LAPADA members. Quality
period furniture, ceramics, silver, plate, metals, treen,*

clocks, barometers, books, pictures, maps, prints, textiles, kitchenalia, lighting and furnishing accessories from the 17th–20thC. Open Mon–Sat 10–5pm Sun 12–5pm. Closed Christmas Day, Boxing Day & New Year's Day. Please ring for brochure, giving location and parking information.

Matlock Antiques, Collectables & Riverside Café, 7 Dale Road, Matlock, DE4 3LT
Tel: 01629 760808
bmatlockantiques@aol.com
www.matlock-antiques-collectables.cwc.net
Proprietor W. Shirley. Over 70 dealers. Open 7 days a week 10am–5pm. Sun 11am–5pm. Call in to buy, sell or browse. We have a centre with a warm and friendly atmosphere, selling a wide range of items. Including collectables, mahogany, pine, oak, pictures, books, linen, kitchenalia, china, clocks, clothes and jewellery.

DEVON

Quay Centre, Topsham, Nr Exeter, EX3 0JA
Tel: 01392 874006
office@quayantiques.com www.quayantiques.com
80 dealers on 3 floors. Antiques, collectables and traditional furnishings. Ample parking. Open 7 days, 10am–5pm. All major cards accepted.

GLOUCESTERSHIRE

Antiques Centre Gloucester, 1 Severn Road, The Historic Docks, Gloucester, GL1 2LE
Tel: 01452 529716 www.antiques.center.com
Open Mon–Sat 10am–5pm, Sun 1pm–5pm.

HAMPSHIRE

Dolphin Quay Antique Centre, Queen Street, Emsworth, PO10 7BU Tel: 01243 379994
chrisdqantiques@aol.com
Open 7 days a week (including Bank Holidays) Mon–Sat 10am–5pm Sun 10am–4pm. Marine, naval antiques, paintings, watercolours, prints, antique clocks, decorative arts, furniture, sporting apparel, luggage, specialist period lighting, conservatory, garden antiques, fine antique/country furniture, French/antique beds.

Lymington Antiques Centre, 76 High Street, Lymington, SO41 9AL Tel: 01590 670934
Open Mon–Fri 10am–5pm, Sat 9am–5pm. 30 dealers, clocks, watches, silver, glass, jewellery, toys & dolls, books, furniture, textiles.

KENT

Castle Antiques, 1 London Road (opposite Library), Westerham, TN16 1BB Tel: 01959 562492
Open 10am–5pm 7 days. 4 rooms of antiques, small furniture, collectables, rural bygones, costume, glass, books, linens, jewellery, chandeliers, cat collectables. Services: advice, valuations, theatre props, house clearance, talks on antiques.

Malthouse Arcade, High Street, Hythe, CT21 5BW
Tel: 01303 260103
Open Fridays and Saturdays Bank holiday Mondays 9.30am–5.30pm. 37 Stalls and cafe. Furniture, china and glass, jewellery, plated brass, picture postcards, framing.

LANCASHIRE

GB Antiques Centre, Lancaster Leisure Park, (the former Hornsea Pottery), Wyresdale Road, Lancaster, LA1 3LA Tel: 01524 844734
140 dealers in 40,000 sq. ft. of space. Porcelain, pottery, Art Deco, glass, books, linen, mahogany, oak and pine furniture. Open 7 days 10am–5pm.

Kingsmill Antique Centre, Queen Street, Harle Syke, Burnley, BB10 2HX Tel: 01282 431953
antiques@kingsmill.demon.co.uk
www.kingsmill.demon.co.uk
Dealers, packers and shippers.

LEICESTERSHIRE

Oxford Street Antique Centre, 16–26 Oxford Street, Leicester, LE1 5XU Tel: 0116 255 3006
osac.leicester@tiscali.co.uk
www.oxfordstreetfurniture.co.uk
Vast selection of clean English furniture ideal for home and overseas buyers, displayed in fourteen large showrooms on four floors, covering 30,000 sq feet. Reproduction furniture and accessories also stocked.

LONDON

Alfie's Antique Market, 13 Church Street,
Marylebone, NW8 8DT Tel: 020 7723 6066
www.alfiesantiques.com
London's biggest and busiest antique market.
Open 10am–6pm Tues–Sat.

Covent Garden Antique Market, Jubilee Hall,
Southampton Street, Covent Garden, WC2
Tel: 020 7240 7405
Every Thursday from 7am. Mobile: 0790 3919 029.

Grays Antique Markets, South Molton Lane,
W1K 5AB Tel: 020 7629 7034
grays@clara.net www.graysantiques.com
Over 200 specialist antique dealers selling beautiful and
unusual antiques & collectables. Open Mon–Fri 10am–6pm.

Palmers Green Antiques Centre, 472 Green Lanes,
Palmers Green, N13 5PA Tel: 020 8350 0878
Mobile: 07986 730155
Over 40 dealers. Specialising in furniture, jewellery,
clocks, pictures, porcelain, china, glass, silver & plate,
metalware, kitchenalia and lighting, etc. Open 6 days a
week, Mon–Sat 10am–5.30pm (closed Tues), Sun
11am–5pm, open Bank Holidays. Removals & house
clearances, probate valuations undertaken, quality
antiques and collectables. All major credit cards accepted.

Spitalfields Antique Market, Commercial Street,
E1 Tel: 020 7240 7405
Every Thursday from 7am. Mobile: 0790 3919 029.

SCOTLAND

Scottish Antique and Arts Centre, Carse of Cambus,
Doune, Perthshire, FK16 6HG Tel: 01786 841203
sales@scottish-antiques.com www.scottish-antiques.com
Over 100 dealers. Huge gift & collectors sections.
Victorian & Edwardian furniture. Open 7 days
10am–5pm. Restaurant.

Scottish Antique and Arts Centre, Abernyte,
Perthshire, PH14 9SJ Tel: 01828 686401
sales@scottish-antiques.com
www.scottish-antiques.com
Over 100 dealers. Huge gift & collectors sections.
Victorian & Edwardian furniture. Open 7 days
10am–5pm. Restaurant.

SURREY

Maltings Monthly Market, Bridge Square,
Farnham, GU9 7QR Tel: 01252 726234
info@farnhammaltings.com
www.farnhammaltings.com
9.30–4.00pm 1st Sat of the month.

EAST SUSSEX

The Brighton Lanes Antique Centre, 12 Meeting House
Lane, Brighton, BN1 1HB Tel: 01273 823121
Mobile: 07785 564337

peter@brightonlanes-antiquecentre.co.uk
www.brightonlanes-antiquecentre.co.uk
A spacious centre in the heart of the historic lanes with
a fine selection of furniture, silver, jewellery, glass,
porcelain, clocks, pens, watches, lighting and decorative
items. Open daily 10am–5.30pm, Sun 12noon–4pm.
Loading bay/parking - Lanes car park.

TYNE & WEAR

The Antique Centre, 2nd floor,
142 Northumberland Street, Newcastle-upon-Tyne,
NE1 7DQ Tel: 0191 232 9832
timeantiques@talktalk.net

WALES

Offa's Dyke Antique Centre, 4 High Street,
Knighton, Powys, LD7 1AT
Tel: 01547 528635/ 520145
Open Mon–Sat 10am–5pm. Wide ranging stock.
Specialists in ceramics and glass, fine art of the 19th &
20th centuries. Country antiques and collectables.

The Works Antiques Centre, Station Road, Llandeilo,
Carmarthenshire, SA1 9NG Tel: 01558 823964
theworks@storeyj.clara.co.uk
www.works-antiques.co.uk
Open Tues–Sat 10am–6pm & Sun 10am–5pm. Open
Bank Holiday Mondays. 5,000sq ft. 60 dealers. Ample
parking. Free tea and coffee.

WARWICKSHIRE

Stratford Antiques Centre, 59–60 Ely Street,
Stratford-upon-Avon, CV37 6LN
Tel: 01789 204180
Every Thursday from 7am. Mobile: 0790 3919 029.

WEST MIDLANDS

Birmingham Antique Centre, 1407 Pershore Road,
Stirchley, Birmingham, B30 2JR
Tel: 0121 459 4587
bhamantiquecent@aol.com
www.birminghamantiquecentre.co.uk
Open 7 days 9am–5pm Mon–Sat and 10am–4pm Sun.
Cabinets available to rent.

YORKSHIRE

St Nicholas Antique Shops, 33–35 St Nicholas Cliff,
Scarborough, YO11 2ES
Tel: 01723 365221/374175
sales@collectors.demon.co.uk
www.collectors.demon.co.uk
International dealers in stamps, postcards, silver, gold,
medals, cigarette cards, cap badges, militaria, jewellery,
commemorative ware, furniture, clocks, watches and
many more collectables.

York Antique Centre, 1a Lendel, York, YO1 8AA
Tel: 01904 641445
Every Thursday from 7am. Mobile: 0790 3919 029.

Key to Illustrations

Each illustration and descriptive caption is accompanied by a letter code. By referring to the following list of Auctioneers (denoted by ⚒), Dealers (⊞) and Clubs (§), the source of any item may be immediately determined. Inclusion in this edition in no way constitutes or implies a contract or binding offer on the part of any of our contributors to supply or sell the goods illustrated, or similar articles, at the prices stated. Advertisers in this year's directory are denoted by (†).

If you require a valuation for an item, it is advisable to check whether the dealer or specialist will carry out this service and if there is a charge. Please mention Miller's when making an enquiry. Having found a specialist who will carry out your valuation is best to send a photograph and description of the item to the specialist together with a stamped addressed envelope for the reply. A valuation by telephone is not possible. Most dealers are only too happy to help you with your enquiry; however, they are very busy people and consideration of the above points would be welcomed.

AAA ⊞ Ad-Age Antique Advertising, Maidstone, Kent
Tel: 01622 670595

ABCM ⊞ A B Coins & Medals, 23-25 'Old' Northam
Road, Southampton, Hampshire, SO14
Tel: 023 8023 3393

ADD ⊞ Addyman Books, 39 Lion Street, Hay-on-Wye,
Herefordshire, HR3 5AD Tel: 01497 821136

AEL ⊞ Argyll Etkin Ltd, 1-9 Hills Place, Oxford Circus,
London, W1F 7SA Tel: 020 7437 7800
philatelists@argyll-etkin.com
www.argyll-etkin.com

AH ⚒ Andrew Hartley, Victoria Hall Salerooms,
Little Lane, Ilkley, Yorkshire, LS29 8EA
Tel: 01943 816363
info@andrewhartleyfinearts.co.uk
www.andrewhartleyfinearts.co.uk

AL ⊞ Ann Lingard, Ropewalk Antiques, Rye,
East Sussex, TN31 7NA Tel: 01797 223486
ann-lingard@ropewalkantiques.freeserve.co.uk

AMB ⚒ Ambrose, Ambrose House, Old Station Road,
Loughton, Essex, IG10 4PE Tel: 020 8502 3951

AME ⊞ American Dream, Unit 10 Stephenson Road,
St Ives, Huntingdon, Cambridgeshire, PE27 3WJ
Tel: 01480 495444 chris2americandream.co.uk
www.americandream.co.uk

AMH ⊞ Amherst Antiques, Monomark House, 27 Old
Gloucester Street, London, WC1N 3XX
Tel: 01892 725552
info@amherstantiques.co.uk
www.amherstantiques.co.uk

AMR ⊞ Amron Antiques Tel: 01782 566895
APC ⊞ Antique Photographic Company Ltd
Tel: 01949 842192 alpaco47@aol.com

ARo ⊞† Alvin's Vintage Games & Toys Tel: 01865 772409
alvin@vintage-games.co.uk
http://www.vintage-games.co.uk

ARP ⊞ Arundel Photographica, The Arundel Antiques
and Collectors Centre, 51 High Street, Arundel,
West Sussex, BN18 9AJ Tel: 01903 885540
cameras@arundel-photographica.co.uk
www.arundel-photographica.co.uk

ASHB ⚒ Stella Ashbrooke Tel: 01948 662050
AU ⊞ Auto Suggestion Tel: 01428 751397
Aur ⊞ Aurum, 310/311 Grays Antique Market,
58 Davies Street, London, W1K 5LP
Tel: 020 7409 0215 aurum@tinyworld.co.uk
www.graysantiques.com

AUTO ⊞ Automatomania, Stands 23 & 24, 284 Westbourne
Grove (corner of Portobello Road),
London, W11 2QA Tel: 07790 719097
magic@automatomania.com
www.automatomania.com

B&R ⊞ Bread & Roses Tel: 01926 817342
BAC ⊞ The Brackley Antique Cellar, Drayman's Walk,
Brackley, Northamptonshire, NN13 6BE
Tel: 01280 841841 antiquecellar@tesco.net
BaN ⊞ Barbara Ann Newman Tel: 07850 016729

BAY ⊞ George Bayntun, Manvers Street, Bath,
Somerset, BA1 1JW Tel: 01225 466000
EBayntun@aol.com

BBA ⚒† Bloomsbury, Bloomsbury House, 24 Maddox
Street, London, W1S 1PP Tel: 020 7495 9494
info@bloomsburyauctions.com
www.bloomsburyauctions.com

BBe ⊞ Bourton Bears help@bourtonbears.com
www.bourtonbears.com

BBR ⚒† BBR, Elsecar Heritage Centre, Elsecar,
Nr Barnsley, South Yorkshire, S74 8HJ
Tel: 01226 745156 sales@onlinebbr.com
www.onlinebbr.com

Bea/Ben ⚒ Bearnes, St Edmund's Court, Okehampton
Street, Exeter, Devon, EX4 1DU
Tel: 01392 207000 enquiries@bearnes.co.uk
www.bearnes.co.uk

BERN ⚒ Bernaerts, Verlatstraat 18-22, 2000
Antwerpen/Anvers, Belgium Tel: (0)3 248 19 21
edmond.bernaerts@ping.be
www.auction-bernaerts.com

Bert ⚒ Bertoia Auctions, 2141 DeMarco Drive,
Vineland, New Jersey 08360, U.S.A.
Tel: 856 692 1881 bill@bertoiaauctions.com
www.bertoiaauctions.com

BET ⊞ Beth, GO 43-44, Alfies Antique Market, 13–25
Church Street, Marylebone, London, NW8 8DT
Tel: 020 7723 5613/0777 613 6003

BEV ⊞ Beverley, 30 Church Street, Marylebone, London,
NW8 8EP Tel: 020 7262 1576/07776136003

BEX ⊞ Daniel Bexfield Antiques, 26 Burlington Arcade,
London, W1J 0PU Tel: 020 7491 1720
antiques@bexfield.co.uk www.bexfield.co.uk

BGe ⊞ Bradley Gent Tel: 07711 158005
www.antiques-shop.co.uk

BI ⊞ Books Illustrated Tel: 0777 1635 777
booksillustrated@aol.com
www.booksillustrated.com

BIB ⊞ Biblion, 1-7 Davies Mews, London, W1K 5AB
Tel: 020 7629 1374 info@biblion.com
www.biblionmayfair.com

BINC ⊞ Bears Inc amanda@bearsinc.co.uk
www.bearsinc.co.uk

BNO ⊞ Beanos, Middle Street, Croydon, London,
CR0 1RE Tel: 020 8680 1202
enquiries@beanos.co.uk www.beanos.co.uk

Bns ⊞ Brittons Jewellers, 4 King Street, Clitheroe,
Lancashire, BB7 2EP Tel: 01200 425555
sales@brittonswatches.com
www.internetwatches.co.uk
www.antique-jewelry.com

BOB ⊞ Bob's Collectables Tel: 01277 650834
BoC NOT TRADING
BOOM ⊞ Boom Interiors, 115-117 Regents Park Road,
Primrose Hill, London, NW1 8UR
Tel: 020 7722 6622 info@boominteriors.com
www.boominteriors.com

BR   See **DN(BR)**

BRIG   ⊞† Briggs, 54 Lupin Ride, Kings Copse, Crowthorne, Berkshire, RG45 6UR Tel: 01344 466022 enquiries@usebriggs.com www.usebriggs.com

BrL   ⊞ The Brighton Lanes Antique Centre, 12 Meeting House Lane, Brighton, East Sussex, BN1 1HB Tel: 01273 823121 peter@brightonlanes-antiquecentre.co.uk www.brightonlanes-antiquecentre.co.uk

BRT   ⊞ Britannia, Grays Antique Market, Stand 101, 58 Davies Street, London, W1Y 1AR Tel: 020 7629 6772 britannia@grays.clara.net

BS   ⊞ Below Stairs, 103 High Street, Hungerford, Berkshire, RG17 0NB Tel: 01488 682317 hofgartner@belowstairs.co.uk www.belowstairs.co.uk

BtoB   ⊞ Bac to Basic Antiques Tel: 07787 105609 bcarruthers@waitrose.com

BUDD   ⚒ Graham Budd Auctions Ltd, London gb@grahambuddauctions.co.uk

BUK   ⚒ Bukowskis, Arsenalsgatan 4, Stockholm, Sweden Tel: +46 (8) 614 08 00 info@bukowskis.se www.bukowskis.se

BUK(F)   ⚒ Bukowskis, Horhammer, Iso Roobertink, 12 Stora Robertsg, 00120 Helsinki Helsingfors, Finland Tel: 00 358 9 668 9110 www.bukowskis.fi

BWL   ⚒ Brightwells Fine Art, The Fine Art Saleroom, Easters Court, Leominster, Herefordshire, HR6 0DE Tel: 01568 611122 fineart@brightwells.com www.brightwells.com

Byl   ⊞ Bygones of Ireland Ltd, Lodge Road, Westport, County Mayo, Republic of Ireland Tel: 98 26132/25701 bygones@anu.ie www.bygones-of-ireland.com

C&R   ⊞ Catchpole & Rye, Saracens Dairy, Jobbs Lane, Pluckley, Ashford, Kent, TN27 0SA Tel: 01233 840840 info@crye.co.uk www.crye.co.uk

c20th   ⊞† www.c20th.com, 9 Brunet Court, 16 Brunet Road, London, SE16 7HU Tel: 07775 704052 simon@c20th.com www.c20th.com

CAB   ⊞† Candlestick & Bakelite, PO Box 308, Orpington, Kent, BR5 1TB Tel: 020 8467 3743 candlestick.bakelite@mac.com www.candlestickandbakelite.co.uk

CAD   ⊞ The Girl Can't Help It!, Sparkle Moore & Cad Van Swankster, Alfies Antique Market, G100 & G116 Ground Floor, 13-25 Church Street, Marylebone, London, NW8 8DT Tel: 020 7724 8984/07958 515614 sparkle.moore@virgin.net www.sparklemoore.com

CaH   ⊞ The Camera House, Oakworth Hall, Colne Road, Oakworth, Keighley, Yorkshire, BD22 7HZ Tel: 01535 642333 colin@the-camera-house.co.uk www.the-camera-house.co.uk

Cai   § Caithness Glass Paperweight Collectors' Society, Mrs Caroline Clark, The Caithness Glass Compay Limited, Inveralmond, Perth, Scotland, PH1 3TZ Tel: 01738 492335/ 01738 637373 collector@caithnessglass.co.uk www.caithnessglass.co.uk

CAL   ⊞ Cedar Antiques Ltd, High Street, Hartley Wintney, Hampshire, RG27 8NY Tel: 01252 843222 or 01189 326628

Cas   ⊞ Castle Antiques www.castle-antiques.com

CAu   ⚒ The Cotswold Auction Company Ltd, incorporating Short Graham & Co and Hobbs and Chambers Fine Arts, The Coach House, Swan Yard, 9-13 West Market Place, Cirencester, Gloucestershire, GL7 2NH Tel: 01285 642420 info@cotswoldauction.co.uk www.cotswoldauction.co.uk

CBB   ⊞ Colin Baddiel, Gray's Mews, 1-7 Davies Mews, London, W1Y 1AR Tel: 020 7408 1239/020 8452 7243

CBGR   ⊞† Chris Baker Gramophones, All Our Yesterdays, 3 Cattle Market, Sandwich, Kent, CT13 9AE Tel: 01304 614756 cbgramophones@aol.com www.chrisbakergramophones.com

CBi   ⊞† Collector Bits Tel: 02476 746981 collectorbits@aol.com www.collectorbits.com

CBP   ⚒†Comic Book Postal Auctions Ltd, 40–42 Osnaburgh Street, London, NW1 3ND Tel: 020 7424 0007 comicbook@compalcomics.com www.compalcomics.com

CCC   ⊞† The Crested China Co, Highfield, Windmill Hill, Driffield, East Yorkshire, YO25 5YP Tel: 0870 300 1 300 dt@thecrestedchinacompany.com www.thecrestedchinacompany.com

CCO   ⊞ Collectable Costume, Showroom South, Gloucester Antiques Centre, 1 Severn Road, Gloucester, GL1 2LE Tel: 01989 562188

CCs   ⊞ Coco's Corner, Unit 4, Cirencester Antique Centre, Cirencester, Gloucestershire Tel: 01452 556 308 cocos-corner@blueyonder.co.uk

CFCC   ⊞ Charlotte Firmin - Artist, Cosmo China, 26 Palace Street, Canterbury, Kent, CT1 2DZ Tel: 01227 784 154 palace@cosmochina.co.uk www.cosmochina.co.uk Also at: 11 Cosmo Place, Bloomsbury, London, WC13 NAP Tel: 020 7278 3374

CFSD   ⊞ Clive Farahar & Sophie Dupre, Horsebrook House, XV The Green, Calne, Wiltshire, SN11 8DQ Tel: 01249 821121 post@farahardupre.co.uk www.farahardupre.co.uk

CGC   ⚒ Cheffins, Vintage Car Department, 8 Hill Street, Saffron Walden, Essex, CB10 1JD Tel: 01799 513131 vintage@cheffins.co.uk www.cheffins.co.uk

ChC   ⊞ Christopher Clarke (Antiques) Ltd, The Fosse Way, Stow-on-the-Wold, Gloucestershire, GL54 1JS Tel: 01451 830476 cclarkeantiques@aol.com www.campaignfurniture.com

CHI   ⊞† Chinasearch, PO Box 1202, Kenilworth, Warwickshire, CV8 2WW Tel: 01926 512402 info@chinasearch.co.uk www.chinasearch.co.uk

CHTR   ⚒ Charterhouse, The Long Street Salerooms, Sherborne, Dorset, DT9 3BS Tel: 01935 812277 enquiry@charterhouse-auctions.co.uk www.charterhouse-auctions.co.uk

Ci   ⊞ Circa, 8 Fulham High Road, London, SW6 Tel: 020 7736 5038

CNM   ⊞ Caroline Nevill Miniatures, 22A Broad Street, Bath, Somerset, BA1 5LN Tel: 01225 443091 www.carolinenevillminiatures.co.uk

COB   ⊞† Cobwebs, 78 Northam Road, Southampton, Hampshire, SO14 0PB Tel: 023 8022 7458 www.cobwebs.uk.com

CoC   ⊞ Comic Connections, 4a Parsons Street, Banbury, Oxfordshire, OX16 5LW Tel: 01295 268989 comicman@freenetname.co.uk

CoHA   ⊞ Corner House Antiques and Ffoxe Antiques, Gardners Cottage, Broughton Poggs, Filkins, Lechlade-on-Thames, Gloucestershire, GL7 3JH Tel: 01367 252007 jdhis007@btopenworld.com enquiries@corner-house-antiques.co.uk www.corner-house-antiques.co.uk

COO   ⊞ Graham Cooley Tel: 07968 722269

Cot   ⊞ Cottage Collectibles, Long Street Antiques, 14 Long Street, Tetbury, Gloucestershire, G18 8AQ Tel: 01666 500850/07967 713512 sheila@cottagecollectibles.co.uk

CP ⊞† Cat Pottery, 1 Grammar School Road, North Walsham, Norfolk, NR28 9JH Tel: 01692 402962

CPCC § Cigarette Packet Collectors Club of GB, Barry Russell, Talisker, Vines Cross Road, Horam, Heathfield, East Sussex, TN21 0HF Tel: 01435 812453

CS ⊞ Christopher Sykes, The Old Parsonage, Woburn, Milton Keynes, Buckinghamshire, MK17 9QM Tel: 01525 290259 www.sykes-corkscrews.co.uk

CTO ⊞† Collector's Corner, PO Box 8, Congleton, Cheshire, CW12 4GD Tel: 01260 270429 dave.popcorner@ukonline.co.uk

CUF ⊞ The Cufflink Shop, Stand G2 Antiquarius, 137 Kings Road, London, SW3 4PW Tel: 020 7352 8201

CWO ⊞ www.collectorsworld.net, PO Box 4922, Bournemouth, Dorset, BH1 3WD Tel: 01202 555223 info@collectorsworld.biz www.collectorsworld.net www.collectorsworld.biz

DA ➤ Dee, Atkinson & Harrison, The Exchange Saleroom, Driffield, East Yorkshire, YO25 6LD Tel: 01377 253151 info@dahauctions.com www.dahauctions.com

DAD ⊞ decorative arts @doune, Scottish Antique & Arts Centre, By Doune, Stirling, Scotland, FK16 6HD Tel: 01786 834401/07778 475974 decorativearts.doune@btinternet.com www.decorative-doune.com

DAL ➤ Dalkeith Auctions Ltd, Dalkeith Hall, Dalkeith Steps, Rear of 81 Old Christchurch Road, Bournemouth, Dorset, BH1 1YL Tel: 01202 292905 how@dalkeith-auctions.co.uk www.dalkeith-auctions.co.uk

Dall ⊞ P&R Dallimore Antique Collectibles, Cheltenham, Gloucestershire Tel: 01242 820119 rdalli5760@aol.com

DaM ⊞ Martin's Antiques & Collectibles Jackiem743710633@aol.com www.martinsantiquescollectibles.co.uk

DD ➤ David Duggleby, The Vine St Salerooms, Scarborough, Yorkshire, YO11 1XN Tel: 01723 507111 auctions@davidduggleby.com www.davidduggleby.com

DE ⊞† Decades, 20 Lord St West, Blackburn, Lancashire, BB2 1JX Tel: 01254 693320

DeA ⊞ Delphi Antiques, Powerscourt Townhouse Centre, South William Street, Dublin 2, Republic of Ireland Tel: 00 353 679 0331

DEB ⊞ Debden Antiques, Elder Street, Debden, Saffron Walden, Essex, CB11 3JY Tel: 01799 543007 info@debden-antiques.co.uk debden-antiques.co.uk

DeJ ⊞ Denim Junkies www.denimjunkies.com

DgC ⊞ Dragonlee Collectables Tel: 01622 729502

DHa ⊞ Diane Harby Antique Lace & Linen, Grays Antique Market, Davies Street, London, W1Y 2LP Tel: 020 7629 5130

DHJ ⊞ Derek H Jordan chinafairings@aol.com www.chinafairings.co.uk

DMC ➤ Diamond Mills & Co, 117 Hamilton Road, Felixstowe, Suffolk, IP11 7BL Tel: 01394 282281

DN ➤ Dreweatt Neate, Donnington Priory, Donnington, Newbury, Berkshire, RG14 2JE Tel: 01635 553553 donnington@dnfa.com www.dnfa.com/donnington

DN(BR) ➤ Dreweatt Neate, The Auction Hall, The Pantiles, Tunbridge Wells, Kent, TN2 5QL Tel: 01892 544500 tunbridgewells@dnfa.com www.dnfa.com/tunbridgewells

DN(HAM) ➤ Dreweatt Neate formerly Hamptons Fine Art Auctioneers, Baverstock House, 93 High Street, Godalming, Surrey, GU7 1AL Tel: 01483 423567 godalming@dnfa.com www.dnfa.com/godalming

DNW ➤† Dix-Noonan-Webb, 16 Bolton Street, Piccadilly, London, W1J 8BQ Tel: 020 7016 1700 auctions@dnw.co.uk www.dnw.co.uk

Do ⊞ Liz Farrow T/As Dodo, Stand F071/73, Alfie's Antique Market, 13–25 Church Street, London, NW8 8DT Tel: 020 7706 1545

Dob § Dobwalls Toy Museum, Dobwalls Adventure Park, Dobwalls, Nr. Liskeard, Cornwall, PL14 6HD Tel: 07771 752215

DOL ⊞ Dollectable, 53 Lower Bridge, Chester, CH1 1RS Tel: 01244 344888 or 679195

DORO ➤ Dorotheum, Palais Dorotheum, A-1010 Wien, Dorotheergasse 17, 1010 Vienna, Austria Tel: 515 60 229 client.services@dorotheum.at

DPC § Devon Pottery Collectors' Group, Mrs Joyce Stonelake, 19 St Margarets Avenue, Torquay, Devon, TQ1 4LW

DRE ⊞ Dreamtime, Shop 7 Georgian Village, 30–31 Islington Green, London, N1 8DU Tel: 020 8880 6695

DRU ⊞ Drummonds Architectural Antiques Ltd, The Kirkpatrick Buildings, 25 London Road (A3), Hindhead, Surrey, GU26 6AB Tel: 01428 609444 info@drummonds-arch.co.uk www.drummonds-arch.co.uk

DSG ⊞ Delf Stream Gallery, Bournemouth, Dorset Tel: 07974 926137 nic19422000@yahoo.co.uk www.delfstreamgallery.com

DStA ➤ David Stanley Auctions, Stordon Grange, Osgathorpe, Leicestershire, LE12 9SR Tel: 01530 222320 tools@davidstanley.com www.davidstanley.com

DuM ➤ Du Mouchelles, 409 East Jefferson, Detroit, Michigan 48226, U.S.A. Tel: 313 963 6255

DW ➤† Dominic Winter Book Auctions, The Old School, Maxwell Street, Swindon, Wiltshire, SN1 5DR Tel: 01793 611340 info@dominicwinter.co.uk www.dominicwinter.co.uk

E ➤ Ewbank Auctioneers, Burnt Common Auction Rooms, London Road, Send, Woking, Surrey, GU23 7LN Tel: 01483 223101 antiques@ewbankauctions.co.uk www.ewbankauctions.co.uk

EAL ⊞ The Exeter Antique Lighting Co., Cellar 15, The Quay, Exeter, Devon, EX2 4AP Tel: 01392 490848/07702 969438 www.antiquelightingcompany.com

Ech ⊞† Echoes, 650a Halifax Road, Eastwood, Todmorden, Yorkshire, OL14 6DW Tel: 01706 817505

EE ⊞ Empire Exchange, 1 Newton Street, Piccadilly, Manchester Tel: 0161 2364445

EHCS § The European Honeypot Collectors' Society, John Doyle, The Honeypot, 18 Victoria Road, Chislehurst, Kent, BR7 6DF Tel: 020 8289 7725 johnhoneypot@hotmail.com www.geocities.com/tehcsuk

EMH ⊞ Eat My Handbag Bitch, 37 Drury Lane, London, WC2B 5RR Tel: 020 7836 0830 contact@eatmyhandbagbitch.co.uk www.eatmyhandbagbitch.co.uk

ET ⊞ Early Technology, Monkton House, Old Craighall, Musselburgh, Midlothian, Scotland, EH21 8SF Tel: 0131 665 5753/07831 106768 michael.bennett-levy@virgin.net www.earlytech.com www.rare78s.com www.tvhistory.tv

EV ⊞ Marlene Evans, Headrow Antiques Centre, Headrow Centre, Leeds, Yorkshire Tel: 0113 245 5344

F&C Finan & Co, The Square, Mere, Wiltshire, BA12 6DJ Tel: 01747 861411 post@finanandco.co.uk www.finanandco.co.uk

FAC Faganarms, Box 425, Fraser, MI 48026, U.S.A. Tel: 00 1 586 465 4637 info@faganarms.com www.faganarms.com

FHF Fellows & Sons, Augusta House, 19 Augusta Street, Hockley, Birmingham, West Midlands, B18 6JA Tel: 0121 212 2131 info@fellows.co.uk www.fellows.co.uk

FMN Forget Me Knot Antiques, Antiques at Over the Moon, 27 High Street, St Albans, Hertfordshire, AL3 4EH Tel: 01923 261172 sharpffocus@hotmail.com

FOF Fossack & Furkle, PO Box 733, Abington, Cambridgeshire, CB1 6BF Tel: 01223 894296/ 07939078719 fossack@btopenworld.com www.fossackandfurkle.freeservers.com

FOSS Fossil Shop, The Blue Slipper, 24 St John's Road, Sandown, Isle of Wight, PO36 8ES Tel: 0778 8834586 tony@fossilshop.co.uk www.fossilshop.co.uk

FOX Fox Cottage Antiques, Digbeth Street, Stow on the Wold, Gloucestershire, GL54 1BN Tel: 01451 870307

FRa Fraser's, 399 Strand, London, WC2R OLX Tel: 020 7836 9325/836 8444 sales@frasersautographs.com www.frasersautographs.com

FRD Fragile Design, 8 The Custard Factory, Digbeth, Birmingham, West Midlands, B9 4AA Tel: 0121 693 1001 info@fragiledesign.com www.fragiledesign.com

FST Frank Scott-Tomlin, The Old Ironmongers Antiques Centre, 5 Burford Street, Lechlade, Gloucestershire, GL7 3AP Tel: 01367 252397

G(L) Gorringes, inc Julian Dawson, 15 North Street, Lewes, East Sussex, BN7 2PD Tel: 01273 478221 clientservices@gorringes.co.uk www.gorringes.co.uk

G&CC Goss & Crested China Club & Museum, incorporating Milestone Publications, 62 Murray Road, Horndean, Hampshire, PO8 9JL Tel: (023) 9259 7440 info@gosschinaclub.demon.co.uk www.gosscrestedchina.co.uk

GAC Antiques Centre Gloucester, 1 Severn Road, The Historic Docks, Gloucester, GL1 2LE Tel: 01452 529716 www.antiques.center.com

GAK Keys, Off Palmers Lane, Aylsham, Norfolk, NR11 6JA Tel: 01263 733195 www.aylshamsalerooms.co.uk

GAU Becca Gauldie Antiques, The Old School, Glendoick, Perthshire, Scotland, PH2 7NR Tel: 01738 860 870 webuy@scottishantiques.freeserve.co.uk

GAZE Thomas Wm Gaze & Son, Diss Auction Rooms, Roydon Road, Diss, Norfolk, IP22 4LN Tel: 01379 650306 sales@dissauctionrooms.co.uk www.twgaze.com

GBM GB Military Antiques, 17-18 The Mall, 359 Upper Street, Islington, London, N1 0PD Tel: 020 7354 7334 info@gbmilitaria.com www.gbmilitaria.com

GBr Geoffrey Breeze Antiques Tel: 01225 466499/ 077 404 35844 antiques@geoffreybreeze.co.uk www.antiquecanes.co.uk

GGD Great Grooms Antiques Centre, 51/52 West Street, Dorking, Surrey, RH4 1BU Tel: 01306 887076 dorking@greatgrooms.co.uk www.greatgrooms.co.uk Also at: Riverside House, Charnham Street, Hungerford, Berkshire, RG17 0EP Tel: 01488 682314 hungerford@greatgrooms.co.uk

GGv G.G. van Schagen Antiquair Tel: 00 31 229 275692 g.schagen@wxs.nl

GH Gardiner Houlgate, The Bath Auction Rooms, 9 Leafield Way, Corsham, Nr Bath, Somerset, SN13 9SW Tel: 01225 812912 gardiner-houlgate.co.uk www.invaluable.com/gardiner-houlgate

GIL Gilding's Auctioneers and Valuers, 64 Roman Way, Market Harborough, Leicestershire, LE16 7PQ Tel: 01858 410414 sales@gildings.co.uk www.gildings.co.uk

GLAS Glasstastique By appointment only Tel: 0113 287 9308 or 07967 345952 sales@glasstastique.com www.glasstastique.com

GLEN Glenda - Antique Dolls, A18-A19 Grays Antique Market, Davies Mews, London, W1Y 2LP Tel: 020 8367 2441/020 7629 7034 glenda@glenda-antiquedolls.com www.glenda-antiquedolls.com

GM Philip Knighton, 1c South Street, Wellington, Somerset, TA21 8NR Tel: 01823 661618 philip.knighton@btopenworld.com

GOv Glazed Over Tel: 0773 2789114

GRo Geoffrey Robinson, GO77-78, GO91-92 (Ground floor) Alfies Antique Market, 13–25 Church Street, Marylebone, London, NW8 8DT Tel: 020 7723 0449 info@alfiesantiques.com www.alfiesantiques.com

GTH Greenslade Taylor Hunt Fine Art, Magdelene House, Church Square, Taunton, Somerset, TA1 1SB Tel: 01823 332525

GTM Gloucester Toy Mart, Ground Floor, Antique Centre, Severn Road, Old Docks, Gloucester, GL1 2LE Tel: 07973 768452

H&G Hope & Glory, 131A Kensington Church Street, London, W8 7LP Tel: 020 7727 8424

HA Hallidays, The Old College, Dorchester-on-Thames, Oxfordshire, OX10 7HL Tel: 01865 340028/68 or 07860 625917 antiques@hallidays.com www.hallidays.com

HAL John & Simon Haley, 89 Northgate, Halifax, Yorkshire, HX1 1XF Tel: 01422 822148/360434 toysandbanks@aol.com

Hal Halls Fine Art Auctions, Welsh Bridge, Shrewsbury, Shropshire, SY3 8LA Tel: 01743 231212

HAld Henry Aldridge & Son Auctions, Unit 1, Bath Road Business Centre, Devizes, Wiltshire, SN10 1XA Tel: 01380 729199 andrew@henry-aldridge.co.uk www.henry-aldridge.co.uk

HAM See **DN(HAM)**

HarC Hardy's Collectables Tel: 07970 613077 www.poolepotteryjohn.com

HARP Harpers Jewellers Ltd, 2/6 Minster Gates, York, YO1 7HL Tel: 01904 632634 york@harpersjewellers.co.uk www.vintage-watches.co.uk

HeA Heanor Antiques Centre, 1–3 Ilkeston Road, Heanor, Derbyshire, DE75 7AE Tel: 01773 531181/762783 sales@heanorantiquescentre.co.uk www.heanorantiques.co.uk

HEG Stuart Heggie Tel: 01227 471162 or 0783 3593344

HEI NOT TRADING

HEM Hemswell Antique Centre, Caenby Corner Estate, Hemswell Cliff, Gainsborough, Lincolnshire, DN21 5TJ Tel: 01427 668389 info@hemswell-antiques.com www.hemswell-antiques.com

HER Hermitage Antiques Tel: 01384 296544

HERR The Herrs Antiques, 2363 Henbird Lane, Lancaster, PA 17601, U.S.A. Tel: 717 569 2268 trishherr@aol.com donmherr@aol.com

HEW ⊞ Muir Hewitt Art Deco Originals, Halifax Antiques Centre, Queens Road Mills, Queens Road/Gibbet Street, Halifax, Yorkshire, HX1 4LR Tel: 01422 347377 muir.hewitt@virgin.net www.muirhewitt.com

HILL ⊞ Hillhaven Antique Linen & Lace Tel: 0121 358 4320

HIP ⊞† Hilary Proctor, Vintage Modes, Shop 6 Admiral Vernon Antiques Market, 141-151 Portobello Road, London, W11 2DY Tel: 07956 876428 hproctor@antiquehandbags.fsnet.co.uk

HL ⊞ Honiton Lace Shop, 44 High Street, Honiton, Devon, EX14 1PJ Tel: 01404 42416 shop@honitonlace.com www.honitonlace.com

HO ⊞ Houghton Antiques, Houghton, Cambridgeshire Tel: 01480 461887 or 07803 716842

HOB ⊞ Hobday Toys Tel: 01895 636737 wendyhobday@freenet.co.uk

HOK ➤ Hamilton Osborne King, 4 Main Street, Blackrock, Co. Dublin, Republic of Ireland Tel: 1 288 5011 blackrock@hok.ie www.hok.ie

HOLL ➤ Holloway's, 49 Parsons Street, Banbury, Oxfordshire, OX16 5NB Tel: 01295 817777 enquiries@hollowaysauctioneers.co.uk www.hollowaysauctioneers.co.uk

HOM ⊞ Home & Colonial, 134 High Street, Berkhamsted, Hertfordshire, HP4 3AT Tel: 01442 877007 homeandcolonial@btinternet.com www.homeandcolonial.co.uk

HOP ⊞† The Antique Garden, Grosvenor Garden Centre, Wrexham Road, Belgrave, Chester, CH4 9EB Tel: 01244 629191/07976 539 990 antigard@btopenworld.com www.antique-garden.co.uk

HOW ⊞ John Howard at Heritage, 6 Market Place, Woodstock, Oxfordshire, OX20 1TA Tel: 01993 811332/0870 4440678 john@johnhoward.co.uk www.antiquepottery.co.uk www.atheritage.co.uk

HSR ⊞ High Street Retro, 39 High Street, Old Town, Hastings, East Sussex, TN34 3ER Tel: 01424 460068

HTE ⊞ Heritage, 6 Market Place, Woodstock, Oxfordshire, OX20 1TA Tel: 01993 811332/0870 4440678 dealers@atheritage.co.uk www.atheritage.co.uk

HUM ⊞ Humbleyard Fine Art, Unit 32 Admiral Vernon Arcade, Portobello Road, London, W11 2DY Tel: 01362 637793 or 07836 349416

HUX ⊞ David Huxtable, Saturdays at: Portobello Road, Basement Stall 11/12, 288 Westbourne Grove, London W11 Tel: 07710 132200 david@huxtins.com www.huxtins.com

HYD ➤ Hy Duke & Son, The Dorchester Fine Art Salerooms, Weymouth Avenue, Dorchester, Dorset, DT1 1QS Tel: 01305 265080 www.dukes-auctions.com

HYP ⊞ Hyperion Collectables

IQ ⊞ Cloud Cuckooland, 12 Fore Street, Mevagissey, Cornwall, PL26 6UQ Tel: 01726 842364 or 07973 135906 Paul@cloudcuckooland.biz www.cloudcuckooland.biz

IW ⊞ Islwyn Watkins, Offa's Dyke Antique Centre, 4 High Street, Knighton, Powys, Wales, LD7 1AT Tel: 01547 520145

J&J ⊞ J & J's, Paragon Antiquities, Antiques & Collectors Market, 3 Bladud Buildings, The Paragon, Bath, Somerset, BA1 5LS Tel: 01225 463715

J&S ⊞ J.R. & S.J. Symes of Bristol Tel: 0117 9501074

JAA ➤ Jackson's International Auctioneers & Appraisers of Fine Art & Antiques, 2229 Lincoln Street, Cedar Falls, IA 50613, U.S.A. Tel: 319 277 2256/800 665 6743 sandim@jacksonsauctions.com www.jacksonsauction.com

JAd ➤ James Adam & Sons, 26 St Stephen's Green, Dublin 2, Republic of Ireland Tel: 00 3531 676 0261 www.jamesadam.ie/

JAM ⊞ Jam Jar Tel: 078896 17593

JAS ⊞ Jasmin Cameron, Antiquarius, 131–141 King's Road, London, SW3 4PW Tel: 020 7351 4154 or 077 74 871257 jasmin.cameron@mail.com

JBa ⊞ John Bartholomew Tel: 01580 241556

JBB ⊞ Jessie's Button Box, Bartlett Street Antique Centre, Bath, Somerset, BA1 5DY Tel: 0117 929 9065

JBe ➤ John Bellman Auctioneers, New Pound Business Park, Wisborough Green, Billingshurst, West Sussex, RH14 0AZ Tel: 01403 700858 jbellman@compuserve.com

JCH ⊞ Jocelyn Chatterton, 126 Grays, 58 Davies Street, London, W1Y 2LP Tel: 020 7629 1971 jocelyn@cixi.demon.co.uk www.cixi.demon.co.uk

JDJ ➤ James D Julia, Inc., P O Box 830, Rte.201 Skowhegan Road, Fairfield ME 04937, U.S.A. Tel: 00 1 207 453 7125 www.juliaauctions.com

JeH ⊞ Jennie Horrocks, Top Banana Antiques Mall, 1 New Church Street, Tetbury, Gloucestershire, GL8 8DS Tel: 07836 264896 info@artnouveaulighting.plus.net www.artnouveaulighting.co.uk

JFME ⊞ James Ferguson & Mark Evans Tel: 0141 950 2452/ 077 699 72935 or 01388 768108/ 07979 0189214 james@dec-art.freeserve.co.uk mark@evanscollectables.co.uk www.evanscollectables.co.uk

JHo ⊞ Jonathan Horne, 66c Kensington Church Street, London, W8 4BY Tel: 020 7221 5658 JH@jonathanhorne.co.uk www.jonathanhorne.co.uk

JHS ⊞ Jonathan Harris Studio Glass Ltd, Woodland House, 24 Peregrine Way, Apley Castle, Telford, Shropshire, TF1 6TH Tel: 01952 246381/588441 jonathan@jhstudioglass.com www.jhstudioglass.com

JMC ⊞ J & M Collectables Tel: 01580 891657 or 077135 23573 jandmcollectables@tinyonline.co.uk

JNic ➤ John Nicholson, The Auction Rooms, Longfield, Midhurst Road, Fernhurst, Surrey, GU27 3HA Tel: 01428 653727 sales@johnnicholsons.com

JPr ⊞ Antique Textiles & Lighting, 34 Belvedere, Lansdown Hill, Bath, Somerset, BA1 5HR Tel: 01225 310795 antiquetextiles@aol.co.uk www.antiquetextiles.co.uk

JTS ⊞ June & Tony Stone Fine Antique Boxes, PO Box 106, Peacehaven, East Sussex, BN10 8AU Tel: 01273 579333 rachel@boxes.co.uk www.boxes.co.uk

JuC ⊞ Julia Craig, Bartlett Street Antiques Centre, 5–10 Bartlett Street, Bath, Somerset, BA1 2QZ Tel: 01225 448202/310457 or 07771 786846

JUJ ⊞ Just Jewellery Tel: 01926 854745

JUN ⊞† Junktion, The Old Railway Station, New Bolingbroke, Boston, Lincolnshire, PE22 7LB Tel: 01205 480068/480087 or 07836 345491 junktionantiques@hotmail.com

JWK ⊞ Jane Wicks Kitchenalia, Country Ways, Strand Quay, Rye, East Sussex Tel: 01424 713635 or 07754 308269 janes_kitchen@hotmail.com

KTA ➤ Kerry Taylor Auctions, in association with Sotheby's, St George Street Gallery, Sotheby's, New Bond Street, London, W1A 2AA Tel: 00785 734337 fashion.textiles@sothebys.com

KWCC § James Sadler International Collectors Club, Customer Services, Churchill China PLC, High Street, Tunstall, Stoke on Trent, Staffordshire, ST6 5NZ Tel: 01782 577566 diningin@churchillchina.plc.uk www.james-sadler.co.uk

L	⚒	Lawrence Fine Art Auctioneers, South Street, Crewkerne, Somerset, TA18 8AB Tel: 01460 73041 www.lawrences.co.uk
L&E	⚒	Locke & England, 18 Guy Street, Leamington Spa, Warwickshire, CV32 4RT Tel: 01926 889100 info@leauction.co.uk www.auctions-online.com/locke
L&L	⊞	Linen & Lace, Shirley Tomlinson, Halifax Antiques Centre, Queens Road/Gibbet Street, Halifax, Yorkshire, HX1 4LR Tel: 01484 540492/01422 366657
LaF	⊞	La Femme Tel: 07971 844279 jewels@joancorder.freeserve.co.uk
LAS	⊞	Reasons to be Cheerful, Georgian Village, 30–31 Islington Green, London, N1 8DU Tel: 0207 281 4600
LAY	⚒	David Lay (ASVA), Auction House, Alverton, Penzance, Cornwall, TR18 4RE Tel: 01736 361414 david.lays@btopenworld.com
LBe	⊞	Linda Bee, Art Deco Stand L18–21, Grays Antique Market, 1–7 Davies Mews, London, W1Y 1AR Tel: 020 7629 5921
LBM	⊞	NOT TRADING
LBr	⊞	Lynda Brine By Appointment only lyndabrine@yahoo.co.uk www.scentbottlesandsmalls.co.uk
LCC	⊞†	London Cigarette Card Co Ltd, Sutton Road, Somerton, Somerset, TA11 6QP Tel: 01458 273452 cards@londoncigcard.co.uk www.londoncigcard.co.uk
LEI	⊞	Joyce M. Leiby, PO Box 6048, Lancaster, PA 17607, U.S.A. Tel: 717 898 9113 joyclei@aol.com
LENA	⊞	Lena Baldock, Mint Arcade, 71 The Mint, Rye, East Sussex, TN31 7EW Tel: 01797 225952
LF	⚒	Lambert & Foster, 77 Commercial Road, Paddock Wood, Kent, TN12 6DR Tel: 01892 832325
LFi	⊞	Laurence Fisher Tel: 07977 368 288
LFNY	⊞	Laura Fisher Antique Quilts & Americana, 1050 Second Avenue, Gallery #84, New York, NY 10022, U.S.A. Tel: 212 838 2596 laurafisher@netlink1.net www.laurafisherquilts.com
Lfo	⊞	Lorfords, 57 Long Street, Tetbury, Gloucestershire, GL8 8AA Tel: 01666 505111 or 07815 802862 toby@lorfordsantiques.co.uk www.lorfordsantiques.co.uk
LGU	⊞	Linda Gumb, Stand 123, Grays Antique Market, 58 Davies Street, London, W1K 5LP Tel: 020 7629 2544 linda@lindagumb.com
LHA	⚒	Leslie Hindman, Inc., 122 North Aberdeen Street, Chicago, Illinois 60607, U.S.A. Tel: 312 280 1212 www.lesliehindman.com
Lim	⊞	Limelight Movie Art, N13–16 Antiquarius Antiques Centre, 131–141 King's Road, Chelsea, London, SW3 4PJ Tel: 01273 206919 info@limelightmovieart.com www.limelightmovieart.com
LIT	⊞	Little Treasures, Petersfield, Kemnay, Aberdeenshire, Scotland, AB51 5PR Tel: 01467 642332 emily@littletreasures.uk.com www.littletreasures.uk.com
LJ	⚒	Leonard Joel Auctioneers, 333 Malvern Road, South Yarra, Victoria 3141, Australia Tel: 03 9826 4333 decarts@ljoel.com.au or jewellery@ljoel.com.au www.ljoel.com.au
LT	⚒	Louis Taylor Auctioneers & Valuers, Britannia House, 10 Town Road, Hanley, Stoke on Trent, Staffordshire, ST1 2QG Tel: 01782 214111
LULU	⊞	Lulu Guinness, 3 Ellis Street, London, SW1X 9AL Tel: 020 7823 4828 www.luluguinness.com
LUNA	⊞	Luna, 23 George Street, Nottingham, NG1 3BH Tel: 0115 924 3267 info@luna-online.co.uk www.luna-online.co.uk
MAL	⚒	Mallams, 26 Grosvenor Street, Cheltenham, Gloucestershire, GL52 2SG Tel: 01242 235712
Mal(O)	⚒	Mallams, Bocardo House, 24 St Michael's Street, Oxford, 0X1 2EB Tel: 01865 241358 oxford@mallams.co.uk
MAR	⚒	Frank Marshall R & Co., Marshall House, Church Hill, Knutsford, Cheshire, WA16 6DH Tel: 01565 653284
MARK	⊞†	20th Century Marks, Whitegates, Rectory Road, Little Burstead, Near Billericay, Essex, CM12 9TR Tel: 01268 411 000 info@20thcenturymarks.co.uk www.20thcenturymarks.co.uk
MB	⊞	Mostly Boxes, 93 High Street, Eton, Windsor, Berkshire, SL4 6AF Tel: 01753 858470
MCa	⊞	Mia Cartwright Tel: 07956 440260 mia.cartwright@virgin.net
MCC	⊞	M.C. Chapman Antiques, Bell Hill, Finedon, Northamptonshire, NN9 5NB Tel: 01933 681260
McD	§	UK McDonald's & Fast Food Collectors Club, c/o Lawrence Yap, 110 Titheherlands, Harlow, Essex, CM19 5ND bigkidandtoys@ntlworld.com
McP	⊞	R & G McPherson Antiques, 40 Kensington Church Street, London, W8 4BX Tel: 020 7937 0812 rmcpherson@orientalceramics.com www.orientalceramics.com
MDe	⊞†	Mike Delaney Tel: 01993 840064 or 07979 910760 mike@vintagehornby.co.uk www.vintagehornby.co.uk
MDL	⊞†	Michael D Long Ltd, 96–98 Derby Road, Nottingham, NG1 5FB Tel: 0115 941 3307 sales@michaeldlong.com www.michaeldlong.com
MEM	§	Memories UK, Mabel Lucie Attwell Club, Abbey Antiques, 63 Great Whyte, Ramsey, Nr Huntingdon, Cambridgeshire, PE26 1HL Tel: 01487 814753 www.mabellucieatwellclub.com
MFB	⊞	Manor Farm Barn Antiques Tel: 01296 658941 or 07720 286607 mfbn@btinternet.com btwebworld.com/mfbantiques
MGA	⊞	M. G. Antiques Tel: 01489 783724
MIL	⊞	Millennia Antiquities Tel: 01204 690175 or 07930 273998 millenniaant@aol.com www.AncientAntiquities.co.uk
MINN	⊞	Geoffrey T. Minnis, Hastings Antique Centre, 59–61 Norman Road, St Leonards-on-Sea, East Sussex, TN38 0EG Tel: 01424 428561
MiW	⊞	Mike Weedon, 7 Camden Passage, Islington, London, N1 8EA Tel: 020 7226 5319 or 020 7609 6826 info@mikeweedonantiques.com www.mikeweedonantiques.com
MLa	⊞	Marion Langham Tel: 028 895 41247 marion@ladymarion.co.uk www.ladymarion.co.uk
MLL	⊞	Millers Antiques Ltd, Netherbrook House, 86 Christchurch Road, Ringwood, Hampshire, BH24 1DR Tel: 01425 472062 mail@millers-antiques.co.uk www.millers-antiques.co.uk
MMa		Madeleine Marsh
MMc	⊞	Marsh-McNamara Tel: 07790 759162
MPC	⊞	M C Pottery Tel: 01244 301800 Sales@Moorcroftchester.co.uk www.Moorcroftchester.co.uk
MRW	⊞	Malcolm Welch Antiques, Wild Jebbett, Pudding Bag Lane, Thurlaston, Nr Rugby, Warwickshire, CV23 9JZ Tel: 01788 810 616 www.rb33.co.uk
MSB	⊞	Marilynn and Sheila Brass, PO Box 380503, Cambridge, MA 02238-0503, U.S.A. Tel: 617 491 6064 shelmardesign1@aol.com
MSh	⊞	Manfred Schotten, 109 High Street, Burford, Oxfordshire, OX18 4RG Tel: 01993 822302 www.antiques@schotten.com

MTMC § Muffin the Mule Collectors' Club, 12 Woodland Close, Woodford Green, Essex, IG8 0QH Tel: 020 8504 4943 www.Muffin-the-Mule.com

MUL ⚒† Mullock & Madeley, The Old Shippon, Wall-under-Heywood, Nr Church Stretton, Shropshire, SY6 7DS Tel: 01694 771771 or 01584 841 428 auctions@mullockmadeley.co.uk www.mullockmadeley.co.uk

MUR ⊞ Murray Cards (International) Ltd, 51 Watford Way, Hendon Central, London, NW4 3JH Tel: 020 8202 5688 murraycards@ukbusiness.com www.murraycard.com/

MURR ⊞ Murrays' Antiques & Collectables Tel: 01202 823870

NAR ⊞† Colin Narbeth & Son Ltd, 20 Cecil Court, Leicester Square, London, WC2N 4HE Tel: 020 7379 6975 Colin.Narbeth@btinternet.com www.colin-narbeth.com

NAW ⊞ Newark Antiques Warehouse Ltd, Old Kelham Road, Newark, Nottinghamshire, NG24 1BX Tel: 01636 674869/07974 429185 enquiries@newarkantiques.co.uk www.newarkantiques.co.uk

NEW ⊞ Newsum Antiques, 2 High Street, Winchcombe, Gloucestershire, GL54 5HT Tel: 01242 603446/07968 196668 mark@newsumantiques.co.uk www.newsumantiques.co.uk

NFR ⊞ The 40's Room, 34 North Street, Bridgetown, Cannock, Staffordshire, WS11 0BA Tel: 07971 174387 info@cc41homefrontdisplays.co.uk Also at: Unit 40 Rugeley Antiques Centre, Main Road, Brereton, Rugeley, Staffordshire, WS15 1DX Tel: 01889 577166

NSal ⚒ Netherhampton Salerooms, Salisbury Auction Centre, Netherhampton, Salisbury, Wiltshire, SP2 8RH Tel: 01722 340 041

NW ⊞ Nigel Williams Rare Books, 25 Cecil Court, London, WC2N 4EZ Tel: 020 7836 7757 nigel@nigelwilliams.com www.nigelwilliams.com

OD ⊞ Offa's Dyke Antique Centre, 4 High Street, Knighton, Powys, Wales, LD7 1AT Tel: 01547 528635/520145

OH ⊞ Old Hat, 66 Fulham High Road, London, SW6 3LQ Tel: 020 7610 6558

OIA ⊞ The Old Ironmongers Antiques Centre, 5 Burford Street, Lechlade, Gloucestershire, GL7 3AP Tel: 01367 252397

OLA ⊞ Olliff's Architectural Antiques, 19–21 Lower Redland Road, Redland, Bristol, Gloucestershire, BS6 6TB Tel: 07850 235 793 marcus@olliffs.com www.olliffs.com

OLD ⊞ Oldnautibits, PO Box 67, Langport, Somerset, TA10 9WJ Tel: 01458 241816 or 07947 277833 geoff.pringle@oldnautibits.com www.oldnautibits.com

Oli ⚒ Olivers, Olivers Rooms, Burkitts Lane, Sudbury, Suffolk, CO10 1HB Tel: 01787 880305 oliversauctions@btconnect.com

ONS ⚒ Onslow's Auctions Ltd, The Coach House, Manor Road, Stourpaine, Dorset, DT8 8TQ Tel: 01258 488838

OTA ⊞† On The Air, The Vintage Technology Centre, The Highway, Hawarden, (Nr Chester), Deeside, Cheshire, CH5 3DN Tel: 01244 530300 or 07778 767734 www.vintageradio.co.uk

OTB ⊞† The Old Tackle Box, PO Box 55, High Street, Cranbrook, Kent, TN17 3ZU Tel: 01580 713979 or 07729 278 293 tackle.box@virgin.net

OW ⊞ See **STa**

PBA ⚒ Paul Beighton, Woodhouse Green, Thurcroft, Rotherham, Yorkshire, S66 9AQ Tel: 01709 700005 www.paulbeightonauctioneers.co.uk

Penn ⊞ Penny Fair Antiques Tel: 07860 825456

PEZ ⊞ Alan Pezaro, 62a West Street, Dorking, Surrey, RH4 1BS Tel: 01306 743661

PF ⚒ Peter Francis, Curiosity Sale Room, 19 King Street, Carmarthen, Wales, SA31 1BH Tel: 01267 233456 nigel@peterfrancis.co.uk www.peterfrancis.co.uk

PFK ⚒ Penrith Farmers' & Kidd's plc, Skirsgill Salerooms, Penrith, Cumbria, CA11 0DN Tel: 01768 890781 info@pfkauctions.co.uk www.pfkauctions.co.uk

Pin ⊞ Gazzas Pinballs Tel: 07753 949887 garypound@go.com www.gazzaspinballs.co.uk

PLB ⊞ Planet Bazaar, 149 Drummond Street, London, NW1 2PB Tel: 020 7278 7793 info@planetbazaar.co.uk www.planetbazaar.co.uk

POLL ⊞ Pollyanna, 34 High Street, Arundel, West Sussex, BN18 9AB Tel: 01903 885198 or 07949903457

POS § Postcard Club of Great Britain, c/o Mrs D. Brennan, 34 Harper House, St James Crescent, London, SW9 7LW Tel: 020 7771 9404

Pott ⚒ Potteries Specialist Auctions, 271 Waterloo Road, Cobridge, Stoke on Trent, Staffordshire, ST6 3HR Tel: 01782 286622

PPH ⊞ Period Picnic Hampers Tel: 0115 937 2934

PPL ⊞ The Pen and Pencil Lady Tel: 01647 231619 penpencilady@aol.com www.penpencilady.com

PrB ⊞ Pretty Bizarre, 170 High Street, Deal, Kent, CT14 6BQ Tel: 07973 794537

PSA ⊞ Pantiles Spa Antiques, 4, 5, 6 Union House, The Pantiles, Tunbridge Wells, Kent, TN4 8HE Tel: 01892 541377 psa.wells@btinternet.com www.antiques-tun-wells-kent.co.uk

Q&C ⊞ Q & C Militaria, 22 Suffolk Road, Cheltenham, Gloucestershire, GL50 2AQ Tel: 01242 519815 or 07778 613977 qcmilitaria@btconnect.com www.qcmilitaria.com

Qua ⊞ Quadrille, 146 Portobello Road, London, W11 2DZ Tel: 01923 829079/020 7727 9860

RaA ⊞ Race Art, 33 Westgate Street, Southery, Norfolk, PE38 0PA Tel: 01366 377069 simon@race-art.com www.race-art.com

RAND ⊞ Becky Randall, c/o 36 Highfield Road, Wilmslow, Buckinghamshire, MK18 3DU Tel: 07979 848440

RBA ⊞ Roger Bradbury Antiques, Church Street, Coltishall, Norfolk, NR12 7DJ Tel: 01603 737444

RdeR ⊞ Rogers de Rin, 76 Royal Hospital Road, London, SW3 4HN Tel: 020 7352 9007 rogersderin@rogersderin.co.uk www.rogersderin.co.uk

REK ⊞ Rellik, 8 Golborne Road, London, W10 5NW Tel: 020 8962 0089

ReN ⊞ Rene Nicholls, 56 High Street, Malmesbury, Wiltshire, SN16 9AT Tel: 01666 823089

REPS ⊞ Repsycho, 85 Gloucester Road, Bishopston, Bristol, Gloucestershire, BS7 8AS Tel: 0117 9830007

RER ⊞ Lucias Red Roses, Admiral Vernon Antique Markets, 67 & 68 Portobello Road, Shops 57 & 58, London, W11 Tel: 01793 790 607 or 07778 803 876 sallie_ead@lycos.com www.vintagemodes.co.uk

RET ⊞ Retro-Spective Tel: 07989 984659 retro_spective1@hotmail.com

ROSc ⚒ R. O. Schmitt Fine Art, Box 1941, Salem, New Hampshire 03079, U.S.A. Tel: 603 893 5915 bob@roschmittfinearts.com www.antiqueclockauction.com

RTo ⚒ Rupert Toovey & Co Ltd, Spring Gardens, Washington, West Sussex, RH20 3BS Tel: 01903 891955 auctions@rupert-toovey.com www.rupert-toovey.com

RTT ⊞ Rin Tin Tin, 34 North Road, Brighton, East Sussex, BN1 1YB Tel: 01273 672424 rick@rintintin.freeserve.co.uk

RTW ⊞ Richard Twort Tel: 01934 641900 or 07711 939789

RUSS ⊞ Russells Tel: 023 8061 6664

RW ⊞ Robin Wareham

S ⚒ Sotheby's, 34-35 New Bond Street, London, W1A 2AA Tel: 020 7293 5000 www.sothebys.com

S(NY) ⚒ Sotheby's, 1334 York Avenue at 72nd St, New York, NY 10021, U.S.A. Tel: 212 606 7000

S(O) ⚒ Sotheby's Olympia, Hammersmith Road, London, W14 8UX Tel: 020 7293 5555

S(P) ⚒ Sotheby's France SA, 76 rue du Faubourg, Saint Honore, Paris 75008, France Tel: 33 1 53 05 53 05

S(S) ⚒ Sotheby's Sussex, Summers Place, Billingshurst, West Sussex, RH14 9AD Tel: 01403 833500

S&D ⊞ S&D Postcards, Bartlett Street Antique Centre, 5–10 Bartlett Street, Bath, Somerset, BA1 2QZ Tel: 07979 506415 wndvd@aol.com

SA ⊞ Sporting Antiques, 9 Church St, St Ives, Cambridgeshire, PE27 6DG Tel: 01480 463891 johnlambden@sportingantiques.co.uk www.sportingantiques.co.uk

SAAC ⊞ Scottish Antique Centre, Abernyte, Perthshire, Scotland, PH14 9SJ Tel: 01828 686401 sales@scottish-antiques.com www.scottish-antiques.com

SaB ⊞ Sara Bernstein Antique Dolls & Bears, Englishtown, New Jersey 07726, U.S.A. Tel: 732 536 4101 santiqbebe@aol.com www.saraberinsteindolls.com

SAND NOT TRADING

SAS ⚒† Special Auction Services, Kennetholme, Midgham, Reading, Berkshire, RG7 5UX Tel: 0118 971 2949 www.invaluable.com/sas/

SAT ⊞ The Swan at Tetsworth, High Street, Tetsworth, Nr Thame, Oxfordshire, OX9 7AB Tel: 01844 281777 antiques@theswan.co.uk www.theswan.co.uk

SBL ⊞ Twentieth Century Style Tel: 01822 614831

SBT ⊞ Steinberg & Tolkien Vintage & Designer Clothing, 193 Kings Road, London, SW3 5EB Tel: 020 7376 3660

SCH ⊞ Scherazade Tel: 01708 641117 or 07855 383996 scherz1@yahoo.com

SDP ⊞ Stage Door Prints, 9 Cecil Court, London, WC2N 4EZ Tel: 020 7240 1683

SEA ⊞ Mark Seabrook Antiques, PO Box 396, Huntingdon, Cambridgeshire, PE28 0ZA Tel: 01480 861935 enquiries@markseabrook.com www.markseabrook.com

SER ⊞† Serendipity, 125 High Street, Deal, Kent, CT14 6BB Tel: 01304 369165/01304 366536 dipityantiques@aol.com

SHER ⊞ Sherwood Golf Antiques Tel: 07968 848448 sherwoodgolf@btinternet.com

SJH ⚒ S.J. Hales, 87 Fore Street, Bovey Tracey, Devon, TQ13 9AB Tel: 01626 836684

SK ⚒ Skinner Inc, The Heritage On The Garden, 63 Park Plaza, Boston, MA 02116, U.S.A. Tel: 617 350 5400 www.skinnerinc.com

SK(B) ⚒ Skinner Inc, 357 Main Street, Bolton, MA 01740, U.S.A. Tel: 978 779 6241

SMI ⊞† Skip & Janie Smithson Antiques Tel: 01754 810265 or 07831 399180 smithsonantiques@hotmail.com

SOR ⊞ Soldiers of Rye, Mint Arcade, 71 The Mint, Rye, East Sussex, TN31 7EW Tel: 01797 225952 rameses@supanet.com chris@johnbartholomewcards.co.uk www.rameses.supanet.com

SOU ⊞ Source, 11 Claverton Buildings, High Street, Widcombe, Bath, BA2 4LD Tel: 01225 469200/07831 734134 shop@source-antiques.co.uk www.source-antiques.co.uk

SPA ⊞ Sporting Antiques, 10 Union Square, The Pantiles, Tunbridge Wells, Kent, TN4 8HE Tel: 01892 522661

SPF ⚒ Scarborough Perry Fine Art, Hove Auction Rooms, Hove Street, Hove, East Sussex, BN3 2GL Tel: 01273 735266

SpM ⊞ The Girl Can't Help It!, Sparkle Moore & Cad Van Swankster, Alfies Antique Market, G100 & G116 Ground Floor, 13-25 Church Street, Marylebone, London, NW8 8DT Tel: 020 7724 8984 or 07958 515614 sparkle.moore@virgin.net www.sparklemoore.com

SRA ⚒† Sheffield Railwayana Auctions, 4 The Glebe, Clapham, Bedford, MK41 6GA Tel: 01234 325341 www.sheffieldrailwayana.co.uk

SRi ⊞ Steve Ribbons Tel: 01484 684043 Dogsinprint@btinternet.com

SSF ⊞ Suffolk Sci-Fi and Fantasy, 17 Norwich Road, Ipswich, Suffolk, IP1 2ET Tel: 01473 400655 or 07885 298361 symon@suffolksci-fi.com www.suffolksci-fi.com

SSL ⊞ Star Signings Ltd, The Burbeque Gallery, 16A New Quebec Street, London, W1H 7DG Tel: 020 7723 8498 starsignings@btconnect.com

STA ⊞ George Stacpoole, Main Street, Adare, Co. Limerick, Republic of Ireland Tel: 00353 (0)6139 6409 stacpoole@iol.ie www.georgestacpooleantiques.com

STa ⊞ Starbase-Alpha, Unit 19-20, Rumford Shopping Halls, Market Place, Rumford, Essex, RM1 3AT Tel: 01708 765633 starbasealpha1@aol.com www.starbasealpha.cjb.net

SUW ⊞ Sue Wilde at Wildewear Tel: 01395 577966 compacts@wildewear.co.uk www.wildewear.co.uk

SWB ⊞† Sweetbriar Gallery Paperweights Ltd., 56 Watergate Street, Chester, CH1 2LA Tel: 01244 329249 sales@sweetbriar.co.uk www.sweetbriar.co.uk www.sweetbriarartglass.co.uk

SWO ⚒ Sworders, 14 Cambridge Road, Stansted Mountfitchet, Essex, CM24 8BZ Tel: 01279 817778 auctions@sworder.co.uk www.sworder.co.uk

T&D ⊞ Toys & Dolls, 367 Fore Street, Edmonton, London, N9 0NR Tel: 020 8807 3301

TAC ⊞ Tenterden Antiques Centre, 66–66A High Street, Tenterden, Kent, TN30 6AU Tel: 01580 765655/765885

TASV ⊞ Tenterden Antiques & Silver Vaults, 66 High Street, Tenterden, Kent, TN30 6AU Tel: 01580 765885

TB ⊞ Millicent Safro Tender Buttons, 143 E.62nd Street, New York, NY10021, U.S.A. Tel: 212 758 7004 Author of BUTTONS

TCG ⊞ 20th Century Glass, Nigel Benson Tel: 07971 859848 nigelbenson@20thcentury-glass.com

TDG ⊞ The Design Gallery 1850–1950, 5 The Green, Westerham, Kent, TN16 1AS Tel: 01959 561234 sales@thedesigngalleryuk.com www.thedesigngalleryuk.com

TEN ⚒ Tennants, The Auction Centre, Harmby Road, Leyburn, Yorkshire, DL8 5SG
Tel: 01969 623780 enquiry@tennants-ltd.co.uk
www.tennants.co.uk

TH ⊞† Tony Horsley, PO Box 3127, Brighton, East Sussex, BN1 5SS Tel: 01273 550770

THE ⚒ Theriault's, PO Box 151, Annapolis, MD 21404, U.S.A. Tel: 410 224 3655 info@theriaults.com
www.theriaults.com

TIC ⊞ NOT TRADING

TIN ⊞ Tin Tin Collectables, G38-42 Alfies's Antique Market, 13-25 Church Street, Marylebone, London, NW8 8DT Tel: 020 7258 1305
leslie@tintincollectables.com
www.tintincollectables.com

TL ⊞† Telephone Lines Ltd, 304 High Street, Cheltenham, Gloucestershire, GL50 3JF
Tel: 01242 583699 info@telephonelines.net
www.telephonelines.net

TMA ⚒ Tring Market Auctions, The Market Premises, Brook Street, Tring, Hertfordshire, HP23 5EF
Tel: 01442 826446
sales@tringmarketauctions.co.uk
www.tringmarketauctions.co.uk

TMi ⊞ T. J. Millard Antiques, 59 Lower Queen Street, Penzance, Cornwall, TR18 4DF
Tel: 01736 333454 or
chessmove@btinternet.com

TML ⊞ Timothy Millett Ltd, Historic Medals and Works of Art, PO Box 20851, London, SE22 0YN
Tel: 020 8693 1111 or 07778 637 898
tim@timothymillett.demon.co.uk

TOL ⊞ Turn On Lighting, Antique Lighting Specialists, 116/118 Islington High Street, Camden Passage, Islington, London, N1 8EG
Tel: 020 7359 7616

TOP ⊞ The Top Banana Antiques Mall, 1 New Church Street, Tetbury, Gloucestershire, GL8 8DS
Tel: 0871 288 1102
info@topbananaantiques.com
www.topbananaantiques.com
Also at: 32, 46 & 48 Long Street, Tetbury
Tel: 0871 288 1110 & 0871 288 3058

TRM(D) ⚒ Thomson, Roddick & Medcalf Ltd, 60 Whitesands, Dumfries, Scotland, DG1 2RS
Tel: 01387 255366 trmdumfries@btconnect.com
www.thomsonroddick.com

Tus ⊞ Tussie Mussies, The Old Stables, 2b East Cross, Tenterden, Kent, TN30 6AD Tel: 01580 766244
tussiemussies@btinternet.com
www.tussiemussies.co.uk

TWI ⊞† Twinkled, High St Antiques Centre, 39 High Street, Hastings, East Sussex, TN34 3ER
Tel: 01424 460068 info@twinkled.net
limehouseblues47@aol.com www.twinkled.net
Also at: 1st Floor, Old Petrol Station, 11–17 Stockwell Street, Greenwich, London, SE10 9JN Tel: 020 8269 0864
Also at: 2nd Floor, 61a Faraday Way (off Westfield St), Westminster Ind Estate, London, SE18 5TR Tel: 07940 471569

TYA ⊞ Tony Young Autographs, 138 Edward Street, Brighton, East Sussex, BN2 0JL
Tel: 01273 732418

UD ⊞ Upstairs Downstairs, 40 Market Place, Devizes, Wiltshire, SN10 1JG Tel: 01380 730266 or
07974 074220 devizesantiques@btconnect.com

VAU ⚒† Vault Auctions Ltd, PO Box 257, South Norwood, London, SE25 6JN
Tel: 01342 300 900 contact@vaultauctions.com
www.vaultauctions.com

VEC ⚒† Vectis Auctions Ltd, Fleck Way, Thornaby, Stockton-on-Tees, Cleveland, TS17 9JZ
Tel: 01642 750616 admin@vectis.co.uk
www.vectis.co.uk

VICT ⊞† June Victor, Vintage Modes, S041-43, Alfies Antique Market, 13-25 Church Street, London, NW8 8DT Tel: 020 7723 6066 or 07740704723

VK ⊞ Vivienne King of Panache
Tel: 01934 814759 or 07974 798871
Kingpanache@aol.com

VRG ⊞ Vintage & Rare Guitars (Bath) Ltd, 7–8 Saville Row, Bath, Somerset, BA1 2QP Tel: 01225 330 888
enquiries@vintageandrareguitars.com
www.vintageandrareguitars.com
Also at: Vintage & Rare Guitars (London), 6 Denmark Street, London, WC2H 8LX
Tel: 020 7240 7500

VS ⚒† T. Vennett-Smith, 11 Nottingham Road, Gotham, Nottinghamshire, NG11 0HE
Tel: 0115 983 0541 info@vennett-smith.com
www.vennett-smith.com

VSP ⚒ Van Sabben Poster Auctions, Appelsteeg 1-B, NL-1621 BD, Hoorn, Netherlands
Tel: 31 (0)229 268203
uboersma@vansabbenauctions.nl
www.vansabbenauctions.nl

WAA ⊞ Woburn Abbey Antiques Centre, Woburn, Bedfordshire, MK17 9WA Tel: 01525 290666
antiques@woburnabbey.co.uk
www.discoverwoburn.co.uk

WAC ⊞ Worcester Antiques Centre, Reindeer Court, Mealcheapen Street, Worcester, WR1 4DF
Tel: 01905 610680
WorcsAntiques@aol.com

WAL ⚒† Wallis & Wallis, West Street Auction Galleries, Lewes, Sussex East, BN7 2NJ Tel: 01273 480208
auctions@wallisandwallis.co.uk
grb@wallisandwallis.co.uk
www.wallisandwallis.co.uk

WAm ⊞ Williams Amusements Ltd, Bluebird House, Povey Cross Road, Horley, Surrey, RH6 0AG
Tel: 01293 782222 or 07970 736486
adrian@williams-amusements.co.uk
www.williams-amusements.co.uk

WeA ⊞ Wenderton Antiques By appointment only
Tel: 01227 720295

WEBB ⚒ Webb's, 18 Manukau Rd, Newmarket, PO Box 99251, Auckland, New Zealand
Tel: 09 524 6804
auctions@webbs.co.nz www.webbs.co.nz

WiB ⊞ Wish Barn Antiques, Wish Street, Rye, East Sussex, TN31 7DA Tel: 01797 226797

WilP ⚒ W&H Peacock, 26 Newnham Street, Bedford, MK40 3JR Tel: 01234 266366

WL ⚒ Wintertons Ltd, Lichfield Auction Centre, Fradley Park, Lichfield, Staffordshire, WS13 8NF
Tel: 01543 263256
enquiries@wintertons.co.uk
www.wintertons.co.uk

WO ⊞ Woodville Antiques, The Street, Hamstreet, Ashford, Kent, TN26 2HG Tel: 01233 732981
woodvilleantiques@yahoo.co.uk

Woo ⊞ Woolworths, 9 High Street, Tenterden, Kent, TN30 6BN Tel: 01580 763209

WOS ⊞ Wheels of Steel, Grays Antique Market, Stand A12–13, Unit B10 Basement, 1-7 Davies Mews, London, W1Y 2LP Tel: 0207 629 2813

WP ⊞† British Notes, PO Box 257, Sutton, Surrey, SM3 9WW Tel: 020 8641 3224
pamwestbritnotes@aol.com
www.britishnotes.co.uk

WW ⚒ Woolley & Wallis, Salisbury Salerooms, 51–61 Castle Street, Salisbury, Wiltshire, SP1 3SU
Tel: 01722 424500/411854
enquiries@woolleyandwallis.co.uk
www.woolleyandwallis.co.uk

YT ⊞ Yew Tree Antiques, Woburn Abbey Antiques Centre, Woburn, Bedfordshire, MK17 9WA
Tel: 01525 872514

Index to Advertisers

Index

Bold numbers refer to information and pointer boxes

GRAYS | ANTIQUE MARKETS

Over 200 dealers in "the best antique markets in the world"

Antique & Fine Jewellery, Antiquities, Asian & Islamic Art, Ceramics & Glass, Clocks & Watches, Coins & Medals, Costume Jewellery, Dolls, Teddy Bears & Toys, Gemstones & Minerals, Handbags & Compacts, Linen & Lace, Militaria, Pewter & Early Oak, Perfume bottles & Limogés boxes, Prints & Paintings, Silver & Objet d'Art, Vintage Fashion & Accessories. Bureau de Change, Engravings & Repairs. The Victory Café

Open Monday - Friday 10am-6pm 020 7629 7034
South Molton Lane, Mayfair, London, W1
BY BOND STREET TUBE
www.graysantiques.com